2001-2002

EVANGELICAL SUNDAY SCHOOL LESSON COMMENTARY

FIFTIETH ANNUAL VOLUME
Based on the
Evangelical Bible Lesson Series

Editorial Staff
Lance Colkmire — Editor
Bill George — Editor in Chief
Daniel F. Boling — General Director of Publications

Lesson Exposition Writers

Eugene C. Christenbury	Jerald Daffe
Rodney Hodge	Oliver McMahan

Published by
PATHWAY PRESS
Cleveland, Tennessee

Lesson treatments in the *Evangelical Sunday School Lesson Commentary* for 2001-2002 are based upon the outlines of the Pentecostal-Charismatic Bible Lesson Series prepared by the Pentecostal-Charismatic Curriculum Commission (formerly the Curriculum Commission of the National Sunday School Association).

Copyright 2001

PATHWAY PRESS, Cleveland, Tennessee
ISBN: 0-87148-896-5

Printed in the United States of America

TABLE OF CONTENTS

INTRODUCTION TO THE 2001-2002 COMMENTARY

The *Evangelical Sunday School Lesson Commentary* contains in a single volume a full study of the Sunday school lessons for the months beginning with September 2001 and running through August 2002. The 12 months of lessons draw from both the Old Testament and the New Testament in an effort to provide balance and establish relationship between these distinct but inspired writings. The lessons in this 2001-2002 volume are drawn from the third year of a seven-year cycle, which will be completed in August 2006. (The cycle is printed in full on page 16 of this volume.)

The lessons for the *Evangelical Commentary* are based on the Evangelical Bible Lesson Series Outlines, prepared by the Pentecostal-Charismatic Curriculum Commission. (The Pentecostal-Charismatic Curriculum Commission is a member of the National Association of Evangelicals.) The lessons in this volume are drawn from the Old and New Testaments; and taken together with the other annual volumes of lessons in the cycle, they provide a valuable commentary on a wide range of Biblical subjects. Each quarter is divided into two units of study.

The 2001-2002 commentary is the work of a team of Christian scholars and writers who have developed the volume under the supervision of Pathway Press. All the major writers, introduced on the following pages, represent a team of ministers committed to a strictly Evangelical interpretation of the Scriptures. The guiding theological principles of this commentary are expressed in the following statement of faith:

1. WE BELIEVE the Bible to be the inspired, the only infallible, authoritative Word of God.

2. WE BELIEVE that there is one God, eternally existing in three persons: Father, Son, and Holy Spirit.

3. WE BELIEVE in the deity of our Lord Jesus Christ, in His virgin birth, in His sinless life, in His miracles, in His vicarious and atoning death through His shed blood, in His bodily resurrection, in His ascension to the right hand of the Father, and in His personal return in power and glory.

4. WE BELIEVE that for the salvation of lost and sinful men, personal reception of the Lord Jesus Christ and regeneration by the Holy Spirit are absolutely essential.

5. WE BELIEVE in the present ministry of the Holy Spirit by whose cleansing and indwelling the Christian is enabled to live a godly life.

6. WE BELIEVE in the personal return of the Lord Jesus Christ.

7. WE BELIEVE in the resurrection of both the saved and the lost—they that are saved, unto the resurrection of life; and they that are lost, unto the resurrection of damnation.

8. WE BELIEVE in the spiritual unity of believers in our Lord Jesus Christ.

USING THE COMMENTARY

The *Evangelical Sunday School Lesson Commentary* for 2001-2002 is presented to the reader with the hope that it will become his weekly companion through the months ahead.

The fall quarter 2001 continues a seven-year cycle of lessons which will be completed with the summer quarter 2006. The 28 quarters of studies, divided into two or more units each, draw from both the Old and New Testaments. Also a number of studies will be topical in nature as attention is focused on contemporary issues. A complete listing of the themes that will be included in the seven-year cycle is printed on page 16 of this volume.

Quarterly unit themes for the 2001-2002 volume are as follows:

• Fall Quarter—Unit One: "Christian Living (Romans and Galatians)"; Unit Two: "Christian Discipleship"

• Winter Quarter—Unit One: "The Gospel According to Luke"; Unit Two: "Message of the Early Church"

• Spring Quarter—Unit One: "Leadership (Joshua and Judges)"; Unit Two: "The Church"

• Summer Quarter—Unit One: "Psalms (Part 1)"; Unit Two: "Learning From Samuel, Elijah and Elisha"

The lesson sequence used in this volume is prepared by the Pentecostal-Charismatic Curriculum Commission.

The specific material used in developing each lesson is written and edited under the guidance of the editorial staff of Pathway Press.

STUDY TEXT: At the opening of each week's lesson, you will see printed the study text. These references point out passages of Scripture that are directly related to the lesson, and it is advisable for you to read each one carefully before beginning the lesson study.

TIME and PLACE: A time and place is given for most lessons. Where there is a wide range of opinions regarding the exact time or place, the printed New Testament works of Merrill C. Tenney and Old Testament works of Samuel J. Schultz are used to provide the information.

PRINTED TEXT and CENTRAL TRUTH: The printed text is the body of Scripture designated each week for verse-by-verse study in the classroom. Drawing on the study text the teacher delves into this printed text, exploring its content with the students. The central truth states the single unifying principle that the expositors attempted to clarify in each lesson.

DICTIONARY: A dictionary, which brings pronunciation and clarification to difficult words or phrases, is included with many lessons. Pronunciations are based on the phonetic system used by Field Enterprises Educational Corporation of Chicago and New York in *The World Book Encyclopedia*. Definitions are generally based on *The Pictorial Bible Dictionary*, published by Zondervan Publishing Company, Grand Rapids, Michigan.

EXPOSITION and LESSON OUTLINE: The heart of this commentary—and probably the heart of the teacher's instruction each week—is the exposition of the printed text. This exposition material is preceded by a lesson outline, which indicates how the material is to be divided for study. These lesson outlines are not exhaustive but, rather, provide a skeleton for the teacher to build upon.

GOLDEN TEXT HOMILY: The golden text homily for each week is a brief reflection on that single verse. As the word *homily* implies, it is a discourse or sermon on a particular point. The homily may often be used effectively to help apply the lesson to life.

SENTENCE SERMONS: Two or more sentence sermons—popular and pithy single-line thoughts on the central truth of the lesson—are included each week.

EVANGELISM APPLICATION: The evangelism application relates the general theme of the week's lesson to the ongoing task of evangelism. The theme of the lesson (but not necessarily of the lesson text) is used to make this application. At times the emphasis of the section bears on direct evangelism of class members who may not be Christians; at other times the emphasis bears upon exhorting the class members to become more involved in evangelizing others.

ILLUMINATING THE LESSON: In this section, illustrative material is provided for the teacher to use to support the lesson at whatever point seems most appropriate.

DAILY BIBLE READINGS: The daily Bible readings are included for the teacher to use in his own devotions throughout the week, as well as to share with members of his class.

TRUTH SEARCH: This is a new tool offered in each lesson for teachers who want to take a more interactive approach to teaching. Truth Search provides a three-step plan:

1. *Focus*: Begin by grabbing the students' attention with an activity that relates to their lives and focuses their attention on the lesson theme.

2. *Explore*: Do a verse-by-verse, discussion-based study of the Scripture passage.

3. *Respond*: Challenge the students to respond to the day's lesson in a specific way.

EXPOSITION WRITERS

Writers for the expository materials for the 2001-2002 volume are as follows:

The lesson expositions for the fall quarter (September, October, November) were written by the Reverend Dr. Oliver McMahan (B.A., M.Div., D.Min., Ph.D.), who is former dean of students and associate professor at Northwest Bible College, Minot, North Dakota, and former dean of Jimmy Swaggart Theological Seminary. Presently, he is associate dean and director of the doctoral ministry and associate professor of pastoral care and counseling at the Church of God Theological Seminary, Cleveland, Tennessee. Dr. McMahan earned his bachelor of arts degree at West Coast Bible College, his master of divinity and doctor of ministry from Brite Divinity School at Texas Christian University, and his doctor of philosophy at Georgia State University.

An ordained minister in the Church of God, Dr. McMahan has served his denomination as pastor, educator, personal counselor and a member of the Council of 18.

Dr. McMahan has written a number of articles for the *Church of God Evangel* and is a contributor of definitions and articles for the *Complete Biblical Library*. He is the author of the books *Becoming a Shepherd*, *Scriptural Counseling* and *Deepening Discipleship*.

Lesson expositions for the winter quarter (December, January, February) were written by the Reverend Dr. Eugene C. Christenbury (B.A., M.A., M.S., Ed.D.).

Dr. Christenbury earned his bachelor of arts and master of arts degrees at George Peabody College for Teachers and his doctorate of education from the University of Tennessee. He also earned the M.S. degree in religion from the Church of God

Theological Seminary, Cleveland, Tennessee. An ordained minister in the Church of God, Dr. Christenbury has served as state youth and Christian education director, pastor, and assistant superintendent at the Home for Children in Sevierville, Tennessee. He is retired after serving as senior adjunct professor of education at Lee University, Cleveland, Tennessee.

Dr. Christenbury is a member of Phi Delta Kappa and the Council on Public Education of Religious Studies. Recognized for his academic and religious knowledge, he is a popular speaker at Lee University and in the broader church community.

Lesson expositions for the spring quarter (March, April, May) were written by the Reverend Rodney Hodge (A.B.), an ordained minister who has served as minister of music for 30 years at Northwood Temple Pentecostal Holiness Church in Fayetteville, North Carolina. He holds degrees from Emmanuel College and the University of Georgia and did graduate studies in history at the University of Georgia.

Reverend Hodge has written numerous Bible study programs, as well as dramas and music productions, and has produced an entire series of theater productions for church use.

The Reverend Hodge presently writes adult Sunday school literature for the International Pentecostal Holiness Church.

Lesson expositions for the summer quarter (June, July, August) were written by the Reverend Dr. Jerald Daffe (B.A., M.A., D.Min.), who is professor of pastoral ministries and coordinator of pastoral ministries major of the Department of Bible and Christian Ministries, Lee University, Cleveland, Tennessee.

Dr. Daffe earned his bachelor of arts degree at Northwest Bible College, a master of arts degree at Wheaton College Graduate School, and his doctorate of ministry degree at Western Conservative Baptist Seminary. An ordained minister in the Church of God, Dr. Daffe has served in the pastoral ministry for 10 years and has been a faculty member at Northwest Bible College and Lee University for over 28 years.

Dr. Daffe has been recognized and listed in *Outstanding Educators of America 1974-75* and *Outstanding Young Men of America 1984*. He also received the Excellence in Teaching (1990) and the Excellence in Advising (1999) awards at Lee University. Recognized for his professional knowledge and communicative skills, Dr. Daffe is a popular speaker at camp meetings, retreats, seminars, and churches in many denominations. In addition to many magazine articles and Sunday school lessons, his two latest books are *Life Challenges for Men* and *Revival: God's Plan for His People.*

GOLDEN TEXT HOMILY WRITERS

Fred A. Abbott
Church of God State Youth and
  Christian Education Director
Yakima, Washington

Timothy J. Bass
Church of God State Youth and
  Christian Education Director
Greenwood, Indiana

Richard Y. Bershon, Ph.D.
Chaplain, State Veterans Home and
  V.A. Medical Center
Hot Springs, South Dakota

Ralph Brewer (Retired)
Former Pastor, Church of God
Cramerton, North Carolina

Noel Brooks, D.D. (Retired)
Writer, *Adult Sunday School Teacher Quarterly*
International Pentecostal Holiness Church
Oklahoma City, Oklahoma

Lance Colkmire, M.A.
Editor, *Evangelical Sunday School Lesson Commentary*
Pathway Press
Cleveland, Tennessee

Charles W. Conn, Litt.D.
President Emeritus of Lee University and Official Historian of the Church of God
Cleveland, Tennessee

Greg Copley
Church of God State Youth and Christian Education Director
Jackson, Mississippi

Jerald Daffe, D.Min.
Associate Professor
Department of Bible and Christian Ministries
Lee University
Cleveland, Tennessee

Stephen P. Darnell, Th.D.
Church of God State Youth and Christian Education Director
Weatherford, Texas

Brady Dennis (Retired)
Former Church of God State Overseer
Greenville, South Carolina

Richard Fowler
Pastor, Church of God
Corbin, Kentucky

Carl R. Hobbs, Ed.D
Associate Pastor, Church of God
Cleveland, Tennessee

Bill Issacs
Church of God State Youth and Christian Education Director
Doraville, Georgia

Willie F. Lawrence, D.D.
Founder/Director
Messianic Jubilee Ministries
Palmetto, Florida

Lee Roy Martin, M.Div.
Pastor, Church of God
Cleveland, Tennessee

Aaron D. Mize, Chaplain I
Mississippi State Prison
Parchman, Mississippi

Chuck Noel
Church of God State Youth and Christian Education Director
Akron, Ohio

O.W. Polen, D.D. (Retired)
Former Editor in Chief
Pathway Press
Cleveland, Tennessee

Jerry Puckett
Director of Printing
Pathway Press
Cleveland, Tennessee

Richard D. Raines
Evangelist, Church of God
Valdosta, Georgia

John E. Renfro, Chaplain
ACPE Supervisor in Training
Quillen VA Medical Center
Mountain Home, Tennessee

Homer G. Rhea, L.H.D.
Editorial Coordinator
Church of God School of Ministry
Cleveland, Tennessee

Philip Siggelkow, Director
Church of God Prayer Power Partners
Saskatchewan, Canada

Jack D. Smith
Associate Pastor and Pastor of Senior Adults
Church of God
Cleveland, Tennessee

Robert B. Thomas, D.Litt.
Director of Special Projects in the
  School of Religion
Lee University
Cleveland, Tennessee

Dennis W. Watkins
Director of Legal Services
Church of God International Offices
Cleveland, Tennessee

Fred H. Whisman (Retired)
Former Cost Analyst
Pathway Press
Cleveland, Tennessee

Keith Whitt, M.Div.
Pastor, Church of God
Huntington, West Virginia

G. Faye Whitten, D.Min.
Evangelist
Doraville, Georgia

Charles G. Wiley
Pastor, Church of God
New Boston, Texas

TRUTH SEARCH WRITERS

Bob Bayles, Ph.D.
Professor, Lee University
Cleveland, Tennessee

Lance Colkmire, M.A.
Editor, *Evangelical Sunday School
  Lesson Commentary*
Pathway Press
Cleveland, Tennessee

Doug Murray, M.Div.
Teacher, Lee University
Cleveland, Tennessee

Richard D. Raines
Evangelist, Church of God
Valdosta, Georgia

SCRIPTURE TEXTS USED IN LESSON EXPOSITION

Deuteronomy
34:9	March 3

Joshua
1:1-3, 6-11, 16, 17	March 3
3:3-7	March 10
4:20-24	March 10
5:13-15	March 10
14:6, 9-13	March 17
15:16-19	March 17
24:2, 3, 11, 14-17, 20-24	March 24

Judges
4:1-4, 6-10, 14-16	April 7
13:3, 5	April 14
16:4, 17-21, 28-30	April 14

1 Samuel
1:9-16, 19, 20, 24-28	July 7
2:27, 28, 31, 34	July 14

1 Samuel (Cont.)
3:2-5, 8-10, 19-21	July 14
8:4-7, 9, 10, 19-22	July 21
10:17, 20, 21, 23, 24	July 21
12:3, 4, 6, 7, 11-13, 16-20, 23	July 28

1 Kings
18:20-24, 27-29, 36-39	August 4
21:2-4, 7, 14-19, 27-29	August 11

2 Kings
2:2, 6, 8-11, 14, 15, 19-22	August 18
5:1, 9-12, 14-16, 20, 25-27	August 25

Psalm
1:1-6	June 2
2:7-12	June 9

1 Peter

4:10	November 25
4:12-14	May 26

1 John

1:5-7	April 28

1 John (Cont.)

2:3-6	April 28
4:7-12, 19-21	November 18

Revelation

19:1-6	May 26

SCRIPTURE TEXTS USED IN GOLDEN TEXT HOMILIES

Deuteronomy

30:19	June 2

Joshua

1:7	March 17
3:7	March 10
24:15	March 24

1 Kings

18:21	August 4

Psalm

16:7	April 7
23:1	June 9
33:18	June 16
34:19	June 23
73:28	June 30
75:6, 7	March 3

Proverbs

4:23	April 14
11:3	August 25

Matthew

16:18	April 21
20:26, 27	November 25
25:40	August 11

Mark

16:15	May 12

Luke

2:11	December 23
2:52	December 2
4:18, 19	December 16
9:23	November 4
12:12	February 10
15:10	January 6
16:13	January 13
24:34	January 27

John

13:34, 35	November 18
14:27	December 30

Acts

2:36	February 3
2:39	May 19
13:26	February 17
14:22	May 26

Romans

3:28	September 9
6:11	September 16
6:23	September 2
8:2	September 23
10:12	October 7
12:1	October 14
12:2	July 21

1 Corinthians

11:26	January 20
15:20	March 31

2 Corinthians

2:14	September 30

Galatians

2:20	October 21
5:1	October 28

Ephesians

3:20, 21	May 5
4:1	July 14

Philippians

1:20	February 24
3:14	August 18

1 Thessalonians

5:17	July 7

1 Timothy

4:12	November 11
4:8	July 28

Hebrews

4:15	December 9
13:1	April 28

ACKNOWLEDGMENTS

Many books, magazines, and newspapers have been used in the research that has gone into this 2001-2002 *Evangelical Commentary*. A few of the major books that have been used are listed below.

Bibles

King James Version, Oxford University Press, Oxford, England
New American Standard Bible (NASB), A.J. Holman Co., Publishers, New York, New York
New English Bible (NEB), Oxford University Press, Oxford, England
New International Version (NIV), Zondervan Publishing House, Grand Rapids, Michigan
New King James Version (NKJV), Thomas Nelson Publishers, Nashville, Tennessee
The Berkeley Version, Zondervan Publishing House, Grand Rapids, Michigan

Commentaries

Clarke's Commentary, Abingdon-Cokesbury, Nashville, Tennessee
Commentaries on the Old Testament (Keil & Delitzsch), Eerdmans Publishing Co., Grand Rapids, Michigan
Ellicott's Bible Commentary, Zondervan Publishing House, Grand Rapids, Michigan
Expositions of Holy Scriptures (Alexander MacLaren), Eerdmans Publishing Co., Grand Rapids, Michigan
The Broadman Bible Commentary, Volumes 10 and 11, Broadman Press, Nashville, Tennessee
The Expositor's Greek Testament, Eerdmans Publishing Co., Grand Rapids, Michigan
The Interpreter's Bible, Abingdon Press, New York, New York
The Letters to the Corinthians, William Barclay, Westminster Press, Philadelphia, Pennsylvania
The Pulpit Commentary, Eerdmans Publishing Co., Grand Rapids, Michigan
The Wesleyan Commentary, Eerdmans Publishing Co., Grand Rapids, Michigan

Illustrations

A-Z Sparkling Illustrations, Stephen Gaukroger and Nick Mercer, Baker Books, Grand Rapids, Michigan
Dictionary of Illustrations for Pulpit and Platform, Moody Press, Chicago, Illinois
I Quote, George W. Stewart Publishers, Inc., New York, New York
Knight's Master Book of New Illustrations, Eerdmans Publishing Co., Grand Rapids, Michigan
Notes and Quotes, The Warner Press, Anderson, Indiana
1,000 New Illustrations, Al Bryant, Zondervan Publishing Co., Grand Rapids, Michigan
Quotable Quotations, Scripture Press Publications, Wheaton, Illinois
The Encyclopedia of Religious Quotations, Fleming H. Revell Co., Old Tappan, New Jersey
The Pointed Pen, Pathway Press, Cleveland, Tennessee
The Speaker's Sourcebook, Zondervan Publishing House, Grand Rapids, Michigan
3,000 Illustrations for Christian Service, Eerdmans Publishing Co., Grand Rapids, Michigan
Who Said That?, George Sweeting, Moody Press, Chicago, Illinois

General Reference Books

Harper's Bible Dictionary, Harper and Brothers Publishers, New York, New York
Pictorial Dictionary of the Bible, Zondervan Publishing House, Grand Rapids, Michigan
The International Standard Bible Encyclopedia, Eerdmans Publishing Co., Grand Rapids, Michigan
The Interpreter's Dictionary of the Bible, Abingdon Press, Nashville, Tennessee
The World Book Encyclopedia, Field Enterprises Education Corp., Chicago, Illinois
Word Pictures in the New Testament (Robertson), Broadman Press, Nashville, Tennessee

Evangelical Bible Lesson Series (1999-2006)

Fall Quarter September, October, November	Winter Quarter December, January, February	Spring Quarter March, April, May	Summer Quarter June, July, August
1999 Unit One—Beginnings (Genesis) Unit Two—Personal Ethics	**1999-2000** Unit One—Gospel of the King (Matthew) Unit Two—Growing Spiritually	**2000** Unit One—Ruth & Esther Unit Two—Divine Healing Unit Three—Great Prayers of the Bible	**2000** Unit One—Acts (Part 1) Unit Two—Family Relationships
2000 Unit One—Providence (Exodus) Unit Two—Spiritual Warfare Unit Three—Worship	**2000-2001** Unit One—Faith for the 21st Century Unit Two—Jesus the Servant (Mark)	**2001** Unit One—The Kingdom of God Unit Two—Law & Gospel (Leviticus-Deuteronomy)	**2001** Unit One—Acts (Part 2) Unit Two—Evangelism
2001 Unit One—Christian Living (Romans & Galatians) Unit Two—Christian Discipleship	**2001-2002** Unit One—The Gospel According to Luke Unit Two—Message of the Early Church	**2002** Unit One—Leadership (Joshua & Judges) Unit Two—The Church	**2002** Unit One—Psalms (Part 1) Unit Two—Learning From Samuel, Elijah & Elisha
2002 Unit One—Wisdom From Job, Proverbs, & Ecclesiastes Unit Two—God's Great Promises	**2002-2003** Unit One—Jesus the Son of God (John) Unit Two—Gifts of the Spirit	**2003** Unit One—Kings of Israel (Samuel, Kings, Chronicles) Unit Two—Second Coming	**2003** Unit One—Heaven & Hell Unit Two—Psalms (Part 2)
2003 Unit One—Judgment & Comfort (Isaiah) Unit Two—Values & Priorities	**2003-2004** Unit One—1 & 2 Corinthians Unit Two—Lesser-Known People of the Bible	**2004** Unit One—Jeremiah & Lamentations Unit Two—Out of Exile (Ezra & Nehemiah)	**2004** Unit One—Prison Epistles Unit Two—Revival & Renewal
2004 Unit One—God's Sovereignty (Ezekiel) Unit Two—James	**2004-2005** Unit One—1 & 2 Thessalonians Unit Two—Pastoral Epistles	**2005** Unit One—Minor Prophets I (Hosea-Micah) Unit Two—Redemption	**2005** Unit One—Faith (Hebrews) Unit Two—Daniel
2005 Unit One—Minor Prophets II (Nahum—Malachi) Unit Two—Parables of Jesus	**2005-2006** Unit One—Peter & Jude Unit Two—Numbers	**2006** Unit One—People Who Met Jesus Unit Two—Christian Formation (inc. Fruit of the Spirit)	**2006** Unit One—1, 2, 3 John Unit Two—Studies in Revelation

The month of September begins the fall quarter series of lessons, which is divided into two distinct units of study. Unit One (lessons 1-9) is presented under the theme "Christian Living (Romans and Galatians)." These lessons focus on how believers can lead victorious lives by walking in the Holy Spirit.

Unit Two (lessons 10-13) is a four-lesson study on "Christian Discipleship," challenging Christians to go deeper in their relationship with Jesus.

As a teacher, you must examine your own walk with God as you prayerfully prepare to teach these lessons through your example as well as your words.

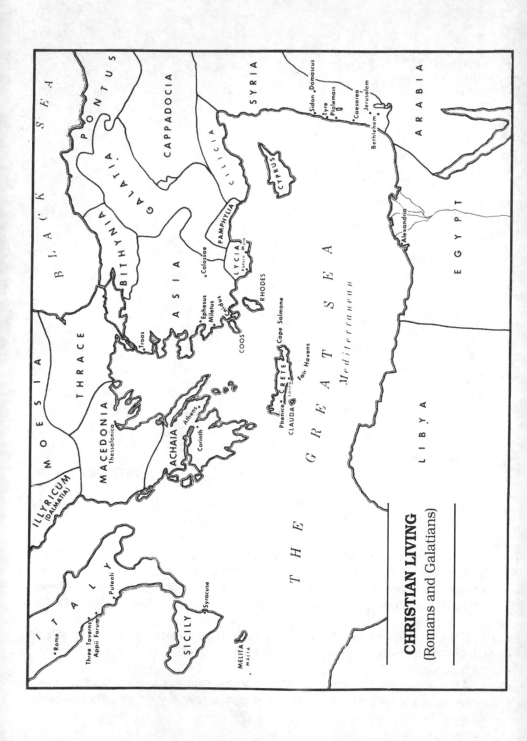

CHRISTIAN LIVING
(Romans and Galatians)

Need for Salvation

Study Text: Romans 1:1 through 3:31
Objective: To acknowledge the sinfulness of every person and proclaim Jesus Christ as the power of God for salvation.
Time: The Epistle to the Romans was written between A.D. 56 and 58.
Place: The Epistle to the Romans was written in the city of Corinth in Greece.
Golden Text: "The wages of sin is death; but the gift of God is eternal life through Jesus Christ our Lord" (Romans 6:23).
Central Truth: All people need the salvation Christ has provided.
Evangelism Emphasis: Jesus Christ died to provide salvation for every person.

PRINTED TEXT

Romans 1:16. For I am not ashamed of the gospel of Christ: for it is the power of God unto salvation to every one that believeth; to the Jew first, and also to the Greek.

17. For therein is the righteousness of God revealed from faith to faith: as it is written, The just shall live by faith.

18. For the wrath of God is revealed from heaven against all ungodliness and unrighteousness of men, who hold the truth in unrighteousness;

19. Because that which may be known of God is manifest in them; for God hath shewed it unto them.

20. For the invisible things of him from the creation of the world are clearly seen, being understood by the things that are made, even his eternal power and Godhead; so that they are without excuse.

2:17. Behold, thou art called a Jew, and restest in the law, and makest thy boast of God,

18. And knowest his will, and approvest the things that are more excellent, being instructed out of the law;

19. And art confident that thou thyself art a guide of the blind, a light of them which are in darkness,

20. An instructor of the foolish, a teacher of babes, which hast the form of knowledge and of the truth in the law.

21. Thou therefore which teachest another, teachest thou not thyself? thou that preachest a man should not steal, dost thou steal?

22. Thou that sayest a man should not commit adultery, dost thou commit adultery? thou that abhorrest idols, dost thou commit sacrilege?

23. Thou that makest thy boast of the law, through breaking the law dishonourest thou God?

24. For the name of God is blasphemed among the Gentiles through you, as it is written.

3:10. As it is written, There is none righteous, no, not one:

11. There is none that understandeth, there is none that seeketh after God.

12. They are all gone out of the way, they are together become unprofitable; there is none that doeth good, no, not one.

19. Now we know that what things soever the law saith, it saith to them who are under the law: that every mouth may be stopped, and all the world may become guilty before God.

20. Therefore by the deeds of the law there shall no flesh be justified in his sight: for by the law is the knowledge of sin.

LESSON OUTLINE

I. GENTILES NEED SALVATION

   A. Power of Righteous Faith

   B. Power of Corruption

II. JEWS NEED SALVATION

   A. Failure of the Law

   B. Circumcision of the Heart

III. ALL NEED SALVATION

   A. All Have Sinned

   B. All Are Guilty Before God

LESSON EXPOSITION

INTRODUCTION

The first three chapters of Romans burst on the scene and explode with a powerful message: Everyone has failed God, and the only answer is the salvation God has provided through His Son, Jesus Christ. Paul, all too familiar with the prideful climb of human achievement he experienced in his own life of religious piety, admits that all human efforts are insufficient to gain the favor of God. According to God's standards, every person fails completely and deserves eternal punishment.

Not a very persuasive message for today's pampered generation. Today's generation wants to hear how good they are, not how much they have failed. But in Romans 1—3, Paul records God's message to mankind, not mankind's message for God. What do we do when we are completely guilty? Turn in faith to a God who completely provided His Son for our salvation.

Paul's list of sinners would have

been surprising for many of his readers. The Jews thought their adherence to the Law, their heritage and their nationality would save them. The Gentiles had not been confronted with the reality of their sin. The intellectuals had reasoned themselves into innocence. The Gnostics thought they had reached such a high level of imagination that they were beyond sin.

Paul was writing to Rome—the center of sophistication, power, commerce and politics in his day. Rome was a fortress dedicated to the achievement of humanity. No army could defeat her, no intellect could challenge her, and no people could transcend her. The city and her people held the world in their hands. Her rulers spoke for the world and, in Rome's eyes, even for the "gods."

Assaulting the imagination, achievement and religion of Rome was Paul, crying out, "You have all sinned!" "You have all failed in the eyes of God!" "No one is exempt!" "There is absolutely no one who is righteous—no, not even one!"

Paul then moved from the message of failure to declare that God's mercy never fails. The message of mercy is only as effective as our understanding of sin and failure. If we do not feel we have sinned, we will not see our need for mercy, much less be grateful. The self-vindicating sinner will not receive God's mercy because the need for mercy will not even be seen.

The peril of missing God's mercy is that mercy is the foundation of salvation. Though salvation is supplied and mercy is applied, sin propels the prideful soul past God's grace. The individual who refuses to admit and repent of sin rejects God's salvation at the same time. Paul boldly approached the Romans about their sin in order that he might even more powerfully say that salvation was available to all.

I. GENTILES NEED SALVATION
(Romans 1:16-23)

A. Power of Righteous Faith
(vv. 16, 17)

16. For I am not ashamed of the gospel of Christ: for it is the power of God unto salvation to every one that believeth; to the Jew first, and also to the Greek.

17. For therein is the righteousness of God revealed from faith to faith: as it is written, The just shall live by faith.

Ashamed sets the personal tone for Paul in the Book of Romans. The gospel of Christ is not shameful, as many of the Jews believed. Rather, the gospel is the answer for shameful sinners.

When Paul said he was not ashamed of the gospel, he was really emphasizing that he was not ashamed of Christ.

Salvation is a personal story provided by a personal God. When we reject the gospel, we actually reject Christ himself. The person who says, "I love Christ, but I do not need to repent; neither do I need to believe the gospel message of repentance and salvation," is actually rejecting Christ himself.

Faith admits sin and accepts Christ. Living without shame is a process of faith, a relationship with the Christ of the gospel. Faith recognizes sin, moves to faith in God's mercy, and then moves to faith in God's salvation through Christ. Like water that brings life to a parched land, faith gives life to a person and produces the ability to have even more faith. The fountain of the river of faith begins with the headwaters of admission that one is a sinner.

Without any faith, the sinner stands guilty before God. The irony is that many sinners remained wrapped up in self-justification. Justification from God begins with faith to confess one's personal sin. Faith and righteousness before God are so interrelated that refusal of one automatically means the rejection of the other.

B. Power of Corruption (vv. 18-23)

(Romans 1:21-23 is not included in the printed text.)

18. For the wrath of God is revealed from heaven against all ungodliness and unrighteousness of men, who hold the truth in unrighteousness;

19. Because that which may be known of God is manifest in them; for God hath shewed it unto them.

20. For the invisible things of him from the creation of the world are clearly seen, being understood by the things that are made, even his eternal power and Godhead; so that they are without excuse.

The message about the sinfulness of humanity and the righteous requirements of God are revealed by God's creation. Observing nature indicates there is a Creator God who is to be worshiped. However, the corrupted self-righteousness of individuals keeps them from worshiping God. And failure to worship God leads to a corrupted relationship with creation.

Just as *faith* leads to more faith, *corruption* leads to more corruption. Corruption of creation's message about God leads humanity to corruption of the heart. This self-corruption is revealed and perpetuated by worshiping the creature rather than worshiping the Creator.

The corruption of the heart leads to a corrupted relationship with creation, all of which is unnatural. Loving, worshiping and serving God through Jesus Christ is the most natural thing a person can do. Self-indulgence and dependence upon this world is unnatural and does not fit with God's intention for creation and humanity.

The mind is the ultimate fatality of the self-indulgent corruption of creation. The mind continues to function, but in a dysfunctional way. What is right is thought to be wrong, and what is wrong is thought to be right. The mind convinces the person to turn away from God and then to consequently turn one's world away from God.

The picture of the sinner's condition in Romans 1:18-32 covers the entirety of a person's personality and existence. One's surroundings are affected. The heart, affections, emotions and mind of a person are affected. Finally, one's personal and social behavior is affected. One's spiritual condition affects every aspect of his or her life and personality. The "don't talk about religion," "what I believe doesn't matter" talk of the sinner is a deception. What someone believes about God and the gospel of Jesus Christ is the primary factor that determines all of that person's life, not just in eternity but on earth.

II. JEWS NEED SALVATION
   (Romans 2:17-29)

A. Failure of the Law (vv. 17-23)

17. Behold, thou art called a Jew, and restest in the law, and makest thy boast of God,
18. And knowest his will, and approvest the things that are more excellent, being instructed out of the law;
19. And art confident that thou thyself art a guide of the blind, a light of them which are in darkness,

20. An instructor of the foolish, a teacher of babes, which hast the form of knowledge and of the truth in the law.
21. Thou therefore which teachest another, teachest thou not thyself? thou that preachest a man should not steal, dost thou steal?
22. Thou that sayest a man should not commit adultery, dost thou commit adultery? thou that abhorrest idols, dost thou commit sacrilege?
23. Thou that makest thy boast of the law, through breaking the law dishonourest thou God?

Paul's declaration about the sinfulness of everyone is directed toward the Jewish readers of Romans 2. The Jews in Paul's day tried to hide their imperfection and sin behind the veil of the Law. Though the Law was from God, the Jews of the Law were not automatically perfect before God. In fact, the Law immediately made the Jews sinners. They felt they had kept the Law perfectly, even though they had personally failed to keep all the Law. Further, their presumption about the Law had led to pseudo piety and pompous claims about perfection.

Paul presses their presumptions by unveiling their imperfection—they had not kept every part of the Law. This meant complete failure before the law of God. The problem with prideful presumption about one's own piety is the lack of admission of one's true, sinful condition and the failure to properly receive the work of salvation based on God's own work.

B. Circumcision of the Heart
   (vv. 24-29)

(Romans 2:25-29 is not included in the printed text.)

24. For the name of God is blasphemed among the Gentiles through you, as it is written.

"The Gentiles have been better Jews than you have been!" is the final message directed at the Jews in Romans 2. One of the clearest marks of the Jews was circumcision. However, Paul cited the Old Testament principle of circumcision of the heart (Jeremiah 4:4; 9:26). God would much rather have circumcision of the heart than physical circumcision. Spiritual circumcision was the true test of one's relationship before God, not physical circumcision.

Paul declared to the Jews that the Gentiles who had been circumcised "in the Spirit" were truly the children of God. And the persistence of the Roman Jews about physical circumcision was a distraction from the true message of circumcision of the heart.

At the core of the failure of the Jews was not just the revelation of the Law but the revelation of their own boasting. Not only were they failing to keep every part of the Law, they were boasting about their walk with God (Romans 2:17). Pride turns godly praise (v. 29) into human boasting. The Jews were so self-confident about their religious piety. They had caught others about the Law, presuming the guilt of others but pre-empting any thought that they could be guilty of the same things. True praise is based upon the heart, not the deception of the mind.

III. ALL NEED SALVATION
(Romans 3:9-20)

A. All Have Sinned (vv. 9-18)

(Romans 3:9, 13-18 is not included in the printed text.)

10. As it is written, There is none righteous, no, not one:

11. There is none that understandeth, there is none that seeketh after God.

12. They are all gone out of the way, they are together become

unprofitable; there is none that doeth good, no, not one.

In verses 10-12, Paul used Psalm 14:1-3 to lament with David that all have sinned. This psalm of the sinner had a repeated introductory and concluding refrain, with four internal depictions that chanted the condition of the sinner. The introductory and summary refrain was that no one was righteous, not even one single individual.

The refrain is ironic because the concept of righteousness was created to describe the conduct of devout followers of God. However, there was no one who was doing what the concept demanded. God created a wonderful way of life for people to live in, and not even one person had found it.

The first internal chant lamenting the sinner was about the impact of sin upon the mind—"there is none that understandeth." For all the intellectual capability of the Romans, they had to come to realize they knew nothing about the ways of God. The Gentile Romans lived in a city that had created the foundational understandings for modern government and law. The Jewish Romans had perfected a system of moral teaching that rivaled the proficiency of the Romans. But neither group had any understanding of true, Biblical righteousness.

The second internal lament about sin was that no one was even headed in the right direction—"there is none that seeketh after God." Not only did each person lack understanding, but no one had even truly tried to come under God's righteousness. Everyone's pursuit of righteousness was tainted by self-indulgence, turned toward sensual perversion and terminated by sinful corruption.

The third internal lament declared no one was even on the right path—"they are all gone out of the way." By the third lament, the progressive intensity of everyone's failure is obvious.

First, no one understands; second, no one even cares; third, no one is even on the right track. Even if someone should begin to care, everyone is so far off track they have no hope of getting back on the right road to righteousness. Paul chose this psalm, no doubt, because it sings of how far everyone has sunk into the hopeless maze of sin, with no hope of finding a way out.

Finally, the song of the sinner laments the degenerative condition of everyone—"they are together become unprofitable." The first three laments identify the sentence that everyone lives under from which there is no way out. The fourth lament says the situation is steadily growing worse. There is no way out . . . the walls are closing in . . . and finally the walls will crush the individual. *Unprofitable* does not mean that the sinner merely is unproductive. Rather, the sinner is self-destructive.

In the repeated refrain in the last portion of verse 12, Paul recapitulates that everyone has sinned, they do not understand their condition, still worse they do not care, they are not even on the right track, and they are headed for destruction.

Verses 13-18 are a collection of other quotations from the Old Testament. Each quotation is a psalm about sin, describing both the sinner and the destructiveness of sin. Verses 13 and 14 (from Psalms 5:9; 140:3; 10:7) emphasize the sinfulness and death executed by the tongue. Verses 15-17 (from Proverbs 1:16; Isaiah 59:7, 8) describe the sinner's feet and where they take the sinner. Verse 18 (from Psalm 36:1) gives the concluding reason why the sinner sins—the sinner does not fear God.

It is interesting that Paul used songs about sin to describe sin. In Romans 2 Paul said the boasting of the pious Jews of Rome was actually corrupted praise. In chapter 3, Paul used worship and praise songs to describe the condition of the sinner. True praise includes not only glory to God but admission of humanity's sinful condition apart from God. Worship and adoration in the Scripture elevates God and confesses the individual's need for God. Psalms that describe the blessings given to the saints first of all declare the source of the blessing and the dependence of the child of God.

B. All Are Guilty Before God
   (vv. 19, 20)

19. Now we know that what things soever the law saith, it saith to them who are under the law: that every mouth may be stopped, and all the world may become guilty before God.

20. Therefore by the deeds of the law there shall no flesh be justified in his sight: for by the law is the knowledge of sin.

The Law is the instrument of condemnation, issuing a guilty verdict upon every person. The irony was that the Jews used the Law for their own vindication! The Gentiles ignored the Law, thinking they had beaten it. Paul declared that no one is exempt from the guilt mandated by the Law. God created the Law. Therefore, the sentence of guilt stood . . . eternally.

The Law was God's instrument to describe and define the distance between God and humanity. This distance is called sin. God measures the distance by naming the acts of sin found in the Law. Immorality is not just personal failure; it is the gulf between humanity and God. The expanse of sin cannot be crossed. Humanity has never been able to build a bridge that can cross the gulf of sin.

The mouths of people trying to explain their way out of guilt, express the depth of their remorse, or expound upon the unfairness of the Law are but futile attempts to sway the righteous judge, God. The Law is the master prosecutor. Paul burst into the lives of the Romans telling them that what they thought was their best defense for proving their own righteousness was actually the source of their own indictment and guilt.

In summary, Romans 1—3 burns with a message that people do not like to hear. In fact, the natural inclination is to resist the message of sin. Every ounce of human ingenuity tries to proclaim the achievement of men and women, not their failures. Praise easily becomes human, religious piety because pride so easily displaces devotion. God is made by individuals in their own image rather than God making people in His own image.

The only answer for humanity is belief in Christ. The gospel is the message that Christ is the bridge that overcomes the expanse of sin separating humanity from God. Not one effort of mankind has ever contributed to redemption; Christ finally and exclusively provided the antidote for the fatal disease of sin.

If a person is to receive salvation, there are four important truths he or she must realize. The first is that salvation is between a person and Christ, and one cannot be ashamed of Christ. A person cannot be compromised by others who elevate themselves above the simple faith of trusting in Christ. Salvation is never complicated; it is a simple belief. The simple belief is that Christ provides everything a person needs for salvation.

The individual's sinfulness is a second realization. The sinner's efforts at self-cleansing are not only futile, but they even make the situation worse. The only answer is admission of sin and acceptance of Christ.

God's mercy is a third realization. Having rejected the piety of others and admitted one's own sinfulness, the sinner now can accept God's mercy.

Confession of sin is the connection to God's mercy.

Finally, the life of faith is a concluding realization. At each passage in Romans 1—3, faith moves a person from one stage to the next. Faith moves a person past shame. Faith confronts the individual about confession of sin. Faith opens the manifold mercy of God before the believer. "From faith to faith" (1:17) Paul has declared the path of godly righteousness to follow.

GOLDEN TEXT HOMILY

"THE WAGES OF SIN IS DEATH; BUT THE GIFT OF GOD IS ETERNAL LIFE THROUGH JESUS CHRIST OUR LORD" (Romans 6:23).

The worst avalanche on record occurred on December 13, 1916, during World War I on the Austrian-Italian front. Thousands were buried alive.

The slightest vibration—a pistol shot or the crack of a whip—may start an avalanche on its downward, destructive plunge. There is a Swiss legend which says that the dulcet tones of a cello once triggered a major slide.

Avalanches are surpassed in destructiveness by sin and evil: "The wages of sin is death." Myriads topple and fall before sin's onslaughts, sinking helplessly in the maelstrom of vice.

Without Christ we are powerless to cope with sin. Martin Luther wrote:

Did we in our own strength confide,

Our striving would be losing;

Were not the right Man on our side,

The Man of God's own choosing.

The promise is unfailing: "When the enemy shall come in like a flood, the Spirit of the Lord shall lift up a standard against him" (Isaiah 59:19).—*Knight's Illustrations for Today*

SENTENCE SERMONS

ALL PEOPLE need the salvation Christ has provided.
—**Selected**

ABSOLUTE CANDOR is an indispensable requisite to salvation.
—**A.W. Tozer**

JESUS CHRIST died to provide salvation for every person.
—**Selected**

LOOKING at the wound of sin will never save anyone. What you must do is look at the remedy.
—**Dwight L. Moody**

EVANGELISM APPLICATION

JESUS CHRIST DIED TO PROVIDE SALVATION FOR EVERY PERSON.

To have provided salvation at all was a mighty act. Just as great, if not greater, was the fact that Christ provided salvation for every person who would repent and accept Christ as Savior. The sacrifice of Christ made possible both salvation and the provision of salvation.

Christ went to the cross, bearing its shame. He was disfigured and ridiculed on the cross (Isaiah 52) and He took the punishment of sinners on the cross (Isaiah 53). Every person needed salvation. Therefore, Christ provided salvation for all through His death on the cross.

The depth of Christ's provision exceeded the depth of humanity's sin.

The extent of the Cross surpassed the breadth of all of sin. The authority of the Cross was far greater than the threat of any sin.

ILLUMINATING THE LESSON

Elizabeth Brenner, a small-business owner in California, recalls a company where she worked as an office assistant many years ago: "It was a family-owned kitchen. And every day at lunch, the owner would formally dish out a bowl of white rice to all his employees. People might have their sandwiches and fast-food hamburgers too, but everyone took a little of that rice. I felt it created an old-fashioned civility" *(Moses on Management: 50 Leadership Lessons From the Greatest Manager of All Time, by D. Baron and L. Padwa).*

In a similar way, Christ, though He was the Son of the heavenly Father, provided nourishment from one source for all humanity's need for redemption.

DAILY BIBLE READINGS

M. God Requires Obedience.
   Deuteronomy 5:28-33
T. God Offers Restoration.
   Isaiah 1:18-20
W. God Provides Salvation.
   Isaiah 53:1-6
T. Christ Our Mediator.
   1 Timothy 2:1-7
F. Christ Our High Priest.
   Hebrews 7:23-28
S. Christ Is Coming.
   2 Peter 3:8-13

TRUTH SEARCH:
Creatively Teaching the Word

Aim: Students will pray against strongholds of sin in the local community.

Items needed: Marker board, marker

FOCUS

Write the Ten Commandments on the marker board: (1) Have no other gods. (2) Have no idols. (3) Don't misuse God's name. (4) Keep the Lord's day holy. (5) Honor parents. (6) Do not murder. (7) Do not commit adultery. (8) Do not steal. (9) Do not give false testimony. (10) Do not covet.

Discuss these questions:

• *In recent years there have been court battles regarding the placement of the Ten Commandments in public buildings. Why do you think some people oppose the display of these commandments?*

• *If you were to watch a typical evening of prime-time TV programming, how many of the Ten Commandments would you likely see violated?*

• *Just think about this question: How many of these commandments have you broken?*

EXPLORE

Divide the class into small groups of three or four students each. Assign half of the groups Romans 1:18-25; assign verses 26-32 to the other groups. Have the groups answer the following questions about their particular passage.

Romans 1:18-25

1. What causes God to be filled with wrath?

2. Could anyone legitimately argue, "I'm innocent because no one has ever told me about God"? Why or why not?

3. Describe the downward spiritual spiral described in verses 21-25.

4. How does the Bible label what the world calls "sexual freedom"?

5. What is the great deception described in verse 25?

Romans 1:26-32

1. What lifestyle is pictured in verses 26 and 27? Is it described as an acceptable alternative or a sinful practice?

2. Divide the sins listed in verses 29-31 into two categories: sins of the heart and sins of action. Which ones are more evil?

3. According to verse 32, what is the price of sin?

4. Why do people knowingly practice sin and even approve those who practice sin?

Bring the groups back together and discuss their answers.

RESPOND

Prepare to present Romans 3:10-12 as a choral reading by asking the class to say "No, not even one," after you read each verse. Then do the reading. **Everyone in our community has sinned, yet some of us have repented. However, many have not turned to Christ, and some people even enjoy flaunting their sin.**

Have the class identify areas in your community that are strongholds of sin. Then have different individuals take turns praying about these areas one at a time while the others agree in prayer.

Justification Through Faith

Study Text: Romans 3:21 through 4:25
Objective: To recognize our need of justification and obtain righteousness through faith in Jesus Christ.
Time: The Epistle to the Romans was written between A.D. 56 and 58.
Place: The Epistle to the Romans was written in the city of Corinth in Greece.
Golden Text: "We conclude that a man is justified by faith without the deeds of the law" (Romans 3:28).
Central Truth: Sinners are made righteous through faith in Christ Jesus.
Evangelism Emphasis: Sinners are made righteous through faith in Christ Jesus.

PRINTED TEXT

Romans 3:21. But now the righteousness of God without the law is manifested, being witnessed by the law and the prophets;

22. Even the righteousness of God which is by faith of Jesus Christ unto all and upon all them that believe: for there is no difference:

23. For all have sinned, and come short of the glory of God;

24. Being justified freely by his grace through the redemption that is in Christ Jesus:

25. Whom God hath set forth to be a propitiation through faith in his blood, to declare his righteousness for the remission of sins that are past, through the forbearance of God;

26. To declare, I say, at this time his righteousness: that he might be just, and the justifier of him which believeth in Jesus.

4:1. What shall we say then that Abraham our father, as pertaining to the flesh, hath found?

2. For if Abraham were justified by works, he hath whereof to glory; but not before God.

3. For what saith the scripture? Abraham believed God, and it was counted unto him for righteousness.

4. Now to him that worketh is the reward not reckoned of grace, but of debt.

5. But to him that worketh not, but believeth on him that justifieth the ungodly, his faith is counted for righteousness.

16. Therefore it is of faith, that it might be by grace; to the end the promise might be sure to all the seed; not to that only which is of the law, but to that also which is of the faith of Abraham; who is the father of us all.

18. Who against hope believed in hope, that he might become the father of many nations; according to that which was spoken, So shall thy seed be.

19. And being not weak in faith, he considered not his own body now dead, when he was about an hundred years old, neither yet the deadness of Sara's womb:

20. He staggered not at the promise of God through unbelief; but was strong in faith, giving glory to God;

21. And being fully persuaded that, what he had promised, he was able also to perform.

22. And therefore it was imputed to him for righteousness.

LESSON OUTLINE

I. RIGHTEOUSNESS BY FAITH

　A. Righteousness Manifested by Faith

　B. Righteousness Decreed by Faith

　C. Righteousness Applied by Faith

II. JUSTIFICATION NOT BY WORKS

　A. Righteousness Through Faith

　B. Righteousness Not by Works

　C. Righteousness Before Works

III. JUSTIFICATION AVAILABLE TO ALL

　A. Promise to All Who Believe

　B. Justification From God

　C. Resurrection Power Available to All Who Believe

LESSON EXPOSITION

INTRODUCTION

Paul proclaims the manifestation of God's righteousness in Romans 3:19—4:25 after laying out the mire of human sinfulness in 1:16—3:18. He compares God's righteousness and humanity's sinfulness, declaring righteousness the winner. As deep as sin was, God's righteousness is deeper. As condemning as the verdict of guilt, even more liberating is God's declaration of righteous amnesty. As futile as attempts at self-righteousness were, so even greater is the fulfillment of the success of God's righteousness.

The righteousness of God cannot be stopped because it has already been provided. His righteousness can be rejected, but that does not stop the fact that God has already provided it. A person can say, "God, I don't want Your righteousness," and thereby not receive it. Nevertheless, because of His mercy, God still continues to offer righteousness to all who will receive it.

The righteousness of God is powerful in itself. However, the fact that God would make His righteousness manifest to sinful humanity is indeed a miracle. For many religions of the world, a supreme being must remain unapproachable to maintain "divine" status. By contrast, not only can the God of Scripture be approached, He took the first step through His Son. Still further, His very own righteousness is made available, continually, to repentant sinners.

Another aspect of God's righteousness is that it involves the Son of the heavenly Father. It is a personal righteousness, not a philosophy. It is even more than a "way of life." It is a personal, family investment by the God of heaven and earth. God did not send a messenger or even a prophet to communicate and provide His righteousness. He sent His very own Son. The righteousness itself is His Son. God's righteousness is a personal provision, not a religious ritual. To know and receive God's righteousness requires knowing God through His Son.

While people have always tried to substitute their own goodness for God's provision of righteousness, God has provided the opportunity to participate in His righteousness and receive eternal life. Divine righteousness comes through a relationship with Christ. The relationship God desires is one of faithfulness, love and faith, fulfilling the requirements of righteousness and built upon eternal foundations. Outside of relationship with God, righteousness is an empty quest that ends in failure.

I. RIGHTEOUSNESS BY FAITH (Romans 3:21-31)

A. Righteousness Manifested by Faith (vv. 21, 22)

21. But now the righteousness of God without the law is manifested, being witnessed by the law and the prophets;

22. Even the righteousness of God which is by faith of Jesus Christ unto all and upon all them that believe: for there is no difference.

Other religions, even Judaism, made righteousness a pursuit, a quest, a journey. But Paul declared that the righteousness of God has already been *manifested*—"completely revealed and made available." God has made righteousness immediately available, not rigidly distant.

Even before Christ's sacrifice, the Word of God in the Books of the Law and the Prophets referred to the righteousness of God provided in Christ. However, the Roman Jews had come to believe that fulfilling the Law through a life of religious piety provided righteousness. On the contrary, godly righteousness has already been provided through relationship with Christ.

A critical distinctive of righteousness in Christ is its provision to all people. The righteousness of the Law was reduced to an exclusive group of moral achievers. On the contrary, the righteousness of Christ is available to anyone who will have faith in Christ. Flowing from that relationship comes confession of sin, moral character and worship to God. Christ is the source of righteousness. The Law only presented the quest for an unachievable goal.

B. Righteousness Decreed by Faith (vv. 23-26)

23. For all have sinned, and come short of the glory of God;

24. Being justified freely by his grace through the redemption that is in Christ Jesus:

25. Whom God hath set forth to be a propitiation through faith in his blood, to declare his righteousness for the remission of sins that are past, through the forbearance of God;

26. To declare, I say, at this time his righteousness: that he might be just, and the justifier of him which believeth in Jesus.

Many readers stop at verse 23. They feel the goal of the verse is to reflect the condition of lost humanity. However, the description of sin and the hopelessness of the sinful life is completed at verse 20. From verse 21, Paul changes the topic to the real hope in God's righteousness.

The real power of verse 23 is that it sets the stage for verse 24, the contrasting provision of God's righteousness. While everyone remains short of God's standard, God has already made provision for receiving the standard.

The first word of verse 24 is powerful. *Being* indicates a currently existing condition. The timing of God's provision of righteousness is already completed. That is, at the same time a person is short of God's standard, God has already provided justification. When a person confesses his or her sin, he or she is accepting a gift already made available to them. God does not begin to provide justification when a person repents; He has already provided the justification and waits for a person to accept it. God has already taken the first step.

The price of the justification is just as powerful as the timing. God, in His Son, has already provided and paid for our justification. Paul told the Romans, in essence, "While you have been trying to pay for something, God has already purchased it for you."

The price was personal to the heavenly Father. He reached into the depths of what was most valuable to Him—He presented His dearest possession, His only Son. Essentially, He was paying for our righteousness through a personal investment, out of His own family.

Even deeper are the depths of the price paid by the Son of God. Christ reached deep within Himself and presented all of Himself. His price was total, claiming His very life. The price of His own life is the declaration of the value of our justification.

The heavenly Father gave His Son and the Son gave His life. While impossible to take the possession of the Father and the life of the Son, it was not impossible that they would give of themselves freely. Something freely given always meets the price demanded.

The "blood" (v. 25) declares the provision of justification. The gospel does not have to be manufactured or propped up. Christ's sacrifice speaks for itself. A "declaration" was an official event at which a new reality was introduced. It may have been a verdict at court, a price that had to be paid, or a new relationship such as an adoption. Once declared, it stood. The blood shed by Christ in His sacrifice at Calvary declared and thereby established the reality of the Father's provision of justification.

C. Righteousness Applied by Faith (vv. 27-31)

(Romans 3:27-31 is not included in the printed text.)

Prerequisite for the price of justification to be applied to a life is faith in Christ. Faith, in effect, says, "I accept the purchase and sacrifice of the Son for my justification."

Even if a gift is paid for, it can still be rejected. The tragedy of disbelief is that it is the rejection of a relationship. The blessing of faith is that it is the entry into a relationship relationship with the Father and the Son, who both freely gave to complete justification. When justification is received, relationship is realized. The blood made possible the bond of faith with the Father through the Son.

II. JUSTIFICATION NOT BY WORKS (Romans 4:1-12)

A. Righteousness Through Faith (vv. 1-3)

1. What shall we say then that Abraham our father, as pertaining to the flesh, hath found?

2. For if Abraham were justified by works, he hath whereof to glory; but not before God.

3. For what saith the scripture? Abraham believed God, and it was counted unto him for righteousness.

Paul brings the Romans, particularly the Jews, back to the relationship they had with Abraham, who was the father of the nation of Israel. Out of his seed came a bond relating all of them to one another. With Abraham, the religion of Israel was a relationship between each of them, spanning many generations. The Jewish people felt they were linked to God through Abraham's relationship with God.

Recognizing that the link with God for the Jews of Rome went back to Abraham, Paul told them that Abraham's link with God was only made possible by faith. The Jews had set up a series of works they had to do to achieve "Abraham-like" relationship with God, when in fact Abraham himself knew God through faith.

Abraham clearly had depended on God for every stage of his life. He depended on God when he was in a new land, when he had to defeat his enemies and the enemies of Lot, when he had to have a son to continue his generations, and when he had to obey God even to the point of offering up his son.

The Jews had become bound by achievement and ritual, depending on their own efforts than the acts of God. Paul declared that Abraham was not an achiever before he was a believer. The greatness of Abraham was his faith, not his accomplishments; his relationship with God, not his own abilities; his dependence on God, not the number of people who depended on him.

B. Righteousness Not by Works (vv. 4-8)

(Romans 4:6-8 is not included in the printed text.)

4. Now to him that worketh is the reward not reckoned of grace, but of debt.

5. But to him that worketh not, but believeth on him that justifieth the ungodly, his faith is counted for righteousness.

The individual who "works" for relationship with God does so out of obligation, not grace. Obligation expects a reward. The principle of *work* is based on debt. Work is done to create a debt. Out of the debt, a reward is given.

Heaven is not a reward as much as it is a gift. A blessing is not a return on an investment but a gift. Answers to prayers are not the result of our "doing our part." Rather, answers to prayer flow from the gracious heart of the heavenly Father.

God is not a broker bargaining for our salvation. We are not auctioneers bidding for God's favor. Faith in God's gift of eternal life is our righteous inheritance.

The bond between the heavenly Father and His children is faith, not debt. Our "work" as believers is the result of our relationship with God, not part of our quest for that relationship. "Stop working for your salvation," was Paul's declaration. The adoption into the family of God was already accomplished through Christ. Being righteous before God is a realization of faith, not a debt that grows out of doubt.

In verses 6-8, Paul quoted Psalm 32:1, 2 to confirm that David, as well as Abraham, enjoyed the blessedness of forgiveness by faith rather than by works.

C. Righteousness Before Works (vv. 9-12)

(Romans 4:9-12 is not included in the printed text.)

Being right comes from believing right, working it out does not work, and Abraham was righteous before he was circumcised—these were the principles Paul was teaching the Romans. Faith, not circumcision, was the heritage of the Jews. Faith, not trying to be "good enough," is the heritage of the Christian. The believer becomes good because of what Christ has already done.

God does not want lazy or irresponsible believers. Righteousness is not cheap. However, the price of our righteousness is already paid by Christ. We work for Christ because we *are* Christians—not to become Christians. Irresponsibility is to persist in putting Christian labor before loving the Father.

Paul reviewed the history of Abraham, pointing out that Abraham received the promises of God (Genesis 12) and believed them without first being circumcised.

Circumcision had become for the Jews the necessary act to become part of the people of God. But the father of their faith, Abraham, was justified before he was circumcised. The lesson: Belief proceeds action. The prescription: Faith empowers work. The message: Righteousness is a relationship of trust that leads to faithful service.

III. JUSTIFICATION AVAILABLE TO ALL (Romans 4:13-25)

A. Promise to All Who Believe (vv. 13-16)

(Romans 4:13-15 is not included in the printed text.)

16. Therefore it is of faith, that it might be by grace; to the end the promise might be sure to all the seed; not to that only which is of the law, but to that also which is of the faith of Abraham; who is the father of us all.

Promise empowers; law creates debt. The promise of the heavenly Father is more powerful than His law because His promise flows from His love and grace. The Law was a temporary instructor required by the sinfulness of humanity. Grace gives and gives, making salvation available to generation after generation ("sure to all the seed," v. 16). Grace does not need to be prompted or pumped. Grace flows from the loving heart of God.

One requirement—faith—is necessary to receive redemption for sin, salvation and the righteousness of the heavenly Father. A lifetime of service, worship, adoration and discipleship is to follow faith. Faith is not really a requirement as much as a response. God offered His wonderful gift of righteousness, and each person can receive the gift by responding in faith relationship with the Father.

The problem for the Jewish believers in Rome was that they had accepted the concept that only a select group who had completed a certain number of steps were even eligible to be considered by God as candidates to receive His righteousness. Paul says that God's righteousness is given on the basis of faith, and faith can be exercised by anyone. All are eligible to be righteous in God.

B. Justification From God (vv. 17-22)

(Romans 4:17 is not included in the printed text.)

18. Who against hope believed in hope, that he might become the father of many nations; according to that which was spoken, So shall thy seed be.

19. And being not weak in faith, he considered not his own body now dead, when he was about an hundred years old, neither yet the deadness of Sara's womb:

20. He staggered not at the promise of God through unbelief; but was strong in faith, giving glory to God;

21. And being fully persuaded that, what he had promised, he was able also to perform.

22. And therefore it was imputed to him for righteousness.

"Fully persuaded" (v. 21) described Abraham's faith. "Fully persuaded" is translated from a Greek word that was comprised of two words, *plethos* and *phero*. *Plethos* emphasized something being fully accomplished versus something empty or incomplete. *Phero* emphasized bringing and applying something that leads the way. When Paul says Abraham's faith was a full persuasion about God, the emphasis was upon Abraham's complete commitment to God that led his life.

Faith means that God is the first priority, leading our life. Openly applied, completely filling our life and moving our life forward, faith in God is fully trusting in Him. This full faith is the basis of our righteousness.

Abraham was fully persuaded of God's action, not his own work. He was so committed to what God was doing that it changed his own behavior. Abraham did work, but it was based on his persuasion of God, not the persuasion of his own efforts.

Accompanying Abraham's persuasion was glory to God (v. 20). Again, his focus was on God's work before his own work. The Law had worshipers working their way up to praise through a series of sacrifices. The way of faith had worshipers responding to what God had done and promised. Law required praise; faith responded with praise. The former did not require a sincere heart; the latter could only be given by a truly devoted heart.

C. Resurrection Power Available to All Who Believe (vv. 23-25)

(Romans 4:23-25 is not included in the printed text.)

Justification was the ultimate tribute to the life of faith. The Law led to guilt and shame; faith led to promise and justification. The dead seed of Abraham (vv. 17, 19) was brought to life by faith, while the Law could only produce a barren womb. In the halls of eternal justice, the Law would only prosecute. Faith would defend, justify and release.

The Roman Gentiles were well aware of the importance of justification. Law was the core of their society. Whereas the Hebrews sought a sign and the Greeks sought men of knowledge, the Romans relied on a system of justice to govern life and society. Principles of Roman law remain as foundational for principles of law and government in many countries around the world today.

The Roman Jews were also well aware of the importance of justification. For centuries they had observed the sacrifices and worship called for by the Law in order to submit to the requirements of religious practice dictated by the Law. This system and way of life remains even to this day.

Faith breaks in upon the centuries-old practices of Roman law and the foundations of Jewish ritual to finally do what they could not do—provide a means whereby a person can be justified before an almighty God. Though perfected for human government, Roman law still lacked eternal authority. Though from God, the law of the Old Testament could only fulfill sacrificial obligation. Springing from the love of God, the faith relationship between the repentant sinner and God himself breaks the shackles of eternal guilt and rewrites the criminal record of the saint, declaring that the believer is fully, eternally justified. Having been justified, the Christian is now free to serve God in a righteous relationship.

GOLDEN TEXT HOMILY

"WE CONCLUDE THAT A MAN IS JUSTIFIED BY FAITH WITHOUT THE DEEDS OF THE LAW" (Romans 3:28).

Justification is one facet of the great salvation diamond (there are other facets!). One of the clearest definitions of *justification* is that of John Wesley: "The plain Scriptural notion of justification is *pardon*, the forgiveness of sins. It is that act of God the Father, whereby, for the sake of the propitiation (or atoning sacrifice) made by the blood of His Son, 'he showeth forth his righteousness (or mercy) by the remission of sins that are past.' This is the easy, natural account of it given by St. Paul throughout this whole epistle. . . . And from the time we are 'accepted through the Beloved,' 'reconciled to God through his blood,' He loves and blesses and watches over us for good, even as if we had never sinned" (*Works of John Wesley*, Vol. 5).

Paul took pains to insist that this great blessing is received solely by faith, "faith in his blood" (v. 25), and "apart from the deeds of the law" (*NKJV*), or, as the *New English Bible* renders it, "apart from success in keeping the law" (v. 28).

Paul described this great experience of "justification by faith alone" (as Luther translated it, and never ceased to insist) as a "blessedness": "David also describeth the blessedness of the man, unto whom God imputeth righteousness without works, saying, Blessed are they whose iniquities are forgiven, and whose sins are covered. Blessed is the man to whom the Lord will not impute sin" (Romans 4:6-8).

No wonder Luther said when he grasped this truth and entered into this experience, "I felt that the gates of Paradise had opened to me," and that John Wesley, on the evening of May 24, 1738, in Aldersgate Street, London, felt his heart "strangely warmed." And no wonder that Philip Doddridge, in retrospect, could sing:

O happy day that fixed my choice
On Thee, my Saviour and my God!
Well may my glowing heart rejoice,
And tell its raptures all abroad.

It is a superlatively wonderful thing to know "the blessedness" of free and full forgiveness through the precious blood of Jesus by faith alone.—**Noel Brooks**

SENTENCE SERMONS

SINNERS are made righteous through faith in Christ Jesus.

—Selected

THE DOCTRINE of justification is the foundation that supports all of the other benefits we receive through Christ.

—Erwin W. Lutzer

JUSTIFICATION means "just-as-if-I-never-sinned."

—*Drapers Book of Quotations for the Christian World*

INDIVIDUALS ARE justified *judicially* by God (Romans 8:33); *meritoriously* by Christ (Isaiah 53:11); *mediately* by faith (Romans 5:1); *evidentially* by works (James 2:14, 18-24).

—**William Evans**

EVANGELISM APPLICATION

SINNERS ARE MADE RIGHTEOUS THROUGH FAITH IN CHRIST JESUS.

Righteousness is not a commodity that can be brokered by human talent, resources or ingenuity; it is a condition that is created only by God. Righteousness is not an achievement that can be claimed by religion, devotion or sincerity; it is the result of God's action. Righteousness is not an alternative lifestyle that can be "picked up" or "cast aside" by human choice, preference or convenience; it is God's choice of grace for each person to accept or reject on his or her own.

The glorious news is that God does transform sinners into saints. An impossible task according to human ability, God has made turning the unrighteous into the righteous part of His work. If a sinner repents of sin, the glorious conversion from being guilty to becoming godly takes place. Christ becomes Lord of that person's life and sins are forgiven.

ILLUMINATING THE LESSON

The old adage "Is the cup half-full or is it half-empty?" raises an important perspective for the believer. If the cup is perceived as only being partially filled, or half-empty, the believer has missed the point of Christ's provision.

The cup—the believer—cannot be both corrupted with sin and pure in Christ. The measure of the cup is not nearly as important as the quality of the contents of the cup. The heavenly Father stands ready with a "pitcher" of the grace of Christ to pour into the believer.

The quantity of the cup is important nevertheless. Once the Father pours in the provision of the Son, the believer is not partially full but abundantly full. In fact, the abundance of the grace of God is such that the pouring never stops. The cup is filled and then overflows with God's grace because the flow never stops. Once the filthiness of sin is removed, the cup begins receiving the grace and salvation of the Lord. The believer can put a "lid" on the cup or remove himself or herself from the flow, thereby not receiving from the Lord. The awful presence of sin can be allowed to corrupt the contents once again. However, the abundant provision of God is like a cup that is overflowing, not half anything.

DAILY BIBLE READINGS

M. Delight in God's Way.
   Psalm 1:1-6
T. God Loves Righteousness.
   Psalm 11:1-7
W. A Life of Faith.
   Habakkuk 2:1-4
T. Live by Faith.
   Romans 5:1-11
F. Saved Through Faith.
   Ephesians 2:1-9
S. Saved Through Mercy.
   Titus 3:1-8

TRUTH SEARCH:
Creatively Teaching the Word

Aim: Students will ask Christ to help them see themselves as He sees them, then put their faith in His ability to justify them.

Item needed: Hand mirror

FOCUS

Have the students name different excuses a person might use to try to justify himself in the following situations:

- Arriving late for work
- Being stopped for speeding
- Screaming at a family member
- Missing Sunday school

We all try to justify our actions at times. Sometimes our excuses are valid; many times they are not. Today's lesson is about justification—being declared righteous before God.

EXPLORE

Have a volunteer read Romans 3:21-31 aloud. Then discuss these questions:

- *According to verse 23, what is the status of every individual before God?*
- *What cannot make a sinner righteous? What can make a sinner righteous (vv. 22, 23)?*
- *What does it cost someone to be made righteous by Jesus (v. 24)?*
- *Since God is a just God, He must punish sinfulness. So how can God be just and yet make sinners righteous at the same time (vv. 25, 26)?*
- *Can a person be justified by keeping all the laws of God? Why or why not (vv. 27, 28)?*

Have a volunteer read Romans 4:1-8 aloud. Then discuss the following questions:

- *How was Abraham declared righteous (vv. 1-3)?*
- *Name the ways in which the justified person is blessed (vv. 7, 8).*

Have another volunteer read verses 16-25. Then discuss these questions:

- *How widespread has God made the offer of justification (vv. 16, 17)?*
- *Why was Abraham's faith "credited to him for righteousness" (vv. 19-22)?*
- *How does a person receive justification today (vv. 23, 24)?*

RESPOND

Pick up the mirror. As you look in the mirror, describe how you *wish* you looked—ways in which you would like your appearance to be different.

I was just kidding myself, wasn't I?

Do we sometimes do the same thing with God—pretending we "look good" spiritually, trying to justify ourselves?

The truth is that justification cannot take place until we come to God "just as I am, without one plea, but that Thy blood was shed for me."

Conduct a time of silent prayer in which students will (1) ask Christ to help them see themselves as He sees them and (2) trust Him to justify them.

Freedom From Sin's Power

Study Text: Romans 6:1-23
Objective: To realize that believers are dead to sin and live for Christ in newness of life.
Time: The Epistle to the Romans was written between A.D. 56 and 58.
Place: The Epistle to the Romans was written in the city of Corinth in Greece.
Golden Text: "Reckon ye also yourselves to be dead indeed unto sin, but alive unto God through Jesus Christ our Lord" (Romans 6:11).
Central Truth: Believers can live righteously in Christ, because they are no longer enslaved to sin.
Evangelism Emphasis: Sinners can be set free from sin through Christ.

PRINTED TEXT

Romans 6:1. What shall we say then? Shall we continue in sin, that grace may abound?

2. God forbid. How shall we that are dead to sin, live any longer therein?

3. Know ye not, that so many of us as were baptized into Jesus Christ were baptized into his death?

4. Therefore we are buried with him by baptism into death: that like as Christ was raised up from the dead by the glory of the Father, even so we also should walk in newness of life.

5. For if we have been planted together in the likeness of his death, we shall be also in the likeness of his resurrection:

6. Knowing this, that our old man is crucified with him, that the body of sin might be destroyed, that henceforth we should not serve sin.

7. For he that is dead is freed from sin.

8. Now if we be dead with Christ, we believe that we shall also live with him:

9. Knowing that Christ being raised from the dead dieth no more; death hath no more dominion over him.

10. For in that he died, he died unto sin once: but in that he liveth, he liveth unto God.

11. Likewise reckon ye also yourselves to be dead indeed unto sin, but alive unto God through Jesus Christ our Lord.

12. Let not sin therefore reign in your mortal body, that ye should obey it in the lusts thereof.

15. What then? shall we sin, because we are not under the law, but under grace? God forbid.

16. Know ye not, that to whom ye yield yourselves servants to obey, his servants ye are to whom ye obey; whether of sin unto death, or of obedience unto righteousness?

17. But God be thanked, that ye were the servants of sin, but ye have obeyed from the heart that form of doctrine which was delivered you.

18. Being then made free from sin, ye became the servants of righteousness.

22. But now being made free from sin, and become servants to God, ye have your fruit unto holiness, and the end everlasting life.

23. For the wages of sin is death; but the gift of God is eternal life through Jesus Christ our Lord.

LESSON OUTLINE

I. DEAD TO SIN
    A. Grace Is Separate From Sin
    B. Burial Leads to Life
    C. Death Leads to Freedom

II. ALIVE TO CHRIST
    A. No More Dominion of Sin
    B. Reckon Yourselves Free
    C. Yield Yourselves Under Grace

III. SERVANTS TO RIGHTEOUSNESS
    A. Servants Brought From Sin
        to Righteousness
    B. Fruit Unto Holiness
    C. Gift of Eternal Life

LESSON EXPOSITION

INTRODUCTION

Servant, slave, shackled, imprisoned, bound—these are words that describe the life of sin. The lost (those who refuse the salvation of the Lord) think they are free. Freedom, according to the sinner, is the ability to do what you want, when you want and wherever you want. Sin is not freedom. Sin is deception. Life becomes a lie. Sin does not create freedom; it only perpetuates imprisonment.

Paul knew all too well the shackles of sin. Driven by religiosity, endeavoring to demonstrate his "righteous" achieving, Paul's life was a cycle of sinful, flesh-based pursuit. He had deceived himself—he was not living for the glory of God.

The only solution to the deception of sin is death to sin through Jesus Christ. Release from the dungeon of deception is achieved through the sacrifice of Christ on the cross and the spiritual death of the believer to sin. As much as Paul knew the stronghold of sin, he also preached the liberation of grace. The Law could only penalize the sinner and point to sin. Grace purchased freedom from sin and life in Christ.

The Christian must have an accurate understanding of the strength of sin in order to receive the depth of God's grace. A major part of the deception of sin is the minimizing of what must be done to sin. Paul said in Romans 6 that sin must be put to death through Jesus Christ.

"Die to sin if you want to live in newness of life in Christ" was Paul's message to the Romans. The believer not only believes in Christ, but also joins with Christ in the process of death, burial and resurrection. The believer does not die on a literal cross but a spiritual one. Nevertheless, the reality of the Christian's spiritual death is just as real as the physical death of Christ on the cross. And that spiritual death is the result of the death and sacrifice of Christ on the cross.

The doctrine of the resurrection was a challenge to Jews and Gentiles in Rome. Many in Judaism and in Roman society did not believe in the resurrection. They were aware of the reality of capital punishment—the sentence of death for transgressions of ancient or Jewish law. However, many had little tolerance for the belief that there would be a resurrected body after death. Existence after death for many was at best mystical or surreal. If it did exist, it was unknowable. Therefore, Paul confronted the Romans' thinking when he taught that the sinful nature of the believer could be rendered dead spiritually and that a resurrection of the body, even spiritually, could take place.

I. DEAD TO SIN (Romans 6:1-7)

A. Grace Is Separate From Sin
    (vv. 1, 2)

1. What shall we say then? Shall we continue in sin, that grace may abound?

2. God forbid. How shall we that are dead to sin, live any longer therein?

What happens to sin when salvation occurs? Sin led to the need for grace. Sin created the need for the cross. Sin is a reminder of the reality of the Enemy. Should sin continue in order to point people to God? Absolutely not, was Paul's response in Romans 6. Sin is dangerous. Sin is deceptive. Sin must be dealt with and delivered unto death.

Grace does not depend on sin, and neither does anything else in the Christian life. Grace is freely given from the heart of God, and it is dependent upon no one or nothing—especially not sin. Grace is not fed or sped by sin. Grace deals the death-blow to sin.

The existence of sin brings the need for grace, but the existence of grace brings the termination of sin. The believer can reject grace and thereby invite the existence of sin. However, the existence of sin is not necessary for the presence of grace. The greater the presence of grace, the lesser becomes the presence of sin.

B. Burial Leads to Life (vv. 3-5)

3. Know ye not, that so many of us as were baptized into Jesus Christ were baptized into his death?

4. Therefore we are buried with him by baptism into death: that like as Christ was raised up from the dead by the glory of the Father, even so we also should walk in newness of life.

5. For if we have been planted together in the likeness of his death, we shall be also in the likeness of his resurrection.

Sin and grace are not private issues. They are both inextricably connected to the Savior. The believer does not wage private wars against sin. When a person becomes a Christian, Christ enters the field of battle. Sin is defeated, and grace is the weapon used by the Savior to defeat the Enemy.

Christ died to make the victory of grace and death of sin possible. The believer is baptized into the death and victory of Christ. Water baptism is not salvation, but it illustrates the faith of the believer in Christ. Faith is putting to death the wages of sin. Just as an individual is submerged in baptism—just as Christ was submerged in death on the cross—so the believer buries sin and the power of sin. Just as the believer is lifted out of the water in baptism—just as Christ was lifted out of the tomb at His resurrection—so the believer is lifted to victory over sin and into the newness of life in God's grace. Further, just as baptism is a commitment of the baptismal candidate to Christ, so Christ commits the believer to a new life of victory over sin.

The road of death to sin and victory through grace must be traveled. "Walk in newness of life" (v. 4) is the directive Paul gave. A road may lead to a wonderful destination, but one will never get there without beginning the journey. Sin will continue to live if the believer does not walk away from it. Rejecting God's grace in Christ is like stopping by the roadside and picking up an animal corpse. The dead corpse is the life of sin. That life is not necessary to experience God's favor. What is necessary is to continue on the road of Christ's provision and walk away from the death of sin.

C. Death Leads to Freedom (vv. 6, 7)

6. Knowing this, that our old man is crucified with him, that the body of sin might be destroyed, that henceforth we should not serve sin.

7. For he that is dead is freed from sin.

The mind is the motivation for the motion of the believer's walk. In other words, filling one's mind with the knowledge of Christ's victory (instead of dwelling on sin and its power) is the catalyst to continue the believer on the walk of victory. The importance of acknowledging the victory in one's mind was the reason Paul said "knowing this" (v. 6). This knowledge came from experience. Paul was essentially saying, "You have experienced this and therefore should keep this experience alive in your minds!" The Romans needed to fill their minds with the fact that their sin had already been dealt with by Christ.

When Christ died on the cross, the sin of the Romans was actually on the cross. "Crucified with him" (v. 6) literally means "co-crucified." When Christ hung on the cross, sin was not somewhere else waiting to be slain. Sin was put on the cross with the Savior.

Crucifixion was a merciless, brutal death. But the cross was more than a means of execution. It was the annihilation of life, the destruction of whatever was suspended on its cruel beams. The elevation of the victim was an assurance to any observer of the weight of the punishment. The view of the cross was the witness to onlookers that there was no question as to the outcome. This picture of crucifixion sent word to the Romans that there was absolutely no doubt as to the destiny of sin. The cross set that destiny to be death!

Unless the Romans put sin on the cross, they might be tempted to think that sin could survive past the provision of Christ. They might allow sin to keep them captive. As long as sin was alive, they could not be free. But when sin was placed on the cross, then the death of sin was sure. With that death, they would no longer have to be tortured and enslaved by sin.

II. ALIVE TO CHRIST (Romans 6:8-14)

A. No More Dominion of Sin (vv. 8-10)

8. Now if we be dead with Christ, we believe that we shall also live with him:

9. Knowing that Christ being raised from the dead dieth no more; death hath no more dominion over him.

10. For in that he died, he died unto sin once: but in that he liveth, he liveth unto God.

Sin was with Christ on the cross, but the believer is with Christ at the empty tomb. The sin of the believer is hanging on the cross, but the believer is walking with Christ. "Crucified with him" (v. 6) means that the "old man" (v. 6) of sin was "co-crucified" on the cross. The phrase "live with him" (v. 8) means that the believer "co-lives" with Christ.

Again, Paul says the Romans had to "know" certain things about their life in Christ. In verse 6 they needed to know that the old man of sin was co-crucified on the cross. In verse 9 they needed to know that the new man was co-living with Christ.

The two words translated as "knowing" in verses 6 and 9 are different in the Greek text. The word in verse 6 is from the root *ginosko*, meaning "knowledge from experience." The word in verse 9 is *eido*, meaning "knowledge from perception."

The two terms work together. The experience of having the old man of sin die on the cross of Christ leads to the perception that sin has no control over the believer. Remembering the experience of the past makes possible the perception of the future. Though sin is dead, the memory of the funeral must not die. The believer must know and continue to know what the death of sin was like. It was liberating; it was invigorating; it was life-giving. Knowing how dead sin was produces the knowledge that sin cannot rule anymore.

The perception of sin's conquered state cuts through the deception of the Enemy. When the Enemy lies, the believer knows there is no basis for the lie. When the Enemy accuses, the believer perceives that the accusation is without basis. When the Enemy roars, the believer knows there is no power to the threat.

B. Reckon Yourselves Free (vv. 11, 12)

11. Likewise reckon ye also yourselves to be dead indeed unto sin, but alive unto God through Jesus Christ our Lord.

12. Let not sin therefore reign in your mortal body, that ye should obey it in the lusts thereof.

Reckoning is the next step after knowing. Reckoning is the use of knowledge. Paul moves the Romans from a memory to a perception and now to action. The activation of knowledge disarms the Enemy. Any person becomes convinced of something if it is repeated often enough in the mind, even if it is not true. The Romans had neglected to reinforce Christ's work in their lives. As a result, their minds had wandered. They had lost their confidence. They had become convinced they were powerless to sin. Further, they had been open to the belief that sin was required to activate grace.

The Roman believers had to once again become convinced of what Christ had done for them. They really had the victory. They really could resist sin. They really could consider sin a dead issue for themselves. However, they had to focus on that victory in their minds. Otherwise their minds would wander where the carnal mind always wanders—back to the slavery of sin. They needed to constantly remind themselves that sin was behind them, the Cross was before them, and the living Christ was beside them.

C. Yield Yourselves Under Grace (vv. 13, 14)

(Romans 6:13, 14 is not included in the printed text.)

The effect of neglect is highlighted in Paul's use of the term *yield.* If the believer did not remember with the mind and then reckon with that knowledge, the result would be to slide to the side of the works of sin. *Yield* literally means "to place to the side of" or "be placed at the side of." Like a boat that moves to the shore if left to drift, the believer will wind up on the shoreline of sin if the mind is left to wander, lacking focus upon the death of sin and the newness of life in Christ.

The Romans were asking, "How much can we sin?" "Isn't sin necessary to some extent?" "Doesn't sin just make grace that much richer?" Paul was responding by saying, "Sin is dead. And if you don't get your mind back on Christ's victorious life, you'll naturally drift back to sin."

The Romans were to place themselves next to the righteousness of God. The yielding of righteousness required focusing the mind, following the Cross and obeying the Master, all principles Paul emphasized in verses 1-14.

III. SERVANTS TO RIGHTEOUSNESS (Romans 6:15 23)

A. Servants Brought From Sin to Righteousness (vv. 15-18)

15. What then? shall we sin, because we are not under the law, but under grace? God forbid.

16. Know ye not, that to whom ye yield yourselves servants to obey, his servants ye are to whom ye obey; whether of sin unto death, or of obedience unto righteousness?

17. But God be thanked, that ye were the servants of sin, but ye have obeyed from the heart that form of doctrine which was delivered you.

18. Being then made free from sin, ye became the servants of righteousness.

Grace is applied by obedience.

Obedience is the key that Paul has been building toward. Knowing, reckoning and yielding are a succession of admonitions. Each leads to the other. The more the believer knows and focuses, the more he or she will be able to reckon and act upon. The more one reckons and acts upon, the more one will be able to place himself or herself next to the Savior and His righteousness. And the way to remain next to Him is through obedience.

Obedience is the evidence of a grace-led life. Without grace, full obedience is impossible. Without grace, the saint struggles to follow even the slightest command. There is a resistance of the soul that slides back toward the rebelliousness of the carnal man. Only when sin is put to death can grace become the platform for full obedience. As long as the Christian believes that a little sin is necessary or that a person has to sin, or, still further, that sin will help me be even more grateful—all notions which Paul has been attacking—obedience will be the struggle of self merely trying to be a better person. On the contrary, with sin put to death, the believer then becomes a representative of what can happen when a person completely depends on God's grace. The Christian is free to follow the Lord in obedience.

The result of applied grace is "yielding unto righteousness"—actually, placing oneself next to righteousness, as discussed earlier. Grace brings the believer closer to the Master. The closer one is to Him, the more obedience becomes an act borne of freedom rather than a struggle against sin.

B. Fruit Unto Holiness (vv. 19-22)

(Romans 6:19-21 is not included in the printed text.)

22. But now being made free from sin, and become servants to God, ye have your fruit unto holiness, and the end everlasting life.

Holiness is a fruit, not a root. In other words, the Christian does not become holy in order to receive grace. Rather, because grace is present, holiness is a natural outcome. The root that bears holiness is the presence of grace and the absence of sin.

Holiness is not at the beginning of the Christian life; it is at the end, the result of the Christian life. At the beginning, the root of sin is replaced with grace. Sin has died on the cross and grace is in its place. Grace then—through the process of death to sin, something already accomplished on the cross (vv. 1-5)—feeds the believer and produces the "fruit" (v. 22) of holiness.

C. Gift of Eternal Life (v. 23)

23. For the wages of sin is death; but the gift of God is eternal life through Jesus Christ our Lord.

The whole process of victory over sin and the ultimate result of eternal life are not based on the believer winning the battle over sin. Christ removed sin from the battlefield when He left sin hanging on the cross.

Yes, the believer can forget, allow and yield to sin. But sin has already been put to death. Rather than a force and weapon of evil used by the Enemy to overcome the believer, sin is a corpse the believer keeps pulling up out of the graveyard of Golgotha. Sin is the badge of self-centered, works-based, depending-on-self religion.

God gives the victory. God gives holiness. And, ultimately, God gives eternal life. The primary obstacle that blurs the Christian's vision of God's grace and gift is sin. That is why Paul so strongly appealed to the Romans to put sin to death.

GOLDEN TEXT HOMILY

"RECKON YE ALSO YOURSELVES TO BE DEAD INDEED UNTO SIN, BUT ALIVE UNTO GOD THROUGH JESUS CHRIST OUR LORD" (Romans 6:11).

How do we look upon our true sense of identity and nature after we have been born again? I often wonder if most of us fail to realize the change within our nature and the new power of God within when Jesus became our Savior and Lord.

There are some important truths we must live by after we have been born again. They are new truths. Some of these truths relate to our past. It is vitally important to know what the Bible says about our past and to confess these truths. What about the truths that have to do with the subjects of forgiveness, justification, reconciliation and regeneration? We are to live by them.

Then there are truths that relate to the believers' future. We know there is life after death. There is heaven awaiting. Our bodies will be resurrected into glorified bodies. We will someday see Jesus face-to-face. On and on the list could go.

But what about Biblical truths that relate to us today and are good for us today—not in the past, not in the future, but now! In this selected study verse, Paul is giving us an important truth to know, to confess, and to live by every day.

Here is the truth: As born-again believers we are to be dead to the power of sin that once reigned in our bodies. We do not have to continue under the rule of Satan. The Bible tells us the power of sin has been rendered dead. We are now free from that power that once was within us. In the name of Jesus that power is now dead.

But one of the major problems we have is that Satan tells us we are not free from his power and that we have no choice but to yield to his sway. May God help us to confess with our mouths and believe in our hearts that this claim of Satan is a lie.

If we truly believe that in Christ we are alive to God, then we are to "reckon"—or "calculate," or come to a fixed and settled conclusion—that sin is no longer in charge. Sin cannot be in charge if Christ is Lord.

Verse 9 tells us if we can firmly believe that death no longer has any power over our resurrected Christ, then "likewise" we should know to believe that sin has no legal power over the believer.

It is true that the devil tempts us to sin, but it is nothing more than a temptation. That is all Satan can do to us. For in Christ we have the choice and power to say no. Why? Because we have reckoned ourselves to be dead to the power of sin and alive to God.

Because of the wonderful work of Christ in the earth, we as believers are no longer alive to sin, and we are no longer dead to God. It is now just the opposite. We are—and let us not forget it—dead to sin and alive to God. All because of Christ and faith.—**Excerpts from the** *Evangelical Sunday School Lesson Commentary*, **Vol. 34**

SENTENCE SERMONS

BELIEVERS can live righteously in Christ, because they are no longer enslaved to sin.

—Selected

MAN is really free only in God, the source of his freedom.

—Sherwood Eddy

THE UNION of faith and freedom is the essential genius of Protestantism.

—Justice W. Nixon

SINNERS can be set free from sin through Christ.

—Selected

EVANGELISM APPLICATION

SINNERS CAN BE SET FREE FROM SIN THROUGH CHRIST.

Part of the bondage of sin is to think that you will never be able to be released. The dungeon of the deceiver, Satan, is real. The Enemy entraps a person with a web of unrighteousness, lust and depravity. The worst part of sin is to think that there is no escape, to feel like the misery can never end, or to be convinced that you were destined to depravity with no hope of deliverance.

The power of the cross of Christ is the message that you can be set free from sin! Freedom is the removal of the shackles of sin. Freedom is the restoration of relationships broken by rebellion. Freedom is the ability to abide in the commandments of God and live as God really intended life to be lived. Christ, through the cross, has already set the repentant sinner free from sin.

ILLUMINATING THE LESSON

Beside every sawmill is a pile of wood that appears worthless. The shavings and chips created by the saw are set aside because the boards,

planks and poles are the products that are the most useful.

One day someone took the scraps of wood, added some lighter fluid, compressed them all together, and the world had a new product—compressed logs. These logs burn longer, burn cleaner, and generate more heat than traditional logs.

In the same way, people who appeared to be worthless because of sin can be made into great servants through God's grace.

DAILY BIBLE READINGS

M. Set Free From Sin.
   Leviticus 16:6-10, 20-22
T. Avoid Sin.
   Leviticus 18:1-5
W. Sanctified by God.
   Ezekiel 37:24-28
T. Forsake the Old Life.
   Mark 8:34-38
F. New Life in Christ.
   2 Corinthians 5:11-21
S. Living by Faith.
   Galatians 2:17-21

TRUTH SEARCH:
Creatively Teaching the Word

Aim: Students will ask Christ to free them from spiritual bondages.

Items needed: Marker, marker board, chain, padlock, key

FOCUS

Have two men and two women come forward. Label one man the master; the other, his slave. Do the same with the women. Ask the masters to imagine that the other two really are their slaves. Have them name some of the commands they would give their slaves. Then have them return to their seats.

In reality, all of us have experienced slavery. The Bible says we all were born as slaves of sin.

EXPLORE

Have students name the two critical questions posed in Romans 6:1, 2. Write these on a marker board as follows:
• *Should we keep on sinning so grace might increase?*
• *How can we live in sin if we are dead to sin?*

Let the students answer those questions.

We are not to continue in sin so God might multiply grace. Instead, God wants us to die to sinful practices.

Have someone read verses 3 and 4. Then ask for two testimonies in which people tell when, where, and why they were baptized.

Going under the water symbolizes Jesus' death on the cross and the believer's death to sin. Being raised from the water symbolizes Christ's resurrection and the believer's new life in Christ.

Have everyone read verses 5-7 aloud with you.
• *In what sense are Christians "freed slaves"?*
• *Compare Christ's death with the death to sin that the believer experiences.*

Have everyone read verses 8-10 aloud with you.
• *If we die with Christ, what promise do we have?*
• *How do we know it is possible to die to sin?*

Read verses 11-14 to the class.
• *Where does sin want to reign? Why?*
• *Name various ways in which the parts of one's body can function as "instruments of wickedness" (v. 13, NIV).*

Read verses 16-18.
• *According to verses 16-18, what type of slavery is pleasing to God?*
• *Is it possible to be a slave to two masters at once? Why or why not?*

Read verses 19-23 aloud. On the board, make two columns: one is titled "Slave to Sin"; the other, "Slave to Righteousness." Drawing from verses 19-23, have students name the characteristics of each type of slave. Write those on the board. Then have students name the rewards of being each type of slave. Add that information to the list. The two lists should look something like this:
• Slave to Sin: *unrighteous, filled with sin, ashamed; reward—eternal death*
• Slave to Righteousness: *holy, free from sin, servant of God; reward—everlasting life*

RESPOND

Have a volunteer come forward. Bind his wrists together with a chain, then secure the chain with a padlock.

Is there any area of your life in which you feel chained to unrighteousness? If so, you can confess it and call out for Christ's help as we pray together. He is the key to your victory.

Display the key and open the lock. Then lead students in a prayer of submission to Christ.

Freedom in the Spirit

Study Text: Romans 7:7 through 8:17

Objective: To examine Paul's description of the struggle with sin and walk in the freedom the Spirit provides.

Time: The Epistle to the Romans was written between A.D. 56 and 58.

Place: The Epistle to the Romans was written in the city of Corinth in Greece.

Golden Text: "The law of the Spirit of life in Christ Jesus hath made me free from the law of sin and death" (Romans 8:2).

Central Truth: By walking in the Spirit, believers are free from sin's dominion.

Evangelism Emphasis: Only Jesus Christ can free sinners from sin's power.

PRINTED TEXT

Romans 7:7. What shall we say then? Is the law sin? God forbid. Nay, I had not known sin, but by the law: for I had not known lust, except the law had said, Thou shalt not covet.

12. Wherefore the law is holy, and the commandment holy, and just, and good.

13. Was then that which is good made death unto me? God forbid. But sin, that it might appear sin, working death in me by that which is good; that sin by the commandment might become exceeding sinful.

21. I find then a law, that when I should do good, evil is present with me.

22. For I delight in the law of God after the inward man:

23. But I see another law in my members, warring against the law of my mind, and bringing me into captivity to the law of sin which is in my members.

24. O wretched man that I am! who shall deliver me from the body of this death?

25. I thank God through Jesus Christ our Lord. So then with the mind I myself serve the law of God; but with the flesh the law of sin.

8:1. There is therefore now no condemnation to them which are in Christ Jesus, who walk not after the flesh, but after the Spirit.

2. For the law of the Spirit of life in Christ Jesus hath made me free from the law of sin and death.

3. For what the law could not do, in that it was weak through the flesh, God sending his own Son in the likeness of sinful flesh, and for sin, condemned sin in the flesh:

4. That the righteousness of the law might be fulfilled in us, who walk not after the flesh, but after the Spirit.

9. But ye are not in the flesh, but in the Spirit, if so be that the Spirit of God dwell in you. Now if any man have not the Spirit of Christ, he is none of his.

10. And if Christ be in you, the body is dead because of sin; but the Spirit is life because of righteousness.

11. But if the Spirit of him that raised up Jesus from the dead dwell in you, he that raised up Christ from the dead shall also quicken your mortal bodies by his Spirit that dwelleth in you.

12. Therefore, brethren, we are debtors, not to the flesh, to live after the flesh.

13. For if ye live after the flesh, ye shall die: but if ye through the Spirit do mortify the deeds of the body, ye shall live.

LESSON OUTLINE

I. THE STRUGGLE WITH SIN
  A. Sin's Deception of the Law
  B. Sin by the Commandment
  C. War of Sin

II. NO CONDEMNATION IN CHRIST
  A. Deliverance by Christ
  B. No Condemnation
  C. Walk After the Spirit

III. LIVE BY THE SPIRIT
  A. The Spirit Is Life
  B. The Bond of the Spirit
  C. Suffering and Glory

LESSON EXPOSITION

INTRODUCTION

No human individual can defeat sin. Sin is greater than any person, human resistance or finite morality. In fact, before a person can even begin the moral battle against sin, it is already present within a person from birth. At best, people only struggle with sin, delay its effects, dodge its attacks and deflect its assaults.

While sin is a struggle for humanity, it is a stricken foe for the Savior. Just because humanity struggles with sin does not mean that the Lord struggles with sin. Though Christ came through the Incarnation unto the earth, dwelling on earth, fully God and fully man, He overcame sin. Sin deceives, condemns and destroys. However, sin is defeated.

How can sin be defeated but still give people so much trouble? Basically, until Satan is finally defeated, he will use sin as his weapon. Sin is of great consequence, bringing destruction and death. But at the same time, sin is defeated. It is like an enemy that is mortally wounded, still alive but reeling and spinning. Though the wound is fatal, the beast is still able to move and swing terrible blows at his opponent. In the same way, though he was dealt the mortal wound at Calvary, Satan still swings the weapon of sin in the face of the believer.

In Romans 7—8, passages that must not be separated, Paul tells the story of sin and the Spirit. Sin is the result of the fall of Adam, and the work of the Spirit is the abiding presence of the Lord. Paul declares to the Romans that even though sin may put up a fight, life in the Spirit is present, available victory for the believer. The defeated foe still attempts to wage warfare, but the Spirit holds off the fighting of the enemy. While the message of Romans 7 is that sin struggles against us and we therefore struggle against sin, the struggle is not defeat. The message of Romans 8 is that nothing can defeat the believer.

I. THE STRUGGLE WITH SIN
   (Romans 7:7-23)

A. Sin's Deception of the Law
   (vv. 7-11)

(Romans 7:8-11 is not included in the printed text.)

7. What shall we say then? Is the law sin? God forbid. Nay, I had not known sin, but by the law: for I had not known lust, except the law had said, Thou shalt not covet.

The Law (the Ten Commandments) pointed to sin and sin violated the Law. The culprit was not the Law. The Law identified the corruption. The Romans, both Jews and Gentiles, knew the power of law. Roman law was the basis of much of known law, even to this day. The law of the Old Testament was the basis of the Jewish way of life. Paul strips away the lie that the Law was the problem. The problem with sin is sin. All the Law did was identify the sin.

Paul further points to the perversion of sin. Sin took the Law and distorted its message. "Deceive" (v. 11) means "to completely lose your way." Sin used the Law to confuse the issues, confound the purposes and condemn the saints. The problem between the Law and sin was not the Law but the way sin used the Law to deceive the believer. The deception of the Law by sin ultimately "slew" Paul (v. 11). Paul had lost his way so extensively that it resulted in his spiritual death.

"I was alive without the law once," was the sobering cry of Paul in verse 9. But when the Law came, Paul continued, "sin revived, and I died." The Law was not sin, but it was used by sin. Nevertheless, the consequences of the deception are striking. Paul's whole life was affected by the deception of sin. And the weapon sin used to deceive Paul was the Law. Paul tried to use his obedience to the Commandments, his adherence to principles and his allegiance to statutes as his first line of defense. Instead, he was defenseless. The Law is not a defense but only a beacon, shining a light upon sin. It would take more for Paul to be victorious over sin.

B. Sin by the Commandment
   (vv. 12-14)

(Romans 7:14 is not included in the printed text.)

12. Wherefore the law is holy, and the commandment holy, and just, and good.
13. Was then that which is good made death unto me? God forbid. But sin, that it might appear sin, working death in me by that which is good; that sin by the commandment might become exceeding sinful.

The Law is holy! Paul settles the issue. Rules are not the problem; sin is the problem. Sin manipulates the rules for the purpose of deceiving people.

Sin's destiny is the death of the individual. The pointed description by Paul is that sin was "working death in me" (v. 13). Sin defeats long before it kills. Sin demoralizes long before it executes. Sin destroys long before it assassinates the struggling soul that tries to battle sin alone.

The irony of sin's deception is that it used a good thing to accomplish something bad. "The law is spiritual" is Paul's conclusion in verse 14. But the Law was used by sin within Paul as a weapon of death (v. 13). Sin is so deceptive that it not only disguises itself as good, but it uses that which is good to accomplish something terrible.

Paul knew the overwhelming, twisted devices of sin. Paul had been betrayed by sin. He had trusted in the Law, something pure and holy (v. 12). But using the Law was no match for the sinful devices of the Enemy. While pursuing perfection under the Law, Paul had been deceived into "all manner of concupiscence [evil desire]" (v. 8). He had been betrayed, not by the Law, but by his trust in the Law. As a result, he was "sold under sin" (v. 14). What Paul had trusted had "sold him out."

Sold emphasizes the depth of sin's cruel deception of Paul. Rather than a onetime sale, the term refers to a once-and-for-all sale. By human standards, the sale was irreversible. What Paul had trusted had been used by sin to condemn him to slavery. In fact, at one time, sin had changed Paul's identity and sold him as a slave.

C. War of Sin (vv. 15-23)

(Romans 7:15-20 is not included in the printed text.)

21. I find then a law, that when I should do good, evil is present with me.
22. For I delight in the law of God after the inward man:
23. But I see another law in my members, warring against the law

of my mind, and bringing me into captivity to the law of sin which is in my members.

The war of sin that had so cruelly sold Paul out occurred within Paul. Sin was not some force surrounding Paul, pushing him into a corner. No, Paul had come to realize that "evil is present with me" (v. 21).

Evil had come close to Paul through the Law. He loved the Law. He "delighted" in the Law and drew the Law into his "inward man" (v. 22). But sin used the Law to war within Paul. Sin won the war within Paul because he, even with the Law, could not defeat sin. This is Paul's climactic description of the power of sin.

Sin had defeated the powerful Law in which Paul had put his trust. He became a prisoner of his own false hope—such was the deception of sin.

II. NO CONDEMNATION IN CHRIST (Romans 7:24—8:4)

A. Deliverance by Christ (7:24, 25)

24. O wretched man that I am! who shall deliver me from the body of this death?
25. I thank God through Jesus Christ our Lord. So then with the mind I myself serve the law of God; but with the flesh the law of sin.

The cry "O wretched man that I am!" crossed over the history of the Jewish nation, transcended the Pharisaic tradition and overshadowed the deeds of a "righteous" man. Paul had fallen so deeply and had been so severely shattered by the blows of sin that he had become encased in "the body of this death" (v. 24). In this passage, Paul was doing more than just describing the result of sin. He was drawing from the catastrophic consequences of sin in his own life. His was not a cold, objective description but a pitiful confession of a conquered man.

Paul's cry was a question: "Who will deliver me?" The answer to sin is not a philosophy nor a principle. Sin is conquered only by a Conqueror. Paul uses 24 verses in chapter 7 leading the reader to the death chamber of sin. In one transition, from verse 24 to 25, he delivers the straightforward truth that Jesus Christ conquers sin. Though sin's plot was complicated and cruel, the conclusion is simple and clear—"through Jesus Christ" (v. 25).

Paul identifies the Conqueror, the victory and the battleground in verse 25. The Conqueror is Jesus Christ. The victory comes through God's work in Paul's mind. The battleground where sin lies defeated is Paul's flesh. Sin is defeated "through Jesus Christ our Lord."

B. No Condemnation (8:1)

1. There is therefore now no condemnation to them which are in Christ Jesus, who walk not after the flesh, but after the Spirit.

"No condemnation," Paul declares in Romans 8. Declare it and abide in it! The walls of sin's dungeon cannot hold the Spirit of God. Therefore, Paul says, "Walk after the Spirit." There need be no doubt, no fear and no intimidation in the believer's life. There is no condemnation to those who are "in Christ Jesus."

The most striking aspect of Paul's confident conclusion is that it is so definite. Paul did not struggle to say "no condemnation." Even though he had miserably failed, he was no longer under condemnation. Despite his "concupiscence" (7:8), he was no longer under condemnation. Regardless of his former slavery to sin (v. 14), he was no longer under condemnation. Paul was not grasping for the victory—he already possessed it. He was walking in Jesus Christ after the Spirit. Therefore, he was free from the stain of sin, no longer labeled as a slave to sin.

The possibility to return to sin was also clear. Paul indicated that to walk after the flesh was to not be in Christ. To walk in the flesh was to return to condemnation and the control of sin. The walk of the flesh was a return to dependence upon the Law to overcome the power of sin. But Paul's emphasis turned from the walk of the flesh to the walk in the Spirit.

C. Walk After the Spirit (vv. 2-4)

2. For the law of the Spirit of life in Christ Jesus hath made me free from the law of sin and death.

3. For what the law could not do, in that it was weak through the flesh, God sending his own Son in the likeness of sinful flesh, and for sin, condemned sin in the flesh:

4. That the righteousness of the law might be fulfilled in us, who walk not after the flesh, but after the Spirit.

Paul repeats the message of Romans 7:25 and 8:1, explaining in fuller detail just how he had received his freedom from the "law of sin and death" (v. 2). Christ's work, described as "through Jesus Christ" in 7:25, is now described as "the law of the Spirit of life through Christ Jesus" (8:2). Christ's work made Paul "free from the law of sin and death." The Spirit of God accomplished what the law of sin could not do.

The victory of Christ's work was accomplished within Paul. Just as the defeat of sin had occurred within Paul, the victory over sin had then occurred within him as well. Again, the Law was involved. Paul explained that the "righteousness of the law [was] fulfilled in us" (v. 4).

The work of Christ on the cross was not just a principle but a powerful work of the Spirit. The Spirit of God took the work of Christ on Calvary and applied it within the heart of Paul. The law of the Commandments was insufficient to overcome the death of sin. However, the Spirit became a "law"—a law of life. Just as light overcomes darkness, the law of the Spirit's life overcame the death of sin's deception.

Paul had hoped the law of statutes and commandments from the Old Testament could overcome sin. But sin only used the Law to further deceive and buy Paul's spiritual death. Nevertheless, within him, at the same place where his faith in the Law had auctioned him into slavery, Paul now stood in freedom because the law of the Spirit's life was greater than sin.

III. LIVE BY THE SPIRIT
(Romans 8:5-17)

A. The Spirit Is Life (vv. 5-11)

(Romans 8:5-8 is not included in the printed text.)

9. But ye are not in the flesh, but in the Spirit, if so be that the Spirit of God dwell in you. Now if any man have not the Spirit of Christ, he is none of his.

10. And if Christ be in you, the body is dead because of sin; but the Spirit is life because of righteousness.

11. But if the Spirit of him that raised up Jesus from the dead dwell in you, he that raised up Christ from the dead shall also quicken your mortal bodies by his Spirit that dwelleth in you.

Rather than going back and forth between victory and defeat, Paul said to the Romans that they were "not in the flesh, but in the Spirit" (v. 9). If the Spirit of God was in them, they were not "in the flesh" at the same time.

The presence of the Spirit of God and the consequential absence of the spirit of death by sin results in the reality of a resurrected body. First, the body of sin dies—the slavery of sin ceases. The believer's walk in the

Spirit renders sin to death. The second part of the process is the indwelling presence of the same Spirit that raised Christ.

The Cross and the empty tomb mark the boundaries of the believer's victory. The same Spirit that raised Christ from the dead now gives life to the "mortal body" that had been defeated by sin. In Romans 6:5 Paul told the Romans they had been "planted together in the likeness" of Christ's death. They shared the crucifixion death of Christ when their sins were put to death. Now he told them that they shared in the resurrection power of Christ as they continued to walk in the power of the Spirit.

B. The Bond of the Spirit (vv. 12-15)

(Romans 8:14, 15 is not included in the printed text.)

12. Therefore, brethren, we are debtors, not to the flesh, to live after the flesh.

13. For if ye live after the flesh, ye shall die: but if ye through the Spirit do mortify the deeds of the body, ye shall live.

Victory is a bond of obligation to Christ. The debt of the flesh and sin is death, but the debt to Christ is life in the Spirit. Freedom in Christ does not mean a person can do whatever seems best to the individual. Deliverance from sin's bondage means the believer is accountable to God for the consequences of that freedom. Sin holds a person's allegiance through deception; in contrast, the Lord through the Holy Spirit acquires a person's faithfulness through a life-giving bond.

The debt to the Lord described in verse 12 is the cry of sonship in verses 14 and 15. A father-son relationship is the bond of life in Christ. Deception and an auction block of slavery is the bond of sin. Paul was celebrating freedom from sin. He was rejoicing in the bond with the heavenly Father. He was not only a slave of sin set free, but also a son secure in the Father's love.

C. Suffering and Glory (vv. 16, 17)

(Romans 8:16, 17 is not included in the printed text.)

How did Paul know what he had experienced was real? How did he know that he was indeed released from the slavery of sin? How could Paul know that his sonship of the heavenly Father was legitimate? Sonship is not speculation but a surety sealed by the Spirit of God. The work of the Spirit of God is to convey the truth of the believer's heavenly heritage. The Spirit communicates love, confidence and parental affection from the heavenly Father to each believer. Just as a natural child senses the emotions of a loving father, so the Spirit conveys the heart of the heavenly Father to the Christian.

The three-part message of the Spirit to the child of God is captured in verse 17:

First, the Father gives what His children could not otherwise have except through Him—freedom from sin and newness of life. The believer is an heir of God's work.

Second, the believer's victory is rooted in the work of Christ's suffering on the cross. The cross is the place where sin was conquered.

Third, the glory of Christ is the resurrection reality that replaces the lordship of sin.

Believers are children of the heavenly Father! He gives us a new life and a new identity. What good is a new life if we are still branded by the devil and society with the same old name? Being a child of the heavenly Father, being an heir of the Father's inheritance, and being able to call the Father by His dearest name, "Abba" (v. 15), is real living!

GOLDEN TEXT HOMILY

"THE LAW OF THE SPIRIT OF LIFE IN CHRIST JESUS HATH MADE ME FREE FROM THE LAW OF SIN AND DEATH" (Romans 8:2).

Freedom is perhaps the most arousing and revolutionary word of the centuries. For it, a thousand wars have been fought and countless brave men have died. To be enslaved politically, socially, economically or spiritually is an abhorrent idea.

In Romans 8:2, two laws are contrasted—"the law of the Spirit of life in Christ Jesus" and "the law of sin and death." The law of sin and death means slavery and condemnation, while the law of the Spirit of life means freedom and peace.

Over 2,000 years ago, Jesus visited the synagogue in Nazareth. Taking the scroll of Isaiah, He stood up and read: "The Spirit of the Lord is upon me, because he hath anointed me to preach the gospel to the poor; he hath sent me to heal the brokenhearted, to preach deliverance to the captives, and recovering of sight to the blind, to set at liberty them that are bruised, to preach the acceptable year of the Lord" (Luke 4:18, 19).

This passage beautifully illustrates the true mission of Christ to the world. God sent His Son as the Great Emancipator to break the fetters of sin and release us from the bondage of the devil. The Spirit-anointed Christ not only declares our spiritual freedom, but pledges all the power and resources of heaven in maintaining it.

Through faith in Christ's atoning death and the power of the Holy Spirit, new life is imparted to the believer (2 Corinthians 5:17; John 1:12). It is the power of the Holy Spirit that breaks the neck of sin and delivers us from the dominion of evil. The Spirit of life, the same Spirit that raised Christ from the dead, has made us free from sin so that we may become the servants of righteousness (Romans 6:18).—**Ralph Brewer**

SENTENCE SERMONS

BY WALKING in the Spirit, believers are free from sin's dominion.

—Selected

WE MUST NOT be content to be cleansed from sin; we must be filled with the Spirit.

—John Fletcher

ONLY JESUS CHRIST can free sinners from sin's power.

—Selected

THE SPIRIT'S CONTROL will replace sin's control. His power is greater than the power of all your sin.

—Erwin W. Lutzer

EVANGELISM APPLICATION

ONLY JESUS CHRIST CAN FREE SINNERS FROM SIN'S POWER.

One way or another, sin will conquer every person. The vilest sinner is in the clutches of carnal pursuit. The most pious religious follower is deceived by demonstrations of ecclesiastical exercise. Oddly, many times sin is so deceptively powerful that the two conditions are mixed. That is, the carnal individual is inwardly envious of religious devotion, depressed because a "spiritual" standard is not met. The religious disciple is all too sadly carnal within, driven by fleshly passions.

The break from the cycle of sin occurs when a person realizes the only way to be set free is through Christ. Every other attempt is manipulated by sin. Whatever or whomever a person may believe in other than Christ will be turned into a deceptive magnet of sin, pulling the individual even deeper into sin. Christ is the only way to defeat sin because He put sin to death on the cross. Rejecting Christ is like lifting the corpse of sin out of the tomb of Calvary. Believing in Christ is accepting the only way to be set free from that corpse.

ILLUMINATING THE LESSON

In April 1985, Coca-Cola introduced a different version of its original formula, thinking the old Coke had too sharp of a "sting" in its taste. The company thought the old formula was dated and had lost its effectiveness. It was felt that the new, revised formula would be more satisfying to customers. So convinced were the speculators they took the old Coke off the market. How wrong they were! Customers were immediately dissatisfied and the old Coke, labeled "Coca-Cola Classic," was reinstated, outselling the "new Coke" by six to one by October of that year.

There is no substitute for death to sin except life in Christ. That formula is the only true victory over sin. Both Christians and sinners so easily decide that Christ's way is in the way. Alternative lifestyles, faddish interpretations of Scripture and new waves of devotion attempt to produce newness of life, but they fail. Not only do they fail, but they also become tools of deception used by Satan to take a person even farther away from God. The original truth is the person of Christ, and the original method of delivery is the Holy Spirit.

DAILY BIBLE READINGS

M. Recognizing Personal Sinfulness.
   Psalm 51:1-12
T. Repentance Is Needed.
   Isaiah 1:10-18
W. Refreshed by the Spirit.
   Isaiah 44:1-8
T. Power to Overcome.
   2 Corinthians 10:1-6
F. Triumphant Through Christ.
   Colossians 2:6-15
S. The Fight of Faith.
   1 Timothy 6:11-16

TRUTH SEARCH:
Creatively Teaching the Word

Aim: Students will praise Christ for freedom from condemnation.

Items needed: A poster board sign reading "Condemned," marker board, marker, index cards, pencils

FOCUS

Have the "Condemned" sign hanging on a classroom wall as students enter. When it's time for class to begin, talk about the sign.
• *If you had seen this sign hanging on the front door of the church, would you have wanted to come inside? What does it mean when a building is condemned?*
Bring a student forward and have him or her hold the sign.
• *What does it mean when a person is condemned by a court of law? How serious of an offense does it take for a person to be condemned to death by execution?*
The truth is that the person holding the sign has been condemned to die. So have I, and so have each one of you.

EXPLORE

Have a volunteer read Romans 7:7-10 aloud.
• *What purpose does the law of God serve?*
The Law teaches us that we have sinned.
• *What does sin bring about?*
Sin leads to death, but Paul wanted to live. However, he had a problem.
Have a volunteer read Romans 7:14-23 aloud.
• *What did Paul want to do? What did he not want to do? What was he doing?*
• *Why do you think Paul was having such a tremendous struggle with sin?*
Have the entire class read verse 24 aloud together.
The good news is that Paul did
not remain in this dilemma forever. In verse 25 he declared that he found victory "through Jesus Christ our Lord."
Ask everyone to read Romans 8:1-17 to themselves.
On the marker board write two headings: "Life in the Flesh" and "Life in the Spirit." Have the students name characteristics of each of those lifestyles as seen in Romans 8:1-17. List their findings on the board. The lists might look something like this:
• Life in the Flesh: *condemned, controlled by sin, filled with carnal thoughts, anti-God, rebellious, not pleasing to God, not belonging to Christ, debtors to the flesh, dead, in bondage to fear*
• Life in the Spirit: *no condemnation, free, filled with the righteousness of Christ, spiritually minded, life, peace, dead to sin, indwelled by the Spirit, victorious over sin, led by God, adopted by God, heirs of God, joint-heirs with Christ, sufferers with Christ, glorified in Christ*
To live in the flesh is to live in condemnation. Eternal death will be the final result. To live in the Spirit is to live without condemnation. Eternal glorification will be the final result.

RESPOND

Hand out an index card to each student. Instruct them to write their name on one side of the card, then draw an X through it.
You have sinned, and your sin condemned you to die. However, if you have received Christ, you are no longer living under condemnation because Jesus took your condemnation upon Himself.
Have everyone read Romans 8:1 with you, then rip their index cards in half. In conclusion, lead students in a concert of praise for freedom from sin.

Victorious in Christ

Study Text: Romans 8:18-39

Objective: To know believers have a glorious future in heaven and be confident in God's provision for victorious living.

Time: The Epistle to the Romans was written between A.D. 56 and 58.

Place: The Epistle to the Romans was written in the city of Corinth in Greece.

Golden Text: "Thanks be unto God, which always causeth us to triumph in Christ" (2 Corinthians 2:14).

Central Truth: Christ gives believers victory over the difficulties of life.

Evangelism Emphasis: Jesus can give sinners hope for the future.

PRINTED TEXT

Romans 8:22. For we know that the whole creation groaneth and travaileth in pain together until now.

23. And not only they, but ourselves also, which have the first-fruits of the Spirit, even we ourselves groan within ourselves, waiting for the adoption, to wit, the redemption of our body.

24. For we are saved by hope: but hope that is seen is not hope: for what a man seeth, why doth he yet hope for?

25. But if we hope for that we see not, then do we with patience wait for it.

26. Likewise the Spirit also helpeth our infirmities: for we know not what we should pray for as we ought: but the Spirit itself maketh intercession for us with groanings which cannot be uttered.

27. And he that searcheth the hearts knoweth what is the mind of the Spirit, because he maketh intercession for the saints according to the will of God.

28. And we know that all things work together for good to them that love God, to them who are the called according to his purpose.

31. What shall we then say to these things? If God be for us, who can be against us?

32. He that spared not his own Son, but delivered him up for us all, how shall he not with him also freely give us all things?

33. Who shall lay anything to the charge of God's elect? It is God that justifieth.

34. Who is he that condemneth? It is Christ that died, yea rather, that is risen again, who is even at the right hand of God, who also maketh intercession for us.

35. Who shall separate us from the love of Christ? shall tribulation, or distress, or persecution, or famine, or nakedness, or peril, or sword?

36. As it is written, For thy sake we are killed all the day long; we are accounted as sheep for the slaughter.

37. Nay, in all these things we are more than conquerors through him that loved us.

38. For I am persuaded, that neither death, nor life, nor angels, nor principalities, nor powers, nor things present, nor things to come,

39. Nor height, nor depth, nor any other creature, shall be able to separate us from the love of God, which is in Christ Jesus our Lord.

LESSON OUTLINE

I. HOPE FOR A GLORIOUS FUTURE
   A. Worth Hoping For
   B. Hope of Creation
   C. Hope by the Spirit
II. LIVING ACCORDING TO GOD'S WILL
   A. Intercession of the Spirit
   B. Calling of God's Purpose
   C. Foreknowledge and Calling
III. TRIUMPHANT THROUGH GOD'S LOVE
   A. God Is for Us
   B. Who Can Be Against Us?
   C. More Than Conquerors

LESSON EXPOSITION

INTRODUCTION

Christians are the most hopeful group of individuals on earth. No other people have more reason to have hope. No other group has been given as powerful a means by which to have hope. And no other population has had their hope so vindicated. This hope can be called the ultimate, victorious hope.

Victorious hope faces the reality of the battles of life. Tragic experiences, broken relationships and shattered promises cannot conquer the hope of the believer. Hope takes into account all the assaults of life and overcomes each one of them.

Victory is the best solution for a hopeful soul. Explanations about why a hope is reasonable might only defer hope, making the soul more anxious waiting to see if the hope is real. An emotional lift feels good and helps temporarily, but eventually it might only prop up hope as a short-term deception. No, hope must be victorious. Hope is good only if it guarantees the hopeful that what was promised will come to pass.

Romans 8 drives home a threefold message about the confident victory of the believer's hope: (1) The victory is made real through the work of the Holy Spirit within the believer. The Spirit works within to make the Christian hopeful, rather than just hoping. (2) The victory is birthed in the will of God, not the mind of the believer. (3) The victory is wedded to the believer through the love of God. God's encompassing love protects the believer from losing hope.

I. HOPE FOR A GLORIOUS FUTURE (Romans 8:18-25)

A. Worth Hoping For (v. 18)

(Romans 8:18 is not included in the printed text.)

The victorious hope of the believer is a worthy hope. Worth is established by comparative value. For example, something is valuable in the marketplace because compared to other items it has the greater value. The hope of the believer is compared to the glory of the resurrected Christ being revealed. The hope of the Christian is laid alongside the glory of Christ on the scales of discipleship. In the opposite side of the scale are the sufferings of this present life and the warfare that must be waged against sin. The comparison is not even close. The weight of worth and value falls on the side of hope and glory. Hope in Christ is an investment of a lifetime that gives real, lasting value to life.

Paul informed the Romans that the glorious hope of Christ is "in us." Hope was deposited in the Romans. Not in their buildings, philosophies or governments, all symbols of the glory of Rome. Constructing an empire that would be a lasting tribute was not only the hope of the Ceasar but also of every Roman citizen. The hope of the Christian was a work within.

B. Hope of Creation (vv. 19-22)

(Romans 8:19-21 is not included in the printed text.)

22. For we know that the whole creation groaneth and travaileth in pain together until now.

While Roman citizens, culture and government sought to capture nature through mighty edifices and ancient engineering marvels, creation was responding with groans of imperfection. The Romans thought they had turned wood, stone and water to another level of genius and productivity. However, Paul pointed out that creation was still imperfect, given to corruption, corrosion and catastrophe.

The groaning of creation begins with the expectation of creation about the believer. Paul was certainly not a pantheist, believing in the animation of creation. That is, he did not believe that creatures and plants had souls or could talk. However, he was pointing out that creation points to an expectation—the expectation that the children of God would live according to the destiny that the Spirit had called them unto.

"Earnest expectation" (v. 19) comes from an ancient term containing three separate words joined together. The combined word literally means "to stretch your head in one direction." The meaning of the term was to focus completely on one thing.

Being created by God, nature looks for the work of God to be fully accomplished in believers. What the Romans had tried to do through nature, God was performing in nature through the believers. Nature's perfection was the goal of the Romans; the believer's perfection was the goal of the Lord. The perfection of the believer, the "manifestation of the sons of God" (v. 19), is God's expectation for nature. And nature is stretched with expectation for God to manifest His glory through believers.

C. Hope by the Spirit (vv. 23-25)

23. And not only they, but ourselves also, which have the firstfruits of the Spirit, even we ourselves groan within ourselves, waiting for the adoption, to wit, the redemption of our body.

24. For we are saved by hope: but hope that is seen is not hope: for what a man seeth, why doth he yet hope for?

25. But if we hope for that we see not, then do we with patience wait for it.

"Groaning" is a fitting description for nature and Christians. The word *groan* (vv. 22, 23, 26), along with the term *travaileth* (v. 22), emphasizes a process similar to childbirth. The pain is real, and the purpose is worthy.

The end result of the groaning is threefold: (1) the "firstfruits of the Spirit," (2) the "adoption" as children of God, and (3) the "redemption of our body." All three highlight the tangible results of the work of the Spirit. This was important because then as now, there were persons in the Roman church and other churches who completely spiritualized the Christian walk. They were essentially saying that the Spirit was unseen and His work intangible. It was only "spiritual."

Paul responds to the "spiritualizers" by saying that the Spirit's work is tangible and fruitful. "Firstfruits" were the buds that came out in the early harvest, demonstrating that the crops were fruit-bearing. Firstfruits were tangible and visible. They were the actual fruit in its first form. In the same way, the Holy Spirit bears fruit. The tangibility of the fruit is in the effect on the person's literal body.

The physical body feels the effects of adoption and redemption. The phrase "of our body" is a direct reference to the literal, physical nature of the process. As a person begins to walk after the Spirit, old habits cease and new ones develop. As a person's life is pointed to the Savior, old speech patterns are left behind and new ones are acquired. As the individual gains ground in discipleship, old relationships are replaced with new ones. All of these changes are expressed in the mind, emotions, behavior and context of the believer's life.

The Holy Spirit uses "patience" (v. 25) to help the believer through the bodily trials brought on by discipleship. The term for "patience" in the ancient text comes from a twofold concept that means "to remain under." Patience is the virtue and ability given by the Holy Spirit to remain under the agenda and affirmation of the Holy Spirit.

Patience is not a person's own hard-fought endurance that holds mind, body and emotions in check. Rather, patience is a relationship. Patience says, "I will remain in relationship with God," rather than saying, "It will take everything I have to keep from giving up." Patience says, "I will continue to receive my strength from my heavenly Father," rather than, "I may be alone, but I can make it on my own." Patience says, "The Holy Spirit is my Comforter and sustainer," rather than, "I'll figure a way to make it through."

II. LIVING ACCORDING TO GOD'S WILL (Romans 8:26-30)

A. Intercession of the Spirit (vv. 26, 27)

26. Likewise the Spirit also helpeth our infirmities: for we know not what we should pray for as we ought: but the Spirit itself maketh intercession for us with groanings which cannot be uttered.

27. And he that searcheth the hearts knoweth what is the mind of the Spirit, because he maketh intercession for the saints according to the will of God.

In times of infirmity the Holy Spirit intercedes. *Infirmity* means "to be with-

out strength." Lying there helpless and hopeless, agonizing through the travail of discipleship, giving birth to the work of God, the believer is not alone.

Helpeth is a beautiful term that culminates much of what Paul says in chapter 8 about relationships. *Help* does not emphasize the deed but the depth of relationships. Rather than saying, "The believer receives help," Paul's emphasis is, "The Spirit himself comes alongside the believer, giving help at the very time it is needed— when the believer is without strength." The relationship is the reason and the substance of the help. The Helper, namely the Holy Spirit, is the difference.

The weakness of the believer is underscored by the inability to pray. He experiences not only a lack of strength, but a lack of words. The travail of life can so surround the believer that prayer becomes a circle of confusion. Even a groan becomes hard to utter. In the midst of the absence of prayer, Paul paints a picture of the Holy Spirit being present as a powerful Intercessor.

Groanings are not meaningless— they are momentous. At the most crucial times in our lives, when words are not enough, God still communicates. And we can still communicate with God. The transmission sent by travail is straight from the deepest part of who we are.

The articulations of a groan are not without meaning. In fact, the Holy Spirit assures that the communication of the heartfelt cry is "according to the will of God" (v. 27). When we cannot communicate with God, the Holy Spirit comes alongside of us and breathes prayer into us. In fact, the Spirit not only makes it possible for us to groan, but He groans with us.

B. Calling of God's Purpose (v. 28)

28. And we know that all things

work together for good to them that love God, to them who are the called according to his purpose.

The Spirit knows what we need to say to the Father, and as a result we know what the Father has purposed for us. The intercession of the Spirit is based on the Spirit's knowledge of what the heavenly Father wants to hear from the believer. That intercession also informs the believer about what the Father desires the believer to know about His work. The Spirit helps when we do not know what to say to the Father so we can know what the Father is saying to us.

The believer knows the work of God through the work of the Spirit. Verses 26 and 27 powerfully describe the intercession of the Spirit that brings the believer's deepest travail to God. Through that work of the Spirit, the believer comes to know the fuller work of God. That fuller work encompasses not only the believer, but "all things" (v. 28) that surround the believer and that the believer experiences.

Once again, creation, circumstances and conditions that are tangible and real are part of the work of the Spirit. Countering the "hyper spiritualizers" who separated the effect of the Spirit's work from "things," Paul declares that "all things work together for good" for the believer. What a powerful declaration! God's work in behalf of the believer does not just involve some of the believer's experiences and surroundings, but all of them.

At the crossroads of the Spirit and the groaning of the disciple, Paul presents the heart of the work of the Father, the Son and the Spirit. Love is the capstone of the believer's victorious hope. Flowing from the middle of verse 28 comes one of the most profound expositions of God's love in all of Scripture.

C. Foreknowledge and Calling
   (vv. 29, 30)

(Romans 8:29, 30 is not included in the printed text.)

Several facets of God's victorious love are presented by Paul. The first aspect of God's love is its purposefulness. Instead of randomly and carelessly showing His love, God applies His love with forethought and intention. The purposes of God are the direction of His love. God's love is not wasted on mistakes, misses and missteps. God's love is right on target, right where it is needed, right on time for the believer.

God's knowledge of the believer does not drive Him away from the believer, but to the believer. Paul is not saying that the Father predetermines the believer by what He knows. Instead Paul is emphasizing that God calls and provides justification and glory to those who love Him.

III. TRIUMPHANT THROUGH GOD'S LOVE (Romans 8:31-39)

A. God Is for Us (vv. 31, 32)

31. What shall we then say to these things? If God be for us, who can be against us?

32. He that spared not his own Son, but delivered him up for us all, how shall he not with him also freely give us all things?

With Christ comes the world. The one fact that the Father gave up His Son proves that the Father gives the believer victory over "all things."

As a lawyer giving his concluding arguments, Paul lays out a convincing case. In Romans 7 he reviewed the condition of lost humanity, admitting that the law had failed to conquer sin. He then reviewed the triumph of Christ over sin and the new life that is possible by walking in the Spirit (8:1-17). Now he details the clear demonstration of the Spirit's compassion and wisdom in times when even the Christian would be weak under the weight of discipleship

in a corrupt world. As a final argument, Paul summarizes all that he
had said and wins the verdict by simply saying, "God gave His Son."

The gift of the Father in Christ is
the proof that all things have been
conquered by Christ and come under
the provision of the Father. At this
point in the text, love becomes victory.
God gave His Son because He loved
the world (John 3:16). Those who will
love the Father and Son will be given
all things in the world, not to do as
they please but to overcome all
things. God's love brought the victory
of the Son so that the love of the
saints for the Father and Son would
bring them victory.

B. Who Can Be Against Us?
   (vv. 33-35)

**33. Who shall lay anything to
the charge of God's elect? It is God
that justifieth.**
**34. Who is he that condem-
neth? It is Christ that died, yea
rather, that is risen again, who is
even at the right hand of God, who
also maketh intercession for us.**
**35. Who shall separate us from
the love of Christ? shall tribulation, or distress, or persecution,
or famine, or nakedness, or peril,
or sword?**

The world can charge the believer,
prosecute the believer and even condemn the believer, but the Christian
will still be innocent because of Jesus
Christ. The words *charge, justifieth* and
condemneth (vv. 33, 34) were all legal
terms from the halls of ancient justice.
The Roman governmental law and the
Jewish Old Testament law were both
addressed by Paul's arguments. The
love of the Father for the saints and the
love of the believers for the Father
would stand up in both courts of law.

Paul moves from the court of law to
the courtroom of life. The terms *tribulation, distress, persecution, famine,*

nakedness, peril, and *sword* (v. 35) are
all descriptive of life circumstances
and events. Paul's terms are in
ascending order. That is, each term
describes a greater degree of assault
upon the believer. First comes the
rumblings of tribulation. Next comes
the increased pressure brought on by
distress. Further, distresses might
increase to the level of persecution.
More painful still are the times that
require sacrifice, pain and famine. Not
only might a person have to do without, but things may be taken away so
the person is left in nakedness. Even
more severe is to be in actual danger
and peril of life. Finally, the culmination of danger is to actually be killed,
as typified by the sword.

Nevertheless, even in the courtroom
of life—from the first signs of trouble
and tribulation all the way through to
the actual assault of evil—the love of
God keeps the believer safe and in
relationship with the Father.

C. More Than Conquerors (vv. 36-39)

**36. As it is written, For thy sake
we are killed all the day long; we
are accounted as sheep for the
slaughter.**
**37. Nay, in all these things we
are more than conquerors through
him that loved us.**
**38. For I am persuaded, that
neither death, nor life, nor angels,
nor principalities, nor powers, nor
things present, nor things to come,**
**39. Nor height, nor depth, nor
any other creature, shall be able to
separate us from the love of God,
which is in Christ Jesus our Lord.**

Verse 36 completes the list started
in verse 35. Going beyond the sword,
beyond death and even beyond this
present world, Paul continues the conclusion of his argument that God's love
covers all and always connects the
believer to the Father, Son and Spirit.

Death cannot separate the believer
from the love of God. Paul quotes

from Psalm 44:22 to describe a cruel death in which the believer was defenseless. The assault of sin came as upon sheep who could not defend themselves against a slaughter.

What kind of victory can a person have after death? A victory that is greater than overcoming one's foe! "More than a conqueror" is the concept Paul uses to describe the victory of God's love over death. Death destroys the body, but love conquers both body and soul. The price of death is only temporary, but the reward of the Father's love is eternal. Death can only take away a person's future, but God's love covers past, present and eternity.

The dimensions of eternity, the seen and unseen, the mortal and the spiritual are all covered by Paul in verses 38 and 39. None of the things listed can conquer the believer. The guarantee of the believer's hope is the Father's love. That guarantee is so sure that it provides something more than victory. The guarantee comes from, is sustained by and provides an eternal relationship between the child of God, the Father, Son and Holy Spirit.

SENTENCE SERMONS

CHRIST gives believers victory over the difficulties of life.
—Selected

THE FIRST STEP on the way to victory is to recognize the Enemy.
—Corrie ten Boom

JESUS can give sinners hope for the future.
—Selected

THE TRIUMPHANT Christian does not fight for victory; he celebrates a victory already won. The victorious life is Christ's business, not yours.
—Reginald Wallis

EVANGELISM APPLICATION

JESUS CAN GIVE SINNERS HOPE FOR THE FUTURE.

Hope for the sinner usually becomes a cycle of anticipation of what might be, to assimilation of what could not be, and to accusation about what should be. The sinner has a hope, but it is a hope that disappoints and even betrays. So the sinner is left in despair.

The wonderful story of Christ is that hope has already been provided. Hope through Christ is a future agenda based on a past accomplishment. Christ purchased the price of hope, conquered the foe of hope, and resurrected the death of hope. The future of Christ's hope is guaranteed because He is already there, in the future, working in behalf of the repentant sinner.

ILLUMINATING THE LESSON

Victory is not always obtained through overwhelming power. There is power in subtle features such as patience. Overwhelming the Enemy may be in the ability to stand rather than advance. Perhaps most fruitful in the pursuit of victory is knowing how to receive the love of the heavenly Father. The Father's love was demonstrated through the defeat of sin, but it was also manifested in the sacrifice of His Son. While scurrying to advance, achieve and assault the Enemy, the believer would do well to learn how to rest in the security of the Father's love.

Albert Einstein conquered the formidable formulas of physics and related sciences. However, the key was not always his hard work or even his ingenuity. Often it was in his ability to withdraw and rest in the knowledge that the victory would eventually come. When he was especially struggling with the theory of relativity, it was when he stepped outside to walk through the woods with a friend that the key struck him. As he strolled, Einstein casually discussed the theory in the context of being with a friend for a warm chat and walk together. Suddenly the idea that would break the theory of relativity wide open burst into his mind, and he knew it. He rushed back to his office and quickly wrote the critical insight.

Friendship and love can be the source of many breakthroughs for the believer, especially when surrounded by the heavenly Father's love.

DAILY BIBLE READINGS

M. Delight in God's Will.
   Psalm 40:1-8
T. New Heavens and New Earth.
   Isaiah 65:17-25
W. God's Everlasting Love.
   Jeremiah 31:1-6
T. Adopted by God's Love.
   Ephesians 1:3-12
F. Knowing God's Will.
   Colossians 1:9-13
S. Victorious King.
   Revelation 19:11-16

TRUTH SEARCH:
Creatively Teaching the Word

Aim: Pray for God's help in difficulties students are currently experiencing.

Items needed: Several newspapers

FOCUS

Pass out copies of the newspapers to various students. Ask them to locate articles reporting bad-news situations and to prepare to summarize those articles for the class. Next, have them present their summaries. Then discuss these questions:

• *Why is there so much bad news in our world?*

• *If you were writing the stories of your life, would there be any bad news included?*

In today's class we're going to discover good news about God's plan for believers when we face trying times.

EXPLORE

Divide the class into small groups of three or four students each. Assign half of the groups Romans 8:18-27; assign verses 28-34 to the other groups. Have the groups answer the following questions about their particular passage.

Romans 8:18-27

1. *List some of "the sufferings of this present time." Why are those sufferings "not worthy to be compared with the glory which shall be revealed in us"?*

2. *What is all of creation waiting for? When will the groaning and travails of creation finally come to an end?*

3. *According to verse 23, what evidence has God given believers that we will one day be fully redeemed? (Also see 2 Corinthians 1:22.)*

4. *In what ways does the Holy Spirit help the believer in times of difficulty (vv. 26, 27)?*

Romans 8:28-34

1. *Restate the promise of verse 28 in your own words.*

2. *According to verse 29, what does God want His followers to become? How could this relate to sufferings in the believer's life?*

3. *Verse 31 says God is "for us." According to verse 32, how did God prove this?*

4. *What does verse 34 say Christ is now doing on behalf of the suffering believer?*

Bring the groups back together and discuss their answers.

Next, have everyone stand to take part in the following responsive reading (vv. 35-39). The students' part is to read, "If God be for us, who can be against us?"

Students: "If God . . . "

Teacher: "Who shall separate us from the love of Christ?"

Students: "If God . . . "

Teacher: "Shall tribulation, or distress, or persecution, or famine, or nakedness, or peril, or sword?"

Students: "If God . . . "

Teacher: *(Read verse 36.)*

Students: "If God . . . "

Teacher: *(Read verse 37.)*

Students: "If God . . . "

Teacher: *(Read verses 38 and 39.)*

Students: "If God . . . "

RESPOND

No matter what you are facing today, God is for you. If you are a Christian, Christ is interceding on your behalf and the Holy Spirit is ready to help you pray. And you have friends here who want to help you to pray.

Ask those students who are currently experiencing trials to stand. Then have those who are nearby to lay their hands on them and pray for them.

God's Sovereign Choice

Study Text: Romans 9:1 through 11:36

Objective: To study God's sovereign plan for His people and rejoice in God's mercy and kindness.

Time: The Epistle to the Romans was written between A.D. 56 and 58.

Place: The Epistle to the Romans was written in the city of Corinth in Greece.

Golden Text: "There is no difference between the Jew and the Greek: for the same Lord over all is rich unto all that call upon him" (Romans 10:12).

Central Truth: God calls all people, both Jews and Gentiles, to salvation through Christ.

Evangelism Emphasis: God desires all people to be saved.

PRINTED TEXT

Romans 9:30. What shall we say then? That the Gentiles, which followed not after righteousness, have attained to righteousness, even the righteousness which is of faith.

31. But Israel, which followed after the law of righteousness, hath not attained to the law of righteousness.

32. Wherefore? Because they sought it not by the faith, but as it were by the works of the law. For they stumbled at that stumblingstone.

10:5. For Moses describeth the righteousness which is of the law, That the man which doeth those things shall live by them.

8. But what saith it? The word is nigh thee, even in thy mouth, and in thy heart: that is, the word of faith, which we preach;

9. That if thou shalt confess with thy mouth the Lord Jesus, and shalt believe in thine heart that God hath raised him from the dead, thou shalt be saved.

10. For with the heart man believeth unto righteousness; and with the mouth confession is made unto salvation.

11. For the scripture saith, Whosoever believeth on him shall not be ashamed.

12. For there is no difference between the Jew and the Greek: for the same Lord over all is rich unto all that call upon him.

11:25. For I would not, brethren, that ye should be ignorant of this mystery, lest ye should be wise in your own conceits; that blindness in part is happened to Israel, until the fulness of the Gentiles be come in.

26. And so all Israel shall be saved: as it is written, There shall come out of Sion the Deliverer, and shall turn away ungodliness from Jacob:

27. For this is my covenant unto them, when I shall take away their sins.

28. As concerning the gospel, they are enemies for your sakes: but as touching the election, they are beloved for the fathers' sakes.

29. For the gifts and calling of God are without repentance.

30. For as ye in times past have not believed God, yet have now obtained mercy through their unbelief:

31. Even so have these also now not believed, that through your mercy they also may obtain mercy.

32. For God hath concluded them all in unbelief, that he might have mercy upon all.

LESSON OUTLINE

I. CHOSEN BY GOD'S MERCY
  A. God's Mercy Upon Israel
  B. God's Mercy Upon the Gentiles
  C. Mercy Applied by Faith

II. SAVED BY FAITH
  A. Salvation Is Here
  B. Belief Is in the Heart
  C. Salvation Is Available to All
  D. Salvation Is Based in the Word

III. RESTORED BY GOD'S KINDNESS
  A. Restoration for the Gentiles
  B. Restoration for Israel
  C. Restoration for All

LESSON EXPOSITION

INTRODUCTION

Christianity is not a club. Selective membership, specialized rights and social elitism were all left at the cross of Christ. Christ did not die only for a privileged class.

The first word in the line of salvation is *mercy*. Rather than choosing who would lose out, God's mercy built a bridge of salvation to all. Rather than sealing the fate of some and rewarding the destiny of others, God's mercy was showered on the just and the unjust.

In Romans 9 Paul wept for those of Israel who could not see past their own rights to the kingdom of God. He mourned that some of his fellow believers in Israel were stuck on the notion that salvation was set aside for a special sect. Grief overran Paul when he was reminded of those of Judah who would exclude others in order to preserve "their way" of salvation. So Paul tore down the myth of exclusive religion.

"Faith is the key" was the essence of Paul's message to the Romans. "Believe and you will be saved" was the herald, not "Be born into a certain nationality and you will be blessed." Rather than the color of one's culture, Paul said that holiness of heart mattered most. Faith in the Word of God, captured in the heart and spoken by the lips in testimony, was the formula. The answer was not to be born and reared under the flag of a nation or religion. Salvation was available to anyone.

The gospel pulls people together rather than apart. The force of the gospel attracts individuals to the Father rather than dividing them from Him. Restoration of both the Gentiles and Israel is God's heart's desire.

In Romans 10 Paul cited the Old Testament Law to remind the Jews that God's love was of the heart and not heritage. Paul conveyed the heart of God by declaring that Christ died for all the Romans. Creed, color or class did not limit the sufficiency of Christ. The heart of God was free of bias when it came to the compassion of the Savior. Salvation flowed from the mercy of God upon all.

I. CHOSEN BY GOD'S MERCY
  (Romans 9:6-8, 16-24, 30-32)

A. God's Mercy Upon Israel (vv. 6-8)

(Romans 9:6-8 is not included in the printed text.)

Israel was part of God's provision. Paul felt so deeply for Israel that he declared to the Romans, "I could wish that myself were accursed from Christ for my brethren, my kinsmen according to the flesh" (v. 3). However, being children of Israel did not necessarily mean they were children of God (v. 6).

Jews had nullified their claim to be true children of God by their own choice. Just as Esau had chosen to reject his promise (see vv. 12, 13), so many of Israel had refused their promise in Jesus the Messiah. Further, the position of Esau over Jacob did not guarantee the promise to Esau. He still rejected the promise and lost his inheritance.

Position, power and bloodline were all given to Israel. The people of Israel were God's first choice. They had the first opportunity to receive the Savior. The church began first in Jerusalem. Nevertheless, they had rejected Christ's salvation. God extended mercy to Israel, even the first opportunity to know the salvation of the Lord.

B. God's Mercy Upon the Gentiles (vv. 16-24)

(Romans 9:16-24 is not included in the printed text.)

The mercy of God is the source of God's provision. That was clearly the message of Paul. Salvation does not come through an individual's own ability to will something into being, or human power to "run" in power and strength. Rather, salvation is "of God that sheweth mercy" (v. 16). Citing Pharaoh, Paul said God has used all kinds of individuals to accomplish His purposes throughout history. Using the illustration of a potter's clay, Paul instructed the Romans that God uses the same clay to produce what He wills. Thankfully, by His mercy, He included the Gentiles in His call to salvation (v. 24).

Paul recognized the great patience of God to work with the Gentiles. Calling the Gentiles "vessels of wrath fitted [for] destruction," Paul laid out the great "longsuffering" of God as the only thing that gave the Gentiles an opportunity to receive salvation (v. 22). It was God's merciful choice that gave Gentiles the calling of salvation (v. 24).

God's mercy did not just let the Gentiles have access to the way of salvation, but it also fashioned the vessels of the Gentiles into something glorious for His greater purposes. Through God's mercy, the Gentiles were made vessels suitable for the "riches of his glory" (v. 23). God's

economy of mercy moved the Gentiles from His wrath to His riches.

C. Mercy Applied by Faith (vv. 30-32)

30. What shall we say then? That the Gentiles, which followed not after righteousness, have attained to righteousness, even the righteousness which is of faith. 31. But Israel, which followed after the law of righteousness, hath not attained to the law of righteousness. 32. Wherefore? Because they sought it not by the faith, but as it were by the works of the law. For they stumbled at that stumblingstone.

Paul presents a dilemma and solution. The dilemma presents the essential condition of both the Gentiles and the Jews. The dilemma was that the Gentiles were receiving righteousness, but the Jews, who should have received righteousness, were not.

The condition of the Gentiles was that they started with unrighteousness and ended up with righteousness. The Gentiles were vile, ungodly, blasphemous and pagan. They worshiped other gods and did not care about the living God. They followed a hedonistic and perverted lifestyle. Nevertheless, the Gentiles "attained to righteousness" (v. 30). The undeserving Gentiles, who had been uncaring and uninvolved with the ways of God, received the righteousness of God through faith.

The condition of the Jews was that they started with what they thought would bring righteousness, "the law of righteousness," but they did not receive righteousness. They were devout, sincere and very religious. They obeyed the Law, offered sacrifices and prayed many prayers. They had received the tradition, the heritage and the history. The Jews "followed after the law of righteousness" but had not "attained" it (v. 31).

The solution was faith and not works. The Jews had depended on the works of the Law. They had placed their trust in their ability to satisfy the requirements of the Law themselves. Their mistake was to trust their own efforts. The solution would have been to believe in the work of the Messiah to satisfy the Law in their behalf.

The Messiah was a "stumblingstone" (v. 32)—an opportunity to some and a barrier to others. As an opportunity, the stumbling stone could have been a cornerstone. A cornerstone was a very important foundation stone upon which a building could be built. The Jews could have built a great spiritual house on the foundation stone of Jesus Christ. Instead, they rejected Him, and the stumbling stone became a barrier, blocking the Jews from making any further progress.

II. SAVED BY FAITH
(Romans 10:5-17)

A. Salvation Is Here (vv. 5-8)

(Romans 10:6, 7 is not included in the printed text.)

5. For Moses describeth the righteousness which is of the law, That the man which doeth those things shall live by them.

8. But what saith it? The word is nigh thee, even in thy mouth, and in thy heart: that is, the word of faith, which we preach.

In their zeal for God, the Jews missed the righteousness God had provided. Paul explained that instead of receiving what God had already provided, the Jews sought to "establish their own righteousness" (v. 3). They had bypassed God's provision by a lack of submission to the righteousness God had provided. *Self-centered, self-righteous* and *self-seeking* attempts to achieve God's righteousness their own way had robbed them of what was already there for them.

Paul took the reader back to Moses to illustrate the opportunity that the Jews had missed (vv. 6, 7). Upon giving God's law, Moses appealed to the people not to act as though the commandments of God were hard to receive or out of their reach. Instead, Moses declared that the commandments of God were close to them, even in their hearts (Deuteronomy 30:11-14). Paul was demonstrating that God had long appealed for the hearts of the Jews but they had instead given Him their works. Paul's heart was indeed saddened because his people had rejected a gift in order to work a plan.

God had already placed the key to the heart of God's righteousness within the heart of the people. Paul said the "righteousness . . . of faith speaketh" (Romans 10:6). The "word of faith" was in their heart and in their mouth (v. 8). The Jews, Paul's "brethren" (9:3; 10:1), had sought for righteousness for so long, and God was making it available to them through faith.

God is always accessible. Religion makes it so hard to come to God. It places so many steps, stages and stipulations between people and God. In reality, God comes to individuals that they might be saved. God offers His Son as a gift of salvation for whosoever will believe on Him. God places His word and means of faith in the heart and on the lips of any person who will respond to His Son, believing on Jesus Christ for their salvation.

B. Belief Is in the Heart (vv. 9, 10)

9. That if thou shalt confess with thy mouth the Lord Jesus, and shalt believe in thine heart that God hath raised him from the dead, thou shalt be saved.

10. For with the heart man believeth unto righteousness; and with the mouth confession is made unto salvation.

The word translated "confess" was used in the Roman judicial system. A person would stand before the Roman tribunal and publicly declare the position that he was taking. The crowd gathered would be judges, witnesses and representatives. The decisions made would affect the speaker's property, family and destiny. The statements made in the confession, once spoken in the court setting, established a position that became a matter of public record.

Public and private faith are both important. Faith is a matter of the heart, but it must be declared in the marketplace of the world. The mouth reveals to the public that you have faith, and faith must be vocalized to be fully formed. Others will not know your faith fully until you "confess" it. You will not know the full force of your faith until you verbalize it in the public arena. God expects your faith to be completed by your public confession.

Private faith is even more important than public faith. The power to proclaim one's faith comes from the fire that burns within the heart of one's private faith. In the heart of the believer, faith is formed in a furnace of devotion and consecration. The faith of the heart must be established first, before any genuine public confession of faith. Public faith is guaranteed by the presence of private faith in the heart.

C. Salvation Is Available to All
   (vv. 11-13)

11. For the scripture saith, Whosoever believeth on him shall not be ashamed.

12. For there is no difference between the Jew and the Greek: for the same Lord over all is rich unto all that call upon him.

The term *ashamed* addresses the effect upon the person who believes in the heart unto righteousness and confesses salvation publicly. This person will not be discredited by others, as the case could be with a public, legal confession. Some tribunal will not later prosecute the person

for making an illegal claim. The person will not be singled out and separated from others who are righteous, as though the person is not as good as they are.

Faith unifies the free grace of the Master with even the most undeserving. The Jews were the only people singled out by God in history to receive His law and former covenant. Yet, the privilege to confess the righteousness of God was not given to the Jews alone. The privilege was given to those who believed in Jesus Christ.

The term *difference* comes from a concept meaning "that which divides between." The term in the Greek text was *diastole*, from which the modern term *distill* comes. To distill something is to separate so as to purify. The Gentiles who confessed faith in Christ would not be "distilled" out as though they were impure and undeserving. Christ was enough! In fact, Christ not only gave the Gentiles the privilege of salvation, but He also enriched them. He made them "rich" in His abundant mercy and righteousness, not because of bloodline or position but because they believed in Christ and called on Him.

D. Salvation Is Based in the Word
   (vv. 14-17)

(Romans 10:14-17 is not included in the printed text.)

Paul emphasizes the role of the Word of God in bringing people to belief in Christ. Though faith in the heart is important, the heart must be fed the Word of God. Though the public confession of faith is important, the believer must have something to declare—the Word of God. Though the Word of God is powerful, it must be proclaimed for people to hear it. When people hear the Word, that Word enters their heart. Within their heart the Word declares into private faith. As a result of the private faith, the Word is then proclaimed publicly.

Preachers proclaiming the Word become the catalysts for the formation of faith. Preaching is not just a manner of public speaking. It is the event through which faith begins to be formed. Preaching is the fulfillment of a faith process that God requires in order for persons to be made righteous.

III. RESTORED BY GOD'S KINDNESS
(Romans 11:11-32)

A. Restoration for the Gentiles
(vv. 11-24)

(Romans 11:11-24 is not included in the printed text.)

God's judgment isn't made final until a person has passed from this life to the next. As long as someone continues to live, he or she has the opportunity to receive the righteousness of God through faith in Christ. The reconciling love of God drives His arms open to anyone who will believe in His Son. Though the Jews had rejected Christ, they could still come unto Him and receive righteousness by faith.

Paul used the illustration of grafts in an olive tree to illustrate God's reconciliation. The Gentiles were wild olive branches that could not bear fruit. Through Jesus Christ, God grafted them into a fruit-bearing olive tree (v. 17). Paul admonished the Gentile readers to be grateful they had been grafted in. The Jews had been good branches on the olive tree but had broken themselves off by their own attempts at self-righteousness through the Law. However, God desired to graft the Jews back into the tree if they would only submit to Him (vv. 23, 24).

B. Restoration for Israel (vv. 25-29)

25. For I would not, brethren, that ye should be ignorant of this mystery, lest ye should be wise in your own conceits; that blindness in part is happened to Israel, until the fulness of the Gentiles be come in.

26. And so all Israel shall be saved: as it is written, There shall come out of Sion the Deliverer, and shall turn away ungodliness from Jacob:

27. For this is my covenant unto them, when I shall take away their sins.

28. As concerning the gospel, they are enemies for your sakes: but as touching the election, they are beloved for the fathers' sakes.

29. For the gifts and calling of God are without repentance.

The peril of religious piety could strike the Gentiles just as easily as it had overtaken the Jews. Paul knew all too well that pride was no respecter of persons. If the Gentiles were not cautious to preserve the humble submissiveness of their faith, they too would lose the righteousness of Christ. The Gentiles had to be especially careful to preserve their faith because they had received salvation only by the mercy of God. They could least afford to be forgetful because they were still outside of God's historical election.

Though they had rejected Christ, the Jews were still the "beloved" (v. 28) of the heavenly Father. The Father's watchful eye of mercy was upon the Jews. His passion for the Jews' salvation had not diminished. He longed for the day Israel would receive Christ as Messiah. Paul admonished the Roman Gentiles to have the same longing as a way to make sure they never forgot the grace by which they had been grafted into the righteousness of God.

C. Restoration for All (vv. 30-32)

30. For as ye in times past have not believed God, yet have now obtained mercy through their unbelief:

31. Even so have these also now

not believed, that through your mercy they also may obtain mercy. 32. For God hath concluded them all in unbelief, that he might have mercy upon all.

Mercy has the power to mold the believer into a vessel of ministry. As the Gentiles recognized the mercy of God that had allowed them to receive God's righteousness, and as they retained the same longing for the redemption of Israel, they would become vessels of mercy to Israel. The mercy they extended to the Jews would increase the chances that they would one day believe and be restored to the righteousness of God. In fact, the mercy of God would, in part, flow through the mercy of the Gentiles. And, the Gentiles should have known all too well how vital mercy was.

GOLDEN TEXT HOMILY

"THERE IS NO DIFFERENCE BETWEEN THE JEW AND THE GREEK: FOR THE SAME LORD OVER ALL IS RICH UNTO ALL THAT CALL UPON HIM" (Romans 10:12).

Christ is "rich unto all." We are assured in God's Word of the "unsearchable riches of Christ" (Ephesians 3:8), and we are counseled to buy of Him "gold tried in the fire, that [we may] be rich" (Revelation 3:18).

If all things are ours, it is because we are Christ's, and Christ is God's. He, who redeems and rules, supplies the needs of His ransomed ones. Unlike some of the wealthy of this world, God is not rich for Himself; He is rich for us. And His riches are boundless and inexhaustible.

The limitations of nationality have been abolished. Christ is Savior and Lord of all people. His riches are for all who call on His name.

In Himself, Christ has the (1) riches of revelation; (2) the riches of redemption; (3) the riches of replenishment,

owing to the nature and perpetuity of the spiritual dispensation of grace; and (4) the riches of resurrection, inasmuch as the true riches endure unto life eternal.

These wonderful facts should encourage every hearer of the gospel to submit to the Lordship and to seek the true riches of Jesus Christ, the Son of God.

Isn't it wonderful that salvation is brought within the reach of everyone? "The same Lord over all is rich unto all that call upon him. For whosoever shall call upon the name of the Lord shall be saved" (vv. 12, 13).—**O.W. Polen**

SENTENCE SERMONS

GOD CALLS all people, both Jews and Gentiles, to salvation through Christ.

—Selected

GOD'S MERCY is boundless, free and through Jesus Christ our Lord, available to us now in our present situation.

—A.W. Tozer

ETERNAL LIFE does not begin with death; it begins with faith.

—Samuel M. Shoemaker

GOD soon turns from His wrath, but He never turns from His love and kindness.

—Charles H. Spurgeon

EVANGELISM APPLICATION

GOD DESIRES ALL PEOPLE TO BE SAVED.

Religion desires to make salvation an exclusive club. Depravity desires to make salvation an undesirable, old-fashioned idea. Depression desires to make salvation an unattainable possession that only a privileged few are fortunate enough to receive. In the midst of all the efforts to push salvation away from humanity, God desires that all people be saved.

God's desire is an active force of mercy. His mercy calls unto the soul and reaches into the heart. God sends His Word by His Spirit and through His preachers to provide the message that begins the journey of faith in Christ. God moves throughout the earth, drawing all people to His saving grace. People can criticize, reject and disbelieve God's mercy, but He still desires and seeks them out.

ILLUMINATING THE LESSON

A story about two stonecutters illustrates how two people with the same opportunity can have two very different perspectives. The stonecutters were asked what they were doing. The first said, "I'm cutting this stone into blocks." The second replied, "I'm on a team that's building a cathedral."

The Jews and Gentiles both had the opportunity to have faith in Jesus Christ. The Jews viewed Christ as a stumbling block. He was an obstacle to their religion and a threat to their establishment. The Gentiles accepted Christ as the key to a new way of life. To them He was a cornerstone. He set them free from the bondage of sin.

He gave them access to the heavenly Father. He made them channels of life and ministry.

Perspective is an essential to faith. Position does not guarantee righteousness. One may be in the right place, even at the right time. One may have the right opportunity with just the right people. One may have the right name and pedigree. However, if an individual does not have the perspective of faith in Jesus Christ, that person will continue to be out of place with God.—**D. Baron,** *Moses on Management*

DAILY BIBLE READINGS

M. Called to Follow God.
Genesis 12:1-9

T. God's Power Displayed.
Exodus 9:13-24

W. Restored by God.
Ezekiel 36:22-28

T. Chosen to Bear Fruit.
John 15:12-17

F. Redeemed From Sin.
1 Corinthians 6:9-11

S. Rejoicing in God's Mercy.
1 Timothy 1:12-17

TRUTH SEARCH:
Creatively Teaching the Word

Aim: Students will ask God to fulfill His purpose in their lives.

Items needed: One pipe cleaner for each student, modeling clay, a large rock

FOCUS

• *Do you ever ask a child, "What do you want to be when you grow up?"*
• *When you were a child, did anyone ever ask you that question? If so, how did you respond?*
• *Did you ever ask God, "What do You want me to be when I grow up?" Do you still ask God what He wants you to become?*

EXPLORE

God has a plan for every person's life. Let's read about it.

Have a volunteer read Romans 9:17.
• *For what purpose did God raise up Pharaoh as leader of Egypt?*

Have another volunteer read verses 18-21.

Now take the piece of clay in your hand, kneading it as you talk.

God is the potter, we are the clay. It is His desire to make each of us a vessel of honor who obediently follows His leading. However, if we decide to live in rebellion, we will become vessels of dishonor whom He will one day have to destroy.

Have a third volunteer read verses 22-24 as you continue working with the clay.

Some Jews become vessels of honor, others become vessels of dishonor. Some Gentiles become vessels of honor, others become vessels of dishonor. What kind of vessel are you becoming?

Set the clay aside. Have someone read verses 30-33.
• *To become a vessel of honor, we must obtain the righteousness of God. How is it obtained, according to verse 30?*

• *How is righteousness not attained, according to verse 31?*

Display the rock.
• *What is the stumbling stone that causes most Jews (as well as many other peoples) to fail to receive God's righteousness?*

No one can ever be good enough to become righteous in God's sight. It only comes through in His Son— the cornerstone who is a stumbling block for so many. The good news is, "Whosoever believeth on him shall not be ashamed" (v. 33).

Ask everyone to read Romans 10:9-17 to themselves.
• *According to verses 9 and 10, how does a person gain salvation?*
• *According to verses 12 and 13, who can be saved?*
• *What is the source of saving faith (vv. 14-17)?*

Pick up the stone. **If you will put your faith in Christ, letting Him be your rock of salvation instead of a stumbling block, you will be saved.**

Pick up the clay with your other hand. **With your life committed to Christ, He will make you into a vessel of honor.**

RESPOND

Hand out a pipe cleaner to every student.

These pipe cleaners remind me of two truths: First, Christ will cleanse you from your sins when you put your faith in Him. Second, He can then shape you into a vessel of honor.

Ask the students to shape the cleaner into a symbol that demonstrates something God needs to do in their lives today. (For example, you might tie a knot in it to show you need to become more closely tied to God through a more consistent prayer life.)

Once students have crafted their symbols, let them silently offer prayers of commitment. Then challenge them to use the pipe cleaners as reminders of their commitments.

Freedom to Serve

Study Text: Romans 12:1 through 13:14

Objective: To recognize there is freedom in serving Christ and commit to a life of loving service.

Time: The Epistle to the Romans was written between A.D. 56 and 58.

Place: The Epistle to the Romans was written in the city of Corinth in Greece.

Golden Text: "I beseech you therefore, brethren, by the mercies of God, that ye present your bodies a living sacrifice, holy, acceptable unto God, which is your reasonable service" (Romans 12:1).

Central Truth: Serving others is a means of serving Christ.

Evangelism Emphasis: Serving Christ includes witnessing to the lost.

PRINTED TEXT

Romans 12:1. I beseech you therefore, brethren, by the mercies of God, that ye present your bodies a living sacrifice, holy, acceptable unto God, which is your reasonable service.

2. And be not conformed to this world: but be ye transformed by the renewing of your mind, that ye may prove what is that good, and acceptable, and perfect, will of God.

13:1. Let every soul be subject unto the higher powers. For there is no power but of God: the powers that be are ordained of God.

2. Whosoever therefore resisteth the power, resisteth the ordinance of God: and they that resist shall receive to themselves damnation.

3. For rulers are not a terror to good works, but to the evil. Wilt thou then not be afraid of the power? do that which is good, and thou shalt have praise of the same:

4. For he is the minister of God to thee for good. But if thou do that which is evil, be afraid; for he beareth not the sword in vain: for he is the minister of God, a revenger to execute wrath upon him that doeth evil.

5. Wherefore ye must needs be subject, not only for wrath, but also for conscience sake.

6. For this cause pay ye tribute also: for they are God's ministers, attending continually upon this very thing.

7. Render therefore to all their dues: tribute to whom tribute is due; custom to whom custom; fear to whom fear; honour to whom honour.

8. Owe no man any thing, but to love one another: for he that loveth another hath fulfilled the law.

9. For this, Thou shalt not commit adultery, Thou shalt not kill, Thou shalt not steal, Thou shalt not bear false witness, Thou shalt not covet; and if there be any other commandment, it is briefly comprehended in this saying, namely, Thou shalt love thy neighbour as thyself.

10. Love worketh no ill to his neighbour: therefore love is the fulfilling of the law.

11. And that, knowing the time, that now it is high time to awake out of sleep: for now is our salvation nearer than when we believed.

LESSON OUTLINE

LESSON EXPOSITION

INTRODUCTION

Consecration, commitment and *continuance* are all words vital to the Christian's life. *Consecration* is the worshipful act of giving one's life to God. *Commitment* is the follow-up of consecration that activates one's consecration into service. *Continuance* is the statement to the world that accompanies commitment, saying that one's consecration lasts over time.

The Romans needed to take the fire of faith in their hearts and convert it into devoted service. Paul went back to the altar to address their service to God. The altar of their salvation would become the table of their service. The place where they initially started with the Lord would be the foundation of their ministry. Their start would be their sustenance.

Paul put ministry in the context of worship. The Romans' labor would be their song unto the Lord, their acts of ministry would be their altar of praise, and their works of service would be their worship of sacrifice. Uniting ministry with worship would produce the kind of discipleship that God had willed for His people from the beginning.

All too often modern-day disciples of the Lord divorce acts of service from worship. The Sunday-morning worship experience is not translated into six more days of service unto the Lord. The experience in the sanctuary of praise is not converted to service in a desperate society.

Paul not only provides the principle of ministry as worship, but he also specifies how it is done. It happens through (a) performing personal acts of worship (vv. 1, 2), (b) taking inventory of self as a foundational result of sincere worship (vv. 3-5), and (c) carrying out worshipful service in daily life (vv. 6-21).

Romans 12 stands at a pivotal juncture in the Book of Romans. If Paul had stopped writing at the end of chapter 11, we would have had an excellent treatise on the history and theology of the Christian faith, especially in the context of the faith of Israel, the work of the Cross and the provision of the heavenly Father. However, Roman culture was the most pragmatic of the ancient era. The Romans were achievers, conquerors and builders.

Paul's description of the construction of the Christian life would have been incomplete if he had stopped with the blueprint of doctrine. To reach the Romans he had to provide the actual implementation of the edifice of discipleship. Romans 12 takes the power of doctrine and shows how to build the Christian life into a devoted instrument of service to the Lord.

The acts of service commanded in Romans 12 were penned in the context of severe persecution of the early church. The Romans had imprisoned Paul himself. How can one be a

Christian when every force of society attacks and binds one's every effort? Paul answers in Romans 13 by talking about consecration once again. Service is an act of worship, and submission in society is an act of worship as well.

Without the conversion of worship to service in society, salvation becomes a shell of what God intended. The saint of God becomes shackled by hesitancy. The believer becomes frustrated and unfulfilled. God's desire is that His people be free to serve Him, moving their acts of worship to acts of service applied in a godless society.

I. CONSECRATE YOURSELF TO CHRIST (Romans 12:1-8)

A. Consecration Is Foundational for Freedom (v. 1)

1. I beseech you therefore, brethren, by the mercies of God, that ye present your bodies a living sacrifice, holy, acceptable unto God, which is your reasonable service.

With the "amen" of the last verse of chapter 11, Paul turns his attention to the application of the riches of God (v. 33) into Christian service. Beginning at 12:1, Paul describes the altar of service. The language of verse 1 is the language of the Temple. *Present* is the description of a follower of God bringing a sacrifice to the Temple. *Sacrifice* is the actual event in which the sacrifice is consumed on the altar. *Service* means "to be given over to the hire of God." In other words, the sacrifice itself becomes the property of God, to use as He sees fit.

Verse 1 is an admonition to which the Romans had to respond. Their life of service unto God could only be offered by themselves. In the Old Testament law, the priests and Levites performed the sacrifices, but each person and family in Israel was responsible for bringing their own animals and crops for sacrifice. In the same way, the sacrifice of oneself could only be done when the person brought himself or herself to the altar.

Christ is the great Mediator who made access to the altar possible by making the one sacrifice that was acceptable to the Father. However, none of the work of Christ could be applied until the Romans' sacrifice was brought to the altar. Paul urged the Romans to bring themselves to the altar.

B. Consecration Sets You Apart for Service (v. 2)

2. And be not conformed to this world: but be ye transformed by the renewing of your mind, that ye may prove what is that good, and acceptable, and perfect, will of God.

Sacrifices in the Old Testament had to be without blemish. Otherwise, a sacrifice could not be wholly consecrated to God. The impurities on a sacrifice symbolized the presence of the world, and God would not accept such a sacrifice.

In the same manner, the marks of the world upon the believer affect the sacrifice of self and service unto the Lord. The believer is not to be "conformed" to this world's system of morals, religion or pseudo-spirituality. The word *conformed* is the equivalent of the Old Testament sacrifice that was blemished and unfit for sacrifice.

Conformed is translated from the Greek term *suschematizo*. The emphasis is on the external features and characteristics by which a person might be identified. Paul appealed to the Romans not to take the markings that would identify them as believers with the world.

The phrase "be ye transformed" stands opposite of "be not conformed." This phrase is translated from the Greek term *metamorphousthe,* from which we get *metamorphosis,* and it emphasizes a change to a permanent state. Transformation is a true change that affects the character and quality of a person. It is not just an external change.

Renewing the mind is the heart of genuine transformation. The Greek term for *renew* is *anakainoo*, which indicates being turned into a new and different kind of person. *Renewal* is not just a reshaping but the replacement of a person. Renewal is not just a new application of an old reality but the beginning of a different way of life.

Transformation and renewal are the key elements in making the sacrifice of self for service acceptable to the heavenly Father. Just as the animals and grain offerings were prepared and thereby became acceptable for sacrifice, the renewal and transformation process makes the believer ready to be received and used by God.

C. Consecration Applies God's Gifts (vv. 3-8)

(Romans 12:3-8 is not included in the printed text.)

Gifts for service come from God. The substance of the gifts is never superseded by the source of the gift, who is God. The ownership of the gifts is retained by the originator of the gifts, who is God. The use of gifts does not depend on the person who becomes gifted, but on the One who creates and bestows the gifts.

The believer's relationship with God is the key to unlocking the genuine potential of God's gifts. The devotion of the sacrifice in verses 1 and 2 makes possible the distribution of gifts to individuals in the body of believers. "Measure of faith" (v. 3) and "grace" (v. 6) emphasize the manner of devotion required for the reception of the gifts of God.

II. OBEY ESTABLISHED
    AUTHORITIES (Romans 13:1-7)

A. God Establishes Authorities (vv. 1, 2)

1. Let every soul be subject unto the higher powers. For there is no power but of God: the powers that be are ordained of God.

2. Whosoever therefore resisteth the power, resisteth the ordinance of God: and they that resist shall receive to themselves damnation.

Paul moves from the personal sacrifice of service to the public application of that sacrifice. Sacrifice in society does not come easy. Spirituality does not evolve into witness overnight. There are many obstacles to testifying triumphantly after being at the altar before God.

Rulers and authorities of Rome dominated the attempts of the early church to fully function in service to God and others. What was difficult to understand became a difficult teaching for Paul. The devotion of Romans 12 was understandable because the altar of sacrifice was part of the heritage of the church. However, the discussion of Romans 13 was almost incomprehensible because the courts of Rome were a threat to the church and part of the peril believers faced almost daily.

Presenting oneself at the altar and humbling oneself at the court—what could the two possibly have in common? Both were acts unto God. The "living sacrifice" (12:1) was matched by the "be subject unto the higher powers" (13:1). "Acceptable unto God" (12:1) was matched by "ordained of God" (13:1). Ironically, service and the subsequent use of gifts from God in chapter 12 could have been distorted by pride and rebellion except for the altar of sacrifice unto God. In a similar way, the response to the government of Rome may have been pride and rebellion except for the act of subjecting unto the government as an act of submission to God.

Governments are to be seen by believers as part of the "ordinance of God" (13:2). *Ordinance* includes a root concept, *tasso*, which means "to set in a certain order or arrangement." "Ordained" (v. 1), "subject" (v. 1), and "resisteth" (v. 2) all include the same concept. Essentially, Paul was teaching that God has set powers in a certain order. Subjecting to government authorities is not agreeing with a government as much as it is placing oneself in the hands of God, who has established all earthly authorities. The focus is on God. The governments are instruments of God and so are believers.

B. God's Use of Authorities (vv. 3, 4)

3. For rulers are not a terror to good works, but to the evil. Wilt thou then not be afraid of the power? do that which is good, and thou shalt have praise of the same:
4. For he is the minister of God to thee for good. But if thou do that which is evil, be afraid; for he beareth not the sword in vain: for he is the minister of God, a revenger to execute wrath upon him that doeth evil.

God's order for the governmental context in which believers serve God is an order that will eventually be used of God for good. Paul did not endorse everything a government might do neither did he suggest that God endorses governments. The government may not be good, but God will eventually use the circumstances of the government for His purposes.

Paul said the Christian must not do evil in response to a government. *Evil* emphasizes "acts that are inconsistent with God's will." A Christian might do evil in the name of rebellion against a government, committing personal sin in the process. The believer must also be careful not to interfere with what God may be doing in relationship to a government. God accomplishes His overall purposes in the midst of world governments, and the believer must be careful to act consistently with God's will and action.

C. Our Response to God (vv. 5-7)

5. Wherefore ye must needs be subject, not only for wrath, but also for conscience sake.
6. For this cause pay ye tribute also: for they are God's ministers, attending continually upon this very thing.
7. Render therefore to all their dues: tribute to whom tribute is due; custom to whom custom; fear to whom fear; honour to whom honour.

Verse 5 emphasizes that believers must be subject to authorities, not only to avoid punishment but for the sake of conscience. Believers are to fulfill the requirements of the government as a faithful response to God. The sacrifice and devotion of Romans 12:1, 2 is to be fulfilled in part by responding to government with "dues," "tribute" (taxes), "custom" (revenue), "fear" (respect), and "honour" (13:7). The first three acts—*dues, tribute* and *custom*—are acts required by governmental law. The last two acts—*fear* and *honour*—are attitudes of one's conscience before God that reflect faithful devotion to Him.

Paul was not speaking of following laws that require the Christian to act sinfully. Rather, he was referring to acts that fulfilled one's devotion to God.

III. SERVE WITH LOVE
(Romans 13:8-14)

A. The Obligation to Love (v. 8)

8. Owe no man any thing, but to love one another: for he that loveth another hath fulfilled the law.

The law of God's love is to guide the believer in fulfilling the laws of governments. Fulfillment of a government's law is not just about facts but about faithfulness. Following a government's mandates is not just about what is required but about God's law of personal righteousness.

Christians are to be more than citizens; they are to be ambassadors of God's law of love.

B. Love Fulfills the Law (vv. 9, 10)

9. For this, Thou shalt not commit adultery, Thou shalt not kill, Thou shalt not steal, Thou shalt not bear false witness, Thou shalt not covet; and if there be any other commandment, it is briefly comprehended in this saying, namely, Thou shalt love thy neighbour as thyself.

10. Love worketh no ill to his neighbour: therefore love is the fulfilling of the law.

Paul summarizes the principles that godly laws are based on—preservation of the family, respect for life, recognition of property and truthfulness. All of these laws of earthly governments and the Old Testament are fulfilled by the law of the second great commandment—"Thou shalt love thy neighbour as thyself."

Regarding governmental laws that fell short of the high standards of Old Testament law, Paul appealed to the Romans to respond with the higher laws of God's principles and ultimately the highest law—the law of the second great commandment. Believers were not to respond with evil; a corrupt government should not make a believer corrupt.

C. The Expediency to Love
   (vv. 11-14)

(Romans 13:12-14 is not included in the printed text.)

11. And that, knowing the time, that now it is high time to awake out of sleep: for now is our salvation nearer than when we believed.

Loving God in the midst of (and sometimes in spite of) a worldly government was a matter of urgency for Paul. Paul knew that believers then and now would easily fall and do evil because of the corruption and pressure of worldly governments. The greatest bondage would not be a government's prison but evil's penitentiary. The slavery of a government would not be as great as the shackles of sin. The corruption of law would not be nearly as confining as the corruption of one's conscience.

The influence of government corruption can be paralyzing. Paul compared it to being in a "sleep."

"Awake" is not just a call to Christian service but a cry to Christian conscience. The believer is to be led by God's love, reflecting a liberated conscience, when fulfilling the requirements of a government. What begins on the altar of personal sacrifice in 12:1, 2, is to be fulfilled in service to God in the world.

GOLDEN TEXT HOMILY

"I BESEECH YOU THEREFORE, BRETHREN, BY THE MERCIES OF GOD, THAT YE PRESENT YOUR BODIES A LIVING SACRIFICE, HOLY, ACCEPTABLE UNTO GOD, WHICH IS YOUR REASONABLE SERVICE" (Romans 12:1).

The language of Romans 12:1 is that of sacrificial ritual. In the Old Testament the animal of offering was slain and its blood shed. The New Testament, however, calls for a new kind of sacrifice: the believer is to be crucified with Christ, yet raised to new life in Christ (Galatians 2:20; see Romans 6:4-11). The offering is to be not only "living," but "holy [and] acceptable unto God." These several qualities stand in sharp contrast to the rampant vice so intimately associated with pagan ceremony.

Holiness is both the fundamental character and the governing principle of the believer in his concern to please God. Pursuit of it is the responsible course ("reasonable service") upon which we are enjoined; and it is, furthermore, the basis for that renewal of the mind (Romans 12:2) so urgent to victorious Christian living in the world.—**Excerpts from the *Evangelical Sunday School Lesson Commentary*, Vol. 27**

SENTENCE SERMONS

SERVING OTHERS is a means of serving Christ.

—**Selected**

MINISTRY that costs nothing accomplishes nothing.

—**John Henry Jowett**

SERVING CHRIST includes witnessing to the lost.

—**Selected**

HE WHO HELPS in the saving of others saves himself as well.

—**Hartman Von Aue**

EVANGELISM APPLICATION

SERVING CHRIST INCLUDES WITNESSING TO THE LOST.

One of the greatest sins a believer can commit is self-centeredness. Devotion is not only for personal edification; it is also preparation for edifying others. Devotion is serving Christ, but it is incomplete until others are served.

The altar of sacrifice was a public place where a private act was committed in order that both personal and public service to God were represented. Service to God, even in the most holy of settings, was never seen as complete if it was cut off from its corporate dimension. The very principle of sacrifice was to fulfill the call to be a blessing to many.

Christ's example is the ultimate representation of One who served others while serving God. The Cross was both a fulfillment of obedience to the heavenly Father and reaching out for others. Similarly, the believer is to be aware of the need to sacrifice for the Lord and at the same time use that sacrifice as a platform of service to others.

ILLUMINATING THE LESSON

Romans 13 poses an awesome question: "Can the believer utilize the surroundings in which God has placed him/her?" The first task of the believer is to look for ways God can utilize resources outside the believer to accomplish His will.

Dell Computers revolutionized the business world by taking an approach that maximizes outside resources. Instead of trying to be self-sufficient, Dell uses outside suppliers, shippers and advertisers that can be linked with their company. Dell has no central sales buildings or marketing facilities. Networking with outside agencies is the heart of the Dell success story.

In a similar way, the believer can partner with God in using surrounding resources for God's glory.

DAILY BIBLE READINGS

M. Bound by Love.
Exodus 21:1-6

T. God's Holy People.
Deuteronomy 7:6-11

W. Obey Rulers.
1 Samuel 12:13-24

T. Honor Governmental Leaders.
Matthew 22:15-22

F. Serving Others With Love.
Ephesians 6:5-9

S. Sanctify Christ in Your Heart.
1 Peter 3:8-17

TRUTH SEARCH:
Creatively Teaching the Word

Aim: Each student will ask the Lord to help him or her become a living sacrifice in one particular area of weakness.

Items needed: News magazines and newspapers, marker board, marker

FOCUS

Hand out the various publications around the room. Give students a few minutes to look for stories that depict people exercising forms of power over others. Stories about crime, political power, war, sporting events, and court decisions are just a few of the possibilities. Have them give brief reports.

Next, have students search for stories depicting acts of service. Such stories will probably be harder to find. Have them give brief reports.

The way of the world is to gain power and to use it—and even abuse it. The way of the Lord is to seek out opportunities to serve others.

EXPLORE

Write the following key words from Romans 12:1, 2 on the marker board: "a living sacrifice," "reasonable service," "not conformed, but transformed."

Then have a volunteer read Romans 12:1, 2 aloud. Next, discuss these questions:

• *The term "reasonable service" can be translated as "act of worship." According to Romans 12:1, what is the greatest act of worship one can perform?*
• *What does it mean to be a "living sacrifice"?*
• *How can a person be transformed from a power seeker to a sacrificing servant?*

Romans 12:3-8 describes some of the gifts God gives to the church to help members serve one another. Here's a list. Write the following words on the board: *prophesying, serving, teaching, encouraging, giving to the needy, leading, showing mercy.*

• *According to verses 3-5, how should these gifts be used? How should they not be used?*

For each of the gifts listed on the board, have the class describe a way in which it could be exercised with the wrong attitude. (For instance, the prophet could have an attitude of being spiritually superior.) Next, have the class describe how the gift could be exercised with a spirit of servanthood. (For instance, the teacher can approach a class period as a time for teacher and students to learn together.)

In verses 9-16, Paul describes what it means to live a transformed life of service to others. But how would this passage be written if it were describing the person who is conformed to the world?

Divide the class into small groups of two or three students each. Give an index card and a pencil to each group. Assign each group one of the following sets of verses: 9 and 10, 11 and 12, 13 and 14, 15 and 16. (If your class is small, some groups can be given more than one pair of verses.) Have each group rewrite their verses as if they were written to describe the person who is not living as a servant of the Lord. (For instance, verse 13 could read, "Ignore the needs of others; refuse to show hospitality to anyone.")

When they're finished, have the groups read their work.

Sadly, what we've just heard is the common way of living in today's world.

RESPOND

Challenge the students to focus on Romans 12:13-16 and ask themselves, "Which one of these commands is most difficult for me to follow right now?" Then ask them to commit that problem to the Lord, yielding themselves to Him as a living sacrifice.

Faith: Foundation for Christian Living

Study Text: Galatians 2:15 through 3:14
Objective: To comprehend that faith is the basis of the Christian life and continue living for Christ by faith.
Time: The Epistle to the Galatians was written between A.D. 49 and 55.
Place: The Epistle to the Galatians was probably written at Antioch or Ephesus.
Golden Text: "I am crucified with Christ: nevertheless I live; yet not I, but Christ liveth in me: and the life which I now live in the flesh I live by the faith of the Son of God, who loved me, and gave himself for me" (Galatians 2:20).
Central Truth: The Christian life is a life of faith.
Evangelism Emphasis: Sinners must have faith in Christ to be saved.

PRINTED TEXT

Galatians 2:15. We who are Jews by nature, and not sinners of the Gentiles,

16. Knowing that a man is not justified by the works of the law, but by the faith of Jesus Christ, even we have believed in Jesus Christ, that we might be justified by the faith of Christ, and not by the works of the law: for by the works of the law shall no flesh be justified.

19. For I through the law am dead to the law, that I might live unto God.

20. I am crucified with Christ: nevertheless I live; yet not I, but Christ liveth in me: and the life which I now live in the flesh I live by the faith of the Son of God, who loved me, and gave himself for me.

21. I do not frustrate the grace of God: for if righteousness come by the law, then Christ is dead in vain.

3:1. O foolish Galatians, who hath bewitched you, that ye should not obey the truth, before whose eyes Jesus Christ hath been evidently set forth, crucified among you?

2. This only would I learn of you, Received ye the Spirit by the works of the law, or by the hearing of faith?

3. Are ye so foolish? having begun in the Spirit, are ye now made perfect by the flesh?

4. Have ye suffered so many things in vain? if it be yet in vain.

5. He therefore that ministereth to you the Spirit, and worketh miracles among you, doeth he it by the works of the law, or by the hearing of faith?

6. Even as Abraham believed God, and it was accounted to him for righteousness.

10. For as many as are of the works of the law are under the curse: for it is written, Cursed is every one that continueth not in all things which are written in the book of the law to do them.

11. But that no man is justified by the law in the sight of God, it is evident: for, The just shall live by faith.

12. And the law is not of faith; but, The man that doeth them shall live in them.

13. Christ hath redeemed us from the curse of the law, being made a curse for us: for it is written, Cursed is every one that hangeth on a tree:

14. That the blessing of Abraham might come on the Gentiles through Jesus Christ; that we might receive the promise of the Spirit through faith.

LESSON OUTLINE

LESSON EXPOSITION

INTRODUCTION

Tried and convicted with no possibility of parole, the guilty person stands before the court. No ordinary court, the jurisdiction of this Judge covers the entire universe for all of time. Not the typical judge, this Sovereign declares with perfect wisdom and eternal righteousness.

Nevertheless, suddenly it becomes apparent that the guilty defendant is not standing alone. Standing next to him all the time has been One whose radiance fills the courtroom. His countenance is matched only by the honor bestowed upon the Judge. This One who stands with the defendant sentenced to eternal punishment is shining with love in His eyes.

The One standing with the convicted says, "I will take his place." The Judge looks with eyes of love, as a Father to a Son, at the Intercessor, standing with the one found guilty. The Intercessor says to the Judge, "Father, I fulfill the judgment You have placed upon this guilty one. I give My life that this one convicted may live for Thee."

The courtroom of eternity is hushed with reverent awe at what has taken place. Nevertheless, another one stands in the courtroom, screaming foul accusations, lies and cursings at the defendant, the Intercessor and the Judge. But it is too late. The gavel of perfect justice strikes the anvil on the bar of eternal jurisprudence, and the decree is sounded for all to hear: "The penalty is paid. He who was bound in sin and shame is now set free. Further, not only is the pardon granted, but the convicted has been further granted a decree of adoption so that he now becomes My child."

The scenario just described is not fictional. On the contrary, it is the story of the redemption of every repentant sinner.

Suddenly the scene changes. Anyone may reject the provision of the Son and the Father. Every person has the prerogative to say, "I do not want to be a child of the heavenly Father." However, the provision has been made for all who will accept it.

Paul wrote to a people in Galatia who had not yet fully realized the great gift of freedom and adoption that the heavenly Father had provided for them. The Galatians were being persuaded by other teachers that they had to do something in order to merit the freedom of God from sin. They did not realize that the freedom was based upon the work of the Father and the Son. The basis of freedom was adoption. The legal proceedings were transcended by the love of the heavenly Father for His children adopted through the work of His holy Son.

I. HAVE FAITH IN CHRIST
(Galatians 2:15-21)

A. Justification by Faith (vv. 15, 16)

15. We who are Jews by nature, and not sinners of the Gentiles,

16. Knowing that a man is not justified by the works of the law, but

by the faith of Jesus Christ, even we have believed in Jesus Christ, that we might be justified by the faith of Christ, and not by the works of the law: for by the works of the law shall no flesh be justified.

To illustrate the power of faith, Paul compares faith in Christ with the privileges of the Jews. The Jews had been given more insight into the ways of God than any other people on earth. They had personally witnessed more of the miracles of God than any other nation ever would. They had experienced the power and mercy of God like no other group in time. The Jews had been blessed with an access to God that no other people or nation had.

Nevertheless, privilege does not purchase the blood of perfect sacrifice for sins. Even the Jews needed to confess their sins and have faith in the sacrifice of Christ. If any people could claim the works, ritual and worship that God required, it was the Jews. But even with all their background, revelation and testimony, they still could only receive salvation by faith in Christ.

B. Sin and Death by the Law and Works (vv. 17-19)

(Galatians 2:17, 18 is not included in the printed text.)

19. For I through the law am dead to the law, that I might live unto God.

Paul illustrates the complete inadequacy of the Law by referring to the death as the only acceptable relationship with the Law. Paul stresses that he is dead to the Law. Then he goes further, saying that the Law itself brought him to death to the Law. The Law, by itself, ultimately produces spiritual death.

In verses 17 and 18 Paul indicates that even after believing in Christ, the Law is not an acceptable option. The false teachers in Galatia had evidently persuaded some of the Galatians that

a combination of living for Christ and following the Law was possible.

While the believer can utilize principles within the Law, the Law is not the source of the believer's salvation. The Law is not a source of God's grace. Instead, it reveals the sinfulness of humanity and points to the need to believe in Christ. The Law represents the insufficiency of an individual to satisfy God's judgment without Christ.

The blessing of death to the Law is that it releases a person to receive life in Christ. The definite result of remaining with the Law is death, and the definite requirement for life in Christ is death to the Law.

False teachers had convinced the Galatians they could and even needed to return to the Law after receiving Christ. Paul sought to spare the Galatians from returning to the mire of the mandates of the Law and the false sense of security that came with personal adherence to it. Death to the Law was the means by which they had realized the grace of Christ, and returning to the Law would bring them under the grip of the Law's death.

C. Life Through Faith in Christ (vv. 20, 21)

20. I am crucified with Christ: nevertheless I live; yet not I, but Christ liveth in me: and the life which I now live in the flesh I live by the faith of the Son of God, who loved me, and gave himself for me.

21. I do not frustrate the grace of God: for if righteousness come by the law, then Christ is dead in vain.

The life Paul lived as a believer did not depend on the Law but on Christ. Paul's life in Christ was not fed by the air he breathed but by the faith he maintained.

The contrast between Paul's relationship with the Law and with Christ highlights the true nature of faith in Christ's work. Paul related to the Law by trying to satisfy its requirements. Paul related to Christ by accepting what Christ gave to him. The Law demanded; Christ gave. The Law required; Christ reconciled. The Law took from Paul; Christ freely gave to him.

Death to the Law is the cross of the believer. The Law is the human effort to do enough, earn enough and accomplish enough to receive salvation from God.

After failing to earn salvation through the Law, Paul forsook it and quit depending on his own works. When Paul died spiritually to human effort, he began to breathe in the life of Christ. That breath was the power of faith to rely upon Christ's gift of salvation.

II. CONTINUE IN FAITH
(Galatians 3:1-9)

A. The Spirit Continues in Faith
(vv. 1-3)

1. O foolish Galatians, who hath bewitched you, that ye should not obey the truth, before whose eyes Jesus Christ hath been evidently set forth, crucified among you?
2. This only would I learn of you, Received ye the Spirit by the works of the law, or by the hearing of faith?
3. Are ye so foolish? having begun in the Spirit, are ye now made perfect by the flesh?

False teachers had convinced the Galatians that the Law was as necessary as the work of Christ and the Holy Spirit. While there is value in the teachings and wisdom of the Law, it can never bring salvation. In no way is it equal to the work of Christ and the Spirit. The Cross and the wind of the Spirit are far superior to the Law. In fact, they fulfill the Law. The Law could never produce life, but the Cross and the Spirit freely apply life to the repentant believer.

Individuals, not ideas, feed heresy. A heretical concept is powerless unless a false teacher propagates it. That is why Paul's admonition is much more about the persuasiveness of the teachers than their teachings. The teaching was lethal enough to the faith of the Galatians. Yet, Paul said, in essence, "Why did you let people convince you of this false teaching?" The Galatians were more convinced by the teachers than their teachings. The emphasis on the teachers demonstrates the fleshly nature of the heresy. Heresy inevitably elevates the heretical teacher and diminishes Christ.

The heresy centered on a rejection of the work of the Holy Spirit. The Spirit works as the wind. In fact, the word *Spirit* in both the Old and New Testaments, is literally the term for "wind" or "breath." The breath of the Spirit had produced faith in the life of the Galatians, but their reliance on works rather than faith showed they were now rejecting the Spirit. They had become convinced that faith must be achieved by visible works rather than received by the unseen wind of the Spirit.

The irony is that the Galatians had once experienced the reality of the life of faith in Christ made possible by the Spirit. However, now they were persuaded that the experience that began their life of faith was no longer legitimate and had to be replaced.

The precious experience of initially believing in Christ through the power of the Spirit must be revisited regularly. The early feeling of the freshness of salvation, brought on by the life-giving work of the Holy Spirit, must be nurtured. The maturation of the believer is a process of perfecting the principles of faith and the Spirit that were present at initial believing.

B. Ministry Continues in Faith
(vv. 4, 5)

4. Have ye suffered so many things in vain? if it be yet in vain.

5. He therefore that ministereth to you the Spirit, and worketh miracles among you, doeth he it by the works of the law, or by the hearing of faith?

The Galatians were not new to the faith. They had been tried and tested in their faith. They had sacrificed for their faith. However, somehow they had been persuaded to depart from reliance upon faith in Christ. Part of the reason is captured in the nature of heresy. As mentioned, heresy typically focuses on teachers and the work of individuals rather than the work of God in the Christ and the Spirit.

Paul points to the work of the Spirit and the miracle-working power of God. These are works that cannot be repeated by individuals.

The life of faith looks beyond the works of humanity. The work of the Spirit is far above the works of men and women. Divine miracles are completely beyond human ingenuity and invention. Faith looks beyond human effort and relies upon what humanity could never do.

C. Abraham Continued by Faith (vv. 6-9)

(Galatians 3:7-9 is not included in the printed text.)

6. Even as Abraham believed God, and it was accounted to him for righteousness.

Abraham, the father of the Jewish nation, was a man of faith. The enduring testimony of Israel was not the Law, but the faith of Abraham.

Abraham's faith was more than a subjective experience. God affirmed his faith. God declared Abraham righteous and blessed both Israel and other nations because of his faith. The righteousness and blessings given were not the result of Abraham's following the Law; after all, the Law came after Abraham had already died.

Paul claimed the heritage of Abraham for the Galatians rather than the heritage of the Law. The faith of Abraham was even a blessing to the Galatian believers (v. 9). Abraham believed, and his faith was the key to receiving from God. In the same way, the Galatians' faith in God was the passage to their position as children of the heavenly Father.

III. LIVE BY FAITH (Galatians 3:10-14)

A. The Curse of the Law (v. 10)

10. For as many as are of the works of the law are under the curse: for it is written, Cursed is every one that continueth not in all things which are written in the book of the law to do them.

The curse of the Law made a person a casualty. To depend on the Law for salvation after believing on Christ was a critical mistake. It meant stepping into a lethal entrapment of the Enemy.

The curse of the Law was the manner in which a person was made guilty before God. The text Paul quotes from is Deuteronomy 27:26. Verses 15-25 cite a number of violations of the Law for which a person would be "cursed," then verse 26 says in summary that any violation of the Law would result in the person being cursed. This meant being brought up to God for divine judgment—judgment that would be severe and punitive.

The concept of the "curse" left no room for reconciliation or retribution. Finality marked the curse. Its purpose was to pronounce a sentence of exile from God and others.

Continual focus on the Law as the means of salvation would only separate the Galatians from God and each other. Legalism is the kin of elitism. Legislative Christianity is divisive religion. Law as salvation is the elimination of love.

Loving Christ and keeping His commandments (John 15) is required after salvation. But keeping the commandments to earn salvation creates the curse of the Law.

B. Living in Faith (vv. 11, 12)

11. But that no man is justified by the law in the sight of God, it is evident: for, The just shall live by faith.

12. And the law is not of faith; but, The man that doeth them shall live in them.

Salvation through Christ is always possible, but redemption through the Law is never possible. "No man" definitively clarifies the position of God that Christ is the only way. "In the sight of God" clarifies that God has made the Cross salvation's door. "It is evident" indicates that salvation through Christ has been openly revealed by God, not hidden to be found by an elite few but available to all.

Being in right relationship before God—justified—is the quest of every heart. Created to be in right relationship with God, individuals never fit into their divine destiny until they become "just" before God. The fulfilling nature of the just relationship between a person and God is powerfully illustrated when compared with the curse. The end result of the works of the Law is to hang as a curse before God with no reconciliation to the Father. The result of the Cross is to receive the salvation of the crucified Christ, thereby receiving full access to the Father.

In verse 11 Paul quoted Habakkuk 2:4, citing the lifestyle of faith. The word *live* highlights the integration of faith in Christ into the living of the believer. Paul's case against the Law and for faith in Christ reaches its climax with the comparison between the death of works and the life of faith.

C. The Blessing and Promise of Faith (vv. 13, 14)

13. Christ hath redeemed us from the curse of the law, being made a curse for us: for it is written, Cursed is every one that hangeth on a tree:

14. That the blessing of Abraham might come on the Gentiles through Jesus Christ; that we might receive the promise of the Spirit through faith.

Just as the ancient Greek term for *curse* literally meant "to hang in judgment," so Christ actually hung on the cross. But His crucifixion was unjust. He was placed on the cross in violation of the Law. The folly of the Law was that it would curse even the innocent.

In verse 13 Paul quoted from Deuteronomy 21:23, which says it is a curse to be hung on a tree. Once the person had died, the Law stated that the body had to be taken down and buried that day. Otherwise, a further violation of the Law would occur when the body began decomposing and became a threat to the health of others. Decomposition was the display of God's judgment upon nature. Christ's later resurrection demonstrated victory over that law of judgment.

Why would a person go back to depending on one's own efforts rather than believing on Christ for salvation? Finite morality reverses the order of salvation. The Christian believes first in Christ and then acts morally as a result of that faith. The reversal is to be deceived into thinking that acting morally comes first and then real faith follows. The deception is to legitimize faith through obedience. Obedience to Christ is necessary but secondary to faith in Christ. The just live in obedience to the commandments of God through faith in Him.

GOLDEN TEXT HOMILY

"I AM CRUCIFIED WITH CHRIST: NEVERTHELESS I LIVE; YET NOT I, BUT CHRIST LIVETH IN ME: AND THE LIFE WHICH I NOW LIVE IN THE FLESH I LIVE BY THE FAITH OF THE SON OF GOD, WHO LOVED ME, AND GAVE HIMSELF FOR ME" (Galatians 2:20).

The Christian life has so many paradoxes in comparison to the worldly way of living.

For example:

- To have friends we must first be friendly (Proverbs 18:24).
- To find ourselves, we must lose ourselves (Luke 9:24).
- To be forgiven, we must first forgive (6:37).
- To receive, we must first give (6:38).
- To be exalted, we must first humble ourselves (14:11).
- If we are to live, we must first die (John 12:24).

Facing crucifixion was a horrible struggle for Christ. Finally, He submitted Himself to the will of His Father.

As believers, only as we become submissive to God's will can the Christlife become an enriching experience. Otherwise it will remain always a struggle.

God does not take away our individualism. His life in us is called a "treasure in earthen vessels" (2 Corinthians 4:7). He provides for our every need, answers for our questions, comfort in our sorrows, and healing for our sicknesses as He works His plan in us.—**Fred H. Whisman**

SENTENCE SERMONS

THE CHRISTIAN LIFE is a life of faith.

—Selected

TRUE FAITH commits us to obedience.

—A.W. Tozer

TRUE FAITH needs neither evidence nor research.

—Jewish Proverb

OUR FAITH grows by expression. If we want to keep our faith, we must share it; we must act.

—Billy Graham

EVANGELISM APPLICATION

SINNERS MUST HAVE FAITH IN CHRIST TO BE SAVED.

What the sinner may be able to do on his or her own is not enough. Fulfilling codes of morality is not enough. One's résumé of accomplishments is not enough. One person's acts of kindness are not enough.

Salvation is not measured according to human standards. Salvation is a divine act that begins and ends with God. The sinner must confess sins, declare Jesus as risen and testify of Christ as Lord. However, the drawing of the Holy Spirit is required to even begin the process of confession, declaration and testimony. The sinner can only receive the divine gift of salvation by faith through the divine work of the Son of God.

ILLUMINATING THE LESSON

The depths of human sin are unimaginable. Consider the Holocaust of World War II, in which millions were brutalized and executed.

In the book *In My Hands*, taken from *Reader's Digest*, January 2000, Irene Opdyke chronicles one particular moment of horror:

Then the prisoners were forced out through a gate, while the SS guards beat them with their rifle butts. In vain, women tried to protect their small children from blows; men tried to shield their old fathers. If someone stumbled and fell, shots rang out.

We watched in a paralysis of horror. We could do nothing but watch. Then I saw an officer make a flinging movement with his arm, and something rose up into the sky like a fat bird. With his other hand he aimed his pistol, and the bird plummeted to the ground beside its screaming mother. The officer shot the mother too. . . . We would say, "Behold, This is the worst thing man can do."

When one considers the depravity of humankind, it is easy to see why humanity's efforts to save itself only fail. The only way of salvation is through faith in Jesus Christ.

DAILY BIBLE READINGS

M. Grace and Faith.
   Genesis 6:1-8
T. Faith and Righteousness.
   Genesis 15:1-6
W. Trust in God.
   Proverbs 3:5-8
T. Faith Brings Hope.
   1 Peter 1:3-9
F. Continue in the Faith.
   Colossians 1:21-29
S. Faith Pleases God.
   Hebrews 11:1-6

TRUTH SEARCH:
Creatively Teaching the Word

Aim: Students will ask God to help them live by faith in Christ's righteousness instead of their own.

Items needed: Marker, marker board

FOCUS

Begin with a four- or five-minute brainstorming exercise in which students name all the traffic laws they can. Jot down a key word or two from each law on the marker board. Possible responses include these:

- Come to a complete stop at all stop signs.
- Don't break the speed limit.
- Don't pass on a solid line.
- Don't litter.
- Yield the right-of-way.
- Don't park in a no-parking zone.
- Always wear a seatbelt.

If a perfect driver award was being handed out today, would you win?

Do you think it's possible to drive year after year without ever breaking a single traffic law?

If only perfect drivers were allowed on the road, probably all of us would have to give up our driver's license. And if only perfect people— people who have never broken any of God's laws—could go to heaven, none of us would ever make it. Thank God that He has made a better way.

EXPLORE

Have a volunteer read Galatians 2:16 aloud.

- *According to this verse, what cannot be accomplished by obeying the Old Testament laws?*
- *According to this verse, how can a person be justified?*

Have another volunteer read verse 20.

- *How was Paul both alive and dead at the same time?*
- *What role was faith playing in Paul's life?*

Ask students to read verse 21 to themselves, then restate it in their own words. For example: "If I could keep God's laws perfectly, Christ's death was a total waste, and I do not need God's grace."

Next, have everyone read Galatians 3:1, 2 to themselves.

- *What was the wrong idea that some of the Galatians were believing?*
- *According to verse 3, how does one's walk with Christ begin? How must it continue?*

The message Paul was giving to the Galatians was nothing new. Centuries before Christ came to earth, "Abraham believed God, and it was accounted to him for righteousness" (v. 6).

- *According to verse 10, what will happen to the person who tries to be justified by the Law but who fails to keep the Law perfectly?*
- *According to verse 13, where has the curse of the Law been placed?*
- *According to verses 11 and 14, how does a person receive justification and the promise of the Spirit?*

RESPOND

Ask everyone to pull a coin out of their pocket or purse, then read the four-word phrase printed on it: "In God we trust."

Is that true? Does our country promote trust in God over trust in self? One look at a bookstore's array of self-help books will give you the answer—society teaches us to put our hope in ourselves. But God's Word tells us, "The just shall live by faith." Not faith in self—but faith in Jesus Christ.

Challenge students to ask themselves if they have been trying to do good on their own rather than relying on faith in Christ. Then lead a prayer in which you ask Christ to help everyone lean on Him.

Freedom of God's Children

Study Text: Galatians 3:15 through 6:10
Objective: To evaluate the role of the Law and faith in God's plan of redemption and rejoice in the freedom we have as God's children.
Time: The Epistle to the Galatians was written between A.D. 49 and 55.
Place: The Epistle to the Galatians was probably written at Antioch or Ephesus.
Golden Text: "Stand fast therefore in the liberty wherewith Christ hath made us free, and be not entangled again with the yoke of bondage" (Galatians 5:1).
Central Truth: Christ sets believers free from legalism to live by the Spirit.
Evangelism Emphasis: Christ sets sinners free from the bondage of sin.

PRINTED TEXT

Galatians 3:19. Wherefore then serveth the law? It was added because of transgressions, till the seed should come to whom the promise was made; and it was ordained by angels in the hand of a mediator.

21. Is the law then against the promises of God? God forbid: for if there had been a law given which could have given life, verily righteousness should have been by the law.

22. But the scripture hath concluded all under sin, that the promise by faith of Jesus Christ might be given to them that believe.

23. But before faith came, we were kept under the law, shut up unto the faith that should afterwards be revealed.

24. Wherefore the law was our schoolmaster to bring us unto Christ, that we might be justified by faith.

5:1. Stand fast therefore in the liberty wherewith Christ hath made us free, and be not entangled again with the yoke of bondage.

13. For, brethren, ye have been called unto liberty; only use not liberty for an occasion to the flesh, but by love serve one another.

14. For all the law is fulfilled in one word, even in this; Thou shalt love thy neighbour as thyself.

16. This I say then, Walk in the Spirit, and ye shall not fulfil the lust of the flesh.

17. For the flesh lusteth against the Spirit, and the Spirit against the flesh: and these are contrary the one to the other: so that ye cannot do the things that ye would.

18. But if ye be led of the Spirit, ye are not under the law.

19. Now the works of the flesh are manifest, which are these; Adultery, fornication, uncleanness, lasciviousness,

20. Idolatry, witchcraft, hatred, variance, emulations, wrath, strife, seditions, heresies,

21. Envyings, murders, drunkenness, revellings, and such like: of the which I tell you before, as I have also told you in time past, that they which do such things shall not inherit the kingdom of God.

22. But the fruit of the Spirit is love, joy, peace, longsuffering, gentleness, goodness, faith,

23. Meekness, temperance: against such there is no law.

24. And they that are Christ's have crucified the flesh with the affections and lusts.

25. If we live in the Spirit, let us also walk in the Spirit.

LESSON OUTLINE

I. PURPOSE OF THE LAW

  A. Moving From Transgression to Promise

  B. Preference of Faith Over the Schoolmaster

  C. Children of God and Not the Law

II. GUARD YOUR FREEDOM

  A. The Necessity of Standing to Be Free

  B. The Entanglements That Restrict Freedom

  C. The Necessity of Running to Be Free

  D. Abusing Leads to Losing Freedom

III. BE LED BY THE SPIRIT

  A. Walk in the Spirit to Walk Away From Lust

  B. Walking, Working and Bearing Fruit

  C. The Spirit Leads to Life

LESSON EXPOSITION

INTRODUCTION

Whose child are you? That is the question Paul posed to the believers in the church at Galatia. Paul asked them if they were children of the Law or children of faith. If they were children of Abraham, then they had to claim faith, not the Law, as their heritage.

Do you hide your family background or do you flaunt it? Many feel they have a lot of explaining to do, and in some cases some hiding, when it comes to their family.

Tragically, some people have grown up in such a dysfunctional family that terms of endearment such as "Daddy" or "Mom" are hard to say,

much less accept. Others have lived in a number of family units because of death, divorce or other tragedies, making the idea of family confusing.

Paul wanted to drive the message home to the Galatians that Almighty God was also their heavenly Father. Despite the distortions of today, the family concept of God as our Father and Jesus Christ as our elder brother are very important concepts for communicating the depth of the Christian message. The message is more than writing on a page; it is a relationship written in the heart of every believer.

I. PURPOSE OF THE LAW
(Galatians 3:19-29)

A. Moving From Transgression to Promise (vv. 19, 20)

(Galatians 3:20 is not included in the printed text.)

19. Wherefore then serveth the law? It was added because of transgressions, till the seed should come to whom the promise was made; and it was ordained by angels in the hand of a mediator.

Paul said to the Galatians that the Law, though full of codes, principles and statutes, was given for a secondary purpose. The primary purpose of God's plan was the work of Christ as the mediator for our sins. The Law was not the solution for sin; it was a secondary, temporary measure provided until the work of Christ was completed. The promise of the heavenly Father was that sinners who believed upon His Son for the mediation of their sin could receive redemption.

An interesting aspect of verse 19 was the mention of angels. Paul was perhaps combating a teaching of the Judaizers or Gnostics that attempted to make Christ subservient to angels and/or spirit beings. Paul was indicating that angels served Christ and His role of mediator. Paul did not elaborate on the nature of the angels' participation except to say that they ordained the promises regarding Christ the mediator. *Ordained* indicated a protective role in which they assisted in the fulfillment of the promise of Christ. The reference may have been to spiritual warfare between angelic and spirit beings.

B. Preference of Faith Over the
   Schoolmaster (vv. 21-25)

(Galatians 3:25 is not included in the printed text.)

21. Is the law then against the promises of God? God forbid: for if there had been a law given which could have given life, verily righteousness should have been by the law.

22. But the scripture hath concluded all under sin, that the promise by faith of Jesus Christ might be given to them that believe.

23. But before faith came, we were kept under the law, shut up unto the faith that should afterwards be revealed.

24. Wherefore the law was our schoolmaster to bring us unto Christ, that we might be justified by faith.

Not only the angels but the Law itself was subservient to Christ. The elitism of the Judaizers had belittled the Galatian believers, attempting to shame them for their faith in Christ. The Law was peddled as being more valuable and worthy than faith in Christ.

Paul did not dismiss the Law but put its value in proper perspective. The Law was valuable because of the way it served the promises of God in Christ. The Law could not produce life, but it could guide individuals to Christ.

The purpose of the Law was not to provide a measurement by which a person could applaud obedience but to demonstrate the need for a way of salvation that was unachievable by anyone except Christ.

The work of the Law is fulfilled with faith in Christ. Works of service after faith in Christ are not done to earn a position of merit but are the fruit of faith in Christ. The believer does not work *for* faith but *because* of faith in Christ.

Faith in Christ is the application of the believer's relationship with Christ and the heavenly Father. The possibility of that relationship was created by the Father, through Christ. It is applied to the believer by faith in Christ. The role of faith testifies to the supremacy of Christ's work, just as the angels and the Law testified and were subservient to Christ.

C. Children of God and Not the Law
   (vv. 26-29)

(Galatians 3:26-29 is not included in the printed text.)

Paul's theology of salvation was rooted in his understanding and experience as one of the "children of God" (v. 26). Breaking through with the declaration that he seemingly had been longing to cry out, Paul bridges the faith of the believer to the family of God. Faith is a relationship that is as deep as family relationships. A child is dependent on a parent for conception, sustenance, nurture, identity and so many other aspects of life itself. In the same way, faith is the birthing of the believer into the family of God.

The Judaizers tried to create second-class believers out of those who did not depend on the Law but instead depended solely on faith in Christ. Paul abolished Christian elitism by declaring we are all on the same level, "all one in Christ Jesus" (v. 28). Culminating his arguments, Paul said that believers are not only children of God but "heirs" (v. 29) of God's promise which began with Abraham. In other words, believers are children with a highly favored stature, qualified through Christ to receive the promises of the heavenly Father.

II. GUARD YOUR FREEDOM
(Galatians 5:1-15)

A. The Necessity of Standing to Be Free (v. 1)

1. Stand fast therefore in the liberty wherewith Christ hath made us free, and be not entangled again with the yoke of bondage.

"You have to take a stand in order to remain a child of God" is the message of Paul in chapter 5. While the work of establishing the relationship of the believer as a child of God was accomplished by Christ, the task of staying in that relationship involves the believer.

Stand was a military term in ancient times. The soldier held ground that had been won. In the spiritual realm, Christ defeated the territory of the Enemy, and the believer is to occupy the reclaimed domain. Standing is part of the warfare. The Enemy's attacks still have to be thwarted.

The ground of victory is called *liberty*. Liberty is the ability to be faithful to the heavenly Father. It is the empowering of the individual spiritually to become mighty in Spirit.

Opposite the liberty of the believer is the bondage of the Law. The Law places a person in a "seesaw" going back and forth, trying to achieve moral victory through human obedience. Rather than obedience flowing from faith in Christ's work, bondage practices morality based first on human allegiance. The bondage is the deception of a temporary high created through successful obedience, then a resulting low when disobedience and imperfection set in. In the end, the Law produces a lethal sense of depravity, imperfection and sinfulness.

Paul described the bondage as being *entangled*, emphasizing personal stress, agony and anxiety. Character is questioned; identity is marred; confidence is eroded.

The liberty and stand of the believer are mightier than the bondage of sin and the Law. The character of the believer is patterned after the image of Christ. The identity of the believer is as a child of God. The confidence of the believer is based on the work of Christ.

B. The Entanglements That Restrict Freedom (vv. 2-6)

(Galatians 5:2-6 is not included in the printed text.)

Beginning at verse 2, Paul amplified what he meant by "entangled" in verse 1. Verses 2-6 identify the specific practice of relying on circumcision for salvation. He was addressing persons who had not yet been circumcised and were considering circumcision, those who had already been circumcised, and females who believed in reliance on circumcision and the Law above faith in the work of Christ.

Circumcision and reliance on the Law above the sacrifice of Christ had several consequences. First, Christ's sacrifice was of no profit to that person (v. 2). Second, the person would have to be perfect to all the Law to be truly moral (v. 3). Third, grace would be of no effect to that person (v. 4). Fourth, the person would not be relying on the work of the Holy Spirit (v. 5). Finally, the person would not truly experience the work of Christ's love (v. 6).

C. The Necessity of Running to Be Free (vv. 7-10)

(Galatians 5:7-10 is not included in the printed text.)

Paul compared the Galatians' disobedience to Christ to a runner. Some interpret *run* (v. 7) to a runner in a race. Others interpret it as a runner attacking the enemy in battle. The second interpretation would be more in line with *stand*, a military term in verse 1. As part of the stand against an enemy, a soldier may have to run toward the enemy in order to attack. Regardless of the interpretation, Paul emphasized that the Galatians had become disobedient to Christ.

D. Abusing Leads to Losing Freedom (vv. 11-15)

(Galatians 5:11, 12, 15 is not included in the printed text.)

13. For, brethren, ye have been called unto liberty; only use not liberty for an occasion to the flesh, but by love serve one another.

14. For all the law is fulfilled in one word, even in this; Thou shalt love thy neighbour as thyself.

Evidently, one of the end results of the controversy between the believers and the Judaizers was a lack of love in relationships. The Judaizers and their converts had become elitists, claiming moral and spiritual superiority to others. However, the believers in Christ were not immune to the same temptation. No doubt on both sides, the temptation may have been to be critical of others in order to demonstrate morality or spirituality.

Faith must be guided by love. Faith may bring salvation to the individual, but love brings harmony to the body of Christ. Love fulfilled and summarized all of the Law. Christ died not only to fulfill the debt of sin but also to fulfil the obligation to love. Whereas sin was to be put to death, love was to come alive—both because of Jesus Christ.

III. BE LED BY THE SPIRIT (Galatians 5:16-26)

A. Walk in the Spirit to Walk Away From Lust (vv. 16-18)

16. This I say then, Walk in the Spirit, and ye shall not fufil the lust of the flesh.

17. For the flesh lusteth against the Spirit, and the Spirit against the flesh: and these are contrary the one to the other: so that ye cannot do the things that ye would.

18. But if ye be led of the Spirit, ye are not under the law.

The departure from the lust of the flesh takes place with the walk of the Spirit. The Law had no life because it did not provide the Spirit of God. Following the Spirit leads the believer away from the lust of the flesh.

The lust of the flesh and the walk in the Spirit do not coexist. Following the flesh wars against life in the Spirit. Paul appealed to the desire of the Galatians—to be able to follow Christ's commandments.

B. Walking, Working and Bearing Fruit (vv. 19-23)

19. Now the works of the flesh are manifest, which are these; Adultery, fornication, uncleanness, lasciviousness,

20. Idolatry, witchcraft, hatred, variance, emulations, wrath, strife, seditions, heresies,

21. Envyings, murders, drunkenness, revellings, and such like: of the which I tell you before, as I have also told you in time past, that they which do such things shall not inherit the kingdom of God.

22. But the fruit of the Spirit is love, joy, peace, longsuffering, gentleness, goodness, faith,

23. Meekness, temperance: against such there is no law.

Paul listed "works of the flesh" in verses 19-21. This list carefully outlines the pattern of passion embedded in the lustful walk of the flesh.

Adultery means marital unfaithfulness, especially of a sexual nature. *Fornication* indicates premarital and overall sexual distortion. *Uncleanness* literally means "without cleansing." *Lasciviousness* means unbridled and unrestrained passion and lust.

Idolatry, from a term which emphasized appeal to the eyes, means the worship of an object. *Witchcraft* indicates the desire to manipulate the supernatural. *Hatred* is open hostility. *Variance* indicates strife and contention. *Emulations* (from the Greek, *zelos*) in the context of verse 20 means to allow something to boil over into wrongful acts.

Wrath is a passion to cause harm to others. *Strife* is a self-centered, political action that creates factions. *Seditions* are desires to create divisions. *Heresies* are sects that capture and overthrow other groups. *Envyings* are persistent desires to corrupt and destroy others. *Murders* means the slaying of others.

Drunkenness means to come under the control of alcohol or other substances. *Revellings* (from the Greek, *komos*) describes open, drunken parades, many times held in honor of a deity. The term emphasizes a group, not just an individual, that is openly displaying its intoxication.

The definitions of the aspects of the fruit of the Spirit (vv. 22, 23) are also insightful. *Love* is love from God for others. *Joy* is the deep, abiding sense of tranquillity and confidence that comes from gratefulness. *Peace* means harmony and the absence of wrath and rage.

Longsuffering means the ability to control passion with prolonged patience. *Gentleness* is kindness of heart. *Goodness* refers to kind acts toward others that result from godly virtue.

Faith is an abiding conviction and trust in the truth. *Meekness* is to be dominated by gentleness and mildness. *Temperance* is self-control—the mastery of one's passions and desires.

Besides listing the terms, Paul emphasized how what occurs on the inside of the person would result in actions by the person outwardly. In verse 16, *Spirit* and *lust* indicate what occur inside a person. *Walk, flesh* and *works* indicated outer actions. In verse 17, the same terms are used as in verse 16, with *ye would*, indicating the inner person, and *do*, indicating outer actions. In verse 18, the term *Spirit* indicates the inner person, and *law* indicates outside actions. In verse 19, the process of what occurred inside a person moving to the outside is indicated by the term *manifest*— "the revealing or coming to light of something."

The manifestation process is indicated by the manner in which Paul listed the lusts of the flesh. He presented them in eight paired sets. Fornication produced adultery. Lasciviousness produced uncleanness. Witchcraft produced idolatry. Variance produced hatred. Wrath produced strife. Seditions produced heresies. Envyings produced murders. Drunkenness produced revellings.

Standing in the middle of the eight sets is the term *emulations* (v. 20). It is critical to understanding the manifestation process. As mentioned earlier, *emulations* is literally "the boiling over of something." In other words, inner conditions boil over into manifest actions.

The listing of the fruit of the Spirit strategically matches the meanings and order of the pairs of inner lusts and works of the flesh. Love overcomes fornication and adultery. Joy overcomes lasciviousness and uncleanness. Peace overcomes witchcraft and idolatry. Longsuffering overcomes variance and hatred. Gentleness overcomes emulations. Goodness overcomes wrath and strife. Faith overcomes seditions and heresies. Meekness overcomes envyings and murders. Temperance overcomes drunkenness and revellings.

Paul stressed emotions of the heart when he talked about hatred, variance, wrath, strife, longsuffering and goodness. He focused on conditions of the spirit when he listed idolatry, witchcraft, seditions, heresies, peace and faith. He emphasized actions and behaviors when he listed uncleanness, lasciviousness, envyings, murders, joy and meekness. Finally, he highlighted relationships when he listed adultery, fornication, drunkenness, revellings, love and temperance.

The greatest result of the presence of the Spirit is the impact made upon relationships. The list of sins starts with adultery and ends with revellings, both extreme violations of relationships. The list of the fruit of the Spirit starts with love and ends with temperance, both qualities that show concern and sensitivity toward others in relationships. The process of spirituality emphasized in verses 16-26 is eventually illustrated with a call to those who are "spiritual" to restore others—especially those "overtaken in a fault"—and to "bear . . . one another's burdens" (6:1, 2).

C. The Spirit Leads to Life (vv. 24-26)

(Galatians 5:26 is not included in the printed text.)

24. And they that are Christ's have crucified the flesh with the affections and lusts.

25. If we live in the Spirit, let us also walk in the Spirit.

Getting rid of the lusts of the flesh is not the complete solution for the believer. The cure for sin must include the infusion of the presence of the Spirit. A genuine crucifixion of the flesh requires living and walking in the Spirit.

GOLDEN TEXT HOMILY

"STAND FAST THEREFORE IN THE LIBERTY WHEREWITH CHRIST HATH MADE US FREE, AND BE NOT ENTANGLED AGAIN WITH THE YOKE OF BONDAGE" (Galatians 5:1).

Spiritual freedom is different from the liberty that the world is seeking. The freedom Christ gives can only be achieved through the divine presence of God.

A person cannot enter into this liberty without faith in Jesus Christ. "Therefore being justified by faith, we have peace with God through our Lord Jesus Christ" (Romans 5:1). By faith we can enter into the presence of God, enjoy a personal relationship with Him, and be heirs of every promise in His Word. Such liberty and relationship bring "joy unspeakable and full of glory" (1 Peter 1:8).

The greatest liberty Christ gives is forgiveness of our sins. Then we become adopted sons and daughters in the kingdom of God. Our lives change, we have a new purpose and new goals. This newfound liberty draws us to exalt Christ as the answer to the suffering of this world. We have peace within and the hope of redemption.

How different is the liberty that the world is seeking. The world seeks to be more promiscuous, rebellious and humanistic. Such "freedom" does not bring liberty, but bondage. A person becomes a slave to his own appetite. The only true freedom a person can achieve is found in the liberty Christ gives.—**Jerry Puckett**

SENTENCE SERMONS

CHRIST sets believers free from legalism to live by the Spirit.
—Selected

FREEDOM is a need of the soul. It is in striving toward God that the soul strives continually after a condition of that which only God can give.
—Whittaker Chambers

HE THAT IS GOOD is free, though he be a slave; he that is evil is a slave, though he be a king.
—Saint Augustine

CHRISTIANITY promises to make

men free; it never promises to make them independent.

—William Ralph Inge

EVANGELISM APPLICATION

CHRIST SETS SINNERS FREE FROM THE BONDAGE OF SIN.

The bondage of sin is real. Sin makes you do what you never thought you would do, and go where you never thought you would go, and farther than you ever wanted to go.

Praise the Lord that the person and work of Christ overcame the force of sin. As great as the power of sin is, Christ has at every point broken that power. Breaking sin's bondage is not a matter of ability or availability but rather applicability. The ability to break sin has already been accomplished by Christ. Christ has already allocated the availability of the breaking. However, the applicability of the breaking of sin is in the hands of the individual. If a person refuses to repent of sin, then the victory over sin will not be applied.

ILLUMINATING THE LESSON

The trials and tests of life can burn upon the believer like the hot rays of the noontime sun. We all face difficulties in life; but Christ, through the Holy Spirit, gives us the ability to live victoriously.

Elizabeth C. Clephane was a 19th-century Scottish woman who was physically frail. Because she was such an overcomer and influence for good in her region of Scotland, she was affectionately known as "Sunbeam" by many far and wide.

Clephane penned the words to the hymn "Beneath the Cross of Jesus," in which she pictured the cross as a haven for weary souls who needed the strength and solace that only Christ could give. She wrote:

> Beneath the cross of Jesus
> I fain would take my stand,
> The shadow of a mighty rock
> Within a weary land;
> A home within the wilderness,
> A rest upon the way,
> From the burning of the noon-
> tide heat,
> And the burden of the day.
>
> **—from Kenneth W. Osbeck,**
> ***Singing With Understanding***

DAILY BIBLE READINGS

M. The Law Is Perfect.
  Psalm 19:7-11
T. The Law Protects.
  Psalm 37:27-34
W. The Law Counsels.
  Psalm 119:17-24
T. Freedom Through Christ.
  John 8:31-36
F. Wisdom of the Spirit.
  1 Corinthians 2:6-16
S. Use Freedom Wisely.
  1 Peter 2:11-16

TRUTH SEARCH:
Creatively Teaching the Word

Aim: Students will evaluate the fruit being produced in their lives.

Items needed: Remote control, brown bottle, mirror, dollar bill, computer mouse, poster boards, markers

FOCUS

Display the following items: remote control, brown bottle, mirror, dollar bill, computer mouse.

Discuss these questions:
* *What does each of these things have in common?*

These items symbolize things that can imprison us: television, alcoholic beverages, ourselves, money, the Internet.
* *How could a person tell if he or she was in bondage to one of those things?*
* *What are some other things that could enslave a person?*

Let's see how the Bible says we can be set free from the world's grip.

EXPLORE

Have everyone read Galatians 5:1 aloud together.

Once Christ has set a person free from the bondage of sin, Christ wants that person to walk in liberty.

Ask everyone to read verses 6-9 to themselves.
* *What were some teachers telling Galatian believers that they needed to do?*
* *What was Paul's advice?*

The Christians did not need circumcision. Instead, they needed to walk in liberty through faith in Jesus Christ.
* *In verse 16, what promise is given to those who will walk in the Holy Spirit?*

Divide the class into four groups. Give a poster board and some markers to each group.

Have group one write the works of the flesh from verse 19—*adultery,* *fornication, uncleanness, lasciviousness* (wild living)—at the top of their sheet. Have group two write *idolatry, witchcraft, hatred* and *variance* (v. 20) at the top of their sheet. Have group three write *wrath, strife, seditions* and *heresies* (v. 20) at the top of their sheet. Have the fourth group write *envyings, murders, drunkenness* and *revellings* at the top of their sheet.

Have the groups write on the posters various ways and places in which these evils are being expressed in the local community. Then bring the groups back together and have them report their findings.
* *Verse 19 calls all these evils "works of the flesh." What does that mean?*
* *What does the flesh war against (v. 17)? Why does the flesh sometimes win?*
* *What stern warning is given in verse 21?*

Have everyone read verses 22 and 23 aloud with you.

On the back of group one's poster, write the words *love* and *joy.* **True love is not expressed through sexual sins. The joy of the Spirit fills the emptiness that wild living can never satisfy.**

On the back of group two's poster, write the words *peace* and *longsuffering.* **Instead of the dissatisfaction and misery that comes through idolatry and the occult, the Spirit gives peace. The Spirit produces patience that does not lead to hatred and fighting.**

On the back of group three's poster, write the words *goodness* and *faith.* **The goodness of the Spirit precludes wrath and strife. Meanwhile, the Spirit produces faithfulness in the believer which**

fights against heresies that cause division.

On the back of group four's poster, write the words *meekness* and *temperance*. **There is no room for envy that leads to murder when the Spirit's meekness is present. And the self-control given by the Spirit enables the believer not to participate in drinking and wild parties.**

• *According to verse 24, what is the only way for the Christian to deal with the flesh?*

• *What does it mean to live and walk in the Spirit (v. 25)?*

RESPOND

The flesh constantly wars against the Spirit. Has the flesh won any battles in your life lately?

Have everyone stand. Ask the students to repeat the following verses after you read each one—verses 16, 24 and 25.

Finally, lead a prayer of submission to the Holy Spirit.

Challenges of Discipleship

Study Text: Matthew 10:1-42
Objective: To examine the challenges Christ's disciples will encounter and respond courageously.
Time: The Gospel According to Matthew was written between A.D. 50 and 70. It covers a period of about 37 years, from 4 B.C. to A.D. 33.
Place: The Gospel According to Matthew was probably written at Antioch.
Golden Text: "If any man will come after me, let him deny himself, and take up his cross daily, and follow me" (Luke 9:23).
Central Truth: Every Christian should have confidence in God when facing opposition.
Evangelism Emphasis: Every Christian has been called, commissioned and empowered to be a witness.

PRINTED TEXT

Matthew 10:1. And when he called unto him his twelve disciples, he gave them power against unclean spirits, to cast them out, and to heal all manner of sickness and all manner of disease.

5. These twelve Jesus sent forth, and commanded them, saying, Go not into the way of the Gentiles, and into any city of the Samaritans enter ye not:

6. But go rather to the lost sheep of the house of Israel.

7. And as ye go, preach, saying, The kingdom of heaven is at hand.

8. Heal the sick, cleanse the lepers, raise the dead, cast out devils: freely ye have received, freely give.

16. Behold, I send you forth as sheep in the midst of wolves: be ye therefore wise as serpents, and harmless as doves.

17. But beware of men: for they will deliver you up to the councils, and they will scourge you in their synagogues;

18. And ye shall be brought before governors and kings for my sake, for a testimony against them and the Gentiles.

19. But when they deliver you up, take no thought how or what ye shall speak: for it shall be given you in that same hour what ye shall speak.

20. For it is not ye that speak, but the Spirit of your Father which speaketh in you.

22. And ye shall be hated of all men for my name's sake: but he that endureth to the end shall be saved.

32. Whosoever therefore shall confess me before men, him will I confess also before my Father which is in heaven.

33. But whosoever shall deny me before men, him will I also deny before my Father which is in heaven.

34. Think not that I am come to send peace on earth: I came not to send peace, but a sword.

35. For I am come to set a man at variance against his father, and the daughter against her mother, and the daughter in law against her mother in law.

36. And a man's foes shall be they of his own household.

37. He that loveth father or mother more than me is not worthy of me: and he that loveth son or daughter more than me is not worthy of me.

38. And he that taketh not his cross, and followeth after me, is not worthy of me.

39. He that findeth his life shall lose it: and he that loseth his life for my sake shall find it.

LESSON OUTLINE

LESSON EXPOSITION

INTRODUCTION

What is the initial act that begins the great journey in life with Christ? Most definitely the heavenly Father laid out the plan. And absolutely vital is the role of the Holy Spirit. But what event connects the believer with the Savior, places the Christian in the plan of the Father, and provides the work of the Holy Spirit? The vital link is the call of Christ. Christ's call comes to every believer from the depths of eternity to give direction to daily living.

The call of Christ communicates mission, meaning and motivation; it conveys health, healing and holiness; it creates vision, victory and foundation. The call of Christ is not just for preachers, evangelists or prophets in the Kingdom, but for every person who professes to be a citizen of the Lord's dominion.

The call of Christ came with a price and requires a price. Matthew powerfully describes the nature, direction and meaning of the call of Christ in chapter 10. As Christ taught the disciples, dealt with opposition and fulfilled His divine mission, He unveiled the message of His call to the believer. The price and provision of the call came from Christ, but the hearers and responders were the believers. The message of the call is about both Christ and all those who would listen to His voice.

The eternal goal of every believer is heaven, but the mission of every believer is to heed the call of Christ. While many benefits come to the believer as a result of Christ's work, the call of Christ puts the believer to the work of the Kingdom. Confession begins the journey of Christianity, but the call determines the direction of the sojourn.

I. ACCEPT CHRIST'S CALL (Matthew 10:1-16)

A. Called to Go (vv. 1-6)

(Matthew 10:2-4 is not included in the printed text.)

1. And when he called unto him his twelve disciples, he gave them power against unclean spirits, to cast them out, and to heal all manner of sickness and all manner of disease.

5. These twelve Jesus sent forth, and commanded them, saying, Go not into the way of the Gentiles, and into any city of the Samaritans enter ye not:

6. But go rather to the lost sheep of the house of Israel.

The 12 disciples were ordinary men. Even those who eventually would be used of God in penning the Gospels were not much different from others of their day. That is, they were no different until they heard and responded to the call of Christ.

Each disciple had an original call, but chapter 10 records a revitalization and advancing of their original callings. Whereas before they were called to follow—for example, Matthew 4:19—now they were called to serve. A disciple not only learned from the

Lord, but he also put into action what he had learned. In a sense, until he actually practiced what he had learned, he was only a student. Jesus promoted His students to the position of disciple when He called unto them to serve.

The call to serve was a call to go. The call from the Lord does not always demand a physical transition, but it always demands another level of relationship with Him.

With the disciples' call came the power to defeat unclean spirits and to minister healing and care to hurting people. They were given a specific mission to reach specific people—the Jews.

B. Called to Minister (vv. 7, 8)

7. And as ye go, preach, saying, The kingdom of heaven is at hand.

8. Heal the sick, cleanse the lepers, raise the dead, cast out devils: freely ye have received, freely give.

A message focusing on the work of God accompanies the believer's call. A call without a God-centered message will become self-serving and distorted.

The work of God that the disciples declared was fourfold: (1) healing persons of physical illness; (2) overcoming isolation and impurities, which characterized the life of lepers; (3) overcoming the ultimate tragedy of death; and (4) bringing victory and deliverance over the work of Satan and his evil host.

The call to go was a flow of ministry that came from the Lord through the disciples unto the world. The connection to God that brought the flow of God's work was established through the Lord's calling and the disciples responding to the call.

C. Called to Effectiveness (vv. 9-16)

(Matthew 10:9-15 is not included in the printed text.)

16. Behold, I send you forth as sheep in the midst of wolves: be ye therefore wise as serpents, and harmless as doves.

Call not only brings connection to ministry but also direction and effectiveness to ministry. Power without wisdom is like a car without a steering wheel. Ministry without godly direction is like a boat without a rudder.

The necessity of godly direction was found in the disciples' depth of inability. They were unable to produce their own power, find their own direction or protect themselves—all characteristics of sheep. Not only were they in a condition like sheep, but they were facing opposition that would slaughter them.

Be as wise as serpents. In responding to God's call to serve, the disciples had to exercise caution in ways that a serpent was cautious as it proceeded through a wilderness. They had to calculate their steps and count the cost. They had to be aware of pitfalls and dangers. They had to minister, aware that danger could approach at any time.

Be as harmless as doves. If the disciples did not effectively respond to the call of God, they could do damage to others. Therefore, just as a tender dove, the disciples were to minister with gentleness, humility and grace. Ministry without the proper sense of God's call becomes abusive and self-serving.

II. EXPECT OPPOSITION
(Matthew 10:17-31)

A. Testimony in the Midst of Opposition (vv. 17, 18)

17. But beware of men: for they will deliver you up to the councils, and they will scourge you in their synagogues;

18. And ye shall be brought before governors and kings for my sake, for a testimony against them and the Gentiles.

God's call placed the disciples in the real world. Call was not immunity. The attacks of the enemy and the circumstances of the real world would affect the disciples. Christ's admonition was so strong; He said to them, "Beware of men [the opposition]." *Beware* was a sobering term that indicated real danger was present. The implication was that failure to heed the warning would possibly place them in potential harm. So it is no wonder that the call included wisdom.

Wisdom was necessary because at times harm and danger could distract the disciples from full effectiveness. This could divert the attention of the people from God to the disciples. That is, unwise actions could cause the disciples to fall into danger, thus putting the focus on the foolishness of the disciples rather than the power of the gospel.

B. The Testimony of the Holy Spirit (vv. 19, 20)

19. But when they deliver you up, take no thought how or what ye shall speak: for it shall be given you in that same hour what ye shall speak.

20. For it is not ye that speak, but the Spirit of your Father which speaketh in you.

The testimony of the Holy Spirit would reach beyond the opposition and resistance of the enemy. While cautious, the ministry of the disciples would not be without power. Rather, in the midst of caution, while the disciple was heeding the command to "beware," the Holy Spirit would reveal to the disciple exactly what to say and do.

Still today there are dangers in the midst of the call; yet there is also the constant provision, especially through the Holy Spirit, to match every danger.

C. The Extent of Opposition (vv. 21-25)

(Matthew 10:21, 23-25 is not included in the printed text.)

22. And ye shall be hated of all men for my name's sake: but he that endureth to the end shall be saved.

The Lord continued to speak of the presence of danger, but He then emphasized personal responsibility. Though the Holy Spirit offers insight, power and protection, the disciple is still responsible for taking advantage of the Holy Spirit's availability and

intercession. Rather than being pictured as a mighty warrior, the picture of the overcomer is one who *endures*.

Endurance is the defining quality of the disciple who faithfully responds to the call of the Lord. Endurance is the ability to encounter opposition time after time, face even continual confrontation, and just as consistently depend upon the Holy Spirit for intercession, wisdom and power each time.

Jesus' reminder in verse 22 was that the ultimate reason for the opposition would be Christ and not the disciples themselves. They were not fulfilling their own destiny but a destiny that began with Christ and would end with Christ. Jesus said, "Ye shall be hated . . . for my name's sake." The reputation and the responsibility for the believer's call were Christ's and not the Christian's.

D. God's Care and Our Confidence (vv. 26-31)

(Matthew 10:26-31 is not included in the printed text.)

Not only did Christ bear the consequences for the call, He also bore the care required by the call. Though the disciples may suffer because of the call, they would be cared for in their suffering. Just as the heavenly Father was aware of the fallen sparrow, so He was aware of the disciples' needs. "The very hairs of your head are all numbered," Christ declared (v. 30).

At the same time that a believer may be encountering the greatest suffering because of the call, Christ is ministering care. When the believer responds to the call of Christ to serve, his or her "value" (v. 31) in the kingdom of God is established. Every living person is of value to the Lord. However, the promise is given to believers who are faithful to God's call to discipleship.

III. PUT CHRIST FIRST (Matthew 10:32-39)

A. Confession of Discipleship (vv. 32, 33)

32. Whosoever therefore shall confess me before men, him will I confess also before my Father which is in heaven.

33. But whosoever shall deny me before men, him will I also deny before my Father which is in heaven.

The stand of the disciple is more than matched by the stand of Christ for the disciple. Christ would not arbitrarily call a person to discipleship and service and then leave him alone. As Christ had already mentioned, He would provide wisdom, power and the intervention of the Holy Spirit. Further and much deeper still, Christ would speak in behalf of the heavenly Father for the disciple.

Christ's advocacy for the disciple to the heavenly Father was an important example to the ministering disciple. It was difficult for the disciple to witness and minister to others. There were many obstacles to overcome. However, by comparison, the gulf of sin and shame that stood between the heavenly Father and the sinner were impossible barriers that Christ nevertheless overcame in order to represent the believer to the heavenly Father.

The fact that Christ represents believers to the Father should be a powerful motivation to us to represent Christ to a hostile world. The power to witness, the wisdom to live as a disciple, and the motivation of Christ's example to live as a living testimony are all constantly provided. However, Christ offered a solemn warning to those who reject all that He offers and denounce Him. Unless they repent, those people will not be acknowledged by Christ to the Father.

B. Commitment of Discipleship (vv. 34-37)

34. Think not that I am come to send peace on earth: I came not to send peace, but a sword.

35. For I am come to set a man at variance against his father, and the daughter against her mother, and the daughter in law against her mother in law.

36. And a man's foes shall be they of his own household.

37. He that loveth father or mother more than me is not worthy of me: and he that loveth son or daughter more than me is not worthy of me.

The call of discipleship and service is to place Christ in the central place of priority before all else. The call is not to eliminate everything and everyone in our lives, but to make the rest secondary.

Christ radically called the disciples to prioritize their discipleship by listing two of the most common desires of people that compete for central place in one's life. First, Christ mentioned the desire for peace. It is only natural to desire to live a restful and peaceful life, but Christ must be the center even if it means a storm may arise. Second, Christ mentioned family. It is only natural to desire to live in harmony and faithfulness to one's family, but Christ must be the center even if it means that family must wait on Christ. One's relationship with Christ is *the* priority.

C. Cross of Discipleship (vv. 38, 39)

38. And he that taketh not his cross, and followeth after me, is not worthy of me.

39. He that findeth his life shall lose it: and he that loseth his life for my sake shall find it.

Ultimately the call to discipleship is a cross for life. While the cross symbolizes suffering, its greater meaning is discipleship. Yes, Christ suffered on the cross. However, the purpose of His suffering was to make discipleship possible.

Following the Lord means identifying with and appropriating the cross of Christ to one's own life. The value of discipleship, as expressed by the word *worthy*, is wrapped up in the value of the cross. If a person does not see the cross as valuable, then that person may very well not see discipleship as being valuable.

The difficulty of the cross is that it is the giving up of one's life. Christ gave His life on the cross. In response, the believer must give his or her life on the cross of discipleship. Gain in discipleship is measured by losses—the losing of one's life. However, not just the loss of life but the loss of life for a purpose—that is, "for my sake" (v. 39).

"Taking" is the barometer of "following" (see v. 38). It is only when a person takes up his cross that he fully follows the Lord. The Lord requires a lot, but He also gives a lot. In order to receive a lot, a person must give a lot. The scales are never balanced because Christ has given and provided more than anyone can ever repay. However, Christ gave Himself fully and, in that sense, the disciple can give of self fully.

GOLDEN TEXT HOMILY

"IF ANY MAN WILL COME AFTER ME, LET HIM DENY HIMSELF, AND TAKE UP HIS CROSS DAILY, AND FOLLOW ME" (Luke 9:23).

Salvation and discipleship are two parts of the same thing—our relationship with the Lord Jesus.

Jesus said in effect, "If you are going to come after Me and find life, then count the cost: You must deny yourself, take up the cross daily, and follow Me."

The first step in following Christ is to deny oneself. Jesus' birth, life and death were a continual act of self-denial or self-emptying.

Our Lord requires total allegiance to Him, regardless of the cost on our part. To follow Him, we must be willing to lay aside all conflicting loyalties and interests. The *Amplified Bible* makes Christ's words quite plain: "If any person wills to come after Me, let him deny himself [disown himself, forget, lose sight of himself and his own interests, refuse and give up himself] and take up his cross daily and follow

Me [cleave steadfastly to Me, conform wholly to My example in living and, if need be, in dying also]" (Luke 9:23).

Jesus does not ask anything of His disciples that He was not willing to do. He bore the cross! When we bear our cross, we say yes completely to Him and no completely to self, the world, and the enemy of our soul.

Bible Themes From Matthew Henry gives a beautiful description of "The Cross of Discipleship": "Every disciple of Christ has a cross and must count on it. As each has his special duty to be done, so each has his special trouble to be borne, and everyone feels most from his own burden. Crosses are the common lot of God's children, but of this common lot each has his particular share. That is our cross which infinite wisdom has appointed for us, and a sovereign providence has laid on us, as fittest for us. It is good for us to call the cross we are under our own, and entertain it accordingly. We are apt to think we could bear another man's cross better than our own. But that is best which is, and we ought to make the best of it. Every disciple of Christ must take up that which the wise God had made his cross."

True discipleship demands commitment, self-denial, obedience and crossbearing. Our total commitment to Christ brings peace and joy in this present world and everlasting life in the world to come.—**Brady Dennis**

SENTENCE SERMONS

EVERY CHRISTIAN should have confidence in God when facing opposition.

—Selected

DISCIPLESHIP MEANS DISCIPLINE. The disciple is one who has come with his ignorance, superstition, and sin to find learning, truth, and forgiveness from the Savior. Without discipline we are not disciples.

—V. Raymond Edman

EVANGELISM APPLICATION

EVERY CHRISTIAN HAS BEEN CALLED, COMMISSIONED AND EMPOWERED TO BE A WITNESS.

Without Christians witnessing, the world would be without the full witness of the gospel that God intended before the second coming of the Lord. The role of the witnessing disciple is vital to God's end-time plan. As powerful as the Word and Spirit are, as irreplaceable as the work of Christ may be, and as incomparable as the authority of the heavenly Father may be, the role of the witnessing disciple is necessary. Without the witnessing disciple fulfilling God's plan, many will not hear the gospel message.

Witnessing is not a club but a commission. That is, witnessing was never intended to be done by just a few exclusive members of an elite group. On the contrary, every believer is to consciously seek to be used by God and take every opportunity presented to be a witness for Christ.

ILLUMINATING THE LESSON

The committed disciple has a confidence that abides even in the midst of great persecution and spiritual struggle. Christ wanted His disciples to know that confidence. The author of the well-known hymn "Onward Christian Soldiers," Sabine Baring-Gould, penned additional verses to the song that are not printed in many hymnals. One of these additional verses communicated the great confidence that can abide in the hearts of believers as they go forward in witness for the Lord:

Crowns and thrones may perish,
kingdoms rise and wane,
But the Church of Jesus
constant will remain;
Gates of hell can never 'gainst
that Church prevail;
We have Christ's own promise,
which can never fail.

—Kenneth W. Osbeck,
Singing With Understanding

DAILY BIBLE READINGS

M. Called to Discipleship.
1 Kings 19:19-21
T. Faithful to the End.
2 Kings 2:1-8
W. Rewarded for Faithfulness.
2 Kings 2:9-14
T. The Cost of Discipleship.
Luke 14:25-33
F. Called to Humility.
John 13:12-16
S. Jesus Prays for His Disciples.
John 17:13-19

TRUTH SEARCH:
Creatively Teaching the Word

Aim: Students will respond positively to Christ's call on their lives.

Items needed: Classified advertising section of newspaper, paper, pencils

FOCUS

Read a variety of help-wanted advertisements from the newspaper. After you read each one, ask the group if they would be interested in applying for that particular job.

Read the following ad last: "Help wanted: Expect long hours, lots of travel, hand-to-mouth living. Be prepared for danger, hatred and frequent opposition. Twelve positions available."

Would you accept that kind of position? That was the job Jesus called His 12 disciples to perform. Let's learn about the call of Christ.

EXPLORE

Divide the class into groups of three to five students each. Assign each group one of the following sets of verses—Matthew 10:1-16, 17-31, or 32-39—and have them work together in writing answers to the following questions.

Matthew 10:1-16

1. What did Jesus call and equip His disciples to do (vv. 1, 8)?
2. Where were the disciples commanded to go (vv. 5, 6)?
3. List the items the disciples were not to bring with them (vv. 9, 10). Why were they not to bring those things along?
4. According to verses 11-15, what kind of reception could the disciples expect from some towns? From other towns?
5. How were the disciples to act as sheep? How were they to act as doves (v. 16)?

Matthew 10:17-31

1. Why did Jesus tell the Twelve to "beware of men" (vv. 17, 18)?

2. How would the Spirit help them when they were arrested (vv. 19, 20)?
3. What kind of division might happen in some families (v. 21)?
4. Why would the disciples be hated (vv. 22-25)?
5. List various ways in which Christ reassured the disciples about their mission (vv. 26-31).

Matthew 10:32-39

1. What promise did Christ offer in verse 32?
2. What warning did Christ give in verse 33?
3. In what sense does Christ wield "a sword" when He calls believers to follow Him (vv. 34-37)?
4. What does it mean to carry one's cross (v. 38)? How important is it to do so?
5. In what way must believers lose their lives, and in what way must they find their lives (v. 39)?

Have the groups report their answers to the class. Then, as time allows, let the class discuss various instances when Jesus' words came to pass—times when the disciples healed the sick, cast out demons, experienced persecution, faced death, and so on.

RESPOND

Jesus has a calling for each of our lives. Your calling may not be exactly the same as the ministry of the Twelve, but it is similar. Answer the following questions in your mind as I ask them:
- *Am I ministering to the needy people God has brought into my life?*
- *When the Lord gives me an opportunity to say something for Him, do I speak up?*
- *When I am with nonbelievers, do I take a stand for the Lord?*
- *Am I trusting in the Lord's ability to care for me as I go about His business?*
- *Am I faithfully serving the Lord before my family?*

Jesus said, "If you do not take your cross and follow me, you are not worthy of me" (see v. 38). My calling may not be exactly the same as your calling, but it is similar. I must faithfully carry out the tasks the Lord gives me to do, and you must do the same.

Close with a time of quiet prayer in which everyone can talk to the Lord about their calling.

The Disciple's Personal Life

Study Text: Psalm 119:9-16; Ephesians 6:18; 1 Thessalonians 5:17; 1 Timothy 2:1-4, 8; 4:6-16; 2 Timothy 2:15

Objective: To understand and practice the personal disciplines of following Christ.

Golden Text: "Be thou an example of the believers, in word, in conversation, in charity, in spirit, in faith, in purity" (1 Timothy 4:12).

Central Truth: A disciple lives a disciplined lifestyle.

Evangelism Emphasis: Discipleship includes witnessing to the lost.

PRINTED TEXT

2 Timothy 2:15. Study to shew thyself approved unto God, a workman that needeth not to be ashamed, rightly dividing the word of truth.

Psalm 119:9. Wherewithal shall a young man cleanse his way? by taking heed thereto according to thy word.

10. With my whole heart have I sought thee: O let me not wander from thy commandments.

11. Thy word have I hid in mine heart, that I might not sin against thee.

12. Blessed art thou, O Lord: teach me thy statutes.

13. With my lips have I declared all the judgments of thy mouth.

14. I have rejoiced in the way of thy testimonies, as much as in all riches.

15. I will meditate in thy precepts, and have respect unto thy ways.

16. I will delight myself in thy statutes: I will not forget thy word.

1 Timothy 2:1. I exhort therefore, that, first of all, supplications, prayers, intercessions, and giving of thanks, be made for all men;

2. For kings, and for all that are in authority; that we may lead a quiet and peaceable life in all godliness and honesty.

3. For this is good and acceptable in the sight of God our Saviour;

4. Who will have all men to be saved, and to come unto the knowledge of the truth.

8. I will therefore that men pray every where, lifting up holy hands, without wrath and doubting.

Ephesians 6:18. Praying always with all prayer and supplication in the Spirit, and watching thereunto with all perseverance and supplication for all saints.

1 Thessalonians 5:17. Pray without ceasing.

1 Timothy 4:12. Let no man despise thy youth; but be thou an example of the believers, in word, in conversation, in charity, in spirit, in faith, in purity.

13. Till I come, give attendance to reading, to exhortation, to doctrine.

14. Neglect not the gift that is in thee, which was given thee by prophecy, with the laying on of the hands of the presbytery.

15. Meditate upon these things; give thyself wholly to them; that thy profiting may appear to all.

16. Take heed unto thyself, and unto the doctrine; continue in them: for in doing this thou shalt both save thyself, and them that hear thee.

LESSON OUTLINE

I. STUDY THE BIBLE
   - A. God Approves Study of His Word
   - B. The Word's Work in Us
   - C. Our Response to the Word

II. CONTINUE IN PRAYER
   - A. Praying for All Persons
   - B. Praying in the Spirit
   - C. Continual Prayer

III. PRACTICE A GODLY LIFESTYLE
   - A. Focused on a Godly Lifestyle
   - B. The Example of a Godly Lifestyle
   - C. The Personal Pursuit of a Godly Lifestyle

LESSON EXPOSITION

INTRODUCTION

The disciple's life is hid in God—safe, protected and secure. However, while outside influences, powers and forces may not be able to penetrate God's protection to destroy the believer, corruption can occur from within, underneath the armor of God.

Picture the soldier of the Cross described in Ephesians 6. All the armor and weaponry is fit and secure. However, underneath the armor is a soldier who is not fit. Physically, mentally and especially spiritually, the soldier has become out of shape, weak and without the will to fight. His or her vitality is gone.

Many believers mistake vitality with value. Just because what they possess through Jesus Christ is of eternal value, they assume that vitality is automatic. Vitality is like breathing. In fact, one understanding of vitality is life and breath. Unless a person continues to constantly breathe, there will be no life. By the same token, if the disciple does not continually "breathe" in the Word, prayer and the ministry of the Holy Spirit, spiritual decline will

occur. And the personal life of the believer will eventually be revealed publicly.

I. STUDY THE BIBLE (2 Timothy 2:15; Psalm 119:9-16)

A. God Approves Study of His Word (2 Timothy 2:15)

15. Study to shew thyself approved unto God, a workman that needeth not to be ashamed, rightly dividing the word of truth.

Study is not an option but a virtue for the believer. *Study* comes from a Greek term which means "to hasten," but also from a more primary root word meaning "feet" or "to sit at one's feet." Both connotations of the word indicate more than just the academic pursuit of data. The student Paul had in mind was someone who was zealously sitting at the feet of a master teacher, learning and applying what the teacher said.

Learning is based on relationship. The teacher pours himself into the student. The student receives because the teacher is giving. However, learning is transmitted and received from one person to another.

Disciples are developed, not distributed. Discipleship is not a master blueprint in which steps are followed and end results are guaranteed. Discipleship is a process of give-and-take. Back and forth the learning takes place in the midst of the relationship between master teacher and disciple.

Paul said to study in order "to shew thyself approved unto God." He did not say to study only to know more, do more or even be more. All of those components—knowing, doing and being—are necessary, but secondary to the primary goal of being approved by the teacher. *Approved* comes from the Greek term *dokimos*, which is akin to our modern English term *document*. To document something means to show the evidence or proof of something. Paul meant that our learning should strive for the goal of hearing Christ, the Master Teacher, say, "Well done."

Resulting from the relationship are two very important realities. First, the disciple will not be "ashamed." In other words, the disciple will be confident rather than timid or tentative. Second, the disciple will know how to use the Word with discernment. That is, the disciple learns not only what the Word says, but also how to properly use it.

B. The Word's Work in Us
(Psalm 119:9-12)

9. Wherewithal shall a young man cleanse his way? by taking heed thereto according to thy word.

10. With my whole heart have I sought thee: O let me not wander from thy commandments.

11. Thy word have I hid in mine heart, that I might not sin against thee.

12. Blessed art thou, O Lord: teach me thy statutes.

Not only must the disciple use the Word, but the Word must also be allowed to use the disciple. In other words, the believer should allow the Word of God to make an impact on his or her life. The Word of God provides wisdom, insight, direction and comfort.

The psalmist wrote that he had received cleansing, commandment, protection and teaching from the Word. The cleansing power of the Word is sufficient even for the lusts and temptations of youth. The commandments of the Word give direction, especially when the believer is tempted to stray from God. The protection of the Word addresses even the conflicts and confusion that can beset the believer's heart and mind. The teaching power of the Word communicates the thoughts and intents of the Master Teacher.

The key to applying the work of the Word is the completeness of the commitment of the heart. The heart is the gateway to the Word—the passage through which the Word enters the individual. The psalmist in sincere devotion declared, "With my whole heart have I sought thee" (v. 10). Devotion is vital to the development of a Word-centered life.

Too many people are content to simply know about the Word. However, the Word of God needs to get into the life of the disciple through application, study and meditation. The power of the Word will not come to an individual until that person comes to the Word.

C. Our Response to the Word
(vv. 13-16)

13. With my lips have I declared all the judgments of thy mouth.

14. I have rejoiced in the way of thy testimonies, as much as in all riches.

15. I will meditate in thy precepts, and have respect unto thy ways.

16. I will delight myself in thy statutes: I will not forget thy word.

The psalmist describes the pursuit of the Word in a sixfold manner: declaration, rejoicing, meditation, respect, delight and remembrance. By examining the list in reverse order, we see a process of pursuit that begins with remembrance and ends with declaration.

First, the disciple must remember the Word of God. This requires making the study of the Word a priority. The second step is to delight in the Word—to enjoy going to the Word and receiving from it. Next comes the step of giving respect to the Word. Respecting is being attentive and responsive to the Word rather than just "putting in time" by going to the Word.

Fourth is meditating on the Word. Meditation is to allow the Word to remain inside and penetrate the areas of one's life. Next is to rejoice in the Word. Getting into the Word, and letting the Word get into one's heart, is a worshipful experience. Finally, the disciple's devotion to the Word breaks out into declaration. By its very nature, the Word is not intended to be contained by a person but to be communicated by the believer to others.

II. CONTINUE IN PRAYER
(1 Timothy 2:1-4, 8; Ephesians 6:18; 1 Thessalonians 5:17)

A. Praying for All Persons
(1 Timothy 2:1-4, 8)

1. I exhort therefore, that, first of all, supplications, prayers, intercessions, and giving of thanks, be made for all men;
2. For kings, and for all that are in authority; that we may lead a quiet and peaceable life in all godliness and honesty.
3. For this is good and acceptable in the sight of God our Saviour;
4. Who will have all men to be saved, and to come unto the knowledge of the truth.
8. I will therefore that men pray every where, lifting up holy hands, without wrath and doubting.

Prayer is not a private matter. Though the disciple may pray in one's "closet" of prayer, that prayer reaches out to others who are in need. The prayer transcends borders of pride, prejudice and persecution. It goes far across the miles of land, ocean and continents.

Especially to be targeted in prayer are those who are a threat to the person praying—the "kings" and "authorities" of Paul's time. Believers are called to intercede on behalf of those who are in leadership.

The expression "lifting up holy hands" (v. 8) comes from the Old Testament. In Isaiah 1, God indicated He was tired of and would not receive the worship and prayers of Judah. The reason was that when they lifted their hands in worship, their hands were stained with human blood—a symbol of broken and violent relationships with others (v. 15). Both in Isaiah 1 and in Paul's use of the phrase, right and loving relationships with others was vital to the acceptability of prayer and worship before God.

B. Praying in the Spirit
(Ephesians 6:18)

18. Praying always with all prayer and supplication in the Spirit, and watching thereunto with all perseverance and supplication for all saints.

The Holy Spirit is the believer's partner in prayer. The importance of the Holy Spirit's role in prayer is emphasized by Paul: One is to pray *always* with *all* kinds of prayer and supplication, and it is to be done "in the Spirit." *In* indicates that the prayer is to be surrounded by the activity of the Spirit. The believer does not pray alone. The Holy Spirit is one's companion in prayer.

Supplication emphasizes the desires expressed in prayer. Prayer is not just the reciting of words. It is intended to be reaching within one's heart and praying with emotion, desires and genuine intent.

C. Continual Prayer
(1 Thessalonians 5:17)

17. Pray without ceasing.

The activity of prayer is to be as much a lifestyle as an event. Prayer is to be an attitude as much as an action, and a constant as much as a communication. The heart, mind, soul and spirit of a person are to be totally involved in prayer. Prayer is to be an abiding consciousness and communication with God.

God sometimes causes a divine interruption in the day of the disciple to try to put that person in the frame of mind and attitude of prayer. God communes with the disciple at any time and all the time. The disciple is to correspondingly commune with God "without ceasing."

III. PRACTICE A GODLY LIFESTYLE
(1 Timothy 4:6-16)

A. Focused on a Godly Lifestyle
(vv. 6-11)

(1 Timothy 4:6-11 is not included in the printed text.)

Paul exhorted Timothy to "godliness" as a faithful disciple of the Lord. Paul's exhortation was for the purpose of directing Timothy beyond the earthly goals of discipleship and godliness to the eternal and heavenly rewards of being faithful.

Paul first described discipleship as a process of learning—being nourished in "the words of faith and of good doctrine" (v. 6). Second, discipleship is the process of discerning and refuting teachings that are not sound, based on myth and fable. Third, discipleship means investing in eternal spiritual priorities. Fourth, discipleship bears the qualities of work, endurance and trust.

B. The Example of a Godly Lifestyle
(vv. 12, 13)

12. Let no man despise thy youth; but be thou an example of the believers, in word, in conversation, in charity, in spirit, in faith, in purity.

13. Till I come, give attendance to reading, to exhortation, to doctrine.

Whether the believer is aware of it, likes it or tries to deny it, he or she is a constant example to others. The example will either point others to Christ or away from Him.

Being an example does not come without resistance and obstacles. The particular obstacle Timothy faced was his youth. He was a pastor whom some might criticize for being too young. The power of Christian example could overcome their criticism, but Timothy had to be faithful as a disciple.

Paul further describes the nature of discipleship in this passage, presenting a ninefold description: the content of one's words, "conversation" (conduct), love for others, spiritual devotion, faith, a pure lifestyle, the study of God's Word, ministry to others and sound teaching ("doctrine").

Vital to the process of Christian formation was the relationship between Paul and Timothy. By saying that he was coming, Paul was communicating that Timothy was going to be held accountable by Paul for his walk with Christ.

C. The Personal Pursuit of a Godly Lifestyle (vv. 14-16)

14. Neglect not the gift that is in thee, which was given thee by prophecy, with the laying on of the hands of the presbytery.

15. Meditate upon these things; give thyself wholly to them; that thy profiting may appear to all.

16. Take heed unto thyself, and unto the doctrine; continue in them: for in doing this thou shalt both save thyself, and them that hear thee.

Timothy was a gifted young man who had been chosen by Paul to pastor the church at Ephesus. Paul had labored long and hard at Ephesus. He began the church, pastored it himself, and remained in touch with the church. Paul thought enough of Timothy's life and ministry that he appointed Timothy pastor.

When Paul used the term *neglect* (v. 14), he was indirectly using the illustration of a fire. In 2 Timothy 1:6, he urged Timothy to "stir up" the gift of God. The term *stir up* was used in other ancient literature to describe the stirring of the embers of a fire in order to keep the fire going. The gifting of God is similar. It must be stirred in order to be maintained. It must not be neglected.

Paul urged Timothy to give himself wholly to the things of God. He was to focus on personal development, not looking at others or other priorities before looking to God. Timothy was to continually learn the things of God and live out the Christian life. Through his faithfulness as a disciple, Timothy would both save himself and his hearers.

GOLDEN TEXT HOMILY

"BE THOU AN EXAMPLE OF THE BELIEVERS, IN WORD, IN CONVERSATION, IN CHARITY, IN SPIRIT, IN FAITH, IN PURITY" (1 Timothy 4:12).

The apostle Paul was cognizant of Timothy's relative youthfulness with regard to his responsible position in the church. Paul did not believe lack of chronological age was necessarily a hindrance to effective Christian service. He exhorted his younger protégé to excel in those qualities in which youth are prone to be deficient, thereby to serve as an example to the believers.

Timothy was to be an example "in word"—that is, in language or manner of speaking. The speech of unbelievers often contains profanity, filth, gossip and malice. Unfortunately, Christians may acquire some of the speech patterns of the society in which they live. It is well to remember the teaching of our Lord, "Let your communication be, Yea, yea; Nay, nay: for whatsoever is more than these cometh of evil" (Matthew 5:37).

The word translated "conversation" in the golden text means much more than our modern English word. It means "manner of life, behavior or conduct." Not only should the Christian be an example in speech but also in actions.

"Charity" is a translation of the word *agape*, which means "affection, goodwill, love or benevolence." In this context it refers to that love of believers toward believers as a result of their relationship to Christ.

The Christian is to be an example "in faith"—believing in God, who is the Creator and ruler of the universe, the bestower of salvation, and other blessings promised in the Scriptures. The word *faith* may also mean "faithfulness or fidelity," of which the believer should also be a model.

Finally, the Christian's conduct is to flow from a life of "purity" that is undefiled by this world. If a believer is to be an effective witness for Christ, he must be a Christlike example.—**Richard Y. Bershon**

SENTENCE SERMONS

A DISCIPLE lives a disciplined lifestyle.

—Selected

THE BIBLE is God's chart for you to steer by, to keep you from the bottom of the sea, and to show you where the harbor is and how to reach it without running on rocks and bars.

—Henry Ward Beecher

HE WHO RUNS from God in the morning will scarcely find Him the rest of the day.

—John Bunyan

PRAYER IS a sincere, sensible, affectionate pouring out of the soul to God, through Christ in the strength and assistance of the Spirit, for such things as God has promised.

—John Bunyan

EVANGELISM APPLICATION

DISCIPLESHIP INCLUDES WITNESSING TO THE LOST.

The disciple's faithfulness to the Lord includes faithfulness to witness. The disciple's personal development includes the development of witness. The disciple's empowerment includes the power to witness.

Discipleship is incomplete and jeopardized when witnessing to the lost is excluded. Witnessing is not without price; nevertheless, it is part of the price of discipleship.

The lost are dependent on the witness of disciples. Believers must pray for the lost, study the Word to equip themselves to win the lost, and declare the Word in order to reach the lost.

ILLUMINATING THE LESSON

Discipleship is a constant task. Each day is a day for discipleship development. Lina Sandell was a great Scandinavian songwriter who was a major influence in the 19th-century revival there. Though she was frail of stature, she had profound insight into the day-to-day faithfulness required of a disciple. In a song titled "Day by Day," she wrote:

> Day by day and with each
>   passing moment,
> Strength I find to meet my
>   trials here;
> Help me then in ev'ry
>   tribulation
> So to trust Thy promises,
>   O Lord,
> That I lose not faith's sweet
>   consolation
> Offered me within Thy holy
>   Word.
> Help me, Lord, when toil and
>   trouble meeting,

> E'er to take, from a Father's
>   hand,
> One by one, the days, the
>   moments fleeting,
> Till I reach the Promised Land.

—from Kenneth W. Osbeck,
Singing With Understanding

DAILY BIBLE READINGS

M. Make the Word Your Pattern.
   Psalm 119:129-135
T. Live a Holy Life.
   Daniel 1:8-17
W. Be Faithful in Prayer.
   Daniel 6:4-13
T. Learn God's Word.
   Acts 17:10-12
F. Live Worthy of Your Calling.
   Ephesians 4:1-6
S. Pray in God's Will.
   1 John 5:13-15

TRUTH SEARCH:
Creatively Teaching the Word

Aim: Students will evaluate their practice of spiritual disciplines, and commit to strengthen weak areas.

Items needed: Paper, pencils, marker board, marker

FOCUS

Have everyone stand. Lead them in doing some simple exercises, such as stretching their arms upward and outward, bending over and touching their toes, walking around the room, and jogging in place. Then have everyone sit down.
• *How many of you exercise regularly? What type of exercise program are you following?*
• *How many of you have ever started an exercise program, then quit? Why did you quit?*

Physical conditioning is important, but there is a more important form of exercise we're going to explore today. In 1 Timothy 4:7, 8, Paul wrote, "Exercise . . . unto godliness. For bodily exercise profiteth little: but godliness is profitable unto all things, having promise of the life that now is, and of that which is to come."

EXPLORE

In today's lesson we'll explore three forms of godly exercise that can help us become more like Christ.

Divide the class into groups of three or four students each. Assign each group one of the following sets of Scripture passages to explore: (1) Psalm 119:9-16; (2) 1 Timothy 2:1-4, 8; Ephesians 6:18; 1 Thessalonians 5:17; and (3) 1 Timothy 4:6-16.

Psalm 119:9-16

1. List all the different terms the psalmist uses to describe the Word of God in this passage. What can you learn from this list?
2. List all the ways the psalmist

said he would respond to the Word of God. What can you learn from this list?
3. What benefits can be gained through the study and application of the Word (vv. 9, 11)?

1 Timothy 2:1-4, 8; Ephesians 6:18; 1 Thessalonians 5:17

1. List the various forms of prayer in which believers are to engage (1 Timothy 2:1-4).
2. How should these prayers be offered (v. 8)?
3. Rewrite this verse in a way that a 12-year-old could easily understand (Ephesians 6:18).
4. How is it possible to practice this verse (1 Thessalonians 5:17)?

1 Timothy 4:6-16

1. Describe the person who is not spiritually healthy (vv. 6-8).
2. In what ways is the believer to be a witness to others (v. 12)?
3. How can a person stay in good physical condition (vv. 13-15)?
4. What are the benefits of a consistent walk with Christ (v. 16)?

Bring everyone back together and discuss their findings.

RESPOND

Write the following on the board:
• Meditate on God's Word.
• Pray regularly—intercede, make requests, and give thanks.
• Faithfully live out God's Word, serving as an example to others.
Which of these areas are strengths in your life right now? Is there a weak area?

Ask the students to locate one of the verses from today's study that highlights a spiritual discipline that needs to be strengthened. Then have them use the words of that verse in a prayer of commitment. (For instance, "Lord, help me to hide Your Word in my heart and meditate on it.")

Love: Mark of the Disciple

Study Text: John 13:34, 35; 15:9-14, 17; 1 Corinthians 12:31 through 13:7; 1 John 4:7-12, 19- 21

Objective: To know that love is the signature of Christ's disciples and demonstrate His love by what we do and say.

Golden Text: "A new commandment I give unto you, That ye love one another; as I have loved you, that ye also love one another. By this shall all men know that ye are my disciples, if ye have love one to another" (John 13:34, 35).

Central Truth: Love for others characterizes a true disciple of Christ.

Evangelism Emphasis: Christ's love motivates disciples to share the gospel.

PRINTED TEXT

John 13:34. A new commandment I give unto you, That ye love one another; as I have loved you, that ye also love one another.

35. By this shall all men know that ye are my disciples, if ye have love one to another.

15:9. As the Father hath loved me, so have I loved you: continue ye in my love.

10. If ye keep my commandments, ye shall abide in my love; even as I have kept my Father's commandments, and abide in his love.

11. These things have I spoken unto you, that my joy might remain in you, and that your joy might be full.

12. This is my commandment, That ye love one another, as I have loved you.

13. Greater love hath no man than this, that a man lay down his life for his friends.

14. Ye are my friends, if ye do whatsoever I command you.

17. These things I command you, that ye love one another.

1 Corinthians 13:4. Charity suffereth long, and is kind; charity envieth not; charity vaunteth not itself, is not puffed up,

5. Doth not behave itself unseemly, seeketh not her own, is not easily provoked, thinketh no evil;

6. Rejoiceth not in iniquity, but rejoiceth in the truth;

7. Beareth all things, believeth all things, hopeth all things, endureth all things.

1 John 4:7. Beloved, let us love one another: for love is of God; and every one that loveth is born of God, and knoweth God.

8. He that loveth not knoweth not God; for God is love.

9. In this was manifested the love of God toward us, because that God sent his only begotten Son into the world, that we might live through him.

10. Herein is love, not that we loved God, but that he loved us, and sent his Son to be the propitiation for our sins.

11. Beloved, if God so loved us, we ought also to love one another.

12. No man hath seen God at any time. If we love one another, God dwelleth in us, and his love is perfected in us.

19. We love him, because he first loved us.

20. If a man say, I love God, and hateth his brother, he is a liar: for he that loveth not his brother whom he hath seen, how can he love God whom he hath not seen?

21. And this commandment have we from him, That he who loveth God love his brother also.

LESSON OUTLINE

LESSON EXPOSITION

INTRODUCTION

What are you known for? If someone were to give your eulogy today, what outstanding characteristics about you would be cited? More than reputation, what would be your witness and legacy?

Legacies linger. You may not think people will remember very much about you, but they will. In fact, you have a living legacy. People remember things about you now. People remember your demeanor, your looks, your words, even the tone of your words. Your attitudes and actions are remembered. Your witness or absence of witness for Christ is remembered.

The thought that so much about you is remembered by others may be frightening. There are things we would rather people forget. Memories can be terrible. We tend to remember tragic events, fights we regretted and sins that have long been repented of.

When Christ was preparing to leave His disciples in John 13, He not only spoke about their remem-

brance of Him, but He also challenged the disciples regarding their own legacy. Christ had ministered, keeping in mind the testimony He would leave behind. While the disciples could not leave a memory that would match Christ's, they could nonetheless leave a powerful, life-changing testimony.

The testimony the Lord exhorted the disciples to leave behind was a testimony about both Himself and themselves. He wanted them to be known for the love of God that had penetrated their lives and the love they had for one another. The disciples' testimony would be a reflection of their obedience to the command of love (John 13:34) that Christ had taught them.

Obedience to the command to love God and one another was more than a reaction to a command; it was an action that would change the lives of others.

I. COMMAND TO LOVE (John 13:34, 35; 15:9-14, 17)

A. Love Is the Mark of the Disciples (13:34, 35)

34. A new commandment I give unto you, That ye love one another; as I have loved you, that ye also love one another.
35. By this shall all men know that ye are my disciples, if ye have love one to another.

The command to love was "new" in that it was fresh, powerful and illustrated by Christ himself. Christ had preached about love before. However, He was now connecting His past teaching with His current modeling of love at the Last Supper and with the future testimony of the disciples. Love was now "new" for the disciples because they were to be the body of Christ and the means by which the gospel would be sent.

The heart of the gospel is love. The lives of the disciples had been transformed through Christ's love for them. "As" (v. 34) indicated that the love and work of Christ was not just history, but the source of the disciples' ability to love one another.

The love that the disciples were to have was no private matter. It came from a source outside of them—God. The model for the love they were to follow came from the Lord Jesus Christ. The motivation to love one another came from the command of Christ. Their love would not be love until they received it and extended it beyond themselves individually.

Love would be the primary means by which others would know the disciples were genuine followers of Christ. Love would say they had not only been with Christ, but they had learned from Him. Love would say they not only heard His words, but they were putting His words into practice. Love would say they had not only been acquainted with Him, but they knew Him very closely. Finally, love would say they had not only witnessed what Christ had done, but they were now witnesses themselves of Christ.

B. God's Love in the Disciples (15:9-12)

9. As the Father hath loved me, so have I loved you: continue ye in my love.

10. If ye keep my commandments, ye shall abide in my love; even as I have kept my Father's commandments, and abide in his love.

11. These things have I spoken unto you, that my joy might remain in you, and that your joy might be full.

12. This is my commandment, That ye love one another, as I have loved you.

Christ continued from the new commandment and mark of love in John 13:34, 35 to the new commandment and corresponding joy of love in John 15:9-12. The mark of love in chapter 13 indicated the effect of love upon others. The joy of love in chapter 15

indicated the effect of love upon the disciples personally, emphasizing the presence of Christ in their lives.

Christ would be connected with the disciples as a vine is connected with its branches, a concept which He had just discussed (vv. 1-8). The connecting point that grafted them to Christ would be the love they had for Him and the love He had for them. Flowing from the Vine through the branches would be the nourishment of joy.

The presence of Christ and His love would bring complete joy. The full measure of the Lord's joy would fill their lives.

The contingency of the disciples' love, joy and witness would be obedience to the commands of Christ. Obedience was not just a response to a command but also their connection to relationship with Christ.

C. Disciples Loving One Another (vv. 13, 14, 17)

13. Greater love hath no man than this, that a man lay down his life for his friends.

14. Ye are my friends, if ye do whatsoever I command you.

17. These things I command you, that ye love one another.

Relationship is the ultimate dimension of Christianity. Christ had taught the disciples about the effect of their love upon a disbelieving world—they would be witnesses through their love for one another. Christ also taught them about the effect of their love upon themselves personally—they would be filled with the fullness of God's joy. Christ was ultimately pointing to the quality of relationship He would continue to have with them. Their obedience would lead to friendship.

The friendship and obedience of verse 14 were based on the action of Christ in verse 13. He had laid down His life for the disciples. Christ had not yet been to the cross, but He knew the cross was coming and that He was willing to be the ultimate sacrifice.

Verse 17 indicates that friends of Christ must love others. Too many Christians are only receivers and not transmitters of Christ's love. They may specialize in obedience to commandments of the Lord but fall short in loving others. The reality is that failure to love others is the ultimate disobedience and rejection of the teachings of Christ. Not only does one then stand alienated from others but also alienated from a full, loving relationship with Christ.

II. CHARACTERISTICS OF LOVE
(1 Corinthians 12:31; 13:1-7)

A. Preeminence of Love Over Self
(12:31; 13:1-3)

(1 Corinthians 12:31 and 13:1-3 are not included in the printed text.)

First Corinthians 13 is not just about love, but about the role of love in the body of Christ. The stage for chapter 13 is set by chapter 12, especially verses 25-27, where Paul taught that the gifts of the Spirit come from God and are given to the body of believers. The effective and godly operation of the gifts of the Spirit demands sensitivity and caring for one another. Paul extends care to love when he introduces chapter 13 by saying in 12:31 that the "more excellent way" is for believers to work together in love. The opposite is for members of the body to be divided.

The possibility of division in the Body is the topic of 13:1-3. When members of the body are more concerned about self than others, those members are "nothing" (vv. 2, 3). Even if God indeed has gifted the unloving members, they and the personal benefit of their gifts are worth "nothing." Love regulates the personal effectiveness of the gifts. Love is greater than giftedness.

B. Preeminence of Love Over Corruption
(13:4-6)

4. Charity suffereth long, and is kind; charity envieth not; charity vaunteth not itself, is not puffed up,

5. Doth not behave itself unseemly, seeketh not her own, is not easily provoked, thinketh no evil;

6. Rejoiceth not in iniquity, but rejoiceth in the truth.

Love is not only preeminent over self-centeredness; love is also to be preeminent over corruption. Verses 4-6 stress the effect of the lack of love—to bring "evil" upon other people. If genuine love abides within a person, person-to-person corruption will be eliminated. People cannot force a believer to not love them.

C. Preeminence of Love Over Circumstances (v. 7)

7. Beareth all things, believeth all things, hopeth all things, endureth all things.

By citing circumstances, Paul completes his initial review of things that might be used by someone to keep him or her from loving. Genuine love is preeminent over all circumstances. There is no circumstance that can force the believer not to love. The inclusiveness of this principle is set forth by Paul when he repeats four times in verse 7 that in "all" circumstances, love is still the commandment of the Lord.

III. PRIORITY OF LOVE
(1 John 4:7-12, 19-21)

A. Priority to Love One Another (vv. 7-9)

7. Beloved, let us love one another: for love is of God; and every one that loveth is born of God, and knoweth God.

8. He that loveth not knoweth not God; for God is love.

9. In this was manifested the love of God toward us, because that God sent his only begotten Son into the world, that we might live through him.

Love was the motive when the heavenly Father sent His only begotten Son to the world. The road that leads to salvation began with the love of the Father. John appeals to the readers to not forget the roots of their Christian experience, the love of the Father.

The existence of the love of the Father within them is identifiable by the love believers have toward one another. What an amazing system— love revealed by love . . . divine love revealed by the presence of human love. In fact, love between brothers and sisters in Christ reveals spiritual life and heritage. Life given by God is revealed in love between members of the Body because spiritual birth naturally leads to Christian love.

Finally, the relationship between the Father and His children is revealed through love. The term *know* (vv. 7, 8) signifies relational knowledge, not intellectual knowledge. The believer's love for other Christians reflects that the believer is in close relationship with God. The loving believer has a deep, abiding relationship with the heavenly Father.

B. Priority of God's Love Within Us (vv. 10-12)

10. Herein is love, not that we loved God, but that he loved us, and sent his Son to be the propitiation for our sins.

11. Beloved, if God so loved us, we ought also to love one another.

12. No man hath seen God at any time. If we love one another, God dwelleth in us, and his love is perfected in us.

The love of believers for one another is not human in origin. The love of God that brought His Son to earth and the cross is the same love that the believers are to have for one another. Just as the water in a river is connected with the source of the headwaters of that river, so the believer's love is connected with the Father's love. The waters of the river of God's love are the same downstream as they are upstream.

Even though God is not seen, His love is seen through believers when they love one another. Love is the reflection of God's image. The world sees God's love through Christians.

C. Proof of God's Love (vv. 19-21)

19. We love him, because he first loved us.

20. If a man say, I love God, and hateth his brother, he is a liar: for he that loveth not his brother whom he hath seen, how can he love God whom he hath not seen?

21. And this commandment have we from him, That he who loveth God love his brother also.

When one believer sees another, God is seen through that person. The rejection of God's presence, as revealed through another believer, is essentially a forecast of the absence of love for God himself.

Some might desire to love God directly and then work on loving believers. However, John says that love for believers now is prerequisite to really loving God at all. The believer cannot love God and then test whether or not he or she loves other believers. Rather, love for other believers is the test as to whether or not a person was or even could genuinely love God himself.

GOLDEN TEXT HOMILY

"A NEW COMMANDMENT I GIVE UNTO YOU, THAT YE LOVE ONE ANOTHER; AS I HAVE LOVED YOU, THAT YE ALSO LOVE ONE ANOTHER. BY THIS SHALL ALL MEN KNOW THAT YE ARE MY DISCIPLES, IF YE HAVE LOVE ONE TO ANOTHER" (John 13:34, 35).

It definitely is easier to say the words "I love you" than to fulfill them. That's because love requires a commitment of actions which goes far beyond our emotions. This can be vividly seen in 1 Corinthians 13. Verses 4-7 provide us with a definition comprised of attitudes and actions.

When Jesus gave the commandment for believers to love one another, that is what He intended. The manner in which He loved us through sacrificial commitment is what we are to demonstrate with fellow believers. This should cause us to step back, take a deep breath and evaluate this dimension of Christian behavior. Are we revealing that type of love toward one another?

This new commandment of Christ emphasizes the difference which He makes in our lives. It also speaks of the bond which is to be the trademark of believers around the world. Here we see that Christ's body, the church, is much more than a loose fellowship in which membership can be taken for granted. Instead, its members are to constantly be demonstrating their commitment to Him and to each other. The greatest witness on a daily basis never consists of our words alone. It's our actions toward each other, confirming our words, that speaks of the difference there is in being a disciple of Christ.—**Jerald Daffe**

SENTENCE SERMONS

LOVE FOR OTHERS characterizes a true disciple of Christ.

—Selected

LOVE is the medicine of all moral evil. By it the world is to be cured of sin.

—Henry Ward Beecher

IT IS LOVE that asks, that seeks, that knocks, that finds, and that is faithful to what it finds.

—Saint Augustine

EVANGELISM APPLICATION

CHRIST'S LOVE MOTIVATES DISCIPLES TO SHARE THE GOSPEL.

Human love for others may assist in the sharing of the gospel for a while, but eventually discouragement, temptations and the cares of life will spoil human love. Love for social causes that endeavor to improve the plight of people may move a person to witness to others, but the immensity of the task will eventually overwhelm the believer's witness.

The experience of Christ's love supplies the beginning and continuing power of the believer's witness. The closer the believer is to the love of Christ, the closer the believer will be able to get to the world in order to witness to others about Christ's love. Christ's love is fostered through a rich devotional life.

Witness begins before the saint even meets the sinner. Witness begins with the experience of Christ's love.

ILLUMINATING THE LESSON

Visitors fail to return to a church when they do not feel the love of the people.

God-directedness is certainly the first priority of the church, but the second priority should be love-directed toward one another. If the transmission of God's love depends on the believers' love for others, how much of God's love does a visitor receive through the congregation? The visitor may leave having been introduced to the love of Christ but never being introduced to the love of the saints. Sinners have a responsibility to accept Christ's love, but saints have a responsibility to share the love of Christ. One person said, "People do not care how much you know until they know how much you care."

DAILY BIBLE READINGS

M. Love at All Times.
Exodus 23:1-9
T. Love Your Neighbor.
Leviticus 19:9-18
W. Love Covers All Sin.
Proverbs 10:6-12
T. Love Your Enemies.
Matthew 5:38-48
F. Encourage Others to Love.
Hebrews 10:19-25
S. Demonstrate Practical Love.
1 John 3:11-18

TRUTH SEARCH:
Creatively Teaching the Word

Aim: Students will explore the priority of love, then pray for one another in small groups.

Items needed: Enough note cards for every class member to have one. Write one letter—L, O, V, or E—on each card, making a similar number of cards for each letter.

FOCUS

As students enter, randomly pass out one note card to each person. When it's time for class to begin, ask students to get in groups based on the letters they have (for example, everyone with a letter L should be together).

- *Everyone's in their own group, right? How does this remind you of how we sometimes act at church?*
- *What are some of the different groups that sometimes divide a church?*
- *Is it possible for the local church to get together as one united body of believers?*

Have groups exchange cards so that the word *LOVE* can be spelled in each group.

The one thing that can unite the church is love.

EXPLORE

Have the four groups stay together as study groups. Each group should explore one of the following passages: (1) John 13:34, 35; 15:9-14, 17; (2) 1 Corinthians 12:31—13:7; (3) 1 John 4:7-12, 19-21.

John 13:34, 35; 15:9-14, 17

1. According to John 13:34, how much are Christians supposed to love each other? What does this mean?

2. Why is love the distinguishing mark of genuine Christians?

3. How does John 15:10, 14 explain the relationship between loving God and obeying God?

4. Can a person truly love God without loving other Christians? Why or why not?

1 Corinthians 12:31—13:7

1. What is the "more excellent way" (12:31)?

2. Why is love more valuable than the gifts of tongues, prophecy, faith and martyrdom?

3. According to 1 Corinthians 13:4-7, what are the things love does not do?

4. Compare the characteristics of love (vv. 4-7) with the fruit of the Spirit (Galatians 5:22, 23). How are the lists similar? What does this signify?

1 John 4:7-12, 19-21

1. What is the evidence that a person has been "born of God" (vv. 7, 8)?

2. Why is the sacrificial death of Christ the greatest possible expression of love (vv. 9, 10)?

3. According to verses 11 and 12, how can Christians help people to "see" God? How can we hinder people from seeing God?

4. Why is it impossible to love God without loving other people (vv. 19-21)?

When the groups have finished working, bring everyone back together to discuss their findings.

- *Of all the things that make up a church, is anything more important than love?*

RESPOND

Loving one another is not a choice—it is a command. Let's let the Holy Spirit increase our love for one another right now.

Lead everyone in singing a simple song of unity (such as "Bind Us Together" or "I Love You With the Love of the Lord"). Then ask everyone to get in groups of three or four people each—people they usually do not sit with at church. Ask the students to share prayer requests within their groups and then pray for each other.

Learning to Be a Servant

Study Text: Matthew 20:20-28; John 13:1-9, 12-17; Romans 15:1-3; Philippians 2:3-8

Objective: To realize that disciples are called to be servants and follow Christ's example.

Golden Text: "Whosoever will be great among you, let him be your minister; and whosoever will be chief among you, let him be your servant" (Matthew 20:26, 27).

Central Truth: Serving others is an essential part of discipleship.

Evangelism Emphasis: Witnessing to the lost is an essential part of discipleship.

PRINTED TEXT

John 13:4. He riseth from supper, and laid aside his garments; and took a towel, and girded himself.

5. After that he poureth water into a bason, and began to wash the disciples' feet, and to wipe them with the towel wherewith he was girded.

12. So after he had washed their feet, and had taken his garments, and was set down again, he said unto them, Know ye what I have done to you?

13. Ye call me Master and Lord: and ye say well; for so I am.

14. If I then, your Lord and Master, have washed your feet; ye also ought to wash one another's feet.

15. For I have given you an example, that ye should do as I have done to you.

16. Verily, verily I say unto you, The servant is not greater than his lord; neither he that is sent greater than he that sent him.

17. If ye know these things, happy are ye if ye do them.

Matthew 20:25. But Jesus called them unto him, and said, Ye know that the princes of the Gentiles exercise dominion over them, and they that are great exercise authority upon them.

26. But it shall not be so among you: but whosoever will be great among you, let him be your minister;

27. And whosoever will be chief among you, let him be your servant:

28. Even as the Son of man came not to be ministered unto, but to minister, and to give his life a ransom for many.

Romans 15:1. We then that are strong ought to bear the infirmities of the weak, and not to please ourselves.

2. Let every one of us please his neighbour for his good to edification.

3. For even Christ pleased not himself; but, as it is written, The reproaches of them that reproached thee fell on me.

Philippians 2:3. Let nothing be done through strife or vainglory; but in lowliness of mind let each esteem other better than themselves.

4. Look not every man on his own things, but every man also on the things of others.

5. Let this mind be in you, which was also in Christ Jesus:

6. Who, being in the form of God, thought it not robbery to be equal with God:

7. But made himself of no reputation, and took upon him the form of a servant, and was made in the likeness of men:

8. And being found in fashion as a man, he humbled himself, and became obedient unto death, even the death of the cross.

1 Peter 4:10. As every man hath received the gift, even so minister the same one to another, as good stewards of the manifold grace of God.

LESSON OUTLINE

I. CHRIST, OUR EXAMPLE
   A. Power of a Servant Example
   B. Obligation of a Servant Example
   C. Commission of a Servant
II. THE MEASURE OF GREATNESS
   A. The Greatness of Ministry
   B. The Greatness of a Servant
   C. The Greatness of a Life of Service
III. MOTIVES FOR SERVING
   A. Strengthening Others
   B. Humble Obedience
   C. Stewards of God's Gift to Us

LESSON EXPOSITION

INTRODUCTION

What was Christ's greatest test while He walked on the earth? Jesus was tempted in the wilderness. That was certainly a trying time. The Pharisees, Sadducees, scribes, lawyers and rulers challenged His authority. The skeptics questioned His ministry and His deity. These trials and many others weighed heavy on the Savior. However, no challenge was greater than living as a servant.

Though Christ was himself God, possessing power over all creation, He was obedient to the heavenly Father's command to be a servant. Servanthood was not an option but a necessity. Bowing to serve others was the succeeding posture after sitting at the right hand of the heavenly Father. Hanging on the cross as the servant of sacrifice was the next step for the Miracle Worker who walked upon earth.

Servanthood is demonstrated in various ways, but Jesus chose ancient practice that placed Him in the unquestionable role of a servant. He knelt to wash the disciples' feet. Jesus washed the feet of those who were to serve Him so they might in turn serve one another and a watching world.

The key to greatness is servanthood. Christ's passage upon earth as the incarnate Son of the heavenly Father was incomplete until He had offered the example of washing the disciples' feet. Humble service was the prelude to saving sacrifice. Bowing before the disciples was the preamble to being lifted up before all mankind. Bathing the soil from the feet of His followers was prerequisite to leading the way to eternal salvation.

I. CHRIST, OUR EXAMPLE
   (John 13:1-9, 12-17)

A. Power of a Servant Example (vv. 1-9)

(John 13:1-3, 6-9 is not included in the printed text.)

4. He riseth from supper, and laid aside his garments; and took a towel, and girded himself.

5. After that he poureth water into a bason, and began to wash the disciples' feet, and to wipe them with the towel wherewith he was girded.

John passes through the Last Supper with one reference but then opens up the astounding events that followed immediately after. Verses 1-3 indicate the setting was the deception of Judas, birthing the betrayal of Christ. In the face of betrayal, Christ responded by bending His knee. The steps that Judas would take would be with feet washed by the Savior. What must have gone through the mind of Christ? Verses 1-3 tell us that Jesus had the purpose and call of the Father on His mind. A servant filled with the purpose of God is able to pour out the waters of service wherever He may lead.

Verses 4 and 5 convey the purposefulness of Jesus. He went directly to the task. He did not question, groan or complain. With profound compassion, He laid aside His garments that prevented Him from kneeling, probably gathering His robe together and tying it to His side, so that He could kneel. He tied a large towel around His waist and lap. He placed a basin at the disciples' feet, each in turn, one by one, washing their feet and then wiping them with His towel. The implication of the text is that a reverent hush overtook the room, the disciples disbelieving and yet profoundly moved by the Lord's example of servanthood.

Christ provided the way of salvation on the cross, but when He bent His knee before Judas and washed his feet, Christ paved the pathway of servitude. The power generated by His example would provide the foundation for the cross and the launching of the disciples into lifelong mission. The attitude of Christianity would forever be set.

What is the excuse of the modern Christian for not serving? *Someone has done us wrong?* Jesus washed Judas' feet, knowing what he would do. *The power of the Enemy is too great; we don't have time to serve one another?* Jesus took time between the Last Supper and the cross to wash each foot of the disciples. *We have more important things to do?* Jesus' agenda included the priority of menial service to those He led.

B. Obligation of a Servant Example (vv. 12-15)

12. So after he had washed their feet, and had taken his garments, and was set down again, he said unto them, Know ye what I have done to you?

13. Ye call me Master and Lord: and ye say well; for so I am.

14. If I then, your Lord and Master, have washed your feet; ye also ought to wash one another's feet.

15. For I have given you an example, that ye should do as I have done to you.

For centuries the obligation of washing the saints' feet has been

sidelined and compromised. Yet, the words of John 13:12-15 are some of the clearest in Scripture. Right after washing their feet, Jesus turned to the disciples and gave them a command. He clearly said that what He had just done, they were to do.

A command would be proof enough of Jesus' intention and the seriousness of His words. But Christ said it was more than a command—the commitment to servanthood and foot washing was an obligation. They owed it to Jesus.

Jesus told His disciples to "do" as He had "done" (v. 15). Salvation was not at stake, but servanthood certainly was. The principle of washing the saints' feet is applicable to various acts of servanthood—for example, acts of benevolence, physical assistance to others and waiting upon others. However, washing the saints' feet as a literal sacrament was also intended.

The obligation that rang out through Christendom from the room where the Last Supper had just been held was certainly not limited to the sacrament of washing the saints' feet. Obligation to servanthood was as serious as the cross and as powerful as the empty tomb. The evidence of Jesus' servanthood that evening obliges all believers to serve one another.

C. Commission of a Servant (vv. 16, 17)

16. Verily, verily I say unto you, The servant is not greater than his lord; neither he that is sent greater than he that sent him.

17. If ye know these things, happy are ye if ye do them.

Jesus commissioned His disciples to be servants through the commission of example. Refusing to follow Jesus' example of service would have been to refuse their commission as His disciples.

The obligation they had received from Christ's example of service as exemplified in foot washing was not a debt for what they had received from Him. They did not owe Him finances or a blessing. They did not owe Him for any healing they had received. They would not owe Him even for the forgiveness of sins they would receive because of the cross. Christ had commissioned them to be His followers, and He had given them an example of being a servant. They were to be servants simply, yet powerfully, because He had served them.

The heavenly Father had commissioned Christ. Jesus knew He had "come from God" (v. 3). In fact, a major part of John's emphasis was not just service but the commission of the servant. The driving force of Christ's service was the commission of the heavenly Father.

II. THE MEASURE OF GREATNESS (Matthew 20:20-28)

A. The Greatness of Ministry (vv. 20-26)

(Matthew 20:20-24 is not included in the printed text.)

25. But Jesus called them unto him, and said, Ye know that the princes of the Gentiles exercise dominion over them, and they that are great exercise authority upon them.

26. But it shall not be so among you: but whosoever will be great among you, let him be your minister.

As Jesus was nearing Jerusalem, He taught the disciples about servanthood. In fact, Matthew records this as the last teaching Jesus would give before going to Jerusalem for the Crucifixion. No doubt, Matthew was highlighting the prominence that servanthood had in Jesus' ministry.

The context of this passage had invited the question, *Which is more important, power or servitude?* The mother of the sons of Zebedee asked Jesus to make her two sons the second and third in authority and power in His kingdom (vv. 20, 21). Jesus responded by saying she did not really understand the implications of what she was asking (vv. 22, 23). His power would lead Him to the cross. His power was based on service, and the ultimate expression of His obedient service was the sacrifice of the cross.

Servitude is the ultimate power of Christ. Jesus explained to His disciples that the power of the world is based on position and the self-centered use of that position (vv. 25, 26). According to the world, power flows from position. However, Jesus said the power of His disciples would not be position but service.

Minister (v. 26) was the Greek term *diakonos*, which is the root of the modern term *deacon.* The term *diakonos* suggests the ability to accomplish something through that which is common or ordinary. The way of the world requires position and special privileges, talents and resources. However, the way of Christianity is fulfilling the will of the Son and the heavenly Father through humble service.

B. The Greatness of a Servant (v. 27)

27. And whosoever will be chief among you, let him be your servant.

Chief refers to the person who holds the position of leadership over others and is perceived to have the greatest amount of power. Jesus said the greatest position is the position of the servant.

Jesus was saying that the disciples' desires should not be for position, power or achievement. Rather, they should have a passion for serving others and making necessary sacrifices. The disciples had erupted with "indignation" (v. 24) when the mother of the sons of Zebedee had requested special positions of authority for her sons. Their reaction was near violent, the full meaning of the term *indignation.* Their reaction revealed the passion they had for power. Jesus confronted them with the passion to follow His power of service.

C. The Greatness of a Life of Service
(v. 28)

28. Even as the Son of man came not to be ministered unto, but to minister, and to give his life a ransom for many.

The depth of Christ's response was His own life. In a brief response, Jesus captured His teaching and His destiny. He singled out the lasting decision the disciples would make. Would they be servants or power brokers? Would they bypass the cross in their pursuit of a crown? Or would they lay aside ambition in order to take up the "towel" of service?

Receiving is not the first mark of the Christian. How much the believer receives does not measure the strength of faith. Tragically, Satan has deceived many believers into thinking their first right as a believer is to be served. On the contrary, the believer is not first to be ministered to but first to minister to others. In fact, the believer is to give his or her life in service to Christ and others. Christ served in this way, in service to others and the heavenly Father. Jesus sought our ransom, not our riches, so that we as believers would not be spoiled saints but ministering servants.

III. MOTIVES FOR SERVING
(Romans 15:1-3; Philippians 2:3-8; 1 Peter 4:10)

A. Strengthening Others
(Romans 15:1-3)

1. We then that are strong ought to bear the infirmities of the weak, and not to please ourselves.

2. Let every one of us please his neighbour for his good to edification.

3. For even Christ pleased not himself; but, as it is written, The reproaches of them that reproached thee fell on me.

In summarizing his great theological treatise to the Romans, Paul ended the book, beginning in Romans 12, by focusing on the practical ways the believers are to live out their freedom in Christ. Paul emphasized relationships between believers, the abiding presence and victory of the love of God, the gifts God has given believers, and many other important aspects of the Christian life. In the teaching of the book, Paul referred to the sacrifice of being a servant.

Just as with Christ at the washing of the disciples' feet, Paul referred to the obligation of servitude when he used the term *ought.* Just as Christ taught about laying aside power and position, Paul said that those who are strong must lead the way as servants. Just as Christ appealed to the power of His own example, Paul pointed to the example of the Savior as a primary motivation for being a servant. Paul especially challenged the readers when he clarified that the great challenger to servitude is self-centeredness—just as Christ taught the disciples that He came not to be ministered to but to minister.

B. Humble Obedience
(Philippians 2:3-8)

3. Let nothing be done through strife or vainglory; but in lowliness of mind let each esteem other better than themselves.

4. Look not every man on his own things, but every man also on the things of others.

5. Let this mind be in you, which was also in Christ Jesus:

6. Who, being in the form of God, thought it not robbery to be equal with God:

7. But made himself of no reputation, and took upon him the form of a servant, and was made in the likeness of men:

8. And being found in fashion as a man, he humbled himself, and became obedient unto death, even the death of the cross.

The mind of Christian service stems from the mind of Christ. Not only does Philippians 2 address the acts of Christ but also the mind, motivation and will of Christ. Service does not just happen. Christlike will, determination and commitment are required. The term that captures the mind of Christ is *obedience*.

The cost of obedient servitude is one's own life. The powerful message of Philippians 2 is that Christ's incarnation and mission are captured in that one word—*servant* (v. 7). Position, power and self are the enemies of Christian service. The central motivation for service is commission from the heavenly Father. The form Christ took in order to complete the mission of the heavenly Father was a servant.

C. Stewards of God's Gift to Us
(1 Peter 4:10)

10. As every man hath received the gift, even so minister the same one to another, as good stewards of the manifold grace of God.

Service is a reflection of God's grace unto us and the ministry of other believers unto us. Peter prefaced his emphasis upon being a servant by saying, "Above all, love each other deeply" (v. 8, *NIV*). He described their love as hospitality and grace.

Serving one another with love and hospitality was so important to Peter because believers are stewards of God's love to them. The service of Christ was an investment by the heavenly Father into the life of each believer, and this investment must be given to others. When a Christian serves someone else, Christ's service flows through that believer to the other person.

Servant must become synonymous with *Christian*. When Christ walked the earth, when He knelt after the Last Supper, and when He hung on the cross, He had the form of a servant. When the believer walks in the world, relates to others and testifies about following Christ, the message of servitude must come through. The obligation to be a servant does not come from some philosophical concept of what a believer should be. The debt to

serve comes from the theology of the New Testament. The debt to serve comes from the knee of Jesus, bowed to wash the disciples' feet. The debt to serve comes from and with the cross of Christ.

GOLDEN TEXT HOMILY

"WHOSOEVER WILL BE GREAT AMONG YOU, LET HIM BE YOUR MINISTER; AND WHOSOEVER WILL BE CHIEF AMONG YOU, LET HIM BE YOUR SERVANT" (Matthew 20:26, 27).

Two of the disciples of the Lord had their mother to request that they sit on the right and left hand of Christ in His kingdom. They thought this was the way to get in high position and power—to get what they wanted. For this was the way the Gentiles gained control of their subjects and reached high authority (vv. 20-25).

Not so with Christ's kingdom, for it was not in His power to grant such a request, but by the Father only. Christ gave the answer to their request in verses 26, 27.

Servants of Christ are to be willing to serve in any capacity—be it a humble position, a hard duty, or a tough situation. Christians are to serve faithfully until the Master changes their duty.

Christ came to this world as a servant. He set the greatest example of servanthood by giving His life a ransom for our sins.—**Charles G. Wiley**

SENTENCE SERMONS

SERVING OTHERS is an essential part of discipleship.

—Selected

LIFE IS a lot like tennis—the one who can serve best seldom loses.

*—Draper's Book of Quotations
for the Christian World*

WITNESSING to the lost is an essential part of discipleship.

—Selected

NO ONE is useless in this world who lightens the burden of it for anyone else.

—Charles Dickens

EVANGELISM APPLICATION

WITNESSING TO THE LOST IS AN ESSENTIAL PART OF DISCIPLESHIP.

The Lord reached out to the lost, not only for the sake of the lost but also as an example to His disciples. The Lord's last word to the disciples in the Gospel of Matthew was to go and make other disciples (28:19, 20). The Lord taught, modeled and commanded that His disciples reach out to the lost.

When Christ described the Last Judgment in Matthew 25:31-46, He emphasized whether or not the disciples reached the lost. Christ said that at the Judgment the disciples would not be asked about their personal spirituality as much as they would be asked if they had reached out to the lost and hurting. The agenda of the lost is the agenda by which all disciples will most critically be judged. The first question the Lord will ask, in essence, will not be, "How well did you do for yourself?" He will ask, "How well did you reach out to others?"

ILLUMINATING THE LESSON

"Rescue the Perishing" was a powerful song written by Fanny J. Crosby. Ira Sankey, song leader for D.L. Moody, sang the song continually in Moody's evangelistic campaigns.

Crosby, who was blind, was one of the greatest American hymn writers and poets of all time. She gave the following account when she wrote this hymn:

"It was written in the year 1869. Many of my hymns were written after experiences in New York mission work. This one was thus written. I was addressing a large company of working men one hot summer evening, when the thought kept forcing itself on my mind that some mother's boy must be rescued that night or not at all. So I made a pressing plea that if there was a boy present who had wandered from his mother's home and teaching, he should come to me at the end of the service. A young man of 18 came forward and said, 'Did you mean me? I promised my mother to meet her in heaven, but as I am now living, that will be impossible.' We prayed for him and he finally arose with a new light in his eyes and exclaimed in triumph, 'Now I can meet my mother in heaven, for I have found God.' . . .

"While I sat in the mission that evening, the line came to me, 'Rescue the perishing, care for the dying.' I could think of nothing else that night. When I arrived home, I went to work on the hymn at once, and before I retired it was ready for the melody" (taken from *Singing With Understanding*, by Kenneth W. Osbeck).

DAILY BIBLE READINGS

M. The Listening Servant.
    1 Samuel 3:1-10
T. The Wise Servant.
    Isaiah 11:1-10
W. The Righteous Servant.
    Isaiah 42:1-4
T. The Prepared Servant.
    Matthew 24:42-47
F. Be a Trustworthy Servant.
    Luke 16:10-13
S. Advice to the Lord's Servant
    2 Timothy 2:15-26

TRUTH SEARCH:
Creatively Teaching the Word

Aim: Students will understand that serving one another is a commandment, and will respond by performing an act of servanthood.

Items needed: Apron, broom, bandana; optional: towels and basins of water

FOCUS

Have someone prepared to carry in each of the following items as you request them.

Bring in the royal robe! Have the helper bring in the apron, and you put it on.

Bring in the royal crown! Have the helper bring in the bandana, and you tie it around your head or neck.

Bring in the royal scepter! The helper brings in the broom and hands it to you.

Wouldn't it look strange if the Queen of England were to dress like this in public? Who ever heard of a person of royalty appearing as a servant?

Have your helper read aloud Matthew 20:27.

EXPLORE

Have the class read aloud Matthew 20:20-28 in the following fashion: one person reads the words of Jesus, another person reads the words of Zebedee's wife, and a third person reads the rest of the text. Then talk about it.

1. What did the mother of James and John request? Did she really know what she was asking for (vv. 21, 22)?

2. Instead, what did Jesus say that James and John could expect? What did He mean by this (vv. 22, 23)?

3. What was the problem all the disciples were experiencing (vv. 24, 25)?

4. How did Jesus define greatness (v. 26)?

5. How did Jesus display His spirit of servanthood (v. 28)?

According to Jesus, Christian living requires serving God through serving others.

Now have the class read aloud John 13:1-17 in the following fashion: one person reads the words of Jesus, another person reads the words of Simon Peter, and a third person reads the rest of the passage. Then discuss the questions below.

1. What did Jesus want to show His disciples? In what stage of Jesus' life on earth did this event take place (v. 1)?

2. Realizing what Jesus knew about Judas, what made Jesus' actions even more amazing (vv. 2-4, 10, 11)?

3. Why did Peter resist the Lord's actions? What caused Peter to change his mind (vv. 6-9)?

4. What did Jesus command His disciples to do (vv. 13-15)?

5. What did Jesus promise His disciples if they would obey His command (vv. 16, 17)?

Footwashing is an act of obedience to Christ and an act of servanthood. And it symbolizes the daily washing of the blood of Jesus that purifies the believer.

RESPOND

Look around this room. God commands each one of us to be a servant to every one else we see.

If feasible, separate the men from the women and conduct a footwashing service, encouraging believers to pray for one another as they wash each other's feet.

If this is not practical, have members break into pairs and perform another important act of service—listening to each other's needs and praying for each other.

The lessons for the winter quarter (December, January, February) are presented in two units under the themes "The Gospel According to Luke" (lessons 1-9) and "Message of the Early Church" (lessons 10-13).

Unit One explores the life of Christ as expressed through the inspired words of Luke.

Unit Two focuses on four important episodes from the Book of Acts, portraying the bold witnessing of Peter, Stephen and Paul.

As you and your students explore the stories of Christ (from Luke) and the accounts of individuals boldly telling Christ's message (from Acts), may the Holy Spirit inspire you and your students to be faithful witnesses.

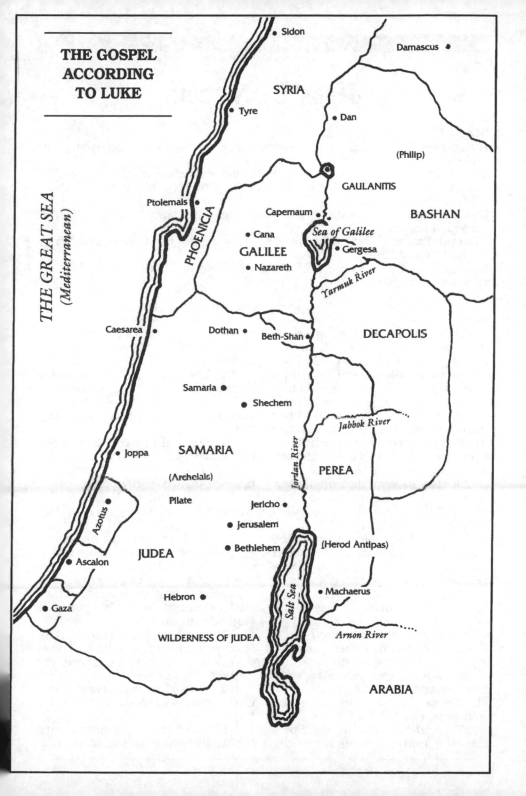

THE GOSPEL ACCORDING TO LUKE

THE GREAT SEA
(Mediterranean)

Sidon

Damascus

SYRIA

Tyre

Dan

(Philip)

Ptolemais

GAULANITIS

PHOENICIA

Capernaum

BASHAN

Cana

Sea of Galilee

GALILEE

Gergesa

Nazareth

Yarmuk River

Caesarea

Dothan

Beth-Shan

DECAPOLIS

Samaria

Shechem

Jabbok River

Joppa

SAMARIA

Jordan River

(Archelaus)

PEREA

Azotus

Pilate

Jericho

Ascalon

Jerusalem

JUDEA

Bethlehem

(Herod Antipas)

Hebron

Machaerus

Gaza

Salt Sea

WILDERNESS OF JUDEA

Arnon River

ARABIA

Jesus' Early Years

Study Text: Luke 2:21-52

Objective: To examine and appreciate how Jesus developed in wisdom and favor with God and man.

Time: The Gospel of Luke was probably written between A.D. 58 and 70.

Place: The Temple in Jerusalem was the site of both events in today's lesson.

Golden Text: "Jesus increased in wisdom and stature, and in favour with God and man" (Luke 2:52).

Central Truth: Christians should follow Jesus' example of obedience to His heavenly Father.

Evangelism Emphasis: Christians who live in obedience to God are effective witnesses.

PRINTED TEXT

Luke 2:21. And when eight days were accomplished for the circumcision of the child, his name was called JESUS, which was so named of the angel before he was conceived in the womb.

22. And when the days of her purification according to the law of Moses were accomplished, they brought him to Jerusalem, to present him to the Lord;

23. (As it is written in the law of the Lord, Every male that openeth the womb shall be called holy to the Lord;)

24. And to offer a sacrifice according to that which is said in the law of the Lord, A pair of turtledoves, or two young pigeons.

25. And, behold, there was a man in Jerusalem, whose name was Simeon; and the same man was just and devout, waiting for the consolation of Israel: and the Holy Ghost was upon him.

26. And it was revealed unto him by the Holy Ghost, that he should not see death, before he had seen the Lord's Christ.

27. And he came by the Spirit into the temple: and when the parents brought in the child Jesus, to do for him after the custom of the law,

28. Then took he him up in his arms, and blessed God, and said,

29. Lord, now lettest thou thy servant depart in peace, according to thy word:

30. For mine eyes have seen thy salvation,

31. Which thou hast prepared before the face of all people;

32. A light to lighten the Gentiles, and the glory of thy people Israel.

33. And Joseph and his mother marvelled at those things which were spoken of him.

40. And the child grew, and waxed strong in spirit, filled with wisdom: and the grace of God was upon him.

49. And he said unto them, How is it that ye sought me? wist ye not that I must be about my Father's business?

50. And they understood not the saying which he spake unto them.

51. And he went down with them, and came to Nazareth, and

was subject unto them: but his mother kept all these sayings in her heart.

52. And Jesus increased in wisdom and stature, and in favour with God and man.

DICTIONARY

Consolation of Israel—Luke 2:25—God's promise of the Messiah.

LESSON OUTLINE

I. PARENTAL OBEDIENCE TO GOD'S WORD

A. The Name

B. The Presentation

C. The Sacrifice

II. RECOGNIZED AS THE SAVIOR

A. The Testimony of Simeon

B. The Testimony of Anna

III. JESUS GROWS IN OBEDIENCE

A. The Early Development

B. The Visit to Jerusalem

LESSON EXPOSITION

INTRODUCTION

The greatest personality ever to appear in the arena of human life was Jesus of Nazareth. He has never been equaled in depth of character, breadth of soul, width of interest, or height of influence. He was the most outstanding individual who ever trod the highway of life.

Russell V. DeLong has written in his book, *The Unique Galilean*: "It staggers the imagination to realize that a child could be born in a humble home; that home to be situated in an obscure little hamlet; that hamlet to be located in a very insignificant, small country—and yet, out from that humble home, obscure village, and small country should come One, the impact of whose dynamic personality should change the whole course of history, revolutionize philosophy, overthrow governments, revitalize religion and transform men."

The historian Luke provides much of the information we have about the early years of Jesus. This information forms the basis of today's lesson.

I. PARENTAL OBEDIENCE TO GOD'S WORD (Luke 2:21-24)

A. The Name (v. 21)

21. And when eight days were accomplished for the circumcision of the child, his name was called JESUS, which was so named of the angel before he was conceived in the womb.

The circumcision was a public testimony to Israel, that according to the flesh Jesus was a Jew, made of a Jewish woman, and "made under the law" (Galatians 4:4). Without this He would not have fulfilled the requirements of the Law. Without it He could not have been recognized as the son of David, and the seed of Abraham. It should be remembered that circumcision was absolutely necessary before our Lord could be heard as a teacher in Israel. Without it He would have had no place in any lawful Jewish assembly, and no right to any Jewish ordinance. Without it He would have been regarded by all Jews as nothing more than an uncircumcised Gentile.

The selection of the name *Jesus* is very striking and instructive. It means "Savior." It is the same as

Joshua in the Old Testament. The Son of God came to earth to be not only the Savior, but the King, the Lawgiver, the Prophet, the Priest and the Judge of fallen man. He could have chosen any one of these titles. But He passed on all of them. He selected a name which speaks of mercy, grace, help and deliverance for lost man. It is as deliverer and redeemer that He desires to be known.

B. The Presentation (vv. 22, 23)

22. And when the days of her purification according to the law of Moses were accomplished, they brought him to Jerusalem, to present him to the Lord;

23. (As it is written in the law of the Lord, Every male that openeth the womb shall be called holy to the Lord;).

The 40 days of purification prescribed by the law of Moses having been completed, Joseph and Mary brought the baby Jesus to Jerusalem to present Him to the Lord. The circumcision constituted Jesus a member of the old covenant, but His presentation in the Temple was His formal dedication to the service of the Lord.

C. The Sacrifice (v. 24)

24. And to offer a sacrifice according to that which is said in the law of the Lord, A pair of turtledoves, or two young pigeons.

The mother was directed at the end of 40 days from the child's birth to appear before the Lord with two offerings—one for a sin offering, the other for a burnt offering—according to Leviticus 12:8. In Mary's case, because of her poverty, the offerings consisted of two doves or two pigeons. The one sacrifice expressed a sense of sin, the other a sense of consecration.

II. RECOGNIZED AS THE SAVIOR (Luke 2:25-38)

A. The Testimony of Simeon (vv. 25-35)

(Luke 2:34, 35 is not included in the printed text.)

25. And, behold, there was a man in Jerusalem, whose name was Simeon; and the same man was just and devout, waiting for the consolation of Israel: and the Holy Ghost was upon him.

26. And it was revealed unto him by the Holy Ghost, that he should not see death, before he had seen the Lord's Christ.

27. And he came by the Spirit into the temple: and when the parents brought in the child Jesus, to do for him after the custom of the law,

28. Then took he him up in his arms, and blessed God, and said,

29. Lord, now lettest thou thy servant depart in peace, according to thy word:

30. For mine eyes have seen thy salvation,

31. Which thou hast prepared before the face of all people;

32. A light to lighten the Gentiles, and the glory of thy people Israel.

33. And Joseph and his mother marvelled at those things which were spoken of him.

When Christ was born, religion was at a low ebb in Israel. Abraham's faith had been spoiled by the doctrines of the Pharisees and Sadducees. Yet there was a man in Jerusalem who was righteous in his dealings with men and cautious and scrupulous in observing Jewish law. He was looking for the advent of the Messiah, and the Holy Spirit was upon him.

It is encouraging to know that God never leaves Himself without a witness. It may be small in number at times, but the gates of hell shall never prevail against it. God's true witness may be driven into the wilderness and be a scattered little flock, but it never dies. There was a Lot in Sodom and an Obadiah in Ahab's household, a Daniel in Babylon and a Jeremiah in Zedekiah's court; and when Christ was born, there were godly people like Simeon.

True believers in every age must remember this and take courage. It is a truth that many are apt to forget and, as a result, become despondent. Even Elijah said, "I only, am left; and they seek my life, to take it away." But God said, "Yet I have left me seven thousand in Israel" (1 Kings 19:14, 18). Believers must learn to be more helpful. They must believe that grace can live and flourish, even in the most bleak and discouraging circumstances. There are more Simeons in the world than we think.

The Holy Spirit is mentioned three times in relation to Simeon. We should not fail to note that this was before the death and ascension of Christ, and the outpouring of the Spirit on the Day of Pentecost. We must never forget that Old Testament saints were also taught by the Holy Spirit.

It is interesting to compare the entrance of Christ into the Temple during the days of His ministry with this occasion (v. 27). How different the reception!

In verse 28 Simeon assumed the priest's duty and received the child who was presented. It was appropriate that he should have done so. This is exactly what Jesus did with little children during His ministry 30 years later.

Verse 29 begins what is known as the *Nunc Dimittis*, which equals the most beautiful of the Psalms. Alfred Plummer writes: "Since the fifth century it has been used in the evening services of the church and has been the hymn of dying saints. It is the sweetest and most solemn of all the canticles. Simeon represents himself as a servant or watchman released from duty because that for which he was commanded to watch has appeared" (*A Critical and Exegetical Commentary on the Gospel According to St. Luke*).

According to J.C. Ryle, we see in the song of Simeon how completely a believer can be delivered from the fear of death. He writes concerning Simeon: "He speaks like one for whom the grave has lost its terrors, and the world its charms. He desires to be released from the miseries of this pilgrim state of existence, and to be allowed to go home. He is willing to be absent from the body and present with the Lord. He speaks as one who knows where he is going when he departs this life, and cares not how soon he goes. The change for him will be a change for the better, and he desires that this change may come" (*Expository Thoughts on the Gospels*).

The salvation that Simeon refers to is the salvation for which all men waited, and especially the Jewish people (v. 30; see also Psalm 119:166, 174). It is the only salvation which God has ever provided, mediated through Jesus Christ our Savior. The message of the New Testament is that Christ was indeed "a light to lighten the Gentiles" (v. 32; see also Isaiah 42:6; 49:6). Without Him they were lost in gross darkness and superstition. They did not know the way of life. They worshiped the works of their own hands. The apostle Paul described their philosophers as utterly ignorant of spiritual things: "Professing themselves to be wise, they became fools" (Romans 1:22). The gospel of Christ was like sunrise to Greece and Rome, as well as the whole Gentile world. When the Gentiles received the light of the gospel, it was like a change from night to day.

Christ was indeed "the glory of . . . Israel" (Luke 2:32). Ryle describes it in these words: "The descent from Abraham, the covenants, the promises, the law of Moses, the divinely ordered Temple service—all of these were mighty privileges. But all were as nothing compared to the mighty fact, that out of Israel was born the Savior of the world. This was to be the highest honor of the Jewish nation, that the mother of Christ was a Jewish woman, and that the blood of One made of the seed of David, according to the flesh, was to make atonement for the sin of mankind" (*Expository Thoughts on the Gospels*).

Christ came to unveil God to man, to unveil man to himself, and to reveal to man the possibilities and glory of life. Although He is not recognized by the Jewish people as their Messiah today, He is the most glorious personality that ever appeared in their remarkable history, and some are beginning to accept this fact. He will be the glory of His people Israel when they receive Him as their Messiah.

The *Pulpit Commentary* says of verse 33: "It was not so much that Simeon foretold new things respecting the child Jesus that they marveled; their surprise was rather that a stranger, evidently of position and learning, should possess so deep an insight into the lofty destinies of an unknown Infant, brought by evidently poor parents into the Temple court. Was their secret then known to others whom they suspected not?"

Verses 34 and 35 reveal that the coming of the Messiah necessarily involved an underlying crisis, a separation or judgment. Some welcomed the light; others loved the darkness rather than the light because their works were evil and, by their own conduct, condemned. Judas despaired, Peter repented; one robber blasphemed, the other confessed.

Simeon predicted that Christ would be a mark for all the fiery darts of the Wicked One. He was to be despised and rejected of men. He was to be hated by all sorts of enemies. It is interesting that men who agreed on nothing else have agreed on hating Christ.

Christ was to be the occasion of "the fall . . . of many in Israel"—He was to be a stone of stumbling and rock of offense to many proud and self-righteous Jews, who would reject Him and perish in their sins. Christ was to be the occasion of "rising again of many in Israel"—He was to become the Savior of many who at one time rejected, blasphemed and reviled Him, but afterward repented and believed. Christ was to be the occasion of "the thoughts of many hearts [being] revealed"—His gospel was to bring to light the real character of many people.

In nearly every chapter of the Book of Acts, there is proof that every item in Simeon's prophecy was true.

B. The Testimony of Anna (vv. 36-38)

(Luke 2:36-38 is not included in the printed text.)

All we know of Anna is recorded in these verses. According to F. Godet, "She was another inspired person waiting for the advent of

Messiah. An aged widow, she seems never to have left the Temple, and to have risen as near the ideal of ceaseless service as one in this life could. She also gave thanks to God as with eager eye she gazed upon her Redeemer in the person of the Holy Child. And to all who, like herself, were looking for redemption, she spoke of Jesus as the Redeemer promised and now given. There is not the same melancholy tone about Anna as about Simeon. She speaks about redemption, and will wait for it, while Simeon seems inclined to reach it as speedily as possible by death" (Pulpit Commentary).

III. JESUS GROWS IN OBEDIENCE
(Luke 2:39-52)

A. The Early Development
(vv. 39, 40)

(Luke 2:39 is not included in the printed text.)

40. And the child grew, and waxed strong in spirit, filled with wisdom: and the grace of God was upon him.

Ryle has some interesting observations concerning verse 39: "Two important incidents in our Lord's history come in here, which St. Luke passes over, not necessarily because he was ignorant of them, but simply because he was not inspired to write of them. Those incidents are the visit of the wise men from the East, and the flight into Egypt. Joseph and Mary appear to have returned to Bethlehem after the presentation in the Temple, though it is quite possible that they may have gone to Nazareth for a short time. They probably returned to Bethlehem under a sense of duty, as if the Messiah ought to dwell in the place where it was prophesied He should be born. There at Bethlehem they

were visited by the wise men from the East. From thence, being supplied by their gifts with the means of journeying, they fled into Egypt, to escape the anger of Herod. From Egypt, after the death of Herod, they returned to Nazareth" (Expository Thoughts on the Gospels).

In verse 40 Luke gives the history of 12 quiet years. From these few words Luke evidently understands the humanity of Jesus as a reality. The statement that He "waxed strong . . . filled with wisdom" tells us that the boy Jesus learned as other children learned. He was subject to the ordinary principles of growth and development physically, mentally and spiritually.

In his book The Education of Christ, Sir William Ramsay gives a description of the type of education Jesus received: "No education was ever so well-adapted to train a thoughtful child in the appreciation of his own country, to render its past history living and real to him, to strengthen his patriotic feeling, to make every geographical name and scene full of meaning and historic truth, as the training which every Hebrew boy received. He learned to know one small collection of books thoroughly, and that library gave him a training in literature and in history, in philosophic insight and in religious feeling."

B. The Visit to Jerusalem (vv. 41-52)

(Luke 2:41-48 is not included in the printed text.)

49. And he said unto them, How is it that ye sought me? wist ye not that I must be about my Father's business?

50. And they understood not the saying which he spake unto them.

51. And he went down with them, and came to Nazareth,

and was subject unto them: but his mother kept all these sayings in her heart.

52. And Jesus increased in wisdom and stature, and in favour with God and man.

Passover was the greatest of the Jewish annual feasts. It was a celebration of the Jews' escape from Egyptian bondage when the death angel passed over the houses of the Hebrews protected by the blood of the Passover lamb on doorposts and lintels, striking down all the firstborn of the Egyptians. Attendance at the Passover in Jerusalem was required by law of every male adult Jew, but not of women. It was a mark of Mary's piety that she always accompanied her husband.

At the age of 12 a Hebrew boy was accepted as an adult. He was then called "a son of the Law," was presented on the Sabbath at the synagogue, received from his father a set of phylacteries, and began to wear them when he said his prayers. It meant much to Jesus to attend the Passover at Jerusalem now that He was accepted as an adult.

The picture of Jesus in the Temple is one of the most beautiful portraits painted by Luke. Luke does not say that the doctors asked Jesus any questions, but he says clearly and emphatically that the child Jesus gave to somebody's questions the wisest and most astonishing answers (v. 47).

The words recorded in verse 49 are the first words of which we have record that came from the lips of the Son of God. They are in response to Mary's concern about His absence from them for a period of time.

In commenting on verse 49, Ryle observes: "These words so translated ['about my Father's business'] would admit of being rendered, 'in my Father's house,' and many commentators are strongly in favor of that sense being given to them. But, on the whole, our own English translation cramps and limits our Lord's words by confining their application to one thing, 'my Father's house.' The [KJV] translation 'my father's business' embraces a far wider range of thought, and is more in keeping with the general depth and fullness of our Lord's sayings" (*Expository Thoughts on the Gospels*).

The Jews understood the words Jesus uttered to them, but they did not understand His reference to God as His Father, and to the Temple as His Father's house, or to the work of the Temple as His Father's business.

This is the last time Joseph is mentioned. Jesus learned obedience and lived a normal healthy life as a young man. This is all we know of His life until He entered upon His public ministry, 18 years later, except the single fact that He was a carpenter (Mark 6:3).

GOLDEN TEXT HOMILY

"JESUS INCREASED IN WISDOM AND STATURE, AND IN FAVOUR WITH GOD AND MAN" (Luke 2:52).

How the infinite One could so bereave Himself of His infinitude as to be able to increase in wisdom, we cannot understand. But we cannot understand infinitude at all, and we act wisely when we do not draw hard-and-fast deductions from it. We stand on far firmer ground when we take the statement of the historian in its natural sense, and open our mind to the fact that Jesus Christ, "our Lord and our God," did stoop so far that it was possible for Him to increase in knowledge and in favor with God and with man.

We do not question the reality of His growth in body; why should we doubt, or receive with any reserve, the affirmation that He grew also in mind?

As Jesus increased in years and grew in wisdom, there was in Him an unfolding of moral and spiritual worth which attracted the eyes of men and which satisfied the Spirit of the Holy One himself.—*The Pulpit Commentary*

SENTENCE SERMONS

CHRISTIANS should follow Jesus' example of obedience to His heavenly Father.

—Selected

PEOPLE, LIKE TREES, must grow or die. There's no standing still.

—Joseph Shore

IF YOU REALIZE that you aren't as wise today as you thought you were yesterday, you're wiser today.

—Quotable Quotations

EVANGELISM APPLICATION

CHRISTIANS WHO LIVE IN OBEDIENCE TO GOD ARE EFFECTIVE WITNESSES.

Aunt Sophie, a converted scrubwoman, who said she was "called to scrub and preach," was made fun of by someone who said she was seen talking to a wooden Indian in front of a cigar store. Sophie replied, "Perhaps I did. My eyesight is not good. But talking to a wooden Indian about Christ is not so bad as being a wooden Christian and never talking to anyone about the Lord Jesus."

ILLUMINATING THE LESSON

Some years ago a Grand Truck Line railroad, knowing the danger that ever threatened motorists who carelessly passed indifferently over the railroad crossings, offered a prize of $2,500 to the person who would suggest the three best words to be used as warning words at railroad crossings. The person wise enough and fortunate to win the $2,500 offered these three words which are seen often: "*Stop, Look, Listen.*"

A railroad company paid $833.33 for each of these three simple little words. But they avail nothing for the safety of those crossing railroads unless they are obeyed— unless people stop, unless they look, unless they listen. Destroyed vehicles, mangled bodies, blood spattered along the right of way, the wails of those whose loved ones went to death in the wreck—all testify to the truth of this statement.

God set up many signposts to warn of the dangers and final consequences of sin. With all that God has done and all that friends can do, a soul will be lost unless he will give heed.

DAILY BIBLE READINGS

M. Dedicated to the Lord.
1 Samuel 1:24-28
T. Ready Obedience.
1 Samuel 3:4-10
W. Grow in Wisdom.
Proverbs 1:1-9
T. Called to Service.
Luke 1:76-80
F. Consequences of Disobedience.
Luke 15:11-19
S. Characteristics of a Godly Home.
Ephesians 6:1-4

TRUTH SEARCH:
Creatively Teaching the Word

Aim: Students will identify and commit to two ways they can help young people grow in the Christian faith.

Items needed: Marker board, marker, index cards, pencils or pens

FOCUS

Break the class up into groups of three or four people each. Have students respond to the following questions in their groups:

• *Describe the ways that you were instilled with religious and/or moral values in your upbringing.*

• *How has your practice in rearing children been influenced by your upbringing, or how would it be?*

• *What does our church currently do to nurture children, youth and young believers in Christian faith?*

EXPLORE

Have four volunteers read Luke 2:21-52 aloud in the following fashion: one person reads all the narrative material, the second reads the words of Simeon (vv. 29-32, 34, 35), the third reads Mary's line (v. 48), and the fourth person reads Jesus' reply (v. 49). Then discuss the following questions:

• *Where does most of the action in this passage take place?*

• *What specific things did Joseph and Mary do to raise Jesus in a godly way?*

• *What roles did other members of the faith community play in Jesus' upbringing?*

• *What does verse 44 suggest about the relationships among members of extended families?*

• *What lessons might Mary and Joseph have learned from the events in verses 46-50?*

• *What does verse 51 say about Jesus' relationship with Mary and Joseph?*

Taking three or four minutes for each category, brainstorm ways that each group of people might help youth, children, and those who are young in the faith develop as Christians. Write each idea on the board under the proper category:

• Parents
• Extended Family Members
• Members of the Faith Community

"Jesus increased in wisdom and stature, and in favour with God and man" (v. 52). God the Father entrusted Jesus to earthly parents who would oversee His formative years. As Christians, each of us is entrusted in some way with the raising of the next generation in the faith.

RESPOND

Have each student identify one of the above roles in which they relate to youth in the church—as parent, extended family member, or fellow member of the faith community. On their own index card, invite each student to write down two ways in which they will faithfully commit to help the young people in their lives grow in the faith. Challenge them to include at least one thing that they have not regularly done in the past.

Close with a prayer of dedication concerning these commitments.

Jesus Faces the Tempter

Study Text: Luke 3:21, 22; 4:1-13
Objective: To explore Christ's temptation in the wilderness and appropriate His victory when we are tempted.
Time: The Gospel of Luke was probably written between A.D. 58 and 70.
Place: The Jordan River and the Wilderness of Judea.
Golden Text: "We have not an high priest which cannot be touched with the feeling of our infirmities; but was in all points tempted like as we are, yet without sin" (Hebrews 4:15).
Central Truth: Christians can overcome temptation by the Word of God implanted in their hearts.
Evangelism Emphasis: Christians should testify to sinners of the overcoming power of Jesus.

PRINTED TEXT

Luke 3:21. Now when all the people were baptized, it came to pass, that Jesus also being baptized, and praying, the heaven was opened,

22. And the Holy Ghost descended in a bodily shape like a dove upon him, and a voice came from heaven, which said, Thou art my beloved Son; in thee I am well pleased.

4:1. And Jesus being full of the Holy Ghost returned from Jordan, and was led by the Spirit into the wilderness,

2. Being forty days tempted of the devil. And in those days he did eat nothing: and when they were ended, he afterward hungered.

3. And the devil said unto him, If thou be the Son of God, command this stone that it be made bread.

4. And Jesus answered him, saying, It is written, That man shall not live by bread alone, but by every word of God.

5. And the devil, taking him up into an high mountain, shewed unto him all the kingdoms of the world in a moment of time.

6. And the devil said unto him, All this power will I give thee, and the glory of them: for that is delivered unto me; and to whomsoever I will I give it.

7. If thou therefore wilt worship me, all shall be thine.

8. And Jesus answered and said unto him, Get thee behind me, Satan: for it is written, Thou shalt worship the Lord thy God, and him only shalt thou serve.

9. And he brought him to Jerusalem, and set him on a pinnacle of the temple, and said unto him, If thou be the Son of God, cast thyself down from hence:

10. For it is written, He shall give his angels charge over thee, to keep thee:

11. And in their hands they shall bear thee up, lest at any time thou dash thy foot against a stone.

12. And Jesus answering said unto him, It is said, Thou shalt not tempt the Lord thy God.

13. And when the devil had ended all the temptation, he departed from him for a season.

LESSON OUTLINE

I. JESUS' IDENTITY QUESTIONED
   A. The Testimony
   B. The Insinuation
   C. The Response

II. JESUS' LOYALTY TESTED
   A. The Offer
   B. The Refusal

III. JESUS OVERCOMES TEMPTATION
   A. The Challenge
   B. The Retreat

LESSON EXPOSITION

INTRODUCTION

The Bible clearly reveals the fact that a personal spirit of evil—Satan, the adversary—exists. To deny the personality of Satan is to deny Scripture. It is, moreover, to reflect upon humanity in a way that is unwarranted by the whole plan of revelation. If there is no personal devil, then all the evil things that blot the pages of human history are the outcome of our own human nature. And this is impossible to believe.

In facing the tempter, Jesus consciously and definitely defended His own divine nature. "If You are the Son of God . . . ," said Satan. Well, indeed, did Satan know that all would have to turn on that one question!

Most people experience confusion and misunderstanding about the meaning of *temptation.* In itself temptation is neither good nor evil. It is the battleground on which the struggle between God and Satan takes place. It is both Satan and God's objective to secure our allegiance. From the beginning, God has been engaged in a quest for our love and loyalty. But Satan also has been striving to gain our allegiance.

Man must always be tempted through his desires. But desire is not sin. There could be no temptation if there were no desire. One is not tempted to do what he does not want to do. In the moral struggle, there must be alternatives. Man is not a robot; instead, he is a free moral creature. He can choose between possible outcomes. The struggle is intensified when both conflicting ends seem desirable.

I. JESUS' IDENTITY QUESTIONED
(Luke 3:21, 22; 4:1-4)

A. The Testimony (3:21, 22)

21. Now when all the people were baptized, it came to pass, that Jesus also being baptized, and praying, the heaven was opened,

22. And the Holy Ghost descended in a bodily shape like a dove upon him, and a voice came from heaven, which said, Thou art my beloved Son; in thee I am well pleased.

As far as the record of the Gospels is concerned, this is the only occasion on which John the Baptist and Jesus were in actual personal contact. But there was no lack of clearness in the testimony of the Baptist. He recognized Jesus at once as the Messiah, declared that instead he needed to be baptized by Jesus, and baptized his Lord only after Christ's insistence (Matthew 3:13-15). Then after witnessing the descent of the Spirit upon Him, John loudly and repeatedly proclaimed Jesus as the Lamb of God, the Savior to whom all the Temple sacrifices for generations had pointed. This assurance of His mission from the great prophet must have been a strong reinforcement to our Lord.

However, His chief strengthening for the trials that lay before Him came from the parting of the sky, the descent of the Holy Spirit in the form of a radiant dove, and the voice of the Father from heaven announcing beyond mistake, "Thou art my beloved Son." Then the Father gave His verdict on the life of the Son as far as it had been lived, "In thee I am well pleased." For the first 30 years of Christ's life, "there had been no deflection from the straight path of obedience to the will of God," comments G. Campbell Morgan. "Nothing in the life, nothing in thought, nothing in speech, nothing in deed, nothing in work" had once displeased "the heart of God" (*Crises of the Cross*).

B. The Insinuation (4:1-3)

1. And Jesus being full of the Holy Ghost returned from Jordan, and was led by the Spirit into the wilderness,
2. Being forty days tempted of the devil. And in those days he did eat nothing: and when they were ended, he afterward hungered.
3. And the devil said unto him, If thou be the Son of God, command this stone that it be made bread.

The phrase "into the wilderness" (v. 1) is usually interpreted to mean the Wilderness of Judea. It was located up from the valley of the Jordan, close to the little village of Bethany, and not too far from Jerusalem. It was a desolate, dreary, barren land. It was in the deep gorges of this wilderness that Elijah hid from the wrath of Ahab. Among its hills and valleys, John the Baptist made his early home.

It was to this place that Jesus was driven by the Spirit immediately after His baptism to meet the adversary in lonely struggle. The Baptism was the beginning of Christ's work. It was the inauguration of His mission of salvation. B.H. Carroll has said the Temptation was hell's response to heaven's challenge in the inauguration. But Christ went to the Temptation with full knowledge that His Father approved Him and that the Holy Spirit was present with Him. All the powers of darkness could not overthrow His steadfast might. It was in the wilderness He was to gain the first victory of His messianic ministry.

From Matthew's account (4:2) we might suppose that the temptation of Jesus was preceded by 40 days of fasting, after which the tempter came to Him for the first time; but, from Mark (1:13) and Luke (4:2), we know that this was not the case. Jesus was tempted during the whole period of His fast.

Matthew recorded that Jesus fasted 40 days and 40 nights. Both Moses and Elijah fasted 40 days (Exodus 24:18; 34:28; 1 Kings 19:8). In contemporary times modern fasters have equaled and even surpassed this record and survived.

Jesus fasted because His whole being was engaged in His conflict with the adversary, which lasted the entire 40 days. The onset of hunger after a long fast is a terrible experience, amounting often to a frenzy. It is the severest possible temptation on the physical side.

We do not know how Satan appeared to Jesus. Some believe he came in a materialized bodily form with an audible voice; others believe he came in spirit. We simply do not know. It must be remembered that this account could have come from no one but our Lord himself, and He did not say. However, Hebrews 4:15 says He was "tempted like as we are," and we know how the devil comes to us.

"And the devil said unto him, If thou be the Son of God . . ." (Luke 4:3). This is the essence of the entire struggle in the wilderness. The devil was seeking, at the very beginning of Christ's ministry, to plant in His mind doubts regarding His divine origin, power and mission. Such doubts could have made His work futile. The devil has no more effective weapon than an "if."

Not only did Satan use doubt, but he used it in connection with the physical condition of Jesus and the physical circumstances of the area. The place provided many round, flat pieces of stone which looked much like the round, flat cakes which were the loaves of Palestinian bread. To Christ's famished body, the very appearance of those stones would furnish a temptation. Jesus knew that He had the power—by a word, or even a thought—to transform the stones into healthy, delicious bread. Jesus never used His power selfishly, and He always tried to turn man's mind from lower to higher desires, from barley bread to living bread.

C. The Response (v. 4)

4. And Jesus answered him, saying, It is written, That man shall not live by bread alone, but by every word of God.

Jesus was always ready with a quotation from the Word of God. He used it for comfort, for exhortation, for rebuke. Here He used it to overcome the temptations of the devil.

The first quotation was from Deuteronomy 8:3: "Man doth not live by bread only, but by every word that proceedeth out of the mouth of the Lord." Thus spoke He who was the Bread of Life. He could feed 5,000 (Matthew 14:15-21) and again

4,000 (15:32-38) with a few loaves and fishes. But He would not exercise that power to feed Himself on this occasion, however hungry. As He once said to His disciples, He had "meat" to eat that they knew not of. His "meat" was to do the will of the Father (John 4:32, 34).

This first temptation was to satisfy a bodily desire. Christ conquered it by substituting a spiritual satisfaction. The way to overcome temptations of the flesh is to practice self-denial, to keep the body under subjection, and to remember that "life is more than meat, and the body is more than raiment" (Luke 12:23).

II. JESUS' LOYALTY TESTED
(Luke 4:5-8)

A. The Offer (vv. 5-7)

5. And the devil, taking him up into an high mountain, shewed unto him all the kingdoms of the world in a moment of time.

6. And the devil said unto him, All this power will I give thee, and the glory of them: for that is delivered unto me; and to whomsoever I will I give it.

7. If thou therefore wilt worship me, all shall be thine.

Long ago, Satan whispered to Eve that the tree was "pleasant to the eyes" (Genesis 3:6). He had tempted her through the "lust of the eyes" (1 John 2:16). Now he raised before the eyes of Jesus a vision of unparalleled grandeur. The tempter showed Jesus all the kingdoms of the world. It was a dream of worldwide empire, majesty and power beyond all that even Alexander the Great had attained.

Satan offered to Jesus the empire of the world. It was a tempting prospect. Jesus knew that He was the Messiah, the Prince of the kings of the earth. All this glory was rightfully His. He was to rule over all the nations. It seemed now within His grasp. He would use it (perhaps the tempter whispered) for the best interests of the human race. He would eliminate the avarice, cruelty, lusts and oppression that ruled the world. He would improve the conditions of the poor. He would put a stop to war and violence and bloodshed. He would introduce universal peace and universal happiness, immediately, without self-sacrifice, without labor, without the cross.

It is Satan who suggests the sinful compliance; he conceals its wickedness; he uses it to destroy the soul. And his promises are deceitful: he offers the kingdoms of the world, and their glory, but they are not his to give. He is a liar from the beginning. He promises, but he does not deliver. His deluded followers lose their own soul, and do not always gain the good things of this world. Or, if they gain them, they find their position, riches and pleasures, all bought by sin, are but dust and ashes in the mouth—vanity of vanities. The enjoyment is but a dream; the misery is real.

B. The Refusal (v. 8)

8. And Jesus answered and said unto him, Get thee behind me, Satan: for it is written, Thou shalt worship the Lord thy God, and him only shalt thou serve.

In His refusal, Jesus called the tempter by his name, Satan, the adversary. The tempter had revealed himself now. His previous advances had been insidious. Now he stood confessed as the enemy of God; he claimed the worship due God alone.

Jesus expressed His indignation: "Get thee behind me, Satan." It is right to call an evil thing by its evil name. However, the use of fair names for foul things is one of the deceits of the Wicked One. It tends to hide the danger of sin and helps to entrap unwary souls. A transgression is not an "indiscretion"; a sin is not a "misfortune." Sin is sin.

Again Jesus said, "It is written." The Bible is a many-sided book; its range covers all the needs of man. Whatever our difficulties or confusion, we shall find light and guidance in the Word.

Jesus told the devil, "Thou shalt worship the Lord thy God," quoting from Deuteronomy 6:13. Here is the Christian's victory. God must be first (Matthew 22:37). Nothing can be right that draws us away from our devotion to God.

III. JESUS OVERCOMES TEMPTATION (Luke 4:9-13)

A. The Challenge (vv. 9-11)

9. And he brought him to Jerusalem, and set him on a pinnacle of the temple, and said unto him, If thou be the Son of God, cast thyself down from hence:

10. For it is written, He shall give his angels charge over thee, to keep thee:

11. And in their hands they shall bear thee up, lest at any time thou dash thy foot against a stone.

On this occasion the devil presented a temptation of easy access to success. He tempted Jesus to prove His divine nature, not in the solitude of the desert, but before the gaping, wonder-smitten throng that filled the Temple court. This particular pinnacle, it is believed, overlooked the deep Kidron Valley or the Valley of Hinnom. It is said that James the Just (the brother of Jesus) suffered martyrdom by being hurled from this pinnacle.

From this pinnacle the devil tempted Jesus, "If thou be the Son of God, cast thyself down . . . for it is written, He shall give his angels charge over thee, to keep thee: and in their hands they shall bear thee up, lest at any time thou dash thy foot against a stone." Here again we see the devil's *if*, calculated to provoke a quick, unthinking response and to lure Jesus out of His stronghold.

The devil, taking his cue from Jesus, showed that he could also quote Scripture. But he wrested the quote from its context, purpose and meaning. He quoted Psalm 91:11, 12, but characteristically omitted the last phrase of verse 11: "in all thy ways." This clearly indicates that we are to rely on the ministry of angels when we are in the path of duty, not when we act presumptuously.

B. The Retreat (vv. 12, 13)

12. And Jesus answering said unto him, It is said, Thou shalt not tempt the Lord thy God.

13. And when the devil had ended all the temptation, he departed from him for a season.

In response, Jesus quoted from Deuteronomy 6:16: "Ye shall not tempt [test, try, prove] the Lord your God," the remainder of which states "as ye tempted [tested] him in Massah." *Massah* means "testing." This refers to the incident in Exodus 17:1-7, when the Israelites tested both the Lord and Moses by asking "Is the Lord among us or not?" (v. 7, *NIV*) when they needed water in the wilderness.

God is delighted when we try the spirits, whether they are of God, or when we prove His promises. This kind of testing comes from a heart of trust, a heart that longs to do God's will and reverences its Maker. But to test God by presuming on

His faithfulness, or by seeing how far He can be pushed, incurs His wrath. This kind of testing comes from a heart of pride and unbelief, a heart that is trusting in self, and has "no fear of God" (Romans 3:18). Testing God by blatant disobedience (trying His patience, sinning against light) is a terrible sin.

It is tempting God to put ourselves into dangers to which He has not called us . . . to expect His help in self-chosen ways . . . to look for His miraculous interposition to save us from our own folly. To trust God is faith; to tempt Him is presumption. We cannot trust Him too much while we are walking in the path of obedience and duty, the path He has designated for us; but to choose our own path, to thrust ourselves into perilous situations, to think of forcing Him to perform a miracle, is not faith but fanaticism.

The miracles of Christ were part of the great plan of redemption. They were performed to relieve distress or to increase the faith of His followers—not needlessly, not to display His power or to satisfy curiosity, and not at the bidding of Satan, the Pharisees or Herod. Jesus would not work a miracle from any of these lower motives; it would have been inconsistent with His high and holy character. Such a miracle, if it were possible, would have been the work of a faith like that described by Paul—a faith that, although it could move mountains, was destitute of love, and therefore useless in the sight of God (1 Corinthians 13:2).

One of the amazing things about this last temptation is that even with its long history, ritual and veneration, the Temple was not hallowed by the devil. When servants of the Lord have listened to the devil's voice and fallen for his bait, have they not thrown themselves down from the "pinnacle" of the holy place? Many preachers have reported that some of the most awful thoughts come to them while they are ministering in the church. But we must remember there is no ground hallowed to the devil. There is no place the devil will not try to invade. There is no person that the devil will not follow to the grave to get him or her to doubt God or to rebel against His plan.

And so the devil left Him "for a season" (Luke 4:13). The clear, calm decision of Jesus, the resolute will, had defeated the tempter at all points. So the devil flees now before those who resist him in the strength of Christ (James 4:7).

The battle over, holy angels came and ministered to Jesus (Matthew 4:11). They had watched the struggle, we may be sure, with the deepest, the most intense interest. And now they were dispatched to meet His physical and spiritual needs, as they had met those of Elijah of old (1 Kings 19:4-7). Even so "the angels . . . minister for them who shall be heirs of salvation" (Hebrews 1:13, 14).

Paradoxically, the very promise that the adversary had thrown at Jesus from Psalm 91:11-14, on which He would not presume, now became His in time of need. God gave His angels charge concerning Him and in their hands they bore Him up.

GOLDEN TEXT HOMILY

"WE HAVE NOT AN HIGH PRIEST WHICH CANNOT BE TOUCHED WITH THE FEELING OF OUR INFIRMITIES; BUT WAS IN ALL POINTS TEMPTED LIKE AS WE ARE, YET WITHOUT SIN" (Hebrews 4:15).

When you're going through a time of testing and someone says, "I know just how you feel," that statement might frustrate or even anger you. How can anyone else know exactly what you're feeling?

But when Jesus says, "I know just how you feel," you should take heart. Because He is God, He knows all things; because He became human, He experienced every dimension of life in the flesh. "We do not have a high priest who is unable to sympathize with our weaknesses" (v. 15, *NIV*).

The Old Testament priest would offer animal sacrifices to God on behalf of the people. But Jesus Christ was both the priest and the sacrifice, offering Himself on your behalf.

No wonder the writer continues, "Let us then approach the throne of grace with confidence, so that we may receive mercy and find grace to help us in our time of need" (v. 16, *NIV*).

Are you feeling rejected? "He was despised and rejected of [by] men" (Isaiah 53:3).

Feeling hated? "Like one from whom men hide their faces, he was despised" (v. 3, *NIV*).

Is your body diseased? "Surely he took up our infirmities" (v. 4, *NIV*).

Are you depressed? "Surely he . . . carried our sorrows" (v. 4).

Do you feel trapped by sin? "He was pierced by our transgressions, he was crushed for our iniquities" (v. 5).

Are you filled with worry? "The punishment that brought us peace was upon him" (v. 5, *NIV*).

Are you sick? "By his stripes we are healed" (v. 5).

Have you been physically or emotionally violated? "He is brought as a lamb to the slaughter" (v. 7).

Feeling like you have no hope or future? "Though the Lord makes his life a guilt offering, he will see his offspring and prolong his days, and the will of the Lord will prosper in his hand" (v. 10, *NIV*).

Every test you will ever face is something He has already endured and defeated. Give it to Him.—**Lance Colkmire**

SENTENCE SERMONS

CHRISTIANS CAN overcome temptation by the Word of God implanted in their hearts.
—**Selected**

YOU ARE NOT TEMPTED because you are evil. You are tempted because you are human.
—**Fulton J. Sheen**

TEMPTATIONS discover what we are.
—**Thomas à Kempis**

EVANGELISM APPLICATION

CHRISTIANS SHOULD TESTIFY TO SINNERS OF THE OVERCOMING POWER OF JESUS.

When you face temptation, the worst thing you can do is to stop and consider it. When one stops he is likely to begin to brood—brooding induces self-pity, and self-pity always magnifies the problem.

Giving in to temptation is somewhat like water that is in a swamp. At one time the water in the swamp was sweet and pure. But it runs into a low place and stops, where it stagnates and breeds all manner of unhealthy things.

Life is like that. If you stop when you hit temptation, you begin to stagnate too. But God has eternal power; and, as one fills his mind with God, His power actually flows into the person, giving him the strength to overcome temptation and to continue living for Him. As a result, the Christian can testify to sinners concerning Christ's overcoming power.

ILLUMINATING THE LESSON

Reports the *Denver Post*: "Like many sheep ranchers in the West, Lexy Fowler has tried just about everything to stop crafty coyotes from killing her sheep. She has tried odor sprays, electric fences, and 'scare-coyotes.' She has slept with her lambs during the summer and has placed battery-operated radios near them. She has corralled them at night, herded them at day. But the southern Montana rancher has lost scores of lambs—50 in one year alone.

"Then she discovered the llama—the aggressive, funny-looking, afraid-of-nothing llama. . . . 'Llamas don't appear to be afraid of anything,' she said. 'When they see something, they put their head up and walk straight toward it. That is aggressive behavior as far as the coyote is concerned, and they won't have anything to do with that. . . . Coyotes are opportunists, and llamas take that opportunity away.'"

Apparently llamas know the truth of what James writes: "Resist the devil, and he will flee from you" (4:7). The moment we sense his attack through temptation is the moment we should face it and deal with it for what it is.—**Barry McGee**, *Leadership* **Magazine**

DAILY BIBLE READINGS

M. Fear the Lord.
   Deuteronomy 6:13-19
T. Live by the Word.
   Deuteronomy 8:1-6
W. Love the Lord.
   Deuteronomy 10:12-21
T. Escape From Temptation.
   1 Corinthians 10:9-13
F. Victory Over Temptation.
   Hebrews 4:12-16
S. Draw Near to God.
   James 4:6-10

TRUTH SEARCH:
Creatively Teaching the Word

Aim: Each student will identify an area where they are frequently tempted, and commit to find three passages of Scripture they can use to overcome this temptation.

Items needed: Marker board, marker, index cards, pencils or pens

FOCUS

Divide the class into groups of three or four students each. Have each group make up a situation in which someone is tempted. Then have each group present a short skit for the class in which they act out their situation.

EXPLORE

Have a volunteer read Luke 3:21, 22 and 4:1-13 aloud. Discuss the following questions:
• *According to 3:21, 22 and 4:1, what experiences preceded Jesus being tempted by the devil?*
• *What human need was the devil playing on in trying to get Jesus to succumb to the first temptation (vv. 2, 3)?*
• *In verses 5-7, why do you think the devil's offer could have been tempting to Jesus?*
• *What word did the devil use in both the first and the third temptation (vv. 3, 9)? What was the point?*
• *What common themes can you find in each of Jesus' responses to temptation?*
• *Was this the end of Satan's temptations of Jesus (v. 13)?*

Have a volunteer look up 1 John 2:16 and read it aloud. On the marker board, write the following phrases: Lust of the Flesh, Lust of the Eyes, and the Pride of Life. Ask the class to compare Jesus' temptations with these categories of temptation.

If you have extra time, ask the students to turn to Genesis 3:1-6. Compare the temptations of Eve to the temptations of Jesus. Divide the ways that Eve was lured into taking the fruit in verse 6 into the categories listed on the board.

RESPOND

Give each class member an index card and a pen or pencil. Have each person write on the top of the index card an area in which they are frequently tempted. (They can use words or symbols.) Underneath this, have them write the numbers 1 to 3 down the left margin of the card.

Challenge each person to find, during the week, three passages of Scripture that speak to their area of temptation. Encourage them to memorize at least one verse to use in times of temptation.

Jesus Is the Messiah

Study Text: Luke 4:14-32; 7:19-35
Objective: To review Jesus' claim as the Messiah and acknowledge His lordship over our lives.
Time: The Gospel of Luke was probably written between A.D. 58 and 70.
Place: Jesus' authority was questioned in His hometown of Nazareth.
Golden Text: "The Spirit of the Lord is upon me, because he hath anointed me to preach the gospel to the poor; he hath sent me to heal the brokenhearted, to preach deliverance to the captives, and recovering of sight to the blind, to set at liberty them that are bruised, to preach the acceptable year of the Lord" (Luke 4:18, 19).
Central Truth: Christians acknowledge Jesus as Lord, because He is the Messiah.
Evangelism Emphasis: Jesus came to set the captives free.

PRINTED TEXT

Luke 4:17. And there was delivered unto him the book of the prophet Esaias. And when he had opened the book, he found the place where it was written,

18. The Spirit of the Lord is upon me, because he hath anointed me to preach the gospel to the poor; he hath sent me to heal the brokenhearted, to preach deliverance to the captives, and recovering of sight to the blind, to set at liberty them that are bruised,

19. To preach the acceptable year of the Lord.

20. And he closed the book, and gave it again to the minister, and sat down. And the eyes of all them that were in the synagogue were fastened on him.

21. And he began to say unto them, This day is this scripture fulfilled in your ears.

22. And all bare him witness, and wondered at the gracious words which proceeded out of his mouth. And they said, Is not this Joseph's son?

23. And he said unto them, Ye will surely say unto me this proverb, Physician, heal thyself: whatsoever we have heard done in Capernaum, do also here in thy country.

24. And he said, Verily I say unto you, No prophet is accepted in his own country.

28. And all they in the synagogue, when they heard these things, were filled with wrath,

29. And rose up, and thrust him out of the city, and led him unto the brow of the hill whereon their city was built, that they might cast him down headlong.

7:19. And John calling unto him two of his disciples sent them to Jesus, saying, Art thou he that should come? or look we for another?

20. When the men were come unto him, they said, John Baptist hath sent us unto thee, saying, Art thou he that should come? or look we for another?

21. And in that same hour he cured many of their infirmities and plagues, and of evil spirits; and unto many that were blind he gave sight.

22. Then Jesus answering said unto them, Go your way, and tell John what things ye have seen and heard; how that the blind see, the lame walk, the **lepers are cleansed, the deaf hear, the dead are raised, to the poor the gospel is preached.**

23. And blessed is he, whosoever shall not be offended in me.

DICTIONARY

Nazareth (NAZ-uh-reth)—Luke 4:16—The hometown of Mary and Joseph, nowhere referred to in the Old Testament. Its people had a poor reputation in religion and morals.

LESSON OUTLINE

I. JESUS ANNOUNCES HIS MISSION

  A. The Return to Nazareth

  B. The Scripture Lesson

  C. The Admission

II. JESUS FACES REJECTION

  A. The Question

  B. The Sermon

  C. The Effect

III. JESUS CONFIRMS HIS IDENTITY

  A. John's Concern

  B. Jesus' Response

LESSON EXPOSITION

INTRODUCTION

Dr. J.H. Jowett has well said that "the gospel of a broken heart demands the ministry of a bleeding heart. We bleed to bless." We lose our life to find it; we give to receive; we die to live.

Luke records that following His baptism and His experience with the tempter, Jesus returned in the power of the Spirit to begin His public ministry. His ministry was an expression of His being—God manifest in the flesh. He knew no sin. There was no guile in His mouth. This holy condition of being expressed itself in compassion. He had holy empathy for needy humanity.

Christ's ministry was one of vision. He saw the hungry and fed them; He saw the sick and healed them; He saw the guilty and pardoned them; He saw the impure and cleansed them. Jesus broke through religious exclusiveness to get to needy humanity. This is what Isaiah had said the Messiah would do.

I. JESUS ANNOUNCES HIS MISSION (Luke 4:14-21)

A. The Return to Nazareth (vv. 14-16)

(Luke 4:14-16 is not included in the printed text.)

Nazareth was the hometown of Jesus, so He was well known there. He had grown up in Nazareth and worked in the carpenter shop of Joseph. He had played in the streets and climbed the surrounding hills. He had laughed and cried with His friends. He had studied and prayed in the synagogue. He had experienced all the normal activities of a Jewish boy as He grew in wisdom and stature and in favor with God and man.

The words in verse 16, "As his custom was, he went into the synagogue on the sabbath day," present an incidental notice of an important part of the exemplary life of Jesus. Christ went into the synagogue on the Sabbath Day, thus setting us an example for regular church attendance.

It is also significant that Jesus began His ministry at a synagogue. Next to the Temple, the synagogue was the center of religious life in Palestine. Since there was only one Temple, the Law declared there could be a synagogue wherever there were at least 10 Jewish families in a community. So in almost every town and village the people worshiped in a synagogue. The Temple was designed for sacrifice, the synagogue for teaching. There were no sacrifices in the synagogue.

B. The Scripture Lesson (vv. 17-20)

17. And there was delivered unto him the book of the prophet Esaias. And when he had opened the book, he found the place where it was written,
18. The Spirit of the Lord is upon me, because he hath anointed me to preach the gospel to the poor; he hath sent me to heal the brokenhearted, to preach deliverance to the captives, and recovering of sight to the blind, to set at liberty them that are bruised,
19. To preach the acceptable year of the Lord.
20. And he closed the book, and gave it again to the minister, and sat down. And the eyes of all them that were in the synagogue were fastened on him.

Some have questioned how Jesus, the carpenter from Nazareth, could have been accepted in the synagogue and how He, a supposed layman, had the authority to deliver His message. The answer is simple. In the synagogue service there were three elements. First, there was the act of worship in which prayer was offered. Second, there was the reading of the sacred Scriptures. In this element, seven men from the congregation read from the sacred writings. As they read, the ancient Hebrew language (which was no longer widely understood) was translated by the Targumist into Aramaic or Greek. The Books of the Law were translated one verse at a time; the writings of the Prophets, three verses at a time. Third, there was the element of teaching. Since there was no professional ministry in the synagogue, there was no set person to give an address. The president could invite any distinguished person present (male and Jewish) to speak, after which the male hearers would discuss the message. Thus, Jesus was given opportunities to speak in the synagogues.

It is significant that Jesus attended the service. Although He did not hear or learn anything there which He did not already know, He himself was the substance of what the Law foreshadowed. Moreover, He was the fulfillment of what the prophets foretold. But He did not neglect public worship.

When He stood to read, Jesus was given one of the books of sacred writings, which He opened. The word *opened* would be more properly translated "unrolled." A book in the time of Jesus' earthly ministry was a rolled scroll of parchment. Jesus found the place from which He wanted to read, indicating His familiarity with the Scriptures. He began with what we know as Isaiah 61:1 and continued into the first clause of verse 2.

Jesus was anointed by the Holy Spirit for a sixfold ministry: to evangelize the poor, heal the brokenhearted, release captives, give sight to the blind, free the oppressed, and preach the acceptable year of the Lord (Luke 4:18, 19).

The poor have often been neglected by the church, while there has been no expense spared for elaborate programs to enlist the educated and cultured and to minister to those with material possessions. But one of the beautiful aspects of Christ's ministry was that He spent time working with the poor. To be like Christ, the church must reach the poor with His message.

A lot of misery exists in our world. Many people have broken hearts for various reasons—tyranny, slander, disappointment, bereavement, and especially sin. But this misery is not by divine appointment, as suggested by God's sending His Son to remove it.

Bible scholars apply "deliverance to the captives" to sinners. The sinner is in captivity to Satan, the enemy, and is not free to live as he knows he ought. However, Christ came to deliver the captive, to set him free. This is good news for the sinner.

The Bible portrays the sinner as being dead, sick, diseased, imprisoned and living in darkness. Salvation through the blood of Christ brings deliverance from all of these.

The gospel of Christ is a message for the oppressed. The world of Jesus' day and our world today is full of broken lives shattered by sin, sagging under the burdens of life. Christ was also broken by sin—not His own, but ours. However, His death on the cross became the triumph for all who will accept Him.

"The acceptable year of the Lord" is perhaps an allusion to the Year of Jubilee. Every 50th year, trumpets were blown and proclamation was made throughout the whole land of the liberty of Hebrew slaves, of the remission of debts, and of the restoration of possessions to their original owners.

A year that is acceptable to the Lord is a year in which the Lord accepts sinners on the basis of the salvation which He has provided in Jesus Christ.

The minister, or *chazzan*, who had handed the book to Jesus was the one who received it back again. It was his duty to take the Scriptures from the ark and to put them back again after they had been used. Jesus took His seat, not with the rest of the audience, but in a particular place where it would be recognized at once that He intended to speak. Sitting was the usual Jewish posture for teaching. There was something about Jesus that held the people spellbound for the moment, waiting for Him to speak.

C. The Admission (v. 21)

21. And he began to say unto them, This day is this scripture fulfilled in your ears.

Jesus made a most astonishing assertion. Isaiah's prophecy had been given almost 750 years before this. No Jewish teacher had ever before dared to say that this prophetic scripture was being fulfilled. When Jesus did this He could only be understood by the people as meaning that He was the Anointed One whom Isaiah had prophesied to come. This accounts for the amazement of the people described in verse 22.

II. JESUS FACES REJECTION (Luke 4:22-32)

A. The Question (v. 22)

22. And all bare him witness, and wondered at the gracious words which proceeded out of his mouth. And they said, Is not this Joseph's son?

The people could find no flaw in the exposition of Scripture by Jesus. They could not deny the beauty of the well-chosen language to which they had listened. But their hearts were absolutely unmoved and unaffected. They could only say, "Is not this Joseph's son?"

B. The Sermon (vv. 23-27)

(Luke 4:25-27 is not included in the printed text.)

23. And he said unto them, Ye will surely say unto me this proverb, Physician, heal thyself: whatsoever we have heard done in Capernaum, do also here in thy country.

24. And he said, Verily I say unto you, No prophet is accepted in his own country.

One writer paraphrases Christ's words as follows: "The question which you have just put to me is only the first symptom of unbelief. From surprise you will pass to derision. Thus you will quickly arrive at the end of the path in which you have just taken the first step" (F. Godet, *A Commentary on the Gospel of St. Luke*).

People are apt to despise the highest privileges when they are familiar with them. This is illustrated by the men of Nazareth on this occasion. They could find no fault in the words of Christ. They could point to no inconsistencies in His conduct. But because He had lived among them for 30 years, and His face, voice and appearance were familiar to them, they would not receive Him nor accept His words. They thought, *Could one so well-known be the Christ?*

We are always in danger of undervaluing God's mercies when we have them in such abundance. We often take for granted an open Bible, a preached gospel and the freedom of public worship. We grow up with these so readily available that we often fail to appreciate them properly. We need to remember that even the manna that came down from heaven was eventually scorned by Israel.

In verses 25-27, Jesus reminded the people of Nazareth that God was under no obligation to work miracles among them. He said the prophet Elijah was not sent to the widows of Israel. They were passed over in favor of a Gentile widow at Sarepta (Zarephath). There were many lepers in Israel during Elisha's time, yet Naaman the Syrian was the only leper cleansed. In essence, Jesus told the people of Nazareth that God is no man's debtor, and that if they were passed over in the distribution of His mercies, they had no right to find fault.

C. The Effect (vv. 28-32)

(Luke 4:30-32 is not included in the printed text.)

28. And all they in the synagogue, when they heard these things, were filled with wrath,

29. And rose up, and thrust him out of the city, and led him unto the brow of the hill whereon their city was built, that they might cast him down headlong.

The pride and self-conceit of the people of Nazareth were wounded by the words of Jesus. They could not take it. They were filled with wrath. They thrust Jesus out of their city, and had it not been for an exercise of miraculous power on His part, they would undoubtedly have put Him to a violent death. In what way this miracle was effected we are not told. It is enough for us to know that His enemies could not kill Him against His will, and that when He was finally delivered up to be crucified, it was only because He was willing to allow Himself to be slain.

III. JESUS CONFIRMS HIS IDENTITY (Luke 7:19-23)

A. John's Concern (vv. 19, 20)

19. And John calling unto him two of his disciples sent them to Jesus, saying, Art thou he that should come? or look we for another?

20. When the men were come unto him, they said, John Baptist hath sent us unto thee, saying, Art thou he that should come? or look we for another?

In considering the question John the Baptist asked, we must remember the circumstances he was experiencing. Because John was incapable of seeing evil without rebuking it, he was in prison. He had spoken the truth fearlessly and definitely, rebuking Herod for his sin, and now he was locked away.

Prison was difficult for John for many reasons. He could no longer preach to the masses; he could not witness Christ's ministry for himself. John was accustomed to living in the open air. The sky had been his roof, the fields his bed, the open country his pulpit. To put a man like this in prison was like putting a bird in a cage.

Some have said John asked his question for the sake of his disciples—that their hearts might be opened and their faith in Christ confirmed. The most obvious explanation is simply that John had some misgivings. For a brief period of time he was under a cloud, involved in doubt, tempted to let go the confidence that had brought him such joy when he first saw the Dove descending and abiding on Jesus.

The Bible does not refuse to tell the truth about the failures of God's children. It tells of Abram's thinking that the Egyptians would take his life. It speaks of Elijah's stretching himself beneath the shadow of the desert bush, and asking that he might die. It reveals how Thomas, who had been prepared to die with his Lord, could not believe that He was risen. So why not allow John the Baptist a moment of doubt?

B. Jesus' Response (vv. 21-23)

21. And in that same hour he cured many of their infirmities and plagues, and of evil spirits; and unto many that were blind he gave sight.

22. Then Jesus answering said unto them, Go your way, and tell John what things ye have seen and heard; how that the blind see, the lame walk, the lepers are cleansed, the deaf hear, the dead are raised, to the poor the gospel is preached.

23. And blessed is he, whosoever shall not be offended in me.

In response to John's question, Jesus directed the messengers from John to His works. He did not affirm His messiahship in words as He did to the Samaritan woman and to the man born blind; but He pointed to His works. Jesus adapted His teaching to the circumstances and personalities of each case.

Jesus must have worked many miracles in the presence of John's disciples. He cured diseases, drove out evil spirits, opened blind eyes. These were His proper works—the works attributed to Him by the prophets. They proved that Jesus was the Christ—the Messiah. They were evidences of His divine origin and of His sacred office.

There is no better evidence than that of eyewitnesses. John's disciples were to report what they had seen and heard. This was the best evidence that Jesus was the Christ.

It is interesting to note that Jesus enumerated the things which John was to be told. He was always ready with evidence.

The disciples were to tell what they had seen and heard. This statement implies that besides witnessing miracles, John's disciples had been privileged to hear Jesus preach.

GOLDEN TEXT HOMILY

"THE SPIRIT OF THE LORD IS UPON ME, BECAUSE HE HATH ANOINTED ME TO PREACH THE GOSPEL TO THE POOR; HE HATH SENT ME TO HEAL THE BROKEN-HEARTED, TO PREACH DELIVER-ANCE TO THE CAPTIVES, AND RECOVERING OF SIGHT TO THE BLIND, TO SET AT LIBERTY THEM THAT ARE BRUISED, TO PREACH THE ACCEPTABLE YEAR OF THE LORD" (Luke 4:18, 19).

Has the world ever experienced an individual totally given over to God? A person that knew, felt and did as God wanted at all times? What kind of effect would that person have on the community where you live today?

Consider Jesus and His three-year ministry here on earth. He was totally human and laid aside His divine attributes when He became flesh (John 1:14; Philippians 2:5-8), and He was anointed by the Holy Spirit to do the work of God (Luke 4:18, 19).

What about us who have been born into God's family and have received the infilling of God's Spirit? Do we not have the authorization, ability and anointing from God to . . .

• communicate the gospel (Mark 16:15)

• bring help and healing to those who are hurting (Luke 4:18)

• bind the strong man who is holding people captive (Matthew 12:29)

• intercede for those who are blinded by Satan (2 Corinthians 4:4)

• bring deliverance to those who are oppressed by demons (Matthew 10:8)

• proclaim the coming of the Lord (1 John 2:28; Revelation 3:11)?

Jesus has given us the authority (see Matthew 16:19) and the power (ability) for anointed ministry (Ephesians 3:20).

Through the person of Jesus the world has seen what God can do through a committed person empowered by the Holy Spirit. God wants His people to be anointed ministers in the world today.—**Philip Siggelkow**

SENTENCE SERMONS

CHRISTIANS acknowledge Jesus as Lord, because He is the Messiah.
—Selected

JESUS CHRIST turns life rightside-up, and heaven outside-in.
—Carl F.H. Henry

EVERY GREAT PERSON has first learned how to obey, whom to obey, and when to obey.
—William A. Ward

EVANGELISM APPLICATION

JESUS CAME TO SET THE CAPTIVES FREE.

Christians can learn an important lesson from the experience of Jesus in Nazareth. Knowing that He would be rejected by the people of His hometown, He persevered in presenting the message He came to deliver. After the rejection, He patiently continued His work. Thrust out of one place, He moved to another. Literally being forced out of Nazareth, He went to Capernaum, and there He continued to teach God's Word on the Sabbath. Why? He was anointed to minister, and minister He did, proclaiming freedom to the captive.

This should be the attitude of all Christians who are anointed by the Spirit to work for God. Whatever the work we are called to do, we should continue in it and not give up because of lack of "success." It is our job to faithfully proclaim the message of deliverance; it is Christ's job to set the captive free.

ILLUMINATING THE LESSON

In acknowledging Christ as the Messiah, Dr. J.T. Gordon observes: "I know that He was kingly, for they sought to make Him king. I know that He was eloquent, for He spake as never man spake. I know that He was tenderhearted, for He wept at the grave of Lazarus. I know that He was magnetic, for the multitude sought to touch Him. I know that He was fascinating, for even a social outcast, as low as the woman of Samaria, exclaimed, 'Is not this the Christ?' I know that He was superb in His mental mold, for a Jewish rabbi affirmed, 'Thou art a teacher come from God.' I know that He was observing, for, as He passed by, He saw a man which was blind from his birth. I know that He was popular, for the multitude shouted, 'Hosanna! Hosanna! Blessed is he that cometh in the name of the Lord'" (quoted in *The Peerless Christ*, by Peter Wiseman).

DAILY BIBLE READINGS

M. The Promised Messiah.
   Isaiah 7:10-16
T. The Messiah's Mission.
   Isaiah 61:1-3
W. The Messiah's Messenger.
   Malachi 3:1-4
T. Jesus Is the Christ.
   Matthew 16:13-21
F. Christ Is Exalted.
   Philippians 2:5-11
S. Christ Is Our High Priest.
   Hebrews 9:11-20

TRUTH SEARCH:
Creatively Teaching the Word

Aim: Students will pray that there will be evidence of Christ's lordship that other people can see in them.

Items needed: Marker board, marker

FOCUS

Write the following on the marker board: Jesus said, "Blessed is the man who does not fall away on account of me" (Luke 7:23, *NIV*). Discuss these questions:

• *Do you know anyone who started to follow God but gave up as they began to understand what it means to be under His lordship?*

• *In your life, when is it most difficult to make Jesus "Lord"?*

EXPLORE

Have a volunteer read Luke 4:14-21 aloud. Then discuss these questions:

• *Did Jesus go to the synagogue regularly?*

• *What did Jesus mean by His statement in verse 21?*

• *According to verses 18 and 19, what were the specific roles of the Messiah?*

Have a volunteer read Luke 4:22-32 aloud. Then discuss these questions:

• *Did the people of Nazareth immediately recognize Christ as the Lord?*

• *Where can a true servant of God expect to be rejected?*

• *After stating that His coming fulfilled Old Testament prophecy, did the people immediately try to make Jesus King? Why or why not?*

• *In Capernaum, why were the people astonished by Jesus (vv. 31, 32)?*

Have a volunteer read Luke 7:19-23 aloud. Then discuss the following questions:

• *After John the Baptist's arrest, why did he send messengers to Jesus?*

• *How did Jesus reply to John's question?*

• *Do you think Jesus wants people to search out His true identity?*

RESPOND

Ask the students to reflect upon the fact that other people are looking for evidence of Christ's lordship in them. Allow the students to respond silently to the following questions:

• *When others look at you, do they see someone who has a wholehearted devotion to Christ?*

• *When others look at you, do they see someone who is bound by sinful habits?*

• *When others look at you, do they see someone who views the world differently than most in mainstream society?*

• *When others look at you, do they see someone who has a vibrant relationship with Christ and exhibits newness of life?*

Pray with the students that the lordship of Christ will become evident to anyone who might examine their lives. Most importantly, pray with the students that they will yield themselves to Christ so they can experience the freedom found in submission to Christ.

The Joy Christ Brings (Christmas)

Study Text: Luke 2:1-20
Objective: To review the events surrounding Christ's birth and rejoice because of His coming.
Time: Bible scholars differ on the exact date of the birth of Christ, but it is generally considered to have been 4 or 5 B.C.
Place: Bethlehem
Golden Text: "Unto you is born this day in the city of David a Saviour, which is Christ the Lord" (Luke 2:11).
Central Truth: Christ's birth is a special reason for the world to rejoice.
Evangelism Emphasis: We must take the good news to lost people everywhere.

PRINTED TEXT

Luke 2:1. And it came to pass in those days, that there went out a decree from Caesar Augustus, that all the world should be taxed.

2. (And this taxing was first made when Cyrenius was governor of Syria.)

3. And all went to be taxed, every one into his own city.

4. And Joseph also went up from Galilee, out of the city of Nazareth, into Judaea, unto the city of David, which is called Bethlehem; (because he was of the house and lineage of David:)

5. To be taxed with Mary his espoused wife, being great with child.

6. And so it was, that, while they were there, the days were accomplished that she should be delivered.

7. And she brought forth her firstborn son, and wrapped him in swaddling clothes, and laid him in a manger; because there was no room for them in the inn.

8. And there were in the same country shepherds abiding in the field, keeping watch over their flock by night.

9. And, lo, the angel of the Lord came upon them, and the glory of the Lord shone round about them: and they were sore afraid.

10. And the angel said unto them, Fear not: for, behold, I bring you good tidings of great joy, which shall be to all people.

11. For unto you is born this day in the city of David a Saviour, which is Christ the Lord.

12. And this shall be a sign unto you; Ye shall find the babe wrapped in swaddling clothes, lying in a manger.

13. And suddenly there was with the angel a multitude of the heavenly host praising God, and saying,

14. Glory to God in the highest, and on earth peace, good will toward men.

20. And the shepherds returned, glorifying and praising God for all the things that they had heard and seen, as it was told unto them.

LESSON OUTLINE

I. MIRACULOUS BIRTH
   A. The Census
   B. The Birth

II. ANGELIC ANNOUNCEMENT
   A. The Shepherds
   B. The Angelic Message
   C. The Heavenly Choir

III. JOYFUL RESPONSE
   A. The Decision
   B. The Testimony
   C. The Meditation
   D. The Worship

LESSON EXPOSITION

INTRODUCTION

On September 2, 1945, in Tokyo Bay, Japan, the second and final phase of the world's most terrible war officially came to an end. That day, while millions of people eagerly listened to their radios, General Douglas MacArthur, aboard the *U.S.S. Missouri*, received the notice of surrender from the imperial government of Japan.

But four months later something took place on the deck of the battleship that few people know about. It was Christmastime, and the *Missouri* was home, anchored quietly in the waters of the Naval Shipyard in Brooklyn. A choral group of bluejackets gave a concert of Christmas carols. They didn't begin with a shallow and completely secular jingle like "Santa Claus Is Coming to Town." No, they opened with . . .

O little town of Bethlehem,
How still we see the lie!
Above thy deep and dreamless
  sleep

The silent stars go by;
Yet in thy dark streets shineth
  The everlasting Light;
The hopes and fears of all the
  years
Are met in thee tonight.
       —Phillips Brooks

That song stands for something stronger than what the battleship *Missouri* stands for. The fighting ship represents man's fears, while Brooks' immortal carol represents man's hopes. They are hopes, moreover, that would have died long since, had it not been for what happened at Bethlehem and later at Calvary.

I. MIRACULOUS BIRTH
(Luke 2:1-7)

A. The Census (vv. 1-5)

1. And it came to pass in those days, that there went out a decree from Caesar Augustus, that all the world should be taxed.

2. (And this taxing was first made when Cyrenius was governor of Syria.)

3. And all went to be taxed, every one into his own city.

4. And Joseph also went up from Galilee, out of the city of Nazareth, into Judaea, unto the city of David, which is called Bethlehem; (because he was of the house and lineage of David:)

5. To be taxed with Mary his espoused wife, being great with child.

This Caesar is that Octavius who, after the defeat of Antony and Cleopatra at Actium, took the government of the Roman Empire into his own hands, and was, properly speaking, the first Caesar, or Roman emperor. Luke refers to him as Augustus, which was one of his other names.

In his *Commentary on the Four Gospels*, David Smith has some interesting comments on verse 2: "It has always been known that Quirinius ["Cyrenius"] was the administrator of Syria from A.D. 6 to 9, and that, during that period, he did take a census, one that is actually mentioned in Acts 5:37, but this cannot of course be the census referred to in the story of our Lord's birth. For years this was a problem for Bible scholars, but now from inscriptions discovered in Antioch in 1912, we know that Quirinius governed Syria twice, and that this first governorship covered the period in which our Lord was born."

The Roman census was taken at this time every 14 years. Smith comments on verse 3: "This fact also fits in perfectly with the historical data which are in our possession. Furthermore, had Judaea been then, as in later days, a mere province, her census would have been taken after the Roman method, which enrolled people wherever they had a chance to reside; but since Judaea was still a kingdom, it was taken after the Jewish method, which required each to repair to his ancestral seat and there report himself."

The Romans permitted the Jews to follow their custom. And so it happened that Joseph, the village carpenter of Nazareth, in the northern Palestine province of Galilee, was compelled to travel southward 70 miles to Bethlehem, since he was descended from the great poet-king, David, who was born in Bethlehem (v. 4). This happening, which seems a mere matter of chance, was really ordered by divine providence, fulfilling the clear prophecy of Micah 5:2: "But thou, Bethlehem Ephratah, though thou be little among the thousands of Judah, yet out of thee shall he come forth unto me that is to be ruler in Israel; whose goings forth have been from of old, from everlasting."

Joseph took Mary, soon to become a mother, with him (v. 5). Why? According to R.C.H. Lenski, it was "in order to shield her against slanderous tongues and in order to give her in her condition all the protection and help that she needed, not leaving her in the care of others. Mary herself must also have greatly desired to leave Nazareth with Joseph" (*The Interpretation of St. Mark's and St. Luke's Gospels*).

The word *Bethlehem* means "house of bread," because nearby were large grain fields, and in the city were huge granaries from which the great city of Jerusalem, seven miles to the north, was furnished with bread. Here was to be born the true Bread of the world.

Lenski states that we should not interpret the word *espoused* (*betrothed*) as identical with our word *engaged*. Betrothal was virtually marriage, lacking only that the bridegroom take his bride to his home. The vows of marriage were made at the betrothal, which was always public, and none were needed when the groom took away his bride. Between Luke 1:27 and 2:5 lies Matthew 1:24, and so we see Mary here in the company of Joseph in a betrothal now consummated.

Here we can see clearly God's perfect preparations for the fulfillment of His purpose and prophecies (Micah 5:2; Matthew 2:6), because Mary was in the city of Bethlehem where Jesus was to be born just at the time she gave birth to her first son. It is interesting that nothing is ever said again about the city of Bethlehem in all the Gospel records, or in all the

New Testament epistles, except an indirect reference in John 7:42.

B. The Birth (vv. 6, 7)

6. And so it was, that, while they were there, the days were accomplished that she should be delivered.

7. And she brought forth her firstborn son, and wrapped him in swaddling clothes, and laid him in a manger; because there was no room for them in the inn.

An anonymous writer has imagined himself talking with the keeper of the inn at Bethlehem: "The inn was overcrowded. The families of the lineage of David had been coming in for days, and every room was full. And what was there to specially commend these pilgrims to me? They were of royal descent, but also of fallen fortunes. The man was a mere peasant, a carpenter, as he told me, from the despised town of Nazareth. Which of the distinguished guests in my caravansary—priests, rabbis, wealthy traders—could I displace to make room for him? Shelter in the cave nearby was better for them than to rest under the open sky. There were cattle there and beasts of burden, so the place afforded shelter from the wind; and there was barley straw to rest on."

A Jew has pictured the scene differently, in accordance with the well-known hospitality of the people. "Laid in a manger? True! True! But how beautiful that becomes when understood aright. You think with your ways of life, of a place for cattle only. But have you not seen that the common people and their animals live together in this land—all sorts of domestic animals with their feeding places in the dwellings of the lowly? Ah, I like to think how, when there was no room in the inn, some kind villager said, 'Come to my house,' and so a place was made for Mary's babe in a household manger!" (based on *Sacred Sites and Ways*, by Gustaf Dalman).

The traditional picture is familiar. Arriving in Bethlehem, six miles south of Jerusalem, worn with the long journey and perhaps Mary already suffering her birth pangs, the pair found the little town so crowded with census visitors there was no room for them in the crude inn. Joseph, anxiously inquiring, could find no other shelter for Mary than a stable. This stable was probably one of the many limestone caves of the vicinity, and there the Son of God was born, a humble home for the King of kings; but He came to earth for that very purpose, that He might identify Himself with the lot of the poorest and lowliest. The manger of the stable was probably a stone trough hollowed out of the side of the cave, and this, filled with straw, served as the cradle of the divine Babe. As was Jewish custom, Jesus was wrapped in many long bands of cloth probably by Mary herself.

II. ANGELIC ANNOUNCEMENT (Luke 2:8-14)

A. The Shepherds (vv. 8, 9)

8. And there were in the same country shepherds abiding in the field, keeping watch over their flock by night.

9. And, lo, the angel of the Lord came upon them, and the glory of the Lord shone round about them: and they were sore afraid.

The tidings of Christ's birth first came to shepherds in a field near Bethlehem. These shepherds were simple, unsophisticated pastoral men. They were engaged in their common occupation when they received the wonderful revelation from heaven. They were not standing idly gazing up into the sky, neglecting the work at hand.

The lack of money does not prevent spiritual blessings. James wrote: "Hath not God chosen the poor of this world rich in faith, and heirs of the kingdom which he hath promised to them that love him?" (James 2:5). The things of God's kingdom are often hidden from those whom we think are great, and revealed to the poor. Being a working man does not prevent one from having special communion with God. Moses was keeping sheep, Gideon was threshing wheat, and Elisha was plowing, when they were honored by direct calls and revelations from God.

The glory of the Lord (v. 9) was probably that wonderful light which accompanies the appearance of God and His angels—a light like the Shekinah that flamed above the mercy seat of the ark.

The shepherds should not be blamed for being afraid. The presence of supernatural beings, however lovely and loving they may be, overawes human beings with majesty, dazzles them with splendor, and terrifies them with strangeness.

B. The Angelic Message (vv. 10-12)

10. And the angel said unto them, Fear not: for, behold, I bring you good tidings of great joy, which shall be to all people.

11. For unto you is born this day in the city of David a Saviour, which is Christ the Lord.

12. And this shall be a sign unto you; Ye shall find the babe wrapped in swaddling clothes, lying in a manger.

The angel said to the shepherds, "Fear not." That was heaven's first word to earth after the birth of Jesus. It was the voice of an angel sounding the keynote of the music of hope for sinful men. Christ often used the same comforting words during His ministry.

These were amazing words from the angel. "I bring you good tidings of great joy, which shall be to all people" (v. 10). These words mean that the spiritual darkness which had covered the earth was about to be rolled away. The way to peace and pardon with God was about to be thrown open to all mankind. The head of Satan was about to be bruised. Liberty was about to be proclaimed to the captives, and recovering of sight to the blind. The mighty truth was about to be proclaimed that God could be just and yet, for Christ's sake, justify the ungodly.

Salvation was no longer to be seen through types and figures, but openly, and face-to-face. The knowledge of God was no longer to be confined to the Jews, but to be offered to the whole Gentile world. The first stone of God's kingdom was about to be set up. If this was not "good tidings," there never were things that deserved the name.

The message in verse 11 was that a Savior, who is Christ the Lord, was born in the city of David. In the Old Testament, God is often referred to as One who saves. People need to be saved from the power of sin, the power of Satan, and the ultimate consequence of sin, which is death. They need to be saved from the penalty of sin, which is the wrath of God. Jesus came to deliver us from every evil power, to bestow upon us eternal life in the place of death, and to deliver us from the wrath to come.

The name *Christ* means "anointed." Jesus (the Christ) was anointed by the Holy Spirit for His great work of redemption. It cannot be overemphasized that it was a voice from heaven that declared these wonderful things about the Babe in Bethlehem. These titles were not given to Jesus by His followers, or by Himself, or by later writers, but by an angel of the Lord, sent by God.

In his letter to the Philippians the apostle Paul says that Christ, who was equal with God, "emptied Himself" (2:7, *NASB*). Christ stepped down in order that He might lift mankind up. His deprivation brought about our revelation. If we miss this gigantic truth, we have miserably fumbled the Christmas story. If we glimpse it, even a little, we have at least struck close to the heart of the Nativity. Christmas is the everlasting miracle of the God who stepped down.

Think about it. Christ "emptied Himself." Whatever it means, it signifies that all the poverty, all the frailty, all the hunger, all the thirst, all the physical weakness, all the suffering and humiliation, all the countless restrictions upon Deity that we see in Jesus were the limitations He put upon Himself when He chose the route of childbirth and a developing human nature as the path of His redeeming revelation.

C. The Heavenly Choir (vv. 13, 14)

13. And suddenly there was with the angel a multitude of the heavenly host praising God, and saying,

14. Glory to God in the highest, and on earth peace, good will toward men.

Sing it out that Christ is a universal Savior. Here is the enormity of the gospel: it is for all men under all skies. In the dark night of man's shattering divisions and shivering fears, the gospel shines with a global glory. Not to Jews only, not to Gentiles only, not to whites only, not to people of color only—but to all the human family of beaten, baffled, broken souls comes the grand universalism of God's love and grace. Isaac Watts caught the sweep and magnificence of the good news when he wrote:

Joy to the world! the Lord is come;
  Let earth receive her King;
Let every heart prepare Him room,
  And heaven and nature sing.

III. JOYFUL RESPONSE
   (Luke 2:15-20)

A. The Decision (vv. 15, 16)

(Luke 2:15, 16 is not included in the printed text.)

The shepherds did not debate with themselves who should keep the sheep, but did as they were commanded, and committed their sheep to Him whose pleasure they obeyed.

They found Mary, Joseph, and the Babe. They found the "sign" given them by the angel. After observing the babe in the manger, they sped on their obvious errand.

B. The Testimony (vv. 17, 18)

(Luke 2:17, 18 is not included in the printed text.)

The Lord had made a great revelation to the shepherds and they felt it their duty to pass it on. So they excitedly communicated the wonderful news to everyone they passed on their way back to their flocks. Thus, the humble shepherds were given the honor of being the first Christian preachers.

C. The Meditation (v. 19)

(Luke 2:19 is not included in the printed text.)

Contrast the action of Mary with that of the shepherds. In their surprise and astonishment, they immediately published what they had witnessed. Mary was not astonished because she knew the significance of the Babe to which she had given birth because of previous annunciations to herself and to Joseph. The word *pondered* means "to bring together in one's mind," "to consider." Mary had the words of the angel to her, the song of Elizabeth, the words of the angel to Joseph, and the message of the shepherds to put together, piece by piece, word by word, picture by picture. The roll of the coming years would pass before the mind of Mary as she looked into the face of the Son of God.

D. The Worship (v. 20)

20. And the shepherds returned, glorifying and praising God for all the things that they had heard and seen, as it was told unto them.

The shepherds had the privilege of being the first of all mankind, after Mary and Joseph, who saw with believing eyes the newborn Messiah. They soon returned, "glorifying and praising God" for what they had seen.

GOLDEN TEXT HOMILY

"UNTO YOU IS BORN THIS DAY IN THE CITY OF DAVID A SAVIOUR, WHICH IS CHRIST THE LORD" (Luke 2:11).

This is one of the greatest messages ever delivered. It is a message of contrast between the magnificent and the mundane. It was announced by an angel. However, it was not announced to Caesar or Herod or the high priest, but to shepherds.

The message was that the Savior had been born. The name *Jesus* means "savior," as an angel had told Joseph, "Thou shalt call his name JESUS: for he shall save his people from their sins" (Matthew 1:21). This Savior was called Christ. He was the Anointed One, the Messiah.

The long ages of waiting and anticipation were over. The promises of the prophets were at last fulfilled. "When the fulness of the time was come, God sent forth his Son, made of a woman, made under the law, to redeem them that were under the law" (Galatians 4:4, 5).

This baby lying in a manger was in reality the Lord—the owner and ruler of all things. However, He had laid aside all His splendor and glory and had come to earth to be the Savior, so all His people would be able to share the joys of heaven.—**Richard Y. Bershon**

SENTENCE SERMONS

CHRIST'S BIRTH is a special reason for the world to rejoice.
—Selected

THE SON OF GOD became a man to enable men to become the sons of God.
—C.S. Lewis

SOME BUSINESSMEN say this could be the greatest Christmas ever. I thought the first one was.
—Art Fettig

EVANGELISM APPLICATION

WE MUST TAKE THE GOOD NEWS TO LOST PEOPLE EVERYWHERE.

A city missionary in London was offering Christ to a jockey in a horse-racing stable. "This is no place to talk religion," said the jockey.

"Oh yes it is," replied the missionary. "Jesus Christ was born in a stable, and you can be born again in one."

Before the conversation ended, the plucky little rider knelt there in prayer and accepted the Savior. Why not? No person, no place, is shut out from Jesus Christ's concern.

ILLUMINATING THE LESSON

The tidings of the coming of Christ communicated to the shepherds by the angel of God are no longer confined to the spot and to the period which were made memorable by their disclosure. They have ceased to be "tidings" because they are no longer new. Now they are history. Time itself has been God's commentator.

Centuries have rolled away, and nations have risen and fallen, but the impact of the coming of Christ has only widened and deepened.

Ironically, how many millions of people are there who, on Christmas Day, present gifts in celebration of the birth of Christ, yet who will not let the Master enter one step into their hearts to purify them? Let us beware lest we fall into this error of receiving Christ outwardly but rejecting Him inwardly.

DAILY BIBLE READINGS

M. Sure Prophecy.
   Isaiah 9:2-7
T. Source of Peace.
   Isaiah 53:1-5
W. God's Anointed Son.
   Psalm 2:1-12
T. Miraculous Conception.
   Luke 1:26-35
F. Virgin Birth.
   Matthew 1:18-25
S. Cause for Rejoicing.
   Matthew 2:1-11

TRUTH SEARCH:
Creatively Teaching the Word

Aim: Students will reflect upon the significance of Christ's birth as a source of genuine joy, and praise God for His coming to earth.

Items needed: Marker board, marker

FOCUS

Have students name events in their lives that were joyful. Write each response on the board. Examples might include graduation, wedding day, the start of a new job, or the birth of a child.

Ask the students how significant these occasions of joy would be if Christ had not been born. Would there have been a difference? Why or why not?

EXPLORE

Have a volunteer read Luke 2:1-7 aloud. Then discuss these questions:
• *Why were Joseph and Mary in Bethlehem?*
• *Were the circumstances surrounding Christ's birth fit for a king?*
• *Do you think the lowly place of Jesus' birth brought about any doubts in Joseph and Mary's mind concerning Jesus' divine identity?*

Have a volunteer read Luke 2:8-14 aloud. Then discuss these questions:
• *Did the angels who announced the Savior's birth first appear to the aristocracy? Why or why not?*

• *Was the angel's message intended for the inhabitants of Israel alone? How do you know?*
• *What was the attitude of the angels concerning Jesus' coming to earth?*

Have a volunteer read Luke 2:15-20 aloud. Then discuss these questions:
• *How did the shepherds respond to the angel's message?*
• *How did people respond to the shepherds' testimony?*
• *How did Mary respond to the shepherds' message?*
• *After searching for the child, were the shepherds disappointed in what they found?*

RESPOND

Write the word *Christ* on the board vertically. Have students name blessings brought about through Christ's coming that begin with the letters in the word *Christ.* After brainstorming and writing students' answers down for several minutes, have everyone stand.

Just as the angels declared praise to God for His birth, we should follow their example. Looking at our list on the board, focus on one or two blessings for which you are particularly grateful. Let's raise our hands and lift our voices in praise to God right now.

Lead students in this corporate outpouring of praise.

Jesus Offers Assurance

Study Text: Luke 12:1-40
Objective: To discover that Jesus can calm our fears and accept His assurance.
Time: The Gospel of Luke was probably written between A.D. 58 and 70. It covers a period from A.D. 29 to 33.
Place: Jesus' teaching took place at a Pharisee's house in an undefined location.
Golden Text: "Peace I leave with you, my peace I give unto you: not as the world giveth, give I unto you. Let not your heart be troubled, neither let it be afraid" (John 14:27).
Central Truth: The presence of Jesus brings assurance to the believer's heart and mind.
Evangelism Emphasis: Christians should boldly proclaim Christ to the lost.

PRINTED TEXT

Luke 12:4. And I say unto you my friends, Be not afraid of them that kill the body, and after that have no more that they can do.

5. But I will forewarn you whom ye shall fear: Fear him, which after he hath killed hath power to cast into hell; yea, I say unto you, Fear him.

6. Are not five sparrows sold for two farthings, and not one of them is forgotten before God?

7. But even the very hairs of your head are all numbered. Fear not therefore: ye are of more value than many sparrows.

22. And he said unto his disciples, Therefore I say unto you, Take no thought for your life, what ye shall eat; neither for the body, what ye shall put on.

23. The life is more than meat, and the body is more than raiment.

24. Consider the ravens: for they neither sow nor reap; which neither have storehouse nor barn; and God feedeth them: how much more are ye better than the fowls?

25. And which of you with taking thought can add to his stature one cubit?

26. If ye then be not able to do that thing which is least, why take ye thought for the rest?

27. Consider the lilies how they grow: they toil not, they spin not; and yet I say unto you, that Solomon in all his glory was not arrayed like one of these.

28. If then God so clothe the grass, which is to day in the field, and to morrow is cast into the oven; how much more will he clothe you, O ye of little faith?

29. And seek not ye what ye shall eat, or what ye shall drink, neither be ye of doubtful mind.

30. For all these things do the nations of the world seek after: and your Father knoweth that ye have need of these things.

31. But rather seek ye the kingdom of God; and all these things shall be added unto you.

37. Blessed are those servants, whom the lord when he cometh shall find watching: verily I say

unto you, that he shall gird himself, and make them to sit down
to meat, and will come forth and
serve them.

**38. And if he shall come in
the second watch, or come in
the third watch, and find them
so, blessed are those servants.**

LESSON OUTLINE

I. ASSURANCE IN CONFESSING
   CHRIST
   A. The Futility of Insincerity
   B. The Privilege of Confessing
      Christ

II. ASSURANCE OVER ANXIETIES
   A. The Inadequacy of Material
      Things
   B. The Lessons From Nature
   C. The Father's Knowledge
   D. The Secret of Receiving

III. ASSURANCE IN SERVING CHRIST
   A. The Father's Purpose
   B. The Heavenly Treasure
   C. The Importance of Faithfulness

LESSON EXPOSITION

INTRODUCTION

Some years ago an oil company
executive was in a boat that was
swamped and overturned along the
South Carolina coast. A strong ebb
tide washed him out to sea. Nine
hours later a flood tide cast him
ashore, exhausted but unhurt.

He had clung all that time to a
kapok cushion. Once, when a
shrimp boat came within less than
200 feet of him and passed on
without anyone seeing him, he felt
his last chance was gone. But the
will to "stay up just 10 minutes
longer" was strong, so he kept his
grip on the cushion.

In many a small and large crisis
of life, the chief secret of coming
through is one's capacity to hang
on. Somebody has called it "the
bulldog's art." Whether or not you
approve of this characteristic in a
bulldog depends on whose pant leg
he sinks his teeth into; but, once he
takes hold, you do not have to see
his face to learn whether he is a
bulldog or a mongrel. Shake a
stick at a mongrel, and he will
loosen his grip to grab at the
weapon in your hand. Not so with
the bulldog. He hangs on no matter what. All the distractions that
you may employ to divert his attention are wasted.

When it is a matter of physical
life or death, a person's instinct of
self-preservation kicks in. We naturally grab even a straw if we are
on the point of drowning. On the
spiritual level, we win victories by
hanging on—by holding fast to
Christ.

The secret of a Christian being
able to hold on when times are trying is the assurance that Christ
gives. Just as the disciples became
fearless when they realized Jesus
was with them, so may we today.
We have an assurance in our
hearts that Jesus travels with us
regardless of the external storms.

Christ gives us assurance in the
storm of sorrow. When sorrow
comes to us—and it will—He tells
us of the glory of the life to come.
He changes the darkness of death
into the glory of eternal life.

When doubt and tension and
uncertainty engulf us, Christ gives
assurance. Though the future is
unknown, we as Christians may
face it with certainty, knowing that
we walk with the Master.

I. ASSURANCE IN CONFESSING
   CHRIST (Luke 12:1-12)

A. The Futility of Insincerity (vv. 1-7)

(Luke 12:1-3 is not included in the printed text.)

4. And I say unto you my friends, Be not afraid of them that kill the body, and after that have no more that they can do.

5. But I will forewarn you whom ye shall fear: Fear him, which after he hath killed hath power to cast into hell; yea, I say unto you, Fear him.

6. Are not five sparrows sold for two farthings, and not one of them is forgotten before God?

7. But even the very hairs of your head are all numbered. Fear not therefore: ye are of more value than many sparrows.

While attending a luncheon in the house of a Pharisee, Jesus was bitterly attacked by some scribes and Pharisees, as recorded in Luke 11. Jesus responded by fiercely denouncing the scribes and Pharisees. This caused an even larger crowd to gather. Jesus used this opportunity to speak to the people about some of the more serious problems of life. The theme of His message was "Beware ye of the leaven of the Pharisees, which is hypocrisy" (12:1).

The Pharisees were a group of men that arose during the Maccabean period of Jewish history. Pharisaism developed out of a passion for the divine ideal for the nation of Israel. In the days of Jesus the Pharisees had become degenerate. Having lost their moral and spiritual fervor, they had become hypocrites.

The word *hypocrite* means "one who is wearing a mask"—one who is acting a part with the intention to deceive. It is pretending to be something one is not, and this, warned Jesus, was something which should be shunned, or else it would ruin everything it touched. He compared it to leaven used in bread.

G. Campbell Morgan describes leaven as something which "transforms secretly, slyly, surely, all that it touches, until it changes it into its own nature. Leaven, in its action, is always destructive and never constructive. It sours, spreads, and disintegrates. Leaven is, in itself corruption. Everything it touches is immediately corrupted, and the process of disintegration commences. Hyprocisy is leaven. Hypocrisy is in itself a lie. It is evil, and evil will bring evil out of everything that it touches. To pretend to be, in order to deceive men, what I am not, whether it be good or bad, is to act upon the principle of a lie, until the lie, the lack of truth, the dishonesty, the deception, reacts upon me and I become of the very nature of the lie, which is the master principle of my life" (*The Westminster Pulpit*).

The fear of others is one of the greatest obstacles which can stand between the soul and heaven. "What will people say of me? What will they think of me? What will they do to me?" How often these questions have kept people bound by sin and the devil. Many people would never hesitate to storm an enemy's territory, but will not dare face the laughter of relatives, neighbors, and friends.

If the fear of others can have such a powerful influence in our day, how much greater must its influence have been during the days when Jesus was upon the earth. If it is difficult to follow Christ because of ridicule and critical words, how much more difficult must it have been to follow Him through prisons, beatings and violent deaths. All these things Jesus knew well. No wonder He cried, "Be not afraid" (v. 4).

What is the best defense against the fear of people? The only remedy is given by Jesus. We must replace the fear of man with a more powerful fear—the fear of God. We must turn our eyes from those who can only harm us in this life to Him who can condemn us to eternal death in the life that is to come. Armed with this powerful principle, we do not have to act cowardly. Seeing Him who is invisible, we can see our fear of people melt away. Fear God and there is no one else we need to fear.

Jesus reminded the people of God's providential care for the least of His creatures, assuring them that the same fatherly care extended to each of them who were in the crowd (v. 6). "The very hairs of your head are all numbered" (v. 7). Nothing whatever, whether great or small, can happen to a believer without God's permission.

B. The Privilege of Confessing Christ (vv. 8-12)

(Luke 12:8-12 is not included in the printed text.)

The responsibility of confessing Christ is incumbent on all Christians in every age of the church. It is not for great occasions only, but for our daily walk through this evil world. If we know and love Jesus, we should not be ashamed to let people know it.

Confessing Christ means being openly loyal to Him. It might also mean mockery, persecution and scorn. But this is bearable in anticipation of hearing Christ say on the great Day of Judgment, "This soul is Mine—Mine forever."

Those who refuse to stand up for Him, denying His divine sonship and refusing to accept His provision for salvation, will not hear Jesus stand up for them at the end of their earthly journey. Jesus said, "He that denieth me before men shall be denied before the angels of God" (v. 9). This is not a threat nor an angry condemnation. Instead, it is the sad statement of an inevitable consequence. If a person renounces allegiance to his country, the leader can no longer count him as a citizen. So it is with Christ and His kingdom.

The sin against the Holy Spirit (v. 10) is simply constant opposition to the influence of the Holy Spirit in the heart. The principal work of the Holy Spirit is to reveal the Lord Jesus. If one refuses such witness, one cannot accept Christ and, consequently, cannot be saved. If a person has a desire to be saved, it is an indication that the Holy Spirit is still at work in that individual's heart.

The reason Jesus gives why believers should not fear persecution when they are brought before authorities is that the Holy Spirit will teach them at that time what they ought to say (v. 12). Speaking on the same issue, Jesus later said, "I will give you a mouth and wisdom, which all your adversaries shall not be able to gainsay nor resist" (21:15).

II. ASSURANCE OVER ANXIETIES (Luke 12:22-31)

A. The Inadequacy of Material Things (vv. 22, 23)

22. And he said unto his disciples, Therefore I say unto you, Take no thought for your life, what ye shall eat; neither for the body, what ye shall put on.

23. The life is more than meat, and the body is more than raiment.

The phrase "take no thought" is better translated "be not anxious."

The Greek word for *anxious* means "to be drawn in different directions" or "to divide." A person given to anxiety is one whose strength and attention are always divided. Anxiety is an uneasiness of mind that often arises from concern about some future or uncertain event.

The apostle James described the condition of an anxious person when he said, "A double minded man is unstable in all his ways" (1:8). A divided mind is unstable in its emotions, thought processes, decisions and judgments. Peace of mind requires singleness of mind. The person who worries robs himself of peace of mind by dividing his mind.

Luke 12:22, 23 summarizes all that Jesus taught in the parable of the rich fool (vv. 16-21).

B. The Lessons From Nature
(vv. 24-28)

24. Consider the ravens: for they neither sow nor reap; which neither have storehouse nor barn; and God feedeth them: how much more are ye better than the fowls?

25. And which of you with taking thought can add to his stature one cubit?

26. If ye then be not able to do that thing which is least, why take ye thought for the rest?

27. Consider the lilies how they grow: they toil not, they spin not; and yet I say unto you, that Solomon in all his glory was not arrayed like one of these.

28. If then God so clothe the grass, which is to day in the field, and to morrow is cast into the oven; how much more will he clothe you, O ye of little faith?

Jesus was not implying that we are to sit down and expect God to feed us as He feeds the birds. He said they neither sow nor reap, they have neither storage bins nor barns, and yet God feeds them (v. 24). But we can sow and reap and have barns—and we should. If God cares for the birds who cannot think, how much more will He feed us to whom He has given power to think!

If the Maker of all things provides for the needs of birds, and orders nature so that they have a daily supply of food, we should not fear that He will let His spiritual children starve. If God replenishes the flowers with a fresh supply of living leaves and blossoms every year, we should not doubt His power and willingness to provide His believing children with all the necessary things of life.

C. The Father's Knowledge
(vv. 29, 30)

29. And seek not ye what ye shall eat, or what ye shall drink, neither be ye of doubtful mind.

30. For all these things do the nations of the world seek after: and your Father knoweth that ye have need of these things.

Jesus bids us remember that a Christian should not become as anxious as unbelievers. The nations of the world may well worry about many things because they do not know God. But the man who can say of God, "He is my Father," and of Christ, "He is my Savior," really does not have anything to be anxious about. A clear faith should produce a heart without fear.

Jesus also reminds us of the perfect knowledge of God. He said, "Your Father knoweth that ye have need of [food and clothing.]" That alone should enable us to be content in His love. The man who can say boldly, "The

Lord is my shepherd" is the man who can also say, "I shall not want" (Psalm 23:1).

D. The Secret of Receiving (v. 31)

31. But rather seek ye the kingdom of God; and all these things shall be added unto you.

The prohibition against anxiety does not negate thinking about the future. Looking ahead and making plans are part of Christian prudence. Those who go forward in life without proper deliberation only bring difficulty on themselves. But this kind of carefulness does not include worry; and it was worry that Jesus was censuring.

It is a sin to worry because God always provides. God's provision is divinely decreed, and that makes it as certain as His promise that day and night shall not cease (Genesis 8:22).

When a person truly seeks the kingdom of God, many other things will be true. He or she will be honest and thrifty. The Kingdom-seeker will be able to differentiate between the harmful and the helpful. Most of all, that person will be known by God, watched over by God, and cared for by God.

III. ASSURANCE IN SERVING CHRIST (Luke 12:32-40)

A. The Father's Purpose (v. 32)

(Luke 12:32 is not included in the printed text.)

We do not earn the kingdom of God; instead, we receive it. The humblest handful of believers in the most remote village in the world, as well as the poorest congregation in the most deprived section of town, are part of Christ's little flock. They are guarded and nurtured by Christ himself. They are heirs of the Kingdom, which He has promised to them that love Him.

B. The Heavenly Treasure (vv. 33, 34)

(Luke 12:33, 34 is not included in the printed text.)

Jesus gave a striking exhortation to seek treasure in heaven. "Sell what ye have," said our Lord, "and give alms; provide yourselves bags which wax not old, a treasure in the heavens that faileth not" (v. 33). But this is not all. A heart-searching principle was given to enforce the exhortation: "Where your treasure is, there will your heart be also" (v. 34).

We are to sell—to give up and to deny ourselves—anything that stands in the way of our salvation. We are to make sure that our names are in the Book of Life and lay up for ourselves treasures that will pass the inspection of the Day of Judgment (see 1 Corinthians 3:11-15). This is true wisdom.

C. The Importance of Faithfulness (vv. 35-40)

(Luke 12:35, 36, 39, 40 is not included in the printed text.)

37. Blessed are those servants, whom the lord when he cometh shall find watching: verily I say unto you, that he shall gird himself, and make them to sit down to meat, and will come forth and serve them.

38. And if he shall come in the second watch, or come in the third watch, and find them so, blessed are those servants.

Jesus said we ought to live "like unto men that wait for their Lord" (v. 36). We ought to be like servants who expect their Master's return, fulfilling our duties and doing nothing which we would not like to be found doing when Christ comes again.

Concerning the above passage, J.C. Ryle notes: "The standard of life which our Lord has set up is an exceedingly high one, so high that many Christians are apt to flinch from it and feel cast down. And yet there is nothing here which ought to make a believer afraid. Readiness for the return of Christ to this world implies nothing which is impossible and unattainable. It requires no angelic perfection. It requires no man to forsake his family, and retire into solitude. It requires nothing more than a life of repentance, faith and holiness. The man who is living the life of faith in the Son of God is the man whose 'loins are girded,' and whose 'light is burning.' Such a man may have the care of kingdoms on him, like Daniel, or be a servant in a Nero's household, like some in Paul's time. All this matters nothing. If he lives looking unto Jesus, he is a servant who can 'open unto Him immediately.' Surely it is not too much to ask Christians to be men of this kind. Surely it was not for nothing that our Lord said, 'The Son of man cometh at an hour when you think not'" (*Expository Thoughts on the Gospels*).

GOLDEN TEXT HOMILY

"PEACE I LEAVE WITH YOU, MY PEACE I GIVE UNTO YOU: NOT AS THE WORLD GIVETH, GIVE I UNTO YOU. LET NOT YOUR HEART BE TROUBLED, NEITHER LET IT BE AFRAID" (John 14:27).

The world today has been described as a puzzle with a *peace* missing. This was the kind of world Jesus would leave behind when He ascended to the Father. He would be leaving, but His fol-

lowers would remain as His representatives in a troubled world.

John 14 is a "going-away" message from Jesus to His disciples. He had been with them day and night for about three years. He was concerned about how they would cope when He was no longer with them. The things they would need in His absence were imparted to them. Among those needs was a personal peace. In a falling-apart world someone needs to have it all together. At least three important things about this peace are identified in verse 27.

First, it was His peace. He who calmed the stormy sea was in control of His own element. He who brought peace to the demoniac of Gadara was sensitive to the storms of life but was unaffected by them. He could struggle in Gethsemane and view the cross with an unbelievable peace. It was this peace—His peace—He would give to His followers.

The second truth we observe is that the peace Jesus had would be passed on to His followers as a gift. This means that it was a spiritual endowment, not a human attainment. No amount of money could purchase such a peace. And no amount of personal adjustment can manufacture it. It is a gift and can come only from Christ. He wants to give it—are we ready to receive it?

The third truth is the way Jesus gives. A contrast between the way He gives and the way the world gives is suggested. The giving of the world is manipulative and coercive. His giving is free and unconditional. The gifts of the world are temporary and subject to rust and decay. His gift is eternal and "fadeth not away." Worldly givers give for their own benefit. Christ gives for the benefit of others.

Only Jesus can bring order to a troubled life. The peace He gives is supernatural and from above. But it can be yours for the asking.—**Robert B. Thomas**

SENTENCE SERMONS

THE PRESENCE OF JESUS brings assurance to the believer's heart and mind.

—**Selected**

PEACE IS the deliberate adjustment of my life to the will of God.
—*Quotable Quotations*

ONE OF THE GREATEST hindrances to internal peace which the Christian encounters is the common habit of dividing our lives into two areas—the sacred and the secular.

—*Signposts*

EVANGELISM APPLICATION

CHRISTIANS SHOULD BOLDLY PROCLAIM CHRIST TO THE LOST.

Are you ready for the coming of Christ? Common sense says you will be in this world for only a short time, followed by eternity. Your preparation now will determine your eternal destiny. Christ is seeking volunteers. Will you be one?

Remember that if you perish, it will not be caused by lack of want or willingness in Christ to save you. The very consideration, which is now so encouraging, will one day fill you with inconceivable anguish. "Christ would, but I would not!" Obey the voice that warns you for good.

ILLUMINATING THE LESSON

We must not allow distracting fears for tomorrow to interfere with the calm performance of the duties of the day. Each day has its burdens, difficulties and temptations. However, each day brings its help from God—grace and mercies to His children. Let us give all of our energy to the work of the day—the duty which is present. "Whatsoever thy hand findeth to do, do it with thy might" (Ecclesiastes 9:10).

Let us not allow the day to be darkened and its work marred by gloomy forebodings that may never come. If they do come, God will give us strength to meet them. Let us do our duty and leave the future in His hands, to whom alone the future is known. He has promised to make "all things work together for good to them that love God" (Romans 8:28).

DAILY BIBLE READINGS

M. Assurance of God's Care.
   Psalm 91:1-16
T. Assurance of God's Protection.
   Isaiah 43:1-7
W. Assurance of God's Purpose.
   Jeremiah 29:11-14
T. Assurance of Heaven.
   John 14:1-6
F. Assurance of God's Love.
   Romans 8:31-39
S. Assurance of God's Presence.
   Hebrews 13:5-8

TRUTH SEARCH:
Creatively Teaching the Word

Aim: Each student will identify a specific thing that he or she worries about, and release those worries to God through prayer.

Items needed: Marker board, marker, paper, pens or pencils, colored pencils or markers, pipe cleaners

FOCUS

Write the following words on the marker board:

- Calamities
- Family members
- Finances
- Health
- Job security

Have each class member, on their own piece of paper, rank the above from 5 to 1 in terms of what they are most frequently tempted to worry about (5 being the top). Compare answers by placing each person's rank beside the categories on the board. Add the numbers together for each category to see what ranks the highest and lowest for the entire class.

EXPLORE

Split the class into small groups of three or four students each. Assign half of the groups Luke 12:4-12, and the other half verses 22-34. Have the groups answer the following questions about their particular passage.

Luke 12:4-12

1. According to this passage, what might Jesus' followers be tempted to fear?

2. Who does Jesus say to fear, and why?

3. What promises are given to the followers of Jesus?

4. Which of your own fears and worries does this passage address?

5. What does this passage tell us about the kind of witnesses we need to be for Christ?

Luke 12:22-34

1. According to this passage, what do the people of the world seek after?

2. What does Jesus say we are to seek, and what promise does He make (v. 31)?

3. What examples does Jesus give that would encourage people to trust God for their needs?

4. How does Jesus refer to those who worry about basic needs (v. 28)?

5. Which of your worries does this passage address?

RESPOND

Using the paper they were given earlier, ask each student to sketch something to represent what they worry about most.

Next, invite each person to hold his or her picture before the Lord as you offer a prayer of release. Afterward, each person may bring his or her paper forward to throw in a wastebasket. When they have done this, hand them a pipe cleaner bent at the end to look like a shepherd's staff. Say, **This is to remind you of our Good Shepherd, who has promised to never leave nor forsake us, and has commanded us not to worry.**

Jesus Values the Lost

Study Text: Luke 15:1-31
Objective: To know that Jesus values every person and determine to make His love known.
Time: The Gospel of Luke was probably written between A.D. 58 and 70. It covers a period from A.D. 29 to 33.
Place: Jesus told these parables to a crowd in Jerusalem.
Golden Text: "There is joy in the presence of the angels of God over one sinner that repenteth" (Luke 15:10).
Central Truth: Jesus loves humanity and delights in the salvation of every person.
Evangelism Emphasis: Jesus loves humanity and delights in the salvation of every person.

PRINTED TEXT

Luke 15:3. And he spake this parable unto them, saying,

4. Which man of you, having an hundred sheep, if he lose one of them, doth not leave the ninety and nine in the wilderness, and go after that which is lost, until he find it?

5. And when he hath found it, he layeth it on his shoulders, rejoicing.

6. And when he cometh home, he calleth together his friends and neighbors, saying unto them, Rejoice with me; for I have found my sheep which was lost.

7. I say unto you, that likewise joy shall be in heaven over one sinner that repenteth, more than over ninety and nine just persons, which need no repentance.

8. Either what woman having ten pieces of silver, if she lose one piece, doth not light a candle, and sweep the house, and seek diligently till she find it?

9. And when she hath found it, she calleth her friends and her neighbors together, saying, Rejoice with me; for I have found the piece which I had lost.

10. Likewise, I say unto you, there is joy in the presence of the angels of God over one sinner that repenteth.

17. And when he came to himself, he said, How many hired servants of my father's have bread enough and to spare, and I perish with hunger!

18. I will arise and go to my father, and will say unto him, Father, I have sinned against heaven, and before thee.

19. And am no more worthy to be called thy son: make me as one of thy hired servants.

20. And he arose, and came to his father. But when he was yet a great way off, his father saw him, and had compassion, and ran, and fell on his neck, and kissed him.

21. And the son said unto him, Father, I have sinned against heaven, and in thy sight, and am no more worthy to be called thy son.

22. But the father said to his servants, Bring forth the best robe, and put it on him; and put a ring on his hand, and shoes on his feet.

23. And bring hither the fatted calf, and kill it; and let us eat, and be merry:

24. For this my son was dead, and is alive again; he was lost, and is found. And they began to be merry.

LESSON OUTLINE

I. THE SHEPHERD'S LOVE
   A. The Search for the Lost
   B. The Joy in Finding the Lost
II. THE WORTH OF A SOUL
   A. The Loss
   B. The Discovery
   C. The Reaction
III. THE JOY OF RESTORATION
   A. The Request
   B. The Waste
   C. The Awakening
   D. The Welcome
   E. The Acceptance

LESSON EXPOSITION

INTRODUCTION

The value of a soul does not register with us as it should until a tragedy occurs. In the summer of 1944, a church in a Western state had its annual church and Sunday school picnic at a large private ranch. There was the usual good time with games, food, and even swimming in the private pool. When it came time to leave, one 10-year-old boy could not be found.

Soon everybody joined in the search, calling "Joe, Joe," anxiously throughout the 80-acre orange grove. At last there was only one place left to look—the swimming pool. But he couldn't be there, he must not! But as methodic diving soon proved—he was. Every effort was made to revive him. Everybody was praying fervently, begging God to spare his life. Many who had never or seldom prayed did so.

The boy was dead, but being a Christian, he went to be with Christ.

Does our fervent concern for those who are spiritually lost reveal how much we value them? This question must be answered individually. But God has already revealed how much He values the lost. He sent His Son to redeem us by dying on a cross.

I. THE SHEPHERD'S LOVE
   (Luke 15:3-7)

A. The Search for the Lost (vv. 3, 4)

3. And he spake this parable unto them, saying,

4. Which man of you, having an hundred sheep, if he lose one of them, doth not leave the ninety and nine in the wilderness, and go after that which is lost, until he find it?

Luke begins chapter 15 by saying that the publicans and sinners drew near to hear Jesus, while the Pharisees and scribes complained that Jesus welcomed sinners and ate with them. Publicans were Jews who were considered inferior by the religious leaders. In the words of R.C. Trench, they were "renegades and traitors who, for filthy lucre's sake, had sided with the enemy [the Roman government] and now collected, for a profane heathen treasury, that tribute which was the evident sign of the subjection of God's people to a Gentile yoke" (*Sermons: New and Old*).

The word translated *sinners* means "people devoted to sin" and, especially, "people stained with certain definite vices or crimes." It is the same word often used in affirming that all people are sinners.

"So dealt this great Redeemer

with the sinners he came to redeem," writes Henry W. Clark, "choosing them as the main object of his care, believing unfalteringly that they had power to respond to the touch he laid upon their hearts, holding that his own perfection was before all else the thing on which their shamed souls must gaze. So deals he with earth's sinners still" (*Laws of the Inner Kingdom*).

It was the attitude of the scribes and Pharisees that prompted Jesus to give the three parables in Luke 15.

The people listening to Jesus could identify with the words *sheep* and *shepherd*. They knew that much of Palestine was a shepherd's country. According to S.A. Brooke, "its literature, its hymns, its religious life were full of the shepherd's life, and none in all the crowd but were able to enter with feeling and knowledge into the picture of the lost sheep, and the seeking shepherd, and the joy that filled his heart" (*Short Sermons*).

The Old Testament often refers to God as a shepherd who cares for His own. Isaiah speaks of humanity as sheep that have gone astray, everyone turning to his own way (53:6). He does this in connection with his prediction of the atoning work of Christ. Jesus spoke of people as distressed and scattered because they were like sheep without a shepherd (Matthew 9:36).

The sheep in this parable was lost, not because it intended to be lost, or wanted to be lost, but because it simply wandered away from the flock and could not get back.

J.D. Freeman writes in his book *Concerning the Christ*, "The soul may get lost as a sheep gets lost through heedlessness. We find ourselves in a world of beauty and of pleasure, and we give ourselves to the pursuit of happiness."

Unless the shepherd seeks and finds the lost sheep, it will remain forever lost. In relation to humanity, the incarnation of the Son of God was the girding of Himself for the task of seeking the lost. In fact, all of His life in the flesh was dedicated to following the strays.

Louis Banks tells the story that St. Francis once saw a mountaineer in the Alps risk his life to save a lost sheep. He was so impressed with it that he cried aloud, "O God, if such was the earnestness of this shepherd in seeking for a little animal which had probably been frozen on the glacier, how is it that I am so indifferent in seeking my sheep?" (*The Great Portraits of the Bible*).

B. The Joy in Finding the Lost
   (vv. 5-7)

5. And when he hath found it, he layeth it on his shoulders, rejoicing.
6. And when he cometh home, he calleth together his friends and neighbors, saying unto them, Rejoice with me; for I have found my sheep which was lost.
7. I say unto you, that likewise joy shall be in heaven over one sinner that repenteth, more than over ninety and nine just persons, which need no repentance.

The shepherd's love was an active, working love. He did not sit still at the sheepfold bewailing his lost sheep. He made a search for the sheep. And when he found it he brought it home on his shoulders rather than leaving it in the wilderness.

Christ's love is also an active, working love. He did not sit still in heaven pitying sinners. He left the glory which He had with the Father and humbled Himself to become like us. He came to this world "to seek and to save that which was lost" (Luke 19:10). He never rested until He had opened a door of life to all who are willing to be saved.

The exceeding value of one soul, in God's sight, is revealed in 15:7. God sustains a loss with every sinner that wanders away from Him. And God's great joy comes from the recovery of even one lost soul. As George Hepworth put it, "Heaven and earth cannot be far apart if there is rejoicing in the one place over incidents which occur in the other."

Who are the "ninety and nine just persons which need no repentance"? Some think it means the glorified saints who can sin no more. Others believe it refers to living believers who are walking in Christ. Some think it means people who think themselves righteous and just, like the Pharisees, and fancy they need no repentance. J.C. Ryle believes the last to be true as confirmed by Luke 5:32; 16:15; 18:9; Matthew 9:13; Mark 2:17 (*Expository Thoughts on the Gospels*).

II. THE WORTH OF A SOUL
   (Luke 15:8-10)

A. The Loss (v. 8)

8. Either what woman having ten pieces of silver, if she lose one piece, doth not light a candle, and sweep the house, and seek diligently till she find it?

The second parable is a continuation of the basic truth given in the picture of the shepherd. The shepherd seeking his sheep represents divine tenderness; the humble woman searching for her silver piece with much diligence and painstaking portrays divine earnestness.

The coin in question was not that valuable, yet it did represent about a day's wages for the common laborer. More importantly, it was one-tenth of this woman's life savings, so the coin was very valuable to her. Some think the coin might have been part of a headdress that signified betrothal or the marriage relationship, which would have made the coin even more significant.

B. The Discovery (v. 9)

9. And when she hath found it, she calleth her friends and her neighbors together, saying, Rejoice with me; for I have found the piece which I had lost.

In the parable of the sheep it was "Rejoice with me; for I have found my sheep which was lost." Here it is "Rejoice with me; for I have found the piece which I had lost." In the first part it was the anguish of the shepherd of the sheep that was the central point of the story. In the second part it was the distress of the woman who had lost something. Deep distress was followed by profound joy.

C. The Reaction (v. 10)

10. Likewise, I say unto you, there is joy in the presence of the angels of God over one sinner that repenteth.

This verse shows that the salvation of souls is a matter of special interest to the angels, and that the salvation of each one is carefully observed.

F. Godet writes: "What grandeur belongs to the picture of this humble rejoicing which this poor woman celebrates with her neighbors when it becomes the transparency through which we get a picture of God himself, rejoicing with His elect and His angels over the salvation of a single sinner" (*Pulpit Commentary*).

III. THE JOY OF RESTORATION
(Luke 15:11-24)

A. The Request (vv. 11, 12)

(Luke 15:11, 12 is not included in the printed text.)

The third parable in Luke 15 has been described as "the crown of all parables," as "the gospel within the Gospels," as "the most divinely tender and most humanly touching story ever told on earth." The twofold purpose of this parable is hinted at in verses 1 and 2, namely, Christ's love and compassion for lost sinners, and His rebuke of the Pharisees for their prejudice toward sinners.

Still seeking to make the hardhearted Pharisees and scribes ashamed of their attitude toward the repentant publicans and sinners, Jesus told this story. A certain man—representing the heavenly Father, whose searching love has been shown in the first two parables—had two sons. The younger son represents the publicans and sinners; the older son, the respectable and self-righteous Pharisees and scribes.

The younger son in the story asked his father to give him the portion of the inheritance that would come to him when the father died. Many Bible scholars charge the behavior of the young man to the aggressiveness and enterprise of youth, its impatience with custom and routine, its adventuresome spirit, its imprudence and rashness, its all-too-frequent selfishness and inconsiderate pleasure-seeking.

According to Jewish law, when the father died the younger son would inherit one-third of the movable property, and the older son would receive two-thirds. The father could not change this final disposition of his goods; but while alive he was not obligated to honor the demand of the younger son. This demand did not take into account the feelings of the father. It was recklessly and heartlessly selfish.

Concerning the attitude of the father, Godet writes: "In the father's consenting to the wish of his son, a very solemn thought is expressed, that of the sinner's abandonment to the desires of his own heart (Romans 1:24, 26, 28), the ceasing, on the part of the divine Spirit, to strive against the inclinations of a spoiled heart, which can only be cured by the bitter experience of sin. God gives such a man over to his folly" (*Commentary on the Gospel of Luke*).

B. The Waste (vv. 13-16)

(Luke 15:13-16 is not included in the printed text.)

The young man was very impatient and eager to leave his home. He ignored the pain he was causing his family and traveled to a far country. There he wasted his substance in "riotous living" (v. 13). The word *riotous* here means "abundant, dissolute, profligate." It is living wildly and carelessly, extravagantly and arrogantly, without restraint or control, a life yielding to every debasing desire. It is so easy for a person to sink this low.

God had given this young man his heart's desire and sent leanness to his soul. The worst famine of all is not a famine of bread or thirst, but "of hearing the words of the Lord" (Amos 8:11); and in such a famine even "the fair virgins and young men faint for thirst" (8:13). Through the prophet Jeremiah, God said, "They have forsaken me the fountain of living waters, and hewed them out cisterns, broken cisterns, that can hold no water" (2:13).

How often men must come to the end of their resources before they will throw themselves on the resources of God. Finding himself in want, this young man began to realize the emptiness of sin, how unsatisfactory it is, how false are its promises of pleasure and profit. Actually, he had been in want through all his months of discontent at home, but he did not know it.

The word *joined* (Luke 15:15) suggests that the young man "glued" himself to a citizen of that country. That man gave the prodigal a job—the lowest job he had—feeding swine. The Jews had such a strong loathing for swine that they would not even name them, but called them "the other thing." As Christ mentioned the young man's detestable occupation, a shudder of disgust must have passed through His audience. It was the very bottom of the miry pit of degradation.

The young man, a Jew, had now lost his independence and freedom, which, at first, he started out to fully enjoy. He had been driven to a task which normally would have been revolting to him. Now, he who would not serve his father was compelled to be the servant of a foreign master. He who would not be ruled by God was compelled to serve the devil; he who would not abide in his father's house was sent to the fields among the swine.

C. The Awakening (v. 17)

17. And when he came to himself, he said, How many hired servants of my father's have bread enough and to spare, and I perish with hunger!

The young man went out to find himself, or so he thought. But indulgence and sin so deceived him that he lost himself. Now the suffering of hunger, a consciousness of failure and shame, and hopelessness brought him back to himself. His experience illustrates the fact that life without God is madness. But he had not sunk so low that he could not still say "my father."

D. The Welcome (vv. 18-21)

18. I will arise and go to my father, and will say unto him, Father, I have sinned against heaven, and before thee.

19. And am no more worthy to be called thy son: make me as one of thy hired servants.

20. And he arose, and came to his father. But when he was yet a great way off, his father saw him, and had compassion, and ran, and fell on his neck, and kissed him.

21. And the son said unto him, Father, I have sinned against heaven, and in thy sight, and am no more worthy to be called thy son.

The turning point is between the remorse which says, "What a fool I have been," and the repentance which says, "I will be a fool no longer." Repentance is being sorry, to be sure, but that is not enough; it is "being sorry enough to quit."

The young man properly carried out his resolve when he returned to his father (v. 20). Note the prompt recognition, swift approach, and enthusiastic embrace by the father. The silence of the father on the question of the son's wayward and wicked behavior is most eloquent with love and compassion.

The young man probably had been rehearsing his little speech (v. 21) over and over, all the way back home, and had it letter-perfect. No speech was ever so truly learned by heart.

E. The Acceptance (vv. 22-24)

22. But the father said to his servants, Bring forth the best robe, and put it on him; and put a ring on his hand, and shoes on his feet.

23. And bring hither the fatted calf, and kill it; and let us eat, and be merry:

24. For this my son was dead, and is alive again; he was lost, and is found. And they began to be merry.

Herbert Lockyer writes: "Because of the son's self-chosen alienation and shame, his father thought of him as 'dead.' Perhaps his physical death would have been easier to bear. In the realm of grace, repentance means the passing from the death of sin to the life of righteousness. 'Lost' and 'found,' common to all three pictures, are likewise expressive of the sinner's abandonment of the far country of sin for the Father's home." (*All the Parables of the Bible*).

The prodigal's full restoration to sonship by his father is a perfect picture of the heavenly Father's readiness to completely restore every sinner who comes to Him with a repentant spirit.

GOLDEN TEXT HOMILY

"THERE IS JOY IN THE PRESENCE OF THE ANGELS OF GOD OVER ONE SINNER THAT REPENTETH" (Luke 15:10).

In all of the three parables of grace in Luke 15, there is an emphasis on joy: (1) the joy of the shepherd and his friends and neighbors when, after long seeking, he brought his lost sheep back; (2) the joy of the woman with her friends and neighbors when, after diligent searching with lamp and broom, she found her precious coin; and (3) the joy of the father and his household when, possibly after years of agonized waiting, praying and yearning, the Prodigal Son came home.

In all three parables, the earthly joy with which all of Christ's hearers could identify was a mirror in which was reflected the greater joy that is experienced "in heaven over one sinner that repenteth" (v. 7). Dr. I.H. Marshall says, "The thought is of the angels rejoicing along with God."

Thus Christ gives us a glimpse into heaven, both now and on the day of resurrection. We witness the rejoicing of God himself and of His angelic hosts as they gaze upon the multitude of lost souls found and redeemed and restored. In Job 38:7 the Lord says to Job, "[Where wast thou] when the morning stars sang together, and all the sons of God [meaning the angelic beings] shouted for joy?" Thus it was when God laid the foundations of the earth. Jesus, however, paints a picture of the angelic choirs shouting with even greater joy as they behold the wondrous products of redeeming grace.

Jesus himself (the Good Shepherd) will share that joy, for "he shall see of the travail of his soul, and shall be satisfied" (Isaiah 53:11). He was strengthened in His earthly life and ministry during the years of searching and suffering and dying for the lost, by "the joy that was set before him" (Hebrews 12:2), the hope of rescued sheep, found coins, and reconciled prodigals.

And shall not all who seek with determination and sacrifice for lost sheep, who search diligently with the lamp of the Word and the broom of the Spirit for lost human coins stamped with the image of God, who pray and mourn and wait with hearts of love for lost prodigals, have their part in those joyful celebrations in the eternal presence of God?—**Noel Brooks**

SENTENCE SERMONS

JESUS loves humanity and delights in the salvation of every person.

—Selected

OUR GOD has a big eraser.
—Billy Zeoli

WE ARE MOST like beasts when we kill. We are most like men when we judge. We are most like God when we forgive.
—*Quotable Quotations*

EVANGELISM APPLICATION

JESUS LOVES HUMANITY AND DELIGHTS IN THE SALVATION OF EVERY PERSON.

The father did not say a single word to his son about his profligacy and wickedness. There was neither rebuke nor reproof for the past, nor admonitions for the present, nor irritating advice for the future. The one thing that filled his mind was joy that his son had come home. Is this not the way God accepts sinners when they come to Him?

ILLUMINATING THE LESSON

There is not enough heartbreak over the lost, not enough soul burden, not enough groaning and weeping and fasting and crying. Moreover, and as a consequence, there is not enough deep and genuine conviction for sin among the unsaved of our families and friends. Hypocrites are too comfortable in our presence, and in our meetings. Bickering and backbiting go with too little condemnation. Sour holiness, bitter devotion to persons and cause, lightness in the homes and in the churches, worldliness, love of ease and occupation with social conventionalities among women, covetousness and love of money among men, contentment with the mediocre, delight in nice clothes and comfortable homes, measuring men by the salaries they receive, weighing people by the position they occupy—all these things get by with too little reproof because the light is not bright enough to discover their devilish origin.—**J.B. Chapman,** *The Preacher's Magazine*

DAILY BIBLE READINGS

M. The Lord Is My Shepherd.
   Psalm 23:1-6
T. Winning Souls Is Wise.
   Proverbs 11:27-31
W. Turn From Wickedness.
   Ezekiel 18:24-32
T. Jesus Saves the Lost.
   Matthew 18:10-14
F. Jesus Forgives Sins.
   Mark 2:1-12
S. Jesus Gives Everlasting Life.
   John 3:12-18

TRUTH SEARCH:
Creatively Teaching the Word

Aim: Students will affirm other students and believers in Christ with joy because of what God has done in bringing these brothers and sisters into the faith.

Items needed: A small object of great sentimental or monetary value

FOCUS

Ask students if they have ever lost something that was valuable to them. Allow a few people to share stories of things that they have lost, and discuss how they felt after the loss.

Display an object that is valuable to you, and tell what makes it valuable.

EXPLORE

Have the class think about the following questions:

• *What kind of loss must God experience when His most prized creations reject Him?*

• *How do you think He responds when a lost person is restored to Him?*

Ask a volunteer to read Luke 15:1, 2 aloud.

Divide the class into groups of three or four students each. Have half of the groups explore Luke 15:4-7, and the other half verses 8-10. Have each group answer the following questions that pertain to their passage.

Luke 15:4-7

1. What kind of relationship does this passage suggest a shepherd would have with his sheep?

2. What words are used to describe the feelings of the shepherd after his sheep is found? What actions correspond to these feelings?

3. What parallels can be drawn between the sheep that are not lost and the just persons who need no repentance?

Luke 15:8-10

1. What does the passage suggest about the significance of this coin to the woman?

2. What adjectives describe the way the woman looks for her piece of silver?

3. What does the woman do to demonstrate her excitement over finding her lost silver piece?

4. Have the groups report their findings.

Now select three volunteers to portray the father and the two sons in the story in Luke 15:11-32. As the text is read aloud slowly, have the volunteers stand facing the class and use dramatic facial expressions and body language (only) to convey the emotions of the characters.

Discuss the following questions:

• *How must the father have felt when his son departed?*

• *To the Jews swine were very unclean. What do verses 16 and 17 suggest about the state of the wayward son?*

• *Describe the son's attitude in verses 18, 19 and 21.*

• *What adjectives can be used to describe the father upon his son's return?*

RESPOND

We were all lost at one time. When we realized our condition and turned away from our sins, our heavenly Father welcomed us as His children.

• *What should our attitude as children of God be when one who has been lost is found by Christ?*

Have class members testify about their coming to Christ, and have everyone rejoice with them.

Jesus Teaches About Money

Study Text: Luke 16:9-13; 20:20-26; 21:1-4
Objective: To learn Jesus' teaching about financial stewardship and commit to use money for the glory of God.
Time: The Gospel of Luke was probably written between A.D. 58 and 70.
Place: Jerusalem
Golden Text: "No servant can serve two masters: for either he will hate the one, and love the other; or else he will hold to the one, and despise the other. Ye cannot serve God and mammon" (Luke 16:13).
Central Truth: Christians must be faithful stewards of their financial resources.
Evangelism Emphasis: The generous financial gifts of God's people enable the spread of the gospel.

PRINTED TEXT

Luke 16:9. And I say unto you, Make to yourselves friends of the mammon of unrighteousness; that, when ye fail, they may receive you into everlasting habitations.

10. He that is faithful in that which is least is faithful also in much: and he that is unjust in the least is unjust also in much.

11. If therefore ye have not been faithful in the unrighteous mammon, who will commit to your trust the true riches?

12. And if ye have not been faithful in that which is another man's, who shall give you that which is your own?

13. No servant can serve two masters: for either he will hate the one, and love the other; or else he will hold to the one, and despise the other. Ye cannot serve God and mammon.

20:20. And they watched him, and sent forth spies, which should feign themselves just men, that they might take hold of his words, that so they might deliver him unto the power and authority of the governor.

21. And they asked him, saying, Master, we know that thou sayest and teachest rightly, neither acceptest thou the person of any, but teachest the way of God truly:

22. Is it lawful for us to give tribute to Caesar, or no?

23. But he perceived their craftiness, and said unto them, Why tempt ye me?

24. Shew me a penny. Whose image and superscription hath it? They answered and said, Caesar's.

25. And he said unto them, Render therefore unto Caesar the things which be Caesar's, and unto God the things which be God's.

26. And they could not take hold of his words before the people: and they marvelled at his answer, and held their peace.

21:1. And he looked up, and saw the rich men casting their gifts into the treasury.

2. And he saw also a certain poor widow casting in thither two mites.

3. And he said, Of a truth I say unto you, that this poor widow hath cast in more than they all:

4. For all these have of their abundance cast in unto the offerings of God: but she of her penury hath cast in all the living that she had.

LESSON OUTLINE

I. USE MONEY WISELY
  A. Making Friends
  B. Facing Consequences
  C. Serving Two Masters

II. FULFILL FINANCIAL OBLIGATIONS
  A. The Question
  B. The Response

III. GIVE GENEROUSLY
  A. The Rich Men
  B. The Poor Widow
  C. The Response of Jesus

LESSON EXPOSITION

INTRODUCTION

Jesus does not discourage making money, but exhorts to diligence in business, thrift, and the stewardship of wealth. Satan, however, can pervert these virtues into miserliness. The rich fool, for example, was not accused of dishonesty but of hoarding. Instead of possessing wealth, wealth possessed him.

Jesus did not denounce saving for a rainy day. Even the apostle Paul instructed parents to lay up for their children (2 Corinthians 12:14). Nor did He prohibit capitalism, which promotes business and provides employment.

Jesus condemned greed and covetousness. Our energies and affections ought to be spent on holier things than just how to add to our bank account, or how to increase our real estate holdings.

When a person is only concerned with making a fortune as quickly as he can, he may be tempted to make it according to the methods and practices prevalent in the world around him. He may take the shortest way—along a road thick with lies, theft and lost reputations. He is subject to become hard and ruthless, not caring about the misery he causes.

Paul said, "Charge them that are rich in this world, that they be not highminded, nor trust in riches, but in the living God, who giveth us richly all things to enjoy" (1 Timothy 6:17).

If we follow Christ through the Gospels and listen to His words in regard to money, we hear Him speak of investing it for the Kingdom's sake. He related eternals to earthly (temporal) stewardship. All life is a matter of stewardship. Even success and joy are dividends on wise investments. So it is not what we own that makes or breaks us, but what we do with it.

I. USE MONEY WISELY (Luke 16:9-13)

A. Making Friends (v. 9)

9. And I say unto you, Make to yourselves friends of the mammon of unrighteousness; that, when ye fail, they may receive you into everlasting habitations.

The word *mammon* is the Syriac word for *money*, and is not to be taken as indicating evil in itself. But mammon is unrighteous when it becomes one's life goal.

It is difficult to say what Jesus means by the phrase "mammon of unrighteousness." Some authorities think He means that by wealth much that is unrighteous is accomplished. Dr. G. Campbell Morgan writes: "Money which, in itself, is a non-moral thing, can be used to blast or bless. In any case, there comes a day when it fails. Sixty seconds after a man is dead, he cannot sign a check! Make use of money now. Make friends by means of it, and, when it fails, in that very moment when your hand is no longer able to sign any check, they, the friends you made, shall greet you in the eternal tabernacles. Do not put upon your money the measurement of your own generation, as these men were doing. It fails when your generation ends. You make such out of your money, said Jesus, that, when it fails, they will receive you. How many investments have we made of that kind? Are there any who have gone on who are likely to want to see us when we arrive because of the use we made on their behalf of our wealth?" (*Westminster Pulpit*).

B. Facing Consequences (vv. 10-12)

10. He that is faithful in that which is least is faithful also in much: and he that is unjust in the least is unjust also in much.
11. If therefore ye have not been faithful in the unrighteous mammon, who will commit to your trust the true riches?
12. And if ye have not been faithful in that which is another man's, who shall give you that which is your own?

J.C. Ryle states that verse 10 seems to be used in a proverbial way. "It is an acknowledged truth, that a man's conduct in little things is a sure test of what he is likely to do in great things, and that when a man is unfaithful in small matters, we do not expect him to be faithful in important ones" (*Expository Thoughts on the Gospels*).

Most Bible scholars agree that the "unrighteous mammon" (v. 11) means "money." The "true riches" means treasure in heaven. It is generally agreed that the idea is "He who is dishonest and unfaithful in the discharge of his duties on earth, need not expect to have heavenly treasure, or to be saved."

The argument in verse 12 is like that of verse 11. Ryle writes: "Money is called 'that which is another man's,' because it passes from one to another, and is never our own for long. Eternal life is called 'that which is your own,' because it is the only property which endures forever. Everything else that we have is only a loan from God, and may be withdrawn any day. Grace and peace once given are an everlasting possession. Once ours they are ours to all eternity" (*Expository Thoughts on the Gospels*).

C. Serving Two Masters (v. 13)

13. No servant can serve two masters: for either he will hate the one, and love the other; or else he will hold to the one, and despise the other. Ye cannot serve God and mammon.

Jesus said that we cannot serve two masters. One who tries to serve God and the world has neither success nor joy in either. When bent on worldliness, the double-minded person is haunted by a disturbing conscience that restrains him from going as far as he would, and vexes him with reproaches. When endeavoring to serve God, that person is troubled by halfheartedness and worldly anxiety. He cannot give himself fully to God. Therefore, worship and service are weary rituals.

Decision is the secret of joy in Christ's service. It is the halfhearted believer who brings up an evil report of the good land. The more completely we give ourselves to Christ, the more we will experience "the peace of God, which passeth all understanding" (Philippians 4:7).

The secret of happiness is wholeheartedness. There is no joy on earth like the deep and satisfying gladness of a complete surrender to God as our only Lord and Master.

II. FULFILL FINANCIAL OBLIGATIONS (Luke 20:20-26)

A. The Question (vv. 20-22)

20. And they watched him, and sent forth spies, which should feign themselves just men, that they might take hold of his words, that so they might deliver him unto the power and authority of the governor.

21. And they asked him, saying, Master, we know that thou sayest and teachest rightly, neither acceptest thou the person of any, but teachest the way of God truly:

22. Is it lawful for us to give tribute to Caesar, or no?

The Pharisees were the legalists among the Jews. They were very proud of their accurate observance of the Law. They heaped up minute regulations until their religion became nothing but the observance of trivial rules and empty ceremonies. The big thing in their favor was the fact that they were fierce nationalists. They won the approval of the masses by their determined opposition to Roman rule, even though their opposition had little hope of success. The Pharisees' pompous attitude was revealed in the question they brought to Jesus.

These people did not go to Jesus in sincere search of truth, for they believed themselves to be the fountain of all righteousness. They were really hecklers. They wanted to put Jesus on the spot. They wanted to entrap Him in some admission or statement that would ruin His influence with the people.

Matthew includes the Herodians as part of the group out to get Jesus (see 22:15-17). They were the reigning advocates of the house of Herod. They were also subservient to the Romans. They were the natural opponents of the Pharisees. Regardless of how Jesus answered their question, these two antagonistic parties would detect any flaw.

The delegation called Jesus a teacher from God. This indicated they were hypocritical in their approach, for they did not believe Jesus to be a true teacher, but rather, the opposite. They invited Christ to be bold in His response to their question and to express His real convictions.

This seemed to point out the trickery to which the questioners themselves were accustomed to resort. They implied that Jesus might evade the issue unless encouraged to speak His mind. They knew that He never dodged any issue or refused to come to grips with any problem that confronted Him.

The question in verse 22 was designed to put Jesus on the spot. Whatever answer He gave would be wrong, they thought. To say "no" would give His enemies something with which to denounce Him before Roman justice. To say "yes" would alienate the people, who were suffering under the Roman yoke.

B. The Response (vv. 23-26)

23. But he perceived their craftiness, and said unto them, Why tempt ye me?

24. Shew me a penny. Whose image and superscription hath it? They answered and said, Caesar's.

25. And he said unto them, Render therefore unto Caesar the things which be Caesar's, and unto God the things which be God's.

26. And they could not take hold of his words before the people: and they marvelled at his answer, and held their peace.

The action of Jesus completely baffled the enemies of righteousness. Christ demanded to see the tribute money. He asked them whose head was on the coin. They replied, "Caesar's." By using money bearing Caesar's image (as he who coined the current money was ruler of the land), even the Pharisees acknowledged that he had some authority over them. At once they received an irresistibly conclusive answer to their question: "Render to Caesar the things that are Caesar's, and to God the things that are God's" (v. 25, *NASB*).

As Christians we owe obedience to the civil government under which we live. We may not approve of every law, but we must submit to those laws so long as they do not violate our duty to God.

We also owe obedience to the God of the Bible. No temporal loss and no fear of the powers that be should ever cause us to do things which the Scriptures forbid. We may find our position very trying, and we may have to suffer for conscience' sake, but we must never disobey the unmistakable commands of the Bible. If "Caesar" coins a "new gospel," he is not to be obeyed.

III. GIVE GENEROUSLY
(Luke 21:1-4)

A. The Rich Men (v. 1)

1. And he looked up, and saw the rich men casting their gifts into the treasury.

Almsgiving was common in Jewish life. The law of Moses provided for the support of the poor within the community (Leviticus 19). In later Judaism the righ-

teousness of almsgiving became somewhat professional and legalistic. Collections for the poor were frequent, and there was plenty of chance for ostentatious giving. Alms were of two kinds: (1) food and clothes for daily distribution and (2) coins received on the Sabbath for widows, orphans, strangers and the poor.

In the second court of the Temple, in the court of the women, were 13 chests with inscriptions (identifying to what use the offerings in each were allotted). Glancing up, Jesus noticed the rich men bringing their Temple gifts and ostentatiously placing them in the chests with trumpet-shaped openings. These rich men were making large gifts so all could see.

The hypocrite acts a part before men; he assumes a character which is not really his. He may give large sums in public—he wishes to be seen. He does not feel for the less fortunate; he is not merciful; he really does not care to do good. His one desire is to win the praise of men; he forgets that God sees the heart.

The New Testament has more to say about stewardship than any other subject. Of the 38 parables Jesus gave us, 16 of them deal with material possessions. One of every six verses in Matthew, Mark and Luke discusses the right handling of material goods. Throughout the Bible one finds about 500 references on prayer, fewer than 500 on the subject of faith, but more than 1,000 references regarding material possessions. We must conclude that God regards financial matters as extremely important.

B. The Poor Widow (v. 2)

2. And he saw also a certain poor widow casting in thither two mites.

The Lord was blessed when He saw a poor widow approach timidly and put in the smallest gift which the rabbis allowed—two mites. The mite (called a *lepton*), made of inferior metal, was the smallest of Hebrew coins and worth less than our penny.

The word here translated "poor" was used to describe an extreme pauper. Jesus knew the amount this poor widow gave, just as He knew it was all that she had. One was not permitted to give less than two mites. She could not have kept one.

C. The Response of Jesus (vv. 3, 4)

3. And he said, Of a truth I say unto you, that this poor widow hath cast in more than they all:

4. For all these have of their abundance cast in unto the offerings of God: but she of her penury hath cast in all the living that she had.

J.P. Lange observes: "The two mites of the widow do not escape Him. This is the Master's claim of love. He acknowledges in her unmeasured, almost foolish effort to support the Treasury of God with her last very small means the pious intention, the pure purpose, the offering of the heart which is given to God. The look of the Lord which recognized the pure flame of piety in that widow in the fume and vapor of hypocrisy that was around her, assures us that the Lord sees all the greater and lesser lights of sacrificing love which faithful and pious hearts kindle to God in every place" (*The Life of the Lord Jesus Christ*).

Life is enlarged as we give. Jesus indicates throughout the Gospels that it is the giver who becomes great. There is no abun-

dant life for those who simply await the abundance.

It is reported that John Wanamaker, in the early years of his life, sat one day in his office wondering whether there was someone for whom he could do a service. He suddenly remembered it was the day of the funeral of a woman who had scrubbed their church and kept it clean. He decided to go to her funeral. He finally found the place, and it was the strangest funeral he had ever seen. They had no minister, but friends, one after another, got up and told what this woman had done, what she had meant to them. Wanamaker went back with a new vision of what life may mean; and as he passed by a corner he heard two men, whom he barely knew, talking together most earnestly and apparently in trouble. He turned back and said, "Gentlemen, I fear you are in trouble."

They said, "Yes, Mr. Wanamaker, real trouble."

"What is it?"

"Well, our creditors have us where they can push us to the wall and they seem determined to do it; but if we could get by this corner, we could go on."

"How much would it take to turn the corner?" Mr. Wanamaker asked. And they named a big sum. Mr. Wanamaker said, "I haven't that much cash, but my credit is good for it. I'll help you out." He helped them turn the corner and these two young men laid the foundation for a great banking firm (taken from *The Supreme Beatitude*, by Earle V. Pierce).

It has been said that the nerve going to the pocketbook is the most sensitive nerve in human personality. People are touchy on money matters when they have more than they ought to have, or less than they want, or when they have wrong ideas about money.

Selfishness is the mud that slows down the chariot wheels of the Lord's army. Most people, including Christians, live as if it is more blessed to receive than to give. But human desires are rubber bags; the more we put into them, the more they stretch.

The law of gain is to give. The farmer gains by giving. The businessman gains by giving his product a wider market. The athlete gains strength in proportion to the output in effort. So does the soul of the Christian. The Christian grows as he gives. He matures as he seeks to serve, not to be served.

GOLDEN TEXT HOMILY

"NO SERVANT CAN SERVE TWO MASTERS: FOR EITHER HE WILL HATE THE ONE, AND LOVE THE OTHER; OR ELSE HE WILL HOLD TO THE ONE, AND DESPISE THE OTHER. YE CANNOT SERVE GOD AND MAMMON" (Luke 16:13).

The human body cannot occupy two spaces at the same time. It cannot be in space and in outer space at the same time. It is either here *or* there; it cannot be here *and* there. This principle is not difficult to understand. It is impossible for humans to face forward and backward at the same time. The focus must be either heavenward or earthward—it cannot be both.

Jesus said that we cannot serve God and mammon. The word *mammon* is Chaldean, meaning "that in which we place our trust." In the New Testament it generally refers to money, riches or wealth.

Does Jesus have a problem with money? Does He have a problem

with people who have money? The answer to both of these questions is, "Certainly not!" The concern of Jesus is not how much money we have, but how much of us does our money have.

A closer look at this text will reveal the logic behind the statement of Jesus.

First, we cannot serve two masters because the masters would not tolerate it. The word *master* would be inappropriate in this context. The nature of a master is to command absolute allegiance. God does not tolerate double agents. There is no place in His kingdom for two-faced, double-minded people. The first and fundamental commandment is "Thou shalt have no other gods before me" (Exodus 20:3). To say that there are two gods is the same as saying there is no God. Jesus made it clear that to be His disciple we must forsake all and follow Him.

Second, we cannot serve two masters because we are incapable of doing so. To attempt to serve two masters places us in a love/hate tension. The word *serve* comes from the same root as the word *slave*. This is a strong term in the Greek New Testament, suggesting absolute ownership. There is no co-ownership of slaves. We either belong to God or we belong to the devil. The apostle Paul says, "Do you not know that to whom you present yourselves slaves to obey, you are that one's slaves whom you obey, whether of sin leading to death, or of obedience leading to righteousness?" (Romans 6:16, *NKJV*). An attempt to serve two masters does a disservice to both.

Third, we have the freedom and the responsibility to choose our master. From the beginning, man was faced with the responsibility to make a choice. Adam and Eve chose their master, and we know the consequences of that choice. From that day forward the destinies of man are determined by the choices made. Jesus paid the ransom to free us from the servitude of Satan. The choice is ours!—**R.B. Thomas**

SENTENCE SERMONS

CHRISTIANS MUST BE faithful stewards of their financial resources.
—Selected

MAKE MONEY your god, and it will plague you like the devil.
—Henry Fielding

MAKE ALL you can, save all you can, give all you can.
—John Wesley

EVANGELISM APPLICATION

THE GENEROUS FINANCIAL GIFTS OF GOD'S PEOPLE ENABLE THE SPREAD OF THE GOSPEL.

A lady was filling a box for India when a child brought her a penny. With it the lady bought a tract to put in the box. The tract was at length given to a Burmese chief, and it led him to Christ. The chief told the story of his Savior and his great happiness to his friends. They also believed, and cast away their idols. A church was built there. A missionary was sent, and 1,500 were converted from heathenism. All of these wonderful changes were the result of that little seed.—**Selected**

ILLUMINATING THE LESSON

Sincere love does not count the cost. Perhaps you have heard of the little girl who said to her mother, "I do wish I had some money to give to the poor children."

Her mother, wishing to teach her the lesson of self-sacrifice, said, "Very well, dear. If you would like to go without sugar for a week, I'll give you the money instead; and then you will have some."

The little girl considered the idea for a moment and then said, "Must it be sugar?"

"Why, no, dear, not necessarily. What would you like to go without?"

"Soap, Mamma," was the little girl's answer. "I think I would like to do without soap."

Giving is the sweet perfume of human goodness which an individual cannot pour upon another without getting a few drops on himself. The greatest reward of giving is self-satisfaction, but often more practical and material rewards follow.

DAILY BIBLE READINGS

M. Tithing Established.
   Genesis 14:17-24
T. Sacrificial Giving.
   1 Kings 17:8-16
W. Blessings Promised.
   Malachi 3:8-12
T. Giving Rewarded.
   Luke 6:30-38
F. Giving Cheerfully.
   2 Corinthians 9:1-10
S. Needs Supplied.
   Philippians 4:10-19

TRUTH SEARCH:
Creatively Teaching the Word

Aim: Students will examine the use of money from a Biblical perspective. They will be challenged to ask God to help them cultivate a lifestyle of generosity.

Items needed: A penny for each student

FOCUS

Have each student examine a penny and answer the following questions:
* *Is God concerned about the worth of the coin?*
* *Does the coin have temporary or eternal value?*
* *Could this coin be a person's master?*

In recent years the economy has been the central issue in many political campaigns. "It's the economy, stupid!" was how one politician defined the central issue in a national campaign.
* *Do you think there is a connection between church members' attitudes toward money and the spiritual decline evident in many churches?*

EXPLORE

Have a volunteer read Luke 16:9-13 aloud. Then discuss these questions:
* *According to this passage, can someone justify not paying tithes by saying, "I will pay my tithes when I have more money"?*
* *Does it matter if I handle someone else's money with care?*

* *What connections does Jesus make between finances and eternal matters?*

Have a volunteer read Luke 20:20-26 aloud. Then discuss these questions:
* *What did Jesus' enemies hope to accomplish in this situation?*
* *Is it an act of Christian devotion to pay taxes?*
* *What does it mean to give "to God what is God's"? What would this include?*

Have a volunteer read Luke 21:1-4 aloud. Then discuss these questions:
* *Can a genuine Christian be poor?*
* *In God's eyes, whose offerings count the most?*
* *Restate Christ's words in verse 4 in the form of a principle or a proverb.*

RESPOND

Take the penny in your hand again. What does your personal managing of finances say about your spiritual condition? Are you generous with your finances? Do you faithfully support the kingdom of God through your giving?

Lead a silent prayer where students can confess any shortcomings. Then allow the students to express different ways in which God has blessed them when they've been obedient with their money.

The Lord's Supper

Study Text: Luke 22:1-23
Objective: To recognize the significance of the Lord's Supper and receive the bread and cup with gratitude.
Time: The Gospel of Luke was written between A.D. 50 and 70. It covers a period of about 3 years (A.D. 29-33).
Place: Jerusalem
Golden Text: "As often as ye eat this bread, and drink this cup, ye do shew the Lord's death till he come" (1 Corinthians 11:26).
Central Truth: The Lord's Supper reminds believers of Christ's sacrifice.
Evangelism Emphasis: The Lord's Supper proclaims Christ's sacrificial provision for salvation.

PRINTED TEXT

Luke 22:1. Now the feast of unleavened bread drew nigh, which is called the Passover.

2. And the chief priests and scribes sought how they might kill him; for they feared the people.

3. Then entered Satan into Judas surnamed Iscariot, being of the number of the twelve.

4. And he went his way, and communed with the chief priests and captains, how he might betray him unto them.

5. And they were glad, and covenanted to give him money.

6. And he promised, and sought opportunity to betray him unto them in the absence of the multitude.

7. Then came the day of unleavened bread, when the passover must be killed.

8. And he sent Peter and John, saying, Go and prepare us the passover, that we may eat.

9. And they said unto him, Where wilt thou that we prepare?

10. And he said unto them, Behold, when ye are entered into the city, there shall a man meet you, bearing a pitcher of water; follow him into the house where he entereth in.

11. And ye shall say unto the goodman of the house, The Master saith unto thee, Where is the guestchamber, where I shall eat the passover with my disciples?

12. And he shall shew you a large upper room furnished: there make ready.

13. And they went, and found as he had said unto them: and they made ready the passover.

14. And when the hour was come, he sat down, and the twelve apostles with him.

15. And he said unto them, With desire I have desired to eat this passover with you before I suffer:

16. For I say unto you, I will not any more eat thereof, until it be fulfilled in the kingdom of God.

17. And he took the cup, and gave thanks, and said, Take this, and divide it among yourselves:

18. For I say unto you, I will not drink of the fruit of the vine, until the kingdom of God shall come.

19. And he took bread, and

gave thanks, and brake it, and gave unto them, saying, This is my body which is given for you: this do in remembrance of me.

20. Likewise also the cup after supper, saying, This cup is the new testament in my blood, which is shed for you.

DICTIONARY
goodman—Luke 22:11—owner of the house

LESSON OUTLINE
I. BETRAYAL INSTIGATED
  A. The Time
  B. The Plot
  C. The Man
II. PASSOVER PREPARED
  A. The Directions
  B. The Completion
III. THE LORD'S SUPPER OBSERVED
  A. The Companions of Jesus
  B. The Heart of Jesus
  C. The Hope Expressed

LESSON EXPOSITION
INTRODUCTION

The Lord's Supper is one of the ordinances of the Christian church. First, its observance was commanded by Jesus in the Gospels. Second, the Lord's Supper was practiced in the early church, as described in the Book of Acts. Third, its spiritual significance is clearly expounded by Paul in 1 Corinthians.

The word *sacrament* is not found in the Bible. It comes from a Latin word, *sacramentum.* The Romans used it to describe the oath of allegiance which a person took when he joined the army. The recruit vowed he had renounced his civilian life with its independence and confessed that he belonged absolutely to Caesar. He swore to obey every command of the emperor, whatever the cost, and lead where it would.

The early church used the word *sacrament* in reference to the Lord's Supper. Through regular observance of the Lord's Supper, believers proclaimed to the world that they had renounced their former life of sin and self and now belonged completely to Christ.

According to the New Testament, the Lord's Supper is to be observed only by those who have accepted Christ as their Savior. It is a simple memorial ordinance which was established by the Savior on the night of His betrayal. It exists only for the purpose of enabling His disciples to gratefully remember Him as they take the bread and drink the wine, and thus show forth His death until He returns for them (*The Lord's Supper*, Alfred P. Gibbs).

I. BETRAYAL INSTIGATED
  (Luke 22:1-6)

A. The Time (v. 1)

1. Now the feast of unleavened bread drew nigh, which is called the Passover.

The Passover was the chief of the Jews' annual feasts. It celebrated the "passing over" of the death angel that dreadful night when Israel left Egypt under the command of God and the leadership of Moses (Exodus 12:1-28). It was a memorial of deliverance from death by the blood of a lamb, and from the power of Egypt by the power of God.

B. The Plot (v. 2)

2. And the chief priests and

scribes sought how they might kill him; for they feared the people.

As the sacred feast drew near, the chief priests and scribes sought a way to kill Jesus. The very leaders who should have welcomed the Messiah conspired to kill Him. They should have rejoiced at the appearing of the Lamb of God, yet they were the first to want to put Him to death. They sat in Moses' seat. They claimed to be "guides of the blind" and "lights of them which were in darkness" (see Romans 2:17-20). Instead, they were the leaders in crucifying Jesus.

The behavior of the Jewish religious leaders should be a warning to us. We must beware of attaching excessive importance to religious leaders just because of their office. Position and rank confer no exemption from error. The greatest heresies have been propagated and the greatest abuses introduced into the church by religious leaders.

Respect is due to Christian leaders. But we must insist that all religious leaders adhere to the rules of the Word of God. Is their message Biblical? Is it true? Isaiah said, "To the law and to the testimony: if they speak not according to this word, it is because there is no light in them" (8:20).

C. The Man (vv. 3-6)

3. Then entered Satan into Judas surnamed Iscariot, being of the number of the twelve.

4. And he went his way, and communed with the chief priests and captains, how he might betray him unto them.

5. And they were glad, and covenanted to give him money.

6. And he promised, and sought opportunity to betray him unto them in the absence of the multitude.

As the chief priests and scribes were seeking a way to kill Jesus, Satan entered into the heart of Judas Iscariot to make him an instrument for the execution of this evil plan. Judas was not an unwilling victim under the control of a demon. He gave in to Satan's promptings (see John 13:2). Often Jesus had attempted to awaken Judas to this danger, but covetousness had gripped him so powerfully that no appeal from the Savior ever led him to repentance.

William Evans writes of Judas: "It is quite true that the fall of Judas is foretold in the Scriptures; but the mere fact of prediction does not unconditionally and arbitrarily fix an event. Judas did not betray Jesus because it had been predicted he would do so; it was predicted because Omniscience knew that he would perform that guilty act of betrayal. While the event did follow the prediction, yet it did not follow because of the prediction. God foreknows actions, but does not determine them to the extent that our free will is overthrown" (*From the Upper Room to the Empty Tomb*).

In his book, *These Twelve*, Charles R. Brown observes: "It is a vivid picture of an ugly process of moral decline. Satan had not been resident within the man's soul during all those months of high privilege, but he was a frequent visitor. Now when the end of Christ's earthly ministry was approaching and the disciples felt the nearness of some crisis, there came a definite moral lapse. By an act of treachery and the deliberate transfer of himself from the ranks of Christ's friends into the ranks of the enemies, Judas went down to become at last 'the son of perdition.'"

Judas would know all the places Christ would be likely to frequent. He could bring His enemies to Him when He was virtually alone. They gave Judas 30 pieces of silver. Many Bible scholars believe this money, given to betray the Lamb of God, was taken from the Temple treasury, from the funds used for the purchase of a sacrifice.

Judas Iscariot should be a prime example to every believer in Christ of what not to do. It should be remembered this man was one of Christ's chosen apostles. He followed Him during the total course of His ministry. He forsook all for Christ's sake. He heard Christ preach and saw Him perform miracles. He preached himself. He spoke like the other apostles. There was nothing about him to distinguish him from the other apostles. He was never suspected of being a hypocrite. And yet this man betrayed his Master, then killed himself.

II. PASSOVER PREPARED
(Luke 22:7-13)

A. The Directions (vv. 7-12)

7. Then came the day of unleavened bread, when the passover must be killed.

8. And he sent Peter and John, saying, Go and prepare us the passover, that we may eat.

9. And they said unto him, Where wilt thou that we prepare?

10. And he said unto them, Behold, when ye are entered into the city, there shall a man meet you, bearing a pitcher of water; follow him into the house where he entereth in.

11. And ye shall say unto the goodman of the house, The Master saith unto thee, Where is the guest-chamber, where I shall eat the passover with my disciples?

12. And he shall shew you a large upper room furnished: there make ready.

13. And they went, and found as he had said unto them: and they made ready the passover.

All leaven was most carefully and scrupulously put away during the day on which the Passover must be sacrificed. The Passover lamb was slain by a priest in the Temple. It was roasted whole, its shed blood denoting atonement for sin. It was eaten with unleavened bread, signifying purity, and with bitter herbs, symbolizing the bitterness of Egyptian bondage.

Jesus entrusted Peter and John to prepare the Passover. The mystery involving their mission may have been a precautionary measure. Christ would not want His enemies to know where He was until the time came for His arrest.

In the East it would have been an unusual sight to see a man carry a pitcher of water because this was considered the work of women. One might see a slave doing this kind of work, or, as F.W. Farrar explains it, "unless we have here a reference to the Jewish custom of the master of a house himself drawing the water with which the unleavened bread was kneaded on Nisan 13" (*Cambridge Bible*).

We do not know who the man was because the Bible is silent on it. But Jesus knew this man would be met by His two messengers.

Apparently the man with the pitcher was not the head of the household. And it would seem that the master of the house was a follower of Christ. It should be remembered that it was customary for the Jews to be very hospitable. According to the Talmud, they would not charge for the use of the rooms for the feast.

According to Gustaf Dalman, "The upper stories of the house, especially the rooms erected on the flat roofs, are the 'upper rooms' of which the New Testament speaks. They were not used as the usual family dwelling rooms and could be quickly turned into guest rooms. When they were provided with couches or cushions, as is taken for granted for the Lord's Supper, they could be used for meals as well as for sleeping places. Wooden stands under the cushions and tables proper were usual in the time of Jesus. The reclining position at a proper common meal was taken for granted. Eating in a sitting position was not the custom. At the Passover Feast, even the poorest man must lie at his ease" (*Sacred Sites and Ways*).

B. The Completion (v. 13)

13. And they went, and found as he had said unto them: and they made ready the passover.

We may assume that the following things were required in order to prepare for the Passover Feast: the lamb, the wine, the bitter herbs and the unleavened bread. Those things being there and in place, the upper room was ready. Peter and John found everything as the Lord had promised. We may rest assured that when Christ sends any believer on an errand, He will provide for every condition.

III. THE LORD'S SUPPER
OBSERVED (Luke 22:14-20)

A. The Companions of Jesus (v. 14)

14. And when the hour was come, he sat down, and the twelve apostles with him.

Jesus was concerned that this last sacred hour not be interrupted, so they did not arrive in Jerusalem

from Bethany until the evening. Luke says Jesus sat down with the 12 apostles with Him. This means that Judas was still part of the group.

When the Passover was first instituted, the people ate standing, in remembrance of the haste with which they began the Exodus. As the years went by, it was eaten by reclining in the usual fashion on couches stretched out before low tables.

This is the only feast of the Jews in which Christ is said to have desired to participate. The deep desire was probably the result of His longing to fulfill His mission on earth, that is, to die for the sins of the world. Jesus knew this Passover was to be the prelude to the eternally ordained event by which men would find forgiveness and freedom from sin.

B. The Heart of Jesus (vv. 15, 16)

15. And he said unto them, With desire I have desired to eat this passover with you before I suffer:
16. For I say unto you, I will not any more eat thereof, until it be fulfilled in the kingdom of God.

Why did Jesus have this intense longing? Why had He so eagerly looked forward to that meeting? Was it not because He desired the support of their fellowship for what was before Him? Jesus needed the comfort His followers could give Him, and longed for the opportunity for their sakes. They were to know something of the sorrow of desolation, and He would prepare them for the darkest days to come. He would assure them of His deathless love, and that would comfort them when the shock of His death came. They could look back on this feast, recall His words, and gather strength to suffer and to wait.

It is clear that Jesus was certain of a Kingdom yet to come in which He and His disciples would be gathered together. As believers we do not yet know a complete redemption from the forces of evil and death, but we shall experience such a completed salvation when the Lord returns. When we sit down at the Marriage Supper of the Lamb of God in glory, it will not be on the threshold of the death of our Savior, but at the threshold of an eternal bliss with Him in the Father's house.

C. The Hope Expressed (vv. 17-20)

17. And he took the cup, and gave thanks, and said, Take this, and divide it among yourselves:

18. For I say unto you, I will not drink of the fruit of the vine, until the kingdom of God shall come.

19. And he took bread, and gave thanks, and brake it, and gave unto them, saying, This is my body which is given for you: this do in remembrance of me.

20. Likewise also the cup after supper, saying, This cup is the new testament in my blood, which is shed for you.

From the Greek word for "giving thanks" comes one name for the Lord's Supper, "the Eucharist," or thanksgiving feast.

Concerning the statement "Take this, and divide it among yourselves" (v. 17), Dr. Joseph Parker comments: "This is what my Lord is always saying, 'Divide it among yourselves.' If you have a truth, if you have a vision, if you have a new way of looking at things, divide it among yourselves, do not keep hidden anything under some secret cover of your own" (*The City Temple Pulpit*).

Verse 18 is another emphatic statement calling attention to the solemn character of the feast. As before, Christ refers to the coming kingdom of God through His death on the cross.

With full knowledge of the suffering that lay before Him, Jesus gave thanks. Knowing the dreadful reality of what was symbolized in the bread and cup, He gave thanks.

The statement "This do in remembrance of me" (v. 19) proclaims the formal character of Christ's acts; He was inaugurating a commemoration which He desired to be permanently observed by all who should hold Him in loving memory. The Passover itself was a "memorial" (Exodus 12:14). One thing above all else our Lord would have us remember concerning Himself is His death. No one can possibly participate in the Lord's Supper without at once remembering Christ's sacrifice for our sins.

From verse 20 of the text comes the term "new testament," which is more accurately translated, "the new covenant."

The cup is no more the actual blood of Jesus than the bread is His body. The fruit of the vine is symbolic of the blood He shed for us on Calvary for our redemption, forgiveness, peace, justification and deliverance. Without the shedding of His blood, there would be no remission of sins (see Matthew 26:28; Hebrews 9:22). God covenants not only to forgive us our sins, but to create a new heart within us. "This is the covenant that I will make with them after those days, saith the Lord, I will put my laws into their hearts, and in their minds will I write them; and their sins and

iniquities will I remember no more"
(Hebrews 10:16, 17).

GOLDEN TEXT HOMILY

"AS OFTEN AS YE EAT THIS
BREAD, AND DRINK THIS CUP,
YE DO SHEW THE LORD'S DEATH
TILL HE COME" (1 Corinthians
11:26).

We must be careful to remember that when we observe the
Lord's Supper, it is not to be a
mere ritual. In fact, as the Lord
designed, it is a powerful experience that has immediate significance. In recent months, each
time that I have taken the Lord's
Supper, I have been impressed
with what a powerful experience it
actually is.

Partaking in this outward act is
a confession that we are laying
hold onto all the benefits of the
death of the Lord Jesus Christ.
This encompasses spiritual, mental and physical blessings. We are
remembering, in present tense,
what Jesus Christ did in past
tense. We realize that the work of
Christ on the cross continues to
work on our behalf.

This proclamation of the Lord's
death, according to this wonderful scripture, is made each and
every time we observe this holy
commandment. If we can appreciate how significant this confession is, the Lord's Supper can
have more spiritual meaning and
blessing for us each time we
observe it.—**Dennis W. Watkins**

SENTENCE SERMONS

THE LORD'S SUPPER reminds
believers of Christ's sacrifice.
—Selected

CHRIST on our cross is the way
Calvary really reads.
—C. Neil Strait

LOOK BACKWARD—see Christ
dying for you. Look upward—see
Christ pleading for you. Look
inward—see Christ living in you.
Look forward—see Christ coming
for you.
—Selected

EVANGELISM APPLICATION

THE LORD'S SUPPER PRO-
CLAIMS CHRIST'S SACRIFICIAL
PROVISION FOR SALVATION.

The old sacrifices, of which
Passover is a type, brought sins
continually to remembrance. The
Lord's Supper brings to remembrance Christ and His sacrifice
once and for all for the full and
final remission of sins. The Lord's
Supper reminds us of a group of
the most terrible facts of history—
of sin . . . how God hates sin . . .
that all have sinned and fallen
short of the glory of God.

It reminds us of another group
of facts which thrill and gladden
our souls—that Jesus, our Savior,
died to reconcile us to God . . . that
the claims of the moral law have
been fully met . . . that God can be
just and yet justify sinners.

ILLUMINATING THE LESSON

Some human leaders have built
monuments of stone. The deeds of
the mighty stand engraved in
bronze and stone to remind future
generations of their accomplishments. But Jesus cared not for
physical monuments; His is an
inner kingdom, the kingdom of
love. His covenant is a spiritual
renewal, with His laws put into the
hearts and written in the minds of
those who accept Him as Savior
and Lord. His great victory came,
not by valor on battlefields, but by
humble obedience to death, even
the death of the cross. Here He
conquered sin and hell and the

devil. Through the shedding of His blood, He provided eternal salvation for all who will accept Him. Here He became the living Conqueror through His resurrection.

The Lord's Supper is a memorial of His passion. As we partake of the bread and wine, we do so as a memorial of our Savior, in remembrance of Him.

This sacrament also points forward. It is a lighthouse that heralds the fact of Jesus' coming again. We announce by partaking of the Lord's Supper that Jesus died for us, that He is now a living Christ, that though bodily absent He is spiritually present, that He is now our glorious Savior, and that we will continue to do this until He comes again, when we will need no symbols.

DAILY BIBLE READINGS

M. The Passover Instituted.
   Exodus 12:3-14
T. Israel Obeys the Lord.
   Exodus 12:28-36
W. Keep the Passover.
   Numbers 9:1-5
T. Observe the Lord's Supper.
   1 Corinthians 11:23-34
F. Power in the Blood.
   Hebrews 9:19-28
S. Marriage Supper of the Lamb.
   Revelation 19:1-9

TRUTH SEARCH:
Creatively Teaching the Word

Aim: Students will compare their sacrifices for Christ with His costly sacrifice.

Items needed: A Communion wafer, cup of grape juice, marker board, marker

FOCUS

Ask the students if they can identify with the following statements:
• *Someone in the church has hurt me.*
• *I am just too busy to serve the Lord.*
• *If my boss knew I was a Christian he probably would not promote me.*

In Jesus' day the chief priests and teachers of the Law were concerned about power and public opinion. Judas was concerned about personal gain, but Jesus, the Son of God, was concerned about the salvation of the world. The Lord's Supper is a reminder that Christ faced a hostile world to save us and that His sacrifice was costly. It is also a reminder of our need to be grateful for His saving work on the cross.

EXPLORE

Divide the class into small groups, and assign each of the following passages. Have the groups answer the following questions about their particular passage.

Luke 22:1-6

1. Who did the Jewish religious leaders fear? Why?

2. Is it significant that Judas was referred to as "one of the twelve" (v. 3)? Why or why not?

3. What motivated Judas to betray the Lord?

4. Did Judas demonstrate courage or cowardice?

Luke 22:7-13

1. What kind of preparations would Peter and John have to make for the Passover?

2. Were the events of this Passover accidental or divinely planned? How do you know?

3. What is the central event of the Passover (v. 7)? How would this relate to Jesus?

Luke 22:14-20

1. Was the Passover an event with meaning to Jesus, or simply a religious ceremony to be observed?

2. What "new covenant" (v. 20, NKJV) did Jesus establish at this time?

3. How would you explain the meaning of the bread and the cup to a new believer?

Bring everyone back together and discuss their findings.

Display a Communion wafer and a cup of grape juice.

In becoming the once-and-for-all Passover lamb, Jesus' body was broken and His blood shed on our behalf. He made a total sacrifice.

RESPOND

Ask each student to name one thing they have sacrificed for the cause of Christ. Write each answer on the board.
• *How does the sum total of all the items on the board compare to Christ's sacrifice?*

As the students bow their heads and close their eyes, quietly read Luke 22:17-20 aloud. Then pause for one minute of quiet meditation on the sacrifice of Christ.

Jesus Is the Resurrected Lord

Study Text: Luke 24:13-35
Objective: To explore how Jesus revealed Himself as the risen Lord, and worship and proclaim Him.
Time: A.D. 30
Place: Jerusalem and Emmaus
Golden Text: "The Lord is risen indeed" (Luke 24:34).
Central Truth: The resurrection of Jesus provides assurance of eternal life.
Evangelism Emphasis: The resurrection of Jesus provides victory over sin and death.

PRINTED TEXT

Luke 24:13. And, behold, two of them went that same day to a village called Emmaus, which was from Jerusalem about threescore furlongs.

14. And they talked together of all these things which had happened.

15. And it came to pass, that, while they communed together and reasoned, Jesus himself drew near, and went with them.

16. But their eyes were holden that they should not know him.

17. And he said unto them, What manner of communications are these that ye have one to another, as ye walk, and are sad?

18. And the one of them, whose name was Cleopas, answering said unto him, Art thou only a stranger in Jerusalem, and hast not known the things which are come to pass there in these days?

19. And he said unto them, What things? And they said unto him, Concerning Jesus of Nazareth, which was a prophet mighty in deed and word before God and all the people:

25. Then he said unto them, O fools, and slow of heart to believe all that the prophets have spoken:

26. Ought not Christ to have suffered these things, and to enter into his glory?

27. And beginning at Moses and all the prophets, he expounded unto them in all the scriptures the things concerning himself.

28. And they drew nigh unto the village, whither they went: and he made as though he would have gone further.

29. But they constrained him, saying, Abide with us: for it is toward evening, and the day is far spent. And he went in to tarry with them.

30. And it came to pass, as he sat at meat with them, he took bread, and blessed it, and brake, and gave to them.

31. And their eyes were opened, and they knew him; and he vanished out of their sight.

32. And they said one to another, Did not our heart burn within us, while he talked with us by the way, and while he opened to us the scriptures?

33. And they rose up the same hour, and returned to Jerusalem, and found the eleven gathered together, and them that were with them,

34. Saying, The Lord is risen

indeed, and hath appeared to Simon.

35. And they told what things **were done in the way, and how he was known of them in breaking of bread.**

DICTIONARY
Emmaus (ee-MAY-us)—Luke 24:13—A village located seven miles from Jerusalem.

LESSON OUTLINE
I. DISMAY OF THE DISCIPLES
  A. The Discussion
  B. The Appearance of Jesus
  C. The Conversation With Jesus
II. THE REVELATION OF SCRIPTURE
  A. A Sure Guide
  B. Divine Appointment
III. CHRIST RECOGNIZED
  A. Revealing Identity
  B. Acknowledging Enjoyment
  C. Sharing Enjoyment

LESSON EXPOSITION
INTRODUCTION

The characteristic word of the Christian religion is *resurrection.* It is the one word that can focus and express the very essence of Christianity. Christianity is essentially a religion of resurrection; the church is a community of resurrection; the gospel is the power of resurrection.

It is true that the Cross must stand at the heart of God's program of redemption, but a person may gaze at the Cross for a lifetime and yet miss the gospel that saves. If there had been no Resurrection, there would have been no New Testament. It was with a burning certainty in the resurrection of Christ that men were motivated to pen the gospel record. They knew that the One about whom they were writing had conquered death and was alive forevermore. The

Resurrection was no mere appendix to their faith; it was their faith. It was the seal of victory—Christ had defeated the Enemy.

In the Book of Hebrews we have one of the most moving and meaningful expressions of the Resurrection ever penned. It reads: "Now the God of peace, that brought again from the dead our Lord Jesus, that great shepherd of the sheep, through the blood of the everlasting covenant, make you perfect in every good work to do his will, working in you that which is wellpleasing in his sight, through Jesus Christ; to whom be glory for ever and ever" (13:20, 21).

The author of Hebrews is saying that the same divine creative energy which resurrected Christ is available to every Christian. It is available not only at death, but it is now ever present to help us live in this present world—what thrilling hope!

Every person has in his heart a voiceless question: "If a man die, shall he live again?" In every person's heart there is an answer, sometimes the feeble whisper of a forgotten faith, sometimes the song of the soul's assurance: "This is not the end; man was not made to be lost in the abyss of nothingness."

In the Old Testament there are but a few glimpses of faith in life after death. But then Jesus came. A few humble men walked with Him over the hills of Galilee and camped with Him on Gennesaret's lonely shores; they heard the words of truth fall from His lips, and their deepest loves were awakened and united with His Godlike love. For them, the world and life were completely changed.

These humble men saw their Friend die. At first they were plunged into unutterable grief and despair; then came the Resurrection, and they could cry, "He is alive! His love and power are still with us; He guides and rebukes and inspires us." Christ's words to them on previous occasions came to life: "I am the resurrection and the life" (see John 11:25; 14:6).

Resurrection had become a reality in their hearts. Such is the authentic Christian faith—they knew that nothing in life or death could separate them from the love of God which they had experienced in Christ the Lord.

I. DISMAY OF THE DISCIPLES (Luke 24:13-24)

A. The Discussion (vv. 13, 14)

13. And, behold, two of them went that same day to a village called Emmaus, which was from Jerusalem about threescore furlongs.

14. And they talked together of all these things which had happened.

On a certain day (apparently Sunday after the crucifixion Friday) two men who had been through the terrible days of the trial and death of Christ walked toward Emmaus. It was the first day of a new week, and the two believers, having heard the report of the women concerning Jesus' empty tomb and the appearance of the angels, spoke casually about it.

B. The Appearance of Jesus (vv. 15, 16)

15. And it came to pass, that, while they communed together and reasoned, Jesus himself drew near, and went with them.

16. But their eyes were holden that they should not know him.

As they walked, the two men questioned each other as to what the women's story might mean. As they talked, a Stranger drew near and began to walk with them, apparently adding nothing to the conversation.

We do not know why the disciples failed to recognize Jesus. H.B. Swete suggests: "Either they did not suspect that the stranger was Jesus, or, if the suspicion crossed their minds, it was promptly dismissed. There is nothing psychologically impossible in such a situation if the men were still possessed by the conviction that, in spite of what they had heard, the Lord was still among the dead. It is less easy to understand how they failed to recognize the voice. . . . It must be remembered, however, that these two men, who were not apostles, may never before have come into close contact with the Master" (*The Appearances of Our Lord After the Passion*).

C. The Conversation With Jesus (vv. 17-24)

(Luke 24:20-24 is not included in the printed text.)

17. And he said unto them, What manner of communications are these that ye have one to another, as ye walk, and are sad?

18. And the one of them, whose name was Cleopas, answering said unto him, Art thou only a stranger in Jerusalem, and hast not known the things which are come to pass there in these days?

19. And he said unto them, What things? And they said

unto him, Concerning Jesus of Nazareth, which was a prophet mighty in deed and word before God and all the people.

The countenances of the two men must have reflected their continuing grief. They failed to see Christ through the open tomb. They saw Him merely dying. Jesus had claimed to be God, and His claims seem to be vindicated by His miraculous deeds and life-changing teachings. But then He was crucified. It was a terrible day. The sun was blotted from sight, and there was an earthquake. Christ's body was buried in the tomb of Joseph of Arimathea. The Pharisees smacked their lips and dusted their hands as if to say, "Well, that's that! We have gotten rid of this man who caused us so much trouble." Jesus was apparently defeated.

Despite their confusion, these two disciples had not become bitter. Disappointed and disillusioned as they were, no angry words are recorded.

Jesus, inquiring into the subject of their earnest conversation, elicited from them a summary of the arrest and crucifixion of their Lord, and a confused account of the empty tomb and the vision of angels at the tomb. But they apparently attached no importance to these rumors, and were completely discouraged, all their messianic expectations having been destroyed. "We were hoping," they said despairingly, "that it was He who was going to redeem Israel" (v. 21, NKJV).

II. THE REVELATION OF
    SCRIPTURE (Luke 24:25-29)

A. A Sure Guide (vv. 25-27)

25. Then he said unto them, O fools, and slow of heart to believe all that the prophets have spoken:

26. Ought not Christ to have suffered these things, and to enter into his glory?

27. And beginning at Moses and all the prophets, he expounded unto them in all the scriptures the things concerning himself.

Continuing their journey, conversation continued, during which Jesus allowed the disciples to express their deepest feelings in regard to Him. When they had spoken, He gently chided them for their failure to believe their Lord would come again as He had promised. Their fault lay in their ignorance of prophetic sacred writings available to them, as well as to their interpretation of the writings.

The disciples listened intently to their Visitor as He revealed to them the profound depths of the ancient prophecies.

G. Campbell Morgan said: "They listened to Him as He traced the Messianic note in the music of all the prophets showing that He was David's King, 'fairer than the children of men,' and in the days of Solomon's well-doing, He was 'the altogether lovely one.' He was Isaiah's Child-King with a shoulder strong enough to bear the government; with the name *Emmanuel*, gathering within itself all the excellencies. He was Jeremiah's Branch of Righteousness, executing justice and righteousness in the land. He was Ezekiel's Plant of Renown, giving shade and giving fragrance. He was Daniel's Stone, cut without hands, smiting the image, becoming a mountain, and filling the whole earth. He was the Ideal Israel of Hosea, 'growing as the lily,' casting out its roots as Lebanon. To Joel, the Hope of the People, and the Strength of the Children of Israel; and the Usherer in the Vision of Amos, of the Plowman Overtaking the Reaper, and the Treader of Grapes, Him that soweth seed; and of Obadiah, the 'Deliverance Upon Mount Zion'; and the 'Holiness' to God, of which Micah spoke. He was the One Nahum saw upon the mountains publishing peace. He was the Anointed of whom Habakkuk sang as 'going forth for salvation.' He was the One who brought to the people the pure language of Zephaniah's message, the true Zerubbabel of Haggai's word, forever rebuilding the house of God; Himself the dawn of the day when 'Holiness shall be upon the bells of the horses,' as Zechariah foretold; and He, the 'Refiner,' sitting over the fire; 'the Sun of Righteousness' of Malachi's dream" (*The Crisis of the Christ*).

B. Divine Appointment (vv. 28, 29)

28. And they drew nigh unto the village, whither they went: and he made as though he would have gone further.
29. But they constrained him, saying, Abide with us: for it is toward evening, and the day is far spent. And he went in to tarry with them.

As the two disciples and Jesus neared Emmaus, Jesus "made as though he would have gone further." It had been a walk of about two hours from Jerusalem to Emmaus, but the presence of Jesus must have made the journey seem less tiring. Jesus made no false pretense. He would have gone further had the disciples not implored Him to stay. Thus it was when He was walking on the Sea of Galilee—He likely would have passed by the storm-tossed ship if the frightened ones on board had not cried out to Him (Mark 6:48, 49).

The statement "But they constrained him" (Luke 4:29) is translated by Weymouth as, "They pressed him to remain with them." In response to the question, *How may we get Christ to abide with us?*

William Bright says: "By deepening, as far as may be, our sense of dependence on His mercy, and therewith our consciousness of our own sin. And, in the second place, let us aim at a more thorough consecration of our lives to the service of Him who claims them as His by right, and is able and willing to transform them by His power" (*The Incarnation*).

Any sincere asking for the presence of Christ receives it immediately and completely.

III. CHRIST RECOGNIZED
(Luke 24:30-35)

A. Revealing Identity (vv. 30, 31)

30. And it came to pass, as he sat at meat with them, he took bread, and blessed it, and brake, and gave to them.
31. And their eyes were opened, and they knew him; and he vanished out of their sight.

Jesus sat down with the disciples for a while at a table to remind them of His promises and to reveal Himself. Once in the home, Jesus assumed the place of host. It was He who broke bread, blessed it, and gave it to the others.

It was in the moment of breaking bread that the disciples' eyes were opened and they recognized Him for who He was. What a moment! But then, in an instant, He was gone; He vanished out of their sight.

Somehow, in the breaking of the bread, the eyes of the disciples were opened and they knew it was their Lord. How did they recognize Christ at this point?

Some scholars think it had to do with some well-known and peculiar gesture of the Lord in the act of breaking bread. Others think the recognition of Jesus may have come because of particular words He used blessing the bread. Or it may have been that marks of the nails which had pierced Him on the cross were discovered. Whatever the case, the disciples did not doubt that He who broke bread was their Lord.

B. Acknowledging Enjoyment (v. 32)

32. And they said one to another, Did not our heart burn within us, while he talked with us by the way, and while he opened to us the scriptures?

It is a wonderful confession the disciples made that the presence of Jesus made their hearts burn within them. The need of our day is for more burning hearts, which comes from companionship with our Lord and with His Word.

Look over the men whom Jesus chose to frame the preamble of our whole religious constitution. John the Baptist was a flamboyant spirit, a torchbearer. John the Beloved and James were called "Boanerges" (the sons of thunder); both were men of powerful impulses and passions. Simon Peter was a spasmodic flame, the forerunner of the steady glow. Andrew was a quick and impulsive man. Simon the Zealot's title gives us a clue to his character. Judas Iscariot was a man of enthusiasm, which was not his weak point. Barnabas was a hospitable fireplace; Paul, a beacon burning on a hill. Jesus himself was an enthusiast, called a fanatic by the standpatters of His day. Nothing worthwhile is ever accomplished except by the compulsion of a burning and glowing love.

C. Sharing Enjoyment (vv. 33-35)

33. And they rose up the same hour, and returned to Jerusalem, and found the eleven gathered together, and them that were with them,

34. Saying, The Lord is risen indeed, and hath appeared to Simon.

35. And they told what things were done in the way, and how he was known of them in breaking of bread.

The two disciples wasted no time in returning to Jerusalem. The seven-mile journey to Emmaus had been filled with questioning and sadness, but the return hike to Jerusalem was filled with confidence and incredible joy.

Once in Jerusalem, the two men were told that the risen Lord had appeared to Simon Peter. The Gospels give no details of Christ's appearance to Peter alone, but it is listed by Paul in 1 Corinthians 15:5.

The two disciples shared with those in Jerusalem their blessed conversation with Jesus and how He revealed Himself to them through the breaking of bread. Being with the resurrected Lord had caused the hearts of Cleopas and his companion to burn within them, and now they were passing the flame to others.

GOLDEN TEXT HOMILY

"THE LORD IS RISEN INDEED" (Luke 24:34).

In quick succession the disciples had seen Christ arrested, tried, crucified and buried. They were confused and hurt that the Son of God could be killed on a cross by Roman soldiers. While still shaken over these improbable events, there suddenly came the news that He was risen—He was no longer dead, but alive!

How like the Lord Jesus Christ that in a phenomenal way He had triumphed over evil and death. Testimony to the resurrection of Christ is given by many in Luke 24. Note the following: the Old Testament prophets (vv. 27, 44-48); angels (vv. 4-7); disciples (vv. 9, 12, 33-35); Jesus' foretelling (vv. 7, 25, 26). Yet the final, most conclusive evidence of Christ's resurrection was given by His own post-resurrection appearance to the disciples (vv. 36-43).

"He is risen" is the anthem of the church. It is our hope and expectation that as He lives we shall live also. Jesus said, "I am the resurrection, and the life: he that believeth in me, though he were dead, yet shall he live: and whosoever liveth and believeth in me shall never die" (John 11:25, 26).—**Jack Smith**

SENTENCE SERMONS

THE RESURRECTION of Jesus provides assurance of eternal life.
—Selected

DEATH IS only a horizon; and a horizon is nothing save the limit of our sight.
—Rossiter W. Raymond

THE TRUEST end of life is to know that life never ends.
—William Penn

EVANGELISM APPLICATION

THE RESURRECTION OF JESUS PROVIDES VICTORY OVER SIN AND DEATH.

A Muslim woman said to a missionary, "What did you do to my daughter?" The 16-year-old girl had died a few days before. The missionary, thinking that the mother was accusing him, replied, "Why, we didn't do anything to her!" But the woman said, "Yes, you did! She died smiling, and our people don't die like that" (*The Supreme Beatitude*, by Earle V. Pierce).

The Lord Jesus Christ, by His resurrection, has removed the terrors of death for those who put their trust in Him, and we die smiling. Because the Lord Jesus died and rose again, death has no sting.

ILLUMINATING THE LESSON

The resurrection of Christ is *the* miracle of Christianity. It is the miracle by which the entire Christian faith stands or falls. If Christ did not rise, then He was not what He claimed to be; His death was not an atoning death, and Christians have been deceived for centuries; preachers have been declaring error; the faithful have been deceived by a false hope of salvation.

The Resurrection was verified by the testimony of those who saw Jesus after His resurrection. People spoke with Him, touched Him, and ate with Him.

The Resurrection is really the completion of the atoning death of Christ. It means that we have a sympathetic High Priest in heaven who has lived our life, knows our sorrows and infirmities, and is able to give us power to live the Christ-life day by day. It means that we may know that there is a life to come.

DAILY BIBLE READINGS

M. Delivered From Death.
  Genesis 22:8-18
T. Promise of Resurrection.
  Psalm 16:1-11
W. Jesus Foretells His Resurrection.
  John 2:13-22
T. The Resurrection and the Life.
  John 11:17-27
F. Alive in Christ.
  Romans 6:1-11
S. The Resurrection Witnessed.
  1 Corinthians 15:1-8

TRUTH SEARCH:
Creatively Teaching the Word

Aim: Students will take their spiritual doubts to Jesus.

Items needed: A copy of a sensationalistic tabloid (such as *The National Enquirer*)

FOCUS

Read some of the far-fetched headlines from the tabloid. Ask your students why people buy such publications.

• *Do people really believe what these publications say? Why or why not?*

The purpose of sensationalistic newspapers is not to be as accurate as possible. Instead, their purpose is to make money. Their editors are good at mixing just enough fact with fantasy to sell their product.

If we had been on earth at the time of Christ's resurrection, I wonder if we would have believed a headline that read, "Man Seen Alive Days After His Death"?

EXPLORE

To set the scene for today's study, read Luke 24:1-12 to your students. **One thing was certain—Jesus' tomb was empty. But was He really alive?**

Have three students read verses 13-24 in the following manner: one reads the narrative lines, a second reads the words of Jesus, and a third reads the lines of Cleopas and his friend. Then discuss the following questions:

• *Why didn't Cleopas and his friend recognize Jesus?*
• *What was their state of mind?*
• *What had their hopes been concerning Jesus?*

• *What did they think about the reports of the empty tomb?*

Now have your readers continue reading their parts from verses 25-29.

• *What did Jesus mean by calling the two men "slow of heart" (v. 25)?*
• *Why should they have expected Jesus to rise from the dead (vv. 25, 26)?*
• *How did Jesus show His loving patience toward His unbelieving followers (v. 27)?*
• *Why do you suppose the men were so insistent on this Stranger staying with them (v. 29)?*

After choosing an additional person to read the words of the believers in Jerusalem (v. 34), have the volunteers to read their parts in verses 30-35.

• *What do you suppose caused the two believers to finally recognize Jesus?*
• *What impact had the Scriptures made on the men while Jesus was teaching them?*
• *Even though it was a seven-mile journey back to Jerusalem, what did Cleopas and his friend immediately do? Why?*
• *How did the disciples in Jerusalem respond to the two men's testimony?*

RESPOND

Jesus had told His disciples He would rise again, and the Old Testament declared it, but somehow His followers had not received the message.

All of us sometimes doubt the promises of God. If you are struggling with doubt today, I have a Scripture passage for you. Jesus may have quoted from

Isaiah 53 as He taught the disciples on the road to Emmaus. Let these verses build your faith in Him.

Read aloud Isaiah 53:3-5.

These verses promise spiritual, emotional and physical blessings because of the suffering and resurrection of Jesus. Let's allow Him to renew our faith in His promises.

Encourage the students to pray silently, asking God to strengthen their faith and meet their needs.

Peter's Pentecost Sermon

Study Text: Acts 2:14-41
Objective: To discover the heart of the gospel message and believe in the risen Christ as Savior and Lord.
Time: On the Day of Pentecost in A.D. 30.
Place: Jerusalem.
Golden Text: "Let all the house of Israel know assuredly, that God hath made that same Jesus, whom ye have crucified, both Lord and Christ" (Acts 2:36).
Central Truth: Christians have a glorious message of hope to proclaim to the world.
Evangelism Emphasis: Christians have a glorious message of hope to proclaim to the world.

PRINTED TEXT

Acts 2:14. But Peter, standing up with the eleven, lifted up his voice, and said unto them, Ye men of Judaea, and all ye that dwell at Jerusalem, be this known unto you, and hearken to my words:

15. For these are not drunken, as ye suppose, seeing it is but the third hour of the day.

16. But this is that which was spoken by the prophet Joel;

17. And it shall come to pass in the last days, saith God, I will pour out of my Spirit upon all flesh: and your sons and your daughters shall prophesy, and your young men shall see visions, and your old men shall dream dreams:

18. And on my servants and on my handmaidens I will pour out in those days of my Spirit; and they shall prophesy:

19. And I will shew wonders in heaven above, and signs in the earth beneath; blood, and fire, and vapour of smoke:

20. The sun shall be turned into darkness, and the moon into blood, before that great and notable day of the Lord come:

21. And it shall come to pass, that whosoever shall call on the name of the Lord shall be saved.

22. Ye men of Israel, hear these words; Jesus of Nazareth, a man approved of God among you by miracles and wonders and signs, which God did by him in the midst of you, as ye yourselves also know:

23. Him, being delivered by the determinate counsel and foreknowledge of God, ye have taken, and by wicked hands have crucified and slain:

24. Whom God hath raised up, having loosed the pains of death: because it was not possible that he should be holden of it.

37. Now when they heard this, they were pricked in their heart, and said unto Peter and to the rest of the apostles, Men and brethren, what shall we do?

38. Then Peter said unto them, Repent, and be baptized every one of you in the name of Jesus Christ for the remission of sins, and ye shall receive the gift of the Holy Ghost.

39. For the promise is unto you, and to your children, and to all that are afar off, even as many as the Lord our God shall call.

40. And with many other words did he testify and exhort, saying, Save yourselves from this untoward generation.

LESSON OUTLINE

I. THE SPIRIT HAS COME
  A. The Refutation
  B. The Explanation
  C. The Refuge
II. CHRIST IS RISEN
  A. His Life
  B. His Death
  C. His Resurrection
III. BELIEVE THE GOSPEL
  A. The Exaltation
  B. The Appeal
  C. The Response

LESSON EXPOSITION

INTRODUCTION

It has been said there are two kinds of preachers—men of thoughts and men of thought. The man of thoughts keeps all sorts of books of illustrations, drawers filled with clippings and envelopes stuffed with bright ideas; and when the time comes for the making of a sermon, he places the thoughts in a certain sequence, like so many beads on a string. He brings his beads before his congregation, counts them over, spends 30 minutes doing it, and the people go home thinking they have been listening to a sermon. However, strictly speaking, reciting a string of thoughts is not preaching. Preaching is the unfolding of truth.

One idea is sufficient to make a powerful sermon. A preacher who can take a great idea and unfold it until it glows and hangs glorious before the congregation, and so burns that hard hearts melt and consciences awake and begin to tremble, is a preacher indeed and actually performs the work of the Lord. But the preacher who fills up his or her time with secondhand anecdotes and stale stories never gets down to the place where the soul lives and does not know either the preacher's agony or his reward.

Acts 2 provides an excellent model of the preacher of thought. The preacher is the apostle Peter. Twenty-three verses are devoted to Peter's sermon. Eleven verses are precise Scripture quotations. Eleven others are explanation and exhortation. And one verse is half the words of Scripture and half the words of Peter. Check it out. Peter's sermon is exactly 50 percent quotation of the Word of God.

I. THE SPIRIT HAS COME
   (Acts 2:14-21)

A. The Refutation (vv. 14, 15)

14. But Peter, standing up with the eleven, lifted up his voice, and said unto them, Ye men of Judaea, and all ye that dwell at Jerusalem, be this known unto you, and hearken to my words:

15. For these are not drunken, as ye suppose, seeing it is but the third hour of the day.

One of the first effects of the coming of the Holy Spirit can be seen in the life of Peter. He immediately comes forward as the brave leader of the Christian church.

Some believe that the Feast of Pentecost was attended by more people than the Feast of Passover. On this particular occasion, when news spread of the strange behavior of Jesus' followers, a large crowd gathered near the Upper Room where the believers were worshiping. There were representatives of at least 16 different parts of the Roman Empire. Peter quickly seized the opportunity to preach Christ to the throng.

Because Peter had received the

Holy Spirit, he could break with the past and become a herald with the Resurrection message. He used a new method—"standing up with the eleven" (v. 14). This was not practiced by the rabbis. Before leaving them, Jesus had told the apostles they were not to be called rabbis (Matthew 23:8). Instead of being teachers in the traditional sense, they were to be heralds. Teachers sat; heralds stood.

William Ramsay characterized Peter's sermon as "the outline of an epoch-making address delivered on a memorable occasion"; "it stands in history as the first utterance of the new church, and as such is a document of the highest interest" (*The Church in the Roman Empire Before A.D. 170*).

Rudolf Stier, in his book *The Words of the Apostles*, writes: "It is very remarkable how the living, and, as it were, newly born words of the Spirit, forthwith link themselves to the ancient Scriptures. The old and the new Word form one great whole; and the letter of the Old Testament, both written in the Spirit, and prophesied by the Spirit, only awaited its being livingly brought forward and fulfilled in the New Testament."

The Jews could neither deny nor explain the things they saw and heard. Since it was a feast day, the Jews assumed the disciples had been drinking wine and that their strange behavior was due to drunkenness.

Peter disposed of the false accusation that the believers, who were heard speaking with tongues, were drunk. The fact that it was only 9 a.m. made these critics' explanation ridiculous, for wine was drunk by the Jews with meat only; and basing the custom on Exodus 16:8, they ate bread in the morning and meat in the evening, and so they took no wine until late in the day.

B. The Explanation (vv. 16-20)

16. But this is that which was spoken by the prophet Joel;

17. And it shall come to pass in the last days, saith God, I will pour out of my Spirit upon all flesh: and your sons and your daughters shall prophesy, and your young men shall see visions, and your old men shall dream dreams:

18. And on my servants and on my handmaidens I will pour out in those days of my Spirit; and they shall prophesy:

19. And I will shew wonders in heaven above, and signs in the earth beneath; blood, and fire, and vapour of smoke:

20. The sun shall be turned into darkness, and the moon into blood, before that great and notable day of the Lord come.

Joel indicated that the outpouring of the Holy Spirit was to be a last-day awakening (Joel 2:28-32). Peter quoted this passage as an explanation of the outpouring of the Spirit which began on the Day of Pentecost.

The prophet emphasized the supernatural element of this revival when he prophesied, "I will pour out my Spirit upon all flesh" (Acts 2:17). This was not to be an invasion of an army, nor was it to be the result of human planning and ingenuity. God would take the initiative—He would come to the people. His power would come upon humanity's weakness. Then, men and women, boys and girls can become an instrument for the fulfilling of the divine purpose.

Observe the prominent part played by youth in the spiritual awakening. Twice this is emphasized: "Your sons and your daughters shall prophesy . . . your young men shall see visions." Through the infilling of the Spirit, young men would discern what others do not see. They would proclaim God's message and God's will for the present day.

According to Joel, the Holy Spirit would be given without distinction to sex: "Your sons and your daughters . . . and also upon the servants and upon the handmaids" (Joel 2:28, 29). This prophecy was fulfilled in the Upper Room on the Day of Pentecost. Luke tells us that among those present when the Spirit fell were "the women, and Mary the mother of Jesus" (Acts 1:14). The Holy Spirit is the great equalizer.

Joel prophesied that the coming of the Holy Spirit would be universal—"upon all flesh." All nationalities and races are included. All levels of society are included—the rich and the poor, the sophisticated and the ignorant.

On the Day of Pentecost when the Holy Spirit came, there was a divergent group present. We have no record of either priest or scribe being present. Neither was the outpouring of the Spirit limited to the Twelve chosen by the Lord. For every apostle, there were nine other disciples. The Holy Spirit did not come just to the Twelve but to about 120.

Undoubtedly the coming of the baptism with the Holy Ghost in our day is the most significant development in Christianity. This spiritual awakening has invaded every continent and almost every church.

In verses 19 and 20, Peter quoted Joel's prophecy regarding wonders in the heavens and on the earth—blood, fire, and pillars of smoke. These wonders are linked with the end time and the return of Christ to the earth.

C. The Refuge (v. 21)

21. And it shall come to pass, that whosoever shall call on the name of the Lord shall be saved.

In the midst of His judgments, God always provides a means of escape. As the Spirit's work was for all, so the escape through His provision is for all. To call on the name of the Lord is to respond by obeying God's command or revealed will.

II. CHRIST IS RISEN
(Acts 2:22-31)

A. His Life (v. 22)

22. Ye men of Israel, hear these words; Jesus of Nazareth, a man approved of God among you by miracles and wonders and signs, which God did by him in the midst of you, as ye yourselves also know.

Peter was courteous in his reference to the "men of Israel." He declared that Jesus was certified by God and that He was commended to the people of Israel by His power. He summarized Christ's ministry by referring to miracles, wonders and signs performed in their midst.

B. His Death (v. 23)

23. Him, being delivered by the determinate counsel and foreknowledge of God, ye have taken, and by wicked hands have crucified and slain.

The One whom God had honored, delighted in, and accredited had been slain by the hands of the religious leaders. And Peter, speaking through the enablement of the Holy Spirit, fearlessly declared this fact.

C. His Resurrection (vv. 24-31)

(Acts 2:25-31 is not included in the printed text.)

24. Whom God hath raised up, having loosed the pains of death: because it was not possible that he should be holden of it.

Peter now preached about the final testimony to the deity of Christ—His resurrection. In verses 25-28, he referred to Psalm 16, in which David said, "You will not abandon me to the grave, nor will you let your Holy One see decay" (v. 10, *NIV*). Peter stressed the point that this psalm did not refer to David since David did experience death and corruption, as evidenced by the sight of David's tomb.

The preacher also called attention to the fact that David was not only a king but also a prophet with divine anointing who was given foresight of some future events. The promise of Christ as David's descendant is found in 2 Samuel 7:11-16 and in Psalm 89:3, 4, and gives assurance that the Messiah was to sit on David's throne. Here Peter claimed that Jesus, who was the descendant of David, was the One to whom Jehovah referred, and that He proved it by raising Jesus from the dead. David saw the resurrection of Jesus prophetically. Peter declared that the resurrected Christ was bringing about the manifestations of the Spirit that they could not explain.

III. BELIEVE THE GOSPEL
(Acts 2:32-41)

A. The Exaltation (vv. 32, 33)

(Acts 2:32, 33 is not included in the printed text.)

The fact that God raised Christ is proof that God was satisfied with Him. G. Campbell Morgan writes: "By the resurrection we know that whatever men may think of Jesus, God placed Him over all men from the standpoint of His life and character. He raised Him from the dead also as a testimony to the perfection of His mediation. Furthermore, if by this resurrection there has been revealed God's perfect man, by that self-same resurrection God has rejected all other men" (*The Spirit of God*).

Peter could speak as an eyewitness of the Resurrection, and the strength of his preaching gave a firm attestation of this central doctrine. Having shown the resurrection of Christ to be the subject of ancient prophecy, Peter now proved the same of His exaltation. J.A. Alexander observes: "The argument is rendered still more parallel and uniform by drawing the proof from the Old Testament (Psalm 110:1; Matthew 22:41-46). Here two signal Messianic prophecies were universally recognized and universally ascribed to David, neither of which could be applied to David as its subject, both of which must have respect to the Messiah, and both of which have been fulfilled in Jesus" (*The Acts of the Apostles Explained*).

The exalted Christ "has poured out what you now see and hear" (v. 33, *NIV*), Peter declared. The crowd had seen and heard the apostles speaking in strange languages, evidence of the Spirit's outpouring.

B. The Appeal (vv. 34-40)

(Acts 2:34-36 is not included in the printed text.)

37. Now when they heard this, they were pricked in their heart, and said unto Peter and to the rest of the apostles, Men and brethren, what shall we do?

38. Then Peter said unto them, Repent, and be baptized every one of you in the name of Jesus Christ for the remission of sins, and ye shall receive the gift of the Holy Ghost.

39. For the promise is unto you, and to your children, and to all that are afar off, even as many as the Lord our God shall call.

40. And with many other words did he testify and exhort, saying, Save yourselves from this untoward generation.

The conclusion of Peter's sermon is the inevitable termination of the argument he had been building. The Jews had crucified the Lord of glory as a blasphemer, a false Messiah. God had recognized Him as the true Messiah. It was time for the Jews to acknowledge their error, and to accept God's verdict and believe in Him. Those listening to Peter may have had no personal part in the crucifixion of Christ, but they had not protested against it, and they were part of the whole nation which had allowed it and urged it on.

As Peter preached, the Holy Spirit brought conviction on the hearers. "They were cut to the heart" (v. 37, *NIV*).

Some of the Jews present may have sneered at the claims of Jesus, or kept silent when His foes had abused Him. Others may have had a chance to influence the authorities in His favor but had been too cowardly to do it. All of them as Jews felt the shame for what their people had done and for fear of the consequences of falling into the hands of an angry God. By addressing the apostles as "brethren," they were in a way seeking admission to their fellowship as believers in Jesus. They admitted their guilt and wanted to know what they could do to escape the penalties.

The first step of every convicted sinner must be to turn from his sins and determine not to do them anymore. So Peter began—as John the Baptist began, as Christ himself began—with the exhortation to repentance, to a change of heart and life, not mere regret for the past (v. 38). There was to be an inward change and then submission to the external rite. Baptism is a sign and a symbol of the washing away of our sins. What clean water does with the stains we have accumulated on our hands and bodies, from contact with the physical world, the precious blood of Christ does with the stains from sin in our hearts.

Peter again reminded his audience of the promise of all that Joel foretold, the salvation that Christ came to bring to all people, including the gift of the Holy Spirit. It was for those to whom Peter was speaking, in spite of all their sins, and in spite of their share in the guilt of crucifying Christ. It was also for their children.

Peter was careful to include "all that are afar off" (v. 39), referring to the Gentiles. The Jews thought they were near to God, and the Gentiles far from Him. But Christ had charged the disciples to preach the gospel in all the world. Apparently Peter understood this although he did not always comply.

Peter pleaded, "Save yourselves from this untoward generation" (v. 40)—a generation with crooked ways that had turned and twisted from the straight and true way. Salvation from destruction could come only by accepting Christ as Savior.

C. The Response (v. 41)

(Acts 2:41 is not included in the printed text.)

Three thousand souls were born into the kingdom of God on this first day of the church's history. It could not have happened until the Holy Spirit came upon the apostles. It could not have happened had not the apostle Peter, filled with the Holy Spirit, led his unbelieving audience to behold the Lord Jesus Christ and to recognize Him as the predicted Savior in Scripture.

GOLDEN TEXT HOMILY

"LET ALL THE HOUSE OF ISRAEL KNOW ASSUREDLY, THAT GOD HATH MADE THAT SAME JESUS, WHOM YE HAVE CRUCIFIED, BOTH LORD AND CHRIST" (Acts 2:36).

Pentecost season is a time for the church to remember Peter's powerful statement. This is the proclamation for which the world had waited thousands of years. The creation had groaned in its anticipation. Peter declared that God had made Jesus both Lord and Christ.

"Let all [God's people] know assuredly" that Yahweh, the great God who spoke to Moses, who led His people for generations through times of great honor and through dark and difficult times, had now made His most notable statement to humanity. This magnificent declaration came through the Incarnation. Jesus was Emmanuel—God with us.

God's mark of completion for this action was seen in the outpouring of the Holy Spirit. From this time forward, God would be actively engaged with His people in a more personal and wonderful way than ever before. This was dynamic proof that Jesus had ascended to heaven and was now seated at the Father's right hand.

Through the gift of the Spirit, the hearts of all people would be wooed toward God. Through conviction and encouragement, the Spirit would lead people to confession, repentance and into a right relationship with God—through this same Jesus, whom God has made both Lord and Christ!—**John E. Renfro**

SENTENCE SERMONS

CHRISTIANS HAVE a glorious message of hope to proclaim to the world.

—Selected

THE WORLD HOPES for the best, but Jesus Christ offers the best hope.

—John Wesley White

THE WORD *HOPE* I take for *faith*; and indeed hope is nothing else but the constancy of faith.

—John Calvin

EVANGELISM APPLICATION

CHRISTIANS HAVE A GLORIOUS MESSAGE OF HOPE TO PROCLAIM TO THE WORLD.

Let us preach positive truth—not doubt, but faith. Not condemnation, but victory. Not sin, but salvation. It may come as somewhat of a surprise to you to realize that the apostles did not preach about sin. They preached salvation, victory and a living Christ. Their preaching brought conviction. The people turned from their sin and were delivered from it. But their message was one of hope and faith in the saving grace of the risen Lord, who alone could give power to live without sin.—**Guy P. Duffield Jr.**, *Pentecostal Preaching*

ILLUMINATING THE LESSON

Someone has pointed out the fact that for 1,700 years after the birth of Christ, God got along without the Sunday school, and that He managed 1,850 years without a single Boy Scout. Yet He has never endeavored to get along without preaching. Even a brief study of His dealings down through the years is sufficient to show that when He wished to deliver a message and stir a people, He raised up a human voice to cry forth His word. God's word to Jonah concerning the city of Nineveh is typical: "Preach unto it the preaching that I bid thee" (3:2).—**Guy P. Duffield Jr.,** *Pentecostal Preaching*

DAILY BIBLE READINGS

M. Outpouring of the Spirit.
   Isaiah 44:1-8
T. A New Spirit Within.
   Ezekiel 11:13-20
W. Promise of the Spirit.
   Joel 2:21-32
T. Rivers of Living Water.
   John 7:32-39
F. Made Alive by the Spirit.
   Romans 8:1-11
S. Call Upon the Lord.
   Romans 10:8-17

TRUTH SEARCH:
Creatively Teaching the Word

Aim: Pray for the preaching and teaching ministries of the local church.

Items needed: Marker board, marker, paper, pencils

FOCUS

Before class, write this question on the board: *What is the greatest sermon you have ever heard a preacher deliver?* Encourage the students to think about that question. Then discuss their answers.

• *What made the message outstanding?*

• *How did the message impact your life?*

In today's lesson we're going to explore one of the most powerful messages ever preached.

EXPLORE

Divide the class into groups of three or four students each. Assign each group one of the Scripture passages and set of questions listed below.

Acts 2:1-13

1. *What outward signs signaled the coming of the Holy Spirit (vv. 1-4)?*

2. *As the believers spoke in different languages, what were they saying (vv. 6-11)?*

3. *What wrong idea did some people have about the believers' actions (v. 13)?*

4. *Why do you suppose God chose to send the Holy Spirit on the Day of Pentecost?*

Acts 2:14-35

1. *What was the source of Peter's newfound boldness?*

2. *How did Peter counter the idea that Christ's followers were drunk (vv. 14-18)?*

3. *In what sense was God responsible for Jesus' fate (vv. 22-24)?*

4. *What did David prophesy concerning Jesus (vv. 25-28)?*

5. *In what ways was Jesus superior to King David (vv. 29-34)?*

Acts 2:36-41

1. *What accusation did Peter make in verse 36?*

2. *What was the crowd's initial response to Peter's charge (v. 37)?*

3. *What did Peter urge them to do, and what promises did he offer them (vv. 38-40)?*

4. *Why was there such an incredible response to Peter's message (v. 41)?*

Discuss the students' findings. Now write the following equation on the board:

Spirit-filled preacher + Scripture-filled message = supernatural results.

RESPOND

If we want to see God move in our church, we must have Spirit-filled preachers and teachers who deliver Scripture-filled messages. To help make this happen, God is looking for church members who will pray for God to anoint our spiritual leaders.

Erase the marker board. Then make a list of the people who preach and teach in your church, starting with the pastor. Next, lead a time of intense prayer on behalf of these men and women.

Finally, urge class members to commit to regularly pray for the pastor and church teachers.

Stephen Defends the Gospel

Study Text: Acts 6:1-15; 7:1-60
Objective: To understand that the gospel message will be opposed and determine to proclaim it without fear.
Time: The martyrdom of Stephen took place around A.D. 50.
Place: Jerusalem
Golden Text: "The Holy Ghost shall teach you in the same hour what ye ought to say" (Luke 12:12).
Central Truth: Christians must present the gospel in spite of opposition.
Evangelism Emphasis: Christians must present the gospel in spite of opposition.

PRINTED TEXT

Acts 6:7. And the word of God increased; and the number of the disciples multiplied in Jerusalem greatly; and a great company of the priests were obedient to the faith.

8. And Stephen, full of faith and power, did great wonders and miracles among the people.

9. Then there arose certain of the synagogue, which is called the synagogue of the Libertines, and Cyrenians, and Alexandrians, and of them of Cilicia and of Asia, disputing with Stephen.

12. And they stirred up the people, and the elders, and the scribes, and came upon him, and caught him, and brought him to the council,

13. And set up false witnesses, which said, This man ceaseth not to speak blasphemous words against this holy place, and the law.

15. And all that sat in the council, looking stedfastly on him, saw his face as it had been the face of an angel.

7:51. Ye stiffnecked and uncircumcised in heart and ears, ye do always resist the Holy Ghost: as your fathers did, so do ye.

52. Which of the prophets have not your fathers persecuted? and they have slain them which shewed before of the coming of the Just One; of whom ye have been now the betrayers and murderers:

53. Who have received the law by the disposition of angels, and have not kept it.

54. When they heard these things, they were cut to the heart, and they gnashed on him with their teeth.

55. But he, being full of the Holy Ghost, looked up stedfastly into heaven, and saw the glory of God, and Jesus standing on the right hand of God.

56. And said, Behold, I see the heavens opened, and the Son of man standing on the right hand of God.

57. Then they cried out with a loud voice, and stopped their ears, and ran upon him with one accord.

59. And they stoned Stephen, calling upon God, and saying, Lord Jesus, receive my spirit.

60. And he kneeled down, and cried with a loud voice, Lord, lay not this sin to their charge. And when he had said this, he fell asleep.

LESSON OUTLINE

I. OPPOSITION TO THE MESSAGE
   A. The Success
   B. The Accusation
   C. The Appearance
II. FAITHFULNESS TO THE MESSAGE
   A. The Defense
   B. The Application
III. MARTYRED FOR THE MESSAGE
   A. The Madness
   B. The Manliness
   C. The Murder

LESSON EXPOSITION

INTRODUCTION

Luke, the author of the Book of Acts, did not hesitate to record everything pertinent, whether good or bad, concerning people and institutions. In dealing with the first dissension in the church, there is no attempt to hide any weaknesses, but there is an attempt to provide detailed information as to how the crisis was met and the difficulties overcome.

After being released from prison, the apostles continued to experience much success in preaching the gospel (see Acts 5:12–42). Many were added to the body, and a problem arose due in part to the rapid growth. In Acts 6 a complaint was lodged by the Grecians, or Hellenists, against the Hebrews. The Hellenists were the Jewish members of the church who spoke the Greek language. The Hebrews were the Palestinian Jews who spoke the Aramaic language. The widows who spoke Greek thought they were not receiving their share of the money and food being distributed by the church, so they complained to the apostles.

Facing an emergency, the apostles did a wise thing and called a church council meeting to deal with the situation. They identified the problem and asked that they be given more time to focus their attention on prayer, preaching and teaching. They proposed that seven men be selected to deal with the distribution fund. These men were to be of good reputation, full of the Spirit and of wisdom.

The qualifications they suggested are still necessary when filling any church office—a good reputation, practical wisdom, and a life yielded to the Spirit.

The church accepted the proposal and proceeded to choose seven men—seven perhaps because that number represented completeness to a Jew, or perhaps because the church in Jerusalem at that time was divided into seven congregations.

The apostles showed their approval of the seven by praying and laying hands on them. The laying on of hands by the apostles symbolized the passage of authority and power from one to the other.

All of the men chosen had Greek names. This showed the conciliatory spirit of the church and evident willingness of the Palestinian Jews to avert further trouble. Stephen was one of the men chosen.

I. OPPOSITION TO THE MESSAGE (Acts 6:7-15)

A. The Success (vv. 7, 8)

**7. And the word of God increased; and the number of the disciples multiplied in Jerusalem greatly; and a great company of the priests were obedient to the faith.
8. And Stephen, full of faith and power, did great wonders and miracles among the people.**

Following the action of the apostles and the council, the church in Jerusalem prospered greatly. The apostles were free to do more intensive preaching and teaching, and the church kept growing. Luke was careful to mention that many of the priests entered the ranks of the followers of Christ. For these men to become Christians meant profound conviction and involved real sacrifice. They must have lost their positions and their livelihood. In many cases they lost their friends and became surrounded by bitter foes who persecuted them.

The tremendous growth experienced by the Jerusalem church was primarily because of the presence of the Holy Spirit and the obedience of the early Christians to Christ. This was manifested in their lives through Christian brotherhood, in their fervent zeal for Christ, and in their courageous testimonies. Such conditions will bring about growth in any church and in any Christian congregation.

The name *Stephen* comes from the Greek word *stephanos*, meaning "a crown." In the Greek culture it was the wreath given as a prize for victory, as a festal ornament, or as a public honor for distinguished service or personal worth.

Such a name was appropriate for Stephen, who distinguished himself as a man of high spiritual acclaim and later would wear the honored crown of a martyr.

Luke states that Stephen was "full of faith and power" (v. 8). "He was a released man," writes Lloyd Ogilvie. "Defensiveness, self-justification, and competitiveness were gone. Graciousness became the discernible trait of his personality. He had the disposition of Christ. Faith had gotten him started, grace had kept him growing, and power

was the result" (*Drumbeat of Love*).

Stephen wrought miracles and signs among the people. The wonders were signs; that is, they were proofs and tokens of the reality of his testimony, that Jesus was the Son of God; for the miracles were worked in the name of Christ and with the power which Christ conferred through the Holy Spirit. Stephen was in no degree inferior to an apostle in his spiritual ability and achievement.

B. The Accusation (vv. 9-14)

(Acts 6:10, 11, 14 is not included in the printed text.)

9. Then there arose certain of the synagogue, which is called the synagogue of the Libertines, and Cyrenians, and Alexandrians, and of them of Cilicia and of Asia, disputing with Stephen.

12. And they stirred up the people, and the elders, and the scribes, and came upon him, and caught him, and brought him to the council,

13. And set up false witnesses, which said, This man ceaseth not to speak blasphemous words against this holy place, and the law.

Stephen's opponents were all from outside of Jerusalem, as was Stephen, yet they argued with him. The word *disputing* (v. 9) implies public discussions of an earnest sort, begun usually in a spirit of finding fault. It is somewhat like the heckling of a modern political gathering. But they were not able to resist the wisdom and spirit by which he spoke.

This was in accordance with Christ's promise, which modern Christians do not often claim: "I will give you a mouth and wisdom, which all your adversaries shall not be able to gainsay nor resist" (Luke 21:15).

In commenting on this verse, Paul E. Adolph observes: "We may well conclude that the appointment of the irresistible Spirit-filled Stephen to this ministry of serving tables had brought the inevitable clash between Christians and non-Christians out into the open at just such a point as to spark Christianity into world advance in a manner that the apostles could never have otherwise anticipated. It was the work of the Holy Spirit."

Unable to cope with Stephen in direct confrontation, Stephen's opponents resorted to subterfuge. They enticed some men to say Stephen was speaking blasphemous words against Moses and against God.

The elders (or heads of clans) and the scribes (men versed in the sacred Law) had already become outraged against the apostles because of their influence with the people. Now they were hearing the lie that Stephen had shown disrespect to their Law and glorious Temple in which they took so much pride. The Temple was the center and symbol of their race and nation.

Previously, the religious leaders had dared not use violence on the Christians for fear of the crowds (Acts 5:26). Now because of the rumors, no one protested when they caught Stephen and brought him before the council. Shouting and gloating, the officials shoved innocent Stephen before the revenge-hungry Sanhedrin, who had been waiting for just such a moment (6:12).

The Sanhedrin had been shamed by the reports of the risen Christ. They had also recently been embarrassed twice by Peter and the other apostles. Now they eyed Stephen with disdain. They decided to develop a trumped-up case against him. They wanted their judgment to be swift. The Jews from the synagogue provided their case.

False witnesses were brought in who charged Stephen with speaking against the Temple and the Law. They also claimed Stephen said Jesus would destroy the Temple and alter their customs. Of course all of this was distortion pure and simple.

C. The Appearance (v. 15)

15. And all that sat in the council, looking stedfastly on him, saw his face as it had been the face of an angel.

As the council and the others present observed Stephen, they saw no clinched fists, no tightened lips, no grim stare. As he stood there facing death, God's undeniable peace shined from his face. It was inward illumination of the Holy Spirit as Moses had after he had communed with God. The Holy Spirit enabled Stephen to boldly stand up for Christ.

II. FAITHFULNESS TO THE MESSAGE (Acts 7:44-53)

A. The Defense (vv. 44-50)

(Acts 7:44-50 is not included in the printed text.)

Bible scholars agree that Stephen's defense is one of the most remarkable addresses in the Bible. Luke probably got his material from Paul, on whom it made a deep impression, and who gave it to Luke as he remembered it. Paul was so impressed with the speech that years later he used its method as the plan for his sermon at

Antioch of Pisida (Acts 13:16-41). At Athens he referred to the scripture that Stephen quoted with the same application (compare 17:24 with 7:48-50). In Paul's letters are echoes of Stephen's address (compare Romans 2:29 with Acts 7:51; Galatians 3:19 with Acts 7:53; 2 Timothy 4:16 with Acts 7:60).

Stephen refuted the charge that he had slighted the law of Moses. He expressed his patriotism by emphasizing God's care for the Jews. The speech saw in all Jewish history a mirror of Christ. Joseph, ill-treated by his brothers, became their savior. Moses, scorned by his own people, became their deliverer from bondage. The same Moses, after he had led the Exodus, was mocked and disobeyed by his people, who made the golden calf and would even return into slavery.

B. The Application (vv. 51-53)

51. Ye stiffnecked and uncircumcised in heart and ears, ye do always resist the Holy Ghost: as your fathers did, so do ye.
52. Which of the prophets have not your fathers persecuted? and they have slain them which shewed before of the coming of the Just One; of whom ye have been now the betrayers and murderers:
53. Who have received the law by the disposition of angels, and have not kept it.

The word *stiffnecked* is found only here in the New Testament. Moses had used it in referring to the Hebrews' forefathers. It means "obstinately disobedient to God," "unwilling to bend to His will and purpose."

The Greek word for *uncircumcised* is also found only here in the New Testament. The Jews had

boasted of their circumcision, which indeed was the sign and seal of their covenant with God (v. 8), and despised the uncircumcised Gentiles. Stephen told them that, in God's sight, they were themselves aliens to the covenant in heart and obedient understanding. Inward disposition, not an external observance of outward rites, was the vital thing.

The verb *resist* (v. 51) means "to fling oneself in opposition" against the Holy Ghost. This is an incidental proof of the divinity and personality of the Holy Spirit.

It seems evident from the sudden change in Stephen's tone that his words had cut his hearers to the quick. They were provoked by his truthful indictment of their national sins and by his fearless criticism of their most cherished opinions. He saw the storm rising and faced it with dauntless courage.

In dealing with verse 52, F.F. Bruce writes: "It was the regular lot of true prophets of God in Old Testament times to suffer persecution and sometimes death itself for their faithfulness to the divine commission. There is ample evidence of this in the canonical Old Testament books, and Jewish tradition elaborated the theme, describing, for example, the martyrdom of Isaiah by sawing asunder in the reign of Manasseh and of Jeremiah by stoning at the hands of the people who had forced him to go down to Egypt with them. But much of that opposition to the prophets was due to their attack on Israel's perverted notions of the true worship of God—an attack of which the prophetic passages quoted by Stephen are samples. Stephen placed himself in the prophetic succession by attacking the people at this very point; it is therefore especially relevant that Israel's traditional hostility to the prophets should be mentioned here.

"But did not the Jews of later days reprobate their ancestors' behavior toward the prophets? Yes indeed; 'If we had been in the days of our fathers,' they said, 'we would not have been partakers with them in the blood of the prophets' (Matthew 23:30). They paid tribute to the prophets' memory and built monuments in their honor. But Jesus assured them that even so they were still true sons of their fathers, maintaining the same hostility to the messengers of God (Matthew 23:29-37); and Stephen now repeats the charge. Their fathers had killed the messengers in days gone by who foretold the advent of the Righteous One; they themselves had gone still farther and handed over the Righteous One himself to violent death" (*Commentary on the Book of Acts*).

As the people's fathers had broken the Law by their stubborn disobedience, so also they themselves had broken it by their unspirituality and by their murder of the Righteous One to whom it testified.

Thus Stephen turned the tables on those who had accused him of disregarding and dishonoring the law of Moses.

III. MARTYRED FOR THE MESSAGE (Acts 7:54-60)

A. The Madness (v. 54)

54. When they heard these things, they were cut to the heart, and they gnashed on him with their teeth.

The council and the others in the audience would not permit Stephen to finish his message. They were maddened into a frenzy by his bold charges, and would hear no more. Luke says "they were cut to the heart." The same thing is said of the Sanhedrin after they had heard the statement of Peter and the other apostles in Acts 5:33. It means the cutting of sawteeth; it describes profound anger and fierce indignation. When Luke says "they gnashed on him with their teeth," he means they were like wild beasts, and wanted to tear Stephen limb from limb.

B. The Manliness (vv. 55, 56)

55. But he, being full of the Holy Ghost, looked up stedfastly into heaven, and saw the glory of God, and Jesus standing on the right hand of God.

56. And said, Behold, I see the heavens opened, and the Son of man standing on the right hand of God.

The Holy Spirit enabled Stephen to bear the persecution with great fortitude. While his foes were glaring at him like wild beasts, he looked upward. His gaze was calm and steady, theirs wild and distracted.

Stephen saw the glory of God and Jesus at the Father's right hand. French Arrington writes, "Jesus was standing, not sitting. Since standing is the proper position of a witness, likely his position stresses that the Son of Man was confessing Stephen before the heavenly Father" (*The Acts of the Apostles*).

The title "Son of Man" (v. 56) here given by Stephen to the Lord Jesus was the one which, in the Gospels, Jesus used in referring to Himself almost exclusively. It never appears again in the Book of Acts nor in any of the New Testament Epistles.

C. The Murder (vv. 57-60)

(Acts 7:58 is not included in the printed text.)

57. Then they cried out with a loud voice, and stopped their ears, and ran upon him with one accord.

59. And they stoned Stephen, calling upon God, and saying, Lord Jesus, receive my spirit.

60. And he kneeled down, and cried with a loud voice, Lord, lay not this sin to their charge. And when he had said this, he fell asleep.

Stephen's foes made a big noise and plugged up their ears with their fingers to avoid hearing what he said. Stephen had just charged them with being "uncircumcised in heart and ears" (v. 51). They verified his charge quickly, not waiting for the legal voice of condemnation. They ran upon him; it was a lynching. They cast him out of the city (v. 58) because there was a law against stoning a man to death inside the city limits. After laying their clothes at the feet of a young man named Saul (Paul), they began to stone Stephen. Stephen entrusted himself to his Advocate, asking Jesus to receive his spirit in heaven.

Standing was the customary Jewish attitude in prayer, but Stephen knelt down. He followed his Lord's example; he cried with a loud voice so all might hear him above the noise (v. 60). He echoed Christ's words on the cross, "Father, forgive them; for they know not what they do" (Luke 23:34). In this violent situation, with these cruel and angry men stoning him to death, Stephen "fell asleep" like a little child in its mother's arms.

SENTENCE SERMONS

CHRISTIANS must present the gospel in spite of opposition.

—Selected

WHAT THE WORLD REQUIRES of Christians is that they continue to be Christians.

—Albert Camus

TO BE GLAD INSTRUMENTS of God's love in this imperfect world is the service to which man is called.

—Albert Schweitzer

EVANGELISM APPLICATION

CHRISTIANS MUST PRESENT THE GOSPEL IN SPITE OF OPPOSITION.

The Book of Acts is an unfinished book. In this day and age there may be some Christians who will be called, like Stephen, to lay down their lives for Jesus' sake. The opposition is sharpening and the hostility is emerging, more vicious, more furious, more enraged on every side. We may face in our own day a tremendous outpouring of the hostility of depraved hearts against the message of Jesus Christ and a persecution of its bearers. May God grant that, like Stephen, we will be faithful unto death.**—Ray C. Stedman,** *Birth of the Body*

ILLUMINATING THE LESSON

It is not for us to seek the prominent or conspicuous ministry, but simply to fill the niche prepared for us by the Holy Spirit. This has been expressed well in a poem by an unknown author:

"Father, where shall I work
     today?"
And my love flowed warm and
     free.
Then He pointed me toward a
     tiny spot
And said, "Tend that for Me."
I answered quickly, "Oh, no,
     not that!
Why, no one would ever see,
No matter how well my work was
     done,
In that little place for me."
And the word He spoke, it was
     not stern,
He answered me tenderly:
"Ah, little one, search that heart
     of thine,

Art thou working for them or Me?
Nazareth was a little place,
And so was Galilee."

DAILY BIBLE READINGS

M. Courageous Attitude.
     1 Samuel 17:20-29
T.   Courageous Action.
     1 Samuel 17:40-50
W. Courageous Confrontation.
     1 Kings 18:30-39
T.   Bold Defense.
     Acts 4:13-21
F.   Defend the Faith.
     Acts 26:19-28
S.   Keep the Faith.
     Jude 17-25

TRUTH SEARCH:
Creatively Teaching the Word

Aim: Worship Jesus for being counted worthy to suffer on His behalf.

Items needed: None

FOCUS

Persecution of Christians is alive and well in the 21st century. What is the price some believers pay today for taking a bold stand for Christ? Loss of job or educational opportunities . . . loss of home . . . slavery . . . torture . . . death.

In the Western world, persecution is usually subtler. Nonetheless, it is real.

Discuss the following question:

• *What type of opposition to Christianity have you personally experienced or witnessed?*

There will always be a price to pay for boldly standing up for God.

EXPLORE

Have a volunteer read Acts 6:7-15. Then discuss the following questions:

• *What was the state of the church in Jerusalem at this time (v. 7)?*

• *Stephen was one of the first seven deacons. What made him stand out (v. 8)?*

• *What happened when people tried to come against Stephen's message (vv. 9, 10)?*

• *What lies were told on Stephen (vv. 11-14)?*

• *What is the significance of the fact that Stephen's "face was like the face of an angel" (v. 15, NIV)?*

In Acts 7:51 the high priest asked Stephen if his accusers were telling the truth. But Stephen didn't try to defend himself. Instead, he reminded his hearers of God's covenant with Israel, and Israel's rebellion against God.

• *After mentioning Solomon's building of the Temple, what point did Stephen make (vv. 48-50)? Why would this have upset the religious leaders?*

• *Through their history, how had the people responded to the Holy Spirit? To the prophets? The law of God? The Son of God (vv. 51-53)?*

• *Compare the demeanor of Stephen with the demeanor of the Sanhedrin (vv. 54, 55).*

• *What was the "last straw" that caused the religious leaders to attack Stephen (vv. 56-58)?*

• *What does Stephen's final prayer (v. 60) say about his heart?*

Stephen was martyred because people were offended by his faith in Jesus Christ. That is still the source of persecution today—the believer's unyielding faith in the person and teachings of Jesus.

RESPONSE

Jesus said, "Blessed are you when people insult you, persecute you and falsely say all kinds of evil against you because of me. Rejoice and be glad, because great is your reward in heaven" (Matthew 5:11, 12, NIV).

Ask everyone who has ever been mistreated in any way because of their faith in Christ to please stand.

Now that we're standing, I want us to rejoice because we've been counted worthy to suffer because of our friendship with Christ. Let's praise the Lord together that we are known as His children.

Lead the class in vocally expressing praise to Christ.

Paul Presents Salvation's History

Study Text: Acts 13:14-49
Objective: To identify the gospel throughout history and embrace its eternal truth.
Time: The Jewish synagogue in Pisidian Antioch.
Place: In the A.D. 50s.
Golden Text: "Children of the stock of Abraham, and whosoever among you feareth God, to you is the word of this salvation sent" (Acts 13:26).
Central Truth: For all time, God's plan of salvation is for all people.
Evangelism Emphasis: For all time, God's plan of salvation is for all people.

PRINTED TEXT

Acts 13:16. Then Paul stood up, and beckoning with his hand said, Men of Israel, and ye that fear God, give audience.

17. The God of this people of Israel chose our fathers, and exalted the people when they dwelt as strangers in the land of Egypt, and with an high arm brought he them out of it.

20. And after that he gave unto them judges about the space of four hundred and fifty years, until Samuel the prophet.

21. And afterward they desired a king: and God gave unto them Saul the son of Cis, a man of the tribe of Benjamin, by the space of forty years.

22. And when he had removed him, he raised up unto them David to be their king; to whom also he gave testimony, and said, I have found David the son of Jesse, a man after mine own heart, which shall fulfil all my will.

23. Of this man's seed hath God according to his promise raised unto Israel a Saviour, Jesus.

29. And when they had fulfilled all that was written of him, they took him down from the tree, and laid him in a sepulchre.

30. But God raised him from the dead:

31. And he was seen many days of them which came up with him from Galilee to Jerusalem, who are his witnesses unto the people.

32. And we declare unto you glad tidings, how that promise which was made unto the fathers,

33. God hath fulfilled the same unto us their children, in that he hath raised up Jesus again; as it is also written in the second psalm, Thou art my Son, this day have I begotten thee.

46. Then Paul and Barnabas waxed bold, and said, It was necessary that the word of God should first have been spoken to you: but seeing ye put it from you, and judge yourselves unworthy of everlasting life, lo, we turn to the Gentiles.

47. For so hath the Lord commanded us, saying, I have set thee to be a light of the Gentiles, that thou shouldest be for salvation unto the ends of the earth.

48. And when the Gentiles heard this, they were glad, and glorified the word of the Lord: and as many as were ordained to eternal life believed.

LESSON OUTLINE

I. ROOTED IN ISRAEL'S HISTORY
   A. The Synagogue Meeting
   B. The Basis of Christian Preaching

II. FULFILLED IN JESUS
   A. An Offer
   B. A Warning

III. SENT TO THE GENTILES
   A. The Sin of Jealousy
   B. Turning to the Gentiles

LESSON EXPOSITION

INTRODUCTION

There has never been a period in the world's history when there were so many churches and preachers. Thousands of sermons are preached throughout the world every Lord's Day, and yet there is such a lack of the unadulterated Word of God. In many churches people are being fed pastry instead of bread. For God's church to recover the flush of health known in the early church, the Word of God must be faithfully proclaimed.

If a man or woman will determine that by the grace of God he or she will proclaim the pure Word of God, that preacher will enlarge, not narrow, the scope and power of his or her ministry. The preacher who obeys this call is a preacher unshackled. All of God's power is behind such a preacher.

There is a great need for orthodoxy in our pulpits, but we need orthodoxy plus spiritual power. We need orthodoxy on fire, not on ice. We need hot houses, not ice houses. The letter kills, but the Spirit gives life. We need the truth proclaimed, energized by the irresistible power of the Holy Spirit.

It would be wonderful if all our preachers could say to their people, as Paul said to the Corinthians, "And my speech and my preaching was not with enticing words of man's wisdom, but in demonstration of the Spirit and of power" (1 Corinthians 2:4). The "demonstration" Paul referred to was not the sensationalism that turns some preachers into entertainers. Sensationalism has proved to be a poor substitute for the gospel. When the pulpit becomes a rival of the stage, it will find the experiment disastrous.

Preaching that gets the job done is the kind that Paul did in Pisidian Antioch. When he had finished, his hearers "besought that these [same] words might be preached to them the next sabbath" (Acts 13:42).

I. ROOTED IN ISRAEL'S HISTORY (Acts 13:14-25)

A. The Synagogue Meeting (vv. 14, 15)

(Acts 13:14, 15 is not included in the printed text.)

Pisidian Antioch was a large and important Roman city, situated on the great highway running east and west across Asia Minor. This highway extended from Ephesus to Antioch, the capital of Syria. Many Jews lived there because Antiochus the Great transplanted about 2,000 Jewish families in order to bind together Phrygia and Syria.

The synagogue which Paul and Barnabas attended was probably arranged like all other synagogues, with an "ark" at one end containing the rolls of the Law, with a veil and lamps before it. At the same end sat the rulers of the synagogue, who were responsible for arranging the services. First, the Shema was recited: "Hear, O Israel: The Lord our God is one Lord" (Deuteronomy 6:4). Then came a prayer service.

This was followed by the reading of the day's portion from the Law (the first five books of Moses, which were divided up in a three-year course) and also from the Prophets. Finally someone selected by the synagogue rulers gave a talk on the Scripture passage, which might be followed by a discussion. The synagogue had no regular minister or preacher.

After the reading of the Scriptures, the rulers of the synagogue sent a message to the two strangers who had come to their city and synagogue, inviting them to speak a word of exhortation to the gathering.

B. The Basis of Christian Preaching (vv. 16-25)

(Acts 13:18, 19, 24, 25 is not included in the printed text.)

16. Then Paul stood up, and beckoning with his hand said, Men of Israel, and ye that fear God, give audience.

17. The God of this people of Israel chose our fathers, and exalted the people when they dwelt as strangers in the land of Egypt, and with an high arm brought he them out of it.

20. And after that he gave unto them judges about the space of four hundred and fifty years, until Samuel the prophet.

21. And afterward they desired a king: and God gave unto them Saul the son of Cis, a man of the tribe of Benjamin, by the space of forty years.

22. And when he had removed him, he raised up unto them David to be their king; to whom also he gave testimony, and said, I have found David the son of Jesse, a man after mine own heart, which shall fulfil all my will.

23. Of this man's seed hath God according to his promise raised unto Israel a Saviour, Jesus.

Paul accepted the invitation to address the group promptly. Using appropriate gestures, he invited their attention and began his sermon. According to verse 16, the audience consisted of "men of Israel" (Jews by birth or by proselytization) and Gentile God-fearers ("ye that fear God").

Paul's exhortation took the form of a historical retrospect, as Stephen's defense did. He outlined the course of God's dealings with His people Israel, beginning with His choice of their fathers and deliverance of the people in the Exodus.

F.F. Bruce writes: "In the earliest days of the settlement in Canaan the Israelite worshiper acknowledged that God had chosen the patriarchs, that He had redeemed their descendants, the children of Israel, for Himself in the events of the Exodus, and that He had given them the land of Canaan as their inheritance. To these acts of God, Israelites of later days added His choice of David to be their king" (*The Book of Acts*).

In verse 18 Paul reminded them how God put up with their bad manners in the wilderness for 40 years. They grumbled repeatedly. They were disobedient many times. Even though God chastened them and sent messages to correct them, He put up with their many mistakes.

In dealing with verse 19, Manford George Gutzke writes: "As Paul approached the Jews and as he talked to them in the synagogue in Antioch in Pisidia, he knew, as Jews, they accepted the Old Testament Scriptures. That meant that Paul would preach here as he would not preach in many other places. The Jews believed that God had actually given a covenant to them, and that in terms of that covenant, God would bless them. So Paul reminded them how God took them from the land of Egypt in order to bring them into the land of Canaan" (*Plain Talk on Acts*).

In verse 20, Paul commented on 450 years of history in one sentence. In that 450 years, which we call the period of the judges, the children of Israel were blessed by the ministry and service of each individual judge. In verse 19 He gave them the land; in verse 20 He gave them judges.

The period of the judges, terminating with Samuel the prophet, was followed by the reign of Saul. But King Saul was not the man after God's heart, so his dynasty did not last; he was removed from his kingship and replaced by another.

The replacement for Saul was David. God confirmed His promise of abiding sovereignty because David was "a man after mine own heart" (v. 22).

The words of Psalm 89 record the promises made by God to David. They were written in a day when disaster had overtaken David's house, and the psalmist was bewildered by the contrast between the divine promises and the awful situation that he saw—the crown of David profaned and cast to the ground. The Lord promised, "Thy seed will I establish for ever, and build up thy throne to all generations" (v. 4).

God promised David that from his seed there would be One sitting upon his throne forever and ever. That One would be the eternal Savior. Paul identified the Savior as Jesus, of the seed of David.

In Acts 13:24, 25, Paul declared

that John's baptism of repentance paved the way for the appearance of Jesus. As John himself made clear, he was the Messiah's forerunner. So far did John think himself beneath the Coming One, whose way he was preparing, that he declared himself unfit to untie the laces of His sandals.

II. FULFILLED IN JESUS
   (Acts 13:26-41)

A. An Offer (vv. 26-39)

(Acts 13:26-28, 34-39 is not included in the printed text.)

29. And when they had fulfilled all that was written of him, they took him down from the tree, and laid him in a sepulchre.

30. But God raised him from the dead:

31. And he was seen many days of them which came up with him from Galilee to Jerusalem, who are his witnesses unto the people.

32. And we declare unto you glad tidings, how that promise which was made unto the fathers,

33. God hath fulfilled the same unto us their children, in that he hath raised up Jesus again; as it is also written in the second psalm, Thou art my Son, this day have I begotten thee.

Having established the fact that the Jewish people accepted John the Baptist as a prophet, in verses 26-28 Paul made his next point. He said that the rulers of the Jews, because they did not know Jesus, "nor yet the voices of the prophets which are read every sabbath" (v. 27), fulfilled those very prophecies by condemning Christ to death, though "they found no cause of death in him" (v. 28).

The children of Israel condemned the Messiah even though God had given them the land of

Canaan, then the judges to rule over them, then their first king, Saul. Afterward He gave them another king, David; and then in keeping with His promise, He had given them the Son of David, but they crucified Him. By describing the cross as "the tree" (v. 29), Paul made a connection with Deuteronomy 21:23.

When all was over, and the prophecies of Christ's passion had been fulfilled, His body was taken down and buried. "But God raised him from the dead" (Acts 13:30).

Unless we see the death of Jesus Christ through the Resurrection, we will only know defeat. If we simply observe Him dying, there is nothing for us. But He did not stay dead. He arose from the grave. His resurrection assures us that death has been conquered.

Whatever the doubters and skeptics may say, the apostles and the early church taught and believed that Christ arose from the dead. Without the Resurrection, one cannot explain the existence of the church at all. The church would not have lasted one week if the truth of the Resurrection had not revitalized the disciples. Immediately after the experience of Calvary they were about to separate; their fellowship was disintegrating. The birth and growth of the church is one tremendous evidence of the resurrection of Jesus Christ. Paul told these people that many persons saw Him after He was raised from the dead and could testify it was true.

In commenting on verses 32 and 33, F.F. Bruce writes: "Here then is the good news—that the promise made to the fathers in days gone by has now been fulfilled by God to their children. After long ages of earnest expectation, God had at last raised up to Israel their true Messiah, the Son of David, in accordance with the royal allocation of Psalm 2:7" (*The Book of Acts*).

As Paul neared the end of his sermon, he declared that "through this man" they might have remission of sins and justification from all things by believing on Him (vv. 38, 39).

Forgiveness of sins was a keynote in the preaching of the apostles. Here is the first time we find the verb *justify* in relation to salvation. It is the only time it occurs in the Book of Acts, but it appears many times in Paul's epistles to the Romans and Galatians. To be justified before God is to stand before Him in perfect righteousness without condemnation. Only one has ever been righteous, the Lord Jesus Christ. His righteousness is imputed to believers, or given to us, when we believe on Him. We are justified before God only by faith in Christ.

B. A Warning (vv. 40, 41)

(Acts 13:40, 41 is not included in the printed text.)

Paul warned, "Beware therefore, lest that come upon you, which is spoken of in the prophets" (v. 40). Then he quoted from Habakkuk 1:5, "For I work a work in your days, a work in which ye shall in no wise believe" (v. 41).

The people to whom Paul was talking were in danger of missing their great opportunity. The Lord Jesus Christ was able to do for them everything that God had promised, but it required one thing on their part: they needed to believe and yield to Him.

III. SENT TO THE GENTILES
(Acts 13:44-48)

A. The Sin of Jealousy (vv. 44, 45)

(Acts 13:44, 45 is not included in the printed text.)

As the apostles were leaving the synagogue after Paul's sermon, the congregation of Jews and proselytes crowded around Paul and Barnabas, asking that the same message be preached the next Sabbath. Many of them followed Paul and Barnabas, and the apostles urged them to continue in the faith (vv. 42, 43).

During the week that followed, the message of Paul was no doubt the talk of the town. And the next Sabbath most of the city turned out to hear Paul preach again (v. 44). P.J. Gloag notes: "Not only the Jews, the proselytes, and the devout Gentiles, but the heathen inhabitants of Pisidian Antioch flocked into the synagogue" (*Acts, Volume II*).

The quality of this success was most encouraging. David J. Burrell writes: "Gentiles, Greeks, who looked upon the Jews as a queer, outlandish people, from whom nothing but turbulence could come, were seen following the guidance of one who had been brought up as a Jew into a religion which claimed to be higher than that to which their own learned philosophers had attained. And in quantity also the success of the apostles could not but be gratifying" (*The Gospel of Gladness*).

When the Jews saw the multitudes, they were filled with "envy" (v. 45). This word (translated "jealousy," *NIV*) is from the Greek verb "to boil," transliterated in our word *zeal.* The Jews were "hot with jealousy" because of their fear that the gospel would set aside the distinction between Jew and Gentile and draw away the God-fearers from the synagogue" (French Arrington, *The Acts of the Apostles*). They did

not argue against the apostles because they couldn't. Instead, they angrily and haughtily asserted that Paul and Barnabas were lying. They also blasphemed the name of Christ.

B. Turning to the Gentiles
   (vv. 46-48)

46. Then Paul and Barnabas waxed bold, and said, It was necessary that the word of God should first have been spoken to you: but seeing ye put it from you, and judge yourselves unworthy of everlasting life, lo, we turn to the Gentiles.

47. For so hath the Lord commanded us, saying, I have set thee to be a light of the Gentiles, that thou shouldest be for salvation unto the ends of the earth.

48. And when the Gentiles heard this, they were glad, and glorified the word of the Lord: and as many as were ordained to eternal life believed.

Paul and Barnabas gave a plain answer to the railing of the Jews. It was right and proper that the Jews should have the first opportunity of hearing and believing the good news. But if they would not receive the light themselves, there were others who would appreciate it: it would be offered to the Gentiles.

This was a bold and revolutionary step that would make Christianity what its Founder intended it to be—*the* world religion. This was necessary because it was what Christ commanded.

Paul based his decision for spreading Christianity on the Word of God, quoting Isaiah 49:6. Isaiah had prophesied that the Messiah would bring salvation to all people.

The Gentiles were overjoyed

that the gospel was going to be preached to them. As many as responded in faith were reconciled to God and received eternal life.

By using the term "as many as were ordained to eternal life believed," Luke declared the inclusiveness of the gospel. All who believe in Christ—Gentile and Jew alike—have been predestined for everlasting life.

GOLDEN TEXT HOMILY

"CHILDREN OF THE STOCK OF ABRAHAM, AND WHOSOEVER AMONG YOU FEARETH GOD, TO YOU IS THE WORD OF THIS SALVATION SENT" (Acts 13:26).

Before the foundation of the world, and before heaven or hell ever existed, God had a plan of salvation for every person who would be born into this world because He knew all would sin and come short of the glory of God.

The Law that was given to Moses was not the final plan. The old covenant was not sufficient to atone for mankind's sin and to keep people from sinning.

God instituted a plan of redemption for all people in which God's Spirit comes into the temple of clay and abides. His presence provides power and holiness to keep believers from sinning.

Christ and His gospel is the only way to salvation. Christ gave the Great Commission to preach the gospel to the ends of the world so all people could be saved.—**Charles G. Wiley**

SENTENCE SERMONS

FOR ALL TIME, God's plan of salvation is for all people.
—**Selected**

TO LABEL PEOPLE as worthy and unworthy, as good and bad,

as acceptable and repulsive, is contrary to God's law and thoroughly anti-Christian.
—**George Sweeting**

THE ELECT are the "whosoever wills"; the non-elect are the "whosoever won'ts."
—**D.L. Moody**

EVANGELISM APPLICATION

FOR ALL TIME, GOD'S PLAN OF SALVATION IS FOR ALL PEOPLE.

In modern society, there are many ways by which people get categorized. For instance:
• Are you upper class, middle class or lower class?
• Are you male or female? Single, married, divorced or widowed?
• What is your nationality?
• Are you a white-collar or a blue-collar worker?
• Do you live in the city, a suburb or a rural area?
• Are you a youth, a young adult, a middle-aged adult or a senior adult?

The list could go on and on. But when Christ sees us, His vision cuts through all those labels and focuses on our souls. Each of us is seen by God as a sinner in need of a Savior. And through His perfect plan of salvation, He has made heaven available to each of us.

The real challenge comes when we as His children realize it is our calling to reach out to the unsaved. We must forget the labels of society and see all people as equally lost and equally loved by God. We can do so only through the compassion of Jesus Christ stirring our heart.

ILLUMINATING THE LESSON

Unlike other religions, Christianity does not appeal to blind credulity, to the senses and the passions, nor to the crude superstitions of men. Christianity is based on solid evidence. It contains both reason and fact. It appeals to the emotions but not at the expense of reason. Emotions are the fire under the boiler; but facts and reason are the coal that produce the fire.

It is popular to decry doctrinal sermons, to scorn basic study of Christian evidences, and to rest our religion on what we feel rather than on what we know. Such religion is like the house built on the sand. The religion that is to last will be as careful with its facts, arguments, and logic as is any court of law. This was the way of Paul; and this is the way of continuing God's church.

DAILY BIBLE READINGS

M. A Chosen People.
    Deuteronomy 7:6-9
T. God's Generous Invitation.
    Isaiah 55:1-7
W. A New Covenant.
    Jeremiah 31:31-34
T. The Messenger Sent.
    Mark 1:1-8
F. Preach the Gospel.
    Mark 16:15-20
S. Message of Reconciliation.
    Ephesians 2:11-22

TRUTH SEARCH:
Creatively Teaching the Word

Aim: Pray for different groups in your community who need to hear the gospel.

Items needed: Marker and marker board

FOCUS

In the top left-hand corner of the marker board, write the heading "Ethnic Groups." Have students name the various ethnic groups living in your community, and list them.

In the center of the board, write "Social Classes." Have students name the various social classes (wealthy, upper middle class, and so on) present in your community, and list them.

In the top right-hand corner of the board, write "Religions." Have students name the various religions (Protestant, Catholic, Muslim, and so on) present in your community, and list them.

• *How many of these ethnic groups would feel welcome in our church?*

• *Does our church reach the various social classes in our community?*

• *Do we know how to reach out to people beyond our religious borders?*

EXPLORE

In today's Scripture passage, Paul and Barnabas have begun what is known as the first missionary journey. They have reached the city of Pisidian Antioch.

Have a volunteer read Acts 13:13-15.

• *Where did Paul and Barnabas go to preach?*

The synagogue was the place where local Jews and some Gentiles would gather for prayer,

Scripture reading and teaching.

Have the students silently read verses 16-25; meanwhile, erase the marker board. When they have finished reading, ask the students to name the people Paul mentioned in the first part of his address. Write these on the board in chronological order. The list should look like this: *God, the Jewish people, the judges, the prophet Samuel, King Saul, King David, John the Baptist, Jesus.*

• *Why did Paul lay out this history for his hearers?*

Paul's point was that Jesus Christ is the Messiah whom Israel had been waiting for throughout their history.

Have a volunteer read verses 26-31.

• *To what people group did God first give the message of salvation (v. 26)?*

• *How did the majority of the Jews in Israel respond to Jesus (vv. 27-30)?*

Next, Paul contrasted Jesus with King David. David was still dead and buried, but Jesus had come back to life. Paul said, "The one whom God raised from the dead did not see decay" (v. 37, *NIV*).

Have a volunteer read verses 38-41.

• *What was the central point of Paul's message (v. 38)?*

• *What warning did Paul give (vv. 40, 41)?*

Have a volunteer read verses 42-48.

• *What was the response of the Jews to Paul and the gospel? Why?*

• *How did many of the Gentiles respond to the gospel?*

Have a volunteer read verses 49-52.

• *Why were the disciples "filled with joy" (v. 52) as they left Antioch?*

Paul made it clear that God intended the light of the gospel to be spread to all people everywhere.

RESPOND

The good news of salvation is for every ethnic group, social class and religious group.

Have students take turns leading brief prayers for the different ethnic groups, social classes and religious groups of people in your community, praying that the light of the gospel will shine to all of them. Then close the class with a question.

This week, what will each of us do to shine the gospel to someone different than ourselves?

Paul Gives His Testimony

Study Text: Acts 26:1-29

Objective: To examine Paul's presentation of his testimony and seize every opportunity to witness for Christ.

Time: Around A.D. 60

Place: The Roman palace in Caesarea

Golden Text: "According to my earnest expectation and my hope, that in nothing I shall be ashamed, but that with all boldness, as always, so now also Christ shall be magnified in my body, whether it be by life, or by death" (Philippians 1:20).

Central Truth: Christians must witness of Christ at every opportunity.

Evangelism Emphasis: Christians must witness for Christ at every opportunity.

PRINTED TEXT

Acts 26:1. Then Agrippa said unto Paul, Thou art permitted to speak for thyself. Then Paul stretched forth the hand, and answered for himself:

2. I think myself happy, king Agrippa, because I shall answer for myself this day before thee touching all the things whereof I am accused of the Jews:

3. Especially because I know thee to be expert in all customs and questions which are among the Jews: wherefore I beseech thee to hear me patiently.

4. My manner of life from my youth, which was at the first among mine own nation at Jerusalem, know all the Jews;

5. Which knew me from the beginning, if they would testify, that after the most straitest sect of our religion I lived a Pharisee.

6. And now I stand and am judged for the hope of the promise made of God unto our fathers:

7. Unto which promise our twelve tribes, instantly serving God day and night, hope to come. For which hope's sake, king Agrippa, I am accused of the Jews.

8. Why should it be thought a thing incredible with you, that God should raise the dead?

22. Having therefore obtained help of God, I continue unto this day, witnessing both to small and great, saying none other things than those which the prophets and Moses did say should come:

23. That Christ should suffer, and that he should be the first that should rise from the dead, and should shew light unto the people, and to the Gentiles.

24. And as he thus spake for himself, Festus said with a loud voice, Paul, thou art beside thyself; much learning doth make thee mad.

25. But he said, I am not mad, most noble Festus; but speak forth the words of truth and soberness.

26. For the king knoweth of these things, before whom also I speak freely: for I am persuaded that none of these things are hidden from him; for this thing was not done in a corner.

27. King Agrippa, believest thou the prophets? I know that thou believest.

28. Then Agrippa said unto Paul, Almost thou persuadest me to be a Christian.

29. And Paul said, I would to God, that not only thou, but also all that hear me this day, were both almost, and altogether such as I am, except these bonds.

DICTIONARY

Agrippa (uh-GRIP-pah)—Acts 26:1—ruler of an extensive region with headquarters in Caesarea Philippi.

Festus (FES-tus)—Acts 26:24—Roman governor of Judea who succeeded Felix.

LESSON OUTLINE

I. SEIZING THE OPPORTUNITY
   A. Courtesy
   B. Conduct
   C. Challenge

II. PRESENTING THE MESSAGE
   A. Commission
   B. Culmination

III. CALLING FOR A DECISION
   A. An Appeal
   B. The Reply

LESSON EXPOSITION

INTRODUCTION

An effective witness views adverse circumstances as doors of opportunity. The apostle Paul was a master at doing this. He had every human right to be resentful, but gave no expression to any feeling of resentment as he faced Agrippa. The secret to Paul's life was his confidence in God's wisdom, love and power. So, whether working or waiting, serving or suffering, Paul could rest assured that all would be well.

To understand how Paul received the opportunity to testify before Agrippa, some background information is necessary.

The successor of Felix as governor of Judea was Porcius Festus. He was a firm and capable ruler. After only three days on the job, he left Caesarea and went to Jerusalem, where Paul's enemies on the Sanhedrin told him about the prisoner. They requested that the apostle be sent to Jerusalem to be tried, but their intention was to kill him on the way. However, Festus was too wise to be fooled by this request and commanded them to go to Caesarea and present their charges against the apostle. This they did, accusing Paul of many grievous crimes which they could not prove. These accusations Paul answered with a calm and positive denial.

Festus, unwilling to oppose the leaders of the Jews at the very outset of his term of office, asked Paul if he would go to Jerusalem to stand trial. Confronted with the deadly threat of removal into the hands of his foes, Paul took the course open to every Roman citizen, that of a direct appeal to the emperor at Rome. Such an appeal always had to be granted without delay. No provincial official was allowed to place an impediment in its way. It was the one safeguard against local tyranny throughout the Roman Empire.

Before Paul could be sent to Rome, Festus received a visit from King Agrippa II. He was the son of the Agrippa who had beheaded James and imprisoned Peter. He came with his sister Bernice, an infamous woman who was living with him as his wife. He was ruler of an extensive region whose capital was Caesarea Philippi. Agrippa and Bernice were both Jewish, and Festus thought they might be able to shed some light on Paul's case, so he arranged a hearing for Paul. Paul was invited to present his case before the king and queen, along with the governor and his chief men in the cabinet.

This was probably the most dignified assembly that Paul had ever faced, and perhaps the most magnificent of all five of the apostle's defenses. It has been classed as one of the great speeches of the world. Let us observe Paul as he once again provides a brilliant defense of the gospel of Christ in relation to his own experience.

I. SEIZING THE OPPORTUNITY (Acts 26:1-8)

A. Courtesy (vv. 1-3)

1. Then Agrippa said unto Paul, Thou art permitted to speak for thyself. Then Paul stretched forth the hand, and answered for himself:
2. I think myself happy, king Agrippa, because I shall answer for myself this day before thee touching all the things whereof I am accused of the Jews:
3. Especially because I know thee to be expert in all customs and questions which are among the Jews: wherefore I beseech thee to hear me patiently.

This is one of the most striking scenes in history. There sat King Agrippa with Bernice by his side— his beautiful sister, his partner in shame. With them sat honest Festus, the representative of the power of Rome, well-meaning but plainly puzzled. Before them in chains was a pale man with a strength of character and personality that instantly caught and held the attention of all.

Paul's attitude toward Agrippa is noteworthy, returning courtesy for courtesy. He stated that he was glad to be able to tell his story before one who was an expert in political and ecclesiastical affairs of Palestine.

Paul planned to give a reasoned narrative and exposition of his whole case, so he asked Agrippa to be patient with him. He might have expected that Agrippa would be interested enough to listen to a fairly lengthy statement.

B. Conduct (vv. 4, 5)

4. My manner of life from my youth, which was at the first among mine own nation at Jerusalem, know all the Jews;
5. Which knew me from the beginning, if they would testify, that after the most straitest sect of our religion I lived a Pharisee.

Paul indicated that his early life had been thoroughly Jewish. This fact was well known because his enthusiasm for Judaism amounted to bigotry. His contemporaries knew all about this and could testify if necessary.

C. Challenge (vv. 6-8)

6. And now I stand and am judged for the hope of the promise made of God unto our fathers:
7. Unto which promise our twelve tribes, instantly serving God day and night, hope to come. For which hope's sake, king Agrippa, I am accused of the Jews.
8. Why should it be thought a thing incredible with you, that God should raise the dead?

The Jewish hopes of a Messiah found in the Old Testament influenced all Jewish life. To Paul there was a definite continuity between these hopes and Jesus Christ—in fact, Christ fulfilled those hopes. When properly understood, he felt there was no break between Judaism and Christianity.

Notice how he associated himself with Jews: "our religion" (v. 5), "our fathers" (v. 6), "our twelve tribes" (v. 7). Then he pointed out that he had been accused of entertaining the hope of resurrection, which they believed to be possible. He was showing them the absurdity of the Jews regarding him as a heretic.

Paul's point was that this belief in resurrection had now been validated in that God had already raised up Jesus from the dead, and thereby had shown Him to be Israel's long-expected Messiah. Why should those who believed in the resurrection of the dead refuse to believe that God had in fact raised up Jesus, and so declared Him to be the Son of God?

II. PRESENTING THE MESSAGE
   (Acts 26:18-23)

A. Commission (v. 18)

(Acts 26:18 is not included in the printed text.)

Paul, with complete frankness, told how as a Jewish enthusiast he once was opposed to Christianity. He pointed out the terrible extremes to which he had gone to persecute the Christians, believing he was carrying out God's will (vv. 9-12).

Paul stated that while he was engaged in a frenzy of persecuting zeal, a revolution took place in his life. On a journey to Damascus, a flash of light had blinded him, and the risen Christ had told him, "It is hard for you to kick against the goads" (v. 14, NKJV). This statement suggests there was already in the depths of Paul's mind a half-conscious conviction that the Christian case was true. Perhaps Stephen's arguments were affecting Paul more than he would allow himself to admit. Paul was kicking against the plan of God, just as a stubborn ox would kick against a farmer's *goad* (a pointed rod used to guide animals).

In verse 16 the apostle pointed out that his conversion was intended for a purpose—that he might be of service to God. His commission was to be a witness for Christ. The Lord had told him, "I will rescue you from your own people and from the Gentiles. I am sending you to them to open their eyes" (vv. 17, 18, NIV).

B. Culmination (vv. 19-23)

(Acts 26:19-21 is not included in the printed text.)

22. Having therefore obtained help of God, I continue unto this day, witnessing both to small and great, saying none other things than those which the prophets and Moses did say should come:

23. That Christ should suffer, and that he should be the first that should rise from the dead, and should shew light unto the people, and to the Gentiles.

Paul concluded with a note of consecration. From the time he heard the words "I am Jesus, whom you are persecuting" (v. 15, NIV), Paul knew but one Master. He had been "kicking against the pricks" before his conversion; but after his conversion he no longer rebelled against God's leading, but gladly followed it in service to Christ and others. The vision was given to Paul, not for its own sake, but for the sake of his obedience to

Christ's commission. As George H. Gould notes: "The flashing light, the audible voice, the rent sky, the unhorsed rider, were only as illuminated capitals heading the several paragraphs of that celestial communication, punctuating and intensifying its tremendous import" (*In What Life Consists*).

Of Paul's vision, Samuel H. Giesy writes: "Various other men have had visions, but in this man vision passed over into action" (*The "I Ams" of Christ*). And George A. Gordon has observed: "Paul stands preeminent among men of vision, because his vision was heavenly and because of his unswerving and passionate pursuit of it to the last breath of life" (*Revelation and the Ideal*).

In verse 20 Paul referred to the fact that after his conversion, he immediately proclaimed Jesus as the Son of God—first in Damascus, then in Jerusalem and among the Jews of Judea, and among the Gentiles. With this proclamation went the call to repent, to turn to God, and to perform works which were the natural fruit of true repentance.

Because Paul preached Christ, whose memory the Jews hated, and more especially because he preached the gospel to the Gentiles, admitting them to equal religious privileges with the Jews, the religious leaders wanted Paul dead. F.F. Bruce writes, "Knowing the Jews as he did, perhaps Agrippa understood why they would cherish such animosity toward a former rabbi who offered Gentile believers spiritual privileges on the same footing as the chosen people" (*The Book of Acts*).

Paul did not have the strength to defend himself, and yet God watched over him and kept him (v. 22). He testified to the small

and great, including the king and queen before whom he stood.

His message was nothing new—it was "what the prophets and Moses said would happen" (v. 22, *NIV*). The "prophets and Moses" includes all the Old Testament. Some believe he reversed the usual order because the prophecies say more about the Messiah than do the Books of the Law.

The Jews debated whether the Messiah would come as a man of sorrows or as triumphant and rejoicing conqueror. Paul, by a study of the messianic passages of the Psalms and the Prophets, had convinced himself that the Messiah was to bear the sins and woes of the world.

Christ proved the immortality of the soul by rising from the dead and appearing to many hundreds in convincing evidence of that great truth. The "light" (v. 23) proclaimed by Christ's resurrection was the illumination of the dark valley of the shadow of death by the certainty of immortality. It carried with it all of Christ's teachings regarding God's love and the salvation brought and offered by God's Son.

III. CALLING FOR A DECISION (Acts 26:24-29)

A. An Appeal (vv. 24-27)

24. And as he thus spake for himself, Festus said with a loud voice, Paul, thou art beside thyself; much learning doth make thee mad.

25. But he said, I am not mad, most noble Festus; but speak forth the words of truth and soberness.

26. For the king knoweth of these things, before whom also I speak freely: for I am persuaded that none of these things are

hidden from him; for this thing was not done in a corner.

27. King Agrippa, believest thou the prophets? I know that thou believest.

When Paul got to the doctrine of resurrection, Festus could endure it no longer and interrupted Paul with a loud voice. He spoke loudly to drown out Paul's voice, and also because he was amazed and excited by what Paul had been saying.

Festus, the cynical Gentile, could not grasp the doctrine of resurrection. All Paul's talk about a supernatural vision, God coming down to earth, and the dead rising to life again seemed absolute lunacy to this idolater who was not a student of the Jewish Scriptures. Paul was accustomed to having his message treated as "foolishness" by Gentiles.

John Wesley said, "If a man is indeed alive to God and dead to all things here below; if he continually sees Him that is invisible, and accordingly walks by faith and not by sight; then men of the world account it a clear case: beyond all dispute, 'much learning hath made him mad'" (*Sermons*).

To Festus, Paul appeared to be a religious fanatic who had lost his sanity through much study of the Scriptures. Festus felt Paul was so full of religious enthusiasm that it had become some sort of mania.

Compare Paul's answer to Festus with that of his answer to Ananias the high priest (23:3). "Thou whited wall," Paul had cried indignantly to the high priest. But the apostle answered the Roman governor mildly and courteously, for Festus had no such light as Ananias had.

With calmness, courtesy and restraint, Paul told Festus that he was far from being mad. He emphasized that he was speaking the truth with sobriety, the very opposite of frenzy.

Next, Paul referred to Agrippa's knowledge of Jewish affairs. It was the business of a ruler to know the history of his people and everything that concerned them. Paul's reference to "these things" (v. 26) meant Christ's life, death and resurrection, which was the climax of Paul's address. Christ was crucified in the chief city of the Jews, at a time when it was filled with people attending their chief festival. It is estimated that more than 1 million people in Jerusalem knew all about the tragic event and the glad story of the Resurrection that followed it; and hundreds had actually seen and talked with Christ.

The *Expositor's Greek Testament* says of verse 27: "The question and answer were quite natural as addressed to a Jewish king; it was a belief which Paul could justly presuppose in every Jew, even in one like King Agrippa, educated among the Romans."

The apostle was saying Agrippa could supply corroborating testimony and assure Festus that Paul's arguments were sane and well-founded, that the gospel which he preached contained nothing but what the prophets and Moses did say should come.

B. The Reply (vv. 28, 29)

28. Then Agrippa said unto Paul, Almost thou persuadest me to be a Christian.

29. And Paul said, I would to God, that not only thou, but also all that hear me this day, were both almost, and altogether such as I am, except these bonds.

This is one of the three times in which the New Testament uses the word *Christian*, and always with reference to its being a term of reproach. The others are Acts 11:26 and 1 Peter 4:16. Agrippa jokingly said, "You expect to make me—me, a king—a member of your despised sect, and with only a few minutes' talk." Yet, despite the king's response, "Agrippa recognizes, all unknowingly, one of the sure signs of a Christian, that of the desire to make someone else a Christian too" (G. Campbell Morgan, *The Life of the Christian*).

F.F. Bruce suggests: "The logic of the situation was so plain to the apostle that he could hardly imagine that such an expert in the Jewish religion would not expect the obvious conclusion. But Agrippa was not minded even to appear to lend support to Paul's case" (*The Book of Acts*).

Perhaps Paul held up his shackled wrists as he told Agrippa, "My desire is that Your Majesty and all who are here listening to me would become Christians like myself—except for these chains." Not even a king's nonchalant response to the gospel could keep Paul from obeying the heavenly vision.

SENTENCE SERMONS

CHRISTIANS MUST WITNESS for Christ at every opportunity.
—Selected

EVANGELISM IS just one beggar telling another beggar where to find bread.
—D.T. Niles

THE SALVATION OF a single soul is more important than the production or preservation of all the epics and tragedies in the world.
—C.S. Lewis

EVANGELISM APPLICATION

CHRISTIANS MUST WITNESS FOR CHRIST AT EVERY OPPORTUNITY.

One minister said that he never knew what it meant to be lost until a little girl was lost in the town where he was a pastor. This little girl and her brother went into the woods to look for the cows, but they did not find them. When nightfall overtook them, they got into an argument as to which way their home was. Neither one would give in. Each went his way.

When the little boy arrived home after dark, the mother frantically asked, "Son, where is your sister?"

"She said I was lost and would not come home with me. She went the other way."

The parents knew the beasts would devour the child. News went out for miles around and neighbors gathered to help in the search.

The next morning about daylight the little girl was found unharmed. That day there was much rejoicing in the community.

The minister said it was then that he thought, "We spent all night searching for this little girl, and justly so, and are now rejoicing because she is found. Yet there are hundreds of lost souls in our community—lost to Christ. We have spent no sleepless nights in prayer or in search for them."

ILLUMINATING THE LESSON

Privilege or sacrifice?

"For my own part, I have never ceased to rejoice that God has appointed me to such an office. People talk of the sacrifice I have made in spending so much of my life in Africa. Can that be called a sacrifice which is simply paid back as a small part of a great debt owing to our God, which we can never repay? Is that a sacrifice which brings its own blest reward in healthful activity, the consciousness of doing good, peace of mind, and a bright hope of a glorious destiny hereafter?

"Away with the word in such a view, and with such thought! It is emphatically no sacrifice. Say rather it is a privilege. Anxiety, sickness, suffering, or danger, now and then, with a foregoing of the common conveniences and charities of this life, may make us pause, and cause the spirit to waver, and the soul to sink; but let this be only for a moment. All these are nothing when 'compared with the glory which shall [hereafter] be revealed in [and for] us' (Romans 8:18).

"I never made a sacrifice. Of this we ought not to talk, when we remember the great sacrifice which He made who left His Father's throne on high to give Himself for us, 'who being the brightness of [that Father's] glory, and the express image of his person, and upholding all things by the word of his power, when he had by himself purged our sins, sat down on the right hand of the Majesty on high' (Hebrews 1:3)."
—**David Livingstone**

DAILY BIBLE READINGS

M. Live Above Reproach.
   Genesis 6:5-9
T. Be Discreet and Wise.
   Genesis 41:33-43
W. Have Integrity.
   Job 2:1-10
T. Know Christ.
   Philippians 3:1-10
F. Press Toward the Mark.
   Philippians 3:10-21
S. Hold to the Truth.
   2 Timothy 4:1-8

TRUTH SEARCH:
Creatively Teaching the Word

Aim: Students will ask God to provide them with opportunities for witnessing.

Items needed: A three- or four-foot-long chain, pencil and paper; also, four slips of paper describing parts in two different role plays:

Skit 1, person A: You are a zealous Christian inviting an acquaintance to your exciting Sunday morning church service. You don't want to take no as an answer.

Skit 1, person B: You used to go to church, but a bad experience turned you away from it. The more someone pushes you to go to church, the more excuses you will create and the stronger you will resist.

Skit 2, person A: You are a faithful Christian who has been witnessing—in life and in deed—to a coworker for a long time. Today that person is going to approach you.

Skit 2, person B: You are an unbeliever, yet you have been impressed by the consistent witness of a coworker. You and your spouse are going through a difficult time—your spouse is even talking about leaving—so you've decided to approach your coworker for help.

FOCUS

Begin the class by having students act out the two role plays. In each skit, use actors of the same gender.

After the role plays have been completed, ask the rest of the class to identify the weakness and strengths of the simulated witnessing efforts.

EXPLORE

Today we will study the witness of Paul before King Agrippa and Governor Festus when Paul was on trial for preaching about Christ.

Divide the class into small groups of three to five students each. Have each group discuss one of the passages shown below.

Acts 26:1-8

1. Why did Paul say he felt fortunate to be testifying before Agrippa (vv. 1-3)?

2. What did the Jewish people know about Paul (vv. 4, 5)?

3. What was "the hope" Paul mentioned (vv. 6, 7)? How had this hope brought him to trial?

4. How important would the resurrection of Christ be in Paul's testimony (v. 8)? Why?

Acts 26:12-24

1. According to Paul's testimony, who had called him to be a witness? What had he been specifically called to do (vv. 12-18)?

2. Why had Paul been seized by the Jews (vv. 19-21)?

3. What is the central issue of the gospel (vv. 22, 23)?

4. What was the response of Governor Festus, and why (v. 24)?

Acts 26:24-32

1. What made Paul hopeful that King Agrippa might be more open-minded than Festus (vv. 24-27)?

2. Why do you suppose Agrippa did not receive Paul's message?

3. Describe the prayer of Paul (v. 29).

4. What positive impact did Paul's witness have on the authorities (vv. 30-32)?

Bring everyone back together and discuss their findings.

RESPOND

Loosely wrap the chain around your neck.

Even though Paul was literally in chains, he did not let that hinder him from boldly witnessing for Christ.

• *Is there any kind of "chain" that is hindering your witness for Christ?*

Have students think about their answer to that question, then ask them to pray that their chains—fear, indifference, inconsistency, doubt, and so on—will be broken by the power of Jesus Christ. Lead a time of focused prayer.

The month of March begins the spring quarter (March, April, May) series of lessons, which is divided into two distinct units of study. Unit One (lessons 1-7) is presented under the theme "Leadership (Joshua and Judges)." In a world that is filled with many poor examples of leadership, it is important to understand what God expects of His leaders (and their followers) in the church.

Unit Two (lessons 8-13) is presented under the theme "The Church." These lessons address critical issues, including the nature of the church, the church's purpose, relationships in the church, and the church's future.

As you present this quarter's lessons, may you be the kind of spiritual leader God wants you to be, and may your students become stronger members of the body of Christ.

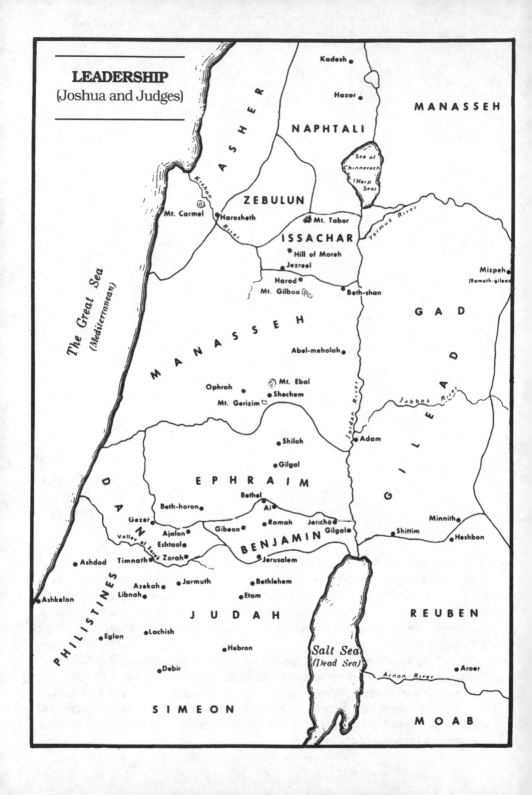

LEADERSHIP
(Joshua and Judges)

ASHER

NAPHTALI

MANASSEH

Kadesh

Hazor

Sea of Chinnereth (Harp Sea)

ZEBULUN

Mt. Carmel

Harosheth

Mt. Tabor

ISSACHAR

Hill of Moreh

Jezreel

Harod

Mt. Gilboa

Beth-shan

Mizpeh (Ramoth-gilead)

Kishon River

Yarmuk River

GAD

The Great Sea (Mediterranean)

MANASSEH

Abel-meholah

GILEAD

Ophrah

Mt. Ebal

Shechem

Mt. Gerizim

Jabbok River

Jordan River

Shiloh

Adam

Gilgal

EPHRAIM

DAN

Beth-horon

Bethel

Ai

Minnith

Gezer

Ramah

Jericho

Ajalon

Gibeon

Gilgale

Shittim

Heshbon

Valley of Sorek

Eshtaole

BENJAMIN

Timnath

Zorah

Jerusalem

Ashdod

Azekah

Jarmuth

Bethlehem

PHILISTINES

Libnah

Etam

REUBEN

Ashkelon

Eglon

Lachish

JUDAH

Hebron

Salt Sea (Dead Sea)

Debir

Aroer

Arnon River

SIMEON

MOAB

God Provides Leaders

Study Text: Numbers 14:6-9; Deuteronomy 34:9; Joshua 1:1-18
Objective: To recognize that God calls and equips leaders and respond to His purposes for our lives.
Time: Around 1405 B.C.
Place: Shittim, which was the last stop of Israel in the wilderness.
Golden Text: "Promotion cometh neither from the east, nor from the west, nor from the south. But God is the judge: he putteth down one, and setteth up another" (Psalm 75:6, 7).
Central Truth: In order to accomplish His purposes, God calls and equips leaders.
Evangelism Emphasis: Godly leaders motivate the church to reach the lost.

PRINTED TEXT

Deuteronomy 34:9. And Joshua the son of Nun was full of the spirit of wisdom; for Moses had laid his hands upon him: and the children of Israel hearkened unto him, and did as the Lord commanded Moses.

Joshua 1:1. Now after the death of Moses the servant of the Lord it came to pass, that the Lord spake unto Joshua the son of Nun, Moses' minister, saying,

2. Moses my servant is dead; now therefore arise, go over this Jordan, thou, and all this people, unto the land which I do give to them, even to the children of Israel.

3. Every place that the sole of your foot shall tread upon, that have I given unto you, as I said unto Moses.

6. Be strong and of a good courage: for unto this people shalt thou divide for an inheritance the land, which I sware unto their fathers to give them.

7. Only be thou strong and very courageous, that thou mayest observe to do according to all the law, which Moses my servant commanded thee: turn not from it to the right hand or to the left, that thou mayest prosper whithersoever thou goest.

8. This book of the law shall not depart out of thy mouth; but thou shalt meditate therein day and night, that thou mayest observe to do according to all that is written therein: for then thou shalt make thy way prosperous, and then thou shalt have good success.

9. Have not I commanded thee? Be strong and of a good courage; be not afraid, neither be thou dismayed: for the Lord thy God is with thee whithersoever thou goest.

10. Then Joshua commanded the officers of the people, saying,

11. Pass through the host, and command the people, saying, Prepare you victuals; for within three days ye shall pass over this Jordan, to go in to possess the land, which the Lord your God giveth you to possess it.

16. And they answered Joshua, saying, All that thou commandest us we will do, and whithersoever thou sendest us, we will go.

17. According as we hear-kened unto Moses in all things, so will we hearken **unto thee: only the Lord thy God be with thee, as he was with Moses.**

DICTIONARY

victuals—Joshua 1:11—Supplies of food.

LESSON OUTLINE

I. CHOSEN TO LEAD
  A. Discipled by Moses
  B. Commissioned by God to Lead
  C. God's Help Prevents Failure

II. RESOURCES FOR LEADERSHIP
  A. Strength and Courage to Lead
  B. Good Success
  C. No Fear

III. MOBILIZED FOR ACTION
  A. Joshua Assumes Authority
  B. The People Respond

LESSON EXPOSITION

INTRODUCTION

Like his predecessor, Joshua was already an old man when he was appointed as Israel's leader of Israel. Moses was 80 years old when he had his "burning bush" experience. Joshua was also an octogenarian when he became Israel's leader, but he was still strong spiritually, physically and mentally. During those 85 years he distinguished himself as a man of rare faith and courage. He had spent his first 40 years as a slave in Egypt, where he was forced to learn obedience to hard taskmasters. When God delivered the Israelites from their bondage, Moses chose Joshua as his minis-ter, or trainee.

Joshua likely had a keen appre-ciation for having been elevated to such a position. According to 1 Chronicles 7:27, he was the oldest son in his family. Had he not been covered by the blood on the door-post on that first Passover, he would have been slain like the many thousands of Egyptian sons. He understood the providence of God in his life.

The first time Joshua is actually mentioned in Scripture is Exodus 17:9: "And Moses said unto Joshua, Choose us out men, and go out, fight with Amalek: to mor-row I will stand on the top of the hill with the rod of God in mine hand." It is obvious that Joshua had already learned obedience to those in authority over him. "He had learned to obey and was thus qualified now to command. . . . There are persons who would like to have authority; they like to supervise others; but they them-selves have never learned to take orders" (Theodore H. Epp, *Joshua— Victorious by Faith*).

Joshua appears to us first as a warrior. He took his orders from Moses and led the armies of Israel against Amalek. Here He fought a physical battle, while Moses fought a spiritual one. The spiri-tual intercession Moses did during the battle was essential for Joshua to win the battle. This is a picture of Christ's intercession for us. To develop as strong Christians and godly leaders, we must under-stand total dependence on the One who makes intercession for us before the throne of God.

Joshua's leadership skills were developed through the mentoring of Moses. It wasn't Moses' strength of character that he emulated, but rather his dependence on and faith in God. Israel was strong only as she obeyed God with prayer, faith and obedience. If any of these three were shortchanged, disaster would occur. The aggressive warfare Joshua would lead Israel in to claim the Promised Land was successful only as an equivalent spiritual battle was fought.

At the end of Deuteronomy, when Moses died and Joshua finally took full command as Israel's leader, we see a man who was (1) called of God to leadership; (2) enlisted to teach submission to those in charge; (3) instilled with a dependence on God to be faithful in every aspect of his life. These are the desired qualities of leadership we will examine as we lead the church in the 21st century.

I.   CHOSEN TO LEAD
     (Deuteronomy 34:9;
     Joshua 1:1-5)

A. Discipled by Moses
   (Deuteronomy 34:9)

9. And Joshua the son of Nun was full of the spirit of wisdom; for Moses had laid his hands upon him: and the children of Israel hearkened unto him, and did as the Lord commanded Moses.

The name *Joshua* literally means "Yahweh is Savior," or "the Lord saves." Centuries later, *Jesus* would be a common derivative of this name. Joshua is first mentioned in Exodus as a warrior. Moses had already seen qualities in Joshua that indicated God was with him, that he could be trusted, that he could fight, and that he would follow orders. By the time of Moses' death, Joshua's strength of character had grown. He was now full of the spirit of wisdom. This would

be a great requirement for the years ahead, for not only would he have to overcome in Canaan, but "also the evil spiritual forces under the direction of Satan who were the actual rulers of these heathen kings" (Epp).

Joshua was not full of the Spirit simply because Moses laid his hands upon him. God chose Joshua to be the next leader of Israel. The anointing of Joshua by Moses was a pivotal point used to empower him with the Spirit in much the same way that the Holy Spirit came upon Jesus at His baptism by John. Jesus was already the Son of God (the Messiah), but the indwelling of the Spirit's fullness came at His baptism. Joshua was already God's choice, but the full anointing came when Moses laid his hands on him.

B. Commissioned by God to Lead
   (Joshua 1:1, 2)

1. Now after the death of Moses the servant of the Lord it came to pass, that the Lord spake unto Joshua the son of Nun, Moses' minister, saying,

2. Moses my servant is dead; now therefore arise, go over this Jordan, thou, and all this people, unto the land which I do give to them, even to the children of Israel.

Joshua had obeyed orders under Moses for 40 years during the wilderness wanderings. In Exodus 24:13 we see him following Moses' every step: "And Moses rose up, and his minister Joshua: and Moses went up into the mount of God." He was patiently learning and preparing for leadership. It is difficult to be second in command. He was near the pinnacle, but not quite there. Moses was the one who was receiving the revelations from

God. No one was interested in what Joshua had to say, except as he carried out orders handed down by Moses. Yet, he was never unfaithful during this time.

Watching Moses, Joshua learned firsthand all the problems that come with leadership. He knew these people, their problems, their lack of faith and their tendency to turn against Moses at the first sign of trouble. His eyes were wide open. He was no starry-eyed youth captivated by the aura of position. He had been one of the two spies who came back with a positive report. It would require intervention by God to take the land. Only the call of God would have motivated him to accept such a challenge.

Joshua would lead 1 million people into a strange land and possess it. Assured of God's help, he could view the work ahead as a positive challenge. With the same guarantee, we can face our daily problems. We may not have to conquer heathen nations, but we still have to overcome difficult situations, human relationship problems and sinful temptations. God will not leave us to endure these on our own, even though there are times we may feel abandoned. By asking for His help, we can be conquerors just as Joshua was.

C. God's Help Prevents Failure
   (vv. 3-5)

(Joshua 1:4, 5 is not included in the printed text.)

3. Every place that the sole of your foot shall tread upon, that have I given unto you, as I said unto Moses.

After 40 years of taking orders from Moses, Joshua unswervingly obeyed the one in spiritual authority over him. This is not to say, however, that he did not have a personal relationship with Jehovah. Exodus 33 indicates that Joshua at times entered into the Tabernacle with Moses. Moses communicated with God, but we are also told that Moses "turned again into the camp: but his servant Joshua, the son of Nun, a young man, departed not out of the tabernacle" (v. 11). Joshua was devoted in his service to Moses, but he was also diligent in his communion with God. This communion served to help him accept his secondary leadership role and obey the orders of Moses.

The promise "I will be with you" was given to Joshua even before Moses' death (see Deuteronomy 31:23) and was reiterated here. As the time drew near for Joshua to take command, the promises of God came more clearly.

"I will be with you" is the same commitment Christ makes to us as believers. We should not fear anything that comes against us. All we have to do is fear God himself and remain in communion with Him. As we see uncertain times approaching, we need not fall into a dismal state of mind. He will be there, no matter what the situation. We merely have to be faithful, obedient and trusting.

II. RESOURCES FOR
    LEADERSHIP (Joshua 1:6-9)

A. Strength and Courage to Lead
   (vv. 6, 7)

6. Be strong and of a good courage: for unto this people shalt thou divide for an inheritance the land, which I sware unto their fathers to give them.

7. Only be thou strong and very courageous, that thou mayest observe to do according to all the law, which Moses my servant commanded thee:

turn not from it to the right hand or to the left, that thou mayest prosper whithersoever thou goest.

At this point, Joshua found himself elevated to the top position of leadership. No longer did he have to go through Moses to receive his orders; from now on he took them directly from the Lord. Even though he had communed with God over the years, he had still been under the authority of Moses. The words spoken here to Joshua by the Lord were spoken to him earlier by Moses. Deuteronomy 31:7, 8 gives the same admonitions through the mouth of Moses as the present text does directly from God. Often we think we must hear God's message for us "directly from the horse's mouth." We forget that God uses those in authority over us to guide us.

Joshua was now in the position to receive direct guidance from God because he had been faithful to follow instructions given by Moses. This brings us to speak of the standards of guidance God gives us. If we are seeking the Lord's leading in a decision, we need not fear we will be led astray if we adhere to several principles:

• Does this decision meet with the criteria of the Word? Is it Scriptural? God will never lead us in directions that contradict the Bible.

• Does this decision agree with the counsel of godly people? We all need strong Christian friends whose integrity we trust. God speaks through these people.

• Do the circumstances fit for this decision? If a decision is in God's will, He will line up the controlling factors for it to come to pass. Otherwise, we should be hesitant to force things to happen.

• Does your spirit bear witness with God's Spirit that this is the right decision? Do you believe in your heart you have found the mind of the Lord?

• Are you at peace with making this decision? When God is in charge, He will give us peace of mind that we are in His will.

When we are faithful to the Lord, we can be assured of His direction, and we can be "strong and of a good courage." He will never leave us dangling without hope. All that was promised to Joshua is equally available to every Christian.

B. Good Success (v. 8)

8. This book of the law shall not depart out of thy mouth; but thou shalt meditate therein day and night, that thou mayest observe to do according to all that is written therein: for then thou shalt make thy way prosperous, and then thou shalt have good success.

All of God's promises are contingent upon obedience. Joshua could trust for perfect guidance as long as he obeyed the commandments of the Law. God's Word is an instruction book. Follow it and there will be success. Wander from it and disaster will surely come. As Moses' assistant, Joshua had observed the victories and failures of Israel for many years. He could look back and see that every time the people met disaster, it was one of their own making. Failure could always be traced to disobedience. The years of training under Moses showed Joshua that God was faithful to do all He said He would do. *Good success* would be his if he maintained careful obedience to God's commandments.

C. No Fear (v. 9)

9. Have not I commanded thee? Be strong and of a good courage; be not afraid, neither be thou dismayed: for the Lord thy God is with thee whithersoever thou goest.

One of the most oft-spoken phrases of the Bible is "Be not afraid." Fear is one of the terrible legacies of man's fall in the Garden. The Lord here reiterated His promise of help to Joshua, knowing that there would be times in the coming years when Joshua would be tempted to give way to human nature.

Winston Churchill is famous for the line "The only thing we have to fear is fear itself." This is not exactly true. The only thing we really need to fear is God. If we fear Him, we need not be afraid of anything else.

III. MOBILIZED FOR ACTION
(Joshua 1:10-18)

A. Joshua Assumes Authority
(vv. 10-15)

(Joshua 1:12-15 is not included in the printed text.)

10. Then Joshua commanded the officers of the people, saying,

11. Pass through the host, and command the people, saying, Prepare you victuals; for within three days ye shall pass over this Jordan, to go in to possess the land, which the Lord your God giveth you to possess it.

Assured of God's help and presence, Joshua responded by taking decisive action. He did not rest on the laurels of his position, but he validated the trust that had been placed in him. The tribes of Reuben and Gad, along with the half-tribe of Manasseh, had earlier asked Moses to let them simply settle east of Canaan. This area contained excellent pastureland for their flocks. Moses agreed to their request, but only if they would help the other tribes conquer the people of Canaan. Perhaps they had already begun to settle in the area and grow complacent. Joshua gave quick orders to pull them from indifference and include them in the campaign.

B. The People Respond (vv. 16-18)

(Joshua 1:18 is not included in the printed text.)

16. And they answered Joshua, saying, All that thou commandest us we will do, and whithersoever thou sendest us, we will go.

17. According as we hearkened unto Moses in all things, so will we hearken unto thee: only the Lord thy God be with thee, as he was with Moses.

The people immediately recognized the authority with which Joshua moved. There was no questioning of his position. He was now their commander. Judson Cornwall writes: "When a word is communicated from God to the people through His leaders, it is a command, not a suggestion, for 'Where the word of a king is, there is power' (Ecclesiastes 8:4). The difference between a shared word and a command is authority" (*Profiles of a Leader*). Joshua had the authority of God on his side. Everyone could see it. Because they saw the anointing on him, they quickly fell in line.

When we commit ourselves to living for the Lord, we must also commit ourselves to obeying those in spiritual authority over us. The kingdom of God will never be advanced when everyone tries to operate individually. God sets up men and women to be leaders over His people. We need to recognize the authority He has given them, and be ready to heed their commands.

There are obviously times when spiritual authority is misused. Some in the modern church delight in commanding others. However, we should not allow these abuses to be a part of godly authority. "The person God commissions to speak on His behalf speaks from a position of divine authority" (Cornwall). We should respect our leaders and give them the chance to operate in strength. When we do, tremendous things can be accomplished for the kingdom of God.

GOLDEN TEXT HOMILY

"PROMOTION COMETH NEITHER FROM THE EAST, NOR FROM THE WEST, NOR FROM THE SOUTH. BUT GOD IS THE JUDGE: HE PUTTETH DOWN ONE, AND SETTETH UP ANOTHER" (Psalm 75:6, 7).

This psalm was written by Asaph, one of David's chief musicians in charge of liturgical music for public worship in Jerusalem. Asaph most likely had heard David tell how God had called him from the sheep pens and promoted him to be the king of Israel and the progenitor of the coming Messiah.

These verses speak to the sovereignty of God. It is God who promotes one individual and demotes another. Generations after David's time, God raised up the Babylonians under King Nebuchadnezzar to punish Israel for her sins. The Babylonians were in turn punished by the Persians.

Closer to our own time, Adolf Hitler and his Nazi hordes brought great disaster on the Jews living in Europe. The Nazis were subsequently devastated by the Allies. In all things good and bad, we see the hand of God working to bring about a restored nation of Israel.

In its most primitive meaning in the Hebrew language, the word *promotion* (v. 6) means "to breed worms." Let us not miss the point here. God in His sovereignty can take one of the lowest forms of animal life—a worm—and exalt it to whatever level He chooses. Remember, Jesus is referred to as a "worm, and no man" in Biblical prophecy (Psalm 22:6) and yet, in the end time, John the Revelator describes Him as "King of Kings, and Lord of Lords" (Revelation 19:16).—**Carl R. Hobbs**

SENTENCE SERMONS

IN ORDER to accomplish His purposes, God calls and equips leaders.

—Selected

THE MAN who follows the crowd will never be followed by a crowd.

—R.S. Donnell

DO NOT trust proud, self-seeking leadership.

—Harold Lundquist

EVANGELISM APPLICATION

GODLY LEADERS MOTIVATE THE CHURCH TO REACH THE LOST.

As godly as Joshua was, we still need to recognize his humanity. Even though he was a chosen leader, he was not perfect. A particular incident helps us see this. In Numbers 11:25, the Lord instructed Moses to choose 70 elders to help administer the daily affairs of the people. The Lord poured out the Spirit on these men. "But two of the seventy—Eldad and Medad— were still in the camp, and when the Spirit rested upon them, they prophesied there" (v. 26, *TLB*). Apparently, these two were not fully obedient, but still the anointing was upon them. When Moses was informed of this, Joshua protested, "'Sir, make them stop!' But Moses replied, 'Are you jealous for my sake? I only wish that all the Lord's people were prophets, and that the Lord would put his Spirit upon them all!'" (vv. 28, 29, *TLB*).

Joshua was wrong to let his frustrations overcome him. He forgot the objective—creating a nation of faithful people. Still, the fact that he was loyal to Moses' leadership is commendable. "Joshua exhibited no jealousy. He did not have a self-seeking spirit. He was concerned only for the honor of the person he served" (Epp). Here we see a man who was fallible just as we are. God is not looking for perfect people to use in building His kingdom; He is looking for those who are willing to be transformed into what He wants them to become.

ILLUMINATING THE LESSON

Moses knew that he could not lead Israel forever and was deeply concerned about who would replace him. He realized that without God's intervention, the people would be "like sheep without a shepherd" (Numbers 27:17, *NIV*).

God instructed him to choose Joshua as a successor. The Lord said, "Take Joshua son of Nun, a man in whom is the spirit, and lay your hand on him" (v. 18, *NIV*). We see from this that the Spirit was operating in Joshua even before becoming Moses' protégé. He had already made himself available to being led by the Spirit. This was the qualification God was looking for in a man.

Over the next years Moses gave Joshua many opportunities to develop the anointing that was upon him. He was not immediately elevated to the top just because of his willingness to be Spirit-led. It took training, proving and mentoring.

The same is true for us. We each have a calling—a place of labor in Christ's kingdom—but we must respond daily to the Spirit and grow in our abilities to lead. If we are faithful in small things, God will elevate us to greater positions or responsibility.

DAILY BIBLE READINGS

M. Anointed Leadership.
   1 Samuel 16:7-13
T. Wise Leadership.
   1 Kings 3:16-28
W. Influential Leadership.
   Daniel 2:46-49
T. Apostolic Calling.
   Matthew 10:1-8
F. Confronted and Changed.
   Acts 9:1-9
S. A Chosen Leader.
   Acts 9:10-19

TRUTH SEARCH:
Creatively Teaching the Word

Aim: Students will seek to discover how God provided leaders in Biblical times and in their local church, and pray for the current leadership of their church.

Items needed: Marker board and colored markers; index cards

FOCUS

Divide your class into two groups: an "Old Testament" group and "New Testament" group. Have each group identify three Biblical instances from their respective Testament when God provided leadership for Israel or the church at a critical time in its history. To stretch their thinking, eliminate Moses, Joshua, Jesus and Paul from their choices. Hint: Responses could be drawn from the Book of Judges, the kings of Israel, Esther, Nicodemus, Peter, many of Paul's associates (Aquila and Priscilla, Timothy), Eunice and Lois. Time: 1 minute.

List these in two columns on your board using a different color for each Testament. For example:

Old Testament	New Testament
Nehemiah	James

Discuss the following questions:
• *What was the crisis or critical event happening? Why was this a crisis?*
• *How did God choose the leader, or what did God do to prepare the leader to respond to the crisis?*
• *What was the outcome of the crisis? How was the issue resolved?*

God always has (and always will) provided leadership for the church, sometimes from unexpected sources. We need to learn to recognize and discern God's hand at work in our local and international church leadership.

EXPLORE

Choose a volunteer and have them read Numbers 14:6-9 aloud to the class. Then discuss the following questions:
• *The context of Numbers 14 is Israel's rebellion against Moses' leadership—eventually getting so severe that God states His intention to destroy them and raise up another nation for Moses. Joshua and Caleb "rent their clothes." What does it mean to "rend clothes" in the Bible? What would be a modern-day equivalent (v. 6)?*
• *Joshua and Caleb describe the Land of Promise as "an exceeding good land" and one that "flows with milk and honey." Since Israel is primarily desert terrain, what did they mean by this (vv. 7, 8)?*
• *What is the link between rebellion and fear, and not receiving the promises of God (v. 9)?*

Choose another volunteer and have them read Deuteronomy 34:9 aloud to the class and discuss the following questions:
• *The context of this verse is the death of Moses and Joshua as his successor. What is the connection between a leader and being full of wisdom (v. 34a)?*
• *What was the result of Joshua's being filled with wisdom (v. 34b)?*

Choose another volunteer and have them read Joshua 1:1-18 aloud to the class and discuss the following questions:
• *The context of Joshua 1 is the transition in leadership from Moses to Joshua. There are often changes or transitions in leadership. What concepts can we see from Joshua 1 that gives us insight on how to make transitions smoothly?*

- *What were God's instructions to Joshua so he could be a successful leader (vv. 6-9)?*
- *What were the consequences of rebellion against Joshua (vv. 17, 18)?*
- *Why do you think such actions were justified? In light of your answers, how should we treat God-ordained leadership today?*

RESPOND

Take a few minutes to identify on the board the leadership of your church. Include the pastor and his/her family, the pastor's council or board, church staff, and any others you may have. Give each person an index card and instruct them to write down the names or groups they see on the board. Take a few minutes to pray specifically for them and then ask the class to commit to praying for these individuals each day of the next week.

Optional: You may wish to suggest a card of encouragement be sent to these people in addition to the prayers.

Principles of Leadership

Study Text: Joshua 3:1 through 5:15
Objective: To analyze and apply Biblical principles of effective leadership.
Time: Around 1405 B.C.
Place: Jordan River
Golden Text: "The Lord said unto Joshua, This day will I begin to magnify thee in the sight of all Israel, that they may know that, as I was with Moses, so I will be with thee" (Joshua 3:7).
Central Truth: Principles for godly leadership are found in the Bible.
Evangelism Emphasis: Being a Christian leader includes a vision for reaching the world for Christ.

PRINTED TEXT

Joshua 3:3. And they commanded the people, saying, When ye see the ark of the covenant of the Lord your God, and the priests the Levites bearing it, then ye shall remove from your place, and go after it.

4. Yet there shall be a space between you and it, about two thousand cubits by measure: come not near unto it, that ye may know the way by which ye must go: for ye have not passed this way heretofore.

5. And Joshua said unto the people, Sanctify yourselves: for to morrow the Lord will do wonders among you.

6. And Joshua spake unto the priests, saying, Take up the ark of the covenant, and pass over before the people. And they took up the ark of the covenant, and went before the people.

7. And the Lord said unto Joshua, This day will I begin to magnify thee in the sight of all Israel, that they may know that, as I was with Moses, so I will be with thee.

4:20. And those twelve stones, which they took out of Jordan, did Joshua pitch in Gilgal.

21. And he spake unto the children of Israel, saying, When your children shall ask their fathers in time to come, saying, What mean these stones?

22. Then ye shall let your children know, saying, Israel came over this Jordan on dry land.

23. For the Lord your God dried up the waters of Jordan from before you, until ye were passed over, as the Lord your God did to the Red sea, which he dried up from before us, until we were gone over:

24. That all the people of the earth might know the hand of the Lord, that it is mighty: that ye might fear the Lord your God for ever.

5:13. And it came to pass, when Joshua was by Jericho, that he lifted up his eyes and looked, and, behold, there stood a man over against him with his sword drawn in his hand: and Joshua went unto him, and said unto him, Art thou for us, or for our adversaries?

14. And he said, Nay; but as captain of the host of the Lord am I now come. And Joshua fell on his face to the earth,

and did worship, and said unto him, What saith my lord unto his servant?

15. And the captain of the Lord's host said unto Joshua, Loose thy shoe from off thy foot; for the place whereon thou standest is holy. And Joshua did so.

DICTIONARY

two thousand cubits—Joshua 3:4—The length of about 10 football fields.

LESSON OUTLINE

I. CHART THE COURSE
  A. Arrival at the Jordan
  B. An Important Three Days
  C. Careful Instructions
  D. A Necessary Preparation—Sanctification
  E. Joshua's Message to the Priests
  F. The Promise
II. LEARN FROM THE PAST
III. ACKNOWLEDGE THE LORD

LESSON EXPOSITION

INTRODUCTION

In the last lesson we examined Joshua's qualifications, preparation and call to lead Israel in the conquest of Canaan. The strategy for success God gave him was based on four major points:

1. Be strong and of good courage, for the battles ahead would not be easy. However, Joshua could rely on God's presence and strength.

2. Always obey God. Never veer from God's distinct and complete instructions.

3. Constantly remind the people of the truths of God's Word lest they quickly forget and retreat to the world.

4. Study God's Word daily for present and future strength, as well as to know the ways of God.

The transition in leadership from Moses to Joshua was smooth because the Lord orchestrated it.

Without God's help, it is always difficult to change leaders. "Leaders don't lead forever, even godly leaders like Moses. There comes a time in every ministry when God calls for a new beginning with a new generation and new leadership" (Warren W. Wiersbe, *Be Strong [Joshua]: Putting God's Power to Work in Your Life*). Moses had led the people out of Egypt, but Joshua would lead them into the Promised Land. It takes more than turning away from sin to follow God; we must also turn toward God and the plan He has waiting for us.

Church leaders today can learn much by studying the transition that took place from Moses to Joshua. It is always difficult when congregations are forced to change leaders. Some "flounder and almost destroy themselves in futile attempts to embalm the past and escape the future" (Wiersbe). By their very nature, people are hesitant to follow a new leader. Very often they become "comfortable in their discomfort," even when they know that change is inevitable. God had prepared the Israelites for Joshua's elevation in position. Not only had He carefully crafted Joshua's character and leadership skills so that he would be accepted, but He had also disciplined and hardened the people through the difficult years in the desert. They were consolidated and ready for the conquest. "A work originated by God and conducted on spiritual principles will surmount the shock of a change of leadership and indeed will probably thrive better as a result" (J. Oswald Sanders, quoted in Wiersbe).

There were three things Joshua was commissioned to do: (1) lead the people into the land; (2) defeat and drive out the enemy; (3) motivate the people to possess their inheritance. These are the same goals leaders should accept in leading the church: (1) They are to lead people out of sin and into abundant life in Christ. The Promised Land is not representative of heaven, but it is representative of a victorious Christian life here on earth. God has "blessed us in the heavenly realms with every spiritual blessing in Christ" (Ephesians 1:3, *NIV*). These blessings are obtainable here on earth. (2) Leaders encourage people to crucify the flesh (Galatians 5:24), "walk in the Spirit" (v. 16) and "resist the devil" (James 4:7). (3) Leaders challenge the church to possess their inheritance by tapping into the "unsearchable riches of Christ" (Ephesians 3:8). Thus their task is the same as that of Joshua.

Driving out the Canaanites was hard and cruel. We see nothing of Christ's later teachings to love our enemy, turn the other cheek, or do good to those who oppose us. Rather, what we do see is brutal obliteration of Israel's enemies. We must remember, however, that the Canaanites were poison. They were pagans with deadly and contagious spiritual infections. Israel would be poisoned and destroyed if these viruses were not eradicated. The holy war that Joshua fought was necessary so Israel could realize her destiny as God's chosen people.

I. CHART THE COURSE
(Joshua 3:1-7)

A. Arrival at the Jordan (v. 1)

(Joshua 3:1 is not included in the printed text.)

The fact that Joshua "rose early" might indicate that the first portion of his day was spent in communion with God. We know if he had not prepared himself through time with the Lord, he could not expect a miracle. The command he received was to march the people to the river.

Tremendous excitement filled the Hebrews when they finally arrived at the Jordan River. They certainly didn't know what Joshua planned to do. They couldn't swim or ford the river because it was at flood stage. There was no way to build boats for so many to cross over. They knew something miraculous was about to happen. They trusted that the God who had done so many miracles through Moses would again act through their new leader, Joshua.

B. An Important Three Days (v. 2)

(Joshua 3:2 is not included in the printed text.)

It probably took one full day for the people to travel the 10-mile journey from Shittim to the Jordan. The second day would have been a time of rest and contemplation before the Lord. They had waited 40 years for this moment. They needed to savor its importance and write it on their hearts. The third day the people received their orders from the officers.

The heathens on the other side of the river in Jericho watched them with trepidation. Why should they fear a people who had no visible means of crossing the flooded river? Yet, how could they rest, knowing the history of how God had miraculously intervened for the Israelites so many times prior to this? It was not a tranquil time for the people of Jericho.

C. Careful Instructions (vv. 3, 4)

3. And they commanded the people, saying, When ye see the ark of the covenant of the Lord your God, and the priests the Levites bearing it, then ye shall remove from your place, and go after it.

4. Yet there shall be a space between you and it, about two thousand cubits by measure: come not near unto it, that ye may know the way by which ye must go: for ye have not passed this way heretofore.

Word was spread among the tribes to follow the ark of the covenant, their ensign and signal. They were to form ranks behind it. The various tribes had an assigned place in the camp, as well as an assigned order in line when they moved from place to place. When the leader of each tribe saw the priests carrying the ark, he was to signal their people to follow.

The ark is mentioned 16 times in chapters 3 and 4. It represents the visible presence of an invisible God. It was God's symbol among them. "The ark going before the people was an encouragement to their faith, for it meant that their God was going before them and opening up the way" (Wiersbe). Dan G. Kent says, "The fact that it was moving to the unusual position of the front of the procession indicated that God was not only with His people but going before them, giving them victory, and giving them the land as He had so often promised" (*Laymen's Bible Book Commentary—Joshua, Judges, Ruth*, Vol. 4). Though it would later be misused (see 1 Samuel 4), at this time the ark guaranteed the presence of the Lord. The people were not to get close to the ark,

remaining about 2,000 cubits (a half mile) behind it. In other words, the presence of God was to be treated with respect and never taken for granted.

D. A Necessary Preparation— Sanctification (v. 5)

5. And Joshua said unto the people, Sanctify yourselves: for to morrow the Lord will do wonders among you.

The entire account of the crossing of the Jordan River was, in essence, a religious ceremony. The initial part of this was a command for the people to sanctify themselves. In a physical sense, this meant that everyone was to bathe their bodies, change their clothing, and the married couples were to restrain from sexual relations. In a spiritual sense, *sanctification* meant that they were to purify their hearts and devote themselves totally to the Lord. "God will not act powerfully on behalf of His people if they are not inwardly clean and aligned with His will" (*The Full Life Study Bible*, notes on Joshua 3:5).

We cannot expect God to bless us when we knowingly harbor sin or waver in our commitment to Him. To *sanctify* means to "set apart." First Corinthians 1:30 says, "But of him are ye in Christ Jesus, who of God is made unto us wisdom, and righteousness, and sanctification, and redemption." Certainly we were in a sense sanctified unto Christ when we were saved. Still, there is a purification aspect required of us. We have to separate ourselves from sin and the world and dedicate ourselves to God.

E. Joshua's Message to the Priests (v. 6)

6. And Joshua spake unto the priests, saying, Take up the ark of the covenant, and pass over before the people. And they took up the ark of the covenant, and went before the people.

When the ark moved, then God was moving before the people. The time for the fulfillment of God's promise had finally arrived. Though no one knew exactly how God would intervene, the people knew that they would soon be on the other side of the Jordan. It is likely that they remembered what had happened when their fathers and mothers had come to the Red Sea. With Pharaoh's army behind, mountains on either side of them, and the sea before them, only God's miraculous power could save them. Now, this new generation was about to witness themselves just how powerful their God was. Every generation needs its own manifestation of God's glory. We cannot live off our parents' experience. We must see God work in our own lives.

F. The Promise (v. 7)

7. And the Lord said unto Joshua, This day will I begin to magnify thee in the sight of all Israel, that they may know that, as I was with Moses, so I will be with thee.

Though Joshua had made a smooth transition to the top leadership in Israel, this was to be his first real test. Was God truly with him? Did he have an equal anointing to that of Moses? The miracle of leading the people through the Red Sea had elevated Moses in the eyes of the people. They saw that he was truly a servant of God. In our present text, God was doing the same thing for Joshua. "Both Moses and Joshua had received their *authority* from the Lord before these miracles occurred, but the miracles from the Lord gave them *stature* before the people" (Wiersbe).

No matter how strong our anointing is from the Lord, the people must recognize it before they will follow. We may have God's authority, but we also need stature from the people we are leading. God was promising to authenticate His servant's commission and standing before all of Israel.

II. LEARN FROM THE PAST
　(Joshua 4:20-24)

20. And those twelve stones, which they took out of Jordan, did Joshua pitch in Gilgal.

21. And he spake unto the children of Israel, saying, When your children shall ask their fathers in time to come, saying, What mean these stones?

22. Then ye shall let your children know, saying, Israel came over this Jordan on dry land.

23. For the Lord your God dried up the waters of Jordan from before you, until ye were passed over, as the Lord your God did to the Red sea, which he dried up from before us, until we were gone over:

24. That all the people of the earth might know the hand of the Lord, that it is mighty: that ye might fear the Lord your God for ever.

The events of the entire day were in the Lord's control. The people acted in obedience, and the natural elements (the water) likewise obeyed the Almighty's command. Under God's guidance,

Joshua instructed one from each tribe to pick up a stone to set up as memorials. Twelve would be used to build a monument at Gilgal (vv. 1-8, 20-24). The other 12 were set in the middle of the river (v. 9). These were to show that their old life was buried and a new life had begun. Memorial stones were a common Old Testament practice, much like historical markers in our own culture. Jacob set up the stone he had used as a pillow at Bethel (Genesis 28:18-22); Samuel set up the Ebenezer stone (1 Samuel 7:12). Later, Joshua would set up stones over the remains of Achan (Joshua 7:25, 26) and also over the king of Ai (8:29).

The men who carried the stones from the river to Gilgal had an arduous task. This was a distance of about eight miles. Gilgal was the first land across the river the people possessed. The stones were to be a reminder in later years. This would be an excellent opportunity for their children to learn about God. Retelling the story would remind them of their heritage of being part of God's chosen people. "To an unbeliever, the heap of stones was simply another stone pile; but to a believing Israelite, it was a constant reminder that Jehovah was his or her God, working His wonders on behalf of His people" (Wiersbe).

In our present text (vv. 20-24), Joshua repeated his instructions to use the stones as teaching tools for future generations. He drew a parallel between what had just happened and what had taken place at the Red Sea a generation earlier. "The individual people were different, and so were their needs and circumstances, but the Lord and His power were just the same. He is worthy of all fear and reverence from those who are His own" (Kent).

As happens as often today, the people eventually turned Gilgal into a shrine and forgot its real meaning. The prophet Hosea would later say, "Is there iniquity in Gilead? surely they are vanity: thcy sacrifice bullocks in Gilgal; yea, their altars are as heaps in the furrows of the fields" (Hosea 12:11). Israel had divided into two separate states by this time, with the northern kingdom worshiping at Gilgal instead of Jerusalem. Both Gilgal and Bethel became places of idolatry (see Amos 5:5). We should never let religious memorials become idols that turn us away from God. We look back to things God has done in the past only to remind us that He can do the same today. History should be an example to follow, not something to languish in.

III. ACKNOWLEDGE THE LORD (Joshua 5:13-15)

13. And it came to pass, when Joshua was by Jericho, that he lifted up his eyes and looked, and, behold, there stood a man over against him with his sword drawn in his hand: and Joshua went unto him, and said unto him, Art thou for us, or for our adversaries?

14. And he said, Nay; but as captain of the host of the Lord am I now come. And Joshua fell on his face to the earth, and did worship, and said unto him, What saith my lord unto his servant?

15. And the captain of the Lord's host said unto Joshua, Loose thy shoe from off thy

foot; for the place whereon thou standest is holy. And Joshua did so.

Joshua personally prepared for the destruction of Jericho. "He was assessing the task before them and thinking through his strategy for the first phase of the actual taking of the land" (Kent). Suddenly, the "captain of the Lord's host" stood before him. This was either a superior rank angel or Christ himself in preincarnate form. When he realized who stood before him, Joshua quickly removed his shoes, despite the fact that he was the leader of Israel. When we come into the presence of God, we are reminded of our lack of righteousness. Like Isaiah's experience in the Temple, Joshua may have said to himself, "Woe is me!" (Isaiah 6:5). What happened here is also reminiscent of Moses' experience with the burning bush (Exodus 3:1-6).

Many years earlier Moses had said, "If your Presence does not go with us, do not send us up from here" (Exodus 33:15, *NIV*). Joshua had already received a promise from God that He would be with him (Joshua 1:5), but this appearance by the powerful being had to be a great encouragement. Leadership, by its very nature, carries with it a sense of loneliness. The old adage, "It's lonely at the top," is true. Notice that Joshua was alone when this incident occurred. Who could he confide in? His solace had to come from God. The Lord did not disappoint him—He assured Joshua of divine protection and guidance.

This encounter gave Joshua assurance that he was ready for what was to come. The spiritual preparations were made. Now it was time for conquest.

GOLDEN TEXT HOMILY

"THE LORD SAID UNTO JOSHUA, THIS DAY WILL I BEGIN TO MAGNIFY THEE IN THE SIGHT OF ALL ISRAEL, THAT THEY MAY KNOW THAT, AS I WAS WITH MOSES, SO I WILL BE WITH THEE" (Joshua 3:7).

I wonder how long Joshua had waited to hear those words. Could it be that Joshua had never even considered himself to ever reach the level of leadership or popularity of Moses?

So often we read the Book of Joshua and we think only of the conquest of the land. We cannot forget that for years he stood in the shadow of Moses. Through all of the journeys of the children of Israel, never do we hear of Joshua causing Moses a problem. Never is Joshua threatening to start a splinter group. What we do see is Joshua supporting Moses to the point of jealousy over Moses being the leader.

Joshua leads the armies in battle. Joshua says, "We can possess the land." Now the Lord says to this man who was a faithful supporter, "I will magnify you in the sight of all Israel." Joshua did not choose this or declare this, but God did. "For promotion cometh neither from the east, nor from the west, nor from the south. But God is the judge: he putteth down one, and setteth up another" (Psalm 75:6, 7). God's time for Joshua had come, and Joshua was ready.

I pray that God will give us, in the body of Christ, men and women with a Joshua spirit . . . men and women who will fill their spot gladly no matter if they are recognized or not . . . men and women who are happy knowing they are in God's will even if it is in the shadow of someone else.—**Richard Fowler**

SENTENCE SERMONS

PRINCIPLES for godly leadership are found in the Bible.
—Selected

YOU DO NOT lead by hitting people over the head—that's assault, not leadership.
—Dwight Eisenhower

A PRIME FUNCTION of the leader is to keep hope alive.
—John Gardner

EVANGELISM APPLICATION

BEING A CHRISTIAN LEADER INCLUDES A VISION FOR REACHING THE WORLD FOR CHRIST.

Three significant things happened at Gilgal: (1) A monument was erected to memorialize God's power and faithfulness. (2) All the males were circumcised. This was a painful procedure and required much time for recovery. Circumcision sealed the people under the covenant. No one had been circumcised during the entire 40 years of wilderness wanderings. Such neglect shows the unbelief that characterized that generation. In contrast, the new generation was a "marked people." Their bodies belonged to the Lord and were not to be used for sinful purposes. The physical operation of circumcision indicated a spiritual operation in the heart. (3) Israel celebrated the Passover. This was only the third time the people had done so since leaving Egypt. The celebration reminded them of God's miracles that had brought them out of bondage.

Some years later, near the beginning of the Book of Judges, we find an interesting statement: "And an angel of the Lord came up from Gilgal to Bochim" (2:1). Outside of God's dwelling in the Holy of Holies in the Tabernacle and later in the Temple, this is the only time God's presence is specifically associated with a place. The angel of the Lord (likely meaning a theophany, or preincarnate visitation of Christ), came from Gilgal to Bochim, where the people were involved in terrible sin. In other words, the people had left the place of dedication (Gilgal), the place of God's presence, and joined the practices of the world.

To rekindle the Lord's work in our hearts, we must go back to the altar, that is, we must go back to our first love. We must rededicate our lives to God (as in circumcision). Finally, we must renew the covenant we first made with God (the Passover). Going back to Gilgal represents going back to the place where we first gave our hearts to Christ and dedicated our lives to Him.

ILLUMINATING THE LESSON

Most Christians aspire to some level of spiritual leadership—teaching a Sunday school class, serving as a deacon or board member, pastoring a great church, leading a denomination, or becoming the spiritual adviser to some famous national leader. Before we can lead in large things, however, we must learn to faithfully follow those in leadership by carrying out lesser assignments as opportunities arise. Joshua proved himself before Moses died. His battle with the Amalekites was a testing ground. His faithfulness to Moses was another. We should do our best with every occasion because we never know when someone is measuring us for a greater assignment.

Imagine what would happen if suddenly you were elevated to a high position of spiritual leadership.

What changes would you need to make? Would you have to study more diligently? Would you have to pray harder? Would you need to seek a greater illumination of the Word and the presence of God in your life? Would you have to change your entire demeanor? If so, you are probably not ready for elevation in leadership. Joshua's transition to leader of Israel was a natural one because he was already a faithful servant of God.

DAILY BIBLE READINGS

M. Knowledge.
   Luke 2:40-52
T. Integrity.
   Luke 4:1-15
W. Compassion.
   Luke 7:11-17
T. Vision.
   John 4:31-38
F. Submission to God.
   John 5:17-23
S. Prayerfulness.
   John 17:1-26

TRUTH SEARCH:
Creatively Teaching the Word

Aim: Students will seek to identify and apply principles of leadership to their personal lives.

Items needed: Dry erase markers, newsprint and easel. A dry erase board can be used in place of newsprint if necessary.

FOCUS

Label the first sheet of newsprint (or one-half the board) "Secular Leaders" and another sheet (or the other half of the board) "Sacred Leaders." Have students name three or four of the world's greatest leaders in each column. For example:

Secular Leaders

Alexander the Great

Queen Victoria

George Patton

Hitler

Sacred Leaders

Abraham

Moses

Esther

Billy Graham

Discussion questions:

• *What was the setting or life story that made each of your choices so important?*

• *What leadership principles do each of your examples have? Why are these important traits?*

• *What are the similarities and dissimilarities between the principles of the "secular" and "sacred" leaders? Are the principles you have identified Biblical and applicable to our lives today?*

EXPLORE

The study text of this lesson is lengthy. The following questions have been developed to facilitate discussion based on the overarching principles found in Joshua 3:1—5:15.

• *What spiritual lesson(s) can be gleaned from the fact that the Jordan would not be parted until the priests stepped into the water (3:13-17)?*

• *God commanded Joshua and Israel to gather 12 stones from the riverbed of Jordan as they were passing over. These stones were used to build an altar that would serve for generations as a reminder of what God had done for Israel. Pentecostals have typically avoided formal "liturgies," yet we have them. What acts or traditions are important for Pentecostals to convey to their children for generations? In other words, what are we doing that makes our children ask questions about their heritage as Christians and Pentecostals?*

• *Circumcision was a sign of God's covenant with Israel, an act that was renewed in 5:1-8 with all those males born in the wilderness wandering. As such, it was preparatory for what God was about to do for and in Israel. How important is it for us today to follow God's Word and do as He instructs us? What are the consequences if we don't?*

RESPOND

This will require a certain level of honesty and transparency on the part of you and your class.

Starting with yourself, identify one principle of leadership discovered in class today and explain to the class how you will seek to incorporate this principle into your everyday life. Then have class members respond accordingly. It is vital you do this first. You may wish to discuss with the class some tangible ways in which any of these can be done throughout the upcoming week.

Responsibilities of Leaders

Study Text: Joshua 14:6-14; 15:13-19
Objective: To acknowledge and accept leadership responsibilities.
Time: Around 1400 B.C.
Place: Gilgal, the first camp of Israel after crossing the Jordan
Golden Text: "Be thou strong and very courageous, that thou mayest observe to do according to all the law, which Moses my servant commanded thee: turn not from it to the right hand or to the left, that thou mayest prosper whithersoever thou goest" (Joshua 1:7).
Central Truth: God uses responsible leaders to advance His kingdom.
Evangelism Emphasis: God uses responsible leaders to advance His kingdom.

PRINTED TEXT

Joshua 14:6. Then the children of Judah came unto Joshua in Gilgal: and Caleb the son of Jephunneh the Kenezite said unto him, Thou knowest the thing that the Lord said unto Moses the man of God concerning me and thee in Kadesh-barnea.

9. **And Moses sware on that day, saying, Surely the land whereon thy feet have trodden shall be thine inheritance, and thy children's for ever, because thou hast wholly followed the Lord my God.**

10. And now, behold, the Lord hath kept me alive, as he said, these forty and five years, even since the Lord spake this word unto Moses, while the children of Israel wandered in the wilderness: and now, lo, I am this day fourscore and five years old.

11. **As yet I am as strong this day as I was in the day that Moses sent me: as my strength was then, even so is my strength now, for war, both to go out, and to come in.**

12. Now therefore give me this mountain, whereof the Lord spake in that day; for thou heardest in that day how the Anakims were there, and that the cities were great and fenced: if so be the Lord will be with me, then I shall be able to drive them out, as the Lord said.

13. **And Joshua blessed him, and gave unto Caleb the son of Jephunneh Hebron for an inheritance.**

15:16. And Caleb said, He that smiteth Kirjath-sepher, and taketh it, to him will I give Achsah my daughter to wife.

17. **And Othniel the son of Kenaz, the brother of Caleb, took it: and he gave him Achsah his daughter to wife.**

18. And it came to pass, as she came unto him, that she moved him to ask of her father a field: and she lighted off her ass; and Caleb said unto her, What wouldest thou?

19. **Who answered, Give me a blessing; for thou hast given me a south land; give me also springs of water. And he gave her the upper springs, and the nether springs.**

DICTIONARY

Kadesh-barnea (KAY-desh-BAR-nee-uh)—Joshua 14:6—The place from which Caleb, Joshua and the other 10 spies went into Canaan and surveyed the land when the Israelites decided not to possess it.

fourscore and five years old—Joshua 14:10—85 years old.

LESSON OUTLINE

I. WHOLLY FOLLOW GOD

  A. Caleb's Wholehearted Faithfulness

  B. Caleb's Inheritance

II. FULFILL YOUR MISSION

  A. Attributing Strength

  B. Taking the Challenge

III. BLESS FUTURE GENERATIONS

  A. The Sons of Anak

  B. Caleb's Legacy

LESSON EXPOSITION

INTRODUCTION

An important distinction should be made between two terms used in the conquest of Canaan—*inheritance* and *possession.* As the conquest of the land was concluding, we read, "So Joshua took the whole land, according to all that the Lord said unto Moses; and Joshua gave it for an inheritance unto Israel according to their divisions by their tribes. And the land rested from war" (Joshua 11:23). Joshua had routed the major enemies and their cities. The biggest part of the job was finished. However, when we get to chapter 13 we read, "And the Lord said unto him, Thou art old and stricken in years, and there remaineth yet very much land to be possessed" (v. 1). The land had been given to the Israelites as an *inheritance*, but it still had to be *possessed.*

In Joshua 1:3, God had said, "Every place that the sole of your foot shall tread upon, that have I given unto you." Responsibility was given to various tribes. They had to possess the land in order to realize their promise.

Our lesson takes place after seven years of war. Israel now controlled the Promised Land as a whole, and Joshua had dismissed the army. He had divided the territories up among the various tribes as God directed, but part of the land had not been conquered. Chapter 13 lists the various peoples, cities and areas left to be subjugated. God's plan was that the various tribes prove their trust in Him by finishing the work with their own efforts. There are things only the miraculous intervention of God can achieve. There are other things we are capable of doing with our own hands. God does not do for us what we should do on our own. If we are in a place of great temptation, we can pray "Lord, deliver me," but nothing will happen. It takes walking away from that place by putting one foot in front of the other. God helps us when we need Him, but some things He expects us to exert human efforts to accomplish.

Caleb was one man who recognized the difference between *inheritance* and *possession.* We will see how he claimed all that had been promised to him 45 years earlier. As an old man he was willing to accept the challenge to take possession of what was his.

The concepts of *inheritance* and *possession* are also valid terms for Christians today. God had given us a wonderful inheritance in Christ. "Our inheritance is in Him. In fact He is our inheritance" (Theodore H. Epp, *Joshua—Victorious by Faith*). Our possession of that inheritance, however, must be appropriated by faith. Also, we must dispossess the enemies of our lives—our sins, our failures, our shortcomings—in order to possess all that He wants us to have.

I. WHOLLY FOLLOW GOD
(Joshua 14:6-9)

A. Caleb's Wholehearted
Faithfulness (vv. 6-8)

(Joshua 14:7, 8 is not included in the printed text.)

6. Then the children of Judah came unto Joshua in Gilgal: and Caleb the son of Jephunneh the Kenezite said unto him, Thou knowest the thing that the Lord said unto Moses the man of God concerning me and thee in Kadesh-barnea.

In Numbers 14:24, God said, "But because my servant Caleb has a different spirit and follows me wholeheartedly, I will bring him into the land he went to, and his descendants will inherit it" (*NIV*). Caleb remained true and faithful all his life. He was 40 years old when Moses sent him into Canaan as one of the 12 spies (Numbers 13). Only he and Joshua came back with a positive report. He desperately tried to convince his unbelieving fellow Israelites that the land could be possessed (13:30; 14:6-9). In response, he and Joshua were nearly stoned to death by the people. Thus, Caleb was no stranger to standing alone on God's promises.

In Joshua 14:10 Caleb reminded Joshua that 45 years had transpired since then. The 85-year-old man could point with pride to the confidence he had in the Lord. He and Joshua were the oldest citizens of Israel. Everyone else in their generation had died in the wilderness. This included all of Caleb's relatives—his father, mother, aunts, uncles and his wife. Only his children and their children would be with him as he claimed his inheritance.

What made Caleb so special? Surely he could see that Israel's enemies were superior in terms of military strength. Caleb didn't look at the enemy, however. Instead, he focused on the supreme strength of God and the prize to be won by trusting Him.

B. Caleb's Inheritance (v. 9)

9. And Moses sware on that day, saying, Surely the land whereon thy feet have trodden shall be thine inheritance, and thy children's for ever, because thou hast wholly followed the Lord my God.

Can you imagine claiming something that was verbally promised to you 45 years earlier? Caleb was an old man who appeared to have very few years left in this life. At age 85, most men would not think of clearing land and building a new home (not to mention the fact that he would have to drive out a whole tribe of people claiming squatter's rights).

Caleb knew he could trust God's promise. Although it took many years to see his promise fulfilled, Caleb never doubted the Lord's integrity. Most people give up quickly when God doesn't immediately answer their cries. How persistent are you in holding on to what you've claimed?

What about your integrity? Have you held true to promises you made five years ago, or 25 years ago? If not, recognize that time should have no bearing on the pledges you make. Whatever you promise to do for others, you should fulfill. Also, have you made commitments to God you haven't fulfilled? Review your life and make an evaluation. If there are things you vowed to do for Christ, set about now to fulfill those vows.

II. FULFILL YOUR MISSION (Joshua 14:10-14)

A. Attributing Strength (vv. 10, 11)

10. And now, behold, the Lord hath kept me alive, as he said, these forty and five years, even since the Lord spake this word unto Moses, while the children of Israel wandered in the wilderness: and now, lo, I am this day fourscore and five years old.

11. As yet I am as strong this day as I was in the day that Moses sent me: as my strength was then, even so is my strength now, for war, both to go out, and to come in.

Caleb was still healthy, vital and strong for his years. He was as much an able warrior in the army of Israel as the day Moses had sent him on the spy mission. He knew why he had retained his vitality. He attributed his health to the Lord because he knew that the Lord would allow him to claim his inheritance. He had accepted the Lord's promises and lived positively to see them fulfilled. "God seemed to prolong Caleb's life as a reminder to a younger generation that He fulfills His word" (*The Word in Life Study Bible*, notes on Joshua 14).

B. Taking the Challenge (vv. 12-14)

(Joshua 14:14 is not included in the printed text.)

12. Now therefore give me

this mountain, whereof the Lord spake in that day; for thou heardest in that day how the Anakims were there, and that the cities were great and fenced: if so be the Lord will be with me, then I shall be able to drive them out, as the Lord said.

13. And Joshua blessed him, and gave unto Caleb the son of Jephunneh Hebron for an inheritance.

Hebron, the area given to Caleb, had been attacked at least once by Joshua and the army of Israel during the years of conquest. Joshua 10:36, 37 informs us that the city and all its inhabitants were destroyed. Still, there were apparently many warriors in the vicinity—the Anakim—whom Caleb must drive out.

Hebron had a long history in the Biblical story, even before it was given to Caleb. In this spot was the cave of Machpelah, the site where Abraham buried Sarah hundreds of years earlier. Hebron was one of the oldest cities of Palestine, occupied since at least 3000 B.C.

Caleb's battle cry, "Give me this mountain," was a bold request for an old man. Still, he was able to drive out the Anakim. This was a direct fulfillment of the faith proclamation he had made 45 years earlier when he tried to convince the other Israelites to go in and take the land: "We should go up and take possession of the land, for we can certainly do it" (Numbers 13:30, *NIV*). Also note that Hebron was one of the specific sections of Canaan explored by the 12 spies (see Numbers 13:22). Caleb may have even then set his sights on the area to claim as his inheritance.

III. BLESS FUTURE GENERATIONS (Joshua 15:13-19)

A. The Sons of Anak (vv. 13, 14)

(Joshua 15:13, 14 is not included in the printed text.)

Despite the fact that the Israelite army under Joshua had attacked Hebron earlier, many of the inhabitants still survived. They probably scattered out in the hills until the army moved to other battles. The three clans of Anak's descendants had to be destroyed. Throughout the history of warfare, the offspring of rulers were killed in order to keep them from trying to revive their ancestors' domain. Although the present text simply says Caleb drove these men from the area, we learn in Judges 1:10 that they were killed. Caleb was carrying out God's commands. To allow descendants of heathen peoples to exist was to invite trouble. Unfortunately, this is the story that unfolds in the Book of Judges.

Several centuries earlier, God had told Abraham that when his descendants entered Canaan, the people they would find there would have to be destroyed because of their sins (see Genesis 15:16). This was not to say that Israel was a righteous people (for they eventually became as wicked as the people they were driving out), but God used them to punish evil.

B. Caleb's Legacy (vv. 15-19)

(Joshua 15:15 is not included in the printed text.)

16. And Caleb said, He that smiteth Kirjath-sepher, and taketh it, to him will I give Achsah my daughter to wife.

17. And Othniel the son of Kenaz, the brother of Caleb, took it: and he gave him Achsah his daughter to wife.

18. And it came to pass, as she came unto him, that she moved him to ask of her father a field: and she lighted off her ass; and Caleb said unto her, What wouldest thou?

19. Who answered, Give me a blessing; for thou hast given me a south land; give me also springs of water. And he gave her the upper springs, and the nether springs.

Caleb was willing to share the blessings of his inheritance. As an old man (probably now 86 to 90 years), he knew his days were limited. His enjoyment of the land he had possessed would only last a short while. He needed to make certain that future generations would claim what he had begun. In reading the story, we see that a nephew (son of his younger brother) accepted the challenge Caleb had initiated to conquer one certain city. Having done such, the nephew won Caleb's daughter as his wife. This girl had her father's tenacity. Caleb did not see her brazen request for additional properties as being selfish, but he saw it as a means to possess her inheritance. He knew that with descendants as strong-willed as this daughter, legacy would be maintained.

A sad element of the national story enters here. Soon after Joshua died, the Israelites lost their will to totally subdue their enemies. This could be the one fault we see in Joshua. Although Joshua was a great leader who was dedicated to God's will, he had not asked divine help in providing a protégé for him to train as leader of the next generation. He had no successor. The job was not completed. Even though he had destroyed many of the Canaanites, many remained in the land after his death. None of us can complete the work of the Lord alone. We must build a heritage of future leaders to continue the work of the Kingdom.

In summarizing the life of Caleb, we see a man who refused to follow the crowd, a man who trusted God wholeheartedly, and one who did not let age factor into his thinking. There are several principles you should follow in order to emulate his attitude and success:

• *Reevaluate your priorities.* What are the priorities of your life? If they do not fit with Biblical objectives, change them. Make certain your life is focused on accomplishing God's will.

• *Have a dream in your heart.* After establishing God's will, set your goals to accomplish that dream.

• *Depend on the Holy Spirit.* Don't try to accomplish your goals on your own. Ask for the Spirit's guidance.

• *Be positive in your expectations.* Believe that you can accomplish what you have set out to do.

In this lesson, we see that Caleb followed this four-point formula. He set his priorities on God's will to take the Promised Land. He had a dream in his heart to accept his inheritance. He depended on the Lord for strength. Finally, he was positive in his expectations. He knew the job was not too great if the Lord intervened.

GOLDEN TEXT HOMILY

"BE THOU STRONG AND VERY COURAGEOUS, THAT THOU MAYEST OBSERVE TO DO ACCORDING TO ALL THE LAW, WHICH MOSES MY SERVANT COMMANDED THEE: TURN NOT FROM IT TO THE RIGHT HAND OR TO THE LEFT, THAT THOU MAYEST PROSPER WHITHERSO-EVER THOU GOEST" (Joshua 1:7).

Moses' death placed the Israelites in a state of uncertainty. God chose Joshua to fulfill Moses' leadership position, and provided him with divine encouragement and instruction through three commands—commands that will help us to be anointed leaders.

1. *Be determined.* We must prevail and be exceedingly courageous in all circumstances. Maintaining a proper mental and spiritual attitude requires continual reliance upon the power of the Spirit, who makes us strong (Luke 24:49).

2. *Be obedient.* God requires more than a proper attitude from us. We must be obedient to Him and those whom He places over us before we can expect others to obey our instructions (see Galatians 6:7).

3. *Persevere.* Faithfulness is what separates great leaders from those who want to be great. It is setting our minds and hearts upon the goal of God's will and continuing on regardless of the circumstances or the cost (Romans 12:2).

These commands enabled Joshua to experience God's blessing, comprehend the truth, and act wisely in his journey. This is the true definition of success. We must learn also to focus on the journey as much as we focus on the destination, because the journey prepares us for the destination.

God never commands without giving the ability to fulfill. These three qualities must be a part of our lives as we fulfill the positions of leadership that are just as important as the one Joshua held. They are important because God and people are counting on us!—**R. Keith Whitt**

SENTENCE SERMONS

GOD USES responsible leaders to advance His kingdom.
                              —Selected

SOME MUST follow, and some command, though all are made of clay.

—Henry Longfellow

COURAGE IS fear that has said its prayers.

—Selected

THE PROCLAIMER of the Kingdom is one who leads men from what they want to what they need.

—Ralph W. Sockman

EVANGELISM APPLICATION

GOD USES RESPONSIBLE LEADERS TO ADVANCE HIS KINGDOM.

Caleb was only one of two individuals (Joshua the other) who truly believed God's promise to Israel. Because of his faith, Caleb was rewarded with great blessings. The rest of the people who came out of Egypt lost their inheritance. They were doomed to wander in the wilderness. We must remember, however, that even though they lost their inheritance, God still provided graciously for them during those years. They settled for God's provision when they could have had a full inheritance of His blessings.

We read where Jesus could do few miracles in His hometown because of the people's unbelief. They refused to see the potential inheritance that was theirs. The same is true for Christians today. Our churches are weak, and our people live spiritually impoverished because we refuse to believe God's promises in the Word and make an effort to possess those promises.

May we begin today to not only claim our inheritance but to also possess it. Activate your faith by believing that God will give you everything He promised. In that way you can be a spiritual leader who will help advance God's kingdom.

ILLUMINATING THE LESSON

Canaan was the inheritance given to Israel, while Christ is our inheritance. In the same way that the Israelites had to go into Canaan and possess the land, we too must possess all that has been given to us. When Christ finished His work at Calvary, He was raised from the dead and ascended to heaven to sit at the right hand of the Father. Ephesians 2:5 says God "made us alive with Christ even when we were dead in transgressions" (*NIV*). Christ conquered the Enemy and gave us life (that was His part of the battle). The next verse says "God raised us up with Christ and seated us with him in the heavenly realms in Christ Jesus" (v. 6, *NIV*). This is our inheritance. We are enthroned with Christ in heavenly places, but we have to possess this inheritance. We appropriate it by faith, and then live our lives with perseverance in prayer and dedication to Christ. "It is our responsibility to conquer sin daily and claim the spiritual blessings that are ours in Christ" (Epp).

DAILY BIBLE READINGS

M. Committed to God.
   Daniel 1:8-17
T. Committed to Family.
   Genesis 14:8-16
W. Committed to Relationships.
   2 Samuel 9:1-13
T. Committed to Mission.
   Acts 16:6-10
F. Committed to the Gospel.
   Romans 1:8-15
S. Committed to Godly Living.
   Ephesians 5:15-21

TRUTH SEARCH:
Creatively Teaching the Word

Aim: To identify, pray for and ease the responsibilities of at least one church leader during the following week.

Items needed: Notepads or index cards, pens, marker board and markers

FOCUS

Sometimes it is difficult to appreciate the great responsibilities a pastor (or other church leader) may have until you have done some of what they do in a given week. Some of the responsibilities a pastor has only he/she can do (e.g., marry, baptize, counsel, money-matters). There are, however, certain duties that we can do to ease the workload of a pastor (or other leader).

Have your class choose a leader in your church—the pastor, secretary or another staff member. Brainstorm what your class feels this person's responsibilities are. REMEMBER: Rule #1 of brainstorming is that no initial answers can be wrong or bad. List everything that is said on the marker board. After your list is as complete as you want it to be, ask the class to identify any responsibilities that may not actually belong to your chosen leader.

Once you have an accurate list of this person's responsibilities, take another colored marker and circle what the class feels someone else could do for this person in the following week. In other words, you are distinguishing primary and secondary responsibilities. The primary responsibilities are what only this leader can (or

should) do. The secondary responsibilities, while important, can be delegated to someone else. It is the secondary responsibilities you need to highlight.

EXPLORE

• *When he was 40, Caleb was sent to spy out the land (Numbers 13), and now, 45 years later, he was asking for his inheritance. Joshua 14:6-14 and 15:13-19 are about the faithfulness of Caleb throughout his life and the rewards given to him by God promised 45 years earlier. What is the connection between faithfulness in leadership and the responsibilities given to leaders?*
• *There seems to be some connection between responsibilities of leaders and accountability of leaders. Discuss this connection. What happens when leaders overemphasize their responsibilities and neglect their accountabilities?*

RESPOND

First, pray in class for the leader identified earlier, asking God to bless this person beyond their human capabilities during the following week.

Second, identify the responsibilities that need to be done during the following week.

Third, solicit volunteers or work as groups; decide who will do what and notify the class of what is being done to identify the leader's workload.

Next week, ask each group or individual to briefly share with the class the results of this assignment.

The Art of Decision Making

Study Text: Joshua 24:1-28
Objective: To understand that life presents many choices and resolve to make godly decisions.
Time: Around 1400 B.C.
Place: Shechem, where Joshua made his farewell address
Golden Text: "Choose you this day whom ye will serve . . . but as for me and my house, we will serve the Lord" (Joshua 24:15).
Central Truth: Leaders should base their decisions on the truth and promises of God's Word.
Evangelism Emphasis: Life's greatest decision is to accept Jesus as personal Savior.

PRINTED TEXT

Joshua 24:2. And Joshua said unto all the people, Thus saith the Lord God of Israel, Your fathers dwelt on the other side of the flood in old time, even Terah, the father of Abraham, and the father of Nachor: and they served other gods.

3. And I took your father Abraham from the other side of the flood, and led him throughout all the land of Canaan, and multiplied his seed, and gave him Isaac.

11. And ye went over Jordan, and came unto Jericho: and the men of Jericho fought against you, the Amorites, and the Perizzites, and the Canaanites, and the Hittites, and the Girgashites, the Hivites, and the Jebusites; and I delivered them into your hand.

14. Now therefore fear the Lord, and serve him in sincerity and in truth: and put away the gods which your fathers served on the other side of the flood, and in Egypt; and serve ye the Lord.

15. And if it seem evil unto you to serve the Lord, choose you this day whom ye will serve; whether the gods which your fathers served that were on the other side of the flood, or the gods of the Amorites, in whose land ye dwell: but as for me and my house, we will serve the Lord.

16. And the people answered and said, God forbid that we should forsake the Lord, to serve other gods;

17. For the Lord our God, he it is that brought us up and our fathers out of the land of Egypt, from the house of bondage, and which did those great signs in our sight, and preserved us in all the way wherein we went, and among all the people through whom we passed.

20. If ye forsake the Lord, and serve strange gods, then he will turn and do you hurt, and consume you, after that he hath done you good.

21. And the people said unto Joshua, Nay; but we will serve the Lord.

22. And Joshua said unto the people, Ye are witnesses against yourselves that ye have chosen you the Lord, to serve him. And they said, We are witnesses.

23. Now therefore put away, said he, the strange gods which are among you, and incline your heart unto the Lord God of Israel.

24. And the people said unto Joshua, The Lord our God will we serve, and his voice will we obey.

LESSON OUTLINE

I. REMEMBER GOD'S
   FAITHFULNESS
   A. Assembly of the Entire Nation
   B. Review of God's Blessings on
      Israel
II. WEIGH THE OPTIONS
   A. Make the Choice
   B. The People Respond
   C. Joshua Reiterates the Choice
III. MAKE WISE CHOICES

LESSON EXPOSITION

INTRODUCTION

In much the same fashion that Moses had done a generation earlier, Joshua brought the people together near the end of his own life. His intention was to lead them in a covenant ceremony of recommitment. The focus was not on Joshua as their leader, but on the faithfulness of God to the people, their necessity of making a decision, and Joshua's concern that they remain separated from the local heathen culture. He could probably already sense their growing attraction to the idol gods of the land when he said, "Throw away the foreign gods that are among you and yield your hearts to the Lord, the God of Israel" (Joshua 24:23, *NIV*).

We might ask, "If God had promised to thoroughly drive out the native Canaanites, why were there still some of them in the Promised Land?" The implication is that God had done all He promised to do, even though there were still heathens in the land. God had kept His part of the bargain; the people had yet to complete their part. They were encouraged to finish the job. It is important to remember the two terms discussed in our last lesson. There

is a vast difference between *inheritance* and *possession*. We saw how Caleb was willing to take for himself (possess) the area of Hebron that had been promised him 45 years earlier. During the years of wilderness wandering (in addition to the seven years of war to conquer the land), Caleb could have been tempted to take the attitude that God had failed him. If the land was his, why didn't he already have it? Caleb recognized that he had a responsibility to possess what had been promised to him. He could not simply expect God to do for him what he knew he could do for himself.

In this final address by Joshua (ch. 24), we feel the pain in his heart as he apparently recognized that the people did not have the determination to possess their inheritance. He knew that if they left even one Canaanite in the land, this Canaanite would contaminate the land and lead to destruction.

It might be said that the greatest indictment against any generation of Christians is the failure to influence the next generation to serve the Lord. Probably Joshua's only fault as a leader was the fact that he did not prepare a successor to lead the nation in serving God. Moses had trained Joshua for many years before passing him the mantle. The Book of Judges reveals there was no one to fill the vacuum when Joshua died.

Instead of condemning Joshua, however, we must remember that it was God's choice to put him under Moses' mentorship. Why didn't God do the same for the next generation? Could it be that it was time for the people to take authority in their own lives to serve the Lord? There comes a time when we too must develop our own relationship with

God. The Lord has no grandchildren. Just as Joshua put the decision before the people to choose whom they would serve, we must make the same choice. Either we live for Christ, or we will fall into the seduction of the heathen gods of our time.

I. REMEMBER GOD'S FAITHFULNESS
(Joshua 24:1-13)

A. Assembly of the Entire Nation (v. 1)

(Joshua 24:1 is not included in the printed text.)

In chapter 23 Joshua had assembled the leaders of the nation and challenged them to be faithful. This had taken place either at Shiloh or at his home in Ephraim. Now, he called the entire nation together at Shechem and repeated his message. The leaders thus received two warnings. *Matthew Henry's Commentary* states that Joshua thought the earlier meeting with the leaders was his final meeting: "Joshua thought he had taken his last farewell of Israel in the solemn charge he gave them in the foregoing chapter, when he said, 'I go the way of all the earth'; but God graciously continuing his life longer than expected, and renewing his strength, he was desirous to improve it for the good of Israel" (notes on Joshua 24:1-24).

Joshua knew he was about to die, but his passion was for the generations that would follow him. If they did not remain faithful, everything he had done would be in vain. He hoped that those in leadership were listening intently, because they would set the course for the rest of the people.

Notice that Joshua chose Shechem for this farewell address.

This was holy ground. Here God promised Abraham that his descendants would inherit this land. Also, Jacob built an altar here after making peace with his brother, Esau (Genesis 33:20).

B. Review of God's Blessings on Israel (vv. 2-13)

(Joshua 24:4-10, 12, 13 is not included in the printed text.)

2. And Joshua said unto all the people, Thus saith the Lord God of Israel, Your fathers dwelt on the other side of the flood in old time, even Terah, the father of Abraham, and the father of Nachor: and they served other gods.

3. And I took your father Abraham from the other side of the flood, and led him throughout all the land of Canaan, and multiplied his seed, and gave him Isaac.

11. And ye went over Jordan, and came unto Jericho: and the men of Jericho fought against you, the Amorites, and the Perizzites, and the Canaanites, and the Hittites, and the Girgashites, the Hivites, and the Jebusites; and I delivered them into your hand.

Here Joshua reviewed the goodness of God to them through the years. The intent of this can be found in the words he had spoken earlier to the nation's leaders: "Ye know in all your hearts and in all your souls, that not one thing hath failed of all the good things which the Lord your God spake concerning you; all are come to pass unto you, and not one thing hath failed thereof" (23:14). God had been faithful to His promises and in His blessings, but Joshua knew that the seeds of discontent were already planted in the people's hearts. He also knew God would not hold back His judgment if they sinned. This review of God's goodness was to give the people a warning against neglect, carelessness and lack of faith in appropriating everything God had given them by inheritance.

God's loving care of Israel over the centuries began with the call of Abraham. It then went through the patriarchs, the deliverance from Egypt, the crossing of the Red Sea and the destruction of Pharaoh's army. Next came the years of provision in the wilderness and the safe crossing into the Promised Land. Joshua then added that God did not give them the land of Canaan because they deserved it. They certainly had not merited His kindness by their actions.

The irony of history is that those who refuse to heed its lessons must relive the same lessons again. Someone has said, "The only thing men learn from history is that they don't ever really learn."

II. WEIGH THE OPTIONS
   (Joshua 24:14-20)

A. Make the Choice (vv. 14, 15)

14. Now therefore fear the Lord, and serve him in sincerity and in truth: and put away the gods which your fathers served on the other side of the flood, and in Egypt; and serve ye the Lord.

15. And if it seem evil unto you to serve the Lord, choose you this day whom ye will serve; whether the gods which your fathers served that were on the other side of the flood, or the gods of the Amorites, in whose land ye dwell: but as for me and my house, we will serve the Lord.

Having enumerated the many reasons for national gratitude to God, Joshua called for a public, solemn pledge of allegiance, faithfulness and obedience to God. "It is

the conjecture of interpreters that upon this great occasion Joshua ordered the ark of God to be brought by the priests to Shechem, which, they say, was about 10 miles from Shiloh, and to be set down in the place of their meeting, which is therefore called 'the sanctuary of the Lord' (v. 26), the presence of the ark making it so at that time" (Matthew Henry). Joshua wanted the people to search their hearts completely. Nothing less than total surrender and soul-searching would suffice for the pledge of allegiance he was requesting.

God never takes away man's right to choose. It was the people's choice whether or not to serve Him, but there was no middle ground. A relationship with God is an exclusive one. He alone must be Lord of all. Because Joshua knew the history of this people's fascination with idol gods, he encouraged them to make a choice.

Joshua had already made the choice to serve God! Notice that he included "my house." The master of a house decided for the entire family, but Joshua was an old man with only a few days left. He was apparently confident that those in his family had made a firm decision to serve God. "Joshua was a ruler, a judge in Israel, yet he did not make his necessary application to public affairs an excuse for the neglect of family religion" (Matthew Henry).

B. The People Respond (vv. 16-18)

(Joshua 24:18 is not included in the printed text.)

16. And the people answered and said, God forbid that we should forsake the Lord, to serve other gods;

17. For the Lord our God, he it is that brought us up and our fathers out of the land of Egypt,

from the house of bondage, and which did those great signs in our sight, and preserved us in all the way wherein we went, and among all the people through whom we passed.

The people immediately declared that they would serve God alone. They seemed aware of the dangers of drifting from God. Reviewing the past not only brought their senses alive to God's goodness, but it also made them conscious of His judgments. They must have remembered the times God had disciplined them when they disobeyed.

Their quick proclamation of loyalty resembles the one their ancestors made at Mount Sinai. God had manifested Himself to the people there in a mighty way. The mountain shook and the people were stricken with fear. The question might be asked, "How long does fear control people?" The answer is only 40 days. Forty days after promising to serve God, Moses came down from the mountain to find the people worshiping the golden calf. Fear alone is a poor motivation for allegiance. Perhaps there was a level of fear in the people now, having just reviewed the mighty acts God had performed on their behalf.

C. Joshua Reiterates the Choice
   (vv. 19, 20)

(Joshua 24:19 is not included in the printed text.)

20. If ye forsake the Lord, and serve strange gods, then he will turn and do you hurt, and consume you, after that he hath done you good.

Joshua was not pleased with their quick response. It was as if they had not thought about the consequences of their decision. "Joshua was too wise to accept a hasty, shallow profession that might be temporary or partial" (Kent). He repeated the challenge again to make sure they understood the gravity of the promises they were making.

III. MAKE WISE CHOICES
   (Joshua 24:21-24)

21. And the people said unto Joshua, Nay; but we will serve the Lord.
22. And Joshua said unto the people, Ye are witnesses against yourselves that ye have chosen you the Lord, to serve him. And they said, We are witnesses.
23. Now therefore put away, said he, the strange gods which are among you, and incline your heart unto the Lord God of Israel.
24. And the people said unto Joshua, The Lord our God will we serve, and his voice will we obey.

The people affirmed their desire three times to serve the Lord (vv. 16-18, 21, 24). Now Joshua was confident that he had impressed on them the severity of their decision. To memorialize the occasion, he took a great stone and placed it under an oak tree as a witness to the people's intention (vv. 26, 27).

To their credit, this generation of Israel was true to its promises made at Shechem. Verse 31 says, "And Israel served the Lord all the days of Joshua, and all the days of the elders that overlived Joshua, and which had known all the works of the Lord, that he had done for Israel." The real problems did not begin until the leaders (Joshua and the elders) had all passed from the scene. This should be a reminder to us today as saints go to their eternal reward. When Christians in the church community die, their influence dies shortly afterward. In an age when older generations are not valued, we should hold our senior saints in highest respect. Their presence sometimes holds back temptation toward evil.

The vows made at Shechem established a great beginning for them in the Promised Land. What a different history Israel would have had, "had each succeeding generation of Israelites reached the same decision and stayed with it" (Epp).

GOLDEN TEXT HOMILY

"CHOOSE YOU THIS DAY WHOM YE WILL SERVE . . . BUT AS FOR ME AND MY HOUSE, WE WILL SERVE THE LORD" (Joshua 24:15).

Instability, insecurity and low morals secretly plague millions of Christian and non-Christian homes in today's world. In every generation since the beginning, the devil has sought to weaken and destroy the home. If he can destroy the home, he can deceive the next generation into dishonoring God. "As the whirlwind passeth, so is the wicked no more: but the righteous is an everlasting foundation" (Proverbs 10:25). "The fear of the Lord prolongeth days: but the years of the wicked shall be shortened" (v. 27). So is the strength of any family, community or nation. When there is a loss of power within the church, it can always be traced back to the neglect of honoring God in the homes of those who are the leaders of that church.

Joshua knew that if the leaders in these homes did not make this commitment as individuals, Israel would be only a short-lived nation in the land of Canaan. He knew that no power can depend on past victories, relationships, charms or forms to give victory today. We can brag and boast about past leaders and their contributions to the cause of Christ, but what will count in this world today will be those who are willing to accept the responsibility TODAY to choose as Joshua did.

If we are to remain a Christian nation, we must proclaim as Joshua did: "As for me and my house, we will serve the Lord" (Joshua 24:15).—**Aaron D. Mize**

SENTENCE SERMONS

LEADERS SHOULD base their decisions on the truth and promises of God's Word.

—Selected

NOT TO DECIDE is to decide.
—Harvey Cox

WHAT YOU DO when you don't have to will determine what you'll be when you can't help it.
—William D. Hersey

EVANGELISM APPLICATION

LIFE'S GREATEST DECISION IS TO ACCEPT JESUS AS PERSONAL SAVIOR.

Eli, the high priest, allowed his two sons to serve as priests, even though they were ungodly men. Finally, when the Lord had enough of their wickedness, He sent an unnamed prophet to Eli with these words: "Wherefore the Lord God of Israel saith, I said indeed that thy house, and the house of thy father, should walk before me for ever: but now the Lord saith, Be it far from me; for them that honour me I will honour, and they that despise me shall be lightly esteemed" (1 Samuel 2:30).

It is a great condemnation by the Lord to be "lightly esteemed." When we allow ourselves to slowly adapt to the heathen practices of the world around us, we reach the danger point of being completely out of the Father's eye—out of His protection and care. King Saul found himself in just such a situation when he visited a sorcerer to find direction in his misery. This was the warning Joshua was giving the nation of Israel.

When a person becomes a Christian, he or she literally marries Christ. We should be very careful in our evangelism to make sure our converts understand the seriousness of the step of faith they are taking. There are untold benefits to the Christian life, but there are great responsibilities as well.

ILLUMINATING THE LESSON

Every young girl dreams of a grand wedding day in a beautifully decorated church, filled with friends and relatives. In prosperous times, the costs of these large weddings can accelerate where thousands of dollars are spent by parents on opulent extras.

There is value in having many friends and family witness the vows of marriage in a solemn occasion. There is also an increased intensity to the meaning of the vows the bride and groom make to one another. This is as it should be. Promising fidelity and love to another should be a public gesture.

Joshua chose to bring the entire nation of Israel together in one final solemn "wedding" ceremony. He asked the people to make a public declaration of their fidelity and faithfulness to God. Certainly the presence of such a giant gathering added meaning to the words spoken.

Even the most solemn promises will be abandoned, however, if there is not a regular renewal of those vows. Just as marriages have to be worked out every day, so do our vows to God. They are not a one-time declaration that carries us through hard times. We must renew our pledges constantly if we stand firm through the temptations and pressures that life brings.

DAILY BIBLE READINGS

M. A Devastating Decision.
Genesis 3:1-6, 14-19
T. Contrasting Decisions.
Genesis 13:1-13
W. A Faithless Decision.
Numbers 14:1-9
T. A Wise Decision.
1 Kings 3:5-14
F. Consider the Cost.
Luke 14:27-33
S. Decide to Obey God.
Acts 5:22-32

TRUTH SEARCH:
Creatively Teaching the Word

Aim: Students will identify and make godly decisions during the next 30 days.

Items needed: These are optional, but very helpful:

1. *Brief video clip of the Holocaust (public library)
2. **Copies of the Supreme Court decision to remove prayer
3. **Copies of the Supreme Court decision to legalize abortion
4. **Copies of the Supreme Court decision (2000) to remove prayer from public high school sporting events

* The public library or local video store should have National Geographic videos on WWII.

** The Supreme Court decisions can be found online or at the public library. Ask for assistance.

FOCUS

Discuss in class some decisions that people have already made today (e.g., what clothes to wear, what to eat, whether or not to even come to church). Remind your class that people make hundreds of decisions (some consciously, some unconsciously) each day.

List on the board the following decisions (or others relevant to your class) made during the 20th century. Discuss the outcomes of those decisions. If you choose to use video clips and/or handouts, distribute them now.

1930s: Not curbing the rising power of Adolph Hitler and Nazism (WWII, Pearl Harbor, atomic weapons, the Holocaust)

1960s: Prayer taken out of the public schools

1970s: Roe vs. Wade (abortion legalized)

1990s: Clergy prevented from *praying at high school graduations; students prevented from praying before high school sports events*

EXPLORE

This is perhaps one of the most well known passages in Scripture, particularly as it relates to families and decisions to follow the Lord. The context is also important: the impending death of Joshua. Emphasize to the class that typically a dying person's last words are very important, and Joshua 24 is no exception. In light of this, discuss the following questions:

• *Why do you think Joshua rehearsed the history of God's blessings on Israel? Is there a connection between this and what Pentecostals call a "testimony service"?*

• *Joshua 24:15 is a key verse in this study. Here Joshua expresses clearly his intention for his entire family to serve the Lord. What are some of the decisions that families make today that will impact generations to come?*

• *The Book of Joshua ends on a positive note, with the children of Israel leaving to possess their inheritance. Yet there is also a sense of sadness as one reads the closing verses. All of the original group that came out of Egypt are now dead. We are left wondering how the stories will be transmitted to the next generation. What is your opinion of this and what implications does this have in your local congregation, especially as the older generation dies? Who is left to tell the stories of the faith to our children?*

RESPOND

Discuss with the class any

impending decisions (within the next 30 days) that need to be made in the church (e.g., business meetings, key financial decisions) or in the community (e.g., school board meetings, referendums, city council meetings). Have the class commit to praying for these meetings and attending them to express their Christian concerns and voice.

Discuss what decisions we, as Christian parents, have made or need to make to ensure our children have a firm foundation in our Christian faith.

Death Destroyed (Easter)

Study Text: 1 Corinthians 15:1-58
Objective: To affirm that Christ has conquered death and live in the hope of eternal life.
Time: Paul wrote 1 Corinthians in A.D. 56 or 57.
Place: Written in Ephesus to the Corinthians
Golden Text: "Now is Christ risen from the dead, and become the firstfruits of them that slept" (1 Corinthians 15:20).
Central Truth: Christ defeated sin and death by His death and resurrection.
Evangelism Emphasis: Faith in Christ is the only way to receive eternal life.

PRINTED TEXT

1 Corinthians 15:20. But now is Christ risen from the dead, and become the firstfruits of them that slept.

21. For since by man came death, by man came also the resurrection of the dead.

22. For as in Adam all die, even so in Christ shall all be made alive.

23. But every man in his own order: Christ the firstfruits; afterward they that are Christ's at his coming.

24. Then cometh the end, when he shall have delivered up the kingdom to God, even the Father; when he shall have put down all rule and all authority and power.

25. For he must reign, till he hath put all enemies under his feet.

26. The last enemy that shall be destroyed is death.

48. As is the earthy, such are they also that are earthy: and as is the heavenly, such are they also that are heavenly.

49. And as we have borne the image of the earthy, we shall also bear the image of the heavenly.

50. Now this I say, brethren, that flesh and blood cannot inherit the kingdom of God; nei- ther doth corruption inherit incorruption.

51. Behold, I shew you a mystery; We shall not all sleep, but we shall all be changed,

52. In a moment, in the twinkling of an eye, at the last trump: for the trumpet shall sound, and the dead shall be raised incorruptible, and we shall be changed.

53. For this corruptible must put on incorruption, and this mortal must put on immortality.

54. So when this corruptible shall have put on incorruption, and this mortal shall have put on immortality, then shall be brought to pass the saying that is written, Death is swallowed up in victory.

55. O death, where is thy sting? O grave, where is thy victory?

56. The sting of death is sin; and the strength of sin is the law.

57. But thanks be to God, which giveth us the victory through our Lord Jesus Christ.

58. Therefore, my beloved brethren, be ye stedfast, unmoveable, always abounding in the work of the Lord, forasmuch as ye know that your labour is not in vain in the Lord.

LESSON OUTLINE

I. CHRIST IS RISEN
   A. The Firstfruits of the Resurrection
   B. The Sin of Adam
   C. Christ's Mediatorial Role
II. BELIEVERS SHALL RISE
   A. The Resurrected Body
   B. The Natural and the Spiritual Body
III. VICTORY OVER DEATH

LESSON EXPOSITION

INTRODUCTION

The resurrection of the dead is a foundational doctrine of Christianity. *Resurrection* means the raising of a body from death, with the person's spirit and soul being reunited with that body.

Three types of resurrection are found in the Bible. The first is *miraculous healings*. In the Old Testament, Elijah raised the widow of Zarephath's son (1 Kings 17:17-23). Elisha did the same with the Shunammite woman's son (2 Kings 4:32-37). There was also the resurrection of a man after his body was placed in a grave where it touched Elisha's bones (2 Kings 13:21). In the New Testament, Jesus raised the widow of Nain's son (Luke 7:12-15), Jairus' daughter (Mark 5:41-43), and His close friend Lazarus (John 11:43, 44). Peter raised Dorcas (Acts 9:40, 41) and Paul raised Eutychus (20:9-12). In none of these situations, however, was the person raised to immortality. They all died again.

The second type is the *resurrection of Jesus Christ*. By His resurrection, the powers of sin, evil and death are defeated. Our faith is based on the Lord's resurrection. Though much of the world disputes

this, there is evidence to affirm that Jesus did bodily rise from the grave. Several indisputable pieces of evidence include: (1) He was really dead; the centurion in charge affirmed this. (2) The tomb was found empty and open, although the tomb had been sealed, a giant stone placed in front of it, and Roman soldiers dispatched to guard it from being tampered with by the Lord's followers (since He had predicted His resurrection). (3) Many testified to seeing Jesus after His resurrection, including as many as 500 at one time. (4) Countless changed lives down through the century affirm that Christ really is alive. *You - theme of*

The third type of resurrection is *witness* the *general resurrection of the saints*. The Old Testament abode of the dead was Sheol. The psalmist fully expected God to ransom his soul from here when he said, "But God will redeem my soul from the power of the grave: for he shall receive me" (Psalm 49:15). Job expressed the same idea: "And though after my skin worms destroy this body, yet in my flesh shall I see God" (19:26). Daniel affirmed that both the good and the evil would be resurrected: "And many of them that sleep in the dust of the earth shall awake, some to everlasting life, and some to shame and everlasting contempt" (12:2). Old Testament Jews firmly believed in a resurrection.

In the days of Jesus' earthly ministry, there were two polarized views concerning resurrection. The Sadducees totally rejected any belief in such. Their entire existence was entrenched in this life. The Pharisees, on the other hand, firmly believed in a resurrection. Before his Damascus-road experience, the apostle Paul had been a devout Pharisee. Though his revelation of the gospel was directly from the Lord himself, Paul's views of the resurrection reflected his early training as a Pharisee. In Acts 23:6, he stated that the reason he was on trial was for affirming the resurrection of the dead.

One note of interest: A strange resurrection also occurred at the moment Christ died on the cross. An earthquake shook Jerusalem, causing the veil in the Temple to split from top to bottom. Matthew records, "The tombs broke open and the bodies of many holy people who had died were raised to life. They came out of the tombs, and after Jesus' resurrection they went into the holy city and appeared to many people" (27:52, 53, *NIV*).

Scholars disagree in their interpretation of this unusual passage. Many think that the bodies of these saints were exposed by the earthquake and came to life for a brief time after the Lord's resurrection. Thus they gave testimony to His greater victory over death. Having made their testimony, they retired to their graves to be ultimately resurrected with the saints. Since they appeared to many, some think that they rose to heaven when Jesus ascended. Whatever the situation, we know little from this vague passage. *Matthew Henry's Commentary* probably gives the proper perspective: "The relating of this matter so briefly is . . . that we must not look that way for a confirmation of our faith" (notes on Matthew 27:50-56). A verse from Luke also affirms this position: "If they hear not Moses and the prophets, neither will they be persuaded, though one rose from the dead" (16:31).

The New Testament teaches firmly a hope of the believer's bodily resurrection from the dead.

Paul states this wonderfully in Philippians 3:20, 21: "For our citizenship is in heaven, from which we also eagerly wait for the Savior, the Lord Jesus Christ, who will transform our lowly body that it may be confirmed to His glorious body" (*NKJV*).

I. CHRIST IS RISEN
(1 Corinthians 15:20-26)

In 1 Corinthians 15, Paul gives a comprehensive treatise on the doctrine of resurrection from the grave. The Christians at Corinth were immature, many of whom vacillated in their thinking on this subject. Though they agreed that Christ had risen from the grave, there were those who had doubts about a general resurrection of believers. Paul unequivocally refutes their doubts by saying, "If there is no resurrection of the dead, then not even Christ has been raised" (v. 13, *NIV*). He then goes on to show that faith without the hope of resurrection is totally in vain (v. 17). The entire chapter attempts to answer three questions: (1) Is there a resurrection of the dead? (vv. 1-34). (2) What kind of body does a resurrected person have? (vv. 35-50). (3) What happens to those who are still alive at Christ's return? (vv. 51-57).

The heart of the gospel is given in a nutshell when Paul states, "That Christ died for our sins according to the Scriptures, that he was buried, that he was raised on the third day according to the Scriptures, and that he appeared to Peter, and then to the Twelve" (vv. 3-5, *NIV*).

A. The Firstfruits of the Resurrection (vv. 20, 21)

20. But now is Christ risen from the dead, and become the firstfruits of them that slept.

21. For since by man came death, by man came also the resurrection of the dead.

There had been resurrections of the dead before Christ's, but none were self-resurrections. Jesus "has truly risen Himself, and He has risen in this very quality and character, as the firstfruits of those who sleep in Him" (Matthew Henry). In the system of sacrifices under the Mosaic Law, *firstfruits* were the first of each harvest—be it fruit, grain, wine, fleece, and so forth. These offerings had to be perfect, free from any blemish. Christ was such an offering. He was literally our "firstborn from the dead" (Colossians 1:18). There need be no other offering, for "if the firstfruit be holy, the lump is also holy: and if the root be holy, so are the branches" (Romans 11:16).

If we were to go to an apple orchard and find the first ripe apple, this would be a sample of what the entire crop would produce. In the same sense, the firstfruits of the resurrection—Jesus Christ—rose from the dead as a sample of all who would follow.

B. The Sin of Adam (vv. 22, 23)

22. For as in Adam all die, even so in Christ shall all be made alive.

23. But every man in his own order: Christ the firstfruits; afterward they that are Christ's at his coming.

Paul goes on to show a connection between the first and second Adam. Since the first Adam introduced mankind to sin and mortality, it would take the resurrection of the Second Adam to conquer sin and again offer mankind immortality. Because of Adam's sin, we share in his death. Because of Christ's resurrection, we share in His resurrection. "All who die, die through the sin of Adam; all who are raised . . . rise through the merit and power of Christ" (Matthew Henry).

The phrase "in his own order" means that it is fitting that Christ should be the first to be resurrected. He is first in honor, rank and dignity, and the resurrection of all others depends on His. The resurrection of believers should follow in due time and order. Paul possibly added this to counteract the Gnostic notion that the resurrection was a spiritual awakening that had already occurred. He strongly condemned such heresy when he wrote to Timothy (see 2 Timothy 2:17-19).

C. Christ's Mediatorial Role
   (vv. 24-26)

24. Then cometh the end, when he shall have delivered up the kingdom to God, even the Father; when he shall have put down all rule and all authority and power.

25. For he must reign, till he hath put all enemies under his feet.

26. The last enemy that shall be destroyed is death.

All three members of the Godhead—Father, Son, and Spirit—are equal and operate in perfect unity, but with different roles. In the scheme of eternity, Jesus Christ is in control of all creation until His work on earth is completed. At that point, He will give His authority back to the Father. Even though He conquered death Himself, there must still be the future resurrection of the saints, or death and the grave would still have power over us. In the final days to come, Christ will strike down Satan and all evil.

"World events may seem out of control and justice may seem scarce, but God is in control, allowing evil to remain for a time until He sends Jesus to earth again. Then Jesus will present to God a perfect new world" (*Life Application Bible*, notes on 1 Corinthians 15:25-28).

Jesus ascended back to heaven after His resurrection and is now "set on the right hand of the throne of the Majesty in the heavens" (Hebrews 8:1). In other words, Jesus, our High Priest, sitting at the right hand of the Father, intercedes for us to the Father. He is head of the church and has the power to protect and build it. When all His enemies are destroyed and the salvation of the church is completed, He will turn His authority back to the Father.

II. BELIEVERS SHALL RISE (1 Corinthians 15:35-49)

A. The Resurrected Body (vv. 35-41)

(1 Corinthians 15:35-41 is not included in the printed text.)

To anyone who doubts God's existence and the truth of the gospel of Jesus Christ, resurrection is a preposterous idea. However, to those who "know that God is almighty and that Jesus Christ is the Son of God and our Savior, the resurrection is not only possible, but real and reasonable" (Manford George Gutzke, *Plain Talk on First and Second Corinthians*).

Paul moves into an explanation of what our resurrected bodies will be like. He tells the Corinthians that we will be immediately recognizable, yet our new bodies will be far superior to anything we can possibly imagine. Our personality and individuality will be intact, but we will be perfected through the work of Christ. These bodies will also be immune to sickness, disease, decay and death.

When a kernel of corn is planted in the earth, the new corn still has the same identity. We will still have our identities after the resurrection, but "it doth not yet appear what we shall be: but we know that, when he shall appear, we shall be like him; for we shall see him as he is" (1 John 3:2). We will be different from what we are now, just like the risen body of Christ was different from His pre-crucifixion one. The Lord's disciples recognized Jesus, but they also recognized something radically different about His resurrected body.

In verse 40 of the text, the word *terrestrial* means "earthly"—that is, made up of earthly matter. "Body of clay" is a perfect definition. On the other hand, *celestial* means "heavenly," or coming from another place. Our new bodies will be unlike anything that can be formed from earthly "clay."

B. The Natural and the Spiritual Body (vv. 42-49)

(1 Corinthians 15:42-47 is not included in the printed text.)

48. As is the earthy, such are they also that are earthy: and as is the heavenly, such are they also that are heavenly.

49. And as we have borne the image of the earthy, we shall also bear the image of the heavenly.

Our resurrected bodies will be like our present bodies only in certain respects—personality, identification, character. They will be different in that they are made of a different type of matter—not earthly clay but an incorruptible composition. Even though what is planted in the earth at death is a corruptible seed, that which comes forth will be incorruptible (v. 42).

It is easy for us to think of "spiritual bodies" as somehow not being real. However, when Jesus appeared to His disciples after His resurrection, they certainly saw Him as very real. He was not an apparition. It was a body that could be handled, touched and experienced, yet it was not human flesh. The substance of our resurrected bodies will not be of elements such as carbon, oxygen, hydrogen, and so forth, but rather of spiritual composition. Spiritual matter is eternal—it will never die.

III. VICTORY OVER DEATH
(1 Corinthians 15:50-58)

50. Now this I say, brethren, that flesh and blood cannot inherit the kingdom of God; neither doth corruption inherit incorruption.

51. Behold, I shew you a mystery; We shall not all sleep, but we shall all be changed,

52. In a moment, in the twinkling of an eye, at the last trump: for the trumpet shall sound, and the dead shall be raised incorruptible, and we shall be changed.

53. For this corruptible must put on incorruption, and this mortal must put on immortality.

54. So when this corruptible shall have put on incorruption, and this mortal shall have put on immortality, then shall be brought to pass the saying that is written, Death is swallowed up in victory.

55. O death, where is thy sting? O grave, where is thy victory?

56. The sting of death is sin; and the strength of sin is the law.

57. But thanks be to God, which giveth us the victory through our Lord Jesus Christ.

58. Therefore, my beloved brethren, be ye stedfast, unmoveable, always abounding in the work of the Lord, forasmuch as ye know that your labour is not in vain in the Lord.

Paul makes a startling indictment to the Corinthian way of thinking when he says "flesh and blood cannot inherit the kingdom of God" (v. 50). In other words, no mortal human being can inherit heaven. There must be a transformation! "No human being in his own physical, sociological human nature can enter the kingdom of God" (Gutzke). Corruptible bodies can only produce corruption!

In verses 51 and 52, Paul explains that not everyone will go through the physical experience of death. The body of a person who dies will return to dust, but it will be raised in an incorruptible state. The Christian who is still alive when Christ returns will be suddenly transformed, in an instant of time, to have a spiritual body as well. All of us (both resurrected and transformed) will have new bodies just like the body of Jesus after His resurrection.

Paul finishes by encouraging his readers to grasp these truths, put them firmly into their body of faith, and never waver in their expectation of what Christ will do for them.

GOLDEN TEXT HOMILY

"NOW IS CHRIST RISEN FROM THE DEAD, AND BECOME THE FIRSTFRUITS OF THEM THAT SLEPT" (1 Corinthians 15:20).

How much would people pay for a formula or process that would arrest the deterioration of their bodies through aging? Many people would give everything they had for a product that would guarantee they would never grow old. Almost since the beginning of mankind, people have sought after the elusive "eternal youth" potion. In our time some people have spent hundreds of thousands of dollars to have their bodies frozen and preserved in liquid nitrogen after they died, in the hope that they could be restored to life and be young again.

The exciting thing is that "eternal youth" is available! There is no question about the factuality of the restoration of Christ from the dead. It was prophesied in the Old Testament, predicted by Christ, mentioned more than 100 times in the New Testament, and was the major theme of the apostles' preaching. The stone was rolled away, the tomb was empty, and Christ appeared to many. Jesus Christ is alive, and He is offering "eternal youth" to all those who will become His disciples.

His resurrection is a pledge and proof of the resurrection of all His followers. "Firstfruits" means that there are more to follow. According to 1 Corinthians 15, our resurrected bodies will be real, perfect, without their present limitations; they will have their own personal characteristics and will never know death.

Praise God for the reality of 1 Corinthians 15:20. Because He lives, we too can live and have "eternal youth"!—**Philip Siggelkow**

SENTENCE SERMONS

CHRIST DEFEATED sin and death by His death and resurrection.
—**Selected**

ALL THAT IS NOT eternal is out of date.
—**C.S. Lewis**

DEATH IS NOT a period but a comma in the story of life.
—**Amos Traver**

EVANGELISM APPLICATION

FAITH IN CHRIST IS THE ONLY WAY TO RECEIVE ETERNAL LIFE.

Paul wrote a wonderful verse to the Romans that affirms our lesson. He said, "If the Spirit of Him who raised Jesus from the dead dwells in you, He who raised Christ from the dead will also give life to your mortal bodies through His Spirit who dwells in you" (Romans 8:11, *NKJV*). This is a tremendous promise that offers great hope to us! However, many of us have a doubting spirit like the people in Corinth had. We believe Christ rose, but we limit His resurrection power. Does this sound confusing? What I'm talking about is not the resurrection of our bodies, but a resurrection of dreams that have died in our hearts.

Is there a loved one who has stooped so low in sin that you've quit praying for him or her? Is there a wounded friendship you've simply allowed to die? Is there a desire in your heart that you've given up on? Is there a sin that you have not been able to overcome?

Jesus has the resurrection power over dreams, hopes, salvations for loved ones, temptations—everything that affects us. His strength is not just over physical death, but also over anything that we've allowed to die. We must restore our trust in His resurrection power, for God has "put all things under his feet" (Ephesians 1:22). Jesus has living power over our dead circumstances! Just believe Him!

ILLUMINATING THE LESSON

In reading 1 Corinthians 15, it's easy to imagine Paul being frustrated with the immature believers at Corinth. How could they not believe in the resurrection of Jesus? How could they not expect a bodily resurrection of the saints? He is incredulous at their ignorance and misguided thinking. This culminates with verse 19, when he says, "If in this life only we have hope in Christ, we are of all men most miserable." In other words, if Christ is just a crutch to get you through the daily trials of human existence— then you've missed out on life altogether! You really don't know Him at all! Your faith is phony and nonexistent.

Paul knew that if these people didn't have hope in Christ for the future, they didn't have a true hope in Him for the present. In other words, they were limiting God's power and promises. The psalmist said of Israel, "Yea, they turned back and tempted God, and limited the Holy One of Israel" (Psalm 78:41). Israel limited God with her doubt and unbelief.

Are we really different today? Do we trust Christ in most areas of our lives, but hold back a small area? Is there a pocket of unbelief in your heart that says God will never undertake here?

Don't limit the power of the resurrected Christ! Always proclaim, "God can! God can!" God can and will do all that we ask and believe!

DAILY BIBLE READINGS

M. Hope of Resurrection.
　　Job 19:23-27
T. Resurrection Foretold.
　　Psalm 16:8-11
W. Order of Resurrection.
　　John 5:24-29
T. Promise of Resurrection.
　　John 11:23-26
F. Resurrection of Believers.
　　Revelation 20:4-6
S. Resurrection of Unbelievers.
　　Revelation 20:12-15

TRUTH SEARCH:
Creatively Teaching the Word

Aim: To make spiritual preparation for death.

Materials needed: Paper, pencils, marker board, markers, poster board cut into the shape of a tombstone (make two or more if you have a large class).

FOCUS

Before class, write the following statement on the marker board: "I'm not afraid to die; I just don't want to be there when it happens."—Woody Allen
• *Can you relate to Woody Allen's statement?*
Most of us try to avoid thinking about our own death. Yet, death is inevitable.

Name things people do to prepare for death (for instance: preparing a will, buying a funeral plot, purchasing life insurance, preplanning their funeral).

Ask students to think about whether or not they have made any of those preparations. Then ask them to name other things people do in preparation for their passing.
• *What spiritual preparations should people make for their death?*

EXPLORE

Divide the class into groups of four or five students each. Assign each group one of the following sets of verses from 1 Corinthians 15 for study: verses 20-26, 35-49, and 50-58. After the groups have finished answering the questions, have everyone come together and discuss their findings.
1 Corinthians 15:20-26
1. *How did death enter the world (vv. 21, 22)?*

2. *Why is Christ called "the first-fruits" (vv. 20, 23)? What does that mean?*
3. *List the different things Christ will do to establish His dominion at the end of time (vv. 23-26).*
4. *Why is death called "the last enemy" (v. 26)?*
1 Corinthians 15:35-49
1. *What does the planting of seed teach about the bodily resurrection (vv. 35-39)?*
2. *Discuss the differences between the earthly human body and the resurrected body (vv. 42-44).*
3. *Who was the last Adam? Contrast the last Adam with the first Adam (vv. 45-47).*
4. *What promise is given to believers in verses 48 and 49?*
1 Corinthians 15:50-58
1. *Explain Paul's statement "Flesh and blood cannot inherit the kingdom of God" (v. 50).*
2. *Describe how and when the believer's body will be changed (vv. 51-53).*
3. *According to verses 54-57, how will death be defeated once and for all? What else will be defeated?*
4. *When we understand God's promises concerning resurrection and immortality, how should we respond, according to verse 58?*

RESPOND

Pass the tombstone and marker around the room. Ask everyone to initial it. (If you have a large class, you should use more than one tombstone and marker.) Once the poster has been returned to you, say the following:
It's inevitable—unless Christ returns first, all of us will die, our bodies will be buried, and

our names etched on a tombstone. However, if we have
made spiritual preparation for
death, it will not sting!

Rip the tombstone(s) in half.

Challenge the students to consider their own spiritual condition. If any have not yet received
Christ's forgiveness, challenge
them to do so today.

Lead a prayer affirming belief in
Christ's resurrection and asking
Him to make every student spiri-
tually prepared for death.

Leadership in Times of Crisis

Study Text: Judges 2:10-15; 4:1-16
Objective: To realize that God provides a strategy for difficult times and look to His Word when dealing with crises.
Time: Around 1250 B.C.
Place: Kishon River near Mount Tabor
Golden Text: "I will bless the Lord, who hath given me counsel" (Psalm 16:7).
Central Truth: Godly leaders solve problems by applying Biblical principles.
Evangelism Emphasis: Sinners are often more receptive to the gospel during crises.

PRINTED TEXT

Judges 4:1. And the children of Israel again did evil in the sight of the Lord, when Ehud was dead.

2. And the Lord sold them into the hand of Jabin king of Canaan, that reigned in Hazor; the captain of whose host was Sisera, which dwelt in Harosheth of the Gentiles.

3. And the children of Israel cried unto the Lord: for he had nine hundred chariots of iron; and twenty years he mightily oppressed the children of Israel.

4. And Deborah, a prophetess, the wife of Lapidoth, she judged Israel at that time.

6. And she sent and called Barak the son of Abinoam out of Kedesh-naphtali, and said unto him, Hath not the Lord God of Israel commanded, saying, Go and draw toward mount Tabor, and take with thee ten thousand men of the children of Naphtali and of the children of Zebulun?

7. And I will draw unto thee to the river Kishon Sisera, the captain of Jabin's army, with his chariots and his multitude; and I will deliver him into thine hand.

8. And Barak said unto her, If thou wilt go with me, then I will go: but if thou wilt not go with me, then I will not go.

9. And she said, I will surely go with thee: notwithstanding the journey that thou takest shall not be for thine honour; for the Lord shall sell Sisera into the hand of a woman. And Deborah arose, and went with Barak to Kedesh.

10. And Barak called Zebulun and Naphtali to Kedesh; and he went up with ten thousand men at his feet: and Deborah went up with him.

14. And Deborah said unto Barak, Up; for this is the day in which the Lord hath delivered Sisera into thine hand: is not the Lord gone out before thee? So Barak went down from mount Tabor, and ten thousand men after him.

15. And the Lord discomfited Sisera, and all his chariots, and all his host, with the edge of the sword before Barak; so that Sisera lighted down off his chariot, and fled away on his feet.

16. But Barak pursued after the chariots, and after the host, unto Harosheth of the Gentiles: and all the host of Sisera fell upon the edge of the sword; and there was not a man left.

DICTIONARY

discomfit—Judges 4:15—To defeat in battle.

LESSON OUTLINE

I. DIAGNOSE THE PROBLEM
   A. A Vacuum of Leadership
   B. From Complacency to Evil
   C. God's Anger
   D. A Continuous Cycle of Sin and Defeat
II. COMMISSION THE PERSONNEL
   A. An Unlikely Candidate for Judge
   B. Carrying Out God's Command
III. IMPLEMENT A PLAN

LESSON EXPOSITION

INTRODUCTION

The Book of Judges takes up precisely where Joshua ends. The great warrior-leader died at age 110 and was buried "in the land of his inheritance" (Joshua 24:29, 30, *NIV*). He had personally possessed his inheritance and effectively led the people throughout his lifetime. For a time the people continued to do as the Lord commanded. As the other elders of Joshua's generation died, however, the people began to drift and forget their purpose.

Because the nation did not have a strong leader like Joshua, it began to lose its grip on the land. Since there were 12 separate tribes, there was no central government. Even though this was a theocracy, the people scattered and lost their spiritual unity. "Instead of exhibiting spiritual fervor, Israel sank into *apathy*; instead of obeying the Lord, the people moved into *apostasy*; and instead of the nation enjoying law and order, the land was filled with *anarchy*" (Warren W. Wiersbe, *Be Available—Judges—Accepting the Challenge to Confront the Enemy*).

The history of the nation of Israel during the era of the Judges is characterized by what might be called the "cycle of spiritual instability." Seven stages are repeated:

1. Faithfulness to God during the leadership of a particular judge
2. Rebellion against God as soon as that judge died
3. God's allowing the people to fall into the hands of an enemy people, resulting in great suffering and oppression
4. A cry to God for help
5. God's raising up a judge and anointing him to deliver the people
6. Miraculous deliverance through the judge
7. Renewed loyalty.

We should note that the enemies who overwhelmed Israel during this period were heathen people God had demanded them to destroy. Rather than destroy them, the Israelites allowed the native Canaanites to live among them, thus causing the cycle of sin to regularly repeat itself. The same pattern is prevalent among many Christians. During a crisis they cry out to the Lord for deliverance. When He comes to their aid, they promise allegiance, love and service. However, they fail to deal with the secret sin that has plagued them. They think that they have control over it, that it won't rise again to bewitch them. Like the alcoholic who says he can still take one drink without its affecting him, they hold on to pockets of rebellion in their hearts. They don't completely destroy the enemy after God has delivered them. Before long, the cycle of spiritual failure has begun anew.

The question might arise as to whether we can ever completely overcome the temptations that plague our Christian lives. The reason God allowed the heathen Canaanites to remain in the Promised Land (without Himself miraculously removing them) was so that the people would exercise their faith and obedience by possessing their inheritance. Had they done so, they would have found Him totally committed to helping them win the victory. The same is true for the Christian. As we move in faith and obedience to overcome temptations and secret sins, we always find Him faithful. It is a daily battle, one where we constantly have to "crucify the flesh" (Galatians 5:24), but as we trust Him, the victory is ours.

Could the Israelites have completely driven out the Canaanites? Yes, because God told them to do so. He never gives a command without also giving the strength and means to complete it. Israel failed because she was attracted to the fleshly, seductive practices of the Canaanite religions. Our failures in defeating our secret sins and temptations result from the fact that we are so attracted to the idolatry the flesh offers us. Israel never drove out her enemies. Many Christians never seem to crucify the flesh. It seems almost too difficult a thing to do, but again—God never commands anything that He doesn't give the strength to accomplish.

I. DIAGNOSE THE PROBLEM (Judges 2:10-15; 4:1-3)

A. A Vacuum of Leadership (2:10)

(Judges 2:10 is not included in the printed text.)

To their credit, the generation that lived under Joshua did remain somewhat faithful to God. It was not until the last of the elders had died that the nation began a massive drift. What caused this drift? The fact that a generation grew up who "knew not the Lord" is an indication that the Word of God was neglected. They had a copy of Deuteronomy in their midst and had been commanded to read it publicly every Sabbatical Year during the Feast of Tabernacles (see Deuteronomy 31:9-13). Joshua had been a great leader because he heeded God's command to him: "This book of the law shall not depart out of thy mouth; but thou shalt meditate therein day and night" (Joshua 1:8). This new generation lost touch with God's Law, and as a consequence began a long slide toward apostasy.

Possibly another factor entering the picture was the seeming cruelty of God's command to exterminate all the peoples of Canaan. However, had the Israelites looked at the history of the region, they would have seen that God had been merciful and patient with these pagans for centuries. It was obvious they were wicked beyond redemption. God knew they would eventually contaminate His people. They were like leaven, permeating everything they touched—much the same as Jesus would later warn of the "leaven of the Pharisees" (Matthew 16:6). The central deities of the Canaanites were Baal and his female counterpart Ashtoreth. The worship of these false gods combined idolatry, immorality and sacrifices offered for agricultural success. They appealed to the flesh, and in the absence of a strong worship of God, their attraction became all the more enticing.

B. From Complacency to Evil (vv. 11-13)

(Judges 2:11-13 is not included in the printed text.)

Joshua's farewell speech and challenge at Shechem was now forgotten. Israel actively embraced foreign religions that were forbidden to her. Matthew Henry calls these idols "dunghill deities" and says of the Israelites: "Whatever they took for their god, they served them and bowed down to them, gave honour to them and begged favours from them." Jehovah was completely forsaken and replaced by the fleshly pleasures Baal and Ashtoreth flaunted.

C. God's Anger (vv. 14, 15)

(Judges 2:14, 15 is not included in the printed text.)

At a certain point in their descent into heathenism, God apparently gave up on the Israelites and "delivered" them into the subjugation of the Canaanites. Thus, they were no longer conquerors, but rather the conquered. Whenever they went to battle, God's hand was now against them. "The Lord was doing exactly what He had warned He would do. And He brought His judgment through the ordinary processes of history, through invasion and oppression" (Kent).

In reading Judges 2, several key factors become apparent in the people's slide into idolatry: (1) They forgot what God had done for them over the years—the deliverance, the sustenance, the victories; (2) they forgot what He had told them to do, that is, actively studying and embracing the law of Moses; (3) they forfeited God's blessings, which God had warned them against (Deuteronomy 28:25, 26). Worse than all of this, however, is that a cycle was begun—one where they never learned from their past.

D. A Continuous Cycle of Sin and Defeat (4:1-3)

1. And the children of Israel again did evil in the sight of the Lord, when Ehud was dead.

2. And the Lord sold them into the hand of Jabin king of Canaan, that reigned in Hazor; the captain of whose host was Sisera, which dwelt in Harosheth of the Gentiles.

3. And the children of Israel cried unto the Lord: for he had nine hundred chariots of iron; and twenty years he mightily oppressed the children of Israel.

The first three judges—Othniel, Ehud and Shamgar—miraculously led Israel out of bondage. After they defeated the enemy that came up against them, peace and faithfulness to the Lord was maintained as long as these particular judges lived. However, as soon as the judge died, the people fell right back into their cycle of sin. Instead of destroying their enemies, Israel made treaties with them. "You will be our servants," they said. Soon, however, they were intermarrying with them. Because of intermarriage, they would quickly combine worship of the heathen gods with the worship of Jehovah. In other words, a new hybrid religion was formed. The gods of any territory or culture have a tendency to mix in with pure worship of God. Whatever culture we live in today, we must be adamant in our fight to keep its heathen practices out of our worship of God.

Chapter 4 begins with Israel again in the depths of sin, and again in bondage—this time to King Jabin of Hazor. His army chief was Sisera, who commanded 900 iron chariots. These were the "nuclear warfare" of a primitive age. "Some chariots even had razor sharp knives extending from the wheels designed to mutilate helpless foot soldiers" (*Life Application Bible*). The Israelites were certainly no match for such armor. After 20 years of dreadful persecution, the people finally turned to God in desperation.

II. COMMISSION THE PERSONNEL (Judges 4:4-10)

A. An Unlikely Candidate for Judge (vv. 4, 5)

(Judges 4:5 is not included in the printed text.)

4. And Deborah, a prophetess, the wife of Lapidoth, she judged Israel at that time.

Here we find God doing as He often does—picking the most unlikely person to become a leader. Deborah was a prophet. A prophet is one who receives revelations directly from God for the people. Sometimes prophecy is predictive, but more often it has to do with immediate situations. Deborah's work was such. There is no recording of her making a predictive statement. Her work was involved with the state of affairs Israel had fallen into. For a woman to become judge in a male-dominated society such as Israel had to be a humbling experience. Isaiah later had a comment on such situations: "As for my people, children are their oppressors, and women rule over them" (Isaiah 3:12). "For God to give His people a woman judge was to treat them like little children, which is exactly what they were when it came to spiritual things" (Wiersbe).

Deborah had special gifts of insight, foresight and wisdom. She served in the judicial process of the land by dispensing justice at the gate. People regularly went to her for advice and settlement of their civil disputes. She was the one voice speaking for God in a dark time.

B. Carrying Out God's Command (vv. 6-10)

6. And she sent and called Barak the son of Abinoam out of Kedesh-naphtali, and said unto him, Hath not the Lord God of Israel commanded, saying, Go and draw toward mount Tabor, and take with thee ten thousand men of the children of Naphtali and of the children of Zebulun?

7. And I will draw unto thee to the river Kishon Sisera, the captain of Jabin's army, with his chariots and his multitude; and I will deliver him into thine hand.

8. And Barak said unto her, If thou wilt go with me, then I will go: but if thou wilt not go with me, then I will not go.

9. And she said, I will surely go with thee: notwithstanding the journey that thou takest shall not be for thine honour; for the Lord shall sell Sisera into the hand of a woman. And Deborah arose, and went with Barak to Kedesh.

10. And Barak called Zebulun and Naphtali to Kedesh; and he went up with ten thousand men at his feet: and Deborah went up with him.

Deborah exercised great authority, as seen in her summoning Barak. She gave him detailed instructions from the Lord as to how to defeat Sisera. "When God wants to glorify Himself through His people, He always has a perfect plan for us to follow" (Wiersbe). Every detail was covered. God never leaves anything out. Barak was to assemble an army of Israelites and draw Sisera's troops into a trap near Mount Tabor. Here the Lord would bring a mighty victory.

Barak accepted his responsibility as general of the army, but not without one great reservation. Deborah must go with him into battle. Was this an expression of unbelief? Or, perhaps could it have been a point of humility on his part? There is no indication that he questioned God's guidance in the situation. Since Deborah agreed to go, there is neither any evidence that she saw his demand as being out of God's will. Considering that weapons were a scarce commodity in Israel, and that there was no regular standing army, Barak's willingness to accept Deborah's plan shows great faith in God. Still, in her granting his wish to accompany the army, the honor for winning the battle would go to a woman and not a man.

III. IMPLEMENT A PLAN
(Judges 4:11-16)

(Judges 4:11-13 is not included in the printed text.)

14. And Deborah said unto Barak, Up; for this is the day in which the Lord hath delivered Sisera into thine hand: is not the Lord gone out before thee? So Barak went down from mount Tabor, and ten thousand men after him.

15. And the Lord discomfited Sisera, and all his chariots, and all his host, with the edge of the sword before Barak; so that Sisera lighted down off his chariot, and fled away on his feet.

16. But Barak pursued after the chariots, and after the host, unto Harosheth of the Gentiles: and all the host of Sisera fell upon the edge of the sword; and there was not a man left.

The "rest of the story" is fascinating. God was totally in charge of the battle. Were Heber the Kenite (v. 11) and his family traitors to Israel? The Kenites (see Judges 1:16) were relatives of the Jews and had joined themselves to God's people years earlier. Some suggest that Heber had aligned himself with the Canaanites because of his trade as an itinerant metalworker. It's possible, however, that he was a spy for Israel and had been sent to set a trap. Also, he may simply have been a neutral who wanted no part of war. Whatever the situation, God had him in the right place at the right time for His purposes.

Sisera depended on his 900 iron chariots for a military advantage, but God sent a strong rain that caused the battlefield to become one giant quagmire of mud. This made it easy for Israelite soldiers to attack and slaughter the enemy. Also, God caused a great confusion to come into the minds of the Canaanites. Part of this was caused by the fact that the battle was fought during what normally was the dry season of the year (June through September). Since Baal was the god of storms, "you can see how the sudden change of weather could have affected the superstitious Canaanites" (Wiersbe).

It became evident that Jehovah God was stronger than any Canaanite deity. Even the enemy could see this. Their only hope was to run for their lives. The story of how Sisera fled like a frightened rabbit (and met his demise at the hand of Jael, Heber's wife—vv. 17-21) further indicates how God knows exactly what He is doing in bringing victory to His people.

GOLDEN TEXT HOMILY

"I WILL BLESS THE LORD, WHO HATH GIVEN ME COUNSEL" (Psalm 16:7).

There were certain qualities in David which enabled him to become one of the greatest leaders of all time and a man after God's own heart.

David was a worshiper: "I will bless the Lord." To bless the Lord means to give praise and adoration to Him. For example, David instructed himself to praise the Lord and then cited the reasons in Psalm 103. When we instruct ourselves to praise Him, the feelings will follow.

David sought the counsel of the Lord. God taught David to trust and follow His instruction and guidance. The generation after Joshua did not seek the counsel of the Lord as their forefathers; therefore, they did not know the Lord nor the work He had done.

David listened to his heart: "My heart instructs me" (Psalm 16:7, NIV). This statement refers directly or indirectly to the Lord who searches our innermost being.

David chose a quiet time to pray in the night seasons. Choosing a time to still our "noisy heart" enables the Holy Spirit to deal with us in communion, correction and guidance. Jesus often spent nights alone on the mountain with the Father and received the counsel He needed for the day. Jesus said, in effect, "I always do the things which I hear the Father saying." So should we all.—**G. Faye Whitten**

SENTENCE SERMONS

GODLY LEADERS solve problems by applying Biblical principles.
—Selected

LET GOD'S problems shine on your problems.
—Corrie Ten Boom

EVANGELISM APPLICATION

SINNERS ARE OFTEN MORE RECEPTIVE TO THE GOSPEL DURING CRISES.

The idols of an existing culture always attach themselves to godly worship. The most deceptive religion to invade the church in the United States today is the gospel of success and prosperity. Christians are so accustomed to the amenities that wealth provides that they have made them their gods. The ideals of self-sacrifice, helping others with humility have been abandoned. Even our efforts at evangelism are tainted. Instead of sharing Christ with the thought of self-abandonment and taking up a cross, we present Him as a perfect relationship to complement our selfish whims. In other words, all our needs will be met without any cost to us.

What are the results of such a false gospel? The divorce rate within the church is the same as in the world. The lack of integrity is the same as in the world. The lowering of standards has followed suit with that of the world. Even though great numbers of people go to church, there is little dedication to Christ.

All is not lost, however. The lesson to be learned from the Judges is that despite their failures, when the people finally did call on God—He responded. The devil will fight prayer more than anything else in a church, because prayer activates God's help and provision. The church can be restored, but we must learn that God will not tolerate worship of anyone except Himself.

ILLUMINATING THE LESSON

The owner of a small used-car business (one that did on-site financing for people with bad credit) was asked about the ethics of charging customers such high interest rates. It somehow seemed unfair to charge the poorer customers, who made up his clientele, more than double what the local banks charged.

His answer was simple: "The customers who come to us have earned the right to be charged a high rate. Most of them are slow to pay their bills, and frequently don't bother at all. They have poor credit because they didn't obey the rules. They deserve the high rates we have to charge them in order to sell them a car."

The same might be said of the Canaanites. When reading the Books of Joshua and Judges, we have a tendency to think it was cruel for the Israelites to invade Canaan with the expressed purpose of destroying the existing heathen nations who lived there. We have to remember, however, that God gave the land of Palestine to Abraham and his descendants. Israel was not sent into Canaan just to murder and plunder an innocent, kindly, "godly" people. No, Israel was to be God's instrument of judgment against sin. The people there had forfeited their rights to the land and even to life itself.

DAILY BIBLE READINGS

M. Intercession in Crisis.
Genesis 18:16-26
T. God Honors Obedience.
Genesis 22:1-13
W. Praise Brings Victory.
2 Chronicles 20:14-22
T. A Crisis Resolved.
Acts 15:1-22
F. Miraculous Deliverance.
Acts 16:25-34
S. Administer Grace in Crises.
2 Corinthians 2:3-11

TRUTH SEARCH:
Creatively Teaching the Word

Aim: Students will pray for church leaders.

Materials needed: Marker, marker board

FOCUS

Write "Spiritual Crises" on the top of the marker board.
• *What kinds of spiritual crises is the church facing today?*

On the left side of the marker board, list the issues named.
• *What should the church be doing to address these issues?*

On the right side of the board, list the ideas named.

According to Scripture, God raises up leaders to help His church face challenges.

EXPLORE

Have everyone open their Bibles to Judges 2, and have a volunteer read verse 10 aloud.
• *Describe the predicament Israel was facing.*
• *How does this crisis compare with the condition of the church today?*

Ask another volunteer to read verses 11-13.
• *Describe the Israelites' relationship with God at this time.*
• *How does this compare with the church's spiritual condition today?*

Read verses 14 and 15 to the class.
• *Because of their sins, how was God acting toward His people?*

In Judges 4 we see this pattern of rebellion against God continuing.

Ask everyone to silently read verses 1-5 from their Bibles.
• *How were the people judged for their rebellion?*

Because God's people cried to Him, He raised up a godly leader to deliver them. She was a judge named Deborah.

Ask a volunteer to read verses 6-10.
• *Describe the military plan Deborah gave to Barak.*
• *How did Barak respond at first? Why? What does this say about Barak's confidence in Deborah?*
• *How did Deborah respond to Barak's request?*

Have someone read verses 12 and 13.
• *Why would Sisera's army have been an imposing sight?*
• *How does this physical display of 900 iron chariots compare with the spiritual foes our church is currently facing?*

Read verse 14 to the class.
• *What was Deborah's response to the sight of 900 iron chariots? Why?*
• *What lesson can the church learn from Deborah's attitude?*

Have someone read verses 15 and 16 aloud.
• *What was the result of the confrontation?*
• *What will cause God to join us in battling spiritual crises?*

RESPOND

Our church needs godly leaders who will guide us during times of crisis.

Name the various leaders in your local church—pastor, pastoral staff, elders, teachers, and so on. Lead the class in interceding on behalf of these individuals.

Next, lead a prayer in which you ask God to raise up more godly leaders in your church.

Finally, encourage the students to regularly pray for the church's leaders.

The Danger of Compromise

Study Text: Judges 13:1 through 16:31
Objective: To acknowledge that leaders can compromise their call, and diligently guard our hearts.
Time: Around 1150 B.C.
Place: Gaza and the Valley of Sorek
Golden Text: "Keep thy heart with all diligence; for out of it are the issues of life" (Proverbs 4:23).
Central Truth: Doctrinal and moral compromise undermine spiritual leadership.
Evangelism Emphasis: Doctrinal and moral compromise undermine effective evangelism.

PRINTED TEXT

Judges 13:3. And the angel of the Lord appeared unto the woman, and said unto her, Behold now, thou art barren, and bearest not: but thou shalt conceive, and bear a son.

5. For, lo, thou shalt conceive, and bear a son; and no rasor shall come on his head: for the child shall be a Nazarite unto God from the womb: and he shall begin to deliver Israel out of the hand of the Philistines.

16:4. And it came to pass afterward, that he loved a woman in the valley of Sorek, whose name was Delilah.

17. That he told her all his heart, and said unto her, There hath not come a rasor upon mine head; for I have been a Nazarite unto God from my mother's womb: if I be shaven, then my strength will go from me, and I shall become weak, and be like any other man.

18. And when Delilah saw that he had told her all his heart, she sent and called for the lords of the Philistines, saying, Come up this once, for he hath shewed me all his heart. Then the lords of the Philistines came up unto her, and brought money in their hand.

19. And she made him sleep upon her knees; and she called for a man, and she caused him to shave off the seven locks of his head; and she began to afflict him, and his strength went from him.

20. And she said, The Philistines be upon thee, Samson. And he awoke out of his sleep, and said, I will go out as at other times before, and shake myself. And he wist not that the Lord was departed from him.

21. But the Philistines took him, and put out his eyes, and brought him down to Gaza, and bound him with fetters of brass; and he did grind in the prison house.

28. And Samson called unto the Lord, and said, O Lord God, remember me, I pray thee, and strengthen me, I pray thee, only this once, O God, that I may be at once avenged of the Philistines for my two eyes.

29. And Samson took hold of the two middle pillars upon which the house stood, and on which it was borne up, of the one with his right hand, and of the other with his left.

30. And Samson said, Let me die with the Philistines. And he bowed himself with all his might; and the house fell upon the lords, and upon all the people that were therein. So the dead which he slew at his death were more than they which he slew in his life.

DICTIONARY

Nazarite (NAZ-uh-rite)—Judges 13:5—An Israelite who consecrated himself or herself and took a vow of separation and abstinence for a particular purpose.

shake myself—Judges 16:20—To shake off bonds or to awaken himself.

grind in the prison—Judges 16:21—To transform grain into flour by pulverizing it between two heavy stones.

LESSON OUTLINE

I. EMPOWERED FOR LEADERSHIP

   A. The Cycle of Sin, Judgment and Repentance

   B. A Child of Promise

   C. A Nazarite Unto God

II. CALLING COMPROMISED

   A. Delilah's Seduction of Samson

   B. Samson's Surrender

III. RESTORED FOR SERVICE

LESSON EXPOSITION

INTRODUCTION

Samson is the classic example in Scripture of people who somehow missed their destiny. Instead of fulfilling all that God had planned for them, these individuals aborted His blueprint altogether. They started with the right motives, ideals and plans—moving for a period of time in the power of their calling. But in the end, they died in total shame. We are quickly reminded of the tragedy of Saul's life. Though he was anointed as the first king of Israel, his life ended in utter failure.

Another man of God who began with great promise was Solomon. How gifted he was in divine wisdom! Yet, because he failed to fulfill his destiny, he would say of his own life in later years, "Vanity of vanities; all is vanity" (Ecclesiastes 1:2).

Samson's story is recorded in Judges 13—16. An angel announced his birth, giving his barren parents detailed instructions about his upbringing. He was to be a Nazarite—meaning that he was to be given completely to God's service for all his life. He could not drink wine or cut his hair. He was never to touch anything dead, nor go to the funeral of a deceased loved one.

Samson knew he had a special calling. Although nurtured by his parents, he was also taught, guided and comforted by the Spirit. He was born for a special purpose—to begin a new era of God's deliverance of Israel. For 20 years he walked upright in that calling. He judged Israel. He was a constant threat to the Philistines, bringing a ray of bright hope for Israel's future. The Holy Spirit would come upon him in great power, causing him to do great exploits.

Without the Spirit, however, Samson was as weak as anyone else. Thus, the miraculous feats were not meant simply to build his ego or standing among the people. They were a precursor to what God had planned—total deliverance for the nation. Samson was supposed to be a picture of what God could do through anyone who was dedicated to holy purposes.

Samson had a fatal flaw in his character—an overwhelming attraction to sinful, heathen women. When he began to seek the company of Delilah, he was flirting with danger. There was a secret sin he held in his heart. Although the Spirit moved upon him in powerful anointing, Samson refused to allow the Spirit to cleanse his inner man. He confused God's anointing with God's approval, which is a terrible mistake for anyone to make.

God fully intended that all the years of Samson's life be filled with great victories. Had he been obedient, the Spirit would have remained with him until his dying hour. Even though the Spirit would move upon him at his death, it was really not a victory. The final slaughter of Philistines was simply about personal revenge, not about honoring the name of the Lord.

If we look carefully, we see a misinterpretation of God's calling even in earlier exploits. Judges 14:19 says, "And the Spirit of the Lord came upon him, and he went down to Ashkelon, and slew thirty men of them, and took their spoil, and gave change of garments unto them which expounded the riddle. And his anger was kindled, and he went up to his father's house." Samson impulsively abused the gifts and anointing God had placed on him. If a man's character does not develop in direct relationship to his gifts, the anointing he has been blessed with will ultimately destroy him. This was exactly what happened to Samson.

I. EMPOWERED FOR LEADERSHIP
    (Judges 13:1-5)

A. The Cycle of Sin, Judgment and Repentance (v. 1)

(Judges 13:1 is not included in the printed text.)

By this time, we have come to see in Judges a monotonous repetition of the sin cycle (see 3:7, 8, 12; 4:1, 2; 6:1; 10:6, 7). What we have here, however, is the last time the cycle is repeated. This episode would continue 40 more years of Philistine domination. Not only was Samson the final judge, he was also the most inconsistent and explosive one.

The Philistines were a fierce seafaring people from Crete or mainland Greece. They migrated to the coastal areas of Palestine in the 12th century B.C. The Israelites had never been able to conquer the Philistine lands because the strong defense included five walled independent cities—Ashdod, Gaza, Ashkelon, Gath and Ekron (see 1 Samuel 6:17). The Philistines eventually began to seize the valleys leading to the central highlands where most Israelites lived. They were a troublesome enemy to Israel, and their defeat did not come until David's time.

B. A Child of Promise (vv. 2, 3)

(Judges 13:2 is not included in the printed text.)

3. And the angel of the Lord appeared unto the woman, and said unto her, Behold now, thou art barren, and bearest not: but thou shalt conceive, and bear a son.

There lived a certain man named Manoah with his wife in the town of Zorah. They were of the tribe of Dan. The Danites had originally settled between Judah and Philistia. Since they were unable to drive out the coastal inhabitants, most of them eventually moved north (see Judges 18; 19). Some chose, however, to remain in their original homeland.

Zorah was a Danite city on the western edge of the hill country, 15 miles west of Jerusalem, and close to the Philistine city Ekron to the west. Manoah and his wife were apparently a godly, though childless, couple. His wife is unnamed, but she is one of five famous barren women in the Bible who finally bore a special son. This group included Sarah, Rachel, Hannah and Elizabeth. Like the birth of Isaac to Sarah, Samson's birth was foretold by an angel. In verse 6, she told her husband she had been visited by "a man of God." The angel had promised her a son who would be a special gift, not only to his parents but also to Israel.

The angel who visited Manoah's wife was likely a *theophany*—an Old Testament manifestation of Jesus Christ himself. "Since it would be the mother who would have the greatest influence on the child, both before and after birth, the angel solemnly charged her what to do" (Wiersbe).

C. A Nazarite Unto God (vv. 4, 5)

(Judges 13:4 is not included in the printed text.)

5. For, lo, thou shalt conceive, and bear a son; and no rasor shall come on his head: for the child shall be a Nazarite unto God from the womb: and he shall begin to deliver Israel out of the hand of the Philistines.

When God wanted to provide a deliverer in Biblical times, He often sent a baby. We are introduced to Moses and Samuel as infants, and also to Jesus as the babe of Bethlehem. The angel promised Manoah's wife a son who must be set apart for God's use—a Nazarite. The vows of a Nazarite indicated a special purpose in God's sight. Samson was to be a Nazarite for his entire life. Numbers 6 relates the particular vows involved in being a Nazarite.

Manoah's wife had to be careful during her pregnancy with everything she ate and drank, so as not to defile the infant (Judges 13:4, 14). "Samson's Nazarite vow wasn't something he voluntarily took: God gave it to him; and his mother was a part of the vow of dedication" (Wiersbe).

The question might arise about Samson's right of choice. If man is a free moral agent, did Samson have any choice in the plans for his life? Certainly! All men have a right to choose whether or not to obey God; all have been foreordained with a plan of God's selecting.

God has a blueprint for your life and mine as well. We either choose to follow Him or our fleshly desires. Samson's blueprint for life was not an easy one; but had he followed it exactly as God had commanded, he would have been greatly rewarded and would have been able to respond as David did when he spoke his last words, "The Spirit of the Lord spake by me, and his word was in my tongue" (2 Samuel 23:2).

In the message given by the angel to Samson's mother, the fact that her son would begin to deliver Israel from the Philistines had to make a great impression. In times of oppression, every woman longed for her son to become a great man in the eyes of his nation. Centuries later, a dream would be on the heart of every Jewish girl—that her son would turn out to be the promised Messiah.

II. CALLING COMPROMISED
(Judges 16:4-6, 16-21)

Though not part of our text, chapters 14 and 15 paint a picture of a man who abused God's anointing on his life. Many of Samson's actions seem rebellious. He disregarded his parents' requests, he followed his own emotions and desires, and he flirted with the people God intended for him to destroy. His marriage to a Philistine showed him to be unstable and unpredictable. Even the Israelites questioned his actions (see 15:11). Our text picks up with his infatuation with the seductress Delilah.

A. Delilah's Seduction of Samson (vv. 4-6)

(Judges 16:5, 6 is not included in the printed text.)

4. And it came to pass afterward, that he loved a woman in the valley of Sorek, whose name was Delilah.

Samson had an insatiable appetite for sex. Verses 1-3 record his visit to a prostitute. Certainly this was a violation of his Nazarite vow, and was one more step into depravity. He still had his strength though, as illustrated by the fact that he carried the city gate of Gaza a great distance (v. 3). In Genesis 22:17 and 24:60, we learn that when one "possessed the gate of his enemies," he metaphorically had defeated them.

Samson was operating under the delusion that his strength made him invulnerable. He never checked to see if he had disobeyed God. Paul's words of warning come to mind: "Wherefore let him that thinketh he standeth take heed lest he fall" (1 Corinthians 10:12).

Delilah lived in the Valley of Sorek not far from Zorah. The Philistines offered to pay her to entice Samson and find the source of his strength. They didn't want to kill Samson, but rather to control him. They intended to use him to further weaken the morale of the Israelites. However, the Israelites had never rallied around Samson. Perhaps they recognized his flaws and saw him as a weak leader. Surely they discerned his inconsistent actions. Also, they seemed to be "comfortable in their misery" under Philistine domination, as illustrated by their attitude in Judges 15:11. Still, the Philistines thought that controlling Samson would increase their domination over their weak neighbors.

Samson should have realized what Delilah was doing when she begged him for the secret of his strength. It is easy to contrast Samson with another Biblical character: Joseph did not hesitate to run when Potiphar's wife enticed him. Samson apparently felt that the normal rules of behavior did not apply to him. He had become a power unto himself. What a selfish delusion! The scandals in the late 20th-century church followed the same pattern as that of Samson. Men who were used greatly by God forgot that He was the source of their strength. They thought they were invulnerable. Oh, how hard was their fall!

B. Samson's Surrender (vv. 16-21)

(Judges 16:16 is not included in the printed text.)

17. That he told her all his heart, and said unto her, There hath not come a rasor upon mine head; for I have been a Nazarite unto God from my mother's womb: if I be shaven, then my strength will go from me, and I shall become weak, and be like any other man.

18. And when Delilah saw that he had told her all his heart, she sent and called for

the lords of the Philistines, saying, Come up this once, for he
hath shewed me all his heart.
Then the lords of the Philistines
came up unto her, and brought
money in their hand.

19. And she made him sleep
upon her knees; and she called
for a man, and she caused him
to shave off the seven locks of
his head; and she began to
afflict him, and his strength
went from him.

20. And she said, The
Philistines be upon thee,
Samson. And he awoke out of
his sleep, and said, I will go out
as at other times before, and
shake myself. And he wist not
that the Lord was departed
from him.

21. But the Philistines took
him, and put out his eyes, and
brought him down to Gaza, and
bound him with fetters of brass;
and he did grind in the prison
house.

Delilah was persistent, perhaps
frightened of what the Philistines
would do to her if she didn't suc-
ceed. Also, the money they offered
her was a great enticement.
Finally she discovered Samson's
secret. "Samson didn't know his
own heart. He thought he possessed enough moral strength to
say no to the temptress, but he
was wrong" (Wiersbe).

Samson arose after his infamous
haircut, fully expecting to have the
strength he had always had, but he
was wrong. Verse 20 is one of the
most poignant and ironic statements in the Bible: "And he wist
not that the Lord was departed
from him." Though the Philistines
knew they had him, they didn't
take any chances. They immediately plucked out his eyes. The
great man of strength was now a
pitiful shadow of what God had
intended him to be.

III. RESTORED FOR SERVICE
   (Judges 16:22-31)

(Judges 16:22-27, 31 is not
included in the printed text.)

28. And Samson called unto
the Lord, and said, O Lord God,
remember me, I pray thee, and
strengthen me, I pray thee, only
this once, O God, that I may be at
once avenged of the Philistines
for my two eyes.

29. And Samson took hold of
the two middle pillars upon
which the house stood, and on
which it was borne up, of the
one with his right hand, and of
the other with his left.

30. And Samson said, Let me
die with the Philistines. And he
bowed himself with all his
might; and the house fell upon
the lords, and upon all the people that were therein. So the
dead which he slew at his death
were more than they which he
slew in his life.

It is always a tragedy when an
individual who has been raised in
a godly home totally fails God.
Samson was now completely
humiliated. He is an example of
those who think they can do as
they please and still expect God's
blessing.

The Philistines deepened Samson's
wound by giving credit to their god,
Dagon, for delivering him into their
hands. They planned a major celebration to praise their idol. The
only thing they overlooked was
that Samson's hair was growing
back. They became even more
careless during the celebration by
bringing him out to make sport of
him (vv. 22-25).

Blinded and led by a boy, Samson
must have had some idea of the
architecture of the temple. Twin pillars supported a major part of the
roof. With a repentant heart,
Samson called on God for one more

empowerment of strength. The story of his pushing the pillars off their pedestals is a familiar one. The result was that more Philistines were killed at this time than during all his other exploits.

Interestingly, his brothers and his father's entire households came to claim his body (v. 31). This was not a happy ending. Surely they mourned over what could have been, had Samson simply obeyed God and submitted his weakness to Him. Still, God achieved His purpose, despite Samson's inconsistency. The foundation was set for David to ultimately conquer the Philistines. Samson apparently repented when he called on God one final time, because he is included in the great "faith hall of fame" (Hebrews 11). This suggests that "all was right between him and his Lord" (Wiersbe).

GOLDEN TEXT HOMILY

"KEEP THY HEART WITH ALL DILIGENCE; FOR OUT OF IT ARE THE ISSUES OF LIFE" (Proverbs 4:23).

The heart represents the very essence of a person's emotions and feelings. It represents the point of origin from which our ideas flow and are made. In this regard our heart represents our ethics. There are many things that can influence our ethics. The movies we watch, the music we hear, the literature we read, and our peers all assist in shaping our ideas and actions. Other things such as our families, relatives and coworkers provide input into how our opinions and decisions are formed.

Proverbs 4:23 suggests that keeping, or guarding, our hearts is of the utmost importance. The *New International Version* says to guard your heart "above all else."

To guard something above all else places ultimate importance on the act of guarding. The writer of our golden text is suggesting that we consider our heart or ethics as the most important thing in our life to guard. Why? If our heart is the seat of our ethics, and if we base our choices on our ethics, then our heart becomes the key player in dictating our daily activities.

God has made available to us His sanctifying grace as a shield around our hearts. As we are obedient to God by placing His will as a priority in our lives, He surrounds our hearts with His wisdom and love. His continual presence in our lives makes it easier to say "yes" to those things that produce a godly ethic.—**Richard D. Raines**

SENTENCE SERMONS

DOCTRINAL AND MORAL COMPROMISE undermine spiritual leadership.
                              —Selected

THE MIDDLE OF THE ROAD is a dangerous location.
                              —Selected

A BROKEN CHARACTER doesn't knit easily.
                    —Megiddo Messenger

EVANGELISM APPLICATION

DOCTRINAL AND MORAL COMPROMISE UNDERMINE EFFECTIVE EVANGELISM.

How do we use the gifts God has blessed us with? Do we seek the approval and adoration of people? Do we want to be put on a pedestal so people will see us as holy? None of us should be proud of ourselves for God's blessings and gifts. The apostle Paul states that the gifts of the Spirit are to be used to build up the church. In Ephesians 4:11, 12, he says, "And he gave some, apostles; and some, prophets; and some, evangelists; and some, pastors and teachers; for the perfecting of the saints, for the work of the ministry, for the edifying of the body of Christ."

The entire body of Christ is supposed to benefit from these gifts. To use the special abilities and anointings for selfish purposes is to disobey God. None of us are islands unto ourselves.

Samson not only failed himself, but he also failed the entire nation of Israel. Our place in Christ's kingdom is integrally related to everyone else in the body. We are to serve others, not ourselves.

ILLUMINATING THE LESSON

By the time of his death, Samson had managed to break all the major tenets of his Nazarite vow. When he went back to the lion's carcass and took honey from it, he defiled himself by touching a dead body (Judges 14:9). When he went to the weeklong wedding feast (14:17), more than likely, wine was involved, and he probably partook of it. After all, he was the groom, and there is no indication of his refusal. The word *feast* actually means "a drinking party." Finally, when he told Delilah that his strength lay in his uncut hair (16:17), he set up a situation for the last part of the vow to be broken. No wonder his life ended in desperation. The writer of Ecclesiastes says it best: "It is better not to vow than to make a vow and not fulfill it" (Ecclesiastes 5:5, *NIV*). God will not be mocked when we promise our lives to Him and then renege on our vows.

What could Samson have accomplished had he fully dedicated himself to the Lord, submitting his weaknesses to God's control? Three questions arise from Samson's life that we all should ask ourselves:

• What sins do you rationalize because they seem harmless? (Samson's weakness was an uncontrolled passion for women.)

• Is there a secret domain of your heart where you allow yourself to fantasize some type of sinful behavior?

• Have you submitted every area of your life to the Lord?

DAILY BIBLE READINGS

M. Consequences of Compromise. 1 Kings 11:1-13
T. Consequences of Godless Leadership. 2 Kings 21:1-14
W. Guard Your Ministry. 1 Timothy 1:12-20
T. Guard Against Failure. Hebrews 12:12-17
F. Endure Temptation. James 1:12-18
S. Kept From Falling. Jude 20-25

TRUTH SEARCH:
Creatively Teaching the Word

Aim: Students will examine their own lives for evidence of spiritual compromise, then ask the Lord for strength to stand firm.

Materials needed: Marker board, marker, bobby pins

FOCUS

Before class, write the following words on the left side of the marker board: *hot, light, love, alive, wise.*
• *What do these words have in common?* (Each is a word that the Bible uses to characterize believers.)

Have students name an opposite for each word. Write each opposing pair as an equation. For instance: *Hot + cold =* _____.
• *How would you solve these equations?*

On the right side of the board, write "the blending of two different things."

I have just written the definition of the word *compromise*. That is what we were trying to do by blending *light* with *darkness*, and *wise* with *foolish*—we were compromising.
• *What results from spiritual compromise?*

EXPLORE

Today we'll explore the story of someone who was born in a time of spiritual compromise. Because the people of Israel had rebelled against God, they had been ruled by the Philistines for 40 years. Finally God sent them a deliverer.

Assign four volunteers the parts of narrator, Manoah, Manoah's wife, and angel, and have them read Judges 13:1-8, 12-14.
• *What kind of restrictions did the Lord place on Manoah's wife?*
• *How was Samson to show that* he was completely dedicated to God?
• *What was God's plan for Samson?*
• *What wise request did Manoah make? How did the Lord respond?*

Read verses 24 and 25 to the class.

Just as God had promised, He had placed His hand on Samson for a special purpose.

Ask the students to read Judges 14:5, 6 and 15:14, 15 to themselves. Then have them explain what the Spirit of the Lord did through Samson.

However, Samson had a problem. He began to be attracted to Philistine women. In Judges 16:1, we read that Samson spent the night with a Philistine harlot. Then he met Delilah.

Assign volunteers the parts of narrator, Samson, Delilah, and the lords of the Philistines, and have them read verses 4-17.
• *When Delilah's intentions of trapping Samson became obvious, why did he continue his relationship with her?*
• *Why did Samson finally tell her the truth about his source of strength?*
• *What can we learn from these verses about our own battle with temptation?*

Have the individuals reading the parts of Delilah and the narrator to read verses 18-21.
• *According to verses 20 and 21, what things did Samson lose because of his sin?*

Adding the part of the Philistine people, have the volunteers read verses 22-30.
• *What was Samson's prayer, and why did God answer it?*
• *Why did Samson die along with his enemies?*

RESPOND

Samson's strength did not come from his hair, but from what his uncut hair represented— submission to the will of God.

Hand a bobby pin to each student, and give the students one minute to bend it out of shape as much as possible. Then challenge them to restore the pin to its original condition.

Let these hairpins remind you that even though Samson turned back to God, his compromise had cost him his integrity, his eyesight, his freedom and his life. Spiritual compromise is just as deadly today.

Challenge the students to search their heart for evidence of spiritual compromise, then close with a prayer of commitment.

Nature of the Church

Study Text: Matthew 16:13-19; 1 Corinthians 12:12-27; Ephesians 3:1-12
Objective: To know that the church is the body of Christ and find our place in His body.
Golden Text: "Upon this rock I will build my church; and the gates of hell shall not prevail against it" (Matthew 16:18).
Central Truth: The church, the body of Christ, is founded on the confession that Jesus Christ is the Son of God.
Evangelism Emphasis: The church proclaims to the lost that Jesus Christ is the Savior.

PRINTED TEXT

Matthew 16:16. And Simon Peter answered and said, Thou art the Christ, the Son of the living God.

17. And Jesus answered and said unto him, Blessed art thou, Simon Bar-jona: for flesh and blood hath not revealed it unto thee, but my Father which is in heaven.

18. And I say also unto thee, That thou art Peter, and upon this rock I will build my church; and the gates of hell shall not prevail against it.

19. And I will give unto thee the keys of the kingdom of heaven: and whatsoever thou shalt bind on earth shall be bound in heaven: and whatsoever thou shalt loose on earth shall be loosed in heaven.

1 Corinthians 12:13. For by one Spirit are we all baptized into one body, whether we be Jews or Gentiles, whether we be bond or free; and have been all made to drink into one Spirit.

14. For the body is not one member, but many.

15. If the foot shall say, Because I am not the hand, I am not of the body; is it therefore not of the body?

16. And if the ear shall say, Because I am not the eye, I am not of the body; is it therefore not of the body?

17. If the whole body were an eye, where were the hearing? If the whole were hearing, where were the smelling?

18. But now hath God set the members every one of them in the body, as it hath pleased him.

19. And if they were all one member, where were the body?

20. But now are they many members, yet but one body.

26. And whether one member suffer, all the members suffer with it; or one member be honoured, all the members rejoice with it.

27. Now ye are the body of Christ, and members in particular.

Ephesians 3:8. Unto me, who am less than the least of all saints, is this grace given, that I should preach among the Gentiles the unsearchable riches of Christ;

9. And to make all men see what is the fellowship of the mystery, which from the beginning of the world hath been hid in God, who created all things by Jesus Christ:

10. To the intent that now unto the principalities and powers in heavenly places might be known by the church the manifold wisdom of God.

LESSON OUTLINE

I. FOUNDED ON CHRIST
   A. Place of the Confession
   B. Public Consensus
   C. The Lord's Deeper Question
   D. Peter's Confession
   E. Peter's Blessedness
   F. The Rock on Which the Church Is Built

II. THE BODY OF CHRIST

III. REVEALS GOD'S WISDOM
   A. The Reason for Paul's Imprisonment
   B. Paul's Great Revelation
   C. Paul's Feelings of Inadequacy

LESSON EXPOSITION

INTRODUCTION

God has always had a body of people who have worshiped Him, though at times their numbers may have been few and their knowledge of Him limited. In the Old Testament, God revealed Himself to Abraham and the race that descended from this particular man. However, the people of God were never intended to be exclusively the genetic offspring of Abraham. The fact that there are many stories of non-Jewish people demonstrating great faith indicates this. Even the bloodline of the Messiah himself was frequently infused with foreigners. Race alone did not qualify one to be among God's chosen.

When Jesus was revealed as the Messiah and the Jews refused to accept Him, the body of individuals who enjoyed a privileged relationship with the Lord became known as "the church." This was the reason for a new covenant—that all mankind, Jew and Gentile alike, might be fused into one family of believers.

The institution of the church in the last 2,000 years, however, does not necessarily constitute God's people, just as the Jews of the Old Testament did not. The true church is not an organization, but a body of believers who have a passion for Christ. It has never been backslidden, cold, lukewarm or compromised.

The first time the word *church* appears in the New Testament is when Christ responded to Peter's confession of who He is (Matthew 16:18). This passage, and the one in 18:17, are the only two times the word appears in the four Gospels, a fact explained in that the church did not begin until the Day of Pentecost (after the death, resurrection and ascension of the Lord). Jesus had declared the church to be His future body when He said, "I will build my church." Paul later clarified the distinction between the old-covenant people of faith and the new-covenant church: "Before this faith came, we were held prisoners by the law, locked up until faith should be revealed. So the law was put in charge to lead us to Christ that we might be justified by faith. Now that faith has come, we are no longer under the supervision of the law" (Galatians 3:23-25, *NIV*).

Jesus purchased the church with His blood (Ephesians 5:25). After the Gospels, the word for "church," *ekklesia,* is used many times, especially in Acts and Paul's letters. It may refer to a local body of believers or to believers everywhere. It may also indicate believers throughout all ages, and as such will not be complete until the total body of the redeemed are caught up together with the return of Christ (see Hebrews 12:23; Revelation 21, 22).

Jesus commissioned the church with His final words in Matthew

28:16-20. He told the disciples to go out and teach men what He had taught them. The Book of Acts is the story of the early church's struggle (and victories) in carrying out His command. Throughout Acts we can see the Holy Spirit operating and directing the Lord's people.

Today, the church is comprised of thousands of denominations, many with opposing ideas and beliefs. The first of our Scripture texts (Peter's confession) has been misused to divide all of Christendom into two factions—Protestantism and Catholicism. However, those who are a part of the true body of Christ will also be identified by their living faith in Christ. For this group, "the gates of hell shall not prevail against it."

I. FOUNDED ON CHRIST (Matthew 16:13-19)

A. Place of the Confession (v. 13)

(Matthew 16:13 is not included in the printed text.)

One doesn't have to stay long in the great cities of the world to realize the darkness that prevails. Satan's armies have used sex, drugs, alcohol, and other vices to kill as much light of truth as possible. The same was true during Jesus' ministry. In that day, Caesarea Philippi was a microcosm of the Roman Empire. Located several miles north of the Sea of Galilee, this pagan stronghold had many idols and temples. As Jesus looked at His motley bunch of disciples, He saw that through them would come the leadership for the body of the Lord, which would ultimately reign over Satan's dominion.

B. Public Consensus (v. 14)

(Matthew 16:14 is not included in the printed text.)

The responses of the disciples reflected the common beliefs of the Jewish mind of the day. In Deuteronomy 18:18, God had said He would raise up a Prophet from among the people who would be like Moses. It had been 400 years since the last great prophet had arisen in Israel. The Jewish culture was expecting a new prophet.

Did Jesus not already know the common opinion of Him? Certainly He did, but He was preparing to teach the disciples a valuable lesson. The religious leaders who hated Jesus had been really vocal in their assessment of Jesus—calling Him a deceiver and in league with Satan—but the masses had not been so vocal. These same common people would certainly have "conversed more familiarly with the disciples than they did with their Master" (*Matthew Henry's Commentary on the Whole Bible*).

Until this time Jesus had not plainly stated who He was, but He let His listeners draw their own conclusions from His actions. By questioning the disciples, He could establish what they believed and how much they were influenced by the public mind.

C. The Lord's Deeper Question (v. 15)

(Matthew 16:15 is not included in the printed text.)

There comes a time when everyone must make a decision about the truth of Christ. This opportunity had come for the disciples. They needed to separate themselves from conjecture and make a solid stand for the Lord's true identity. The people agreed that He was an extraordinary person, but they were unwilling to admit He was the Messiah. The average person will do the same thing today, but such neutrality cannot exist among those who are searching for salvation.

D. Peter's Confession (v. 16)

16. And Simon Peter answered and said, Thou art the Christ, the Son of the living God.

Peter said what all the disciples were thinking, but were not bold enough to proclaim. "Peter's temper led him to be forward in speaking upon all such occasions, and sometimes he spoke well, sometimes amiss" (Matthew Henry). In this instance, the courageous disciple verbalized and crystallized the very reason for the disciples to follow the simple Rabbi from Galilee.

E. Peter's Blessedness (v. 17)

17. And Jesus answered and said unto him, Blessed art thou, Simon Bar-jona: for flesh and blood hath not revealed it unto thee, but my Father which is in heaven.

Jesus called Peter *blessed* because he had come to an understanding of truth. "Contrary to the popular maxim 'Ignorance is bliss,' Peter's bliss was rooted in correct knowledge" (R.C. Sproul, *The Soul's Quest for God*). It was not simply, however, that Peter had discovered the right answer, but how he came upon it. This knowledge came to him by revelation from the Father in heaven.

Anyone could have said Jesus was the Messiah, simply based on speculation and a cursory grasp of Old Testament prophecy. Peter's confession went deeper. He had come to a life-changing understanding—knowledge that had been granted to him from God. "Immediate revelation comes directly from God to the receiver. No

object, book, person, or any other thing acts as a conveyor of the message. It comes directly from the mind of God to the mind of man" (Sproul).

F. The Rock on Which the Church Is Built (vv. 18, 19)

18. And I say also unto thee, That thou art Peter, and upon this rock I will build my church; and the gates of hell shall not prevail against it.

19. And I will give unto thee the keys of the kingdom of heaven: and whatsoever thou shalt bind on earth shall be bound in heaven: and whatsoever thou shalt loose on earth shall be loosed in heaven.

When Peter gave Jesus his answer, he was in essence saying, "You are the full embodiment of God's revelation to mankind." Jesus' response, "upon this rock," are words that have been so misused and misunderstood for the last 2,000 years.

The rock to whom He was referring was Himself—God, embodied in the flesh, and His ultimate sacrifice for man's sins to restore full fellowship with man. Peter's confession of faith is the same confession that those coming to Christ must make to become a part of the church. In confessing Jesus as our Savior and Lord, we are saying: "Lord, I believe You are the Son of God; that You came to restore me from the power of sin; that I can have life, both present and eternal, because of what You have sacrificed for me."

For Catholics all over the world, the implication of Jesus' words was that Peter himself would be the rock on which the church would be built. But nowhere in Scripture is it stated that Peter would have infallible authority over the church.

In fact, in the early church convocations in Acts, it was actually James (the half-brother of Jesus) who presided. As powerful a man of God as Peter was, he had no more authority than any other believer. Also, there is no indication that there would be a series of successors to take Peter's place as leader of the church.

As Protestants, we believe it was the confession Peter made that carried such wonderful authority, not Peter himself. In other words, "Peter, your declaration of My identity is the rock upon which the church will be built." It is Jesus who is the Rock. Paul would call Him "the foundation stone" when writing to the Corinthians: "For no one can lay any foundation other than the one already laid, which is Jesus Christ" (1 Corinthians 3:11, NIV).

When Jesus said, "The gates of hell shall not prevail," He was speaking of the entire realm and authority of Satan. Evil has continually attempted to destroy the church many years earlier. Isaiah had stated something of the same idea: "No weapon that is formed against thee shall prosper; and every tongue that shall rise against thee in judgment thou shalt condemn. This is the heritage of the servants of the Lord, and their righteousness is of me, saith the Lord" (Isaiah 54:17). Throughout the centuries the true church has experienced this. Every power, empire, charlatan and culture that stood against the true church has been unable to stand permanently.

II. THE BODY OF CHRIST
(1 Corinthians 12:12-27)

(1 Corinthians 12:12, 21-25 is not included in the printed text.)

13. For by one Spirit are we all baptized into one body, whether we be Jews or Gentiles, whether we be bond or free; and have been all made to drink into one Spirit.

14. For the body is not one member, but many.

15. If the foot shall say, Because I am not the hand, I am not of the body; is it therefore not of the body?

16. And if the ear shall say, Because I am not the eye, I am not of the body; is it therefore not of the body?

17. If the whole body were an eye, where were the hearing? If the whole were hearing, where were the smelling?

18. But now hath God set the members every one of them in the body, as it hath pleased him.

19. And if they were all one member, where were the body?

20. But now are they many members, yet but one body.

26. And whether one member suffer, all the members suffer with it; or one member be honoured, all the members rejoice with it.

27. Now ye are the body of Christ, and members in particular.

We are representatives of Christ on earth. We are His "body." In the text above, Paul compares the body of Christ to the physical body. Each organ and limb has a special function that is necessary to sustain life. The parts are different in their purpose, but they are components of one composite whole, and all are necessary. As members of the body of Christ, believers must be careful to avoid two potential problems: (1) thinking their talent or function is more important than another member; (2) thinking that they are not important because they play an insignificant or smaller role in the body.

Despite our differences in backgrounds, talents, abilities, resources, and so forth, we must all come to Christ through one common denominator—faith in His shed blood for our salvation. We are all baptized by one Holy Spirit into one body. When we come to Christ, the Holy Spirit breathes life into us and resides within us. This is the meaning of the phrase "born again."

On the evening after His resurrection, Jesus appeared to His disciples. During this unannounced visit He "breathed on them and told them, 'Receive the Holy Spirit'" (John 20:22, *NIV*). He did not discriminate among them, but breathed life into all of them equally. They were all infused with the regenerating power of the Holy Spirit, giving them new life from a resurrected Christ.

Down through the centuries we have certainly attributed more attention to three of those who were present—Peter, John, Matthew—because we have letters written by them. However, we cannot underestimate the value of the others. We know the others also carried the gospel message everywhere they went. They were equal parts of the Lord's body.

Paul emphasized the fact that if an insignificant part of the body is taken away, the whole body becomes flawed, less effective. As co-members of the Lord's body (the church), we should never be jealous of those who have impressive gifts. Neither should we flaunt any gifts we have been given. Instead, we should wisely use what has been given us and encourage others in their value and usefulness.

If we become intimidated by someone else's gifts, or if we feel inadequate in our own gifts, are we not simply questioning God's love for us? Our worship should arise from a vision of God's unmerited love. We must realize that God provides goodness and mercy, and is ready to forgive us all. None of us deserve this grace, no matter how many or how few our gifts.

Many of us find it hard to believe that God truly loves us. This is perhaps the greatest revelation we can receive—that God truly loves us. Our first priority, then, is not to prove our love for God by exaggerated efforts to show our usefulness, but rather to simply allow ourselves to experience how much He loves us. In other words, striving to draw closer to God—"Draw nigh to God, and he will draw nigh to you" (James 4:8)—is first necessitated by receiving a sense of His unconditional love. Real communion with Him thus consists of two things—receiving His love and loving Him in return.

III. REVEALS GOD'S WISDOM
    (Ephesians 3:1-12)

A. The Reason for Paul's
   Imprisonment (vv. 1-3)

    (Ephesians 3:1-3 is not included in the printed text.)

Paul was writing to the Ephesian church from prison. He was under house arrest in Rome because the Jews in Jerusalem hated him and brought false charges against him. What was the source of their hatred? Their pride in their Hebrew heritage. If ever there was a people who were guilty of spiritual pride, it was the Jews. God had chosen to reveal Himself through Abraham's descendants. This was not to say they were any better than everyone else, but simply that they were chosen. One great sin of the Hebrews was their belief that they had exclusive rights to God, that His sovereignty existed only for their purposes.

Paul had been given a wonderful revelation—that God's love extended to all mankind. From the beginning God planned to have only one people, which included both Jews and Gentiles. The Jews knew this from prophecy (Isaiah 49:6; 56:3), but they simply refused to accept it. Thus, when Paul began to preach to the Gentiles the length and breadth of God's love to all, the Jews became furious.

B. Paul's Great Revelation (vv. 4-7)

(Ephesians 3:4-7 is not included in the printed text.)

The Jews might accept that God had some sort of plan for the Gentiles, but they could never believe that they were to become equals. However, Christ broke down the wall of contempt (see Ephesians 2:14, 15) between the peoples of the earth and created one body—the church.

Paul had been a Pharisee himself, walking with all the Jewish pride that had developed throughout the centuries. Before his confrontation with Christ on the road to Damascus, he would probably have spit on a Gentile if one came too close to him. Now, however, after what was revealed to him, he saw himself in a totally different light. He had been visited by Christ and given a new mission in life! *The Living Bible* rendition of 3:7 beautifully demonstrates this: "God has given me the wonderful privilege of telling everyone about this plan of his; and he has given me his power and special ability to do it well."

C. Paul's Feelings of Inadequacy (vv. 8-12)

(Ephesians 3:11, 12 is not included in the printed text.)

8. Unto me, who am less than the least of all saints, is this grace given, that I should preach among the Gentiles the unsearchable riches of Christ;

9. And to make all men see what is the fellowship of the mystery, which from the beginning of the world hath been hid in God, who created all things by Jesus Christ:

10. To the intent that now unto the principalities and powers in heavenly places might be known by the church the manifold wisdom of God.

God had granted Paul the ability and charge to share the gospel with the Gentiles. The Pharisee that Paul had been would have had to step over his cultural pride to be willing to do this. The new Paul, however, was a totally different man. Though he was probably among the most educated of his day, Paul saw himself as "less than the least of all saints." He had been humbled by the revelation of God's love for all mankind. Paul now knew he was useless in himself, but as God empowered him, he could step out and do great things. When we as Christians feel useless, we are likely accurate in our perception, but we must not forget what a difference God can make as He reveals His love toward us.

GOLDEN TEXT HOMILY

"UPON THIS ROCK I WILL BUILD MY CHURCH; AND THE GATES OF HELL SHALL NOT PREVAIL AGAINST IT" (Matthew 16:18).

As the world understands rock, *Rock* was not a good character name for Peter. At first glance, his immovableness, his solidity of character were not obvious. Clearly,

Peter was neither a great pioneer nor a great theologian nor a great scholar, but he was a great child. Because of his confession of Christ, he was the foremost of the Twelve.

Jesus promised that the gates of hell shall not prevail against the church that would be built on confession of Christ. Men talk about the church being in danger. A more foolish cry was never raised. The church is the most precious thing in the universe. It is the bride—the Lamb's wife. His love is toward it, and His omnipotent arm is ever around it. The church on earth is as safe as the church in heaven. The avalanche of atheism is poised over it. The air hurtles with fiery hostilities. The mechanisms of diabolic temptation encroach on eery side. The air quivers with the anger of demons.

Yet the work is God's, and the gates of hell shall not prevail against it. In the very angle of these demonic forces the work shall thrive, for the hidden lines of His protecting power are round about it. "I the Lord do keep it; I will water it every moment: lest any hurt it, I will keep it night and day" (Isaiah 27:3).—**Adapted from *The Preacher's Homiletic Commentary*, Vol. 22**

SENTENCE SERMONS

THE CHURCH, THE BODY OF CHRIST, is founded on the confession that Jesus Christ is the Son of God.

—Selected

JESUS CHRIST IS God's everything for man's total need.
—Richard Halverson

GOD CALLS US not to solitary sainthood but to fellowship in a company of committed men.
—David Schuller

EVANGELISM APPLICATION

THE CHURCH PROCLAIMS TO THE LOST THAT JESUS CHRIST IS THE SAVIOR.

In today's so-called multicultural society, politicians frequently find it difficult to straddle the fence on religious issues. Can a person find eternal life through any other means than Christ? How does a candidate approach a voting constituency that is made up of not only Christians, but also Muslims, Hindus, Mormons, and so forth? If you want to hear a fence-straddler stammer, just ask where these people go after death.

In one of the first sermons Peter preached after the Day of Pentecost, it took an empowered Holy Spirit boldness for him to say: "Neither is there salvation in any other: for there is none other name under heaven given among men, whereby we must be saved" (Acts 4:12). Without the confession that Jesus is the only way to eternal life, there can be no salvation. As the church, we are to proclaim to the lost that Jesus Christ is the Savior.

ILLUMINATING THE LESSON

We should never go to God expecting a fierce, angry father. He is anxious to fellowship with us and ever ready to forgive our sins. He has revealed His pure, unconditional love, and never turns down His children when they come to Him.

However, many among us have a distorted view of God and live in fear that they cannot measure up to what is expected of them. We are like the members of the body Paul was describing, who felt themselves of lesser importance. Frequently, this is caused by distorted relationships in our earthly families.

If your natural father was hard,

critical and non-affirming, it is likely that this will be your view of God the Father. You may have lived in dread of your earthly father and shied away when he was nearby. We often do the same with God. We are afraid of Him because we sense that we have failed Him. We have nagging feelings of inadequacy, that we have been lazy or have done something wrong. We see the Lord much as the man who was given only one talent. He said, "I knew that you are a hard man. . . . So I was afraid and went out and hid your talent in the ground" (Matthew 25:24, 25, *NIV*).

We must overcome this misconception and believe what the Word says—that He loves us. Revelation 3:20 says, "Behold, I stand at the door, and knock: if any man hear my voice, and open the door, I will come in to him, and will sup with him, and he with me." When we recognize this truth, we have no problems understanding our place in the Lord's body, be it great or small.

DAILY BIBLE READINGS

M. God Calls Abraham.
      Genesis 12:1-9
T.   God Calls Israel.
      Deuteronomy 4:32-40
W. God Calls in Love.
      Deuteronomy 7:7-14
T.   The Word Made Flesh.
      John 1:1-18
F.   Christ, the Wisdom of God.
      1 Corinthians 1:20-31
S.   Christ, Head of the Church.
      Ephesians 5:22-32

TRUTH SEARCH:
Creatively Teaching the Word

Aim: Members will affirm one another's importance to the church.

Materials needed: Paper, pencils, marker, marker board

FOCUS

Begin my making a list on the board of all the different groups (outside the church) in which class members are involved. Here are some of the countless possible categories of answers: various sports teams, school organizations, unions, health clubs, vocational groups, computer groups, and political organizations.

• *How are these groups alike? How are they different?*

• *What kind of qualifications does it take to join?*

• *What are the benefits of membership?*

• *How are these groups like the church? How are they different?*

Today's lesson is about that one-of-a-kind organization, the church, that Christ himself created.

EXPLORE

Divide the class into groups of three to five students each. Assign each group one of the following Scripture passages to explore: Matthew 16:13-19; 1 Corinthians 12:12-27; or Ephesians 3:1-12.

Matthew 16:13-19

1. Why did people have so many different ideas about who Jesus was?

2. How did Peter know that Jesus was the Son of God?

3. What is the foundation of the church?

4. How powerful is Christ's church?

1 Corinthians 12:12-27

1. What causes every member of the body of Christ to be equal (vv. 12, 13)?

2. Who determines what roles people are to play in the church (v. 18)?

3. List ways in which the body of Christ is like the human body.

4. When a church is actually functioning as the body of Christ, how do believers relate to one another (vv. 25, 26)?

Ephesians 3:1-12

1. What was the mystery that had been revealed to Paul (vv. 1-6)?

2. What did God call Paul to do (vv. 7-9)?

3. What did God call the church to do (vv. 10, 11)?

4. To whom is the promise in verse 12 directed?

Have each group present their findings to the class. Then write the following on the board:

• The church is built on Jesus Christ (Matthew 16).

• Every member is equally important (1 Corinthians 12).

• Membership is available to all people (Ephesians 3).

RESPOND

Have students break up into groups of four or five students each. Or, if your class has less than 10 students, you might keep the entire group together. Encourage members to affirm each member in their group by stating the positive attributes he or she brings to the local body. Be prepared to make your own affirmation statements about class members.

Next, have everyone stand and hold each other's hands, forming a giant circle. Pray that the Holy Spirit will enable your class to be a unified group that will help bring unity to your entire congregation.

Fellowship of Believers

Study Text: Acts 4:23-37; 1 John 1:5-7; 2:3-6
Objective: To observe characteristics of believers and be productive members of the church.
Golden Text: "Let brotherly love continue" (Hebrews 13:1).
Central Truth: Christianity is a lifestyle of obedience to Christ, prayer and generosity.
Evangelism Emphasis: Sinners will come to know Christ's love by the love Christians show for one another.

PRINTED TEXT

1 John 1:5. This then is the message which we have heard of him, and declare unto you, that God is light, and in him is no darkness at all.

6. If we say that we have fellowship with him, and walk in darkness, we lie, and do not the truth:

7. But if we walk in the light, as he is in the light, we have fellowship one with another, and the blood of Jesus Christ his Son cleanseth us from all sin.

2:3. And hereby we do know that we know him, if we keep his commandments.

4. He that saith, I know him, and keepeth not his commandments, is a liar, and the truth is not in him.

5. But whoso keepeth his word, in him verily is the love of God perfected: hereby know we that we are in him.

6. He that saith he abideth in him ought himself also so to walk, even as he walked.

Acts 4:29. And now, Lord, behold their threatenings: and grant unto thy servants, that with all boldness they may speak thy word,

30. By stretching forth thine hand to heal; and that signs and wonders may be done by the name of thy holy child Jesus.

31. And when they had prayed, the place was shaken where they were assembled together; and they were all filled with the Holy Ghost, and they spake the word of God with boldness.

32. And the multitude of them that believed were of one heart and of one soul: neither said any of them that ought of the things which he possessed was his own; but they had all things common.

33. And with great power gave the apostles witness of the resurrection of the Lord Jesus: and great grace was upon them all.

34. Neither was there any among them that lacked: for as many as were possessors of lands or houses sold them, and brought the prices of the things that were sold,

35. And laid them down at the apostles' feet: and distribution was made unto every man according as he had need.

36. And Joses, who by the apostles was surnamed Barnabas, (which is, being interpreted, The son of consolation,) a Levite, and of the country of Cyprus,

37. Having land, sold it, and brought the money, and laid it at the apostles' feet.

LESSON OUTLINE

I. BELIEVERS OBEY JESUS
   A. True Christian Fellowship
   B. Obedience to God
II. BELIEVERS PRAY
   A. United in Prayer
   B. The Results of Prayer
III. BELIEVERS ARE GENEROUS

LESSON EXPOSITION

INTRODUCTION

The true church of Jesus Christ is characterized by love among the members. On the night before His crucifixion, Jesus told His disciples, "A new commandment I give you: Love one another. As I have loved you, so you must love one another. By this all men will know that you are my disciples, if you love one another" (John 13:34, 35, *NIV*). The Lord insisted that they love one another with brotherly love and recognize their interdependency. The church, operating as Christ intended, is a corporate body made up of many members, all with different talents and gifts that aid each other.

Camaraderie among any group of people must have at least one common denominator. For instance, during the Christmas season the same person might attend several different parties, each based on a mutual element—employees of the same company, members of the same Sunday school class, members of a fraternal or social organization, and so forth. Though the various people come from many backgrounds, they share one thing that brings them together.

For the Lord's disciples, there were many factors drawing them together. These included: three years of walking with Him during His earthly ministry; their mutual cowardice at His crucifixion; their fear of the religious leaders; their being together when He appeared to them after the Resurrection; His breathing life into them through the Holy Spirit; His commission to them just before the Ascension; their infilling with the Holy Spirit on the Day of Pentecost; and the persecution they all endured. There was much to bond them in love and responsibility toward one another.

The shared element uniting the church over the centuries remains the same. It is stated in 1 John 1:3: "That which we have seen and heard declare we unto you, that ye also may have fellowship with us: and truly our fellowship is with the Father, and with his Son Jesus Christ." Every true Christian has found fellowship with the Father through a living relationship with Jesus Christ.

It has recently been shown that there really is nearly no church growth in the United States. Most churches that are getting larger are simply gaining people from other congregations. It's called transfer growth. There is little real evangelism taking place. For people to leave one church body and join another indicates a lack of love and fellowship in the church they leave. In addition, if there is little evangelism in the world, we have to conclude that the world is seeing very little love within the church to attract them.

What did Jesus say would unite believers? "By this shall all men know that ye are my disciples, if ye have love one to another" (John 13:35).

It has been said that the destruction of the American family might be traced "not to government schools nor to video games but to central heating. Before that 'gift,' families had to be warm together, or freeze alone" (R.C. Sproul Jr., "Won't You Be My Neighbor?", *Tabletalk Magazine*, April 1999). The church has been victim of the same destruction. We have become islands unto ourselves, forgetting that the Lord commanded us to love one another.

True fellowship in the church of our Lord is dependent on three things:

1. *An illumination in each heart of the truth of God's Word.* All members must come to the divine illumination that God loves them, that they are God's children. In other words, a true relationship with the Lord precedes spiritual fellowship with others in the church.

2. *An outward extension of love toward others.* Because the members are experiencing and reveling in God's love for them individually, they can and must extend that love to each other. This love will cause them to lift up Christ everywhere they go. As a result, He will "draw all men unto me" (John 12:32). The true church is never wrapped up in itself. It is always looking outwardly to win others to Christ.

3. *A regular renewal through the Holy Spirit.* The Holy Spirit gives life. Without that life-giving force, a church soon slips into a dead lifelessness. At this point, fellowship is purely on a social level.

I. BELIEVERS OBEY JESUS (1 John 1:5-7; 2:3-6)

A. True Christian Fellowship (1:5-7)

5. This then is the message which we have heard of him, and declare unto you, that God is light, and in him is no darkness at all.

6. If we say that we have fellowship with him, and walk in darkness, we lie, and do not the truth:

7. But if we walk in the light, as he is in the light, we have fellowship one with another, and the blood of Jesus Christ his Son cleanseth us from all sin.

After reading this portion of Scripture, we might want to ask ourselves: "Do we have true Christian fellowship? Do we show concern for our fellow believers in this body? Do we really care if someone else in the body has a problem?" If we can't answer "yes" to these questions, then we are apparently deceiving ourselves about our relationship with the Lord. Verse 7 seems to indicate that fellowship with others is a direct result of walking in the light of the Lord.

Fellowship simply means "sharing things in common with others." The word has strong spiritual connotations, which can be both positive and negative. Positively, we have fellowship with the Father and the Son: "That they all may be one; as thou, Father, art in me, and I in thee, that they also may be one in us: that the world may believe that thou hast sent me" (John 17:21). We also share fellowship with the Holy Spirit: "If there be therefore any consolation in Christ, if any comfort of love, if any fellowship of the Spirit . . . ye be like-minded, having the same love, being of one accord, of one mind" (Philippians 2:1, 2). What believers share is a common relationship based on the Holy Spirit dwelling in each of them. "Those who have fellowship with Christ should enjoy fellowship with other believers. This fellowship ought to illustrate the very nature of God Himself" (*Nelson's Bible Dictionary*).

In the negative sense, we are not to have fellowship with unbelievers. This simply means we should not share their ungodly lifestyles. It doesn't mean we are to avoid them altogether. We are obligated to share the gospel with them.

God is light. The opposite of light is darkness. God's light provides us a candle by which we walk through the darkness of this life. Also, since He is light, He exposes anything that lurks in the darkness. Sin cannot continue where His light shines. Thus, if we have a real relationship with the Lord, He is constantly exposing areas of darkness in our lives. To maintain our relationship with Him, we must put aside anything He exposes. If we don't, we are living a lie in claiming a relationship with Him. Such hypocrisy will ultimately be exposed.

B. Obedience to God (2:3-6)

3. And hereby we do know that we know him, if we keep his commandments.

4. He that saith, I know him, and keepeth not his commandments, is a liar, and the truth is not in him.

5. But whoso keepeth his word, in him verily is the love of God perfected: hereby know we that we are in him.

6. He that saith he abideth in him ought himself also so to walk, even as he walked.

A false doctrine pervaded much of the church in John's day. The school of antinomianism taught that because salvation was a free gift of grace, there was no need to forsake sin. Everything was covered by the blood of Jesus. Aligned with these apostates were the Gnostics, who boasted of great spiritual knowledge, yet thought nothing of disobeying the laws of God. In other words, the salvation relationship with Christ overwhelmed any need for obedience to His commands. A ludicrous line from an

old movie describes this type of reasoning: "Love means never having to say you're sorry."

A true believer, however, has imprinted on his heart a desire to obey every word of Christ. "A careful conscientious obedience to His commands shows that the apprehension and knowledge of these things are graciously impressed upon the soul" (Matthew Henry).

Simply put, a true believer will strive with all to obey the will of Christ. Verse 4 shows the very opposite of a sincere believer. Those who disobey Christ while claiming a relationship with Him are nothing but liars, and the truth is not in them. "The attempt to be justified through faith in Christ without a commitment to follow Christ is doomed to failure" (*Full Life Study Bible*, notes on 1 John 2:4).

These verses have a direct relationship to 1 John 1:7 (see point A above). Fellowship with other believers is a divinely mandated element of Christianity, but that fellowship must be with true believers. We can distinguish those who are sincere by their conscientious desire to obey the commands of Christ. Those who unabashedly walk in the flesh should not be part of a believer's close circle of friends.

II. BELIEVERS PRAY
   (Acts 4:23-31)

A. United in Prayer (vv. 23-30)

(Acts 4:23-28 is not included in the printed text.)

29. And now, Lord, behold their threatenings: and grant unto thy servants, that with all boldness they may speak thy word,

30. By stretching forth thine hand to heal; and that signs and

wonders may be done by the name of thy holy child Jesus.

Peter and John had gone to the Temple where they encountered a crippled beggar. Peter took him by the hand and healed him. This immediately gave the two disciples an audience, and Peter preached a fiery sermon. His powerful words inflamed the religious leaders, who arrested them and left them in jail overnight. The next day, the two disciples were brought before the Sanhedrin, and Peter again proclaimed the gospel—Jesus Christ had arisen, He is the Messiah, and there is salvation through no other means but Him. The Sanhedrin threatened them, but finally let them go. They were not yet willing to do bodily injury to the disciples, because the crowds in the streets were so carried away with the miracle of the beggar being healed.

The disciples, however, were sobered by their night in jail. They now realized that there would be great costs for carrying the gospel. This didn't slow them down, but they knew they had to have the Spirit with them to stand firm against increasing opposition. Our text above indicates just what they did to get this boldness—they prayed. Even more important, however, is the fact that they sought out the brethren to join them in prayer. There is a power in corporate prayer that is not available in solitude. "No advancement in gifts or usefulness should make us think ourselves above either the duties or the privileges of the communion of saints" (Matthew Henry).

The nature of God is most perfectly illustrated as believers unite in prayer for a common cause. Verse 24 shows that all were united "with one accord." Our text shows that the early church members had little concern for their own

lives. They knew they were in God's protection. What they prayed for was a "boldness" (v. 29) to speak the truth. "In threatening times, our care should not be so much that troubles may be prevented as that we may be enabled to go on with cheerfulness and resolution in our work and duty, whatever troubles we may meet with" (Matthew Henry).

B. The Results of Prayer (v. 31)

31. And when they had prayed, the place was shaken where they were assembled together; and they were all filled with the Holy Ghost, and they spake the word of God with boldness.

The pressures that come against Christians can deplete any storehouse of spiritual energy. Even in good times, draining takes place from the affairs of daily life.

In verse 31 the gathered believers in Jerusalem received a new filling. Their indwelling by the Holy Spirit in Acts 2 cannot be downplayed, but their need of constant refueling is equally evident.

This fresh filling equipped them for the new problems they were facing. "Fresh fillings with the Holy Spirit are part of God's will and provision for all who have received the baptism in the Holy Spirit" (*Full Life Study Bible*, notes on Acts 4:31). God's presence was manifested in such power that the very building shook.

III. BELIEVERS ARE GENEROUS
    (Acts 4:32-37)

32. And the multitude of them that believed were of one heart and of one soul: neither said any of them that ought of the things which he possessed was his own; but they had all things common.

33. And with great power gave the apostles witness of the resurrection of the Lord Jesus: and great grace was upon them all.

34. Neither was there any among them that lacked: for as many as were possessors of lands or houses sold them, and brought the prices of the things that were sold,

35. And laid them down at the apostles' feet: and distribution was made unto every man according as he had need.

36. And Joses, who by the apostles was surnamed Barnabas, (which is, being interpreted, The son of consolation,) a Levite, and of the country of Cyprus,

37. Having land, sold it, and brought the money, and laid it at the apostles' feet.

Something happened to the people as they united in prayer in those early days. They lost sight of their own needs and regarded each other with great care and concern. As a result, they "shared everything they had" (v. 32, *NIV*). This was not a forced communal living—it was a voluntary one. Their spiritual unity quickly attracted others to them, and the church grew by leaps and bounds.

It should be noted, however, that Scripture never mandates an equal distribution of goods. The Bible does not promote communal living. This was a situation where people shared with one another out of the abundance of their love. People made themselves the extended arms of Christ.

While not promoting a total sharing of everything, churches should still strive to establish covenant community in their congregations. "In too many modern churches, the parishioners have the same ties to one another that fellow shoppers at Sears do, which

is to say, next to none. But a church should be a place where trust, knowledge, and commitment are all cultivated" ("In Season and Out of Season," by Douglas Wilson, *Tabletalk Magazine*, April 1999).

GOLDEN TEXT HOMILY

"LET BROTHERLY LOVE CONTINUE" (Hebrews 13:1).

This admonition to *keep* loving each other as brothers implies that this trait was already prevalent among the early believers. Brotherly love involves treating others as if they are a member of one's own family, enjoying having them around and desiring what is best for them. This is the kind of love that believers should have for one another and that should be manifested in the church.

Brotherly love is an act of obedience. For these believers to continue loving one another was not an option; it was a mandate. Likewise believers today are under this same exhortation. How beautiful would be the congregation of the saints if this love were always manifested.

Brotherly love is at the heart of holiness. This admonition to love cannot be separated from the call to holiness in the previous chapter. There we are reminded of the awe-inspiring holiness of our God, who is a consuming fire, and of our need both to pursue holiness and to become partakers of His holiness.

Brotherly love is a sign of Christian maturity; in fact, it is the ultimate expression of Christlikeness. This kind of love leads believers to pray for one another, bear one another's burdens, forgive one another and build up one another.

Brotherly love is a witness to the world. Jesus had this kind of love in mind when He said, "By this all will know that you are My disciples, if you have love for one another" (John 13:35, *NKJV*).—**Homer G. Rhea**

SENTENCE SERMONS

CHRISTIANITY is a lifestyle of obedience to Christ, prayer and generosity.

—Selected

LOVE LOOKS through a telescope; envy, through a microscope.

—Josh Billings

THE MOST OF US want very much to be loved. Perhaps we are not concerned enough about loving.

—Erwin McDonald

EVANGELISM APPLICATION

SINNERS WILL COME TO KNOW CHRIST'S LOVE BY THE LOVE CHRISTIANS SHOW FOR ONE ANOTHER.

One of the great churches in the United States that has exhibited a true picture of Christian love and outreach is the Brooklyn Tabernacle in New York City. Through recordings of the church's choir, millions around the world have been touched. The pastor, Jim Cymbala, speaks to groups of ministers on how God moved to bring about this New Testament atmosphere. His formula is really quite simple: *prayer*. The story is told in the book *Fresh Wind, Fresh Fire*. Things were not always wonderful for Pastor Cymbala and his wife, Carol. In fact, their situation was demoralizing and nearly hopeless. In the pits of despair, Pastor Cymbala cried out to God for help. This is how God responded: "If you and your wife will lead My people to pray and call upon My name, you will never lack for something fresh to preach. I will supply all the money that's needed, both for the church and for your family, and you will never have a building large enough to contain the crowds I will send in response."

Pastor Cymbala accepted the Lord's promise. The church was built on prayer meetings. Every Tuesday night, thousands of people join together and cry out to God for His presence and help. The fellowship among believers is extraordinary. This is how God meant for all Christians to live—in prayerful unity with one another.

ILLUMINATING THE LESSON

There is a fascinating little-known story in history. Because of Jesus' prophetic words concerning Jerusalem's destruction (see Matthew 24), as well as the cruel treatment from nonbelieving Jews, most Christians had left Jerusalem by the time of the Roman invasion under Titus in A.D. 70. Persecution had dispersed them to all corners of the known world. Still, there was an element of God's protection.

Flavius Josephus, a first-century Jewish historian, tells of a manifestation that occurred while Jerusalem was under siege. He gives this account cautiously, as if fearing it too strange for people to believe: "Then again, not many days after the feast, on the 21st of the month of Artemisium, a supernatural apparition was seen, too amazing to be believed. What I am now to relate would, I imagine, have been dismissed as imaginary, had this not been vouched for by eyewitnesses, then followed by subsequent disasters that deserved to be thus signalized. For before sunset, chariots were seen in the air over the whole country, and armed battalions speeding through the clouds and encircling the cities. Then again, at the feast called Pentecost, when the priests had entered the inner courts of the

Temple by night to perform their usual ministrations, they declared that they were aware, at first, of a violent commotion and din, then of a voice of a host crying, 'We are departing hence'" (*The Complete Works of Flavius Josephus*).

The chariots of heaven announced that God's presence was forsaking the city. When the believers had exited the city, so had the reason for God to be there. It is in the fellowship of Christians that His presence is manifest.

DAILY BIBLE READINGS

M. Obey the Lord.
   Exodus 3:11-17
T. Serve Wisely.
   Exodus 18:13-27
W. Prayer for Victory.
   2 Chronicles 20:1-15
T. Community of Believers.
   Acts 2:42-47
F. Answered Prayer.
   Acts 12:5-16
S. Be Willing to Share.
   1 Timothy 6:6-19

TRUTH SEARCH:
Creatively Teaching the Word

Aim: Students will identify obstacles facing the church and seek God's help in becoming a genuine fellowship of believers.

Materials needed: Index cards, pencils, marker, marker board

FOCUS

Give an index card to each student. Ask each one to write down what he or she thinks is the greatest obstacle facing the church today. Have an assistant collect the cards, divide them according to similar responses, and tally the results. Meanwhile, continue the lesson by discussing these questions:
- *Why are you part of this local church?*
- *What are the strengths of this church?*
- *What would cause more people to want to attend our church?*

In today's lesson we will see what the Bible says the church should be like.

EXPLORE

Divide the class into groups of three to five students each. Assign each group one of the Scripture passages and sets of questions listed below. When they are finished finding their answers, bring everyone back together to discuss their findings.

1 John 1:5-7; 2:3-6
1. Can a person be a genuine believer and intentionally live in darkness (1:5, 6)?
2. How can believers "walk in the light" and in unity with one another (v. 7)?
3. What is the evidence that a person is walking with Christ (2:3-5)?

4. Restate 1 John 2:6 in your own words.

Acts 4:23-31
1. To what does "being let go" (v. 23) refer? (See Acts 3:1-7; 4:1-4, 18-22.)
2. Why did the believers pray so intensely (vv. 23-28)?
3. What did they request from the Lord (vv. 29, 30)?
4. How did the Lord respond (v. 31)?

Acts 4:32-37
1. Describe the attitude of the believers (v. 32).
2. How was the church moving forward (v. 33)?
3. What needs were going unmet among the believers (vv. 34, 35)?
4. Why was Barnabas known as the "son of encouragement" (vv. 36, 37, NIV)?

In summarizing the Bible studies, emphasize that the early church was obedient, unified, prayerful and generous.

RESPOND

Have your helper give the results of the greatest-obstacle survey. Write the results on the board.
- *Do you think the early church ever faced any of these problems?*
- *If our church functions as an obedient, unified, prayerful and generous body, will these obstacles be something we can overcome?*

Ask four volunteers to take turns praying for your local church. The first volunteer should pray for the church to be more obedient; the second, more prayerful; the third, more generous; and the fourth, more unified.

The Church and Divine Power

Study Text: Ephesians 1:15-23; 2:11-22; Colossians 1:24-29
Objective: To recognize and respond to God's divine power at work in the church.
Time: About A.D. 60.
Place: Paul wrote his epistles to the Ephesians and the Colossians from a Roman prison.
Golden Text: "Unto him that is able to do exceeding abundantly above all that we ask or think, according to the power that worketh in us, unto him be glory in the church by Christ Jesus throughout all ages" (Ephesians 3:20, 21).
Central Truth: The Holy Spirit empowers the church.
Evangelism Emphasis: The Holy Spirit empowers believers to witness.

PRINTED TEXT

Ephesians 1:15. Wherefore I also, after I heard of your faith in the Lord Jesus, and love unto all the saints,

16. Cease not to give thanks for you, making mention of you in my prayers;

17. That the God of our Lord Jesus Christ, the Father of glory, may give unto you the spirit of wisdom and revelation in the knowledge of him:

18. The eyes of your understanding being enlightened; that ye may know what is the hope of his calling, and what the riches of the glory of his inheritance in the saints,

19. And what is the exceeding greatness of his power to us-ward who believe, according to the working of his mighty power,

20. Which he wrought in Christ, when he raised him from the dead, and set him at his own right hand in the heavenly places.

Colossians 1:25. Whereof I am made a minister, according to the dispensation of God which is given to me for you, to fulfil the word of God;

26. Even the mystery which hath been hid from ages and from generations, but now is made manifest to his saints:

27. To whom God would make known what is the riches of the glory of this mystery among the Gentiles; which is Christ in you, the hope of glory:

28. Whom we preach, warning every man, and teaching every man in all wisdom; that we may present every man perfect in Christ Jesus:

29. Whereunto I also labour, striving according to his working, which worketh in me mightily.

Ephesians 2:14. For he is our peace, who hath made both one, and hath broken down the middle wall of partition between us;

15. Having abolished in his flesh the enmity, even the law of commandments contained in ordinances; for to make in himself of twain one new man, so making peace;

16. And that he might reconcile both unto God in one body by the cross, having slain the enmity thereby:

17. And came and preached peace to you which were afar off, and to them that were nigh.

18. For through him we both have access by one Spirit unto the Father.

19. Now therefore ye are no more strangers and foreigners, but fellowcitizens with the saints, and of the household of God.

DICTIONARY
dispensation—Colossians 1:25—commission

LESSON OUTLINE

I. EMPOWERED BY GOD

  A. Appreciation for the Ephesian Believers

  B. Prayer for the Ephesians

  C. Opened Eyes of Understanding

  D. Christ, the Supreme Head of the Church

II. PROCLAIMING CHRIST

  A. Paul's Suffering

  B. Christ in You, the Hope of Glory

  C. Good News for All

III. UNITED IN THE SPIRIT

  A. Jew Versus Gentile

  B. Christ, the Means of Peace

  C. Fellow Citizens in God's House

LESSON EXPOSITION

INTRODUCTION

Our lesson deals with exhortations Paul gave to two churches—the church at Ephesus and the church at Colosse. Though his message to both bodies is somewhat the same (and both letters were written from his prison cell in Rome), the conditions of the two congregations were radically different.

The church at Ephesus gives us possibly the best picture of what has been called the "New Testament church." Generally, when someone mentions this phrase, our minds immediately go to the Jerusalem church just after Pentecost. Certainly this was a wonderful time of Holy Spirit empowerment, but the Jerusalem church (comprised of converted Jews) does not represent the full spectrum of how God worked in the first century.

The real story of the spread of Christianity was in the outreach to the Gentiles. The church at Antioch was a model church (where believers first took on the name Christian—Acts 11:26), and there was no doubt of a move of God's power there. However, at Ephesus we get the best long-term view of what life in a body of Christian believers was really like in the apostolic age. More New Testament material deals historically with Ephesus than any other city. We see the progress of this congregation over a time span of at least 40 years. In addition to the Ephesian letter, Paul also wrote 1 and 2 Timothy to the young pastor of this congregation. Finally, John's vision in Revelation both encouraged and warned the believers at Ephesus (Revelation 2:1-7).

The church at Ephesus was established in A.D. 53, near the end of Paul's second missionary journey. He returned one year later on his third journey and stayed three years—preaching, teaching, establishing, grounding and organizing the body of believers there. He was aided greatly by Priscilla and Aquila (his business associates and "evangelistic team"). Later, he established his own protégé, Timothy, as pastor of the thriving congregation.

There are no great problems or schisms dealt with in Paul's letter to the Ephesians. It is almost entirely a letter of encouragement, which will be the focus of our lesson.

The church at Colosse was a different story. Located in Asia Minor 100 miles east of Ephesus, this congregation apparently was founded by Epaphras—a convert of Paul's ministry. Colosse was a place where Judaism, cults, paganism, Greek thought—as well as every other secular philosophy under the sun—all competed to possess people's minds. The result was that the Christians at Colosse mixed and matched ideas of all kinds to form a hybrid form of religion. This is known as *syncretism*, and results in total heresy. The fact that a strong leader like Paul never ministered in person in Colosse meant there was no grounding in pure Christian doctrine. Paul's words of correction would be both strong and loving. He made sure they understood that Jesus is absolutely supreme and Lord of the universe.

I. EMPOWERED BY GOD
    (Ephesians 1:15-23)

A. Appreciation for the Ephesian Believers (v. 15)

15. Wherefore I also, after I heard of your faith in the Lord Jesus, and love unto all the saints.

Paul commended the Ephesian believers for their strong faith in the

Lord. On first reading, one might think it strange that he addressed them so formally—as if he had not earlier spent three years laboring there. It had been some time, however, since his departure from the city (in addition to communications being slow and infrequent), and perhaps he had heard no word from them until recently. He was writing from prison, and his last known meeting with their leaders was at Miletus (Acts 20). Whatever the situation, it was with great joy that he finally received good news of their spiritual growth. His anxiety was relieved, and he expressed great thanks for what he had heard.

It is clear that Paul expected other people to read this letter. Circulating letters to the churches of a region were a common practice by the apostles. Though addressed to one particular body, Paul's words are directly from the Lord. Thus, all believers could benefit from hearing them.

B. Prayer for the Ephesians
   (vv. 16, 17)

16. Cease not to give thanks for you, making mention of you in my prayers;
17. That the God of our Lord Jesus Christ, the Father of glory, may give unto you the spirit of wisdom and revelation in the knowledge of him.

Being held in a Roman jail, Paul likely had great doubts that he would ever return to Ephesus. He did not doubt, however, the power or distance of his prayers. His cry was not that the believers be blessed materially, but rather that they come to a greater knowledge of Jesus Christ.

There is an unlimited vastness to be learned of Christ. Paul desired this ever-increasing revelation for all Christians, as well as for himself. He prayed, "That I may know him, and the power of his resurrection, and the fellowship of his sufferings, being made conformable unto his death" (Philippians 3:10).

The word *revelation* means a deepening understanding of the character of the Redeemer, an illumination of His nature and work. In referring to the *spirit*, Paul likely was referring to the Holy Spirit as the author of all understanding of Christ. He prayed that God would grant a greater outpouring of the Holy Spirit to make them wise and knowledgeable of Christ.

C. Opened Eyes of Understanding (vv. 18, 19)

18. The eyes of your understanding being enlightened; that ye may know what is the hope of his calling, and what the riches of the glory of his inheritance in the saints,

19. And what is the exceeding greatness of his power to us-ward who believe, according to the working of his mighty power.

Philo said, "What the eye is to the body, that is the mind to the soul." Paul wanted the eyes of his readers to be opened to three great revelations of the wonders of Christ:

1. *The hope of his calling.* Paul knew that there lies an inestimable benefit that comes with being a part of Christ's kingdom. As Jesus told His disciples, "I bestow upon you a kingdom, just as My Father bestowed one upon Me, that you may eat and drink at My table in My kingdom" (Luke 22:29, 30, *NKJV*). Paul wanted his readers to see beyond the mundane affairs of life and discern the objects of their hope. They were being invited to dine at the Lord's table forever. An old gospel song describes this well: "Jesus has a table spread where the saints of God are fed. He invites His chosen people, 'Come and dine.'" Paul had caught a vision of this, and he wanted other believers to see the same.

2. *The riches of his inheritance.* Paul was not speaking of material wealth, but rather of spiritual things. These riches are not reserved just for the future life with Christ in heaven, but they include remarkable benefit for the present—peace of mind, joy in the Lord, communion with Christ, fellowship of other believers—an entire spectrum of wealth. "There is a present inheritance in the saints; for grace is glory begun, and holiness is happiness in the bud" (Matthew Henry).

3. *The greatness of His power.* The power Paul speaks of is the power that was exerted in bringing salvation to mankind; it is also the power that keeps the believer. It is ultimately the same power that brings the resurrection of believers from the dead, exalting them with Christ to heaven. God's great power will be manifested toward believers until they reach their ultimate inheritance in glory.

D. Christ, the Supreme Head of the Church (vv. 20-23)

(Ephesians 1:21-23 is not included in the printed text.)

20. Which he wrought in Christ, when he raised him from the dead, and set him at his own right hand in the heavenly places.

God has given Christ total dominion in this world and in the world to come. He is the Messiah, the head of the church, the long-awaited Redeemer of Israel, the One who alone can set a fallen world straight. We can be confident that we have a Savior who is totally in charge. Everything is subject to Christ. Satan cannot hurt us; neither can any dictator, tyrant or nation.

The church is the Lord's body. This is not just one individual, but it is the corporate body of Christ. As members of this body, we should strive to find our place of usefulness within it.

II. PROCLAIMING CHRIST (Colossians 1:24-29)

A. Paul's Sufferings (vv. 24, 25)

(Colossians 1:24 is not included in the printed text.)

25. Whereof I am made a minister, according to the dispensation of God which is given to me for you, to fulfil the word of God.

The Living Bible rendition of verse 24 reads: "But part of my work is to suffer for you; and I am glad, for I am helping to finish up the remainder of Christ's sufferings for his body, the church." Paul saw himself as sharing with Christ in "the fellowship of his sufferings" (Philippians 3:10).

With the phrase "finish up [fill up]," Paul does not indicate that Christ's personal suffering on the cross was insufficient to purchase our salvation. Neither does he indicate that every believer will have to suffer in this life. He does expect, however, that persecutions and suffering are inevitable as the good news is carried to the world. He sees his own life as an example. Even as he penned these words, he was suffering in a Roman jail.

The Christian suffers because of his relationship to Christ. "When we suffer, Christ feels it with us. But this suffering can be endured joyfully because it changes lives and brings people into God's kingdom" (*Life Application Bible*, notes on Colossians 1:24).

B. Christ in You, the Hope of Glory (vv. 26, 27)

26. Even the mystery which hath been hid from ages and from generations, but now is made manifest to his saints:

27. To whom God would make known what is the riches of the glory of this mystery among the Gentiles; which is Christ in you, the hope of glory.

The great mystery of the universe is that Christ, the Son of God, would make His dwelling place in the hearts of men. The Gnostics in Colosse believed that spiritual perfection was a secret available only to a select few through special knowledge. This group was condemned by Paul in 2:8-23 for their endless fables, speculations and moral laxity. Nevertheless, Paul still portrays the hope of the gospel as a mystery.

God's plan had certainly been a secret down through the ages. Some of the Old Testament heroes and prophets caught glimpses of it, but they never had a full understanding. It was finally revealed, and revealed to all, when Christ came to live in the hearts of men. That God would become man and live in vessels of human clay is truly a mystery, but this is truly our "hope of glory."

C. Good News for All (vv. 28, 29)

28. Whom we preach, warning every man, and teaching every man in all wisdom; that we may present every man perfect in Christ Jesus:

29. Whereunto I also labour, striving according to his working, which worketh in me mightily.

The mystery is no longer a secret, nor is it available to only a few. Paul's personal mission was to spread the news everywhere.

The gospel of Jesus Christ is meant for all! This has both positive and negative connotations. However, positively, every man can have eternal life through a relationship with Christ—"For whosoever shall call upon the name of the Lord shall be saved" (Romans 10:13). Negatively, salvation and future life is available only through Christ—"Salvation is found in no one else, for there is no other name under heaven given to men by which we must be saved" (Acts 4:12, NIV).

III. UNITED IN THE SPIRIT
    (Ephesians 2:11-22)

A. Jew Versus Gentile (vv. 11-13)

(Ephesians 2:11-13 is not included in the printed text.)

For centuries Jews had refused to have anything to do with the Gentiles, considering them unclean and beyond redemption. Gentiles likewise hated Jews for their excessive pride and religiosity. Christ revealed that both were wrong, both were equally sinful, and both were helpless to save themselves outside of His saving work.

Paul reminded the Ephesians, who were Gentiles, that they could be just as guilty of spiritual pride as the Jews. The Jews were guilty for thinking themselves to be God's exclusive people, while the Gentiles were guilty for forgetting that, outside of Christ's grace, they were spiritually dead and hopeless.

B. Christ, the Means of Peace
    (vv. 14-18)

14. For he is our peace, who hath made both one, and hath broken down the middle wall of partition between us;

15. Having abolished in his flesh the enmity, even the law of commandments contained in ordinances; for to make in himself of twain one new man, so making peace;

16. And that he might reconcile both unto God in one body by the cross, having slain the enmity thereby:

17. And came and preached peace to you which were afar off, and to them that were nigh.

18. For through him we both have access by one Spirit unto the Father.

Christ shattered the walls that separated people, bringing them peace. Through His death and resurrection, all mankind can become one family. The Cross is the focus of that unity. Though many barriers still potentially isolate us—cultural, financial, racial and language—we can unite under the banner of the Cross. We have equal access to the Father through Jesus Christ, and this is by means of the Holy Spirit. The Holy Spirit helps us see others, though different from ourselves, as brothers and sisters. It is the Spirit who breaks the fetters of hatred.

C. Fellow Citizens in God's House
    (vv. 19-22)

(Ephesians 2:20-22 is not included in the printed text.)

19. Now therefore ye are no more strangers and foreigners, but fellowcitizens with the saints, and of the household of God.

God's house is not a building—it is a gathering of people united by the gospel. In recent years, churches in the United States have worked hard to eliminate racial and cultural barriers. Many can now boast of having many nationalities and racial heritages all worshiping in the same congregation.

The Jews were selected for a special purpose in bringing God's ultimate plan of salvation, but God has no preference of race or heritage. All bow at the foot of the Cross as equals. A true church body is a place where people are united, both in their love for Christ and in their love for one another. Jesus said, "By this shall all men know that ye are my disciples, if ye have love one to another" (John 13:35).

GOLDEN TEXT HOMILY

"UNTO HIM THAT IS ABLE TO DO EXCEEDING ABUNDANTLY ABOVE ALL THAT WE ASK OR THINK, ACCORDING TO THE POWER THAT WORKETH IN US, UNTO HIM BE GLORY IN THE CHURCH BY CHRIST JESUS THROUGHOUT ALL AGES" (Ephesians 3:20, 21).

Are you in a tough spot? Does there seem to be no way out? The apostle Paul was in that kind of predicament when he penned these words found in Ephesians. He was in prison.

When Paul was imprisoned in Philippi, he had learned the power of prayer and praise. At the midnight hour, Paul and Silas prayed. Maybe they had prayed, "Lord, help us to endure this pain"; or, "Heavenly Father, let us be a witness, even in this dungeon"; or, "Jesus, let us feel Your presence"; or, "Dear God, please deliver us from the hands of the Romans."

After they had prayed, they began to worship the Lord. Suddenly, the floor began to vibrate; the walls began to shake; the bars began to rattle; and the doors flung wide open.

God was doing "exceeding abundantly above all" that they had asked. Not only did God help them endure the pain, but He sent them to the jailer's house where they received care. Not only did God let them witness, they were able to win an entire family to Christ. Not only did God reveal His presence, He revealed Himself through an awesome display of power. Not only did God deliver Paul and Silas, He delivered them with style, in a grand miracle that would never be forgotten.

Yes, Paul knew from experience that God is able to do great things. To this saving God belongs all glory, in all places, at all times, forever.—**Lee Roy Martin**

SENTENCE SERMONS

THE HOLY SPIRIT empowers the church.

—Selected

THE HOLY SPIRIT is not a substance to fill an empty receptacle, but a Person to control another person.

—Quotable Quotations

THOUGH EVERY BELIEVER has the Holy Spirit, the Holy Spirit does not have every believer.

—A.W. Tozer

EVANGELISM APPLICATION

THE HOLY SPIRIT EMPOWERS BELIEVERS TO WITNESS.

Paul said that we have been "raised . . . up . . . and made [to] sit together in heavenly places in Christ Jesus" (Ephesians 2:6). By faith, we are already seated at the Lord's table. In the Old Testament, to be invited to the king's table was a wonderful privilege. When David wanted to fulfill his covenant with Jonathan (who had been killed in battle), he sought out his friend's one living descendant— Mephibosheth. David said to Mephibosheth, "Do not fear, for I will surely show you kindness for Jonathan your father's sake . . . and you shall eat bread at my table continually" (2 Samuel 9:7, *NKJV*).

There is tremendous honor and majesty given us by having been raised up to sit with Christ at His heavenly table. Paul's letter to the Ephesians was written to help them grasp the "riches of the glory of his inheritance in the saints" (1:18). He himself knew the joy of feasting at the Lord's table. His miraculous conversion had not been enough. His soul cried out, "Oh, that I might know Him" (see Philippians 3:10). Not only that, he wanted every believer to understand what is available in this Christian life. Are you feasting at the table? Set your heart to "know Him" as Paul did.

The more we know Him, the more we want others to find this same relationship. It was Paul's yearning for Christ that took him all over the Roman Empire building churches. His evangelism was a direct outflow of His desire to know more of Christ. His power to evangelize came through the infilling of the Holy Spirit.

ILLUMINATING THE LESSON

There was a couple who had a beautiful 4-year-old daughter. They were content and happy, but were made even more so with the arrival of a second child, a little boy. The little girl was very excited when her parents brought the infant home from the hospital, but she immediately insisted on having her own private moment with him as soon as he was settled into the nursery. Fearing that there might be sibling rivalry, the parents eavesdropped through a crack in the doorway. What they saw and heard startled them. She lay down beside the infant and placed her face very close to his. Then she said, "Tell me, little brother—what does God feel like? I'm getting older now, and I'm beginning to forget!"

Though the church at Ephesus was a model congregation with a yearning for Christ, a few years later they would receive a warning: "Thou hast left thy first love" (Revelation 2:4). It's easy to "grow up" and become busy in the Kingdom. Like the big sister in the story above, we forget what God feels like. Let us not ever forsake our first love for Christ, but continually renew our affections for Him.

DAILY BIBLE READINGS

M. Blessing of Unity.
     Psalm 133:1-3
T. Christ Foretold.
     Isaiah 11:1-10
W. Filled With the Spirit.
     Ezekiel 36:25-31
T. Preaching With Boldness.
     Acts 4:5-13
F. Courage in Persecution.
     Acts 7:54-60
S. The Bond of Love.
     Colossians 3:12-17

TRUTH SEARCH:
Creatively Teaching the Word

Aim: Students will ask the Holy Spirit to empower them to effectively continue the ministry of Jesus.

Items needed: Marker board, markers, pencils, paper

FOCUS

On the marker board write "Candidates for Ministry." Below this write the numbers 1 through 10. Ask the students to list at least 10 types of people they feel are genuine candidates for Christian ministry. For the purpose of this lesson, *ministry* shall be defined as any action taken by a Christian to meet the financial, physical, mental, emotional or spiritual needs of others.

EXPLORE

Divide the class into small groups of three or four students each. Ask half of the groups to study Ephesians 1:15-23. Ask the other groups to study Colossians 1:24-29. One person in each group should read the assigned passage aloud, and another person should be assigned to write the answers to the following questions about their particular passage.

Ephesians 1:15-23

1. *Why did Paul give thanks for the Ephesian Christians (vv. 15, 16)?*
2. *What did Paul ask God to do for these believers (vv. 17-19)? Which of those things are important for people who want to do ministry today? Why?*
3. *How does Paul define the church (vv. 22, 23)?*
4. *Reflecting on verses 19-21,* why is Christ's power essential for the church to do ministry?

Colossians 1:24-29

1. *How does Paul describe the church (v. 24)? Why?*
2. *What did God call Paul to do (vv. 25-27)?*
3. *What was Paul's goal in preaching and teaching (v. 28)?*
4. *How hard did Paul work in doing ministry (vv. 24, 29)?*
5. *What principles about ministry can we learn from this passage?*

Have the groups present their findings, then have everyone turn to Ephesians 2:19-22 and follow along as you read it.

• *How does Paul describe the church (v. 19)?*
• *What is the foundation of the church (v. 20)?*
• *What is the framework of the church (v. 21)?*
• *What is the element that holds the church together (v. 22)?*

As believers, we are part of the living building called the church, and each of us has a ministry to perform.

RESPOND

Turn the class's attention back to the marker board. List specific ministries that these candidates for ministry can perform. Now ask members to think about tangible ways they can be involved in ministry.

Legitimate, meaningful, Christian ministry requires the empowerment of the Holy Spirit.

Pray for the students to receive the Holy Spirit's empowerment for effective ministry.

Purpose of the Church

Study Text: Mark 16:15-18; Ephesians 4:7-16; 1 Thessalonians 1:2-10
Objective: To understand that people are at the heart of God's purposes for the church and devote ourselves to His mission.
Golden Text: "Go ye into all the world, and preach the gospel to every creature" (Mark 16:15).
Central Truth: The church exists to worship Christ, proclaim the gospel, and disciple believers.
Evangelism Emphasis: The church is mandated to reach the lost for Christ.

PRINTED TEXT

Ephesians 4:11. And he gave some, apostles; and some, prophets; and some, evangelists; and some, pastors and teachers;

12. For the perfecting of the saints, for the work of the ministry, for the edifying of the body of Christ:

13. Till we all come in the unity of the faith, and of the knowledge of the Son of God, unto a perfect man, unto the measure of the stature of the fulness of Christ.

Mark 16:15. And he said unto them, Go ye into all the world, and preach the gospel to every creature.

16. He that believeth and is baptized shall be saved; but he that believeth not shall be damned.

17. And these signs shall follow them that believe; In my name shall they cast out devils; they shall speak with new tongues;

18. They shall take up serpents; and if they drink any deadly thing, it shall not hurt them; they shall lay hands on the sick, and they shall recover.

1 Thessalonians 1:2. We give thanks to God always for you all, making mention of you in our prayers;

3. Remembering without ceasing your work of faith, and labour of love, and patience of hope in our Lord Jesus Christ, in the sight of God and our Father;

4. Knowing, brethren beloved, your election of God.

5. For our gospel came not unto you in word only, but also in power, and in the Holy Ghost, and in much assurance; as ye know what manner of men we were among you for your sake.

6. And ye became followers of us, and of the Lord, having received the word in much affliction, with joy of the Holy Ghost:

7. So that ye were ensamples to all that believe in Macedonia and Achaia.

8. For from you sounded out the word of the Lord not only in Macedonia and Achaia, but also in every place your faith to God-ward is spread abroad; so that we need not to speak any thing.

9. For they themselves shew of us what manner of entering in we had unto you, and how ye turned to God from idols to serve the living and true God;

10. And to wait for his Son from heaven, whom he raised from the dead, even Jesus, which delivered us from the wrath to come.

LESSON OUTLINE

LESSON EXPOSITION

INTRODUCTION

The church is the army of the Lord. It is the fighting military machine that physically represents Christ on this earth. When Jesus descended from heaven in the Incarnation, He marched into the territories that Satan had stolen from God's people, recovering all that had been lost.

In the Old Testament, we see foreshadows of Christ's triumph when rulers of city-states would invade the territories of other peoples, stealing their livestock and taking their women and children as slaves. Even David was subjected to this horror once during his years of fleeing from King Saul.

First Samuel 30 tells how the Amalekites invaded Ziklag, a city that Achish, king of Gath, had given David as a refuge and military base. (Many of Saul's followers had defected to David's camp and lived there.) While David and his men were away with King Achish, the Amalekites invaded Ziklag, burned it to the ground, took all the women and children, and plundered anything that was of value. David pursued the Amalekites, defeated them, and recovered everything that had been stolen, plus much more. David shared the plunder with all his men, even those who had not gone on the raid. He also sent some to the elders of Judah, telling them, "Here is a present for you from the plunder of the Lord's enemies" (30:26, *NIV*). This incident pictured Christ's defeat of Satan and the giving of gifts to His people.

Jesus came down from heaven and defeated Satan, thus recovering all the plunder that had been robbed from mankind. He ascended back to heaven in exaltation, and now He fills the entire universe as a conquering King. He joyously grants gifts to His church (His army) and wonderfully gives His people the power to fulfill their gifts. The gifts come, however, with great expectation on His part. They are to be used to bring power and victory to the church.

I. EQUIPPING BELIEVERS (Ephesians 4:7-16)

A. A Defined Structure in the Kingdom (v. 7)

(Ephesians 4:7 is not included in the printed text.)

Paul tells his readers that every believer has been given a measure of grace to be used in service for the Kingdom. *Grace* simply indicates an ability to perform some task or function that God calls one to do. This thought is reiterated in Romans 12:6, where Paul spoke of "gifts differing according to the grace that is given to us." Those who come to Christ are immediately imparted with a gifting (or grace). All have places to fill in the church and are given free gifts from Christ to be used as He sees fit. Discovering that grace, and living it out, is probably the most important goal a Christian can dedicate himself to.

In any earthly army each recruit is assigned a particular specialty or function. One might be placed in supply, aviation, communications, or a host of other fields. The same is true for the body of Christ. As a believer matures in Christ, that person's specialization becomes more clearly defined and evident.

Sadly, so many in the church never understand their function, often thinking they have no value to Christ. Any high-ranking officer in a military organization, however, will quickly admit to the utter importance of even the most "insignificant" soldier.

B. Christ's Triumph (vv. 8-10)

(Ephesians 4:8-10 is not included in the printed text.)

Paul indicates that not only do we all have gifts of grace, but our particular functions have a miraculous origin. In Psalm 68:18, God is pictured as a conquering king who marches victoriously over an enemy city. The city gates are broken down, the captives are freed, and tribute is demanded from the defeated tyrants. Borrowing from this imagery, Paul speaks of Christ's triumph over Satan. Jesus came down to the earth and was victorious through His incarnation, ministry, death and resurrection. When He ascended back to heaven, He gave gifts to His church. The church is His army. The gifts He gives are assignments of rank, order and function so this army can be mighty in its work.

Just what does "descended first into the lower parts of the earth" (Ephesians 4:9) mean? Christ's descent to earth means He set aside the divine attributes—omniscience, omnipresence, omnipotence— submitting them to the Father's will, in order that He could come down to the earth as a man, and even further down into the earth through His death, thus becoming sin for us. As a result of this sacrificial effort and triumph, He now fills the entire universe as the ultimate King. Sharing His victory with His people, He now lavishes gifts upon His children. Along with the gifts, He also gives believers the power to fulfill those assignments. He *graces* believers with divine help.

The positioning of graces goes even beyond the church. God puts men in high offices in secular governmental affairs. Paul exhorted Timothy to intercede "for kings, and for all that are in authority; that we may lead a quiet and peaceable life in all godliness and honesty" (1 Timothy 2:2). Christ's kingdom extends universally. He has authority over princes, kings, and all other earthly rulers. It is He who places them there. He truly is the victorious ruler of the universe.

C. Special Graces to Church Leaders (v. 11)

11. And he gave some, apostles; and some, prophets; and some, evangelists; and some, pastors and teachers.

The Holy Spirit distributes giftings to all believers, but some are assigned weightier responsibilities. No matter how great or small, however, there is still the necessity for mature and wise use of all giftings. "God has limited the operation of His Spirit and Word by channeling them through redeemed persons;

apart from this, there is no divine impartation, no advocacy, no advice" (Judson Cornwall, *Profiles of a Leader*).

The Holy Spirit channels the administration of the church through human leadership. Leaders thus must lead those who follow them. "It is a sad circumstance to see a congregation more spiritually advanced than their pastor, for this means he can lead them only if they will backtrack to his position in God" (Cornwall).

Though Paul lists giftings in other texts (see 1 Corinthians 12:8-10, 28-30; Romans 12:6-8), here he concentrates on five types of leaders who minister to the church. *Apostles* are those sent on a special mission. The original apostles were those who saw Jesus after His resurrection and were personally commissioned by Him. This included the disciples and Paul (who saw Jesus and was commissioned at the Damascus-road experience). These men all carried a unique influence in the building of the church. Their authority is not repeatable by anyone today. Still, the church continues to have apostles in a general sense—Spirit-led leaders who have a profound effect on the spread of the gospel. Though identifying such men is disputable, still, the likes of Billy Graham and D.L. Moody would be acclaimed by most as having been apostles to their generations.

The gifting of *prophets* is equally disputed in the church today, but God has always had believers who speak under the direct leading of the Holy Spirit, whether their prophecies be an encouragement for the church or some prediction of future events. The main concern of a prophet is the spiritual life and purity of the church.

Evangelists, pastors and *teachers* are less disputed roles, but are of equal importance. Evangelists have the great burden of winning souls. Pastors have the responsibility of leading local church bodies and keeping them focused on Christ. Teachers have the duty to teach Biblically sound doctrine, making sure the church does not move into heresy or error.

D. Purpose of Special Giftings
   (vv. 12, 13)

12. For the perfecting of the saints, for the work of the ministry, for the edifying of the body of Christ:

13. Till we all come in the unity of the faith, and of the knowledge of the Son of God, unto a perfect man, unto the measure of the stature of the fulness of Christ.

Christ gives certain gifts to individuals in the church for the dual purpose of (1) preparing people for service and (2) spiritually building up the people as a body. Since the operation of the Lord's kingdom is done through the instrumentality of men and women, there is great responsibility in preaching, teaching, healing, administration, discipling, discernment and a host of other tasks.

As leaders work together with laity in harmony, the church can progress. Leaders who try to do everything will fail. Those with lesser gifts who refuse to follow will also fail. The church is a body, just like the human body. All parts are necessary.

E. Mature Faith (vv. 14-16)

(Ephesians 4:14-16 is not included in the printed text.)

As the church follows God's plan and order (in terms of giftings), there will be growth and maturity, with wisdom and discernment to avoid Satan's pitfalls. Satan is always present to present a lie, quickly moving in among immature believers to get them caught up in false doctrines and dissensions. If all things are done in proper order, with everyone recognizing each other's roles in the Kingdom, there will come a solidarity in Christian truth that Satan cannot penetrate. True church growth comes when those gifted in special leadership operate wisely under the Holy Spirit's guidance.

II. EVANGELIZING THE LOST (Mark 16:15-18)

A. Preaching the Gospel to Every Creature (v. 15)

15. And he said unto them, Go ye into all the world, and preach the gospel to every creature.

The Great Commission to the church is found here in Mark's Gospel, as well as in Matthew 28:19. The emphasis is on proclaiming the glad tidings that Christ was crucified, raised from the dead and, as a result, has brought salvation to all people. The church's task is to go into all the world and preach this good news to all peoples. Because Christ has tasted death for every individual, every person can have eternal life.

As the history of the early church developed, the idea of the good news going to every creature was a difficult one for many to accept. Centuries of Jewish exclusivism were not easily extracted from even the most dedicated believer's heart. The idea that the gospel was meant for the Gentile world took time to take hold.

B. Salvation Through Grace (v. 16)

16. He that believeth and is baptized shall be saved; but he that believeth not shall be damned.

All who receive the gospel as a revelation from God are given salvation. Romans 10:9 gives the simple formula for receiving the wonderful message of grace: "That if thou shalt confess with thy mouth the Lord Jesus, and shalt believe in thine heart that God hath raised him from the dead, thou shalt be saved."

Water baptism is an outward sign of an inner faith expressed in what Christ has done for the individual. Can one be saved without going through the act of baptism? Certainly the response of the thief on the cross to Jesus' invitation indicates that one's salvation is not based on a ritual. Also, baptism alone without a heartfelt declaration of faith in Christ is insufficient.

Those who refuse the gospel shall be damned. But what happens to those who never hear the gospel? This passage does not address that issue, but it does clearly state that all who *do* hear and refuse will come under judgment.

C. Signs of Believers (vv. 17, 18)

17. And these signs shall follow them that believe; In my name shall they cast out devils; they shall speak with new tongues;
18. They shall take up serpents; and if they drink any deadly thing, it shall not hurt them; they shall lay hands on the sick, and they shall recover.

Signs and wonders should follow those who believe. The early church could not have accomplished all it did without supernatural intervention. Pure doctrine was backed up by power. Paul said, "Truly the signs of an apostle were wrought among you in all patience, in signs, and wonders, and mighty deeds" (2 Corinthians 12:12). He also said, "My speech and my preaching was not with enticing words of man's wisdom, but in demonstration of the Spirit and of power" (1 Corinthians 2:4).

The gospel message, when properly delivered, will see great things happen. The Scriptures never suggest that miracles and wonders were to cease with the immediate period just after Pentecost (see Acts 2:4). Miracles are for today as well. Anyone who denies this truth denies the very power of the gospel.

Driving out demons and healing the sick are needed in great measure today. We should be looking for an even greater move of the Spirit than was ever experienced by Peter or Paul. We have been promised, "Eye hath not seen, nor ear heard, neither have entered into the heart of man, the things which God hath prepared for them that love him" (1 Corinthians 2:9).

Christ's power, authority and presence are totally available to the church today as we spread the gospel and battle satanic forces. If we live righteous lives and expect the miraculous to take place, we will be the mighty conquerors He intended.

III. EXALTING CHRIST
(1 Thessalonians 1:2-10)

A. The Gospel Presented in Power (vv. 2-6)

2. We give thanks to God always for you all, making mention of you in our prayers;
3. Remembering without ceasing your work of faith, and labour of love, and patience of hope in our Lord Jesus Christ, in the sight of God and our Father;

4. Knowing, brethren beloved, your election of God.
5. For our gospel came not unto you in word only, but also in power, and in the Holy Ghost, and in much assurance; as ye know what manner of men we were among you for your sake.
6. And ye became followers of us, and of the Lord, having received the word in much affliction, with joy of the Holy Ghost.

The believers at Thessalonica were a model group. They had true faith, love and hope. They were patient in trials and ever hopeful of an eternal home with Jesus. To a great degree this had been accomplished because the gospel had been preached to them in the power of the Holy Ghost and verified by signs and wonders.

Paul and his coworkers had arrived in Thessalonica in the summer of A.D. 50. They planted a church there, but had to leave because of threats on their lives (see Acts 17:1-10). Paul later sent Timothy to this city to get a report on how well the believers were doing. Timothy returned with a glowing testimony of the strength of their faith (1 Thessalonians 3:1-7). Though they were going through persecution, the Holy Spirit was enabling them to stand up to any pressure.

In verse 4 of the text Paul speaks of the election of God. The believers at Thessalonica were chosen because they had themselves chosen to believe and to live the Christian life to its fullest.

B. Examples to Other Believers (vv. 7-10)

7. So that ye were ensamples to all that believe in Macedonia and Achaia.
8. For from you sounded out the word of the Lord not only in

Macedonia and Achaia, but also in every place your faith to God-ward is spread abroad; so that we need not to speak any thing.

9. For they themselves shew of us what manner of entering in we had unto you, and how ye turned to God from idols to serve the living and true God;

10. And to wait for his Son from heaven, whom he raised from the dead, even Jesus, which delivered us from the wrath to come.

The Thessalonians had received the gospel with great joy and repentance. Although they had to face difficult times of persecution, they stood firm. They had turned from their sin and toward a holy life in Christ. They provided a wondrous example for other churches to follow. Paul was proud of the faith that had been established in this body of believers.

GOLDEN TEXT HOMILY

"GO YE INTO ALL THE WORLD, AND PREACH THE GOSPEL TO EVERY CREATURE" (Mark 16:15).

How great was the detailed care God took to accomplish the eternal plan of redemption! Moses and the Prophets, being moved by the Holy Spirit, carefully took note of those special details announced beforehand.

Now centuries later the charge, the challenge to tell, to preach, to get the message, the plan and gift of eternal life through Christ has come to us. It is ours to take to the world. It is the greatest gift and plan, and the only way man can receive eternal life. What an awesome responsibility! Paul tells us in 2 Corinthians 5:20 "we are ambassadors." We are daily representatives. Christ has made each of us His servant to tell, to teach and to preach His wonderful gospel.

Our heavenly Father longs for willing, loving service offered by those who owe a debt they can never repay. In Deuteronomy 10:12 Moses lists the things the Lord requires: "to fear the Lord thy God, to walk in all his ways, and to love him, and to serve the Lord thy God with all thy heart and with all thy soul." We are required to fear, to walk, to love Him and to serve. Service is the result and emanates from love. It is verified by the devotion of heart and soul. That is a contrast to Deuteronomy 6:5, where Israel is told to love the Lord "with all thine heart, and with all thy soul, and with all thy might."

Did you notice that *might* was left out of service in Deuteronomy 10:12? Service for the Lord does not depend on the strength of the flesh. Service in the might of the flesh is not bound by love. We note that the word *serve* (*bondage*) was used when Jacob served Laban for a wife. It was used also when God told Abraham that his seed would serve in a strange land for 400 years. The apostle Paul calls himself a bond-slave of Jesus Christ (Romans 1:1).

Herein is a new dimension of relationship. Service is required with all the heart and all the soul. That is a total commitment preceded by love. It is without might, but requires a total commitment to an omnipotent and loving Lord.—**Willie F. Lawrence**

SENTENCE SERMONS

THE CHURCH exists to worship Christ, proclaim the gospel, and disciple believers.

—Selected

ALL THE WORLD is my parish.
—**John Wesley**

THE SPIRIT OF CHRIST is the spirit of missions, and the nearer we get to Him the more intensely missionary we will become.
—**Henry Martyn**

EVANGELISM APPLICATION

THE CHURCH IS MANDATED TO REACH THE LOST FOR CHRIST.

Even though God specifically graces some individuals with the gift of evangelism, it is the responsibility of every Christian to help reach the lost for Christ. While those with the gift to evangelize should lead the charge, every believer must join the effort by witnessing through lifestyle and words of testimony.

ILLUMINATING THE LESSON

In God's kingdom, can all be apostles and teachers? No. There are graces appointed to each of us. We dare not assume roles that haven't been granted to us. We must find our places as God intended, play those parts to the best of our abilities, and then watch as the Kingdom functions properly.

For some, rising to the roles God intended is the big challenge. Husbands especially need to take authority and become the priests of their families. The collapse of the American home is due greatly to men not being the spiritual heads they should be. For others, becoming willing to submit to higher authorities and accept lesser roles is what God demands. If we try to carry out ministries and tasks we were never commissioned to do, then we have failed in understanding the entire concept of order and function.

May every Christian discover his place in the Kingdom, and may he step forward to fulfill that role wisely—with love, submission and unity.

DAILY BIBLE READINGS

M. Prepared for Service.
Exodus 4:1-17
T. Tell Good News.
2 Kings 5:1-6
W. Praise the Lord.
Psalm 98:1-9
T. One-to-One Evangelism.
Acts 8:29-38
F. Stewards of God's Grace.
1 Peter 4:7-11
S. Worship the Glorified Christ.
Revelation 1:10-18

TRUTH SEARCH:
Creatively Teaching the Word

Aim: Students will make a commitment to focus on one person this week and pray for an opportunity to witness to that person.

Items needed: An American flag and a Bible

FOCUS

As the class begins, ask for two or three volunteers to testify about their salvation experience. You may want to ask these volunteers before class so they can be prepared. Make sure they include the name of the Christian who had the most influence on them and their decision to accept Christ as Savior.

Next, ask students to lift their hand if they can point to one or two individuals who greatly influenced their decision to accept Jesus Christ.

We all can point to individuals who influenced our decision to follow Christ.

EXPLORE

Have a volunteer read Mark 16:15-18, and then discuss the following questions with the class:
• *What is the significance of the words "all" and "every" in verse 15?*
• *How serious is the mission Christ gave His followers (v. 16)?*
• *What signs did Christ promise in verse 17? Are these works needed today? Why or why not?*
• *What promises did Christ make to His disciples as they carried out their mission (v. 18)? What do you suppose might be the source of these potentially deadly encounters?*
• *Why did Christ promise believers the enablement to heal the sick?*

• *Is it significant that these were Christ's last instructions to His followers?*

Now have a volunteer read 1 Thessalonians 1:4-10.
• *When Paul brought the gospel to the Thessalonians, what characterized his ministry (v. 5)? Why was his witness so powerful?*
• *What was the result of Paul's ministry (v. 6)?*
• *How did the witness of the Thessalonian converts impact others (vv. 7, 8)?*
• *How did the Thessalonians show the authenticity of their walk with Christ (vv. 9, 10)?*

RESPOND

Display the American flag. Explain that it has represented a better way of life and freedom for millions of people for over 200 years.

Now hold the Bible up. Say that the Bible, along with the deliberate intentions of dedicated Christians, spells freedom and a better way of life for anyone bound by sin.

Will you be a witness to someone in your community? God has given you the gift of eternal life. He now expects you to share the good news with others.

Ask each person to get a mental picture of one person whom they would like to witness to this week. Challenge students to pray for these individuals every day this week, then to witness as the Lord provides opportunity. Pray for your students' witnessing efforts.

The Day of Pentecost

Study Text: Deuteronomy 16:9-12; Acts 2:1-39
Objective: To understand the Holy Spirit was at work in Bible times and appreciate that He is working in the world today.
Time: A.D. 30
Place: Jerusalem
Golden Text: "The promise is unto you, and to your children, and to all that are afar off, even as many as the Lord our God shall call" (Acts 2:39).
Central Truth: God's plan is that all believers be filled with the Holy Spirit.
Evangelism Emphasis: The Holy Spirit makes us effective witnesses for Christ.

PRINTED TEXT

Acts 2:1. And when the day of Pentecost was fully come, they were all with one accord in one place.

2. And suddenly there came a sound from heaven as of a rushing mighty wind, and it filled all the house where they were sitting.

3. And there appeared unto them cloven tongues like as of fire, and it sat upon each of them.

4. And they were all filled with the Holy Ghost, and began to speak with other tongues, as the Spirit gave them utterance.

5. And there were dwelling at Jerusalem Jews, devout men, out of every nation under heaven.

6. Now when this was noised abroad, the multitude came together, and were confounded, because that every man heard them speak in his own language.

7. And they were all amazed and marvelled, saying one to another, Behold, are not all these which speak Galilaeans?

8. And how hear we every man in our own tongue, wherein we were born?

12. And they were all amazed, and were in doubt, saying one to another, What meaneth this?

13. Others mocking said, These men are full of new wine.

14. But Peter, standing up with the eleven, lifted up his voice, and said unto them, Ye men of Judaea, and all ye that dwell at Jerusalem, be this known unto you, and hearken to my words:

15. For these are not drunken, as ye suppose, seeing it is but the third hour of the day.

16. But this is that which was spoken by the prophet Joel;

17. And it shall come to pass in the last days, saith God, I will pour out of my Spirit upon all flesh: and your sons and your daughters shall prophesy, and your young men shall see visions, and your old men shall dream dreams:

18. And on my servants and on my handmaidens I will pour out in those days of my Spirit; and they shall prophesy.

37. Now when they heard this, they were pricked in their heart, and said unto Peter and to the rest of the apostles, Men and brethren, what shall we do?

38. Then Peter said unto them, Repent, and be baptized every one of you in the name of Jesus Christ for

the remission of sins, and ye shall receive the gift of the Holy Ghost.

39. For the promise is unto you, and to your children, and to all that are afar off, even as many as the Lord our God shall call.

LESSON OUTLINE

I. MEANING OF PENTECOST
  A. Feast of Weeks
  B. Freewill Offering
  C. Rejoice Before the Lord
  D. Remember Slavery in Egypt

II. OUTPOURING OF THE SPIRIT
  A. The Sound of a Rushing Wind
  B. The Appearance of the Holy Spirit
  C. Tongues on Their Lips

III. INVITATION TO RECEIVE
  A. Doubters and Mockers
  B. Peter's Boldness
  C. In the Last Days
  D. Pricked Hearts
  E. Repentance and Baptism
  F. The Promise

LESSON EXPOSITION

INTRODUCTION

In most respects we think of the birthday of the church as occurring on the Day of Pentecost. Pentecost was certainly the event that completed the church's character by giving it supernatural power. Ever since the events that took place in Acts 2, Pentecost has been applied to the great outpouring of the Holy Spirit, although the word *pentecost* itself simply means "fiftieth."

The Feast of Pentecost was celebrated 50 days after the Feast of Firstfruits (which always took place the day following the Sabbath after Passover). It was also known as the Feast of Weeks, 50 being a week of weeks (49 days) plus one day. It marked the end of the grain harvest.

Because this was one of the three annual feasts requiring every Jew to come to Jerusalem, the city of Jerusalem would become very crowded. This was obviously in God's plan, for when Peter preached his great sermon (Acts 2), the fiery message was immediately disseminated to the far corners of the earth. The 3,000 converts who believed the gospel were the first Christian missionaries as they returned to their various countries.

Warren Wiersbe makes an interesting observation concerning the Feast of Firstfruits and the Feast of Pentecost. At Firstfruits, the priest waved a sheaf of grain before the Lord. On Pentecost, he presented two loaves of bread. Why the two loaves of bread? "The Jewish believers received this baptism at Pentecost, and the Gentile believers in the home of Cornelius" (Warren Wiersbe, *Be Dynamic*). In other words, both Jews and Gentiles in the church were represented by the two loaves.

In a certain sense, the church was actually born when Jesus appeared to His disciples in the Upper Room on the evening following His resurrection. When He "breathed on them, and saith unto them, Receive ye the Holy Ghost" (John 20:22), He was bringing them into the new covenant, and the Holy Spirit was active in this act of grace (3:6, 8). The act of the Holy Spirit enduing the believers with power, however, has to be attributed to the magnificent events of the Day of Pentecost.

Today there are many churches that wear the label "Pentecostal." These all draw their identity from the events that occurred in Acts 2. The infilling of the 120 believers in the Upper Room forms the backbone for the fulfillment of the Great Commission. The Holy Spirit is the absolute source of life for the church, without which there would be no church. Thus, if the church receives its sustenance from the Holy Spirit, we conclude that every believer should seek to experience the baptism of the Holy Spirit.

I. MEANING OF PENTECOST (Deuteronomy 16:9-12)

A. Feast of Weeks (v. 9)

(Deuteronomy 16:9 is not included in the printed text.)

The Feast of Pentecost was to be observed 50 days after the Passover. It appears that the Day of Pentecost as occurred in Acts 2 was on a Sunday. (This is because John 18:28 indicates that the Passover that year was on a Friday.) Thus, the seven weeks plus one day after Passover equates to a Sunday. This was the tradition of the early church, but cannot be proven.

B. A Freewill Offering (v. 10)

(Deuteronomy 16:10 is not included in the printed text.)

At the Feast of Firstfruits a priest would wave a sheaf of grain before the Lord, signifying the beginning of the grain harvest. At Pentecost, the priest presented two loaves of bread. Pentecost celebrated the completion of the harvest. A grain offering was required, though it was called a freewill offering. There was no specified amount put on the size of the offering, this being left to each man's conscience. "It was a grateful acknowledgment of the goodness of God to them in the mercies of these corn-harvests now finished, and therefore must be according as God had blessed them. Where God sows plentifully He expects to reap accordingly" (*Matthew Henry's Commentary*).

C. Rejoice Before the Lord (v. 11)

(Deuteronomy 16:11 is not included in the printed text.)

This feast was to be a time of rejoicing, but it was not an exclusive event. Rather, all people—slaves, bondservants, widows, neighbors, orphans, aliens—were to take part. Likely, everyone in the extended family of a faithful Jewish home would make the trip. This would be a festive time, where goodwill and joy were expressed to everyone. The same level of joy is admonished for the church. Paul said, "Rejoice in the Lord alway: and again I say, Rejoice" (Philippians 4:4).

From a census taken during the time of Nero, it appears that as many as 2.5 million (or more) Jews invaded Jerusalem during the Passover Feast. However, still greater numbers came at Pentecost, for by then the seas were calm and travel was easier from distant lands. This was truly a time of rejoicing, much more so than the solemn observance of Passover.

D. Remember Slavery in Egypt (v. 12)

(Deuteronomy 16:12 is not included in the printed text.)

In the midst of the celebration, the Jews were to recall their past slavery in Egypt. The intensity of the celebration of joy at Pentecost was to be equivalent to the level of pain they experienced in past bondage.

With the coming of the Holy Spirit in Acts 2, there is certainly reason to express gratitude. God now lives in us in power. We are no longer slaves to our sins, but rather free to enjoy the continual presence of Jesus inside us.

II. OUTPOURING OF THE SPIRIT (Acts 2:1-8)

A. The Sound of a Rushing Wind (vv. 1, 2)

1. And when the day of Pentecost was fully come, they were all with one accord in one place.

2. And suddenly there came a sound from heaven as of a rushing mighty wind, and it filled all the house where they were sitting.

On the night before His crucifixion, Jesus had given a promise to His disciples concerning the coming of the Holy Spirit. He had told them to expect a *Comforter* (John 14:26). Because so much had happened since that night, however, they probably did not understand the significance of that promise. Neither did they have any clue as to how the Holy Spirit would make His appearance.

Jesus reiterated the promise just before His ascension in Acts 1:9. Three other clues were added. First, He instructed them not to leave Jerusalem until they had received "the promise of the Father" (1:4). Most of the disciples were actually from Galilee. Had they not been told to stay put, some of them might have begun the journey back to their homes. Jesus also told them they would be filled with power—and then would be witnesses ultimately to the entire world (v. 8). Thus, the second and third clues *power* and *witness*.

The commandment to wait for the promise is often taken out of context in Pentecostal circles. Many believe there must be a period of time between salvation and cleansing of the heart before the Holy Spirit is ready to empower one's life. However, the charge to the disciples had less to do with time than it did with circumstance. Jesus knew how many hearts would be prepared to hear Peter's sermon on the Day of Pentecost. Had the Holy Spirit arrived any earlier, those throngs would not have been in the city. There is nothing in Scripture that would prevent a believer from quickly receiving the fullness of the Holy Spirit.

On the Day of Pentecost the 120 had gathered for prayer and worship. In synagogues throughout the city similar gatherings would have been taking place. None of the others, however, experienced what occurred with this group. The meeting place was the Upper Room—possibly in the home of Mary, mother of John Mark (see Acts 12:12). Though tradition tells us that it was 10 days before the fullness of Pentecost came, this time of prayer was likely somewhat shorter. Since there were 50 days from Passover to Pentecost, by subtracting the three days Jesus was in the tomb, as well as the 40 days mentioned in Acts 1:3, what remains is about one full week.

The sound that came was sudden and extraordinary—that of a "rushing mighty wind." The best comparison might be the sound of a tornado, although there was no actual wind. This was not a natural phenomenon, but a supernatural one.

B. The Appearance of the Holy Spirit (v. 3)

3. And there appeared unto them cloven tongues like as of fire, and it sat upon each of them.

Both *fire* and *wind* were Old Testament symbols of divine presence. Notice, however, that the word *as* is used. There is no reason to believe there were actual flames in the Upper Room, but the intensity of the manifestation of the Spirit had the same effect. Everyone knew something incredible was happening. A presence had invaded the room that could not be denied. The tongues of fire came upon everyone in the room. There were no skeptic spectators present.

Tongues represents speech and the vocal communication of the gospel. Fire indicates purification, or a burning away of all things unholy. The Holy Spirit fell on a group of people who had totally dedicated themselves to God and who were ready now to carry the gospel.

C. Tongues on Their Lips (vv. 4-8)

4. And they were all filled with the Holy Ghost, and began to speak with other tongues, as the Spirit gave them utterance.

5. And there were dwelling at Jerusalem Jews, devout men, out of every nation under heaven.

6. Now when this was noised abroad, the multitude came together, and were confounded, because that every man heard them speak in his own language.

7. And they were all amazed and marvelled, saying one to another, Behold, are not all these which speak Galilaeans?

8. And how hear we every man in our own tongue, wherein we were born?

What occurred next was the fulfillment of Joel 2:28, 29. God finally was pouring out His Spirit on all His people. This also signified the beginning of the last days (see Acts 2:17). The audible and visible signs of the Spirit's presence were already there. Now present was a manifestation from the believers' mouths. The gift of speaking in languages they did not know was powerful evidence that the promise had been fulfilled.

Even more amazing was that these were real languages, evidenced by the fact that people in the streets recognized them. Virtually every land to which the Jews had been dispersed was represented. What is not known is the message that was coming to the people. Likely, it was a presentation of the gospel, proclaiming Jesus to be the Son of God. When Peter stood and preached his powerful sermon, the crowds had likely already been witnessed to by the words spoken directly from the Holy Spirit.

The manifestation of tongues was not a learned one. There was nothing contrived from a human or emotional perspective, though likely everyone involved was experiencing a tremendous sense of anointing and joy. These believers had so completely surrendered their lives (through the days of prayer leading up to this time) that they were willing and useful vessels of divine intervention.

III. INVITATION TO RECEIVE (Acts 2:12-18, 37-39)

A. Doubters and Mockers (vv. 12, 13)

12. And they were all amazed, and were in doubt, saying one to another, What meaneth this?

13. Others mocking said, These men are full of new wine.

Though everyone present was amazed, there were still those who doubted and mocked. This was in spite of the fact that many were hearing their own native languages being spoken. Even more astonishing was that these languages could be discerned above all the noise of so many speaking at once. Also, because of their clothing and demeanor, the disciples were easily recognized as poor men from northern Palestine. No one would have expected strange languages to come from such simple men.

Unless the Holy Spirit moves upon the hearts of men, they will never turn toward God. As Paul said, "The natural man receiveth not the things of the Spirit of God: for they are foolishness unto him: neither can he know them, because they are spiritually discerned" (1 Corinthians 2:14).

B. Peter's Boldness (vv. 14, 15)

14. But Peter, standing up with the eleven, lifted up his voice, and said unto them, Ye men of Judaea, and all ye that dwell at Jerusalem, be this known unto you, and hearken to my words:

15. For these are not drunken, as ye suppose, seeing it is but the third hour of the day.

Since this was a feast day, many assumed that the believers had been drinking too much wine. Somehow, Peter was able to get the attention of all present. He began by addressing the people politely (despite the presence of mockers). A powerful anointing came over Peter, and he was able to speak confidently about what was happening. He had truth on his side, so he could boldly face even those who scoffed.

This was a different man from the one who had just weeks earlier denied the Lord three times. He explained that those with him could not possibly be drunk so early in the day. There were no hard alcoholic beverages available, so to get drunk would have taken many hours.

C. In the Last Days (vv. 16-18)

16. But this is that which was spoken by the prophet Joel;

17. And it shall come to pass in the last days, saith God, I will pour out of my Spirit upon all flesh: and your sons and your daughters shall prophesy, and your young men shall see visions, and your old men shall dream dreams:

18. And on my servants and on my handmaidens I will pour out in those days of my Spirit; and they shall prophesy.

"In the last days" was used in the Old Testament to indicate a period of time when the Lord would move in a mighty way to judge evil, but also provide salvation to His people (see Isaiah 2:2-21; 3:18-26; 4:1-6; 10:20-23). Peter changed the original wording of Joel's prophecy from "afterward" to "in the last days." Peter recognized that the outpouring of the Holy Spirit which had just occurred was the beginning of the final period of God's redemptive program. The entire church age (from Pentecost down to the present and until Christ returns) is thus called the last days.

D. Pricked Hearts (v. 37)

37. Now when they heard this, they were pricked in their heart, and said unto Peter and to the rest of the apostles, Men and brethren, what shall we do?

Peter likely had no idea what the response to his message would be. He was simply moving as the Spirit led him. What happened was overwhelming. The people were shaken to the core, not with guilt, but rather with divinely inspired conviction. On his own, Peter could not have produced this. Only the Holy Spirit working through him did just what Jesus had earlier predicted: "When he comes, he will convict the world of guilt in regard to sin and righteousness and judgment" (John 16:8, *NIV*).

The Spirit convinced the people that Jesus was all He had claimed to be during His earthly ministry. Since Jesus had been crucified and resurrected just a few weeks earlier, His name was likely the talk of everyone in Jerusalem. Now, all the wonderful things the visiting crowds had heard about Jesus were being confirmed. Perhaps, too, many of the same individuals who had clamored for the Lord's arrest were now themselves being arrested by the wooing power of the Spirit. This led them to ask what they should do about their condition of heart. When the Spirit moves, it is not just to bring sorrow for sin, but also to instigate an inner change, a new direction for life.

The fact that Peter called his hearers "brethren" (Acts 2:29) indicates that he was identifying himself with them as having been a Jewish person living in sin. The crowds responded by addressing the disciples as "brethren."

E. Repentance and Baptism (v. 38)

38. Then Peter said unto them, Repent, and be baptized every one of you in the name of Jesus Christ for the remission of sins, and ye shall receive the gift of the Holy Ghost.

Peter was led to give an invitation. He issued the first "altar call" of the church age. He urged the people to repent, to change their minds and look to Jesus as Savior. As David did in Psalm 51, they needed to humble themselves, acknowledge their sin, and turn to a complete dependence on the Lord. He told them to couple their repentance with water baptism, thus declaring publicly what had taken place in their hearts.

F. The Promise (v. 39)

39. For the promise is unto you, and to your children, and to all that are afar off, even as many as the Lord our God shall call.

Peter did not stop with bringing the crowd to salvation. He let it be known that they could have the same power that the 120 had just experienced. This would also continue to be available to all their children and later descendants. Although it is not specifically mentioned by Luke, we assume that many (if not all) of the 3,000 converts won on that day (v. 41) were also filled with the Spirit.

GOLDEN TEXT HOMILY

"THE PROMISE IS UNTO YOU, AND TO YOUR CHILDREN, AND TO ALL THAT ARE AFAR OFF, EVEN AS MANY AS THE LORD OUR GOD SHALL CALL" (Acts 2:39).

It is unlikely that the writer of this scripture had a full conception of just how far the scope of his statements would extend. He may have visualized "to all that are afar off" in the terms of the area of the Middle East or even of the then-known world. But there is no way that he could have fully grasped the vast sweep of the promise of this scripture.

Many times we are too small in our thinking when it comes to the promises of God. Even while we are thinking of the infinite possibilities of what God can accomplish, we are probably underestimating Him.

There is an old saying that "what the human mind can conceive, it can achieve." But God can achieve those things that the human mind can never conceive or comprehend. It is impossible to cast the promises of God in such cosmic terms that they fully explore the range of His power.

Dedication to the cause of Christ and surrender to Him will result in signs following the believer. We have that assurance from God. We only need to take hold of that promise and live for Him whether or not the signs are always visible to us ourselves.—**Excerpts from** ***The Pulpit Commentary*, Vol. 18**

SENTENCE SERMONS

GOD'S PLAN is that all believers be filled with the Holy Spirit.

—Selected

WE MUST NOT be content to be cleansed from sin; we must be filled with the Spirit.

—John Fletcher

ALL THAT HAS been done by God the Father and by God the Son must be ineffectual to us, unless the Spirit shall reveal those things to our souls.

—Charles Spurgeon

EVANGELISM APPLICATION

THE HOLY SPIRIT MAKES US EFFECTIVE WITNESSES FOR CHRIST.

The fact that Jesus told the disciples to "wait for the promise of the Father" (Acts 1:4) has led many to believe that there is a required time of tarrying before being filled with the Holy Spirit. In many Pentecostal churches, we have often mistakenly taught that when a person receives Christ as Savior, he should cleanse his heart and tarry for the Holy Spirit but not expect an immediate filling. However, there is no reason why every new believer should not quickly move forward in his walk to receive the promised blessing.

I personally was one who received the Holy Spirit on the very night of my salvation. There are many things we have to wait for in faith in our Christian walk, but the promise of God to endue us with power is not one of those. Christ wants to baptize us in the Spirit so we can effectively witness for Him.

ILLUMINATING THE LESSON

The Holy Spirit came when all the believers present were in "one accord." It is amazing to see the unity that was in that Upper Room. Throughout the Lord's earthly ministry, the disciples had been a bickering bunch, all vying for the Lord's attention. They were clearly different men now.

Also included among the 120 were Jesus' brothers. They had been adamantly opposed to His ministry, but now had come to believe He was just who He said He was. Two of them, James and Jude, would go on to become leaders in the church. Present, too, were a number of women. Besides Mary, the Lord's mother, were most likely Mary Magdalene, Salome, Joanna, and Mary and Martha of Bethany. Jesus had elevated the position of women, which went against the grain of society at that time.

The requirement for a church to experience a spiritual awakening—a revival of Pentecost—is that there be unity. This starts by individuals forgiving one another and expressing love and concern to those with whom they have had differences. There can never be a real outpouring of the Spirit where there is discord.

DAILY BIBLE READINGS

M. Spirit-Filled Craftsmen.
   Exodus 31:1-6
T. Spirit-Filled Elders.
   Numbers 11:24-29
W. Spirit-Filled King.
   2 Samuel 23:1-5
T. Spirit-Filled Believers.
   Acts 4:23-33
F. Spirit-Filled Gentiles.
   Acts 10:44-48
S. Spirit-Filled Living.
   Galatians 5:16-25

TRUTH SEARCH:
Creatively Teaching the Word

Aim: Students will pray for the Holy Spirit to be poured out in the local church.

Items needed: Pencils, paper, marker board, marker

FOCUS

On the board write, *What does it mean to be Pentecostal?* Divide the class into groups of two or three students each, and give each group a sheet of paper and pencil. The job of each group is to write their best one-sentence response to the question. After three or four minutes, have groups take turns reading their answers.

In Old Testament times, Pentecost began as a holiday known as the Feast of Harvest. Later it developed into a commemoration of the giving of the Law to Moses. But when Christ sent the Holy Spirit to His followers on the Day of Pentecost, the word took on a whole new meaning.

EXPLORE

Ask the students to have their Bibles in hand, ready to take part in today's Scripture study.

• *Before His ascension, what did Jesus promise His disciples in Acts 1:8?*

Have a volunteer read verses 12-14 aloud.

• *What did Christ's followers do after His ascension?*

Verse 15 tells us there were 120 believers together in the Upper Room. They had been together 10 days when the Day of Pentecost arrived.

Have a volunteer read Acts 2:1-4 aloud.

• *What does "they were all with one accord" mean? Why was this important?*

• *What sound did they hear (v. 2)? What was important about the wind?*

• *What did they see (v. 3)? What was the significance of the fire?*

• *What sounds did the disciples make (v. 4)? How were they able to speak in tongues?*

Allow two or three students to testify about their own "Pentecost" experience.

Have a volunteer read verses 5-8.

• *Why do you suppose Christ chose Pentecost as the day to send the Holy Spirit to His followers in Jerusalem?*

• *Why were the people "confounded" and "amazed," and why did they "marvel"?*

• *According to verse 11, what were the believers saying as they spoke in tongues?*

• *According to verses 12 and 13, what were the initial reactions of the crowd?*

In 1 Corinthians 14:22, Paul wrote, "Tongues, then, are a sign, not for believers but for unbelievers" (NIV). This certainly was the case on the Day of Pentecost!

Have a volunteer read Acts 2:14-18.

• *How did Peter respond to the notions that the believers were drunk?*

• *What did Joel prophesy concerning "the last days"?*

• *According to Joel's prophecy, who could be filled with the Holy Spirit?*

The Bible puts no racial, age or gender restrictions on the gift of the Holy Spirit. Instead, this gift is for all Christians.

RESPOND

Think about this: If an unbeliever walks into our church today, do you think he or she will know there is something different—something Pentecostal—about our church?

Spend the last portion of class praying for the Holy Spirit baptism to be poured out in your church. Ask for volunteers to take turns leading in prayer on behalf of specific age groups: children, teens, adults and senior adults.

Future of the Church

Study Text: Matthew 24:9, 10; John 15:18-25; 1 Peter 4:12-16; Revelation 19:1-8

Objective: To consider the future of the church and determine to persevere through difficult times.

Golden Text: "We must through much tribulation enter into the kingdom of God" (Acts 14:22).

Central Truth: The church of the Lord Jesus Christ will prevail over evil.

Evangelism Emphasis: In times of spiritual darkness the church is a light to the unsaved.

PRINTED TEXT

1 Peter 4:12. Beloved, think it not strange concerning the fiery trial which is to try you, as though some strange thing happened unto you:

13. But rejoice, inasmuch as ye are partakers of Christ's sufferings; that, when his glory shall be revealed, ye may be glad also with exceeding joy.

14. If ye be reproached for the name of Christ, happy are ye; for the spirit of glory and of God resteth upon you: on their part he is evil spoken of, but on your part he is glorified.

Matthew 24:9. Then shall they deliver you up to be afflicted, and shall kill you: and ye shall be hated of all nations for my name's sake.

10. And then shall many be offended, and shall betray one another, and shall hate one another.

John 15:18. If the world hate you, ye know that it hated me before it hated you.

19. If ye were of the world, the world would love his own: but because ye are not of the world, but I have chosen you out of the world, therefore the world hateth you.

20. Remember the word that I said unto you, The servant is not greater than his lord. If they have persecuted me, they will also persecute you; if they have kept my saying, they will keep your's also.

21. But all these things will they do unto you for my name's sake, because they know not him that sent me.

Revelation 19:1. And after these things I heard a great voice of much people in heaven, saying, Alleluia; Salvation, and glory, and honour, and power, unto the Lord our God:

2. For true and righteous are his judgments: for he hath judged the great whore, which did corrupt the earth with her fornication, and hath avenged the blood of his servants at her hand.

3. And again they said, Alleluia. And her smoke rose up for ever and ever.

4. And the four and twenty elders and the four beasts fell down and worshipped God that sat on the throne, saying, Amen; Alleluia.

5. And a voice came out of the throne, saying, Praise our God, all ye his servants, and ye that fear him, both small and great.

6. And I heard as it were the voice of a great multitude, and as the voice of many waters, and as the voice of mighty thunderings, saying, Alleluia: for the Lord God omnipotent reigneth.

LESSON OUTLINE

I. TRIALS

  A. Suffering, a Norm for the Christian Life

  B. Suffering, Producer of Joy

  C. The Honor of Suffering for Christ

  D. No Wrongdoing

  E. No Shame in Suffering

II. PERSECUTION

  A. Prophecy of Coming Persecution

  B. Character of Coming Persecution

  C. Hatred of Christ's Disciples

  D. No Excuse for Ignorance

III. TRIUMPH

  A. Alleluia

  B. The Bride Is Ready

LESSON EXPOSITION

INTRODUCTION

There will be trials and persecution in the life of every true Christian. No believer is exempt.

Paul was once so wearied of the struggles he was going through that he said, "We were pressed out of measure, above strength, insomuch that we despaired even of life" (2 Corinthians 1:8). In other words, Paul would have preferred death over dealing with the problems before him.

Paul was mistreated in Ephesus, where the people tried to kill him. He had to stiffly reprove the Corinthians, and he was unsure of their acceptance of him. He was accused of being a poor speaker, and he was even charged with insanity. He was whipped with 39 stripes on five different occasions. He was beaten with rods. He was stoned. He was shipwrecked and nearly drowned. The more he loved people, the more they came against him. Finally he said, "We are troubled on every side, yet not distressed; we are perplexed, but not in despair; persecuted, but not forsaken; cast down, but not destroyed; always bearing about in the body the dying of the Lord Jesus" (2 Corinthians 4:8-10).

Through all of this, Paul could say that the Lord "comforteth us in all our tribulation, that we may be able to comfort them which are in any trouble" (1:4). This verse identified the reason we are allowed to go through suffering and trials: so we may identify with others in their difficulties. Advice is not what people need when they are in trouble. Instead, they need the compassion of someone who has faced similar circumstances. If we have not known loneliness, rejection or heartache, we cannot empathize with a person going through these terrible things. Suffering kills a judgmental attitude.

Paul, Peter and other New Testament believers were able to rejoice in their tribulations because they knew their sufferings were for the benefit of others. Their trials were a type of schooling for dealing with the wicked world where they were sent to minister. Because they saw God prove Himself faithful to them in their struggles, they could encourage others to stand firm.

No one likes to suffer. In America, we have had to endure very little for the cause of Christ. Stagnancy and self-centeredness can result from such a life of ease. Trials can help us truly identify with Christ and with the rest of His body.

However, suffering simply for the sake of suffering is of little use to the believer. Bitterness, disappointment, frustration and cynicism can be the result. We must let God teach us a tenderness toward others when we go through difficulties.

Paul never let the trials he faced harden him toward the people he was sent to serve. At his worst hour, he still blessed the name of the Lord. Praise is the language a true Christian learns while going through a trial. When one hits the very bottom, God is right there.

Finally, there is always a means of escape. As Paul said, "God is faithful, who will not suffer you to be tempted above that ye are able; but will with the temptation also make a way to escape, that ye may be able to bear it" (1 Corinthians 10:13). We can bear whatever comes our way by trusting in the love of the One who saved us.

I. TRIALS (1 Peter 4:12-16)

A. Suffering, a Norm for the
     Christian Life (v. 12)

12. Beloved, think it not strange concerning the fiery trial which is to try you, as though some strange thing happened unto you.

Trials are an element of the normal Christian life. One who doesn't go through discouragement, loss or hurt can never truly identify with Christ.

One may face physical oppression from a vicious world, or the trials may come in the form of emotional trauma through broken relationships, health problems, wayward children, or the death of a loved one. There are many ways to be tried in this life. In most situations, emotional pain is just as real as physical pain.

We do a great disservice to people when we portray Christianity as a life without anguish. Coming to Jesus does not eliminate any of life's woes. We still face the strug-gles that accompany humanity. The difference is that we have a Savior who identifies with everything we go through because He went through these things Himself.

The readers of Peter's letter were facing a trial by fire. It was written about the time that Nero began his heavy persecution of believers (A.D. 62-64). Some would be beaten, others stoned, some killed by the sword, and others even fed to lions. What comes forth from such heavy refinement is pure-gold Christian character (1 Peter 1:7). God permits the times of testing, times in which the soul is allowed to go through fiery trials. He actually allows these seasons in order to prove the believer's love for Him.

B. Suffering, Producer of Joy (v. 13)

13. But rejoice, inasmuch as ye are partakers of Christ's sufferings; that, when his glory shall be revealed, ye may be glad also with exceeding joy.

There is a depth of Christian joy that can only be known by those who endure great trials in this life. One of the greatest times of testing in the life of Christ was on the night before His crucifixion when He tried to get His three closest disciples to tarry with Him in prayer. They could not comprehend His pain and consequently fell asleep.

Countless believers have endured years of agonizing emotional distress as they prayed for lost loved ones to come to Christ. Such pain is actually a cause for rejoicing because it enables the believer to identify with the Lord.

There is a level of blessedness that comes from persecution. Jesus spoke of this in Matthew 5:11: "Blessed are ye, when men shall revile you, and persecute you, and shall say all manner of evil against you falsely, for my sake." The result of enduring such persecution is a great reward in heaven (v. 12). Since this is the final outcome of such trials, believers should rejoice for being given the privilege of going through such testings.

C. The Honor of Suffering for Christ (v. 14)

14. If ye be reproached for the name of Christ, happy are ye; for the spirit of glory and of God resteth upon you: on their part he is evil spoken of, but on your part he is glorified.

There is a special sense of the Lord's presence to bless, help and provide whenever believers are truly afflicted for Christ. Being identified with Him in struggle or heartbreak is therefore a privilege. "This is the highest honour to which any man can arrive in this world, and therefore the apostle says to such, 'Happy are ye'" (*Adam Clarke Commentary*).

Not every problem believers face is a trial for Christ. Sometimes people bring calamity on themselves through selfishness, greed or personal ambition. Some think they are being persecuted for Christ when they are simply paying the consequences of poor decisions. For instance, the person who gets caught up in credit card debt will have to pay the piper for his failure to budget his resources. This is not a case of Christian persecution. Believers are responsible for their behavior and actions. Christians should be honest with themselves in determining where their problems are coming from.

D. No Wrongdoing (v. 15)

(1 Peter 4:15 is not included in the printed text.)

Peter makes it clear that the Christian is to live above reproach. Believers are not to be lawbreakers, but rather peaceful citizens living as honestly and cleanly as possible. Christians are not to meddle in other people's business. Peter regards this activity as being as sinful as murder or robbery.

E. No Shame in Suffering (v. 16)

(1 Peter 4:16 is not included in the printed text.)

If one is truly going through a trial for Christ, then he or she should be happy, for God is allowing this for the individual's growth and strengthening.

When Peter and the other disciples came away from their first frightening arrests by the Sanhedrin, they rejoiced that they were privileged to be counted worthy of being associated with Christ. Acts 5:41 expresses their excitement: "And they departed from the presence of the council, rejoicing that they were counted worthy to suffer shame for his name." They had not sought confrontation, but neither did they avoid it. They knew the truth of the gospel they were proclaiming and were willing to stand firm in their beliefs.

II. PERSECUTION
(Matthew 24:9, 10; John 15:18-25)

A. Prophecy of Coming Persecution (Matthew 24:9)

9. Then shall they deliver you up to be afflicted, and shall kill you: and ye shall be hated of all nations for my name's sake.

Matthew 24 and 25 are known as the Olivet Discourse, which took place in the middle of the week after Jesus' triumphal entry into Jerusalem. Almost from the moment

He came into the city on Palm Sunday, the Pharisees, Sadducees, and other religious leaders harassed Him. His overturning of the money changers' tables in the Temple did nothing to appease their hatred, but rather infuriated them.

On Monday and Tuesday they continued to challenge Him with trick questions from the Law. Their constant harangue led Him to pronounce a series of "woes" against them. He was so burdened over their stubbornness and hypocrisy that He ultimately broke down and cried out, "O Jerusalem, Jerusalem . . ." (see 23:37-39). A tender sorrow overtook Him as He foresaw what terrible events their rebellion would bring. He wanted "all men to be saved and to come to a knowledge of the truth" (1 Timothy 2:4, *NIV*). He longed to gather them to Himself for protection, but they refused His love.

In the opening verses of Matthew 24, as the disciples climbed with Him up the Mount of Olives overlooking the city, they perhaps felt a need to console Him. They made remarks concerning the beauty of the Temple. His response, however, was far from what they expected. He told them of the coming destruction of the Temple, the signs of His second coming, and also signs of the end of the age. These were fearful things, and He also let them know they themselves would become targets of tribulation and persecution. They would be rejected by people of "all nations" (v. 9). "The disciples, targeted 'on account of my name,' would be victims of random violence and tribulation but marked for persecution because of identity with Jesus" (Ed Glasscock, *Moody Gospel Commentary—Matthew*).

Simply being associated with

Christ brings an enmity with Satan. In every generation there are martyrs when the true gospel of Jesus Christ is proclaimed.

B. Character of Coming Persecution (v. 10)

10. And then shall many be offended, and shall betray one another, and shall hate one another.

There is a hint given here (along with verses 11 and 12) as to the kind of persecution believers will face. These include internal betrayal, the proliferation of false prophets, and a terrible callousness from the world. Pain inflicted by the world is less damaging than the hurt that comes from those who are in the church.

C. Hatred of Christ's Disciples (John 15:18-21)

18. If the world hate you, ye know that it hated me before it hated you.

19. If ye were of the world, the world would love his own: but because ye are not of the world, but I have chosen you out of the world, therefore the world hateth you.

20. Remember the word that I said unto you, The servant is not greater than his lord. If they have persecuted me, they will also persecute you; if they have kept my saying, they will keep your's also.

21. But all these things will they do unto you for my name's sake, because they know not him that sent me.

To understand this passage, verse 17 should be included. There the Lord commanded His disciples to love one another. They would have to stick together because they would obviously get enough hatred from the world.

The nature of the gospel is anathema to secular (or even religious) thinking. If believers don't love and support one another, they will be destroyed by the heathen mind-set coming at them.

When the 12 disciples were chosen by Jesus, they were enthralled by His personal charisma and anointing. However, it didn't take long to grasp that following Him would be costly. The religious leaders quickly rose up to oppose everything He taught. Toward the end of the Lord's earthly ministry, most of the peripheral followers had deserted Him. The disciples were already paying a cost for their association with Him. The three days of hiding between the Crucifixion and the Resurrection indicates their level of fear of persecution.

Jesus gave the disciples an interesting equation. The hatred they received from the world would be in direct proportion to their love of Him. They should therefore rejoice when persecution came their way "because that should always be a proof to them that they were in the very path in which Jesus had trod" (*Adam Clarke Commentary*).

D. No Excuse for Ignorance
(vv. 22-25)

(John 15:22-25 is not included in the printed text.)

Prior to the coming of Christ, the penalty for those who would persecute godly people was not as great. Now that Christ was revealed, those who would do such must be held accountable. Ignorance is excusable where there has been no revelation of truth, but when the truth comes, that very ignorance turns to condemnation. "As sin is not imputed where there is no law, so unbelief is not imputed where there is no gospel" (*Adam Clark*

Commentary). A servant who doesn't know right from wrong will be disciplined with fewer stripes than the one who knows better, but still disobeys: "For unto whomsoever much is given, of him shall be much required: and to whom men have committed much, of him they will ask the more" (Luke 12:48).

III. TRIUMPH (Revelation 19:1-8)
A. Alleluia (vv. 1-6)

1. And after these things I heard a great voice of much people in heaven, saying, Alleluia; Salvation, and glory, and honour, and power, unto the Lord our God:

2. For true and righteous are his judgments: for he hath judged the great whore, which did corrupt the earth with her fornication, and hath avenged the blood of his servants at her hand.

3. And again they said, Alleluia. And her smoke rose up for ever and ever.

4. And the four and twenty elders and the four beasts fell down and worshipped God that sat on the throne, saying, Amen; Alleluia.

5. And a voice came out of the throne, saying, Praise our God, all ye his servants, and ye that fear him, both small and great.

6. And I heard as it were the voice of a great multitude, and as the voice of many waters, and as the voice of mighty thunderings, saying, Alleluia: for the Lord God omnipotent reigneth.

The four times in this passage that the word *alleluia* is used are the only times it appears in the entire New Testament. Derived from two Hebrew words, it simply means "praise the Lord." The saints in heaven at this point praise God because the wicked world has finally been judged. The idolatrous city of Babylon has been destroyed, and the blood of all martyred saints has been avenged.

Verses 1-4 show how God has judged His enemies. Both the demonic religious system and the satanic economic-political world empire have fallen. These had caused great persecution and martyrdom to God's people. God now reigns complete, without interference from the Enemy. This doesn't mean there was ever any real threat from Satan's efforts, but now even those barbs and conflicts are complete. The omnipotent God has accomplished His purposes, and as Psalm 97:1 says, "The Lord reigneth; let the earth rejoice." In the past God had allowed evil men and fallen angels to work their wickedness, but now God's will is truly being carried out "[on] earth, as it is in heaven" (Matthew 6:10).

From a historical perspective, this passage gave great hope to believers living in the wicked Roman Empire. Domitian was the Roman emperor at the time of John's exile on Patmos. One of his titles was "Lord and God." "How significant it must have been, then, to John's readers that he used the word *alleluia* four times in the first six verses of this chapter—truly, only Jehovah is worthy of worship and praise" (Warren Wiersbe, *Be Victorious—Revelation*).

Even though these words are apocalyptic in nature, it is refreshing to know there will be an end to sorrows and trials for the believer. Not only that, everything believers have had to endure for Christ will be avenged against Satan in the coming times.

B. The Bride Is Ready (vv. 7, 8)

(Revelation 19:7, 8 is not included in the printed text.)

The church is the bride of Christ. Christ is the groom—the Lamb. It is customary for the bride to be the center of everyone's attention at a wedding, but this is an unusual wedding. The Bridegroom receives all the attention. The bride is dressed in the righteousness of saints. She is fully dressed, spotless in white raiment, and ready for the public ceremony of marriage.

SENTENCE SERMONS

THE CHURCH of the Lord Jesus Christ will prevail over evil.
—Selected

ONE on God's side is a majority.
—Wendell Phillips

VICTORY IS GAINED only through conflict.
—Quotable Quotations

EVANGELISM APPLICATION

IN TIMES OF SPIRITUAL DARKNESS THE CHURCH IS A LIGHT TO THE UNSAVED.

There are several truths from the writings of Jeremiah that will help us in dealing with trials and persecutions:

At our lowest point, God draws near. "Thou drewest near in the day that I called upon thee: thou saidst, Fear not" (Lamentations 3:57). Remember that God is not found "up there," but rather "down here."

God hurts with us in our struggles. "For he doth not afflict willingly nor grieve the children of men" (v. 33).

God is always faithful, and will do right for us. "The Lord is good unto them that wait for him, to the soul that seeketh him. It is good that a man should both hope and quietly wait for the salvation of the Lord" (vv. 25, 26).

Because we are emptied and humbled, we can totally be dependent on God. "And I said, My strength and my hope is perished from the Lord. . . . My soul hath them still in remembrance, and is humbled in me. This I recall to my mind, therefore have I hope" (vv. 18, 20, 21).

When we get our eyes off our problems and afflictions, remind ourselves that God is in charge, and live like we believe it, we can be a light to the unsaved.

ILLUMINATING THE LESSON

The prophet Jeremiah was familiar with terrible trials. In Lamentations 3:7, 9, he said, "He hath hedged me about, that I cannot get out: he hath made my chain heavy. . . . He hath inclosed my ways with hewn stone, he hath made my paths crooked." This is the same prophet who thundered God's word to kings. Nations and armies hung on his words. Still, he faced bitter, despondent times— rejected, lonely, and feeling that God had left him. Notice, however, that this is the same prophet who penned

the great words we use as a hymn: "It is of the Lord's mercies that we are not consumed, because his compassions fail not. They are new every morning: great is thy faithfulness" (vv. 22, 23).

Our greatest trials come right after a victory or period of spiritual revelation. We often are thrust into difficulties and persecutions just after leaps of faith and growth. It seems that God gives us the high points in our walk so we will be prepared for the struggles that are on the way. These hard times force us to rely on God even more.

DAILY BIBLE READINGS

M. God's People Persecuted. Exodus 1:1-14
T. God's People Captive. Psalm 137:1-9
W. Hope for Deliverance. Isaiah 40:1-11
T. Scorned by the World. Matthew 10:17-25
F. Perilous Times Ahead. 2 Timothy 3:1-12
S. More Than Conquerors. Romans 8:35-39

TRUTH SEARCH:
Creatively Teaching the Word

Aim: Students will pray for the persecuted church.

Items needed: None

FOCUS

Persecution of Christians is alive and well in our world. It is believed that more people have been martyred for their faith in Christ during the past 100 years than were martyred during the previous 1,900 years since Christ's death.

The main persecutors today are Communists (as seen in China and North Korea, for example) and radical Muslims (as seen in Egypt and Indonesia, for example).

One eyewitness from a North Korean prison camp said Christians are deprived of rest, told to recant, beaten, and assigned the most difficult and dangerous jobs. Many are taken to the electric treatment room, where they are tortured and killed.

Let's see what God's Word says about the persecution of believers.

EXPLORE

Have everyone turn to 1 Peter 4:12-16, and have a volunteer read the passage.
• *Should "fiery trials" of Christians be seen as unusual (v. 12)?*
• *For what reasons should believers rejoice and be happy when undergoing persecution (vv. 13, 14)?*
• *According to verse 16, how should Christians not respond to persecution? Instead, what is the proper response?*

Now have a volunteer read Matthew 24:9, 10. Then discuss.

• *When Jesus warned His followers about the end times, what did He tell them to expect? Why did He say this would happen?*

The truth of Jesus' words can be seen in the country of Ukraine, where the Communists destroyed countless churches and executed millions of Christians. Numerous believers gave in to the pressure and became informers for the government. Today the Ukraine is no longer controlled by Communists, but the wounds of betrayal have been slow to heal.

Have a volunteer read Jesus' words in John 15:18-21. Then discuss the passage.
• *Where did hatred of Christians begin (v. 18)?*
• *According to verse 19, name one reason the world hates Christians.*
• *According to verse 20, name another reason the world hates Christians.*
• *Why does the world hate Christ and His followers (v. 21)?*

When Paul preached the gospel and did the miraculous in Lystra, the persecution became so intense that they stoned him until they thought he was dead. But after Paul was divinely spared, he told his fellow Christians, "We must through many tribulations enter the kingdom of God" (Acts 14:22, *NKJV*).

Though we may never face stoning or torture, we should all expect to be tested because of our faith in Christ.

RESPOND

On New Year's Eve 1999, a Christian shopkeeper in upper Egypt refused to sell to a Muslim man due to his bad credit record. The Muslim responded by initiating a riot in which 3,000 Muslims burned more than 150 homes and businesses in the Al Kosheh area. The destruction continued for three days and extended to nearby towns. When the violence ended on January 3, 2000, 21 Christians lay dead and at least 44 were wounded (source: *www.persecutedchurch.org*).

It is our responsibility to pray for our suffering fellow believers in Egypt, North Korea, and around the world.

Have students take turns leading in prayer for the persecuted church while everyone else prays in agreement.

INTRODUCTION
TO SUMMER
QUARTER

The lessons for the summer quarter (June, July, August) are presented under two distinct themes: Unit One (lessons 1-5) is titled "Psalms (Part 1)," and Unit Two (lessons 6-13) is titled "Learning From Samuel, Elijah and Elisha."

The lessons from the Book of Psalms center on the greatness of God and His ability to meet every human need. Be sure to allot class time for students to express their needs to God.

"Learning From Samuel, Elijah and Elisha" provides students opportunities to learn how they should and should not lead their lives as they explore various Old Testament stories.

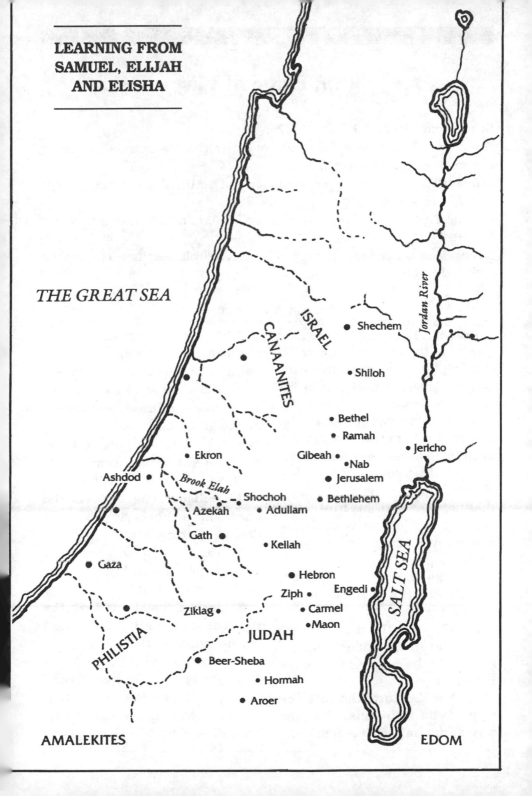

Two Ways of Life

Study Text: Psalms 1:1-6; 37:1-7

Objective: To compare the results of both righteous and godless living and choose a godly lifestyle.

Golden Text: "I have set before you life and death, blessing and cursing: therefore choose life" (Deuteronomy 30:19).

Central Truth: The choices we make will determine our destiny now and for eternity.

Evangelism Emphasis: The choices we make will determine our destiny now and for eternity.

PRINTED TEXT

Psalm 1:1. Blessed is the man that walketh not in the counsel of the ungodly, nor standeth in the way of sinners, nor sitteth in the seat of the scornful.

2. But his delight is in the law of the Lord; and in his law doth he meditate day and night.

3. And he shall be like a tree planted by the rivers of water, that bringeth forth his fruit in his season; his leaf also shall not wither; and whatsoever he doeth shall prosper.

4. The ungodly are not so: but are like the chaff which the wind driveth away.

5. Therefore the ungodly shall not stand in the judgment, nor sinners in the congregation of the righteous.

6. For the Lord knoweth the way of the righteous: but the way of the ungodly shall perish.

37:1. Fret not thyself because of evildoers, neither be thou envious against the workers of iniquity.

2. For they shall soon be cut down like the grass, and wither as the green herb.

3. Trust in the Lord, and do good; so shalt thou dwell in the land, and verily thou shalt be fed.

4. Delight thyself also in the Lord; and he shall give thee the desires of thine heart.

5. Commit thy way unto the Lord; trust also in him; and he shall bring it to pass.

6. And he shall bring forth thy righteousness as the light, and thy judgment as the noonday.

7. Rest in the Lord, and wait patiently for him: fret not thyself because of him who prospereth in his way, because of the man who bringeth wicked devices to pass.

LESSON OUTLINE

I. THE WAY OF THE RIGHTEOUS
   A. A Contrast
   B. A Stability

II. THE WAY OF THE UNGODLY
   A. The Separation
   B. The Punishment

III. TRUST IN THE LORD
   A. Do Not Fret
   B. Commit Your Way
   C. Wait Patiently

LESSON EXPOSITION

INTRODUCTION

The Book of Psalms is a frequent source for devotions, and occasionally we may even recognize the lines of songs that we sing. However, to derive a fuller meaning of what each of the writers is attempting to communicate, we need to understand the nature of Hebrew poetry. In his book, *Psalms: A Thousand Years of Hebrew History,* Laud O. Vaught says:

"Forget that it does not sound like the poetry you learned in school. The Hebrew of the Old Testament is a language 3,000 years old, and we can expect it to be a little different. We were taught to rhyme the sound at the end of a line or within a line.

"Hebrew poetry does not have a rhyme of sound, and it is good for us that it doesn't. If it did, it could not be translated because the sound is different, and we could not change it to Greek or English and have the same sound and meaning.

"Hebrew poetry rhymes in thought rather than sound. If a person wrote a thought and then on the next line wrote the same thought in different words, that was poetry. If someone wrote a thought and then on the next line wrote something directly opposite to the first thought, that too was poetry. But there were also other options. The first line could contain a thought and the second line could be a progression of that thought. Just as in our rhyme of sound, it made the poem easier to remember."

With this understanding of the nature of Hebrew poetry, let's turn our attention to the topic of our discussion. Whether or not our society wants to accept the fact, we are individuals of choice. Who we are and what we do rest upon our choices. Each of us has a will and we choose the path of our actions.

There are various forces that influence our choices. Our family environment or lack of family influences creates either a heritage or a vacuum in our perspective. Our social class provides views upon which we may act in certain settings. Not to be overlooked are the views and lifestyle of a person of influence. This may be a family member, teacher, friend, hero or some type of mentor. But regardless of the factors influencing us, the choices we make are our own.

This first lesson shows a contrast between those who serve God and those who do not. The focal point of this discussion needs to continually be that of choice. Those who are categorized as righteous are continuing to make the choice to serve Christ and follow the Scriptures. In contrast are the ungodly who choose to reject the Lord openly or carelessly neglect Him.

I. THE WAY OF THE RIGHTEOUS (Psalm 1:1-3)

A. A Contrast (vv. 1, 2)

1. Blessed is the man that walketh not in the counsel of the ungodly, nor standeth in the way of sinners, nor sitteth in the seat of the scornful.
2. But his delight is in the law of the Lord; and in his law doth he meditate day and night.

Psalm 1 bears no superscription as to its author. Many believe it to be the words of David. This would be likely in view of David's having authored more of the Psalms than any other person. However, even as the chief author, he wrote slightly less than half of them.

This psalm is as a prelude to the entire collection which follows. It provides a contrast between the godly and ungodly, which can be seen in various ways throughout the book.

Instead of addressing the positive stance of a righteous person, the writer starts with the "thou shalt nots." This thought pattern seems backward, yet it is logical. Vaught said, "There can be no building without an excavation, and there can be no holy living without renunciation of evil."

Righteousness follows a path which carefully avoids ungodliness and opposition to truth. *Walking* may be seen as a passing or casual relationship which allows some influence from those categorized as wicked. *Standing* implies entertaining a continued fellowship with those who regularly follow a pattern of sin in attitude and action. *Sitting* speaks of settling in and being at home with those who are in opposition to God. They mock His Word and those who follow it.

Verse 1 paints a picture which is undeniably clear. If we want to follow righteousness and be in harmony with God, there is a definite separation which must occur. Yes, we will work beside and live next to unbelievers. But their philosophies of life and thought patterns are never to be the umbrella under which we seek shelter.

The contrast comes in verse 2. Here the author states the positive actions. Instead of hearing and thinking the thoughts of the ungodly, we are to find our delight in God's Word. In the Holy Scriptures we are to find happiness as God instructs us how to live our lives to the fullest by maintaining a relationship with Him. Instead of an obedience that reflects reluctance, we are to joyously plunge forward along the path of righteousness.

This lifestyle and attitude doesn't just happen. It is the result of immersing ourselves in the Word of God. Not only do we understand what God wants from us, but we learn of Him. As we read of God's greatness and holiness, it becomes so much easier to understand what He requires of us.

Meditate speaks of more than simply reading or thinking of what is written. It suggests a form of study in which the words are not read aloud but rather half-aloud. Think of it as how many of us try to memorize or implant a thought in our memory. We tend to say it under our breath. It seems to help when we are able to use a form of speech.

Notice how this immersion in God's Word is a 24-hour activity. There's no time when we choose to separate ourselves from His influence.

B. A Stability (v. 3)

3. And he shall be like a tree planted by the rivers of water, that bringeth forth his fruit in his season; his leaf also shall not wither; and whatsoever he doeth shall prosper.

The author uses a tree to further picture the life of the righteous. It is not a tree that grew by chance. Instead, this tree was intentionally planted near the water.

It is easy to see this as a picture of believers. By faith in Jesus Christ we have been transplanted from the wilds of sin and placed in a life-giving environment which enables us to mature and produce fruit.

The tree described has been cultivated for production. Its secure location enables it to stand against the weather patterns that would hinder or even destroy it. This special security describes those who follow the way of righteousness. When the storms of disease, accidents, temptation and common crises assail us, we can stand firm and also continue to be productive.

Inclusion of the leaf that doesn't wither indicates the green foliage of a healthy tree. In a spiritual sense, some Biblical scholars see this as the faith which converts the water of life into strength and fruit production.

The last phrase of verse 3 must be carefully evaluated. Does "whatsoever he doeth shall prosper" mean everything that the God-fearing man or woman attempts to do will be successful? Absolutely not! It isn't a blanket statement that all of the believer's personal and church ventures will never have any setbacks. It does not mean the believer will have all of the money he or she wants.

Instead, this appears to be the description of the freshness which a believer can continually experience in walking with God. New opportunities for service and witness are approached with a vigor which comes from a strong relationship with God. This inner spiritual strength flows outwardly so the whole person reflects the blessings of God.

II. THE WAY OF THE UNGODLY (Psalm 1:4-6)

A. The Separation (v. 4)

4. The ungodly are not so: but are like the chaff which the wind driveth away.

The ungodly are a complete contrast from the godly. The words "are not so" reflect the great difference between the godly and ungodly. It reminds us of the fallacy which the world would have us believe—that all people are God's children and on their way to the same eternal destiny. But this idea ignores the reality which the Scriptures project. Not only do the righteous and ungodly have a different perspective on their current life, but they definitely will not be sharing the same future.

Jesus said, "Enter ye in at the strait gate: for wide is the gate, and broad is the way, that leadeth to destruction, and many there be which go in thereat: Because strait is the gate, and narrow is the way, which leadeth unto life, and few there be that find it" (Matthew 7:13, 14).

Psalm 1 depicts the godly as a deeply rooted tree which reflects its health in its leaves and fruit. But the ungodly are a vivid contrast, being likened to the worthless chaff at threshing time. It has no value and serves no purpose other than being blown away by the wind.

To gain a better picture, one needs to understand the threshing process of this time. Harvested grain was brought to a threshing floor often located on a hilltop. There a breeze would facilitate the separation process. First, the grain stalks were laid on the floor. Then they were beaten to separate the kernels of grain from the heads and individual coverings. Last, the grain and chaff (coverings) were thrown into the air. The heavier kernels fell to the floor while the light chaff was blown away.

The comparison of the ungodly to chaff isn't intended to suggest they have no worth. Rather, it speaks of their being separated from the righteous. Every human has worth due to being the creation of God. However, one's relationship with God determines his or her future.

B. The Punishment (vv. 5, 6)

5. Therefore the ungodly shall not stand in the judgment, nor sinners in the congregation of the righteous.

6. For the Lord knoweth the way of the righteous: but the way of the ungodly shall perish.

These two verses are not popular among those who believe God will send no one to an everlasting place of punishment. They argue that a God of love couldn't possibly subject any of His creation to such a fate. But they fail to understand the totality of God's nature. Yes, He definitely is a God of love; but He is also a holy and just God. Sin separates individuals from God, since He demands holiness. And anyone who disregards His laws then must experience His justice. "Ye shall be holy: for I the Lord your God am holy" (Leviticus 19:2). "He is the Rock, his work is perfect: for all his ways are judgment: a God of truth and without iniquity, just and right is he" (Deuteronomy 32:4).

Psalm 1:5 teaches that the inner worthlessness of unbelievers, caused by sin, makes it impossible for them to receive God's approval. Sinners can never be part of the congregation of the righteous. They may become members of a church, but they will still be exempted from the family of God.

Though people may not always know who qualify as the godly and ungodly, God knows, as verse 6 points out. The Lord approves of the commitment of the righteous, and He takes a personal interest in directing each of their lives.

At the same time, it is not out of character for God to allow the ungodly to perish due to their disregard for or rejection of Him. Their chosen path leads to destruction.

III. TRUST IN THE LORD
   (Psalm 37:1-7)

A. Do Not Fret (vv. 1-4)

1. Fret not thyself because of evildoers, neither be thou envious against the workers of iniquity.

2. For they shall soon be cut down like the grass, and wither as the green herb.

3. Trust in the Lord, and do good; so shalt thou dwell in the land, and verily thou shalt be fed.

4. Delight thyself also in the Lord; and he shall give thee the desires of thine heart.

Just like Psalm 37, the first psalm deals with a contrast of the righteous and the ungodly. Known as a wisdom psalm, it can be divided into four sections. Our lesson uses only the first section, which focuses on commitment.

The seven verses for consideration remind us that trusting in the Lord necessitates much more than words. Its true test comes in times of frustration and crisis. How will we respond when facing the inequities of life?

David begins with a strong "thou shalt not" statement in verse 1. The righteous are to avoid fretting or being envious of the ungodly. First, it's not fitting for a child of God to stoop to such an attitude. Not only does it reflect a lack of trust, but it also speaks of a desire to possess the environment of those who are involved in wrong attitudes and actions.

In verse 2 the psalmist pictures the true situation. For the moment the ungodly appear as luscious and healthy as green grass and other green plants. Yet, this can change so quickly. Grass can be cut down. Most of us think in terms of a mower. However, to a shepherd the better understanding is how quickly plants can wither and lose their vitality due to the lack of water and corresponding heat. The same holds true for those who follow the patterns of evil. Their success and enjoyment will be short-lived. With this in mind, we must remember that there is no need for us to desire God's judgment on them prematurely. Neither are we to become upset to the point of not fulfilling our prescribed course of living.

In contrast, the righteous are to trust in the Lord and turn their attention to the pursuit of good. This path provides security and provision. To more fully understand verse 3, it is important to keep in mind the context. These words were initially written to the people of Israel. "Dwell in the land" refers specifically to their possession of the land of Canaan. Under the leadership of Joshua and through God's miraculous intervention, the Israelites took possession of this land initially promised to Abraham. Though controlled by people much stronger than themselves and sheltered in walled cities, God opened the land to His children.

Their ownership of the land wasn't a guarantee of their continually being in physical possession of it. As Moses closed his 40 years of leadership with farewell addresses, he pointed out the results of disobedience. One might be removed from their land (Deuteronomy 28:63). In contrast was the result of obediently trusting in the Lord and following His laws. Not only would they remain in the land, but enjoy prosperity from its fruits (vv. 9-14).

How does that apply to us who are neither Jews nor living in the Promised Land? First, trusting in the Lord always is beneficial. There continues to be a bright future beyond this life. Second, no one can continue a commitment to Christ without a trust relationship. Third, God provides in this life for those who are His children.

The psalmist's second directive appears in verse 4. Not only are we to trust, but we are to delight in the Lord. This speaks of taking full pleasure in our God. Nothing is more pleasing than our commitment to Him.

God's commitment to us enables righteousness to be our lifestyle.

His commitment to us provides a life and future unlike that of the ungodly. No wonder we should find delight in the Lord.

This type of relationship develops as a result of our commitment to God. We are the means by which the delight continues and grows. And the reward comes in the form of fulfilling our desires. No, this doesn't mean becoming a multimillionaire. While God does grant us material possessions, there is something far greater here. The context is that of relationship with God. As we desire to grow closer to Him, He draws closer to us. As we study His Word to know more of Him, He unveils Himself to us.

These four verses depict an important progression. First, we eliminate the negative attitudes which creep in so easily when viewing the seeming prosperity of the ungodly. Second, we commit ourselves to the practice of trusting and delighting in the Lord. And then we begin to enjoy the fullness of God our Father.

B. Commit Your Way (vv. 5, 6)

5. Commit thy way unto the Lord; trust also in him; and he shall bring it to pass.

6. And he shall bring forth thy righteousness as the light, and thy judgment as the noonday.

This second dimension of trusting in the Lord involves a different way of committing oneself to the Lord. It is much more than saying "Yes, Lord, I will serve You," or "Yes, Lord, I'll go where You want me to go." The commitment desired here is that of rolling the burdens of life onto the Lord. This means commitment on a daily basis. It involves the struggles of work, relationships, family duties, and the occasional crisis which is normal to life. When we trust God by placing our cares in His hands, they become His concerns. When our reliance reaches such a state, our worries and stress diminish.

Verse 6 points to the further results of such a trusting relationship. Sometimes God's people are wrongly charged and frequently misunderstood for their lifestyles and belief. But eventually the righteousness of their cause will be exposed. Notice that no time limit is offered. It may take years or even centuries. Our concern isn't to be with the timetable but with the result. Just as the sun eventually rises and light bursts through the darkness, so will the causes of God's people be vindicated in His time.

C. Wait Patiently (v. 7)

7. Rest in the Lord, and wait patiently for him: fret not thyself because of him who prospereth in his way, because of the man who bringeth wicked devices to pass.

Verse 7 repeats the directive of verse 1. We are not to be individuals who fret over the apparent prosperity of the wicked. Why should we be robbed of our joy and progress as believers due to the temporary apparent success of the ungodly?

Some unbelievers accumulate great amounts of wealth. Others benefit from promotions and consequently wield considerable power. We must not allow these things to hinder our own spiritual progress. Asaph wrote, "But as for me, my feet were almost gone; my steps had well nigh slipped. For I was envious at the foolish, when I saw the prosperity of the wicked" (Psalm 73:2, 3).

Believers are to rest in the Lord. This means being still before Him rather than restlessly wishing for a change. If we are waiting patiently, there is the absence of stress and questioning why God hasn't come on the scene. Instead we know that His will and timing are always right.

Not only does He know what needs to be done but also when it should occur. Individuals who learn to wait patiently on God experience an emotional and physical health benefit as well. The whole person is blessed when we have a proper spiritual commitment to God.

GOLDEN TEXT HOMILY

"I HAVE SET BEFORE YOU LIFE AND DEATH, BLESSING AND CURSING: THEREFORE CHOOSE LIFE" (Deuteronomy 30:19).

The story of one's life may be told in terms of the choices made. Many times the choices we make affect not only our own history but that of many others as well. The choice seems to us to be personal but in the long run turns out to be both personal and social.

A few examples of this from the Bible will illustrate the sobering truth. Adam made a choice. It was a personal decision, yet it has affected the entire human family. Moses chose to suffer affliction with the people of God rather than enjoy the pleasures of sin for a season. Abraham, Isaac, Jacob, Nehemiah, Esther . . . and on and on the list could grow. We know about these people on the basis of how they chose. Their choices continue to influence the unfolding pages of history.

It is the freedom to choose that makes man a morally responsible creature. The freedom to choose means that we are responsible for the choices we make and, for the most part, responsible for the consequences of those choices.

A Chinese proverb states, "Take what you want and pay for it." This makes life similar to a supermarket or smorgasbord. We are free to claim whatever we want but must be prepared to pay the price. Sometimes we get a bargain and at other times we lose.

Looking at the text, one wonders if it really is a choice. Life or death?

Blessing or cursing? What fool would not choose life and blessing?

To add to the weight of this choice, the text admonishes readers and hearers to choose life. If such a choice is logical, why the need to be urged to make the right decision? I am not sure I know the answers to that puzzle. But we do know that this choice confronts mankind every day. And we also know that despite the logic of choosing life and blessing, many have chosen death and cursing.

Life and blessing are available to us all, but they are not thrust or forced upon us. Neither are we doomed to death and cursing. Whichever it is for you it is a matter of choice. Choose wisely, for your choice will affect not only your history but also your eternal destiny.—**R.B. Thomas**

SENTENCE SERMONS

THE CHOICES we make will determine our destiny now and for eternity.

—Selected

THE GREAT THING in the world is not so much where we stand, as in what direction we are moving.

Oliver Wendell Holmes

WE MAKE our decisions, and then our decisions turn around and make us.

—F.W. Boreham

EVANGELISM APPLICATION

THE CHOICES WE MAKE WILL DETERMINE OUR DESTINY NOW AND FOR ETERNITY.

It doesn't make much difference which toothpaste you use. It doesn't really matter that you prefer apples over oranges, or vice-versa.

There are other areas of life where your decisions have far greater impact. Wearing your seat belt, having regular medical checkups and making careful use of your money may have considerable impact in certain situations. An accident, malignant growth or money scheme may bring disaster, if proper choices have not been made earlier.

Of even greater importance are the spiritual choices you make. Choosing sin may be fun for a while, but it eventually brings pain, sorrow and suffering. Will you make the choice which brings eternal life? Or will you choose the path of eternal separation and suffering. The difference rests upon whether or not you choose to accept Jesus Christ as Savior and Lord.

ILLUMINATING THE LESSON

Isn't amazing all the items we trust in the course of our daily work, occasional travel and adventurous endeavors?

1. We trust a piece of metal with wings on its sides (called an airplane) to actually fly us safely to our destination.

2. We trust the cables on the elevator will not break and plunge us out of control to the bottom floor.

3. We trust that the physician or nurse administering a shot or intravenous fluid has not mistakenly selected the wrong medicine.

4. We trust the signal lights are working in the other direction as we rapidly drive through the intersection.

DAILY BIBLE READINGS

M. Choose Between Blessing and Cursing.
   Deuteronomy 11:22-28
T. Choose Between Life and Death.
   Deuteronomy 30:11-19
W. Fear and Honor the Lord.
   Proverbs 3:7-14
T. Choose to Believe in Christ.
   John 3:14-21
F. Choose the Wisdom of God.
   1 Corinthians 1:18-25
S. Choose the Light of God.
   1 John 1:5-7

TRUTH SEARCH:
Creatively Teaching the Word

Aim: Students will affirm or reaffirm their commitment to Christ.

Items needed: Paper, pencils, matches

FOCUS

We like to categorize each other, don't we? And we tend to compare ourselves with those who fit in a different category than we do.

For instance, if I am middle-class, perhaps I long to be upper-class. If I am lower-class, I might want to be middle-class.

God has a simple way of categorizing people. In His eyes, we are either righteous or unrighteous. Incredibly, those who are righteous sometimes envy the unrighteous! Let's check it out.

EXPLORE

Divide the class into groups of three or four students each, and give each group paper and pencil. Have half of the students explore Psalm 1:1-3, while the other half studies verses 4-6.

Psalm 1:1-3

1. *Name three things the righteous person chooses not to do (v. 1).*
2. *What does it mean to "delight" in Scripture (v. 2)?*
3. *What does it mean to "meditate day and night" on God's Word (v. 2)?*
4. *What image does the psalmist use to describe the righteous person (v. 3)? Why is it an appropriate image?*

Psalm 1:4-6

1. *"The ungodly are not so" (v. 4) is a reference back to verse 3. What are the ungodly not like?*

2. *What is chaff (v. 4)? How is the ungodly person like chaff?*
3. *In what two places will unbelievers not be able to stand (v. 5)? Why?*
4. *Contrast the way of the righteous with the way of the wicked (v. 6).*

Have the groups report their findings. Next, have a volunteer read Psalm 37:1-6. Then discuss those verses with the entire class.

• *Why do we sometimes "fret" and become "envious against" sinners (v. 1)?*
• *Why should believers not envy unbelievers (v. 2)?*
• *What command does God give in verse 3? What promise does He make?*
• *What command does God give in verse 4? What promise does He make?*
• *What command does God give in verse 5? What promise does He make (also see v. 6)?*

RESPOND

When we look around us and see wicked people prospering, we can become envious. We can be lured into the false belief that their way is superior. But listen to Psalm 37:18-20. Have a student read this passage.

Light a match, then quickly put it out. Like the flame, the ungodly will burn brightly—but only for a season. Then they will vanish like smoke.

Lead the students in prayer, challenging them to commit themselves to following the way of righteousness.

Our Magnificent Messiah

Study Text: Psalms 2:7-12; 22:1-31; 23:1-6

Objective: To see prophecies about Jesus in the Psalms and worship Him.

Golden Text: "The Lord is my shepherd; I shall not want" (Psalm 23:1).

Central Truth: Christ suffered rejection and crucifixion to obtain salvation for all people.

Evangelism Emphasis: Christ suffered and died to save people from their sins.

PRINTED TEXT

Psalm 2:7. I will declare the decree: the Lord hath said unto me, Thou art my Son; this day have I begotten thee.

8. Ask of me, and I shall give thee the heathen for thine inheritance, and the uttermost parts of the earth for thy possession.

9. Thou shalt break them with a rod of iron; thou shalt dash them in pieces like a potter's vessel.

10. Be wise now therefore, O ye kings: be instructed, ye judges of the earth.

11. Serve the Lord with fear, and rejoice with trembling.

12. Kiss the Son, lest he be angry, and ye perish from the way, when his wrath is kindled but a little. Blessed are all they that put their trust in him.

22:1. My God, my God, why hast thou forsaken me? why art thou so far from helping me, and from the words of my roaring?

2. O my God, I cry in the daytime, but thou hearest not; and in the night season, and am not silent.

6. But I am a worm, and no man; a reproach of men, and despised of the people.

7. All they that see me laugh me to scorn: they shoot out the lip, they shake the head, saying,

8. He trusted on the Lord that he would deliver him: let him deliver him, seeing he delighted in him.

23:1. The Lord is my shepherd; I shall not want.

2. He maketh me to lie down in green pastures: he leadeth me beside the still waters.

3. He restoreth my soul: he leadeth me in the paths of righteousness for his name's sake.

4. Yea, though I walk through the valley of the shadow of death, I will fear no evil: for thou art with me; thy rod and thy staff they comfort me.

5. Thou preparest a table before me in the presence of mine enemies: thou anointest my head with oil; my cup runneth over.

6. Surely goodness and mercy shall follow me all the days of my life: and I will dwell in the house of the Lord for ever.

LESSON OUTLINE

I. SON OF GOD
   A. Sonship
   B. Dominion
   C. Service

II. SUFFERING SAVIOR
   A. Despair
   B. Trust
   C. Scorn

III. COMPASSIONATE SHEPHERD
   A. Satisfaction
   B. Presence
   C. Provision

LESSON EXPOSITION

INTRODUCTION

Who is Jesus?

This ancient question continues even into our 21st century. Was Jesus a philosopher, a great teacher, a miracle worker, a fraud or a liar, just to name a few? Was He a political rebel looking to set up His own kingdom?

When Jesus was brought before Pilate, "they began to accuse him, saying, We found this fellow perverting the nation, and forbidding to give tribute to Caesar, saying that he himself is Christ a King. And Pilate asked him, saying, Art thou the King of the Jews? And he answered him and said, Thou sayest it" (Luke 23:2, 3).

Earlier in Jesus' ministry He asked the disciples, "Who do people say the Son of Man is?" They replied, "Some say John the Baptist; others say Elijah; and still others, Jeremiah or one of the prophets" (Matthew 16:13, 14, *NIV*).

The truth is that Jesus is the Messiah. Though the word *Messiah* is not within the Old Testament, it represents the future expectation held by Israel as they anticipated the coming of "the Anointed One," the King of Israel.

Saul was Israel's first king, divinely appointed. When Samuel anointed Saul, the prophet said, "Is it not because the Lord hath anointed thee to be captain over his inheritance?" (1 Samuel 10:1). However, Saul was not the Messiah.

David followed Saul as the king of Israel. In spite of his failures, he was recognized as "a man after God's own heart" and the ideal king by which all other reigns would be judged. But he was not the Messiah. However, God promised the Messiah would come through David's posterity: "Your house and your kingdom will endure forever before me" (2 Samuel 7:16, *NIV*).

These messianic expectations can be seen in the writings of the various Old Testament prophets such as Jeremiah 33 and Zechariah 9 and 12. They also can be seen in various psalms. Today's lesson looks at passages from three of them.

Our lesson title emphasizes the magnificence of our Messiah. Yet, Jesus' love and compassion for a sinful world caused Him untold agony and death. While we all enjoy worshiping in the presence of our King, Jesus Christ, it is vital that we not neglect the picture of His suffering.

I. SON OF GOD (Psalm 2:7-12)

A. Sonship (v. 7)

7. I will declare the decree: the Lord hath said unto me, Thou art my Son; this day have I begotten thee.

The author of Psalm 2 is unknown. Yet, it is cited more in the New Testament than any other psalm. This is due to its prophetic content of Jesus, the Son of God.

This psalm begins with a description of the nations in tumult against the Lord. It speaks of the kings and their subjects being in a state of rebellion. They have made sin the center of their lives rather than serving God. But, beginning in verse 4, God looks down on this confusion and speaks the words of truth. His holiness brings terror to them. As He sits above them in glory, their finite efforts to rebel causes Him to scoff at them and rebuke them. God rules, and it shall never change.

Then, in verse 7 we see a sudden transition. Without any introduction we find a major declaration: The dominion of the world is given to God's Son. Of special importance is the concept of being the "begotten Son," which brings to mind John 3:16. The question is, What does *begotten* imply in Psalm 2:7?

This verse is not referring to a point in time for Christ's coming into existence. There never has been a time when Christ was not. As part of the Trinity, Christ has always been God. Colossians 2:9 states this succinctly, "For in him dwelleth all the fulness of the Godhead bodily."

From the inclusion of Psalm 2:7 in various New Testament passages, we see the extent of its meaning. While preaching in Antioch the apostle Paul used it in application to the resurrection of Jesus: "God hath fulfilled the same unto us their children, in that he hath raised up Jesus again; as it is also written in the second psalm, Thou art my Son, this day have I begotten thee" (Acts 13:33).

The writer of the Book of Hebrews used this passage in two places. First, in speaking of Christ's superiority to the angels: "For unto which of the angels said he at any time, Thou art my Son, this day have I begotten thee? And again, I will be to him a Father, and he shall be to me a Son?" (1:5). Second, in speaking of Christ's release as High Priest: "So Christ also did not take upon himself the glory of becoming a high priest. But God said to him, 'You are my

Son; today I have become your Father'" (5:5, *NIV*).

These varied references further emphasize the position of Christ as the Son of God and His role both on earth and in heaven. All the rights and authority of God the Father reside in Jesus, the Son of God.

B. Dominion (vv. 8, 9)

8. Ask of me, and I shall give thee the heathen for thine inheritance, and the uttermost parts of the earth for thy possession.

9. Thou shalt break them with a rod of iron; thou shalt dash them in pieces like a potter's vessel.

After seeing the position of Sonship, verses 8 and 9 emphasize Christ's power. The Father gave Him dominion over the earth. However, that dominion wasn't automatic. It involved a specific action on the part of the Son. "Ask of me" meant far more than simply requesting permission to own. It spoke of a willingness to do what was necessary to obtain this dominion.

Of course, we know the specifics of this willingness. God the Father loved the world and wanted to redeem it from sin. But a sinless sacrifice was the only means by which this domination of sin could be accomplished. And this is where the Son became the crucial key. Would He be willing to pay the price of taking on human flesh and then experience the ultimate suffering of crucifixion?

The Son's willingness resulted in His receiving the heathen as His inheritance. *Heathen* refers to the nations of the world or, in other words, the Gentiles. All of them, regardless of their location on the globe, would become the Son's inheritance.

Verse 9 declares that Christ would rule over the Gentiles. The "rod of iron" represents a king's scepter, his symbol of authority and power. The material, iron, emphasizes his strength and ability to overcome. It is reminiscent of the account recorded in 1 Samuel 13:19. To make sure the Israelites would remain weak and unable to mount resistance, the Philistines allowed no blacksmith in Palestine. At one time there were only two metal swords found in the land.

Those nations who yield to the Son will obtain His favor. But those who resist will be destroyed in the same way that a piece of pottery can be smashed to pieces. There will be no contest when Christ chooses to exert His power and punish people's unwillingness to accept His lordship.

C. Service (vv. 10-12)

10. Be wise now therefore, O ye kings: be instructed, ye judges of the earth.
11. Serve the Lord with fear, and rejoice with trembling.
12. Kiss the Son, lest he be angry, and ye perish from the way, when his wrath is kindled but a little. Blessed are all they that put their trust in him.

These last three verses turn the attention away from the Son and place the spotlight on the rulers of the world. This, of course, doesn't take away each person's responsibility for his/her individual choices. But it does highlight the role of those who are in the elevated positions of leadership. Their choices will impact the entire nations they lead.

Verse 10 is a warning to be wise. Kings and their ruling subordinates are to submit themselves to the Son. This isn't political submission, but spiritual. It is fearing the Lord as the sovereign ruler of the heart, mind and body. Verse 12 emphasizes the homage that leaders need to exhibit. "Kiss the Son" refers to a common action by which individuals would reflect their obedience and submission. For example, after anointing Saul to be the first king of Israel, the prophet Samuel kissed him (1 Samuel 10:1). In a dialogue between God and Elijah, God informed Elijah there were still 7,000 people who had not kissed allegiance to the evil ruler, Ahab (1 Kings 19:18).

Verse 12 of the text also emphasizes that failing to offer allegiance to the Son will result in His wrath being unleashed. This holds a double implication. All who reject the Son will experience eternal punishment. However, punishment is sometimes poured out in the physical and political arenas. For example, God's judgment against King Nebuchadnezzar of Babylon resulted in this vaunted king living like an animal out in the fields for seven years (Daniel 4).

God desires people to serve Him with reverence and joy. When we serve the Lord with fear, it doesn't mean to be scared to death. Instead, this is service in the attitude of reverent awe. He is so great, and we are so finite. He is worthy, and we are unworthy. But due to His love we can enjoy fellowship as we obediently serve Him.

II. SUFFERING SAVIOR
(Psalm 22:1-8)

A. Despair (vv. 1, 2)

1. My God, my God, why hast thou forsaken me? why art thou so far from helping me, and from the words of my roaring?
2. O my God, I cry in the daytime, but thou hearest not; and in the night season, and am not silent.

The opening lines of this psalm are best known as the words of Jesus from the cross (Matthew 27:46; Mark 15:34). At about 3 p.m., darkness mysteriously began to replace the light of day. The darkness remained for three hours in the middle of the day. Then, the battered and bruised Messiah cried out these words of despair in a loud voice. Shortly thereafter He died.

These words portray a suffering that far superseded His physical condition. They reflect the agony of Jesus' knowing the Father wasn't going to come to His rescue. Out of necessity God turned His back (so to speak) on His beloved Son. It was the only way for redemption to be provided for this sinful world. Without Christ's suffering the agony of crucifixion and rejection, we could never have the gift of eternal life.

A thousand years before Jesus uttered these words of agony, the psalmist David spoke them in despair. Generally it is believed that he wrote them during a period of deepest gloom when being persecuted by Saul, his father-in-law. Saul repeatedly tried to kill him, forcing David to live as a fugitive. All this occurred after having been anointed as the next king of Israel.

Though knowing God had plans for him, it appeared to David that he had been forsaken. He felt all alone against the oppressor and the unrelenting circumstances.

According to verse 2, the alienation and yearning David felt consumed him day and night. No matter when or how long he cried out, no answer came. Yet, no matter how deserted he felt, David never suggested going his own way. In fact, just the opposite comes through. Three times in the first two verses he cries out, "*My* God." This speaks of a faith that held fast even when surrounded by the most trying circumstances. He continued to demonstrate a reliance on God even though God wasn't offering specific comfort or direction for the moment.

Despair may develop within us when we are beleaguered by circumstances that soar beyond our control. The suffering may appear to be more than we can bear. But that's when our commitment needs to remain firm. God's silence or seeming non-involvement is for a purpose. He never forsakes His children.

B. Trust (vv. 3-5)

(Psalm 22:3-5 is not included in the printed text.)

Immediately after expressing the depths of his despair, David turned to the subject of trust. Though having voiced his complaint very specifically, the psalmist knew the truth about God—He is holy. A review of His people's history emphasized how God does come to the aid of His own. Yet, that doesn't mean there will be no times of difficulty. God's personal holiness is no guarantee against difficult situations. It *does* ensure God will do the right thing at the right time.

In referring to events from the past when Israel placed their trust in God (vv. 4, 5), David could have been thinking of God's deliverance and provision in the events surrounding the Exodus. God heard the cry of the Hebrews while burdened by the oppression of slavery and sent Moses to bring deliverance (Exodus 2:23-25; 3:16, 17). About a year later the Hebrews were pinned between mountains on either side, the Red Sea ahead and the Egyptian army behind. In terror they cried out to the Lord, and He delivered (14:10,13-31).

These verses have a great deal of practical application for us as believers. We can trust God to be with us and deliver by His chosen means. This is demonstrated repeatedly not only in the Scriptures but also in the lives of believers today. As we listen to the testimonies of the saints (young and old), God's unchanging care for His children appears. The challenge for us is to trust in the Lord while waiting for His timetable.

Not to be overlooked in this setting is how Christ trusted His heavenly Father and followed His will even though God sent Him to earth to take on human flesh and die for the sins of the world.

C. Scorn (vv. 6-8)

6. But I am a worm, and no man; a reproach of men, and despised of the people.
7. All they that see me laugh me to scorn: they shoot out the lip, they shake the head, saying,
8. He trusted on the Lord that he would deliver him: let him deliver him, seeing he delighted in him.

David's embattled condition of that time period—nearly 1,000 years before Christ—mirrored the suffering Savior as presented in the Gospel records. He complained of the reproach to the point of describing himself as a lowly worm. Some years previously the women sang of his having killed 10,000 enemy soldiers (1 Samuel 18:7). But now people were mocking him and hurling insults. They shook their heads in disdain, seeing David as nothing more than a fugitive from the king.

In this same way the crowds insulted and jeered at Jesus as He hung on the cross. "Those who passed by hurled insults at him, shaking their heads and saying, 'You who are going to destroy the temple and build it in three days, save yourself! Come down from the cross, if you are the Son of God!'" (Matthew 27:39, 40, *NIV*; see also vv. 41-44).

Neither David nor Jesus were guilty of any wrong that was causing them to suffer. Saul's sin and unrepentant attitude placed David in his dilemma. In Christ's case, it was our sins and those of the rest of the world that put him in the agony of humiliation and suffering.

III. COMPASSIONATE SHEPHERD
(Psalm 23:1-6)

A. Satisfaction (vv. 1, 2)

1. The Lord is my shepherd; I shall not want.
2. He maketh me to lie down in green pastures: he leadeth me beside the still waters.

Psalm 23, the most well-known passage of Scripture with the possible exception of the Lord's Prayer, continues to reveal our magnificent Messiah. It offers comfort in times of crisis and sorrow and reveals the compassion of the Messiah for each of us. However, to grasp the fullness of what is being said, one must have a clear understanding of the relationship between an Eastern shepherd and his sheep. It also necessitates knowing the nature of sheep and the commitment of a true shepherd. There is a difference between the person who cares for sheep because of the money and the one who cares for sheep because of his love for them (see John 10:12, 13).

In verses 1 and 2 the psalmist emphasized the satisfaction the Shepherd provides for His sheep. "I shall not want" must be understood in terms of needs, not all the items on a "want list." Needs of sheep are relatively simple. At the top of the list are the basics of food and water.

Sheep tend to wander and not lie down until their hunger is satisfied. Their natural fear of running water necessitates the shepherd's finding calm water or building a dam with a quiet reservoir. To fulfill the needs of his flock, the shepherd not only has to be knowledgeable of the area but be willing to go the extra mile to bring satisfaction.

In the same way our Messiah, the Good Shepherd, constantly strives to provide the spiritual food and spiritual drink which satisfies and sustains. However, we still have the obligation to partake of it. It is not forced on us. We must choose to be fed from the Word of God and ministered to by the Holy Spirit.

B. Presence (vv. 3, 4)

3. He restoreth my soul: he leadeth me in the paths of righteousness for his name's sake.

4. Yea, though I walk through the valley of the shadow of death, I will fear no evil: for thou art with me; thy rod and thy staff they comfort me.

These verses can be summed up in one sentence: *We're never alone!* What an assurance! Regardless of the situation, God is with us. He wants our soul to be uplifted rather than spiritually anemic or devastated. This means our inner person can experience His daily renewal. The apostle Paul spoke of this in 2 Corinthians 4:16: "For which cause we faint not; but though our outward man perish, yet the inward man is renewed day by day."

Psalm 23:3, 4 emphasizes the Shepherd's presence in directing us to straight paths of righteousness as well as comforting us in the hard places. Because of God's personal holiness, He cannot help but instruct us in the life paths that avoid sin and enable us to follow His likeness. He never allows us to simply wander and flounder on just any path of life. He seeks to direct us in wholesome patterns that keep us from the dangers of the Enemy.

All of us face difficult situations in our lives and then the eventuality of death. Our Shepherd continues to be there and grants us courage to face even that last enemy—death. Notice His weapons. The *rod* speaks of protection. The knobbed end of this club would be embedded with bits of metal which would inflict severe pain and injury on an enemy. The *staff* served many purposes, including protection. The shepherd would sweep the staff across the ground to drive away the snakes which would try to strike the sheep.

C. Provision (vv. 5, 6)

5. Thou preparest a table before me in the presence of mine enemies: thou anointest my head with oil; my cup runneth over.

6. Surely goodness and mercy shall follow me all the days of my life: and I will dwell in the house of the Lord for ever.

These final two verses change the scenario from a shepherd caring for sheep to a host serving guests. From the culture of that time verse 5 represents a special honor being bestowed. For example, a king might hold such a banquet for a favored person. Opponents of the guest might be in attendance or at least nearby to see the festivities. However, they had to remain quiet. At such an occasion the guest would be anointed with perfumed oils, and his supply of food and drink would be brought on a continual basis.

The anointing with oil represented joy and refreshing. The guest of honor would be anointed as a sign of respect. Anointing was also used for a wound or injury. A shepherd would always check each sheep for bites, scratches and other wounds. These would be anointed with oil to soothe and heal.

As we consider verse 6, understand David's situation. Psalm 23 was written during Absalom's rebellion. David and a few family members had fled the capital city of Jerusalem and lived in the wilderness of Judah. He again was a hunted man, but now his perspective was completely different. He said only prosperity and good were pursuing him because God was in control of the situation. Though David didn't know what the end result would be, there was the assurance of his future. Though forced from his earthly palace, he would continue to dwell forever in the house of the Lord! He understood the totality of God's provision even in crisis.

GOLDEN TEXT HOMILY

"THE LORD IS MY SHEPHERD; I SHALL NOT WANT" (Psalm 23:1).

"The Lord is my shepherd, I shall not be in want" is the *New International Version* rendition of this verse. One children's Bible reads, "The Lord is my shepherd. He gives me everything I need." The one who wrote this psalm about the Good Shepherd was himself a shepherd. What kinds of provision did David the shepherd need?

• *Wisdom* and *skill* to protect his sheep from wild animals
• *Physical strength* to care for his sheep
• *Guidance* to help his sheep find food and water
• *Patience* and *diligence* in caring for wayward sheep
• *Protection* from weather and thieves
• *Companionship* as he tended the sheep alone

The Lord met all those needs in David's life, giving him everything he needed. And He promises to meet those same needs in our life if we will follow Him.

• God promises us *wisdom* (James 1:5).
• God promises to meet our *physical needs* (Matthew 6:33).
• God promises *guidance* (Romans 8:14).
• God promises to give us *patience* and *diligence* and other graces (Galatians 5:22, 23).
• God promises us *protection* (Psalm 91).
• God promises us constant *companionship* (Hebrews 13:5).

If the Lord is our Shepherd, we can rely on Him to give us *everything* we need!—**Lance Colkmire**

SENTENCE SERMONS

CHRIST SUFFERED rejection and crucifixion to obtain salvation for all people.
—Selected

WE ARE GOD'S VERY OWN, being redeemed by Him. Every Christian therefore should wear a sign in his heart, "Not for sale!"
—Anonymous

THE VOICE OF SIN may be loud, but the voice of forgiveness is louder.
—D.L. Moody

EVANGELISM APPLICATION

CHRIST SUFFERED AND DIED TO SAVE PEOPLE FROM THEIR SINS.

When thinking about Jesus Christ, it is so easy to concentrate on the positive highlights of His life here on earth. We emphasize the angelic announcement to the shepherds and the Magi seeing His star. But also important is the divine preservation as Joseph is directed through a dream to flee to Egypt from the anger of King Herod.

Then during Christ's ministry we see the phenomenal miracles of thousands who are fed from a few loaves and fishes. Blind eyes receive sight, deaf ears are unstopped, and limbs are restored to health. Plus, His teaching resulted in the crowds' marveling at His words of authority.

But all of these activities comprise an active ministry. The primary purpose for Jesus coming to earth in the form of human flesh was to die for our sins. This represented His passive ministry. He came to be a suffering Savior so we could be freed from the burden, guilt and consequences of our sins.

And that's why He is truly our magnificent Messiah.

ILLUMINATING THE LESSON

Adoniram Judson, the renowned 19th-century missionary to Burma, ministered seven years before having his first convert. During that time he suffered from hunger and other deprivations. For 17 months he was imprisoned and subjected to many forms of mistreatment which left their ugly marks on his body.

Undaunted, he immediately sought to enter another province of the country after being released from prison. He desired to continue ministering the gospel. The ruler refused his request. Not because he thought people would be convinced by Judson's words, but because he feared the scars would impress them to convert to his religion.

DAILY BIBLE READINGS

M. Promised Redeemer.
   Isaiah 9:2-7
T. Smitten Servant.
   Isaiah 53:1-9
W. God's Son, Our Savior.
   Matthew 27:33-43, 50, 51
T. Good Shepherd.
   John 10:11-18
F. Worthy Lamb.
   Revelation 5:8-14
S. King of Kings.
   Revelation 19:11-16

TRUTH SEARCH:
Creatively Teaching the Word

Aim: Students will worship Christ for who He is.

Items needed: Pencils, paper, marker board, marker

FOCUS

Who is Jesus? How might some groups answer that question?

Jehovah's Witnesses: "Jesus is one of the sons of God."

Muslims: "Jesus was a prophet."

Orthodox Jews: "Jesus was a false Messiah."

New Agers: "Jesus was an enlightened being."

There are a lot of false ideas about who Jesus is. Let's see what the Bible says.

EXPLORE

Divide your class into small groups, and have each group answer questions regarding one of the following three passages.

Psalm 2:1, 2, 7-12

1. What is the inheritance of the Son of God (vv. 7, 8)?

2. According to verse 9, in what manner will Christ one day rule the earth?

3. What will be the fate of those who rebel against Christ's rule (vv. 1, 2, 10, 12)?

4. What is the wise way to respond to Christ's rule, and what is the result (vv. 11, 12)?

Psalm 22:1-8

1. How were verses 1 and 2 fulfilled in the life of Christ? (See Mark 15:33, 34.)

2. How were verses 6-8 fulfilled in the life of Christ? (See Mark 15:25-32.)

3. What is the true identity of this One who was abused (v. 3)?

4. What abilities does the Holy One have (vv. 4, 5)?

Psalm 23:1-6

1. What does "I shall not want" mean (v. 1)?

2. Describe the ministry of the Good Shepherd as depicted in verses 2 and 3.

3. Why does the believer need not fear death (v. 4)?

4. List the promises given in verses 5 and 6.

RESPOND

At the top of the board, write the following names for the Son of God: *All-Powerful Ruler, Suffering Savior, Good Shepherd.*

It's incredible to think that one person could fit all of the descriptions we have just studied. This could happen only if that person were the Son of God.

Which of these three titles best fits the dimension of Christ you need to rely on today?

• The *All-Powerful Ruler* who has complete control of the affairs of earth.

• The *Suffering Savior* who understands your struggles and is able to deliver you.

• The *Good Shepherd* who offers you guidance, comfort and eternal life.

Challenge the students to take turns making faith statements based on one of these roles of Christ. Each statement should begin, "Because Jesus is the All-Powerful Ruler (or Suffering Savior or Good Shepherd), I believe He will . . . "

Here are a couple of examples:

• Because Jesus is the Suffering Savior, I believe He will deliver my friend from alcohol.

• Because Jesus is the Good Shepherd, I believe He will help me find a job.

If possible, let everyone make a praise statement.

Our Great God

Study Text: Psalm 33:1-22
Objective: To acknowledge attributes of Almighty God and submit to His sovereignty.
Golden Text: "The eye of the Lord is upon them that fear him, upon them that hope in his mercy" (Psalm 33:18).
Central Truth: God is unchanging in His character.
Evangelism Emphasis: Christians who trust God and worship Him are powerful testimonies to the unsaved.

PRINTED TEXT

Psalm 33:1. Rejoice in the Lord, O ye righteous: for praise is comely for the upright.

2. Praise the Lord with harp: sing unto him with the psaltery and an instrument of ten strings.

3. Sing unto him a new song; play skilfully with a loud noise.

4. For the word of the Lord is right; and all his works are done in truth.

5. He loveth righteousness and judgment: the earth is full of the goodness of the Lord.

6. By the word of the Lord were the heavens made; and all the host of them by the breath of his mouth.

7. He gathereth the waters of the sea together as an heap: he layeth up the depth in storehouses.

8. Let all the earth fear the Lord: let all the inhabitants of the world stand in awe of him.

9. For he spake, and it was done; he commanded, and it stood fast.

10. The Lord bringeth the counsel of the heathen to nought: he maketh the devices of the people of none effect.

11. The counsel of the Lord standeth for ever, the thoughts of his heart to all generations.

12. Blessed is the nation whose God is the Lord; and the people whom he hath chosen for his own inheritance.

13. The Lord looketh from heaven; he beholdeth all the sons of men.

14. From the place of his habitation he looketh upon all the inhabitants of the earth.

15. He fashioneth their hearts alike; he considereth all their works.

16. There is no king saved by the multitude of an host: a mighty man is not delivered by much strength.

17. An horse is a vain thing for safety: neither shall he deliver any by his great strength.

18. Behold, the eye of the Lord is upon them that fear him, upon them that hope in his mercy;

19. To deliver their soul from death, and to keep them alive in famine.

20. Our soul waiteth for the Lord: he is our help and our shield.

21. For our heart shall rejoice in him, because we have trusted in his holy name.

22. Let thy mercy, O Lord, be upon us, according as we hope in thee.

LESSON OUTLINE

LESSON EXPOSITION

INTRODUCTION

Today's lesson, the third in our series from the Psalms, provides us with a variety of challenges. At the forefront stands a huge obstacle. How can finite humans, such as ourselves, grasp even a portion of the greatness of our God? We understand in terms of conceivable spans of time and measurable space. But God defies all the standards of our measurements. For that reason we must strive to comprehend to the best of our ability while trusting the Biblical record and descriptions.

The second challenge then becomes one of fulfilling the need and call to worship our great God. Initially this would seem easier to accomplish due to the worship renewal which has been occurring since the 1960s. At this point we are in the second generation of the movement. Since the inception of the worship renewal, denominations have experimented with new orders of service, creative wording and actions, as well as new musical styles and words. The vast majority of local churches have been impacted in some way. However, that doesn't guarantee either the ability or sincerity of an individual's worship.

A third challenge resides in our taking sufficient time to explore the areas of God's involvement. It begins with our seeing Him as the Creator. Nothing is without His having brought it into existence. Following God's power in creation we move to His providence (involvement) in history. The nations of the world have not been exempt from divine intervention. And then there's God's provision of redemption for sinful humanity. Without this magnificent work, there would be no hope of eternal life.

This lesson provides a foundation for the rest of our theology. In itself theology simply means a study of God. Our expanded use of it refers to the other doctrines of the Bible. Without the understanding of God, it becomes impossible to fully understand these other doctrines.

Also, it seems only reasonable that we would want to know the God who made us and whom we serve. Though our ability to understand is limited by our humanness, it doesn't give us an excuse to be ignorant. Besides, not to learn of the God we serve means we are "junking" the intellectual ability that each of us has been given. We are able to better worship when we concentrate on what we know about our great God!

For many years the song "How Great Thou Art" has been sung as both a special musical presentation and a congregational hymn. It points out the great God we serve and then enables us to respond with the worship due to Him. It follows the concepts presented in Psalm 33.

Before beginning our study, there are several other items for consideration. First, the author of this psalm is not named. This eliminates our knowing either the person or circumstances under which it was written. Second, this psalm is a hymn of praise. Even as we study of God's sovereign power, we should be expressing our praise to Him. Hopefully this wouldn't be just an intellectual experience alone. May it be a time of exalting the God of our salvation! He is worthy of our praise.

I. GREAT IN RIGHTEOUSNESS (Psalm 33:1-5)

A. The Righteous (v. 1)

1. Rejoice in the Lord, O ye righteous: for praise is comely for the upright.

One of the modern translations records this verse as follows: "Sing joyfully to the Lord, you righteous; it is fitting for the upright to praise him" (*NIV*). Worship is a defined activity for the righteous. But who are the righteous?

There are two ways to approach the answer. First, we need to examine how someone becomes righteous or upright. Because of Adam and Eve's sin of disobedience, no one is born upright. The only way for anyone to become righteous is for God himself to declare that person just. Since Christ's death on the cross and resurrection from the grave, to become righteous occurs when the believer is justified in the process of salvation. However, prior to this event God's declaration of righteousness came to those who faithfully committed themselves to obedience to the Law.

Second, we must look at maintaining the status of righteousness before God. To be righteous carries the sense of being straight, following a level path. This speaks of a consistency in one's lifestyle. Instead of straying from truth, the righteous person stays on course. That does not mean the believer

never sins! Only when we reach the state of total perfection will that occur. And that's not possible until our glorification after death. But this state does describe the person who steadfastly strives to be found acceptable in the sight of God. His laws and will supersede the norms of culture and personal desires.

The emphasis on righteousness stems from the very nature of our righteous God. Therefore, those who would be called by His name and receive His favor must strive for likeness with Him.

B. The Praise (vv. 2, 3)

2. Praise the Lord with harp: sing unto him with the psaltery and with an instrument of ten strings.
3. Sing unto him a new song; play skilfully with a loud noise.

In view of God's greatness and the relationship of the righteous to their heavenly Father, praise and worship should be the logical response. It is only fitting for those who partake of God's righteousness to express their joy. How can anyone be in relationship with God and not outwardly demonstrate it?

God's greatness and our neediness provide an initial reason for us to praise Him. But more importantly, the righteous have an obligation to praise and worship the God who declares us upright in His sight. It is an honor to confess the glory and characteristics of our God. Nothing can compare to who He is and the deeds of His hands!

Consider the word *praise*. *Baker's Dictionary of Theology* defines it as "homage rendered to God by His creatures in worship of His person and in thanksgiving for His favors and blessings." For this to genuinely happen, it involves our mind, our will, our emotions and our body. Praise comes from our whole being.

On some occasions this praise breaks forth spontaneously as the Holy Spirit moves upon us or when we have been the benefactor of specific blessings of a physical or tangible nature. These are easy times of praise. On other occasions praise comes with much more hesitation. When our health fails, circumstances are difficult, and people are "doing us wrong," praise becomes a challenge. Instead of brimming with enthusiasm and faith, we may be buried in pain and frustration. That's when we sacrifice our feelings on the altar of truth—looking at who God is and what He has done rather than rely on our feelings. We will to praise and thus surmount the obstacles that would block out our expressions to God.

Verses 2 and 3 point to both instrumental and vocal music as a distinct means for humankind to express praise for our God. The two instruments mentioned were both stringed instruments, but of different size and tone. The harp was the smaller of the two and easily carried. The psaltery (also known as the lyre) might have been larger and capable of producing the deeper base tones.

The author of this psalm also emphasizes ability and exuberance in our praise. To play skillfully means offering the best we are capable of presenting. This would seem to include practicing for a quality offering of praise. Not to be overlooked is the volume and force of that expression. By its very nature, praise can't always be quiet and subdued. The nature and deeds of God are such that the soul wants to burst forth. That doesn't mean each one of us must express praise at the same decibel level or with the same forcefulness. However, praise should rise above our normal expression.

One last aspect of these verses is the "new song." It doesn't mean each of us is to become a songwriter. Rather, this speaks of our regularly praising God for the new blessings which become ours on a daily basis.

C. The Faithfulness (vv. 4, 5)

4. For the word of the Lord is right; and all his works are done in truth.

5. He loveth righteousness and judgment: the earth is full of the goodness of the Lord.

A modern translation presents the second half of verse 4 as follows: "He is faithful in all he does" (*NIV*). God always accomplishes what He chooses to do. Nothing falls beyond the scope of His ability or memory. What an assurance for His children! We never need to worry about God fulfilling His word.

Since these verses are part of viewing God in creation, it reminds us that the principles which were established at the beginning are continuing. The seasons follow each other on a regular basis throughout the millenniums. Imagine the chaos that would reign if the laws of nature would be occasionally jumbled or in some cases reversed. Life as we know it could not be sustained.

Verse 5 reminds how this earth literally teems with the goodness of God. Everything He created is good and orderly. The problems of disorder do not stem from God's inability or lack of righteousness. No! They arise due to the sinfulness of human hearts. They are the result of personal pride and greediness. This is in marked contrast to the righteous conduct of our holy God.

II. GREAT IN POWER
(Psalm 33:6-12)

A. The Creation (vv. 6-9)

6. By the word of the Lord were the heavens made; and all the host of them by the breath of his mouth.

7. He gathereth the waters of the sea together as an heap: he layeth up the depth in storehouses.

8. Let all the earth fear the Lord: let all the inhabitants of the world stand in awe of him.

9. For he spake, and it was done; he commanded, and it stood fast.

The power described in these verses cannot be grasped by our finite minds. God makes something out of nothing by simply speaking it into existence!

We have difficulty comprehending some of the powerful forces around us. The velocity of a storm that flattens everything in its path, the thrust of engines that propel rockets into outer space, and the force of raging waves as they carve their way through the earth are often beyond our imagination. Yet, they are just puny, insignificant forces when placed in comparison with the power of our God.

Verse 6 summarizes the means by which all of creation came into being. It takes us back to Genesis 1, where God repeatedly said "Let . . ." (vv. 9, 11, 20, 24) and "Let there be . . ." (vv. 3, 6, 14). Everything came into being from nothing but through the breath of God.

In Psalm 33:6, "the host of them" refers to the stars and heavenly planets. The writer could not have known their many numbers. Even now new planetary bodies are being discovered. But what appears here is an understanding of their orderliness and constant pattern.

In verse 7 the author refers to "the waters of the sea." In spite of their tremendous power, they stay within the borders defined by God, thus keeping distinct bodies of land and water (see Genesis 1:9, 10). Except on unusual instances when the waters burst forth in what we refer to as "acts of God," they remain a constant treasury of power.

As a result of viewing these two aspects of God's creative power, all the inhabitants of the earth should respond in reverence (v. 8). To a cer-

tain extent we should all fall back in terror. We are so weak and insignificant as to be utterly meaningless to this great God. However, since we are the children of His creation and He loves us, we do not need to be overwhelmed with fear. But we do need to recognize God's omnipotence and sovereignty over this world. This we demonstrate by standing in awe of His being and power.

Verse 9 simply reiterates the creative power of God. Not only do His words and commands bring into existence, but those items remain. There is no temporariness in God's power and ability to create.

B. The Counsel (vv. 10, 11)

10. The Lord bringeth the counsel of the heathen to nought: he maketh the devices of the people of none effect.

11. The counsel of the Lord standeth for ever, the thoughts of his heart to all generations.

These verses raise two questions: (1) Has God been involved in the events of history? (2) Is God currently involved in the affairs of the world? Both of these deserve our consideration.

There are those who deny God's continual working in the events of human history. They believe in God but place Him in a distant, noninvolved position. Such a view was promoted by the deists of the 18th century who said God acts like a clockmaker who winds the clock and lets it run without any further involvement.

Others deny God's continual involvement on the basis of all the cruelty and inequities evident. Their line of reasoning assumes that a loving God who involves Himself in the affairs of the world could never allow these things to happen. What they overlook is the sinfulness of humanity and the fact God gives individuals the freedom to make choices. He didn't make the world as the stage for human robots. It is only through the freedom of choice that God's creations can bring the honor and glory due Him.

Verse 10 speaks plainly of God's intervention in the affairs of humanity. The plans of God will not be overrun by the purposes of the heathen (unbelievers). This doesn't mean God is the checker player who controls every move. Instead it speaks of God's divine will being accomplished regardless of human will. As a result incredible events which defy the patterns of history occur. Most notable would have to be the resurrection of Israel as an independent nation in 1948. For 2,000 years there had been no nation of Israel. Yet, in accord with prophecy, God brought about Israel's rebirth.

Verse 11 projects the unity and continuity of God's plan. His plan of salvation for the world remains steadfast throughout the centuries of time and spans the generations of the people. Unlike humans who change their plans frequently, God maintains His. He consistently projects the same will and purpose to all. This stability of purpose is in direct accord with God's unchanging character. This provides a tremendous assurance!

C. The Chosen (v. 12)

12. Blessed is the nation whose God is the Lord; and the people whom he hath chosen for his own inheritance.

Anytime a nation makes a spiritual commitment to God, other blessings automatically follow. In the case of Israel, God promised them material blessings, long life and possession of their land (Deuteronomy 30:9, 15, 16, 19, 20). Though these blessings were given to His chosen nation which He had developed from Abraham through Isaac, the application is to Gentile nations as well. Anytime a national group of people choose to serve God, there will be a greatly diminished crime rate, material blessings, and the right to ask for God's protection.

Every individual who chooses to serve God becomes His heir. We have the blessings of our relationship with God now, as well as an inheritance to come. The paradox here though is that after death, the greater part of the inheritance is received. The believer inherits an eternal dwelling place and a constant presence with God's Son.

III. GREAT PROTECTOR
(Psalm 33:13-22)

A. His Watchfulness (vv. 13-17)

13. The Lord looketh from heaven; he beholdeth all the sons of men.
14. From the place of his habitation he looketh upon all the inhabitants of the earth.
15. He fashioneth their hearts alike; he considereth all their works.
16. There is no king saved by the multitude of an host: a mighty man is not delivered by much strength.
17. An horse is a vain thing for safety: neither shall he deliver any by his great strength.

God is not of this world. His dwelling place is the heavens, even though His presence permeates the whole earth. This exalted position and ability enables Him to see and know the activities of the entire earth. No place is shielded from His sight or presence. Just think of it—He knows exactly what you and I are doing this very moment. Not only does He know where we are, but He is there with us.

Verses 13 and 14 also emphasize the equality of God's watchfulness. No one is exempted by their geographical location, skin color, occupation, economic level or religious preference. He sees all and desires for each one to be brought into a righteous relationship with Himself.

Verse 15 reminds us of God's creative work within each one. The reference to "hearts" speaks of our mind and emotions. Since God fashioned our hearts, He understands the why behind our thought patterns and emotional responses. So even when we push back thoughts and feelings into the most hidden chambers of our being, He knows how to deal with us. This watchfulness enables Him to seek for the best in our lives. The challenge resides in us. Will we allow Him to will and work within us? Or will we independently seek to go our own way?

Verses 16 and 17 give three examples of power on which people may rely. A king or a president tends to see military might as the means for protection and promoting his own country. A warrior trusts in his own physical strength and the skill with which he uses various weapons. A horse reflects might because for centuries mounted warriors held superiority over foot soldiers. Their strength and speed enabled victory with the possibility of less casualties.

Yet in the broad scheme of events, armies and physical strength and horses aren't the final protectors. None of them provide salvation and eviction from the miry pit of sin. Only God through His plan of salvation provides the greatest safety and victory of life.

B. His Redemption (vv. 18-22)

18. Behold, the eye of the Lord is upon them that fear him, upon them that hope in his mercy;

19. To deliver their soul from death, and to keep them alive in famine.

20. Our soul waiteth for the Lord: he is our help and our shield.

21. For our heart shall rejoice in him, because we have trusted in his holy name.

22. Let thy mercy, O Lord, be upon us, according as we hope in thee.

This passage of Scripture has two key words: *hope* and *trust*. Our spiritual and physical redemption depends on our trusting God as our redeemer. This relationship spans both the good times and the times of crisis. It depends on our understanding that without Him we are utterly helpless.

In verse 18 we see how the Lord has an ever wakeful, undimmed view toward those who stand in reverent awe and trust in His provision. This should always be the attitude of believers. Any other view assumes self-sufficiency. Verse 19 says those who seek and cling to God understand Him to be the deliverer of their souls from spiritual death. They also understand that when physical famine comes to the land due to drought or invading enemies, there is no source of hope other than God's provision.

Verse 20 emphasizes that quiet confidence with which the believer can wait for God's intervention and fulfillment of His will. Probably no one states it any more emphatically than Habakkuk: "Yet I will wait patiently for the day of calamity to come on the nation invading us. Though the fig tree does not bud and there are no grapes on the vines, though the olive crop fails and the fields produce no food, though there are no sheep in the pen and no cattle in the stalls, yet I will rejoice in the Lord, I will be joyful in God my Savior" (Habakkuk 3:16-18, *NIV*).

Regardless of the situation facing us, we can have the assurance of God being our help and shield. One caution needs to be raised: It's not our task to tell God how that deliverance should come. In times of financial difficulty He may make a second job available rather than providing a cash gift. Either way it is provision. There may be occasions of stress and pain, and we desire God to take away the source. But in His wisdom the choice of provision might be the strength to sustain rather than eradicate it.

When we hope in God we refrain from trying to dictate the means of redemption in our lives. Instead we strive to rest in Him, knowing that His wisdom and foresight far exceeds our own. Sometimes this necessitates asking for patience so we can remain quietly under the shelter of His protective wings. That's when we need to take a lesson from a little chick as it snuggles under the encompassing wings of the mother hen. It understands the security there and only rarely peeks out to see the rest of the world.

GOLDEN TEXT HOMILY

"THE EYE OF THE LORD IS UPON THEM THAT FEAR HIM, UPON THEM THAT HOPE IN HIS MERCY" (Psalm 33:18).

To those who fear God and who hope in His mercy, to be under the watchful eye of the Lord is a wonderful place of refuge. In Psalm 11:4 the Scripture teaches us that "His eyes behold, His eyelids test the sons of men" (NKJV), and in 66:7 the Bible states, "His eyes behold the nations." Each time within the Scripture that we read of the "eyes of God" or any derivative thereof, it always carries connotations of God's safety or defense for His children. To the child of God, to know that I am the object of His vision and to know that He keeps me in His sight is a tremendous consolation.

His constant cognizance of all things blankets my life with protection. His omnipotent position is unthreatened. His reign is without end. He is just and altogether righteous. It is out of these inherent traits that He holds the world within His hands. The forces of evil are limited to His discretion. Satan is constrained to His will. God will work all things together for our good and His glory so that even the troubles of life have purpose and meaning. I will not be afraid or dismayed, for through faith in Christ I know He will not fail me. This wonderful place of refuge will forever protect me and serve as my defense. The eye of the Lord is upon me!—**Steven P. Darnell**

SENTENCE SERMONS

GOD IS unchanging in His character.

—Selected

MAN PROPOSES, but God disposes.

—Thomas à Kempis

THE HISTORY of all the great characters in the Bible is summed up in this one sentence: They acquainted themselves with God, and acquiesced His will in all things.

—Richard Ceil

EVANGELISM APPLICATION

CHRISTIANS WHO TRUST GOD AND WORSHIP HIM ARE POWERFUL TESTIMONIES TO THE UNSAVED.

As Christians we should be ready to share what a difference accepting Jesus as Savior and Lord makes in our lives. How can we possibly remain quiet about this cure for sin and opportunity for a new fullness of life?

Words are powerful means of communication. However, they are powerless if our actions and lifestyle fail to corroborate our testimony. People want proof! They want to know the genuineness of our witness.

There's no doubt that we need more people speaking of their faith. But even more importantly, we need people who are living their faith.

Lifestyle evangelism must accompany verbal witness.

Two areas of our daily living will reflect the truthfulness of our words. The first is demonstrating our trust in God. In times of difficulty we rely on the truths and principles of Scripture rather than the norms of our culture. The second is worship. If we claim to be serving such a majestic God, then we should be regularly worshiping Him and proclaiming His worth. Church attendance is only one dimension of it. This worship needs to be evident anytime and anyplace when we focus on His greatness.

So the bottom line is this: Let's testify by our trust and worship.

ILLUMINATING THE LESSON

The passengers on the train were uneasy as they sped along through the dark, stormy night. The lightning was flashing, black clouds were rolling, and the train was traveling fast. The fear and tension among the passengers was evident.

One little fellow, however, sitting all by himself, seemed utterly unaware of the storm or the speed of the train. He was amusing himself with a few toys.

One of the passengers spoke to him. "Sonny, I see you are alone on the train. Aren't you afraid to travel alone on such a stormy night?"

The lad looked up with a smile and answered, "No ma'am, I ain't afraid. My daddy's the engineer."
—**Brethren Quarterly**

DAILY BIBLE READINGS

M. Great in Creation.
   Psalm 8:1-9
T. Great in Might.
   Isaiah 40:18-26
W. Great in Mercy.
   Isaiah 55:1-7
T. Great in Providential Care.
   Matthew 6:24-34
F. Great in Love.
   Ephesians 2:1-10
S. Great in Redemption.
   1 Peter 1:3-12

TRUTH SEARCH:
Creatively Teaching the Word

Aim: Students will reaffirm their hope in Almighty God.

Items needed: Paper, pencils, marker board, marker, eraser

FOCUS

Write *TRUST & HOPE* at the top of the marker board. Then ask the class to name things other than God and His Word in which people put their trust and hope. Their answers might include the stock market, horoscopes, insurance policies, friends, family, money, physical strength, military power, brain power, the government, and so on.

Next, have students name events that could cause these various items to fail. (For instance, divorce could break up a family; recession could ruin the stock market; corruption could topple the government.) As each event is named, erase the corresponding source of hope. When the board has been completely erased, write *GOD* on the board.

Can God ever fail? Let's see what Psalm 33 says about it.

EXPLORE

Divide your class into small groups, and have each group answer questions regarding one of the following three passages. When the groups have finished, have them report their findings to the entire class.

Psalm 33:1-5

1. *According to verse 1, who should praise the Lord? Why?*
2. *What specific means of praise are given in verses 2 and 3?*
3. *Explain the reasons for praise given in verse 4.*
4. *Explain the reasons for praise given in verse 5.*
5. *List specific evidences of God's unfailing love, righteousness,* *faithfulness, and the truthfulness of His Word.*

Psalm 33:6-12

1. *How did God create the earth and heavens (vv. 6, 9)? What does this tell you about God?*
2. *What are people commanded to do in verse 8? Why?*
3. *Compare the plans of people and nations with the plans of God (vv. 10, 11).*
4. *Who are the most blessed people on earth (v. 12)? Why?*

Psalm 33:13-19

1. *How much interest does God have in the affairs of earth and humanity (vv. 13-15)? How do you know?*
2. *Compare military strength with divine power (vv. 16, 17).*
3. *Where should our hope rest, and why (v. 18)?*
4. *What two powerful enemies can God deliver us from (v. 19)? Describe accounts from Scripture when God accomplished such deliverance.*

RESPOND

Have everyone stand and read Psalm 33:20-22 aloud with you:

"Our soul waiteth for the Lord: he is our help and our shield. For our heart shall rejoice in him, because we have trusted in his holy name. Let thy mercy, O Lord, be upon us, according as we hope in thee."

These three verses contain three key words telling us how to respond to the greatness of God. Verse 20 says, "Wait"; verse 21 says, "Rejoice"; verse 22 says, "Hope."

Whatever you need God to do in your life, don't lose your hope in Him. Instead, be willing to wait. And as you wait, rejoice in Him!

Read verses 20-22 aloud together again.

Path to Deliverance

Study Text: Psalm 34:1-22
Objective: To understand God's ability and desire to deliver His people and trust in Him.
Time: Written by David around 1010 B.C.
Place: Probably the wilderness of Judah
Golden Text: "Many are the afflictions of the righteous: but the Lord delivereth him out of them all" (Psalm 34:19).
Central Truth: Christians can be confident in the knowledge that God's deliverance is always timely.
Evangelism Emphasis: Sinners find deliverance from sin when they accept Christ as Savior.

PRINTED TEXT

Psalm 34:1. I will bless the Lord at all times: his praise shall continually be in my mouth.

2. My soul shall make her boast in the Lord: the humble shall hear thereof, and be glad.

3. O magnify the Lord with me, and let us exalt his name together.

4. I sought the Lord, and he heard me, and delivered me from all my fears.

5. They looked unto him, and were lightened: and their faces were not ashamed.

6. This poor man cried, and the Lord heard him, and saved him out of all his troubles.

7. The angel of the Lord encampeth round about them that fear him, and delivereth them.

8. O taste and see that the Lord is good: blessed is the man that trusteth in him.

9. O fear the Lord, ye his saints: for there is no want to them that fear him.

10. The young lions do lack, and suffer hunger: but they that seek the Lord shall not want any good thing.

11. Come, ye children, hearken unto me: I will teach you the fear of the Lord.

12. What man is he that desireth life, and loveth many days, that he may see good?

13. Keep thy tongue from evil, and thy lips from speaking guile.

14. Depart from evil, and do good; seek peace, and pursue it.

15. The eyes of the Lord are upon the righteous, and his ears are open unto their cry.

16. The face of the Lord is against them that do evil, to cut off the remembrance of them from the earth.

17. The righteous cry, and the Lord heareth, and delivereth them out of all their troubles.

18. The Lord is nigh unto them that are of a broken heart; and saveth such as be of a contrite spirit.

19. Many are the afflictions of the righteous: but the Lord delivereth him out of them all.

20. He keepeth all his bones: not one of them is broken.

21. Evil shall slay the wicked: and they that hate the righteous shall be desolate.

22. The Lord redeemeth the soul of his servants: and none of them that trust in him shall be desolate.

LESSON OUTLINE

I. PRACTICE TRUE WORSHIP
   A. Regular Worship
   B. Genuine Worship
II. SEEK GOD'S HELP
   A. Call for Help
   B. Take Refuge
   C. Fear the Lord
III. EXPECT DELIVERANCE
   A. Deliverance of the Righteous
   B. Consequences of the Wicked

LESSON EXPOSITION

INTRODUCTION

None of us is exempt from trouble and tragedy. It never considers our name, title, wealth or family. Disease strikes without warning. Accidents happen so quickly. Relationships that seemed permanent begin to shatter.

So what do we do when crises come? We must turn to our omniscient God who watches over and knows everything we are encountering. Our Savior and Lord, Jesus Christ, knows the frailties and complications of life in this human flesh. And He intercedes to the Father on our behalf.

In the previous lesson the emphasis was placed on the great God we serve and His abilities. Today's lesson looks at the steps the believer must take to receive deliverance from problems.

The path we will be studying has three distinct segments: *worshiping*, *seeking* and *expecting*. Though we will be studying them within the context of deliverance in time of need, they really are basic aspects which should continually be a part of our life in Christ. Through the previous decades all three of them have received a considerable amount of attention. However, the worship emphasis of the past 30-plus years places it in the forefront of familiarity.

Yet, familiarity doesn't guarantee knowledge of the subject. For example, many people are familiar with the VW "bug." But, it doesn't mean we understand the mechanical aspects of the engine. The same applies to worship. We may be involved in some form of it but not at the depth we should be.

The second segment, seeking for God's help, raises some questions for consideration. Do we seek God's help only in crises? Do we seek God only for the big problems and ignore Him when the little difficulties antagonize us? And how do we go about seeking God's help?

Our final segment is expectation. This can prove to be difficult. How can we expect God's deliverance in situations where everything seems hopeless? How can we be people of faith when other believers question our chosen path? These are tough questions that deserve consideration before finding ourselves in the afflictions and difficulties that come to the righteous.

Today's lesson covers the entire 34th psalm, which was written by David, who had fled from King Saul. Hoping to escape and remain anonymous, he went to the Philistine city of Gath. Once his identity was recognized, the king had David brought to him. Fearing for his life, he feigned insanity, knowing the Philistines would not kill one mentally afflicted. So here we find the anointed king of Israel letting spittle run down his beard. His physical antics even went so far as to include marking the gates in some form of physical manner. As a result he was freed. (Read 1 Samuel 21:10-15; 22:1.) With this situation in mind, let's study the verses.

I. PRACTICE TRUE WORSHIP
   (Psalm 34:1-5)

A. Regular Worship (vv. 1-3)

1. I will bless the Lord at all times: his praise shall continually be in my mouth.

2. My soul shall make her boast in the Lord: the humble shall hear thereof, and be glad.

3. O magnify the Lord with me, and let us exalt his name together.

David begins this psalm with a twofold statement: He will worship, and it will be a regular practice. There is to be no time or situation that will preclude this action and relationship. Not only does this statement provide us with a great deal of material for discussion but also a terrific example to follow.

In verse 1 David speaks of blessing the Lord. The word *bless* comes from a root word which includes to kneel in acknowledgment, to praise and to worship. It implies our declaring the worth of God. *Worship* is "my response to God declaring His worth as He has revealed Himself to me."

Verse 1 also reminds us that worship isn't to be limited to a particular time or place. It is not to be confined to the times of service held in the sanctuary.

God's presence isn't limited to our church buildings. He is omnipresent. We need to recognize this and offer our worship throughout the day regardless of the location. It may be a brief moment where we quietly say, "Lord, I worship You." It may be in the form of meditating on Him while performing a variety of household chores. My personal choice is while mowing the lawn. Anytime and anyplace is a good time to worship our great God!

Worship stems from our relationship with God and our knowledge of Him. It should never be dependent on a particular musical background or emotional atmosphere. Worship begins from within and then proceeds outwardly to be evidenced by our words and actions. There's no doubt it is easy to worship as we are surrounded by other worshipers and hear beautiful music extolling the greatness of God. Yet, it is equally easy to worship when we begin to meditate on His greatness and goodness in our own lives.

When David states "I will," he indicates that worship is a personal choice. We decide *if* and *when* we are going to worship. That's why some individuals leave a service with the praise of God on their lips while others leave having done nothing more than fulfill a ritual. All heard and saw the same stimuli. But each made a different choice. This is a truth that worship leaders need to understand. All that can be done is offer an opportunity.

In verse 2 David speaks of boasting in the Lord. We often associate the word *boast* with a person who is bragging about himself, his accomplishments or even possessions. But there is a positive side to boasting when it uplifts the truth without personal benefit. To boast in the Lord means to glory in who He is and what He has done. In reality, that is all any of us have to boast about. Everything we have become, do or possess comes from His empowerment.

The second part of verse 2 projects the benefit that comes to others as a result of our boasting in the Lord. The *humble* referred to here are those who are experiencing some form of affliction. Hearing the testimony of others in worship encourages them to be able to rejoice as well. It encourages them and builds their faith. Our boasts in God enable the hurting to wait and to believe in God's intervention in their lives.

In verse 3 we are encouraged to magnify the Lord. This means to make Him great in the eyes of others. Then together all may praise Him. This reminds us there are individuals who need to once again be reminded of God's greatness. For whatever the reason, they have a dimmed vision. But our magnifying the Lord enables them to once again see Him in all His glory and majesty. There are times when we who have served the Lord for many years may have lost the freshness of our experience. We need others to emphasize to us the need for revitalizing our worship.

B. Genuine Worship (vv. 4, 5)

4. I sought the Lord, and he heard me, and delivered me from all my fears.

5. They looked unto him, and were lightened: and their faces were not ashamed.

These two verses provide a personal testimony of how worship impacted David. How humiliating it must have been for David to feign insanity in order to preserve his life! He could have been very angry with God for allowing such an experience. He could have made some sharp accusations. Instead, he sought the Lord and found deliverance from his fears. Not only did his fears disappear, but verse 5 indicates a radiance came upon his face. All traces of shame were removed, and in its place was the glow that comes from a worship encounter with God.

These two verses could be studied under several possible headings; however, the choice of "genuine worship" reflects the impact that occurs when real worship is offered. The challenge for each of us continues to be doing more than offering only exterior words and actions. They must be accompanied with that commitment and desire for it to be acceptable to God. The issue here isn't liturgical worship versus free style. All of us must remember that the Bible doesn't prescribe a standard style or form of worship. But God does expect there to be a correlation between the interior and exterior.

Genuine worship enables us to see beyond our current circumstances. God becomes the center of our focus and our surroundings become secondary. Worship enables us to experience a relationship of joy and fulfillment separate from our physical situation. Worship helps us to put aside our fears as we lean on our God. Worship opens doors of understanding that previously were shut.

David's testimony provides a superb example of how worship can positively impact a negative situation. The conclusion is that in crises, as we are asking "Why?" we must not forget to offer genuine worship. For in doing so our questions may be answered even while our countenance is changed.

II. SEEK GOD'S HELP
(Psalm 34:6-14)

A. Call for Help (vv. 6, 7)

6. This poor man cried, and the Lord heard him, and saved him out of all his troubles.

7. The angel of the Lord encampeth round about them that fear him, and delivereth them.

As long as we live in these bodies of flesh and are on this earth, there will be difficulties. Some of them will be insurmountable in our own strength. Then we face the question, "What will I do"? The situation may vary our choices, but one remains constant: Will I seek God's help in this problem?

It is wisdom rather than weakness to seek God's help and direction in our times of difficulty. Our heavenly Father desires involvement in our lives during both the good and the bad times. Asking God for help isn't using religion as a crutch. Rather, it speaks of the relationship of a child and his father.

David was in a desperate situation. On one hand the king of Israel, Saul (who was also his father-in-law), wanted to kill him. On the other hand the Philistines had recognized David as the one who only a few years earlier had killed their champion, Goliath. He couldn't flee or fight his way out of this confrontation. His only option was to seek God's help.

Notice how David summarized what took place—the Lord heard and delivered. He credited the Lord with enabling him to escape, though it necessitated his acting out the part of an insane person. The issue here must not be the means. We need to zero in on the fact of God's intervention. David left the Philistine city physically whole and free!

In verse 7 David said, "The angel of the Lord encamps around those who fear him" (NIV). He understood how God surrounds His children and offers protection. But who is the angel of the Lord? A common belief is that this is the preincarnate second person of the Trinity. There are various instances in the Old Testament when the angel of the Lord appeared and offered assistance. For example, on two occasions Hagar, Sarah's handmaiden, was helped by the angel of the Lord (see Genesis 16:7; 21:17). For us this means God cares enough for each one of us to intercede in our behalf.

The story of blind Bartimaeus (Mark 10:46-52) deserves consideration here. Knowing that Jesus was passing by, he called out for mercy. Even when those around rebuked him, Bartimaeus persisted. Jesus heard and stopped. Then He asked, "What do you want me to do for you?" (v. 51, NIV). Surely his need was obvious—he was a blind man. Yet, we see a principle. We need to call on God for help and state our need. Jesus knows what we are in need of even before we ask, yet He wants us to ask (Matthew 6:8). Asking is a vital part of the dependent relationship between child and Father.

B. Take Refuge (vv. 8-10)

8. O taste and see that the Lord is good: blessed is the man that trusteth in him.

9. O fear the Lord, ye his saints: for there is no want to them that fear him.

10. The young lions do lack, and suffer hunger: but they that seek the Lord shall not want any good thing.

The second part of verse 8 has been translated, "Blessed is the man who takes refuge in him" (NIV). Seeking God's help begins with calling for help. But the second step is to take refuge in Him instead of trusting in ourselves or others. We place our total being in God's protective care. This can be very difficult for many believers. For some, their personality gets in the way. Having lived in such a self-sufficient manner, they find it difficult to give up control and hide in God. Others have difficulty due to not understanding what God wants to do for them. They do not possess the full understanding of God's love for them as individuals.

Verse 8 begins with a call to experience. David wanted others to experience the same trust and refuge that was his. It's like somebody wanting us to taste a particular food. That person enjoys it so much that he or she wants you to have the same pleasure in eating. Like the commercial of some years back, the person is saying, "Try it, you'll like it." The psalmist knew that no one who took refuge in the Lord would ever find it to be less than good and the right thing to do.

The phrase "there is no want" (v. 9) does not refer to our wish list. Instead it refers to deficiencies. When we trust in the Lord and take refuge, He supplies our needs. This doesn't mean we will never be short of money or that the cupboards will never be bare. This speaks of His taking us through those crises that stretch our faith and even our physical being. Remember the apostle Paul's words to the Philippian church: "Not that I speak in respect of want: for I have learned, in whatsoever state I am, therewith to be content" (4:11). Then, at the right time and in means we may never expect, our needs will be met.

C. Fear the Lord (vv. 11-14)

11. Come, ye children, hearken unto me: I will teach you the fear of the Lord.
12. What man is he that desireth life, and loveth many days, that he may see good?
13. Keep thy tongue from evil, and thy lips from speaking guile.
14. Depart from evil, and do good; seek peace, and pursue it.

If we desire God's help, there are some requirements on our part. Certain attitudes and actions need to be evident in our lifestyle that demonstrate our relationship with our God. It is not sufficient to simply stand in awe of this great God who holds the universe in the palm of His hand. This awe must become a true religion that reflects the God we serve. With this in mind, the writer calls us to listen to some specific words of ethical wisdom. These instructions can be seen in a variety of places in both the Old and New Testaments.

In verse 11 the writer emphasizes that he will teach us. This indicates that what follows doesn't come naturally. It also points out that just because we become a follower of God doesn't mean these things automatically become a part of our being. Many aspects of our spiritual life need to be cultivated through study of the Word, personal choice and the empowerment of the Holy Spirit.

Before looking at specific areas, the writer inserts a question in verse 12. It could be restated as "Who doesn't want to live a long life full of good?" The obvious answer would be "Very few." To lead a good life, there are some distinct directions to be followed.

First, each of us is to take great care to ensure that we speak truth. The tongue can be a tremendous weapon of division and destruction. It can destroy people's self-image as well as their character and reputation. No wonder James spends so much time in the third chapter of his epistle dealing with its harmful potential. Verse 8 stands out, "But the tongue can no man tame; it is an unruly evil, full of deadly poison." One person's ill-advised comments can result in a divisiveness which hinders the body of Christ from accomplishing its goals.

Immediately following is the pursuit of peace. It involves our not disturbing a peaceful situation as well as attempting to bring peace to conflict. As believers, we should have the peace of God within, which then spills over to wherever we are. The seventh beatitude applies here. Jesus said, "Blessed are the peacemakers: for they shall be called the children of God" (Matthew 5:9). Paul wrote, "Live in peace" (2 Corinthians 13:11). Anyone who does not strive for the wholeness and well-being of Christ's body, while still maintaining truth, can't possibly claim to be living in the fear of the Lord.

III. EXPECT DELIVERANCE
(Psalm 34:15-22)

A. Deliverance of the Righteous
(vv. 15-20)

15. The eyes of the Lord are upon the righteous, and his ears are open unto their cry.
16. The face of the Lord is against them that do evil, to cut off the remembrance of them from the earth.
17. The righteous cry, and the Lord heareth, and delivereth them out of all their troubles.
18. The Lord is nigh unto them that are of a broken heart; and saveth such as be of a contrite spirit.
19. Many are the afflictions of the righteous: but the Lord delivereth him out of them all.
20. He keepeth all his bones: not one of them is broken.

If God is as great as His Word declares and as we believe, then it becomes only logical that we can expect deliverance when in difficulty.

If God loves us and watches over us as His Word states, then it should be normative to experience God's intervention in our problems.

Verse 15 sets the stage for the rest of the verses in this section. It establishes the fact of God's watchfulness and care. He knows what is happening in our lives and hears as we cry out to Him. His children are never in a state of isolation or hidden from view. The Lord's ears are not deafened nor turned to another frequency as we cry out for help. What a consolation! As children of God we have the security of knowing we are always within the sight and hearing of our heavenly Father.

The righteous—God's children—are subject to a wide variety of distresses. We experience fatigue, illness, handicaps and stress. The pressures of family life, making a living and a changing culture impact us. There is also our spiritual enemy, the devil, and all his forces who strive to strip us of our life in Christ either through temptation or direct attack.

Within this framework of many distresses the writer points out that "the Lord is close to the brokenhearted and saves those who are crushed in spirit" (v. 18, *NIV*). How consoling! When we are in our greatest distress and our lowest ebb, He is right there for us. In our hour of need He draws especially close. All we have to do is open ourselves to His comfort and deliverance.

Repeatedly the psalmist emphasizes that our God isn't limited when it comes to deliverance; instead, He delivers believers from all troubles and afflictions (vv. 17, 19). So how do we interpret this? Does it mean He takes away all my problems, heals me every time I am ill, and makes all my days free from conflict? It does not. Just consider the next several years of David's life. He remained a fugitive from Saul, and many years would pass before he finally became the king of all Israel.

Yet, this "man after God's own heart" spoke of deliverance from "all."

This is where we must consider the various aspects of deliverance. Usually we associate it with our problems being removed. And God does do that for His children. However, another form of deliverance is when anxiety and frustration are removed, and in their place God infuses peace and assurance. We are able to face our situation with strength even though the source of pain and disruption remains.

Verse 20 speaks of protecting the bones. To begin with, this is a messianic prophecy that none of Christ's bones would be broken though experiencing crucifixion. Usually the leg bones were broken to heighten the pain while shortening the death process. The application of this verse to the whole topic of discussion must be understood in its reference to the skeletal framework of our bodies. Thus the writer of this psalm was speaking of the whole person. Nothing of our physical, spiritual, mental or emotional being is beyond the scope of His deliverance. He can heal a broken heart just as easily as a broken hand. He can protect our mind just as easily as our body. On and on the comparison list could go. The bottom line is that He can deliver any dimension of the righteous in fulfilling His will.

B. Consequences of the Wicked (vv. 21, 22)

21. Evil shall slay the wicked: and they that hate the righteous shall be desolate.

22. The Lord redeemeth the soul of his servants: and none of them that trust in him shall be desolate.

Even while considering the deliverance of the righteous, a contrast still remains. What about the wicked? What can they expect?

Unlike the righteous who have the hope of God's deliverance, the wicked can only be certain of their death. Evil men and women automatically harbor hatred and animosity toward those who live and promote righteousness. Their sin nature predisposes them to these actions. This in turn causes them to become the recipients of God's judgment. Their sins not only are noticed but punished for being in opposition to truth and God's children.

Evildoers fail to understand that within themselves they possess the seed of their own destruction. Even while seeming to be in control of their own lives, doing what pleases themselves, they are fostering the seed of sin which produces eternal death. This can be seen so clearly in the Book of Habakkuk. The prophet couldn't understand why God would use the heathen to bring punishment to Judah for its sinfulness. In chapter 2 God informed him the Babylonians would not escape punishment for their own sins. Though for the moment they would appear as the conquerors, a time of destruction awaited them. God's holiness would not allow them to continue without retribution.

Psalm 34 closes on the high note of deliverance. The plan of salvation will not fail anyone who chooses to put their trust in God. Through the sacrifices of the Old Testament and now through the sacrificial death of Jesus Christ, there is salvation. God delivers us from a variety of physical, emotional and even intellectual dilemmas. But the greatest deliverance is from sin which destroys. In its place we are declared righteous as a result of confessing our sins and accepting Jesus as Savior and Lord.

GOLDEN TEXT HOMILY

"MANY ARE THE AFFLICTIONS OF THE RIGHTEOUS: BUT THE LORD DELIVERETH HIM OUT OF THEM ALL" (Psalm 34:19).

Sometimes life stinks! There is just no other way to describe those times when life's circumstances bring pain and sorrow without notice. We've all been there. No one is immune; regardless of who you are, you find that trouble knows your name and address.

Peggy was a woman of faith who loved the Lord and served Him with distinction. She always tried to reflect God's goodness and grace in her life. Then Peggy's husband was killed in a hunting accident. The loss was difficult, but God helped and she attempted to move on with her life. Soon Peggy's daughter was stricken with cancer and a son was laid off from his job. Why would a good person like Peggy have to deal with such stress and strain? Why would God permit her life to know such sorrow?

Like Peggy, we all have questions with no answers. Yet, we are comforted to remember the words of the Lord: "For he is faithful that promised. . . . I will never leave thee, nor forsake thee. So that we may boldly say, The Lord is my helper, and I will not fear what man shall do unto me" (Hebrews 10:23; 13:5, 6). Nothing catches God by surprise, for He is faithful. Count on Him!—**Bill Isaacs**

SENTENCE SERMONS

CHRISTIANS CAN BE CONFIDENT in the knowledge that God's deliverance is always timely.

—Selected

VICTORY IS GAINED only through conflict.

—Quotable Quotations

THE REAL PROBLEM is not why some pious, humble believing people suffer, but why some do not.

—C.S. Lewis

EVANGELISM APPLICATION

SINNERS FIND DELIVERANCE FROM SIN WHEN THEY ACCEPT CHRIST AS SAVIOR.

Romans 10:14 says, "How then shall they call on him in whom they have not believed? and how shall they believe in him of whom they have not heard? and how shall they hear without a preacher?" Usually we apply this verse to the need of bringing the gospel to those who have never heard.

But maybe we should expand our application. It's not just hearing of God's love through Jesus Christ. It includes being made aware of the destruction which awaits them unless they come into relationship with Jesus Christ. God's holiness demands justice for sin.

Many sinners know of Jesus Christ and His death on Calvary. But they do not believe God will bring judgment on them for their actions. They are in desperate need to hear the truth and experience deliverance.

We must be the messengers of warning and deliverance!

ILLUMINATING THE LESSON

John Haggai said, "Your pain has a purpose. I can't tell you what that purpose is—that is something you will discover in your own walk with God."

DAILY BIBLE READINGS

M. Give Glory to the Lord.
   Psalm 96:1-13
T. God's Goodness Evokes Praise.
   Psalm 98:1-9
W. Deliverance From Death.
   Psalm 116:1-8
T. Faith Reaches Out.
   Luke 7:1-10
F. Persistent Faith.
   Luke 18:35-43
S. Deliverance Promised.
   Acts 27:13-25

TRUTH SEARCH:
Creatively Teaching the Word

Aim: Students will pray for God to deliver people in need.

Items needed: Rattrap, index cards, pencils

FOCUS

Display the rattrap. Encourage students to talk about times they have tried to catch a mouse or rat.

Once a rat is caught in one of these traps, it usually does not get out alive. That's why these traps haven't changed much over the years—they're deadly.

Use a marker to write *SATAN* on the back of the trap. Show the class.

• *What are some of the deadly traps Satan uses to snare people?*

If we try to escape Satan's lethal traps in our own power, we will be as unsuccessful as the trapped rat. However, none of Satan's devices are stronger than God's power to deliver.

EXPLORE

Have all the students stand and open their Bible to Psalm 34. Lead them in reading verses 1-3 with lots of enthusiasm. Then lead them in lifting their hands and praising the Lord aloud.

This psalm encourages us to praise the Lord by citing many of the ways He delivers us.

• *What is one trap God delivers people from (vv. 4, 5)?*

• *According to verses 6 and 7, why should we not be consumed by fear?*

Ask students who have been delivered from fear to raise their hand. Then encourage a volunteer or two to testify about it.

Have everyone read verse 8 aloud with you. **When we put our trust in the Lord, we find out how good and powerful He is.**

• *What is another trap from which God can deliver (vv. 9, 10)?*

• *Has God ever provided for you when you were in desperate need of food, shelter or clothing?*

Encourage students to offer testimonies of God's provision.

• *According to verse 17, what troubles can God deliver us from?*

• *What clue does verse 18 give concerning what we should do when we are in trouble?*

Encourage individuals to testify about how God saved them from trouble when they approached Him with a broken heart.

• *According to verses 19 and 20, what is a third trap from which God delivers His people?*

Encourage students to testify about being healed by God.

• *The most important deliverance of all is found in verse 22. What is it?*

Encourage students to testify about God saving their soul.

God has delivered people from every kind of satanic trap.

RESPOND

Pass out an index card and pencil to every student. Then have everyone read verse 17 aloud together.

We are going to pray for people who need to be delivered from snares of Satan.

Encourage everyone to think of one person who needs deliverance, then to write down that person's first name. Next have students break into small groups. Ask members to add the names from their partners' lists onto their cards.

Now have the members of each group to pray for one another's requests. Finally, encourage everyone to take the cards home as a prayer reminder.

Faith on Trial

Study Text: Psalm 73:1-28
Objective: To know that God understands our difficulties and determine to seek His help.
Golden Text: "It is good for me to draw near to God: I have put my trust in the Lord God, that I may declare all thy works" (Psalm 73:28).
Central Truth: We must learn to trust God in all circumstances.
Evangelism Emphasis: Christians must warn sinners that God's judgment is certain.

PRINTED TEXT

Psalm 73:1. Truly God is good to Israel, even to such as are of a clean heart.

2. But as for me, my feet were almost gone; my steps had well nigh slipped.

3. For I was envious at the foolish, when I saw the prosperity of the wicked.

4. For there are no bands in their death: but their strength is firm.

5. They are not in trouble as other men; neither are they plagued like other men.

6 Therefore pride compasseth them about as a chain; violence covereth them as a garment.

7. Their eyes stand out with fatness: they have more than heart could wish.

8. They are corrupt, and speak wickedly concerning oppression: they speak loftily.

9. They set their mouth against the heavens, and their tongue walketh through the earth.

10. Therefore his people return hither: and waters of a full cup are wrung out to them.

11. And they say, How doth God know? and is there knowledge in the most High?

12. Behold, these are the ungodly, who prosper in the world; they increase in riches.

13. Verily I have cleansed my heart in vain, and washed my hands in innocency.

14. For all the day long have I been plagued, and chastened every morning.

15. If I say, I will speak thus; behold, I should offend against the generation of thy children.

16. When I thought to know this, it was too painful for me;

17. Until I went into the sanctuary of God; then understood I their end.

18. Surely thou didst set them in slippery places: thou castedst them down into destruction.

24. Thou shalt guide me with thy counsel, and afterward receive me to glory.

25. Whom have I in heaven but thee? and there is none upon earth that I desire beside thee.

26. My flesh and my heart faileth: but God is the strength of my heart, and my portion for ever.

27. For, lo, they that are far from thee shall perish: thou hast destroyed all them that go a whoring from thee.

28. But it is good for me to draw near to God: I have put my trust in the Lord God, that I may declare all thy works.

LESSON OUTLINE

I. FAITH TESTED
   A. The Envy of the Righteous
   B. The Prosperity of the Wicked
   C. The Thoughts of the Righteous
II. SUSTAINED BY TRUTH
   A. The Impact of Worship
   B. The Future of the Wicked
   C. The Recognition of Truth
III. FAITH RENEWED
   A. Our Strength in God
   B. Our Trust in God

LESSON EXPOSITION

INTRODUCTION

How often we have heard this quotation: "If ye have faith as a grain of mustard seed, ye shall say unto this mountain, Remove hence to yonder place; and it shall remove" (Matthew 17:20).

Then there is Hebrews 11:1, the oft-quoted definition of *faith*: "Now faith is the substance of things hoped for, the evidence of things not seen."

We must know these and other important verses on faith. Faith is the means by which we come to Christ and by which we live a victorious life in Him. Today's lesson focuses on those times when doubt attempts to override or undermine our faith.

Faith can be defined as "commitment, confidence and concentrated trust." Faith cannot mature beyond the level of one's commitment. It also cannot be expected to develop and to mature when spiritual commitment swings back and forth or is in an up-and-down cycle.

The confidence aspect of faith enables the believer to endure pain, suffering, loss and even approaching death with peace of mind and heart. It provides the ability to believe in the invisible which is beyond the horizon of current sight and understanding.

The final aspect of the definition is *trust*, but the adjective *concentrated* is added to emphasize the aspect of single reliance. Concentrated or individual trust is a must for a mature, working faith. It means we relinquish control. Regardless of what He asks or where He leads, our trust causes us to comply and confirm the direction.

Circumstances may occur in our lives which severely test the fiber of our faith. Though we may not always appreciate those testings at the moment, they serve as stimuli to cling to the truth we know and trust. None of us can truly know the condition of our faith unless we are tested.

There are times when the inequities of life stand as a major block in our road of faith. Such is the case in today's lesson. The author of this psalm looked around and in his mind questioned why the bad guys appeared to be more blessed than the good guys. It grinded him to the point of placing his faith on trial.

I. FAITH TESTED (Psalm 73:1-15)

A. The Envy of the Righteous (vv. 1-3)

1. Truly God is good to Israel, even to such as are of a clean heart.
2. But as for me, my feet were almost gone; my steps had well nigh slipped.
3. For I was envious at the foolish, when I saw the prosperity of the wicked.

These verses present the problem facing the righteous person of faith. He understands that those whose hearts are pure can be assured of God's favor. However, after making this faith assertion, he presents the problem with which he has been grappling—the success of the wicked. Why do those who aren't serving God have an abundance of material goods? It doesn't seem fair.

In these few verses we see how easy it is for our eyes as well as our mind to become sidetracked. Instead of focusing on God's care and blessing, we begin to compare it with what is happening in the lives of the unrighteous. The common result is envy, which eats away at us until it drains our spirituality. Unless there is a spiritual renewal, it will eventually lead to our spiritual death.

The author refers to this crisis in verse 2. His spiritual feet are slipping. As a result of losing what could be described as a doctrinal foothold, he finds himself in a precarious position. Except for a distinct event which is discussed in verse 17, he could have been in the same condition as the unrighteous whom he envied—separated eternally from God.

This situation reminds us of the necessity to remain focused on the truths of God and His personal care for us. Any comparison outside of this circle will have a negative impact on our relationship with the heavenly Father.

B. The Prosperity of the Wicked
   (vv. 4-12)

4. For there are no bands in their death: but their strength is firm.

5. They are not in trouble as other men; neither are they plagued like other men.

6. Therefore pride compasseth them about as a chain; violence covereth them as a garment.

7. Their eyes stand out with fatness: they have more than heart could wish.

8. They are corrupt, and speak wickedly concerning oppression: they speak loftily.

9. They set their mouth against the heavens, and their tongue walketh through the earth.

10. Therefore his people return hither: and waters of a full cup are wrung out to them.

11. And they say, How doth God know? and is there knowledge in the most High?

12. Behold, these are the ungodly, who prosper in the world; they increase in riches.

In describing the unrighteous, the psalmist Asaph begins with their physical well-being. Verse 4 speaks of their health. A more understandable translation of this verse is as follows: "They suffer no violent pain; their body is well nourished" (*Berk.*). These individuals had healthy bodies, reflecting an abundance of nourishment which came from their prosperity. Another logical result of this description would be longer lives and freedom from intense suffering prior to death.

Verse 5 repeats the concepts of the previous verse. The *New International Version* reads, "They are free from the burdens common to man; they are not plagued by human ills." This would be especially noticeable to the individual who was serving God and at the same time battling illness and other difficulties.

The arrogance of these ungodly ones was very visible. They wore it as a decoration around their necks and allowed violence to be their covering garment. The evil stood forth for all to see on the outside. From the abundance of their hearts, their mouths were speaking boastful and blasphemous words. They did not hesitate to state their positions in opposition to God. Instead of standing in awe of God, these individuals projected themselves as having the right to determine their own values.

How influential were these people? Well, it wasn't just the author of this psalm who was impacted. Verses 10 and 11 say that many individuals were turning toward the teachings of the unrighteous, asking the same questions Asaph penned. Human wisdom appeared more viable to them than divine wisdom. In reality, they were sacrificing life for the foolishness of rebellious humans.

This reminds us of many modern incidents where good people have abandoned true doctrine because of being duped by attractive human reason. It happens when individuals stop seeking the Lord through His Word and worship, and instead substitute the philosophies of humans.

Verse 12 concludes the author's description with a brief summary. The wicked live a carefree life without experiencing all the usual burdens. And in the process they experience material gain.

C. The Thoughts of the Righteous (vv. 13-15)

13. Verily I have cleansed my heart in vain, and washed my hands in innocency.

14. For all the day long have I been plagued, and chastened every morning.

15. If I say, I will speak thus; behold, I should offend against the generation of thy children.

In view of everything he had seen, Asaph began to wonder about his actions. He had taken the time and effort to cleanse his heart and life only to see no visible effect in view of prosperity. His shortsightedness caused him to think materially. Spiritual dimensions weren't part of the consideration. In essence he was thinking, *What good has all this done me?* Inherent in the words spoken is the question, "Why bother if there is no difference?"

Verse 14 further explains his situation. Asaph was experiencing a variety of difficulties. It appears his lot included physical pain and possibly emotional agony. How could a believer's life include so much difficulty?

Though he thought these things, he had not verbalized them. All doubts remained private. His purpose in doing this was to protect others so they would not follow the same downward path of thinking. That was commendable, but it didn't change the upside-down condition within himself.

These verses remind us of the many thoughts and doubts we may harbor. The reasons vary. Like the author, we may not want to discourage other believers. Or we may not want to verbalize our thoughts for fear that others will think we have backslid. Occasionally we resist due to our not knowing exactly how to say it. Or we may fear God's retaliation if we are too candid. Regardless of the reason for the silence, it doesn't change the fact of our dissatisfaction. God sees and knows the inner recesses of our heart.

II. SUSTAINED BY TRUTH (Psalm 73:16-24)

A. The Impact of Worship (vv. 16, 17)

16. When I thought to know this, it was too painful for me;

17. Until I went into the sanctuary of God; then understood I their end.

In verse 16 the writer indicated the inner pain or frustration that resulted from seeing and thinking about what appeared to be a gross injustice. He apparently had thought about the situation over a period of time.

No relief or understanding came until he "entered the sanctuary of God" (v. 17, *NIV*), experiencing the presence of the Lord. This is a reality the ungodly do not know because of their choosing not to be in harmony with Him.

How do we enter into the presence of God? We begin by separating ourselves from the culture around us. It means taking time to allow all the influences of the world to be put aside and rest our attention solely on God—His being and His truths. This can take place in a corporate worship service or in private devotions. When genuine worship occurs, we cannot help but see things differently. New understanding develops as we grasp divine principles. This is more than an emotional high or catharsis. It is worship which affects our mind and heart.

As we focus on God's greatness, He speaks thundering truths which impact the depths of our being. We see beyond the clutter of our surroundings. The blurry vision clears and we see things from a new perspective.

As Asaph worshiped, he understood the future of the ungodly. Right now they were enjoying material prosperity and all its advantages, but it was temporary. Those whom he had so foolishly envied even to the point of spiritual ruin would not enjoy themselves forever. The day of reckoning will produce a far different set of circumstances. The true settling of accounts comes at the end of life.

B. The Future of the Wicked
   (vv. 18-20)

(Psalm 73:19, 20 is not included in the printed text.)

18. Surely thou didst set them in slippery places: thou castedst them down into destruction.

If anyone resides in a slippery spiritual state, it is the ungodly. How ironic! When the righteous man envied their prosperity, he came close to exchanging a foundation secure in the Lord for a slippery state leading to eternal destruction. The future of the wicked consists of God's condemning them to eternal destruction. All their prosperity will be wiped away.

Verse 19 emphasizes the suddenness of the destruction. It is like what happened to the northern 10 tribes of Israel. Economically the country was doing well. God sent prophets warning them of their imminent destruction. They doubted it could be so, but then it happened. The Assyrians swept in, and the words of the prophets were fulfilled (see 2 Kings 17).

Verse 19 of the text also describes what occurs when the ungodly are snatched from the living. It isn't just a gradual process; but rather, they are swept away. Judgment falls on them quickly with little or no warning. It can be seen in the New Testament parable of the rich man (Luke 12:16-21). While he was enjoying the abundance of the harvest and making plans for larger storage facilities, the Lord declared that his life was coming to an end that night.

A historical event that further demonstrates this verse is the fall of Babylon to the forces of Cyrus (Daniel 5). While they were feasting and erroneously relying on gods they had collected from nearby cities, the Persian forces entered the city by diverting the flow of the river. The Babylonians knew the Persian army was moving in their direction but never expected the invasion which conquered their city.

Psalm 73:20 emphasizes again how quickly judgment comes to the ungodly. The author used the example of a dream. One moment the person is lost in a particular fantasy world. But at the point of awakening, a totally different environment becomes his reality. In the same way, the ungodly live in a fantasy of their own making, not knowing the reality of judgment which awaits them at the end.

C. The Recognition of Truth
   (vv. 21-24)

(Psalm 73:21-23 is not included in the printed text.)

24. Thou shalt guide me with thy counsel, and afterward receive me to glory.

It's amazing how our circumstances can impact our thinking. In some cases we are so influenced by what we see, hear and feel that our thinking process becomes negatively impacted. This would seem to have been the case of the psalmist. However, once he dwelt in an environment of God's presence, the truth quickly dominated. After having come to his senses, so to speak, he then faced the foolishness of what had taken place.

In verse 21 Asaph recounted how his heart had become grieved and his spirit embittered over the prosperity of the wicked. In the next verse he described himself as being senseless (foolish) and ignorant, like a brute beast lacking the ability to think properly. Animals follow the path of instinct rather than carefully calculating the truth and then responding appropriately.

The author then emphasized how truth comes to those who cling to God's hand for guidance (vv. 23, 24). He used the concept of holding God's hand to emphasize constantly being in God's presence and allowing Him to guide one's thoughts and actions. As a result there are two benefits.

First, in this life one can walk according to divine counsel. It enables the believer to steer clear of pitfalls unseen by human shortsightedness and blindness. With the believer's hand in God's, the believer will not slip or fall.

The second benefit comes at the end of life when the saints will be brought into God's heavenly presence to enjoy all His glory. As Jesus promised, "that where I am, there ye may be also" (John 14:3).

III. FAITH RENEWED
(Psalm 73:25-28)

A. Our Strength in God (vv. 25, 26)

25. Whom have I in heaven but thee? and there is none upon earth that I desire beside thee.

26. My flesh and my heart faileth: but God is the strength of my heart, and my portion for ever.

How do we keep on track when situations seem to be destroying our hopes, dreams and regular style of life? It's these types of situations that are alluded to in verses 25 and 26. The psalmist understood human

weakness and the loneliness that surrounds those who are steeped in doubt or surrounded by billowing obstacles. No wonder he asked such an important question. Nothing on earth can provide the strength and guidance needed in times of crises. While friends, family and even other Christians will offer support and direction, they in themselves cannot deliver us. And when it comes to spiritual matters, only God can change our inner being. No one in heaven or earth is better than God himself.

The failing mentioned in verse 26 describes the aging process. As the years pass, the body eventually wears out. We all will die. And then we will face the judgment of God. However, the psalmist knew that death would not destroy his union with God. What a change from the beginning of the psalm where he described a spiritual crisis that almost brought disaster. Now he declared a commitment through death.

There are occasions when our faith may grow weak. The important point is for it to be renewed. This comes as we return to God and recognize His strength to be our strength. When we come to the conclusion that nothing supersedes His glory, then our commitment will be renewed. Our faith returns. Nothing can separate us from Him. In the faith chapter, Hebrews 11, we see that none of those individuals were spiritually perfect. Despite their faith lapses, they were included in this showcase chapter of faith.

B. Our Trust in God (vv. 27, 28)

27. For, lo, they that are far from thee shall perish: thou hast destroyed all them that go a whoring from thee.

28. But it is good for me to draw near to God: I have put my trust in the Lord God, that I may declare all thy works.

Verse 27 uses the framework of faithfulness in marriage to describe the relationship which should be followed by the people of God. But in this scenario the ungodly are those who chose to be unfaithful. In essence they prostitute themselves by following after heathen gods and false religious systems. This break in faithfulness can result only in their destruction.

Also contained within this verse is the concept of distancing oneself from God. It may be done by conscious choices of rebellion, or it may be the result of gradually drifting away by neglect. But in either case this distance produces a separation that brings God's judgment. Righteous living comes by drawing close to God and remaining there. As we take shelter in Him we find spiritual fulfillment and security.

And that's exactly what the writer of the psalm chose to do. Notice how Asaph equated drawing near with trusting in God. These two go hand in hand. Anytime we choose to trust in God, we find ourselves drawn closer to Him. His presence surrounds us. The *New International Version* renders the second part of verse 28, "I have made the Sovereign Lord my refuge." This isn't running and hiding in fear. Instead, it is understanding the strength and shelter needed to withstand the temptations and trials of life which would otherwise destroy us.

The final words of the psalm speak of testimony. This is no closet follower of God. Asaph wanted to speak forth the goodness of God and his personal commitment to righteousness.

GOLDEN TEXT HOMILY

"IT IS GOOD FOR ME TO DRAW NEAR TO GOD: I HAVE PUT MY TRUST IN THE LORD GOD, THAT I MAY DECLARE ALL THY WORKS" (Psalm 73:28).

If it is good to draw near to God, why do so many people choose to run away from God?

In Psalm 73, Asaph described some of the reasons people choose not to draw close to God:

• Prosperity making them feel materially self-sufficient (v. 3)

• Good health making them feel physically self-reliant (vv. 4, 5)

• Callousness brought on by a lifestyle of evil (v. 7)

• Ignorance causing them to think God will never bring judgment on them (vv. 8-11)

However, Asaph saw things differently. Realizing that material possessions and physical strength will not last forever, and understanding that God will one day judge all the earth, Asaph declared, "But as for me, it is good to be near God. I have made the Sovereign Lord my refuge" (v. 28, *NIV*).

God is the only safe refuge against financial failure, fading health, a sinful world and coming judgment.—**Lance Colkmire**

SENTENCE SERMONS

WE MUST LEARN to trust God in all circumstances.
—Selected

THE LORD doesn't take us into deep water to drown us, but to develop us.
—Irv Hedstrom

WHEN IT IS DARK ENOUGH, men see the stars.
—Ralph Waldo Emerson

EVANGELISM APPLICATION

CHRISTIANS MUST WARN SINNERS THAT GOD'S JUDGMENT IS CERTAIN.

It's amazing how in the latter decades of the 20th century the church as a whole moved away from teaching and preaching on the reality and certainty of God's judgment for sin. It was as if the "love emphasis" of the hippie culture of the '60s and '70s became the theme of the church.

There's no doubt that God's love is a major part of our message. His love for us resulted in Christ's dying on the cross so we could have forgiveness of sin. Yet God's holiness demands justice for that sin, and that justice comes in the form of judgment. Some of it may occur in this life as God restrains the forces of evil. But all unrepentant sinners will reap eternal judgment when they stand before God and are made accountable for their sins!

If we as Christians do not warn sinners, no one else remains to do so.

ILLUMINATING THE LESSON

Probably one of the most moving stories of faith on trial is that of M.Y. Chan, a Chinese pastor singled out for punishment. For 18½ years he worked in what is called a "night soil" pit. In reality that meant spending from six to eight hours a day standing in human excrement with no protection. Sometimes he stood in this sludge up to his waist.

But his faith remained strong. His church continued to support him in prayer. They continued to witness in his absence until their church grew from 300 at his imprisonment to 5,000 at his release.

DAILY BIBLE READINGS

M. Faith in God Gives Security.
2 Samuel 22:21-31
T. Faith in God Brings Peace.
Isaiah 26:1-4
W. Faith in God Brings Blessedness.
Jeremiah 17:5-8
T. Faith in God Brings Power.
Matthew 21:18-22
F. Faith in God Gives Comfort.
2 Corinthians 1:3-9
S. Faith in God Assures Victory.
1 John 5:1-5

TRUTH SEARCH:
Creatively Teaching the Word

Aim: Students will pray for God to change people's perspective as they worship together.

Items needed: Marker, marker board, eraser, slips of paper, pencils

FOCUS

Pass out slip of paper and a pencil to each student. Ask everyone to write down one excuse a person might give for not coming to church.

Collect the cards and read the various excuses.

Today we're going to study about one man who went to God's house even though he was having serious doubts about whether or not serving God was worth it.

EXPLORE

Have students open their Bible to Psalm 73. Have a volunteer read verses 1 and 2.

• *What did the writer acknowledge about God in verse 1?*

• *What almost happened to the writer?*

While the writer, Asaph, obviously included himself in the category of the clean-hearted, when he looked at the world around him, he almost fell. Let's see why.

Have the students read verses 3-12 to themselves. Then have them name things the writer observed of the ungodly people who lived around him. List them on the board. The list should include the following: the prosperity of unbelievers (v. 3), their pang-free deaths (v. 4), their trouble-free lives (v. 5), their abundance (v. 7), their arrogance (vv. 8, 9), their disrespect for God (vv. 10, 11), their riches (v. 12).

• *Look at the list. Do you think the writer was exaggerating? Why or why not?*

• *According to verses 13-16, in what ways did Asaph respond to his observations?*

Read verses 16 and 17.

• *In the middle of his confusion, what wise thing did Asaph do? How did this help him?*

Have the students read verses 18-22 to themselves. As they read, erase the board.

• *When he entered into worship and began to see things from God's perspective, what truths about unbelievers did Asaph realize?*

• *What did he realize about his earlier ideas concerning the ungodly?*

Read verses 23-26.

• *What blessings are promised to the pure in heart?*

List students' answers on the board. They should include the following: God's presence (v. 23), God's guidance and eternal life (v. 24), divine strength and provision forever (v. 26).

• *In verse 27, what contrast does Asaph draw between the ungodly and the godly?*

• *According to verse 28, what did Asaph decide to do?*

RESPOND

Today there might be people in our worship service who are feeling like Asaph felt—filled with doubt. Wouldn't it be wonderful if those same people left church today with the same new mind Asaph had?

Have the class stand and read verse 28 aloud together: "But it is good for me to draw near to God: I have put my trust in the Lord God, that I may declare all thy works."

Ask a volunteer to pray for God to change hearts in today's worship service. Encourage the others to agree with him or her in prayer.

God Answers Prayer

Study Text: 1 Samuel 1:1-28
Objective: To know that God answers prayer, and persist in prayer.
Time: Around 1080 B.C.
Place: Ramah, probably a short distance north of Jerusalem; Shiloh, about 10 miles north of Bethel
Golden Text: "Pray without ceasing" (1 Thessalonians 5:17).
Central Truth: God responds to the prayers of His people.
Evangelism Emphasis: Believers should pray continually for the salvation of sinners.

PRINTED TEXT

1 Samuel 1:9. So Hannah rose up after they had eaten in Shiloh, and after they had drunk. Now Eli the priest sat upon a seat by a post of the temple of the Lord.

10. And she was in bitterness of soul, and prayed unto the Lord, and wept sore.

11. And she vowed a vow, and said, O Lord of hosts, if thou wilt indeed look on the affliction of thine handmaid, and remember me, and not forget thine handmaid, but wilt give unto thine handmaid a man child, then I will give him unto the Lord all the days of his life, and there shall no razor come upon his head.

12. And it came to pass, as she continued praying before the Lord, that Eli marked her mouth.

13. Now Hannah, she spake in her heart; only her lips moved, but her voice was not heard: therefore Eli thought she had been drunken.

14. And Eli said unto her, How long wilt thou be drunken? put away thy wine from thee.

15. And Hannah answered and said, No, my lord, I am a woman of a sorrowful spirit: I have drunk neither wine nor strong drink, but have poured out my soul before the Lord.

16. Count not thine handmaid for a daughter of Belial: for out of the abundance of my complaint and grief have I spoken hitherto.

19. And they rose up in the morning early, and worshipped before the Lord, and returned, and came to their house to Ramah: and Elkanah knew Hannah his wife; and the Lord remembered her.

20. Wherefore it came to pass, when the time was come about after Hannah had conceived, that she bare a son, and called his name Samuel, saying, Because I have asked him of the Lord.

24. And when she had weaned him, she took him up with her, with three bullocks, and one ephah of flour, and a bottle of wine, and brought him unto the house of the Lord in Shiloh: and the child was young.

25. And they slew a bullock, and brought the child to Eli.

26. And she said, Oh my lord, as thy soul liveth, my lord, I am the woman that stood by thee here, praying unto the Lord.

27. For this child I prayed; and the Lord hath given me my petition which I asked of him:

28. Therefore also I have lent him to the Lord; as long as he liveth he shall be lent to the Lord. And he worshipped the Lord there.

DICTIONARY

Hannah (HAN-nuh)—1 Samuel 1:9—The mother of Samuel; her name means "favor" or "grace."

Shiloh (SHY-low)—1 Samuel 1:9—A city on a hill where the Tabernacle remained for some 400 years.

Belial (Be-LIE-ul)—1 Samuel 1:16—A foolish and reckless person.

Elkanah (el-KAY-nuh)—1 Samuel 1:19—The husband of Hannah and father of Samuel. The name means "whom God has acquired."

ephah (EE-fah)—1 Samuel 1:24—A measure containing a little over a bushel.

LESSON OUTLINE

I. SINCERE PRAYER
   A. The Problem
   B. The Vow
   C. The Clarification

II. ANSWERED PRAYER
   A. The Encouragement
   B. The Fulfillment

III. CONSECRATION TO GOD
   A. The Child's Development
   B. The Child's Presentation

LESSON EXPOSITION

INTRODUCTION

Lesson 6 begins the second unit of the summer quarter. We now switch from Psalms in the Poetical Books to the Historical Books of 1 Samuel, 1 Kings and 2 Kings. Specific attention will be given to events in the lives of three important prophets: Samuel, Elijah and Elisha.

Samuel's prophetic ministry was considerably different from that of Elijah and Elisha in terms of the political environment. When his prophetic ministry began, Israel was a theocracy. This means that the nation depended on God to lead them by speaking through prophets, priests and judges. His wisdom and will were the authority. However, later in Samuel's life the people would be given the monarchy they desired even though warned of the negative impacts.

Samuel's Biblical coverage begins with the circumstances of his birth.

His birth was a direct answer to his mother's prayer. This event provides us with the opportunity to consider the need to persist in prayer and to understand that God answers prayer.

Appeals to pray are common. Repeatedly we are told how revival comes when people pray. Hundreds of books and study guides are available on all aspects of prayer. But the haunting truth remains: The vast majority of believers talk and study more about prayer than actually practicing it. In marked contrast, Hannah, the mother of Samuel, prayed earnestly and persistently.

Not to be overlooked is Samuel's godly father, Elkanah. His righteous actions and support of Hannah must not be minimized or neglected. He stands forth as a husband who was sympathetic to his wife's feelings and did his best to comfort and satisfy her.

As you study and teach this lesson, focus on the fact that God responds to the prayers of His people. Sometimes the answer is "Yes." Other times it's "No." Sometimes it's "Wait a little; it's not the right time." There are even times when God answers positively but in a different way than we had asked. Then the challenge becomes one of both recognizing and accepting His answer.

I. SINCERE PRAYER
   (1 Samuel 1:1, 2, 9-16)

A. The Problem (vv. 1, 2)

(1 Samuel 1:1, 2 is not included in the printed text.)

The narrative of 1 Samuel begins with an introduction of Elkanah. Since genealogy is an important aspect of the Jewish nation, and this story introduces an individual who significantly impacted the national life of Israel, it is only logical that a brief historical picture would be included. In this case the author includes four generations of Elkanah's ancestry.

Verse 1 says Elkanah resided in the hill country of Ephraim, but he was not from the tribe of Ephraim. Though living in that territory of Israel, Elkanah and his ancestors were from the priestly tribe of Levi. This can be seen in the genealogy of the sons of Levi as recorded in 1 Chronicles 6:27. This dispersing of Levi throughout all the other tribes provided ministry to each of them in their individual territories.

After the introduction of Elkanah, the next verses describe the problem. He was involved in a polygamous marriage, having two wives. One wife, Peninnah, had borne children for her husband while the other, Hannah, was barren. This created tremendous difficulties for Hannah. First, society considered barrenness to be the product of sin resulting in God's judgment. Second, her barrenness robbed her of respect within the marriage. A woman's status came from bearing children, especially sons. Third, the other wife didn't let Hannah's barrenness go without comment. Verse 6 says Hannah's "rival [Peninnah] also provoked her severely, to make her miserable, because the Lord had closed her womb" (*NKJV*).

Elkanah did his very best to make Hannah feel loved. He generously gave her double portions for sacrificial worship (v. 5). But as the years passed, the burden and desperation to have a child continued to grow. Hannah had no concept that her current dilemma was from the Lord and intended for His glory and honor.

B. The Vow (vv. 9-11)

9. So Hannah rose up after they had eaten in Shiloh, and after they had drunk. Now Eli the priest sat upon a seat by a post of the temple of the Lord.

10. And she was in bitterness of soul, and prayed unto the Lord, and wept sore.

11. And she vowed a vow, and said, O Lord of hosts, if thou wilt indeed look on the affliction of thine handmaid, and remember me, and not forget thine handmaid, but wilt give unto thine handmaid a man child, then I will give him unto the Lord all the days of his life, and there shall no razor come upon his head.

Yearly Elkanah would travel to Shiloh with his family to worship God. The significance of this city comes from the Tabernacle's being located there for nearly 400 years. It was erected there after Joshua and the Israelites completed the first phase of military conquest against the Canaanites. This act made Shiloh the capital city under the theocratic style of government. This Tabernacle was built during the initial stage of Israel's journey from Egypt to the Promised Land.

On one of the yearly trips to Shiloh after having completed the acts of worship, Hannah's agony burst forth. In her grief she began to pray at the door to the Tabernacle. This was the same location where Eli, the current high priest, would sit. The bitterness of her situation overflowed in a flood of tears. She promised the Lord, "If you will . . . not forget your servant but give her a son, then I will give him to the Lord for all the days of his life" (v. 11, *NIV*). Hannah's vow indicated how deeply she wanted a child by the price she was willing to pay.

Before going any further, understand that God can neither be bribed nor bought! Hannah's vow does not fall under either category. A vow is a voluntary promise to God in which the person offers to follow a particular lifestyle or perform certain actions which will please Him. The vow also includes some hoped-for benefits for the one participating. In Hannah's vow she offered the Lord a sanctified vessel for His service. In return, she would see her shame of barrenness removed. But if it didn't happen, there is no indication that she would be angry with God.

The specific details of Hannah's vow deserve attention. First, she requested a male child. Not only would a son bring Hannah more credibility and honor, but only a male could serve the Lord in ministry at the Tabernacle. Second, she promised to offer this child as a lifetime gift to God. Totally lacking was any concept of personal possessiveness. The last part of Hannah's vow—"there shall no razor come upon his head" (v. 11)—was part of the Nazarite vow. The consecration to God included (1) a refusal to drink wine or eat grapes, (2) no use of the razor, and (3) avoidance of contact with a dead body. Normally this vow was temporary. However, in this case and in that of Samson, it was for a lifetime (Judges 13:4, 5).

Vows were never considered to be a religious duty in the Old Testament. Likewise they are not a religious duty for believers today. They are an option or path a believer may choose in an ongoing relationship with God. No one should ever entertain a vow flippantly or with little thought of the overall consequences. We must remember that the intent of a vow is to be seen as a binding agreement for an edifying purpose which will be consistent with the will of God. Selfish ambitions or greedy desires have no part in a vow to God.

C. The Clarification (vv. 12-16)

12. And it came to pass, as she continued praying before the Lord, that Eli marked her mouth.
13. Now Hannah, she spake in her heart; only her lips moved, but her voice was not heard: therefore Eli thought she had been drunken.
14. And Eli said unto her, How long wilt thou be drunken? put away thy wine from thee.
15. And Hannah answered and said, No, my lord, I am a woman of a sorrowful spirit: I have drunk neither wine nor strong drink, but have poured out my soul before the Lord.
16. Count not thine handmaid for a daughter of Belial: for out of the abundance of my complaint and grief have I spoken hitherto.

While in this time of sincere prayer, Hannah was observed by Eli. He saw her lips moving but heard no sound coming forth. Not only did he assume she was intoxicated, but he rebuked her for the alleged condition. How could this be happening? A righteous, God-seeking woman was being oppressed by the ruling religious officer of the Tabernacle. Why didn't the high priest know the difference between drunkenness and the intense, personal prayer of a righteous woman? One suggested answer is that Eli had witnessed other drunken individuals there and assumed Hannah was another one of those. A second suggestion points to a spiritually insensitive or spiritually blinded Eli. Though holding the spiritual office, he no longer possessed the qualification. Either scenario points to a less-than-positive spiritual environment.

Hannah's response respected his position while at the same time clarified what really was taking place. She emphasized not being intoxicated with any drink deriving from pressing of grapes or brewing of other foods such as grain or dates. For that reason the *New International Version* translates Hannah's statement in verse 15 to read, "I have not been drinking wine or beer." She also pointed out she was not a woman of wretchedness.

The term *Belial* speaks of being scorned due to one's lawlessness or recklessness. Some individuals would have lashed back at Eli for his lack of discernment and sensitivity. But not Hannah. This further demonstrates her spirituality.

Having shared who she wasn't, Hannah then indicated what really needed to be understood—she was expressing her anguish and grief to the Lord. It is understandable why these words would be kept between her and God. No one, including the high priest, needed to be a party to this personal petition. Maybe there is something for us to learn today. Instead of pouring out our troubles to others, we should give them to God.

II. ANSWERED PRAYER
   (1 Samuel 1:17-20)

A. The Encouragement (vv. 17, 18)

(1 Samuel 1:17, 18 is not included in the printed text.)

In defense of Eli, notice his quick correction of the gross error. He joined in desiring that her petition be granted. Instead of continuing her sorrow, he indicated that she should go in peace. The idea was for her to return home and await God's answer. There's no indication of his receiving any affirmation from God that Hannah's prayer would be answered. Rather, he knew the sincerity of her prayer and most assuredly understood the mercy of God.

Having presented herself to God, explaining her actions to Eli, and receiving his encouragement, Hannah left the Tabernacle in faith. The whole situation rested in God's hands. There was nothing more for her to do but trust that God would be merciful.

This portion of the story deserves some special thought for our own petitions. Is there a point in time when intercession for a particular request can be ended and the matter simply left in the hands of God? If the answer is "yes," how do we know when we have reached that point? A second question follows: If we leave our request in the hands of God, do we give this as a testimony to others?

B. The Fulfillment (vv. 19, 20)

19. And they rose up in the morning early, and worshipped before the Lord, and returned, and came to their house to Ramah: and Elkanah knew Hannah his wife; and the Lord remembered her.

20. Wherefore it came to pass, when the time was come about after Hannah had conceived, that she bare a son, and called his name Samuel, saying, Because I have asked him of the Lord.

These two verses summarize how quickly God answered Hannah's prayer. The morning after she prayed in anguish and made the vow, Hannah and Elkanah worshiped the Lord, then returned home. Intercourse between husband and wife resulted in the long-awaited conception of a child. After his birth she named him *Samuel*, which means "asked of God." His name would be a consistent reminder of God's provision for Hannah.

There are other accounts in Scripture of barren women eventually conceiving and birthing a special son; for example, the births of Isaac, John the Baptist and Samson. Yet Hannah's account varies from the others. Hannah initiated the prayer, poured out her sorrow, and put herself in accountability to God. Samuel's miraculous birth and Hannah's rescue from shame and conflict occurred due to her choosing to personally intercede and petition her God.

III. CONSECRATION TO GOD
   (1 Samuel 1:21-28)

A. The Child's Development
   (vv. 21-23)

(1 Samuel 1:21-23 is not included in the printed text.)

The godly character and actions of Elkanah stand out once again in these verses. Verse 21 describes his continuing the yearly practice of taking his family to Shiloh. The yearly sacrifice mentioned here could include such items as paying his annual tithe as well as offering the various sacrifices to the Lord for both himself and his family. Of interest is reference to his vow. This could possibly be a simple indication of fulfilling his spiritual commitment to serve God. Or, if it refers to some particular vow, we have no indication of its nature. Though he concurred with Hannah's vow, it did not become his vow.

Elkanah's agreeing with Hannah's vow to God is significant. In this patriarchal society, the ruling male in a woman's life could disagree with her vow and negate it. A single woman needed the agreement of her father, and a married woman the acceptance by her husband (see Numbers 30:3-8). Though it would be a sacrifice for Elkanah to give up Samuel, he fully supported her desire and vow. He would be giving up the first-born son of his favored wife. Not to be overlooked is the less-than-spiritual household into which this child would be entrusted.

Hannah chose not to accompany the family in the yearly trip to Shiloh until the child, Samuel, was weaned and then could be presented to God in fulfillment of her vow. In that society children were breast-fed until they were 2 to 3 years old. The weaning of the child was a time for celebration, for it signified an important milepost. Since there was a high infant-mortality rate, any child reaching the age of weaning had a significantly better chance of attaining adulthood.

In verse 23 we once again see the wisdom and understanding of Elkanah as a husband. He allowed Hannah to choose what was best for her and the child, knowing that in a few short years she would give Samuel to the Lord. Then she would see him only on their yearly visits. Elkanah said, "Stay here until you have weaned him; only may the Lord make good his word" (*NIV*).

B. The Child's Presentation
(vv. 24-28)

24. And when she had weaned him, she took him up with her, with three bullocks, and one ephah of flour, and a bottle of wine, and brought him unto the house of the Lord in Shiloh: and the child was young.
25. And they slew a bullock, and brought the child to Eli.
26. And she said, Oh my lord, as thy soul liveth, my lord, I am the woman that stood by thee here, praying unto the Lord.
27. For this child I prayed; and the Lord hath given me my petition which I asked of him:
28. Therefore also I have lent him to the Lord; as long as he liveth he shall be lent to the Lord. And he worshipped the Lord there.

Finally the time came for Hannah to fulfill her part of the vow. In the natural this would appear difficult. The child's personality was very evident. He was talking, running and doing all those inquisitive adventures of a 3-year-old. But Hannah didn't allow her motherly instinct to detour her. Notice the absence of any entreaties to lengthen the amount of time she could keep this child. Nor did she attempt to reword the vow for her advantage. Instead she simply followed the agreement exactly as it had been presented to God at Shiloh years before.

Hannah transferred Samuel from her protection to the custody of Eli and the environment of God's house. The tender age of this small child differed so greatly from the normal age of service for Levites. According to divine directive the beginning age for service was 25. In view of whom Samuel would become—leader of the nation of Israel—he came to the Tabernacle at a time when his whole life would be immersed in the presence of a holy God.

The presentation of Samuel entailed more than simply taking him to the Tabernacle and saying an extended good-bye. Hannah brought along three bulls, a measure of flour (a little over a bushel) and a skin of wine. Two of the oxen were for the burnt offering and thank offering which were presented yearly by the family. The third one was for a burnt offering as part of consecrating Samuel to God.

As Elkanah and Hannah brought Samuel to Eli, she identified herself in terms of the previous event a few years before. Just in case Eli didn't remember, she stated how she stood there praying to the Lord. But it was more than the location. She pointed out Eli's presence at that time. Then Hannah introduced Samuel by saying he was God's answer to her petition—she had come to Shiloh and prayed for this child. Then she added, "He shall be lent to the Lord" (v. 28).

The idea of lending Samuel to the Lord is better understood as returning him. God gave Samuel to Hannah and now she was returning him as per her vow. Besides, how could anyone lend to God what was already His? The *New International Version* renders verse 28, "So now I give him to the Lord. For his whole life he will be given over to the Lord."

The last portion of verse 28 says, "And he worshiped the Lord there." Most believe this refers to Samuel. As a little child he wouldn't know the fullness of worship, so most likely it means he learned to worship while growing up in the Tabernacle.

Living a holy life of service is a spiritual act of worship. As Romans 12:1 says, "Therefore, I urge you, brothers, in view of God's mercy, to offer your bodies as living sacrifices, holy and pleasing to God—this is your spiritual act of worship" (*NIV*).

Today's lesson is a tremendous testimony to the power of prayer. It builds our faith, as do contemporary testimonies. However, with the decline of testimony services in many of our Pentecostal churches, we have lost a valuable aspect of both body edification and personal witnessing. The stories of faith from both the past and present no longer are a regular part of believers' memory and discussion. We are losing a building block of faith for both ourselves and our young people.

God isn't different today. He continues to make Himself known in many miraculous ways. Our challenge is to continue speaking publicly of them. If we don't make our stories known, it's possible to produce a generation who either speaks of God's works in the past or assumes God doesn't do miracles today.

GOLDEN TEXT HOMILY

"PRAY WITHOUT CEASING" (1 Thessalonians 5:17).

When you are unable to do anything else, you can pray. Prayer is a privilege that God has given us and cannot be taken away from the believer.

When you pray, things happen: hope is restored, revival takes place, souls are saved, hearts are changed, needs are met, bodies are healed, people are called to carry the gospel into the entire world, and churches grow spiritually.

Prayer is the key to hope. "And he spake a parable unto them to this end, that men ought always to pray, and not to faint" (Luke 18:1). "Ask, and it shall be given you; seek, and ye shall find; knock, and it shall be opened unto you" (Matthew 7:7).

There are two main ways to pray without ceasing: (1) "Rejoice always, pray without ceasing, give thanks in all circumstances; for this is the will of God in Christ Jesus for you" (1 Thessalonians 5:16-18, *NRSV*); and (2) "Always giving thanks to God the Father for everything, in the name of our Lord Jesus Christ" (Ephesians 5:20, *NIV*).

Give thanks to God with joy, always, for everything, in all circumstances.—**Timothy Bass**

SENTENCE SERMONS

GOD RESPONDS to the prayers of His people.

—Selected

PRAYER IS NOT overcoming God's reluctance; it is laying hold of His highest willingness.

—Richard Cheneuix

HURRY is the death of prayer.

—Samuel Chadwick

EVANGELISM APPLICATION

BELIEVERS SHOULD PRAY CONTINUALLY FOR THE SALVATION OF SINNERS.

One of the most vital prayers we can continue to pray is for the salvation of unbelievers. They need to know Christ as their Savior, who cleanses from sin and restores them in their relationship with the heavenly Father. They need to know Christ as Lord of their life as He provides guidance through the challenges and cycles of living.

Our prayer for sinners may include a number of aspects: "Lord, break through sinful rebellion as the Holy Spirit brings conviction." "Lord, send laborers into the harvest of souls who will share Your Word." "Lord, help me to witness of Your love and mercy to those I see daily." "Lord, give me boldness to ask someone if he or she wants to accept You as Savior and Lord."

When we pray for the salvation of unbelievers, we know we are praying according to the will of God, for He is "not willing that any should perish, but that all should come to repentance" (2 Peter 3:9).

ILLUMINATING THE LESSON

When Edmund Gravely died at the controls of his small plane while on the way to Statesboro, Georgia, his wife, Janice, kept the plane aloft for two hours. As the plane crossed the South Carolina/North Carolina border, she radioed for help: "Help, help! Won't someone help me? My pilot is unconscious." Authorities who picked up her distress signal were not able to reach her by radio during the flight because she kept changing channels. Eventually, Mrs. Gravely made a rough landing and had to crawl for 45 minutes to a farmhouse for help.

How often God's people cry out to Him for help but switch channels before His message comes through! They turn to other sources for help, looking for human guidance. When you cry out to God for His intervention, don't switch channels.—**Michael P. Green, *Illustrations for Biblical Preaching***

DAILY BIBLE READINGS

M. Prayer for God's Favor.
1 Kings 8:22-30

T. Repentance and Intercession.
Job 42:1-10

W. Delivered by Prayer.
Psalm 34:1-9

T. Persevere in Prayer.
Luke 11:5-13

F. Believe God When You Pray.
Hebrews 11:1-6

S. Prayer Is Effective.
James 5:13-18

TRUTH SEARCH:
Creatively Teaching the Word

Aim: Students will pray for one another's long-standing prayer requests.

FOCUS

Is there anything you've been praying about for a long time?

Encourage students to name the types of requests they have been praying about for months or years.

Next, ask a student or two to testify about a request God did answer after they prayed about it for months or years.

Today's Bible story is about a woman who kept bringing the same request to God every year.

EXPLORE

Have students turn to 1 Samuel 1 in their Bible, and ask a volunteer to read verses 1-8.

• *According to verse 2, what was similar about Hannah and Peninnah? What was different?*

• *What was Peninnah's attitude toward Hannah?*

• *What was Elkanah's attitude toward Hannah?*

• *What was Hannah's attitude regarding her situation?*

Every year Hannah would make the pilgrimage to the Tabernacle in Shiloh, and no doubt she always asked God for a child. But nothing ever changed.

Have three volunteers read verses 9-18 in this fashion: one reads the narration, another reads Hannah's words, and the third reads Eli's words. Then discuss.

• *How did Hannah feel as she began to pray?*

• *What promise did she make?*

• *What assumption did Eli make?*

• *Put Hannah's response to Eli in your own words (vv. 15, 16).*

• *How did Eli answer her?*

• *How was Hannah different when she left the Tabernacle (v. 18)?*

Read verses 19 and 20 aloud.

The name *Samuel* means "heard of God." Samuel's birth was a miraculous answer to prayer, and his name would be a continual reminder of that fact.

Have the students read verses 21-28 to themselves.

• *When did Hannah bring Samuel to the Tabernacle to live?*

• *How difficult do you suppose it was for Hannah to keep her vow?*

• *When Hannah brought Samuel to the Tabernacle, how did she introduce herself to Eli the priest (v. 26)?*

• *How did Hannah introduce Samuel (v. 27)?*

• *What did Hannah mean when she said, "I have lent him to the Lord" (v. 28)?*

• *What does the end of verse 28 say about Samuel's life at Shiloh?*

• *Why did the Lord wait so long to grant Hannah's request?*

RESPOND

Peninnah ridiculed Hannah; Hannah's age was working against her, and the priest accused her falsely. But she never gave up!

Those of us who have been offering the same prayer for a long time know what it is to face obstacles to our praying. However, God wants us to never give up.

Ask students to divide into groups according to types of long-standing prayer requests (for instance, salvation of a lost loved one, healing of a sick person, restoration of a relationship, and so on). Then have them pray for one another's needs.

God Calls People to Service

Study Text: 1 Samuel 2:12 through 3:21
Objective: To understand that God still calls people to His service and respond to His call.
Time: About 1075-1100 B.C.
Place: Shiloh
Golden Text: "Walk worthy of the vocation wherewith ye are called" (Ephesians 4:1).
Central Truth: God calls Christians to lives of service.
Evangelism Emphasis: God calls Christians to witness to the unsaved.

PRINTED TEXT

1 Samuel 2:27. And there came a man of God unto Eli, and said unto him, Thus saith the Lord, Did I plainly appear unto the house of thy father, when they were in Egypt in Pharaoh's house?

28. And did I choose him out of all the tribes of Israel to be my priest, to offer upon mine altar, to burn incense, to wear an ephod before me? and did I give unto the house of thy father all the offerings made by fire of the children of Israel?

31. Behold, the days come, that I will cut off thine arm, and the arm of thy father's house, that there shall not be an old man in thine house.

34. And this shall be a sign unto thee, that shall come upon thy two sons, on Hophni and Phinehas; in one day they shall die both of them.

3:2. And it came to pass at that time, when Eli was laid down in his place, and his eyes began to wax dim, that he could not see;

3. And ere the lamp of God went out in the temple of the Lord, where the ark of God was, and Samuel was laid down to sleep;

4. That the Lord called Samuel: and he answered, Here am I.

5. And he ran unto Eli, and said, Here am I; for thou calledst me. And he said, I called not; lie down again. And he went and lay down.

8. And the Lord called Samuel again the third time. And he arose and went to Eli, and said, Here am I; for thou didst call me. And Eli perceived that the Lord had called the child.

9. Therefore Eli said unto Samuel, Go, lie down: and it shall be, if he call thee, that thou shalt say, Speak, Lord; for thy servant heareth. So Samuel went and lay down in his place.

10. And the Lord came, and stood, and called as at other times, Samuel, Samuel. Then Samuel answered, Speak; for thy servant heareth.

19. And Samuel grew, and the Lord was with him, and did let none of his words fall to the ground.

20. And all Israel from Dan even to Beer-sheba knew that Samuel was established to be a prophet of the Lord.

21. And the Lord appeared again in Shiloh: for the Lord revealed himself to Samuel in Shiloh by the word of the Lord.

LESSON OUTLINE

I. GOD REJECTS CORRUPT
   LEADERS
   A. Eli's Failure
   B. The Judgment

II. GOD CALLS A SERVANT
   A. Spiritual Darkness
   B. Recognizing God's Voice

III. GOD PREPARES A SERVANT
   A. Message for the Future
   B. Reporting God's Word
   C. Positioning of a Prophet

LESSON EXPOSITION

INTRODUCTION

God *calls* people to service. What does this mean? The concept of calling is grounded in both the Old and New Testaments. The basic meaning is to be summoned or invited. In the Old Testament, God called the Hebrews to enter into covenant relationship with Himself and enjoy the benefits of divine favor as He executed His will on earth. In the New Testament, God calls "whosoever will" to enter into a covenant of forgiveness of sin through the shed blood of Jesus Christ on Calvary. Here too we receive the benefits of this divine relationship while God fulfills His sovereign will in history. In each of these cases the covenant includes responsibilities as well as blessings.

Besides the general calling to all, God calls believers to specific tasks of service. Some individuals are chosen to fulfill positions of leadership such as prophet, evangelist, pastor and teacher. This lesson concentrates on Samuel's calling from God to the position of prophet along with his ministry duties as part of the tribe of Levi.

It is important to understand the nature of this type of calling. In his book, *The Preacher: His Life and Work*, J.H. Jowett says, "In all genuine callings to ministry there is a sense of the divine initiative, a solemn communication of the divine will, a mysterious feeling of commission, which leaves a man [or woman] no alternative." Calling is a compulsion that goes far beyond personal feelings or hunches.

This calling comes in various ways. For some it is the quiet voice of God speaking within their heart. For others it is much more dramatic, as in the case of Samuel. But for all, it creates an intense desire to accomplish what God asks in that moment and thereafter.

However, not every believer accepts the call of God when it initially comes. Some wrestle with it. Others reject it. But no one can forget it. Those who accept God's call enter into a new relationship with their Sovereign Lord. Once again, His will becomes their will.

This lesson also reminds us that a chosen leader can become corrupt. Initially the inner corruption may not be evident. But eventually it becomes exposed to all. God chooses His time and place to bring judgment. The saddest result is the harm it brings to those who are dependent on this individual's ministry to the body. No wonder harsh judgment can befall those who knowingly fail in their calling to lead God's people.

Though some leaders fall, God continues to call individuals to faithfully serve His purposes.

I. GOD REJECTS CORRUPT
   LEADERS (1 Samuel 2:27-35)

A. Eli's Failure (vv. 27-29)

(1 Samuel 2:29 is not included in the printed text.)

27. And there came a man of God unto Eli, and said unto him, Thus saith the Lord, Did I plainly appear unto the house of thy father, when they were in Egypt in Pharaoh's house?
28. And did I choose him out of all the tribes of Israel to be my

priest, to offer upon mine altar, to burn incense, to wear an ephod before me? and did I give unto the house of thy father all the offerings made by fire of the children of Israel?

The corruption of Eli's household quickly comes to light in chapter 2. His two sons, Hophni and Phinehas, reflected an inward evilness. Though having been trained in the proper procedures of ritual while ministering the sacrifices to the Lord, they rejected them to fulfill their own sinful desires. Verses 13-16 indicate a constant pattern of taking their portions of the sacrifices before they were dedicated to the Lord. This contempt for the Lord's offering was a "very great" sin in the sight of the Lord (v. 17).

Verse 22 indicates another sin of this devious duo. Eli's two sons regularly committed immoral acts with the women who participated in the operation of the Tabernacle. How scandalous! More than likely they justified their immoral acts as a form of sacred prostitution like that practiced by some of their heathen neighbors.

In marked contrast was the boy Samuel. Not only was he growing physically, but he was maturing spiritually and socially as well. Both God himself and the people who came in contact with Samuel approved of his character and actions (v. 26). Notice how similar this description is to the development of John the Baptist and Jesus (see Luke 1:80; 2:52). It most closely parallels that of Jesus.

Eli was not ignorant of his sons' sinful actions, nor were the people of Israel (vv. 23, 24). Eli mildly rebuked his sons but took no disciplinary action. As the high priest, he had the power to remove them from office. Why did he take such a weak stance? One can only speculate. Maybe this was a continuance of poor parental discipline over the years. Possibly Eli's advanced age and declining physical abilities contributed to a seeming helplessness. Regardless of the reason he failed to take action, it resulted in Eli's honoring his sons above God (v. 29)!

The time came when God chose to confront Eli with his failures. An unnamed man fulfilling the role of a prophet came with a specific message for him. The phrase "thus saith the Lord" (v. 27) speaks of the prophetic office. His message began with a historical look at the selection of the tribe of Levi to be the ministering tribe. The question asked in verse 27 refers to the 10th plague when God spared the firstborn of the Hebrews. Later the Levites were selected to take their place and be dedicated to God's service (see Numbers 3:41-45).

God further reminded Eli of the particular task of the Levites. They were the instruments through whom the people were able to offer sacrifice unto the Lord. And since God is holy, the servants presenting the offerings needed to be holy. How could they stoop to the depth of taking away from God by reserving the best of the offerings for themselves? Such scorn of God was inconceivable. Though Eli did not personally commit that sin, he was also guilty for allowing that evil to continue. He was guilty for failing to fulfill his duties as a father and as the high priest of Israel. There was no excuse for what was taking place!

B. The Judgment (vv. 30-35)

(1 Samuel 2:30, 32, 33, 35 is not included in the printed text.)

31. Behold, the days come, that I will cut off thine arm, and the arm of thy father's house, that there shall not be an old man in thine house.

34. And this shall be a sign unto thee, that shall come upon thy two sons, on Hophni and Phinehas; in one day they shall die both of them.

What a chilling message of judgment came from this unnamed prophet! In verse 30 Eli was reminded of God's selecting of the tribe of Levi to walk before Him as the spiritual leaders of Israel. But this selection did not mean God would overlook those in the lineage who failed to live a life of obedience and purity. Instead, those who despised His requirements would no longer retain their position of esteem.

The statement "I will cut off thine arm" (v. 31) meant Eli's strength would be cut off, for the arm signifies power. A similar warning was given in Psalm 37:17: "For the arms of the wicked shall be broken: but the Lord upholdeth the righteous."

This judgment against Eli would be accomplished through there being no old men in the lineage (1 Samuel 2:32). Through illness and the sword the youth would be cut down prior to arriving at the maturity of old age. Verse 33 speaks of one who would be spared only to be grievously cut down. The partial fulfillment of this took place years later when Saul ordered the death of 85 priests at Nob. Only one, Abiathar, escaped the massacre (see 22:18-23).

Much closer to home was the judgment that would come upon Eli's two sons. Both of them would die on a single day as a definite sign of God's judgment. This prophecy was fulfilled when Hophni and Phinehas foolishly took the ark of the covenant into battle against the Philistines. The enemy emerged victoriously and took possession of Israel's most sacred piece of furniture (1 Samuel 4).

While delivering the message of judgment, God included a bright note. A faithful priest would arise to replace this corrupt leadership. He would fulfill the heart and mind of God by demonstrating God's character and fulfilling His law. Who is this faithful one? No doubt Samuel receives the first consideration. However, his family lineage did not

remain forever, as promised in 2:35. For this reason the verse must also refer to Christ. He continues forever as the Anointed One.

II. GOD CALLS A SERVANT
(1 Samuel 3:1-10)

A. Spiritual Darkness (vv. 1-7)

(1 Samuel 3:1, 6, 7 is not included in the printed text.)

2. And it came to pass at that time, when Eli was laid down in his place, and his eyes began to wax dim, that he could not see;
3. And ere the lamp of God went out in the temple of the Lord, where the ark of God was, and Samuel was laid down to sleep;
4. That the Lord called Samuel: and he answered, Here am I.
5. And he ran unto Eli, and said, Here am I; for thou calledst me. And he said, I called not; lie down again. And he went and lay down.

This chapter begins with a description of the spiritual darkness that gripped God's people Israel. Doom on the household of Eli was approaching, and there was no prophet in the land through whom the Lord was speaking. Verse 1 says, "In those days the word of the Lord was rare; there were not many visions" (NIV). Conspicuously absent were those special manifestations of divinity that could not be revealed to Israel's corrupted spiritual leader. The only small bright spot was the faithful ministry of a boy named Samuel.

Verses 2 and 3 describe the environment of the Tabernacle. Eli's advancing age negatively impacted his eyesight. He now could barely see. His room was one of those right beside the sanctuary. Samuel, his ministering attendant, apparently slept in a nearby room. This enabled him to hear any summons from Eli and move there quickly. The time of day stands out by the condition of the lamp. Each evening the seven-branched candlestick was lighted and burned from dusk to dawn. Since the light was about to be extinguished, the time of God's calling can be placed at just before dawn.

Twice God called Samuel by name. Each time Samuel assumed it to be Eli and ran into his room. Eli responded the same on each occasion, informing Samuel that he hadn't called and that he should return and rest. The repetition of this scenario was partially due to Samuel's spiritual immaturity. He did not have that personal acquaintance with God which comes by hearing His voice or receiving a vision (v. 7). This was the beginning of a new spiritual experience which would lead to his being the prophet for Israel.

As believers we can identify with Samuel's experience. The first time God speaks to us through that still, small voice within, or when the Spirit begins to initiate the operation of a gift in us, we may find ourselves ignorant of what is taking place. We may attribute God's working to something else. It is at that point when experienced, sensitive believers can immediately help us understand. Or, at the very least, they can steer our thinking and study of the Word in the right direction.

B　Recognizing God's Voice
　　(vv. 8-10)

8. And the Lord called Samuel again the third time. And he arose and went to Eli, and said, Here am I; for thou didst call me. And Eli perceived that the Lord had called the child.

9. Therefore Eli said unto Samuel, Go, lie down: and it shall be, if he call thee, that thou shalt say, Speak, Lord; for thy servant heareth. So Samuel went and lay down in his place.

10. And the Lord came, and stood, and called as at other times, Samuel, Samuel. Then Samuel answered, Speak; for thy servant heareth.

God persisted in His calling of Samuel. At the third call Samuel immediately went to Eli and presented himself, expecting that something was needed of him. Finally, Eli became sensitive to what was occurring. Knowing he had not called Samuel could mean only one other answer: God was beginning to speak directly to him.

Eli's advice and direction were very specific. First, Samuel was to return to his room and lie down. Second, he was to respond in a specific manner if called again. "Speak, Lord" indicates a receptivity to hear what God has to say. "For thy servant heareth" shows a heart of humility and service.

The years of preparation within the Tabernacle were now about to result in a new level of communion with God. What Samuel knew in head and in practice would receive the enlightenment of a personal acquaintance with the God he was serving.

What about us? Will we recognize the voice of God regardless of the varied ways He might select to speak to us? How can we prepare to be sensitive and receptive to God's voice? What are some reasons a believer might not recognize God's call?

III. GOD PREPARES A SERVANT
　　(1 Samuel 3:11-21)

A.　Message for the Future (vv. 11-14)

(1 Samuel 3:11-14 is not included in the printed text.)

What a message Samuel received in this first personal encounter with God! God entrusted this young person with a message of judgment to be fulfilled against Eli and his household. The person who had the task of mentoring Samuel would become the object of God's discipline.

The expression in verse 11 of Israel's ears tingling is one of horror and dread. It can be seen in other passages of Scripture—such as

2 Kings 21:12 and Jeremiah 19:3—when evil was about to come upon God's people. The horribleness of what would soon take place—the victory of the Philistines and their coming into possession of the ark of the covenant—can be seen by the description of both ears tingling in every person within Israel.

In verse 12 God emphasized that all the things previously prophesied would take place as stated. This referred to the message brought by the unnamed prophet in chapter 2. Once He began the process of judgment, it would not stop until completed. There comes a point in time when there can be no second chance or a stopping of events. That is what was facing Eli and his household.

God's message points out how failing to assume responsibility for one's office causes an association with the sins of others. Eli never took the sacrificial meat prior to its being consecrated. He didn't engage in illicit sexual relations. However, he did not stop those who were involved in such behavior. Eli's failure to restrain and to discipline his priestly sons caused him to be contemptible in the sight of God. What made this even worse was Eli's failing to change after he was warned.

How does Eli's failure apply to our own lives? We need to consider who are the individuals accountable to each of us. Do we dialogue with them concerning their spiritual lives? Do we encourage them in the good times and disciple them productively in the difficult scenarios? This applies to our biological and spiritual children.

B. Reporting God's Word (vv. 15-18)

(1 Samuel 3:15-18 is not included in the printed text.)

Imagine the burden that Samuel surely must have felt after hearing the message of coming judgment. How many 12-year-old boys today would be capable of properly handling the situation? But not to be forgotten is God's sovereign knowledge. He knew the strengths and abilities of this boy coming into manhood. He knew what this divinely chosen servant could accomplish.

Notice the progression of events. After the divine visitation ended, Samuel lay down and continued to rest until morning. He fulfilled his duties of opening the doors of the Tabernacle as was his usual pattern. Yet, he was deeply concerned about having to share the vision with his master. No way would Eli not question him. And that's exactly what took place.

Eli called Samuel that morning, and Samuel came and responded, "Here am I." It's the same wording Samuel used during the night. And then Eli asked the all-important question. He wanted to know what God had told Samuel. It appears that Eli had some discernment concerning God's message, for he implored Samuel not to hide it from him. If it were a message of joy, this wouldn't be necessary. But Eli did not stop there. He suggested that failure to share the message of God would be an act of inclusion making Samuel guilty also (v. 17).

Why would Eli make such a strong statement? Surely he did not wish for Samuel to be part of the judgment. More than likely this was a strong lesson in needing to speak forth the word of God regardless of whom it might impact. Messengers of the Lord do not have the option of selecting which audience will hear the divine message. They must speak the word of the Lord regardless of its content or the intended audience.

This lesson needs to be ingrained within anyone who is called of God to any ministry position which entails preaching, teaching or operating of spiritual gifts. Not only are leaders not to hide the heavy truths, but they also are to avoid becoming velvet-mouthed messengers who simply speak that which pleases. They must fulfill the commission and message given by God.

C. Positioning of a Prophet (vv. 19-21)

19. And Samuel grew, and the Lord was with him, and did let none of his words fall to the ground.

20. And all Israel from Dan even to Beer-sheba knew that Samuel was established to be a prophet of the Lord.

21. And the Lord appeared again in Shiloh: for the Lord revealed himself to Samuel in Shiloh by the word of the Lord.

This three-verse summary describes Samuel's development from boyhood to his maturing positioning as a prophet. The first part of verse 19 speaks of his physical and spiritual development. The spiritual aspect can be described no clearer than "the Lord was with him." Not only was there the personal fellowship, but God fulfilled the message given to Samuel in the night. Not letting any "of his words fall to the ground" is symbolic of nothing being wasted or unfulfilled. God never speaks words that are merely fluff and not intended for fulfillment.

Verse 20 indicates how evident it became to the entire nation that a prophet was now being established in their presence. The breadth of this knowledge can be seen by the city locations indicated. Beersheba represented the far south, while Dan was in the far north. Thus all the tribes of Israel from north to south knew that a new spiritual leader was arising in their midst. It signaled a dimension of God's representation that had been lacking for many years.

Samuel was a Levite by tribal lineage. But his ministry task was not limited to that provided by his bloodline. God selected him to fulfill the office of a prophet. The prophet's task includes both predicting future events and forthtelling the words of God that have already been spoken. Prophets provide a constant emphasizing of what God has said in the past and expects His people to follow in the present and the future.

This establishment of Samuel as prophet indicated a renewed presence of God in the nation. Verse 21 speaks of the Lord's coming again to Samuel. This was not the event of his initial calling, but apparently a separate event. God revealed Himself to Samuel "by the word of the Lord." This raises an important aspect for us. We can become so enamored and desiring of the spectacular that we overlook the most powerful revelation of God, His Holy Scriptures.

Samuel's establishment as a prophet began the rise of a line of prophets. He established the school of the prophets and became the spiritual ancestor of prophets whose ministry would span the centuries of Israel's existence.

GOLDEN TEXT HOMILY

"WALK WORTHY OF THE VOCATION WHEREWITH YE ARE CALLED" (Ephesians 4:1).

The term *walk* implies daily living or a lifestyle. Our society today advocates living for the moment much like a sprinter running the 100-yard dash. Our life in Christ must be continuous without ceasing, not as the sprinter running for a short time and then taking a break.

The dictionary defines *worthy* as "useful, valuable, respectable or admirable." *Vocation* is defined as a profession, especially one to which an individual is particularly suited. These traits should be exemplified on the job, and as Christians we must remember that our conduct in every setting will have great impact on all those who observe us. But God's Word is speaking to a different kind of vocation, a higher calling: "But all these worketh that one and the selfsame Spirit, dividing to every man severally as he will. For as the body is one, and hath many members, and all the members of that one body, being many, are one body: so also is Christ" (1 Corinthians 12:11, 12).

As members of the body of Christ we all have important jobs, vocations that require us to live daily at a standard much higher than this world would have us live. We must live every day as respectable, valuable members of the body of Christ.—**Greg Copley**

SENTENCE SERMONS

GOD CALLS Christians to lives of service.

—Selected

IT IS HIGH TIME that the ideal of success should be replaced by the ideal of service.

—Albert Einstein

ONLY A BURDENED HEART can lead to fruitful service.

—Alan Redpath

EVANGELISM APPLICATION

GOD CALLS CHRISTIANS TO WITNESS TO THE UNSAVED.

Most believers never receive a call to the ministry position of prophet, evangelist or pastor. However, every one of us is called to be a witness of our faith in Jesus Christ. How else are the unsaved going to hear the good news of Jesus Christ unless we, His children, spread the message?

Many are afraid to witness due to false conceptions. Some feel they have to know all the potential questions and answers which could be asked by the non-Christian. Others are afraid to witness due to not understanding the Bible as well as they would like. Some are afraid of being rejected or perceived as weird. These are reasonable concerns. But they overlook one major fact. We all have a testimony of how God forgave our sins, gave us life, and has provided a hope for both the present and the future.

Testimonial is one of the most popular methods of advertising products. The effectiveness comes from its having happened to us, so it can't be reasonably challenged. So let's tell the world what Christ has done for us. That's our calling!

DAILY BIBLE READINGS

M. Called to Be a Blessing.
   Genesis 12:1-5
T. Called to Be a Deliverer.
   Exodus 3:1-10
W. Called to Be a Prophet.
   Jeremiah 1:4-10
T. Called to Follow Jesus.
   Luke 5:27-32
F. Called to Be Apostles.
   Luke 6:12-16
S. Called to Be Missionaries.
   Acts 13:1-5

TRUTH SEARCH:
Creatively Teaching the Word

Aim: Students will ask God to help them faithfully follow God's calling on their life.

Items needed: Marker board, marker

FOCUS

Begin class by discussing these questions:

• *Name some people who have been called by God into ministry and who are faithfully carrying out their call.*

• *What makes you think God has ordained those individuals? What evidence do you have that they are being obedient to God?*

Now ask students to think of some people who were called into ministry but have been unfaithful to God.

• *Why do you suppose these people have failed to follow through on their calling?*

Today we're going to look at two people who were called by God to be priests over Israel.

EXPLORE

Have everyone open their Bible to 1 Samuel 2:27-34. Ask a volunteer to read those verses aloud.

On the top of the board write *ELI.* As students respond to the following questions, list phrases that describe Eli. (For instance, you might write "Called by God" in response to the first question.)

• *Was Eli divinely called by God to be a priest (vv. 27, 28)?*

• *What were the priest's duties (v. 28)?*

• *How had Eli and his sons carried out those duties (v. 29)?*

• *What had been God's intention for Eli and his sons (v. 30)?*

• *What judgments did God pronounce against Eli (vv. 31-34)?*

• *Eli had been called of God, but he failed God. Why?*

Read verse 35 to the class.

• *Because of Eli's failure, what did God say He would do?*

Now erase the board. Write *SAMUEL* at the top of the board.

God raised up a boy named Samuel to become the next spiritual leader of Israel.

Have four volunteers to read 1 Samuel 3:1-18 in the following fashion: one reads the narration, another reads the words of the Lord, another reads Eli's lines, and another reads Samuel's words. Then discuss the following questions:

• *According to verse 1, what was the sad spiritual condition of Israel at this time?*

• *What was Eli's physical condition (v. 2)?*

• *Why didn't Samuel know who was calling him?*

• *Why do you suppose it took Eli so long to realize who was calling Samuel?*

• *What instruction did Eli give Samuel regarding the voice he was hearing?*

• *What did God tell Samuel He was about to do (vv. 11-14)?*

• *When Samuel related the message to Eli, how did Eli respond?*

Have a volunteer read verses 19-21. As students respond to the following questions, list phrases that describe Samuel. (For instance, "All his prophecies came to pass" could be the response to the second question.)

• *According to verse 19, what did Samuel do since childhood?*

• *How did the Lord verify Samuel's call to be a prophet-priest (v. 19)?*

- *What reputation did Samuel quickly earn (v. 20)?*
- *What kind of relationship did Samuel have with God (v. 21)?*
- *How was Samuel different from Eli?*

RESPOND

Samuel was called of God for a special purpose, but so was Eli. And so are you.

Erase the board. Write *MY CALLING* on the board.

God calls all people to be Christians. Once we become Christians, He then calls us to particular functions in His kingdom. Are you doing the things God has called you to do?

Have the class divide into small groups of four or five students each. Ask group members to identify specific qualities and gifts they see in each other which God can use for His glory. Then ask members to pray for one another that they would be the Christians God has called them to be.

Consequences of Rejecting God's Will

Study Text: 1 Samuel 8:1-22; 9:15-18; 10:17-25
Objective: To realize that rejecting God's will leads to trouble and follow His plan for our lives.
Time: Around 1050 B.C.
Place: The cities of Ramah and Mizpeh
Golden Text: "Be not conformed to this world: but be ye transformed by the renewing of your mind, that ye may prove what is that good, and acceptable, and perfect, will of God" (Romans 12:2).
Central Truth: It is wise to follow God's will, but foolish to reject it.
Evangelism Emphasis: Faithfulness to God's will makes our Christian testimony more effective.

PRINTED TEXT

1 Samuel 8:4. Then all the elders of Israel gathered themselves together, and came to Samuel unto Ramah,

5. And said unto him, Behold, thou art old, and thy sons walk not in thy ways: now make us a king to judge us like all the nations.

6. But the thing displeased Samuel, when they said, Give us a king to judge us. And Samuel prayed unto the Lord.

7. And the Lord said unto Samuel, Hearken unto the voice of the people in all that they say unto thee: for they have not rejected thee, but they have rejected me, that I should not reign over them.

9. Now therefore hearken unto their voice: howbeit yet protest solemnly unto them, and shew them the manner of the king that shall reign over them.

10. And Samuel told all the words of the Lord unto the people that asked of him a king.

19. Nevertheless the people refused to obey the voice of Samuel; and they said, Nay; but we will have a king over us;

20. That we also may be like all the nations; and that our king may judge us, and go out before us, and fight our battles.

21. And Samuel heard all the words of the people, and he rehearsed them in the ears of the Lord.

22. And the Lord said to Samuel, Hearken unto their voice, and make them a king. And Samuel said unto the men of Israel, Go ye every man unto his city.

10:17. And Samuel called the people together unto the Lord to Mizpeh.

20. And when Samuel had caused all the tribes of Israel to come near, the tribe of Benjamin was taken.

21. When he had caused the tribe of Benjamin to come near by their families, the family of Matri was taken, and Saul the son of Kish was taken: and when they sought him, he could not be found.

23. And they ran and fetched him thence: and when he stood among the people, he was higher than any of the people from his shoulders and upward.

24. And Samuel said to all the people, See ye him whom the Lord hath chosen, that there is none like him among all the people? And all the people shouted, and said, God save the king.

DICTIONARY

Ramah (RAY-muh)—1 Samuel 8:4—Samuel's birthplace and the center of the prophet's circuit.

Mizpeh (MIZ-pah)—1 Samuel 10:17—A town in the inheritance of the tribe of Benjamin.

LESSON OUTLINE

I. GOD'S RULE REJECTED

  A. The Elders' Request

  B. Samuel's Displeasure

II. HAZARDS OF A SELFISH CHOICE

  A. Military Conscription

  B. Forced Labor

  C. Appropriated Property

  D. Heavy Taxation

  E. Refusal To Listen

III. GOD'S MERCY REVEALED

  A. The Situation Reviewed

  B. A King Selected

LESSON EXPOSITION

INTRODUCTION

There is no better way to begin this lesson than to emphasize the Central Truth: It is wise to follow God's will, but foolish to reject it.

No one in his/her spiritually "right mind" would ever consider not doing the will of God. In His sovereignty God knows what is best for us and how we can accomplish His will here on earth.

So then, why would anyone consider the foolish path dictated by someone or anything other than what God authorizes? If we as finite beings can recognize this situation, then surely God must continually be asking it as He observes the foolish deviations of those claiming to be His devoted followers.

But that continues to be the challenge for all of us. We must recognize those influences which not only sidetrack us but also turn us in the wrong direction. Making the task more difficult is the fact of their being rather difficult to recognize. Those influences that ravage our life in Christ usually come as suggestions and whispers which eventually can cause us to turn away from God's will.

One of the most common negative influences is *spiritual anemia*. We speak of the past experiences of our life in Christ as though they are current events. But in reality they are memories—distant in some cases. Lacking is the freshness of new growth in Christ that makes us more effective in His kingdom. In turn, a complacency sets in which allows non-Biblical and non-Christian concepts to lead us astray.

Another negative influence is *peer pressure*. Too frequently we associate or describe peer pressure as a young person's temptation. What a fallacy! All of us can be subjected to peer pressure. It may be in the areas of possessions, positions or even activities. No one, regardless of age, can assume exemption from peer pressure.

A third negative influence is *temptation*. It comes to all. Some temptations come as direct attacks of the forces of evil. These forces want to distract us from serving God and fulfilling His will in our lives. Other temptations are the result of these bodies in which we live. Unless the desires of our bodies are kept within the boundaries of God's Word, we will find ourselves in rebellion against Him. And this is a rejection of God's known will.

Not only can these influences affect us as individuals, but they also can be evident in the life of a larger group of people such as a nation. This is the situation in the life of Israel in today's lesson. Many years have passed since the events discussed in lesson 7 when God called Samuel to the prophetic office. In today's lesson he is about 70 years old.

The story to be reviewed stands out as a classic example of how we can be influenced to move outside of God's will for our corporate lives. Though we usually do not apply this setting to the life of a local congregation, it deserves consideration. Individuals and corporate groups frequently follow some of the same paths.

I. GOD'S RULE REJECTED
(1 Samuel 8:1-9)

A. The Elders' Request (vv. 1-5)

(1 Samuel 8:1-3 is not included in the printed text.)

4. Then all the elders of Israel gathered themselves together, and came to Samuel unto Ramah,

5. And said unto him, Behold, thou art old, and thy sons walk not in thy ways: now make us a king to judge us like all the nations.

For a better grasp of the situation that develops in chapter 8, the last verses of chapter 7 need consideration. Verses 13 and 14 explain that the Philistines were now a subdued foe, and Israel had regained possession of the cities previously captured. Another foe, the Amorites,

were at peace with Israel. This was a time of peace and security. What more could the Israelites want?

Also summarized is Samuel's pattern of ministry (vv. 15-17). Though Ramah continued as his home city, he maintained a three-city circuit of Bethel, Gilgal and Mizpeh in the middle of Palestine. He served as a judge in all those places while continuing his ministry as prophet and priest.

In chapter 8 we see Israel's change from a theocracy to a monarchy. The period of the judges was ending and the era of kings was beginning.

Samuel was advancing in age. He appointed his two sons to serve as judges in Beersheba. Located in the southern part of Palestine, this area was not part of Samuel's normal circuit; also, his age may have kept him from being able to minister in that distant location.

Samuel's two sons were Joel and Abiah. *Joel* means "The Lord is God" while *Abiah* means "The Lord is Father." Those names were an expression of Samuel's heart as well as a hope for his sons' futures. However, neither one of them lived up to their names. Verse 3 says they "walked not in his [Samuel's] ways." Instead, they were much like Eli's sons, Hophni and Phinehas, seeking their own gain rather than ministering to the people.

Joel and Abiah "turned aside after dishonest gain and accepted bribes and perverted justice" (v. 3, *NIV*). While they were not involved in a perversion of worship or sexual immorality as were Eli's sons, Joel and Abiah were not men of spiritual character like their father. One cannot help but wonder why.

It was within this environment that the elders of the tribes of Israel gathered to meet with Samuel in Ramah. They came to request the appointment of a king in Israel. Notice how carefully they crafted their desire with an apparently legitimate reason. They said Samuel was advancing in age and his sons had shown their unworthiness to pick up the mantle of leadership. So, it seemed only reasonable for Samuel to place a king over them who could fulfill the duties of leading and judging the nation.

It is at this point when the real reason behind the request surfaces. The elders wanted Israel to be like other nations (v. 4). They wanted a king. Their desire might be easier to understand if enemies were threatening the borders, but Israel was at peace. Also, the Bible mentions no signs of unrest within the nation. So it boils down to this: being like others took precedence over God's plan and will for them. Identification with neighboring nations had become more important than following faith. Why do God's people so frequently want what the world has, even though it eventually leads to their physical and spiritual harm?

B. Samuel's Displeasure (vv. 6-9)

(1 Samuel 8:8 is not included in the printed text.)

6. But the thing displeased Samuel, when they said, Give us a king to judge us. And Samuel prayed unto the Lord.
7. And the Lord said unto Samuel, Hearken unto the voice of the people in all that they say unto thee: for they have not rejected thee, but they have rejected me, that I should not reign over them.
9. Now therefore hearken unto their voice: howbeit yet protest solemnly unto them, and shew them the manner of the king that shall reign over them.

Why was Samuel so displeased with their request? Was it simply a reaction to what had been said about his advancing age and the conduct of his sons? Was it possible that he didn't know the words of the Law as recorded in Deuteronomy 17:14-20, where instruction was given regarding the time when Israel would have a king?

Samuel's displeasure surely found root in his deep realization of the moral and spiritual forces at work here. He knew God had made provision for the eventual establishment of a king once Israel was established in the land of Canaan. But that was not God's initial desire for them. Samuel knew his nation was at the point of turning to a lesser pattern.

At this crisis juncture Samuel turned to the Lord in prayer. He desperately needed divine direction.

Verse 7 confirms Samuel's concern. The Israelites were rejecting God's direct reign over them.

In verse 8 God reminded Samuel that Israel's actions were not a new pattern. Their rebellion could be seen from the point of their release from Egyptian bondage even to their new life in the Promised Land. The promises of God were hidden under their foolish and selfish desires. Instead of being a people of faith they repeatedly continued to be a people of frustration, desiring the unattainable and the defiling. Remember how they complained for food and water while doubting God would provide? Remember how they wished to return to Egypt even though it was a devastated country?

Though God directed Samuel to grant their request, He also instructed him to protest this desire. He was to warn them of the implications and consequences that would follow. God wanted His people to know ahead of time what they could expect. Thus there would be no occasion for them to complain at a later date that God had not warned them or had failed to look after their best interests.

II. HAZARDS OF A SELFISH CHOICE (1 Samuel 8:10-22)

A. Military Conscription (vv. 10, 11)

(1 Samuel 8:11 is not included in the printed text.)

10. And Samuel told all the words of the Lord unto the people that asked of him a king.

Without hesitation Samuel spoke the words of the Lord to the elders. First he warned of *military conscription*. Their sons would be required to do military service. The soldiers would serve as a standing army in case of war and as servants to the king. The chariots (v. 11) more than likely refer to state carriages rather than war wagons. The horsemen and runners mentioned would be part of the cavalcade accompanying the king on his travels.

B. Forced Labor (vv. 12, 13, 16)

(1 Samuel 8:12, 13, 16 is not included in the printed text.)

The second burden a king would bring is *forced labor*. How ironic! Centuries before, when Israel was in the bondage of forced labor in Egypt, they desired a deliverer. Now, living in freedom, they were setting the stage for a return to conscripted labor. While the military draft included only the males, this burden would rest on Israel's sons and daughters.

The king would use men as field hands to plow and harvest his lands. They would be used to make his instruments of war rather than personally profiting from their own skills. Some women would be used as cooks and bakers to feed those who ate at the king's table and attended his gala events. Others would serve as perfumers, preparing special ointments and oils for the body.

Verse 16 notes that the conscription for forced labor would include the taking of people's household slaves and animals for his own use. Everyone and everything stood to be enslaved.

C. Appropriated Property (v. 14)

(1 Samuel 8:14 is not included in the printed text.)

Samuel also addressed the issue of *property ownership*. This is especially significant when considering Israel's inheriting the land of Canaan. Their properties were to remain within their families. And by now there would have been family histories and traditions tied to individual properties due to Israel's having been in the land for some 400 years.

The king would be selective in which property he took. He would choose the most fertile and productive of the fields, vineyards and olive groves. Even though payment might be given, the family heritage would be broken and their current lives disrupted. Possibly equally galling would be the reason for the appropriation. The king would use the lands for his benefit and to reward his servants. There's no thought of the properties being needed for national defense or a crisis moment. It would just be a matter of the ruler's preference.

D. Heavy Taxation (vv. 15, 17, 18)

(1 Samuel 8:15, 17, 18 is not included in the printed text.)

Why would anyone substitute no taxation for *taxation*, the fourth burden? It is a mind-boggling concept. But that is exactly what Israel desired when pursuing the request for a king. Samuel warned them of an immediate taxation rate of 10 percent. Surely that would have a significant impact on all but the very rich. It appears that most of Israel were of the lower economic class just like most other nations. Why heap such a burden on themselves?

Yet, even while we ask the question, the answer is obvious. There is a human tendency to ignore the cost when attempting to fulfill one's personal desires, and to disregard how that cost might escalate in time.

Little did the people of Israel realize the price that would be paid by their grandchildren and great-grandchildren under the stunning reign of Solomon. They could not imagine that upon Solomon's death their descendants would demand his successor, Rehoboam, to lighten their burden. And when he refused, 10 of the tribes would separate and form their own nation (1 Kings 12:4, 13, 14, 16). Israel stands forth here as a blinded nation lacking both historical and spiritual perspective.

Through Samuel, God warned them that a time would come when they would cry out to Him because of the grievous burden. But then the Lord would turn a deaf ear. He would turn from them and let their backs bear the burden for which they were now asking. When God gives us what we ask in disobedience to Him, there is no reason for rescue, especially after having been warned.

E. Refusal to Listen (vv. 19-22)

19. Nevertheless the people refused to obey the voice of Samuel; and they said, Nay; but we will have a king over us;

20. That we also may be like all the nations; and that our king may judge us, and go out before us, and fight our battles.

21. And Samuel heard all the words of the people, and he rehearsed them in the ears of the Lord.

22. And the Lord said to Samuel, Hearken unto their voice, and make them a king. And Samuel said unto the men of Israel, Go ye every man unto his city.

How did the people respond to Samuel's warning? They refused to listen. Instead, they insisted that Samuel appoint a king over them.

After God again repeated the directive to Samuel to give them their wish (v. 22), the elders were dismissed to their cities to await the appointment of their first monarch. The elders did not offer any qualifications for the new monarch or a particular means for his selection. They left everything in the hands of Samuel. They trusted his judgment and knew him to be a man of spiritual character.

III. GOD'S MERCY REVEALED
(1 Samuel 10:17-25)

A. The Situation Reviewed
(vv. 17-19)

(1 Samuel 10:18, 19 is not included in the printed text.)

17. And Samuel called the people together unto the Lord to Mizpeh.

There's no indication of a time period between the elders' request and God's revealing the man selected to be the first king of Israel. In view of Samuel's advancing age and the people's request, the process was put into motion.

Chapter 9 unfolds the series of events that led to Saul's being the anointed leader. In verses 15 and 16 we see how God prepared Samuel a day in advance. The Lord stated that a man from the tribe of Benjamin would come to him the next day. This man would be God's chosen deliverer.

Notice what God did not tell Samuel. First, there was no mention of Saul's name. Second, there was no physical description even though Saul was "a head taller than any of the others [Israelites]" (9:2, NIV). And even the next day when Saul approached him, God simply informed Samuel that this was the man He had been speaking about. He would reign over God's people and be their anointed deliverer against the Philistines, who would flex their military muscle and become aggressors.

Unknown to Saul, this meeting with Samuel was divinely orchestrated. Unable to find his father's donkeys after three days of searching, one of the servants suggested they seek the aid of the seer rather than simply return home. But what would be revealed exceeded Saul's wildest dreams. Saul would be the new king of his people even though he came from the smallest tribe, Benjamin (see 9:18-21).

Some days later Samuel called for all of Israel to meet at Mizpeh (10:17). This town in the inheritance of Benjamin was the site of other national conventions as well as not being too far from Samuel's home in Ramah. Many years before, Samuel had led Israel to a great victory over the Philistines in Mizpeh (7:5-14). Symbolically it represented the intent for Saul to continue this history of delivering God's people from the Philistines.

Once the tribes gathered, Samuel opened the proceedings by doing a brief historical review (10:18). The people once again heard of the miraculous deliverance of their forefathers from the bondage of Egypt as well as the victories won as they progressed to the land of Canaan and then took it for their inheritance.

Samuel then declared that the request for a king was a direct rejection of God. They were rejecting the One who had delivered them from countless calamities and distresses. And then, without prolonging the discourse, he directed them to come before the Lord by tribe. Each tribe was divided into its various clans or families. (The term *thousands*, v. 19, in the King James Version means "clans.")

Why did Samuel not simply announce the name of God's chosen individual and then present him to the whole nation? That could have been done. But the people needed to be reminded of God's continuing guidance of His people even in the selection of the king.

B. A King Selected (vv. 20-25)

(1 Samuel 10:22, 25 is not included in the printed text.)

20. And when Samuel had caused all the tribes of Israel to come near, the tribe of Benjamin was taken.
21. When he had caused the tribe of Benjamin to come near by their families, the family of Matri was taken, and Saul the son of Kish was taken: and when they sought him, he could not be found.
23. And they ran and fetched him thence: and when he stood among the people, he was higher than any of the people from his shoulders and upward.
24. And Samuel said to all the people, See ye him whom the Lord hath chosen, that there is none like him among all the people? And all the people shouted, and said, God save the king.

The details of the selection method are not given; however, we do know it was through the drawing of lots. Since this had been the means of God's revealing specific choices in the past, it was only logical for it to be utilized in the selection of the king. Previous examples of Israel's presenting herself by tribe, clan and family can be found in the case of Achan's sin (Joshua 7:16-18) and the distribution of the land in Canaan by lot (Numbers 33:54).

Benjamin, the smallest tribe, was chosen from among the 12. Next came the selection of the clan of Matri, then Kish's individual family, and finally the man Saul. But there was one problem—Saul was missing! Only after inquiring of the Lord were they able to locate him hiding among the baggage—the various supplies the people brought for their stay at Mizpeh.

Saul's actions revealed a great deal about his character. His humility stands out. He did not push himself forward and boast about being God's anointed choice as king over God's people. He did not force himself into the limelight to receive the acclamations of the new position. Tragically, within a few years this characteristic would erode and be replaced with a self-dependency that wanted to do things his own way!

The suitability of Saul for the kingship can be underscored from other areas as well as his modesty and shyness. His physical stature would immediately command respect. Anyone who towers above the average height is given credibility without having done or said anything. It is suggested that he may have been between 6' 2" and 6' 4" tall.

There are two other aspects that need to be considered. God chose a man from the tribe of Benjamin. Though known for their military ability, the smallness of this tribe would not provoke jealousy or quarreling between the more populated, powerful tribes such as Judah, Simeon, Dan and Issachar. Also, Saul was a man in the prime of life and had an adult son. This maturity would stand out as a reason to accept and follow his leadership.

Samuel's public presentation of Saul emphasized his physical stature. Their response was a shout of loyalty and homage to the new monarch. The statement "God save the king" (v. 24) may also be interpreted as "May the king live" or "Long live the king." Could they have done anything less? They were receiving exactly what they had asked for!

Verse 25 explains that the king was not simply appointed and then left on his own to determine the rights and limits of the monarchy. Instead, Samuel explained "the manner of the kingdom"—the rights and duties of the king in relationship to God. Israel was still God's people, so the king was responsible to God. Samuel not only spoke of the king's rights and duties for all to hear, but wrote them in a document for future record. It is believed that this document was kept in the tabernacle with the law of Moses.

GOLDEN TEXT HOMILY

"BE NOT CONFORMED TO THIS WORLD: BUT BE YE TRANSFORMED BY THE RENEWING OF YOUR MIND, THAT YE MAY PROVE WHAT IS THAT GOOD, AND ACCEPTABLE, AND PERFECT, WILL OF GOD" (Romans 12:2).

What is the will of God for my life? For many Christians, this is a question with an elusive answer. They know God's will is out there somewhere; they are just not sure where it is or what it is. However, Romans 12:2 gives valuable insight into an area where every Christian can know God's will.

It is God's will that every Christian avoid conforming to the world and its systems. To conform is to allow one's attitudes and actions to be shaped by the society one lives in. Just as pressure and time change carbon into coal, the world will use pressure and time to change believers. It is a gradual process that will cause the Christian to begin to think and act like a non-Christian.

As children of God, we must remember that we are called to transcend societal trends and live a transformed life. We must constantly throw off the characteristics and influences of our world and take on the characteristics of Christ. It is the Lord's will that we consistently renew our minds through worship, the Word and daily fellowship with our Savior. Through this renewal of the mind we give living proof of the good, acceptable and perfect will of God for our lives.—**Chuck Noel**

SENTENCE SERMONS

IT IS WISE to follow God's will, but foolish to reject it.

—Selected

DON'T BOTHER to give God instructions; just report for duty.

—Corrie ten Boom

PUT YOUR MIND in neutral so God can shift you.

—*Decision*

EVANGELISM APPLICATION

FAITHFULNESS TO GOD'S WILL MAKES OUR CHRISTIAN TESTIMONY MORE EFFECTIVE.

According to *The Journal of Education,* when a girl applies for admission to Vassar College, a questionnaire is sent to her parents. A father in a Boston suburb, filling out one of these blanks, came to the question "Is she a leader?" He hesitated, then wrote, "I am not sure about this, but I know she is an excellent follower."

A few days later he received this letter from the president of the college: "As our freshman group next fall is to contain several hundred leaders, we congratulate ourselves that your daughter will also be a member of the class. We shall thus be assured of one good follower."

The Lord Jesus is looking for many good followers. The better we follow the will of God, the better we will be at leading others to Christ.

ILLUMINATING THE LESSON

Life is full of choices and decisions. Some choices are as small as what we will eat or which clothes we will wear. Other decisions are a matter of life or death. Such was Adolph Hitler's choice to expand his power and war against neighboring European countries.

Hitler underestimated the tenacity of the British to continue the fight even though sustaining a heavy aerial bombardment. He underestimated the underground movements which were sustained in occupied countries. Under the constant threat of torture and execution, they sabotaged the Nazis' schemes by conducting counteractive propaganda and sending information to the Allies. Hitler also underestimated his ability to fight a war on two major fronts when invading Russia. The result his armies lost, and Hitler himself lost his life.

DAILY BIBLE READINGS

M. Blessings of Obedience.
Deuteronomy 7:9-15
T. Wait on God.
Psalm 37:1-9
W. Rewards of Right Living.
Proverbs 3:1-10
T. Wisdom of Obeying Christ.
Matthew 7:21-27
F. Obeying the Call of God.
Acts 26:1, 13-20
S. Do God's Will.
James 1:22-27

TRUTH SEARCH:
Creatively Teaching the Word

Aim: Students will ask God to help them follow His plans.

Items needed: Marker board, markers, any kind of instruction manual

FOCUS

Display the instruction manual and tell what it is to be used for.

Do you carefully read an instruction manual and follow it step-by-step? Or do you dive into a project, ignoring instructions until you've made a big mess?

It's one thing to ignore a manual that instructs you how to build something or how to make something work; it's quite another to ignore God's instructions for life.

Display your Bible. **If we decide to go our own way instead of following God's plan, we're headed for serious trouble.**

EXPLORE

Ask the students to open their Bible to 1 Samuel 8 and read verses 1-6 to themselves.

• *How did Samuel's sons compare with their father?*
• *What reasons did the people of Israel give for wanting a king?*
• *How did Samuel feel about their request? Why? What did he do?*

Have a volunteer read verses 7-9 aloud.

• *According to the Lord, whom were the people rejecting by demanding a king?*
• *Why should their request not have been surprising (v. 8)?*
• *What did the Lord tell Samuel to do?*

Ask the students to read verses 11-18 to themselves. Then make a list on the board of ways Israel would suffer because of having a king. Their list should include the following: drafting sons into the military; forcing children into the king's service; taxation on crops and livestock; government takeover of private lands; the Lord turning a deaf ear to their complaints.

• *Of all these burdens, which would be the heaviest?*

Read verses 19-22 aloud.

• *Even after Samuel gave them all these warnings, why did the people still insist on having a king?*
• *God had chosen Israel to be a country set apart unto Himself. So why had it become so important for the Israelites to become like other nations?*
• *What did God tell Samuel to do? Why?*

After God chose Saul to become Israel's first king, the day came for Samuel to present him to the people.

Have a volunteer read 3:17-23 aloud.

• *When it was time to present Saul to Israel, what did Samuel say to the Israelites first (vv. 17-19)?*
• *When Saul was announced as king, what did he do? Why (vv. 21, 22)?*
• *According to verses 23 and 24, what was different about Saul?*
• *How did the people respond to Saul?*
• *What was the last thing Samuel did before he sent the people home (v. 25)?*

All seemed well. Israel had a king who was both striking in appearance and humble, and the people were united behind him. Surely Samuel's warnings won't come to pass! the people must have thought. But how wrong they were! Anytime we chart our own course, trouble eventually comes.

RESPOND

Erase the board. Then write the letter *I*.

God had told the Israelites, "*I* have chosen you to be my own

people—a nation like none other. *I* will be your only king."

Add the letter *N* to spell *IN.* Tragically, Israel decided that fitting *in* with other nations was more important than being God's chosen people.

Add letters to spell *KING.* **So the Israelites demanded they have a human king, and God finally yielded to their request.**

Add letters to spell *ASKING.* **But God knew they were doing more than asking for an earthly king; they were actually rejecting God's leadership. You could say they were asking for trouble.**

Have the students bow their heads and ask themselves if they are completely yielding to God's will. Then lead a prayer of consecration.

A Life Lived Well

Study Text: 1 Samuel 12:1-25
Objective: To observe the value of a godly life and determine to finish well.
Time: About 1050 B.C.
Place: Gilgal
Golden Text: "Godliness is profitable unto all things, having promise of the life that now is, and of that which is to come" (1 Timothy 4:8).
Central Truth: A life of godliness is of great value.
Evangelism Emphasis: Godly living reinforces the Christian's witness of Christ.

PRINTED TEXT

1 Samuel 12:3. Behold, here I am: witness against me before the Lord, and before his anointed: whose ox have I taken? or whose ass have I taken? or whom have I defrauded? whom have I oppressed? or of whose hand have I received any bribe to blind mine eyes therewith? and I will restore it you.

4. And they said, Thou hast not defrauded us, nor oppressed us, neither hast thou taken ought of any man's land.

6. And Samuel said unto the people, It is the Lord that advanced Moses and Aaron, and that brought your fathers up out of the land of Egypt.

7. Now therefore stand still, that I may reason with you before the Lord of all the righteous acts of the Lord, which he did to you and to your fathers.

11. And the Lord sent Jerubbaal, and Bedan, and Jephthah, and Samuel, and delivered you out of the hand of your enemies on every side, and ye dwelled safe.

12. And when ye saw that Nahash the king of the children of Ammon came against you, ye said unto me, Nay; but a king shall reign over us: when the Lord your God was your king.

13. Now therefore behold the king whom ye have chosen, and whom ye have desired! and, behold, the Lord hath set a king over you.

16. Now therefore stand and see this great thing, which the Lord will do before your eyes.

17. Is it not wheat harvest to day? I will call unto the Lord, and he shall send thunder and rain; that ye may perceive and see that your wickedness is great, which ye have done in the sight of the Lord, in asking you a king.

18. So Samuel called unto the Lord; and the Lord sent thunder and rain that day: and all the people greatly feared the Lord and Samuel.

19. And all the people said unto Samuel, Pray for thy servants unto the Lord thy God, that we die not: for we have added unto all our sins this evil, to ask us a king.

20. And Samuel said unto the people, Fear not: ye have done all this wickedness: yet turn not aside from following the Lord, but serve the Lord with all your heart.

23. Moreover as for me, God forbid that I should sin against the Lord in ceasing to pray for you: but I will teach you the good and the right way.

LESSON OUTLINE

I. HONEST LEADER
   A. The Review
   B. The Response

II. WITNESS OF GOD
   A. Deliverance From Bondage
   B. Deliverance From Oppression
   C. Obedience or Rebellion

III. CARING COUNSELOR
   A. Directions for the Future
   B. Commitment to Pray

LESSON EXPOSITION

INTRODUCTION

Today's lesson provides us with an example of a leader in transition. After decades of serving Israel as God's judge, it became necessary for Samuel to step back. God's people, Israel, would now be led by a king fulfilling their desire to be like other people. This placed Samuel in a new position. Would he fuss and fume about the situation? Or would he pick up the reins of responsibility which were still his? What kind of leader would Samuel be?

Leadership entails more than making decisions and being able to lead people. Many people fail to perceive the importance of the spiritual traits of leaders.

What are the spiritual characteristics we need to look for in our leaders? Consider the following: (1) Consistency of service to Christ counts. A true spiritual leader strives to serve Christ both in the limelight and out of the limelight. That person emphasizes Kingdom work rather than personal gain or admiration. (2) Caring for those one leads is more important than one's personal needs. A spiritual leader who understands the shepherding role always places the people's concerns and safety above his or her own. (3) A spiritual leader should model life in Christ. He or she demonstrates the teaching of the Master in the workplace, at home, and in the church. (4) There is the characteristic of longevity. A spiritual leader to be emulated and followed is the person who follows Christ over the long haul of time and through all seasons of life.

Too frequently people become enamored with an individual due to his or her charismatic personality, style of ministry, or ministry results. However impressive these may be, we need to look beyond the obvious. What lies under the surface? Is there a heart which beats with compassion for everyone regardless of skin color, personal ability or economic status? Is there a desire for integrity which pursues truth regardless of the consequences? Is there a foundation in the Word which determines lifestyle?

Today's lesson also provides us with an opportunity to evaluate how we want our individual lives to be viewed as we grow older. It is common to be asked what we would want or hope to have said in our eulogy or placed on the epitaph of our tombstone. But here is a more important concern—will our life's record be without either shame or regret as we grow older?

The central truth of this lesson reminds us of the value there is in godly living. The Old Testament gives us many examples of godliness. Consider Joseph. Though rejected and sold by his brothers, falsely accused by his employer's wife, and imprisoned without just cause, he remained true to God. Not to be overlooked is Job. Even though reduced to poverty and poor health, he clung to his integrity. And how could we forget Jeremiah, who continued to speak God's truth even in the face of disbelief, ridicule and imprisonment. These individuals, along with Samuel, demonstrated lives well-lived.

I. HONEST LEADER
(1 Samuel 12:1-5)

A. The Review (vv. 1-3)

(1 Samuel 12:1, 2 is not included in the printed text.)

3. Behold, here I am: witness against me before the Lord, and before his anointed: whose ox have I taken? or whose ass have I taken? or whom have I defrauded? whom have I oppressed? or of whose hand have I received any bribe to blind mine eyes therewith? and I will restore it you.

Chapter 12 records Samuel's farewell address to the nation of Israel. They were in Gilgal for a renewal of the monarchy. This can be seen as the formal inauguration of Saul. In the preceding days, Saul demonstrated his rightful position as king by leading Israel's army in saving the city of Jabesh-gilead from the Ammonites. Led by Nahash, the Ammonites had offered the city's inhabitants a horrible choice: resist and be killed or surrender and have their right eyes put out (11:2). However, the Spirit of God empowered Saul to save the city.

The successful military encounter could have resulted in tragedy. Some of Saul's supporters remembered there were a few in Israel who had despised their king at the time of his first presentation. Saul's supporters wanted his detractors to be put to death. But Samuel intervened. Instead of celebrating by execution, he directed the Israelites to gather at Gilgal and confirm Saul's monarchy (11:14, 15).

In the process of celebrating and sacrificing unto the Lord, Samuel found an opportunity to give his farewell as Israel's leader. Using the common pattern of historical review, such as is seen in both Moses' and Joshua's farewells, he began with a brief overview of the recent events. He reminded the nation of his fulfilling their request for a king (12:1).

Verse 2 sets the stage for the next verse. The extent of Samuel's ministry was evident by his beginning as a youth and now standing before the people with grown sons and a gray head. This demonstrates his many years of service. Samuel then asked them to evaluate his integrity. He wanted the Israelites to affirm his record of honesty and justice. With this in mind, he asked specific questions. Had they ever known him to seize anyone's property? Had he ever cheated anyone? Were there any instances of his oppressing or using violence against anyone? Could anyone point to his accepting bribes for the purpose of preventing justice?

Knowing that no one could level any of these charges against him, Samuel still willingly offered to right any wrong. This further emphasized the personal godliness of this man. He knew how he had lived his life. But just in case he had erred, he was now willing to right it.

Samuel reminds us that restitution needs to be made, if we have wronged anyone. Not only are we to repent of sins and right our relationship with God, but we must right the wrongs committed against our brothers and sisters in Christ, our neighbors, and even those who are strangers at the time of the offense.

B. The Response (vv. 4, 5)

(1 Samuel 12:5 is not included in the printed text.)

4. And they said, Thou hast not defrauded us, nor oppressed us, neither hast thou taken ought of any man's land.

In our information age we can find statistics of almost any kind. It would be interesting if we knew how many individual cases Samuel decided as he continuously worked his circuit. Surely there were thousands of individual situations spanning several generations. Yet no one could point a finger of blame at his record. What a testimony! Notice the people's answer to Samuel's previous questions. They were very specific in pointing out that he hadn't cheated, oppressed or taken anything from them. His record before them was spotless—a godly life lived before the people.

Hearing this response, Samuel then pointed out who were the witnesses to his personal integrity. First, God himself stood as a knowing witness to the godly life of this selected, faithful servant. Second, the new king also bore witness of Samuel's impeccable lifestyle.

These witnesses were in reality a negative statement against the people. Even though they had no reason for dissatisfaction with Samuel's administration, they still desired a king. Didn't they believe that God could raise up another judge of like character as a successor? Apparently their desire to be like other nations blinded them to God's provision and care for them. It caused them to forget how Samuel came to this position through a miraculous conception and a divine call.

II. WITNESS OF GOD
   (1 Samuel 12:6-18)

A. Deliverance From Bondage
   (vv. 6-8)

(1 Samuel 12:8 is not included in the printed text.)

6. And Samuel said unto the people, It is the Lord that advanced Moses and Aaron, and that brought your fathers up out of the land of Egypt.

7. Now therefore stand still, that I may reason with you before the Lord of all the righteous acts of the Lord, which he did to you and to your fathers.

The witness of God isn't limited to just the present or immediate past.

His provision and involvement in Israel's national life extended back to the events preceding their establishment as an organized nation. With this in mind, Samuel mentioned the placing of both Moses and Aaron in strategic leadership. The Lord providentially protected Moses as a baby and then provided for his royal education as the son of Pharaoh's daughter. The Lord had him become accustomed to desert living while being Jethro's son-in-law, thus enabling Moses to lead Israel in their wilderness years. The divine call of God at the burning bush commissioned him to lead the people from Egyptian bondage.

Aaron's story doesn't have the same drama to it. In fact, we know nothing of the circumstances of his first 83 years. Since there was an art form to being the spokesman in Pharaoh's court, we assume he had some education, experience or exceptional speaking skills. Aaron also became God's choice to be the first high priest, and thus the nation's spiritual leader. But the bottom line is that God placed Aaron in the position to be Moses' spokesman and the spiritual leader.

Samuel wanted Israel to continue to remember how God brought them out of Egyptian bondage. The mere mention of this event brings the 10 plagues to mind. They were to remember how God showed the ineffectiveness of all the Egyptian gods. In fact, each of the plagues was directed against one or more of their 70 gods. God showed there is only one true God when the nation of Egypt was decimated while the Hebrews were left untouched. And, to punctuate it, the Egyptians piled precious gifts on the Hebrews in their haste to send God's people out of the country.

Notice how Samuel repeated the concept of God's placing Moses and

Aaron in leadership and then leading the people out of Egypt. Repetition like this always speaks of a special emphasis. The people were to be conscious of this fact and remember it. This narrative set the stage for Samuel's reminding the Israelites of God's righteous involvement in the lives of their fathers as well as their own. How could anyone overlook the benefits of serving God in lieu of having their own way? For that reason Samuel was putting them on trial by confronting them with all the evidence of God's care for them, beginning with the evidence of deliverance from Egypt.

B. Deliverance From Oppression
(vv. 9-12)

(1 Samuel 12:9, 10 is not included in the printed text.)

11. And the Lord sent Jerubbaal, and Bedan, and Jephthah, and Samuel, and delivered you out of the hand of your enemies on every side, and ye dwelled safe.

12. And when ye saw that Nahash the king of the children of Ammon came against you, ye said unto me, Nay; but a king shall reign over us: when the Lord your God was your king.

From our Biblical perspective Samuel moved from events recorded in the Book of Exodus to the Book of Judges. After settling in the land of Canaan, there came a time when the Israelites forsook the Lord (Judges 2:11, 12). Of special interest is the impact of Joshua even after his death. Israel served God until Joshua's entire generation died. Only when a new generation arose with no tie to him did they forsake God (2:10).

God's response to this rejection was to punish them by allowing their heathen neighbors to oppress them. He allowed His people to experience the dominance of the nations whose

gods they were serving. Notice how this transaction is described as being sold into their enemy's hands (Judges 2:14; 1 Samuel 12:9). Using the term *sold* speaks of an enslavement and loss of freedom.

Verse 9 gives a short list of the enemies that God allowed to oppress Israel. Among them was Sisera, who led an army of 900 chariots against Israel. Next, Samuel mentioned the Philistines and Moabites. Israel's history reveals many encounters with both of these nations.

In verse 10, Samuel reminded Israel of their forefathers seeking the Lord for deliverance. He specifically described their repentance. At times they acknowledged their sin of forsaking the Lord and forsook the gods they had adopted. Then they would ask for deliverance as well as commit themselves to serving the Lord. And God would answer their cry.

Verse 11 provides a partial list of the various judges whom He sent to help them. The first judge listed, *Jerubbaal*, was also known as *Gideon*. The names *Samuel* and *Jephthah* are familiar, but *Bedan* is not. This name doesn't appear in the Book of Judges. First Chronicles 7:17 lists a man by this name as being from the tribe of Manasseh; however, nothing is known of him. It is likely that *Bedan* is actually a reference to *Barak*.

After witnessing of God's continual care for His people and His ability to lead them without a king, Samuel approached the current situation. He suggested that the rising threat of Nahash was the catalyst for their request. The insinuation was why they should fear Nahash in view of what God had already done for them. The king of Ammon provided no greater threat than had the peoples of the past. Why should the Israelites not believe God could raise up a deliverer for this challenge?

This evidence continued to point to their disregard for God as king and desiring a mortal, visible man to be their leader.

C. Obedience or Rebellion (vv. 13-18)

(1 Samuel 12:14, 15 is not included in the printed text.)

13. Now therefore behold the king whom ye have chosen, and whom ye have desired! and, behold, the Lord hath set a king over you.

16. Now therefore stand and see this great thing, which the Lord will do before your eyes.

17. Is it not wheat harvest to day? I will call unto the Lord, and he shall send thunder and rain; that ye may perceive and see that your wickedness is great, which ye have done in the sight of the Lord, in asking you a king.

18. So Samuel called unto the Lord; and the Lord sent thunder and rain that day: and all the people greatly feared the Lord and Samuel.

Samuel pointed out that Israel was at a crossroads. Standing before them was the king they desired and whom God had given them. What would he and the nation do in the coming years? Would they follow a path of obedience to the Lord's commandments, or would they rebel and follow their own wishes? The choice was theirs. However, there were consequences for making the wrong decision.

If the people would attach themselves to God's Word and follow His voice, then the king and the kingdom would continue. But if they rejected His voice and rebelled against His commandments, they would suffer the same fate as generations before them—oppression from their enemies.

How could Samuel emphasize the power of these words? Yes, the people respected Samuel. But standing before them was the king who had led them in a successful mission against the Ammonites (1 Samuel 11). It was difficult for the Israelites to perceive the wickedness of their requesting a human king.

God granted Samuel a miracle to prove the reality of his words. The wheat harvest occurred between the middle of May and the middle of June in Canaan. This period of time is part of a still larger timespan—April to October—when normally no rain would fall. Verse 18 describes what occurred with several brief statements. First, Samuel asked the Lord for this miracle. Second, God answered with thunder and rain. Third, the people responded with awe toward God and His judge, Samuel.

This event reminds us how strongly God wants each of us to know and follow the truth. On occasions He allows us to experience the miraculous to further confirm His words. However, we must also understand that miracles in themselves will not guarantee faith and obedience. Regardless of the evidence God offers, each of us has to make the choice to accept the Lord and to follow His commandments.

III. CARING COUNSELOR
(1 Samuel 12:19 25)

A. Directions for the Future
(vv. 20-22, 24, 25)

(1 Samuel 12:21, 22, 24, 25 is not included in the printed text.)

20. And Samuel said unto the people, Fear not: ye have done all this wickedness: yet turn not aside from following the Lord, but serve the Lord with all your heart.

Even though both Samuel and the people understood the sinfulness of the request for a king,

Samuel did not choose to shun or disregard them. No way can a ministering heart reject a flock simply because of disobedience. Love for people and a sense of purpose keeps a leader on track regardless of the circumstances.

As the spiritual counselor for the nation, Samuel directed Israel not to fear. God wasn't about to rain down judgment. The issue at stake was what would be their lifestyle in the future. He encouraged them to serve the Lord completely. There should be no thought of turning to the idols of their neighbors. Idols are completely useless, having no power to either deliver or provide good things (v. 21). Besides, why should Israel ever want to turn aside from a God who promised to never forsake them (v. 22)? He selected them as His own even though there was nothing distinguishing about them.

Samuel said that God would not forsake Israel because of His reputation among the nations. Other nations knew of God's direction and protection of Israel during the centuries. This reminds us of Moses' dialogue with God after the people rebelled and chose to believe the report of the 10 spies (Numbers 14:11-16). God tested Moses by suggesting He would destroy them and make a new and greater nation out of him. Immediately Moses vetoed the idea, asking what the nations would say about God once they heard of His people's demise. They would doubt His power and ability to see Israel through difficult challenges.

Next, Samuel warned the people not to take God's great mercy and grace for granted. Regardless of the great things God had done for them as a nation, it did not mean His anger would not be unleashed against their wickedness. For that reason, Samuel counseled them to continue to hold the Lord in awe and faithfully serve Him with their whole hearts. Outward conformity in itself would not be satisfactory. Their words and actions were to flow in faith from a sincere heart of love and devotion.

Samuel warned the people that failure to live righteously and avoid wickedness would result in their being consumed, or "swept away" (v. 25, *NIV*). Even the very king they so desired would not stand in the face of evil. He would be consumed with the rest of the nation. Centuries later it came to pass when the Assyrians took away the northern tribes of Israel (2 Kings 17) and the Babylonians took away the southern tribes (2 Kings 25).

B. Commitment to Pray (vv. 19, 23)

19. And all the people said unto Samuel, Pray for thy servants unto the Lord thy God, that we die not: for we have added unto all our sins this evil, to ask us a king.
23. Moreover as for me, God forbid that I should sin against the Lord in ceasing to pray for you: but I will teach you the good and the right way.

There is no doubt of how effective the miracle of thunder and lightning was in the eyes of the people. They were not stupid—this had to be God. As a unit the people appealed for Samuel's intercessory prayer. They saw him as their mediator. Without his intervention they feared they might die.

"All the people" asked Samuel to pray because all of them understood their corporate sin. They saw it as heaping another sin upon previous sins. They could have been speaking of sin in terms of their national history, which included rebellion, disobedience and idolatry. Or perhaps they were thinking of more recent history as they considered their individual lives. Either way, they understood they had committed sin. Absent was any justification or excuses. They stood forth as men and women humbly acknowledging wrong.

Here we see the compassionate counselor in Samuel (v. 23). He committed himself to a practice of praying for the Israelites in the future. There was no thought of praying the requested prayer now, and then leaving people on their own. Instead he saw part of his ministry as praying for Israel. Failure to do so on his part would be sin, for he would be negligent in his call as a priest and judge. But he did not stop there. Instead, he committed himself to teaching them the way of God. There would be no reason for the people to lack in understanding of God's law and will.

Samuel provides a fabulous example of what each Christian institution needs. We need those who will teach the way of the Lord by word and lifestyle. We also need those who will provide prayer support and cover for the rest. Lord, send us teachers and prayer warriors!

GOLDEN TEXT HOMILY

"GODLINESS IS PROFITABLE UNTO ALL THINGS, HAVING PROMISE OF THE LIFE THAT NOW IS, AND OF THAT WHICH IS TO COME" (1 Timothy 4:8).

One of my favorite movies when I was a child was Cecil B. DeMille's *Samson and Delilah*, starring Victor Mature as the Biblical strong man Samson. I had been taught the popular lesson many times in Sunday school, but to see the "real" Samson on television made quite an impression. Watching him jump off his chariot and kill a lion with his bare hands inspired me to immediately run outside and put a full nelson on the neighbor's cat.

This image of Samson stayed with me until many years later when I watched a celebrity golf tournament that included Victor Mature. The once great Samson was now a very elderly gentleman struggling to hit the golf ball a mere 100 yards. His glory days of being a Hollywood strong man had passed.

In 1 Timothy 4:8, Paul is instructing the young minister Timothy that bodily exercise, although having its proper place, is temporary and fleeting. The human body will profit from it for a while, but eventually the decaying of time will take its toll. However, godliness is profitable for now and the future. It keeps one fit in this life and the life to come. It is an attitude and style of life that acknowledges God's claims on the believer and seeks to live in accordance with God's will. It is the spiritual fountain of youth!—**Fred A. Abbott**

SENTENCE SERMONS

A LIFE OF GODLINESS is of great value.

—Selected

CHRISTIANITY IS EITHER relevant all the time or useless anytime.

—Richard Halverson

CHRISTIANITY IS NOT just a phase of life, it is life itself.

—Richard Halverson

EVANGELISM APPLICATION

GODLY LIVING REINFORCES THE CHRISTIAN'S WITNESS OF CHRIST.

When you buy a new car, how important is it to you that the salesperson drive a vehicle of the same brand? When you see the picture of some star on the Wheaties cereal box, do you expect that person is eating it for breakfast? If someone recommends a particular repairman, don't you expect that person to have already used that repairman for their own home, appliances or vehicles?

When a person follows his own advice, it causes a sense of security to arise in his or her recommendation.

It's no different with life in Christ. Your actions provide support for the words of witness which you offer to believers and unbelievers alike. It's the old proof-in-the-pudding theory. In essence you are saying, "Look at my life and see the truth of my words."

ILLUMINATING THE LESSON

During the 1960 Olympics, defending gold medalist Al Oerter and teammate Rink Babka were expected to take the gold and silver medal in the discus throw. Although Babka was very ill the night before the competition, he beat his teammate in the first four throws. On the fifth throw Oerter stepped into the circle, spun around, and threw the discus farther than any other that day. He had snatched victory from defeat and won the gold medal, while Babka took the silver. What no one knew until later was that Babka had noticed and pointed out a flaw in Oerter's technique during the fourth throw. A small adjustment was all Oerter needed, and it cost Babka the gold medal. Babka was not the winner that year, but no one could call him a loser.—**Michael P. Green,** *Illustrations for Biblical Preaching*

DAILY BIBLE READINGS

M. A Righteous King.
     1 Kings 15:9-15
T. Way of the Righteous.
     Psalm 1:1-6
W. A Man Without Fault.
     Daniel 6:4-10
T. Right Living Glorifies God.
     Matthew 5:13-16
F. A Godly Woman.
     Acts 9:36-42
S. Right Living Commanded.
     Ephesians 5:1-10

TRUTH SEARCH:
Creatively Teaching the Word

Aim: Students will evaluate their spiritual lives based on specific guidelines.

Items needed: Thermometer, clock, bathroom scale, paper, pencils

FOCUS

Display the thermometer, clock and bathroom scale.

• *What do these three things have in common?*

Each of these items is a measuring device that can give you good news or bad news—it's according to how you measure up. If you're on a diet but the scale shows you've gained three pounds, that's bad news.

However, if the clock says you're on time, or the thermometer shows your fever has broken, that's good news.

Just as we measure our temporal concerns, so God wants us to regularly measure our spiritual condition. In today's Bible lesson, Samuel challenged the Israelites to measure themselves.

EXPLORE

Pass out paper and pencil to every student. Have them turn to 1 Samuel 12 in their Bible. Ask a volunteer to read aloud verses 1-5.

Samuel the prophet-priest had led Israel for many years. But at the request of the people, he had appointed them a king. In his farewell address, Samuel instructed the people how to live.

• *Samuel pointed to his own life of integrity as a model to follow. On paper, write four ways in which Samuel was a godly example.*

Discuss the students' responses. Then have a student read verses 6-11 aloud.

• *In verse 6, what did Samuel remind the people about?*

• *In verse 7, what did he tell the people to do?*

• *Name specific ways in which the Lord had shown His faithfulness to Israel (vv. 8-11).*

Have the students read verses 12 and 13 to themselves.

• *According to verses 12 and 13, how did the faithfulness of Israel compare with God's faithfulness?*

Have a volunteer read verses 14 and 15. Then have the students make two lists on their paper: (1) things God told the Israelites to do and (2) things God told them not to do.

• *What warning did Samuel give (v. 15)?*

Have a student read verses 16-19 aloud.

• *What did Samuel ask the Lord to do? Why?*

• *How did the people respond to this divine act?*

Have a student read verses 20-25 to the class. Then instruct the students to list additional things the Lord told His people to do and not to do. Discuss their responses.

• *What did Samuel say the Lord would never do (v. 22)?*

• *What did Samuel promise to do (v. 23)?*

• *What warning did Samuel give the people (v. 25)?*

RESPOND

Whether or not you realize it, today you have created a spiritual measurement tool. It is that paper you have been writing on.

Ask the students to read back over the list.

Are you doing all the things this list says you should do? Are you avoiding the errors this list says you should not do? Are you leading a life of integrity like Samuel lived?

Lead a time of quiet reflection of prayer in which you and your students take spiritual inventory.

Taking a Stand for God

Study Text: 1 Kings 18:17-40
Objective: To recognize the worthlessness of false beliefs and commit ourselves to Biblical faith in God.
Time: Around 867 B.C.
Place: Jezreel, Mount Carmel
Golden Text: "How long halt ye between two opinions? if the Lord be God, follow him" (1 Kings 18:21).
Central Truth: Christians must stand firm for God and truth.
Evangelism Emphasis: Uncompromised commitment to Christ is needed to lead the unsaved to Him.

PRINTED TEXT

1 Kings 18:20. So Ahab sent unto all the children of Israel, and gathered the prophets together unto mount Carmel.

21. And Elijah came unto all the people, and said, How long halt ye between two opinions? If the Lord be God, follow him: but if Baal, then follow him. And the people answered him not a word.

22. Then said Elijah unto the people, I, even I only, remain a prophet of the Lord; but Baal's prophets are four hundred and fifty men.

23. Let them therefore give us two bullocks; and let them choose one bullock for themselves, and cut it in pieces, and lay it on wood, and put no fire under: and I will dress the other bullock, and lay it on wood, and put no fire under:

24. And call ye on the name of your gods, and I will call on the name of the Lord: and the God that answereth by fire, let him be God. And all the people answered and said, It is well spoken.

27. And it came to pass at noon, that Elijah mocked them, and said, Cry aloud: for he is a god; either he is talking, or he is pursuing, or he is in a journey, or peradventure he sleepeth, and must be awaked.

28. And they cried aloud, and cut themselves after their manner with knives and lancets, till the blood gushed out upon them.

29. And it came to pass, when midday was past, and they prophesied until the time of the offering of the evening sacrifice, that there was neither voice, nor any to answer, nor any that regarded.

36. And it came to pass at the time of the offering of the evening sacrifice, that Elijah the prophet came near, and said, Lord God of Abraham, Isaac, and of Israel, let it be known this day that thou art God in Israel, and that I am thy servant, and that I have done all these things at thy word.

37. Hear me, O Lord, hear me, that this people may know that thou art the Lord God, and that thou hast turned their heart back again.

38. Then the fire of the Lord fell and consumed the burnt-sacrifice, and the wood, and the stones, and the dust, and licked up the water that was in the trench.

39. And when all the people saw it, they fell on their faces: and they said, The Lord, he is the God; the Lord, he is the God.

LESSON OUTLINE

I. OPPOSING FALSE BELIEFS
   A. The Identification
   B. The Challenge

II. CONFRONTING FALSE BELIEFS
   A. An Opportunity to Prove
   B. An Exercise in Futility

III. FAITH IN GOD VINDICATED
   A. Building the Altar
   B. Preparing the Altar
   C. Hearing From God

LESSON EXPOSITION

INTRODUCTION

The ministry of the prophet Elijah demonstrates the need for spiritually and emotionally strong people who not only will stand up for right but confront wrong. Without that balance it is impossible to be the salt and light which the world needs.

We know very little about Elijah prior to his appearing before Ahab, king of Israel (the northern 10 tribes). He is described simply as Elijah the Tishbite, from Tishbe in Gilead. Gilead is in the northern section of Transjordan, but the location of Tishbe isn't known. *Elijah* means "My God is Jehovah" or "The Lord is my God," and that name fits the kind of man he was.

Elijah stepped into a sinful environment as evidenced by the persons of King Ahab and his queen, Jezebel. The marriage of this duo of disaster very likely came about through a political alliance between their fathers. Joining of ruling households through a marriage tie frequently accompanied military and economic treaties. (An example can be seen in 1 Kings 3:1, where Solomon married Pharaoh's daughter after making an alliance.)

The evil instituted by Ahab and Jezebel is mind-boggling. What Ahab did not do, his former Phoenician princess wife did. Not only did this wicked monarch follow the pattern of the first king of Israel, Jeroboam (1 Kings 16:31), but he fell for and promoted Baal worship. The name *Baal* is much broader than a single deity. It came to represent the supposedly controlling deity of any given area. These gods were thought to control the land and its production. The Baal which Jezebel introduced was the Zidonian god, who was the productive principle in nature. Their rites of worship included immoral sexual relations (14:23, 24), burnt sacrifices (Jeremiah 7:9), and on rare occasions the parents offering their children (Jeremiah 19:5).

The Bible says, "Ahab did more to provoke the Lord God of Israel to anger than all the kings of Israel that were before him" (1 Kings 16:33). Into this environment God sent Elijah. The most wicked king to date would face God's most powerful prophet. This reminds us that God always knows what the times require, and His resources are more than sufficient to meet the challenge.

As God's children today, we are the chosen resources to confront evil here on earth. It isn't enough for us to simply enjoy the blessings of sins forgiven. We are to be of service. And part of serving is standing up for right and confronting evil. If we do not take a stand for God and speak against evil, who will? This does not mean we must become fire-breathing denouncers of evil. Occasionally that may be necessary, as can be seen in the ministry of the prophets Jonah and Amos. But more importantly, it always means to faithfully speak the truth.

We can stand up for God by (1) sharing our testimony of the difference Christ makes in our life; (2) projecting a lifestyle that confirms our words; (3) making our voice known against sin (by writing political leaders and media outlets); and (4) attending city council or county commission meetings that influence the quality of life. Many other ways could be added to the list. The key is to take a stand for God in every way we can.

I. OPPOSING FALSE BELIEFS
(1 Kings 18:17-24)

A. The Identification (vv. 17, 18)

(1 Kings 18:17, 18 is not included in the printed text.)

In chapter 17, Elijah appeared on the scene with a message of judgment. Israel would suffer an extreme drought. No rain or dew would come upon the land until Elijah called for it. During this drought, God miraculously cared for Elijah. First, he hid by the brook in the Kerith Ravine and the ravens brought food twice daily. Then, God directed him to go to Zarephath in Sidon. Here a flour jar and an oil jug continuously produced so the prophet, a widow woman and her son were fed.

In the third year of the drought Elijah once again confronted King Ahab. Immediately upon recognizing the prophet, Ahab spoke of him as being the "troubler of Israel" (18:17, NIV). What else could be expected from a man steeped in his own selfishness and sin? Ahab was blind to the possibility that anyone but Elijah could be responsible for the drought. No conviction prevailed in Ahab's heart as the nation suffered. More than likely, vengeance was the preferred action in Ahab's mind.

Elijah's response dealt directly with the problem. He pointed out that Ahab himself along with Ahab's family stood as the real issue. Their sins had caused this drought. They were the ones who had abandoned God's commandments. They had substituted the worship of the Baals for the worship of God Jehovah.

There are times when standing up for God demands strong and pointed statements. While tact and wisdom are important, velvet-mouthed words of weakness will never do when the situation demands strength.

Elijah clarified the situation and drew the battle lines. Anything less would have caused Ahab's self-righteousness to appear as truth. It also would have made Elijah to appear as the real problem. One other aspect of his reply needs our attention. Elijah did not allow Ahab to put him on the defensive. He knew the truth and boldly identified Ahab as the true issue.

B. The Challenge (vv. 19-24)

(1 Kings 18:19 is not included in the printed text.)

20. So Ahab sent unto all the children of Israel, and gathered the prophets together unto mount Carmel.

21. And Elijah came unto all the people, and said, How long halt ye between two opinions? if the Lord be God, follow him: but if Baal, then follow him. And the people answered him not a word.

22. Then said Elijah unto the people, I, even I only, remain a prophet of the Lord; but Baal's prophets are four hundred and fifty men.

23. Let them therefore give us two bullocks; and let them choose one bullock for themselves, and cut it in pieces, and lay it on wood, and put no fire under: and I will dress the other bullock, and lay it on wood, and put no fire under:

24. And call ye on the name of your gods, and I will call on the name of the Lord: and the God that answereth by fire, let him be God. And all the people answered and said, It is well spoken.

Elijah could have simply engaged in a war of words. But what good would that have accomplished? Ahab's sin created a blindness of the heart which could not be penetrated by an exchange of identifying phrases. Even more importantly, the people of Ahab's kingdom who had embraced their king's sinfulness needed to be confronted with more than the spoken truth. So Elijah immediately took charge of the situation. Under God's divine direction, he took the offensive position. He gave the orders to King Ahab in preparation for a major challenge of true spirituality.

Ahab followed Elijah's directions and gathered all the parties indicated. Besides the whole of Israel, the prophet specifically requested the attendance of two groups of false prophets—450 prophets of Baal and 400 of Asherah (translated "groves" in KJV, v. 19). Since there is no further mention of the prophets of Asherah, it is likely they did not attend the contest. Jezebel might have personally intervened in their nonattendance, and thus their deliverance.

Elijah chose Mount Carmel as the place of confrontation. Carmel is a mountain ridge with various peaks. The tallest rises about 1,800 feet above sea level. The ridge itself runs some 12 miles and contains many caves and ravines. Why Mount Carmel? Suggestions vary, but it is possible that Mount Carmel was the location of a special worship place for the cult of Baal. If so, what a great place for God's dominance to be revealed before all of Israel!

Continuing on the offensive, Elijah impatiently implored the people to consider their situation. How long would they continue to limp between two religious positions? They were wavering back and forth between serving God and the false religions, and it was time for them to make a final decision. Why should they continue in such a spiritually crippled condition?

Notice the people's silent response (v. 21). Apparently they chose to wait and see what unfolded rather than speaking.

To set the stage, Elijah emphasized the numerical representation. He stood alone as the prophet of God. In marked contrast were the 450 prophets of Baal. Elijah's sense of standing alone would be seen several times in the coming days when he was in flight from Jezebel (19:10, 14). His willingness to make a one-man stand spoke loudly to the people of Israel.

The contest rules were very specific. Both sides were to prepare a bull for sacrifice. Each one would be laid on the altar with a wood bed ready for burning. But neither group was to put fire to the wood. Instead, each would petition their God to divinely send the fire necessary to consume the offering. This contest allowed no room for chance. Either there would be divine intervention or there would be proof of a false god. The decision shouldn't be too hard for the people to make under those circumstances.

After hearing the specifics of this contest, the people responded. They perceived it as a wise, logical solution to the dilemma they were in.

Like Elijah's actions, there are times when our taking a stand needs to not only be public but evident to the multitudes. It's easy to stand up when only a few are in attendance. But the challenge becomes much greater when placed in the limelight of the public eye!

II. CONFRONTING FALSE BELIEFS (1 Kings 18:25-29)

A. An Opportunity to Prove (vv. 25, 26)

(1 Kings 18:25, 26 is not included in the printed text.)

Elijah's public confrontation included a sense of politeness in allowing the other side an opportunity to present their god first. Elijah even allowed them the first choice of the two bulls. If they thought one would be more preferable to their god than the other, they had an opportunity to make that decision. They had the first opportunity to demonstrate to Israel the power of their god. However, in this case they would be demonstrating Baal's powerlessness.

This example should speak loudly to us when we have occasions to stand boldly for our God and His righteousness. It is not a time to be rude and obnoxious. Common sense and good manners should prevail. It does not mean we cannot speak pointedly and demonstrate the inadequacies and errors of those in opposition. However, we must take care not to label people and level harsh criticisms which deafen people to the truth of our words and drive them away.

Verse 26 provides us with a brief description of the opening events. After preparing their sacrifice, the false prophets began to solemnly call on Baal to hear their supplication. After many hours of praying, no voice had spoken from heaven and no fire had kindled their sacrifice.

The last sentence of verse 26 reads, "And they danced around the altar they had made" (*NIV*). They were putting tremendous physical effort into this contest. But it was all hopeless, senseless activity. No higher power came to their aid. That's the problem when serving a god of human conception.

Not to be overlooked is the congregation of Israel. The selected site for this contest must have provided for these prophets to be continually observed. For hours the people witnessed the ritual dance of these self-proclaimed prophets, but no divine presence appeared. Surely it caused the contemplation process to begin.

They knew the history of God's working in their national history. The marvelous accounts of His miraculous deliverance could be recited. Maybe they were like others throughout the centuries. Facts about God were known, but only as a historical perspective rather than a current experience.

B. An Exercise in Futility (vv. 27-29)

27. And it came to pass at noon, that Elijah mocked them, and said, Cry aloud: for he is a god; either he is talking, or he is pursuing, or he is in a journey, or peradventure he sleepeth, and must be awaked.

28. And they cried aloud, and cut themselves after their manner with knives and lancets, till the blood gushed out upon them.

29. And it came to pass, when midday was past, and they prophesied until the time of the offering of the evening sacrifice, that there was neither voice, nor any to answer, nor any that regarded.

Hours passed, but still the Baal worshipers heard nothing from their god. At midday Elijah entered the altar area and began to taunt them. Was that really necessary? Yes, in light of the entire situation. These were the men who were leading the worship of Baal in Israel. It was vitally important that there be an eroding of their credibility in front of the entire nation. Decisive moments in the life of a people demand hard measures when dealing with spiritual issues of life and death.

Elijah offered a number of reasons for why no answer was coming. But first he suggested their turning up the volume of their cries for Baal's intervention because their god was so deep in thought or so busy their cries had not penetrated his consciousness. Or perhaps Baal was out of the area and could not be of assistance now. The final idea was that Baal was sleeping and needed to be awakened. All of these scenarios took Baal out of the realm of the divine and left him with nothing more than human abilities. If that was so, how could this be a god anyone would want to serve?

The prophets of Baal responded in a wild frenzy of actions. They began slashing their bodies with knives and swords until they bled. Can you imagine the sight of 450 men madly dancing around the altar? Soon their clothes, hands and faces were smeared with their blood and the blood of others around them. Still, no answer came. All was silent. After all these continued hours of activity and blood loss, they surely were experiencing extreme fatigue. But more importantly, the harsh reality of their deception must have been tormenting them.

There are contemporary examples of futile actions of worship. And it's not limited to pagan ritual in some distant country. In our own churches, actions of legalism which produce a form of righteousness without the power may fall into the category of futile worship. What about going to church and going through all the signs and words of worship but failing to have a personal, growing relationship with Jesus Christ? Insincere worship is futile too.

III. FAITH IN GOD VINDICATED
   (1 Kings 18:30-39)

A. Building the Altar (vv. 30-32)

(1 Kings 18:30-32 is not included in the printed text.)

Now that the day was nearly spent, it became Elijah's turn. He asked the people to come in closer. He wanted them to be complete witnesses of what was about to transpire. They would have the opportunity to both hear and see what would

take place. Not only would this be a personal witness for the people, but it would safeguard against any charges of fraud or trickery.

After the people moved in, Elijah's first task was to repair the altar of the Lord. The history of this particular altar remains unknown. Two viable suggestions are presented by various Biblical scholars. First, this altar could date back to the time prior to the building of the Temple in Jerusalem. During that era, altars to the Lord were constructed in various places throughout the land of Israel (see 1 Kings 3:2). Second, this altar could have been built by pious Israelites who wanted to continue worshiping God properly after Jeroboam's perversion of the northern 10 tribes' worship of God. Jeroboam's changes were effected to further the separation of the tribes after Solomon's death (read 1 Kings 12:27-33). It's possible that with Ahab and Jezebel's forcing Baal worship on the people, this altar was abandoned.

In 18:31 we see some strong symbolism as Elijah took 12 stones to reconstruct the altar. They represented the 12 tribes of Israel. This must speak of the unity God intended for Israel both politically and spiritually. However, God did not force His will on a stubborn, rebellious people. He allowed their desires even though He knew it was not in their best interest.

Once the altar was built, Elijah made a trench around it. The trench's size was sufficient for two measures (about 13 quarts) of grain.

B. Preparing the Altar (vv. 33-35)

(1 Kings 18:33-35 is not included in the printed text.)

The first part of verse 33 chronicles the normal actions of preparing the sacrifice. The wood was put in place. The bull was killed and appropriately placed on the altar. But what follows completely defied logic. Elijah directed that water be poured on the sacrifice and altar. Since there had been a drought for the past three years, some have questioned where this water came from and why it would be necessary. First, the dousing with water would further the thought of this being a legitimate contest. No fire could be hidden in concealed places of the altar and then eventually set the sacrifice on fire. It erased all possibility of deception. Second, water was available from a spring in the area. Even during the most difficult drought it continued to supply water.

Elijah ordered a series of three pourings. This allowed the water to soak in as well as fill all the holes and crevices. The exact size of the jars is not given, though they were called "large" (v. 33, NIV). Surely the containers had been brought by the people from their homes to guarantee having water at this gathering.

Twelve jars/pitchers of water were poured on the altar and its sacrifice. Some of it flowed off into the surrounding trench. Then more water was brought and poured into the trench until it too was filled. The picture provided emphasizes the miraculous intervention which was about to occur.

C. Hearing From God (vv. 36-39)

36. And it came to pass at the time of the offering of the evening sacrifice, that Elijah the prophet came near, and said, Lord God of Abraham, Isaac, and of Israel, let it be known this day that thou art God in Israel, and that I am thy servant, and that I have done all these things at thy word.

37. Hear me, O Lord, hear me, that this people may know that thou art the Lord God, and that thou hast turned their heart back again.

38. Then the fire of the Lord fell and consumed the burnt-sacrifice, and the wood, and the stones, and the dust, and licked up the water that was in the trench.

39. And when all the people saw it they fell on their faces: and they said, The Lord, he is the God; the Lord, he is the God.

Having completed the preparations, Elijah approached the altar and began to pray. This prayer's effectiveness was not based on its length or elaborate wording. Elijah's power came through relationship. The prophet knew the Lord God. He had been relying on God's provision for several years. Elijah was a man of prayer.

Elijah began the prayer with a special invocation. He identified God as the Lord of Abraham, Isaac and Israel. The use of "Israel" rather than "Jacob" was deliberate. Not only was it the name which identified the 10 tribes as a nation, but it spoke of an important historical event. As Jacob anxiously awaited the arrival of his brother, Esau, he encountered God himself. In recognition of his changed heart, God changed Jacob's name to Israel (Genesis 32:28). Elijah wanted that same change of heart for the people of Israel.

Notice the specific petitions which the prophet offered in the hearing of the people. First, he asked that there be a confirmation of who is God in Israel. The people's oscillation between the Lord God and Baal necessitated their coming back to the true knowledge of the Lord God. Second, closely associated was a confirmation of Elijah's position. He was not just a proponent of another god, but the true servant of the Lord. Third, Elijah desired that the people know these actions were not of his own making. Everything taking place here came directly from the command of God.

Verse 37 is the second aspect of the prayer. But in reality it explains or furthers the initial concepts of Elijah's prayer. The purpose of this contest was much more than a matter of head knowledge. There was more at stake here than facts. Everything must lead to the people's experiencing a spiritual renewal of the heart. This application continues to us today. True life in Christ includes a wholesome balance of head knowledge and heart experience. Each supports the other, enabling believers to live courageously in the face of difficulties.

At the end of Elijah's short, distinct prayer, God miraculously answered from heaven by causing fire to fall on the altar. Verse 38 indicates the intensity of the fire that fell. It wasn't a few embers that eventually were successful in catching the water-drenched sacrifice on fire. No! A literal firestorm consumed the wood, the sacrifice, the stones of the altar and the earth around it, and licked up all the water in the trench. What a demonstration of divine power!

When the people saw this, they fell on their faces before the Lord and confessed that Jehovah stood before them as the true God. This confession also indicated that Baal must be a false god.

This scene—the fire of the Lord and the people on their faces—was similar to an event that took place centuries before. On Mount Sinai at the beginning of the priests' ministry, the presence and glory of the Lord appeared after the priests offered the sacrifices. As fire consumed the sacrifice, the people shouted and fell on their faces (Leviticus 9:24).

The fabulous account of God's showing His power on Mount Carmel and the people's confession of Him as the true God came about as Elijah took a stand for God. How does this apply to us as believers? Do we all need to be prophets before taking a stand and making a difference? Of course not! The challenge for each of us is being ready to take a stand for God in any situation where truth needs to be seen.

GOLDEN TEXT HOMILY

"HOW LONG HALT YE BETWEEN TWO OPINIONS? IF THE LORD BE GOD, FOLLOW HIM" (1 Kings 18:21).

There are many people today who serve God halfheartedly, who claim to be Christians, but whose hearts are far from Him. God wants to be Lord of our lives. He is not pleased with the divided heart. Christ stated that we cannot serve God and mammon (Matthew 6:24).

Baal was a god of lust, of sensuousness, of wickedness, of selfish materialism. The people had mixed their worship, carrying on the basic sacrifices and observing the feast days, but they were also worshiping Baal with rituals that promoted sex orgies in the name of religion.

Elijah was telling Israel that the worship of Baal and God could not be mixed. The children of Israel had to make up their minds to serve either the Lord God or Baal.

We see mixed religion today in the form of worship that honors Christ with the lips, but denies the power of the Cross. We see mixed religion where church members worship at the throne of money, pleasure, popularity, fashion, power, and prestige rather than at the throne of God.

We need preachers today who will cry out as did Elijah: "If the Lord be God, follow him: but if Baal, then follow him."—**Selected**

SENTENCE SERMONS

CHRISTIANS must stand firm for God and truth.
—Selected

UNLESS WE STAND for something, we shall fall for anything.
                    —Peter Marshall

ONE MAN on God's side is a majority.
                    —Wendell Phillips

EVANGELISM APPLICATION

UNCOMPROMISED COMMITMENT TO CHRIST IS NEEDED TO LEAD THE UNSAVED TO HIM.

There is no category of part-time Christian. It can never be less than a full-time relationship with our Lord and Master, Jesus Christ. This speaks of commitment on a daily basis regardless of the surrounding circumstances. Neither our health nor our emotional levels are to impact our surrender and service to Him. Sometimes we may be forced to change the types of activities but never the commitment.

This brings us to the necessity of uncompromised commitment. Life in Christ demands our adherence to the principles of holy living. Wrong is always wrong! Right is always right! There's no room for relativism based on the situation. Failure to keep God's standards places us in conflict with our heavenly Father and will render our witness ineffective.

The challenge and opportunity before all of us is to actually live the lifestyle we claim others should adopt. We can't think about confronting the sin in another's life and offering Christ unless they can see the proof in our own!

ILLUMINATING THE LESSON

One of the more interesting accounts of confronting evil comes from the early centuries of church history. Ambrose was the bishop of the church in Milan, Italy. Prior to taking the position, he had distributed his wealth to the poor. Once becoming bishop he gave himself to an intense study of Scripture and theology.

About 390 or 391 the Roman emperor, Theodosius, ordered the massacre of about 7,000 people in Thessalonica. This was in response to the killing of their governor. Ambrose confronted this wrong by refusing to administer Communion to the emperor until he had humbly and publicly repented of this horrible deed.

DAILY BIBLE READINGS

M. Determined to Serve God.
   Joshua 24:14-18
T. Decisive Commitment.
   Ruth 1:11-18
W. Doing a Good Work.
   Nehemiah 6:1-9
T. Demands of Discipleship.
   Luke 14:25-33
F. Declaring the Word Boldly.
   Acts 4:23-31
S. Contend for the Faith.
   Jude 1-4, 20, 21

TRUTH SEARCH:
Creatively Teaching the Word

Aim: Discuss ways to overcome opposition.

Items needed: Five sheets of construction paper, permanent marker, pencils, paper

FOCUS

Write each of the following phrases on a separate sheet of construction paper:
- Opposition #1: "I do not believe God exists."
- Opposition #2: Cults or false doctrines
- Opposition #3: "They are all a bunch of hypocrites."
- Opposition #4: "Christianity doesn't seem relevant."
- Opposition #5: "I will change my lifestyle when I am older."

Show these signs one at a time, asking, "Have you ever encountered this type of opposition to Christianity?" Ask for brief testimonies.

No doubt we all have faced some opposition to Christianity. How should we respond?

EXPLORE

Divide the class into small groups of three or four students each. Each group should appoint a person to read the assigned passage of Scripture aloud and another person to record the group's response to the questions. Assign half of the groups 1 Kings 18:15-24; assign verses 25-39 to the other groups.

1 Kings 18:15-24

1. How was the nation of Israel being plagued (v. 2)?

2. What accusation did Elijah bring against Ahab (v. 17)?

3. According to verses 17-19, who were Elijah's opponents?

4. How did the Israelites respond to Elijah's first challenge (v. 21)?

5. Why do you think the people responded in this manner?

6. How did the people respond to Elijah's second challenge (vv. 22-24)?

7. Why do you suppose the people responded in this manner?

8. Why did Elijah let Baal's prophets go first?

1 Kings 18:25-39

1. What were the specific instructions given to the prophets of Baal?

2. How long did the prophets call on Baal?

3. What was Elijah's response to their rituals?

4. How did they respond to Elijah's taunts?

5. In verse 29, who is the writer speaking of when he says "no one paid attention" (NIV)?

6. Why do you think Elijah poured so much water on the sacrifice?

7. How long was Elijah's prayer?

8. What was the people's response to the miracle?

RESPOND

Elijah was probably more outnumbered than we are. His response to the prophets of Baal was an extreme response not to be used as a rule of thumb when dealing with opponents to Christianity. The point here is that Elijah was confident that what he believed was true, and that opposition can be dealt with in a manner that draws the unbeliever to Christ.

Display the pieces of construction paper again. Discuss ways to deal with these types of opposition to Christianity.

Remember, love is our most powerful weapon, and leading the lost to Christ is the ultimate goal.

Balance MID

Social Injustice Rebuked

Study Text: 1 Kings 21:1-29
Objective: To consider how the abuse of power affects society and stand for social justice.
Time: Around 863 B.C.
Place: Jezreel
Golden Text: "Inasmuch as ye have done it unto one of the least of these my brethren, ye have done it unto me" (Matthew 25:40).
Central Truth: Social justice is commanded by God.
Evangelism Emphasis: Effective evangelism must be accompanied by social justice.

PRINTED TEXT

1 Kings 21:2. And Ahab spake unto Naboth, saying, Give me thy vineyard, that I may have it for a garden of herbs, because it is near unto my house: and I will give thee for it a better vineyard than it; or, if it seem good to thee, I will give thee the worth of it in money.

3. And Naboth said to Ahab, The Lord forbid it me, that I should give the inheritance of my fathers unto thee.

4. And Ahab came into his house heavy and displeased because of the word which Naboth the Jezreelite had spoken to him: for he had said, I will not give thee the inheritance of my fathers. And he laid him down upon his bed, and turned away his face, and would eat no bread.

7. And Jezebel his wife said unto him, Dost thou now govern the kingdom of Israel? arise, and eat bread, and let thine heart be merry: I will give thee the vineyard of Naboth the Jezreelite.

14. Then they sent to Jezebel, saying, Naboth is stoned, and is dead.

15. And it came to pass, when Jezebel heard that Naboth was stoned, and was dead, that Jezebel said to Ahab, Arise, take possession of the vineyard of Naboth the Jezreelite, which he refused to give thee for money: **for Naboth is not alive, but dead.**

16. And it came to pass, when Ahab heard that Naboth was dead, that Ahab rose up to go down to the vineyard of Naboth the Jezreelite, to take possession of it.

17. And the word of the Lord came to Elijah the Tishbite, saying,

18. Arise, go down to meet Ahab king of Israel, which is in Samaria: behold, he is in the vineyard of Naboth, whither he is gone down to possess it.

19. And thou shalt speak unto him, saying, Thus saith the Lord, Hast thou killed, and also taken possession? And thou shalt speak unto him, saying, Thus saith the Lord, In the place where dogs licked the blood of Naboth shall dogs lick thy blood, even thine.

27. And it came to pass, when Ahab heard those words, that he rent his clothes, and put sackcloth upon his flesh, and fasted, and lay in sackcloth, and went softly.

28. And the word of the Lord came to Elijah the Tishbite, saying,

29. Seest thou how Ahab humbleth himself before me? because he humbleth himself before me, I will not bring the evil in his days: but in his son's days will I bring the evil upon his house.

DICTIONARY

Naboth (NAY-both)—1 Kings 21:2—A typical Jewish landowner with an independent spirit who unfortunately owned land near Ahab's palace.

Jezreelite (JEZ-reel-ite)—1 Kings 21:4—An inhabitant of Jezreel, a city favorably situated for climate and fertility. Omri and Ahab fortified it and made it their winter capital and royal residence.

LESSON OUTLINE

I. COVETOUS DESIRE
   A. The Request
   B. The Response

II. ABUSE OF POWER
   A. The Plan
   B. The Production
   C. The Possession

III. CONDEMNATION AND COMPASSION
   A. The Confrontation
   B. The Condemnation
   C. The Conciliation

LESSON EXPOSITION

INTRODUCTION

If we were to sit down and make a list of sins, social injustice probably wouldn't be listed first. Why not? Well, we tend to think of those sins which are emphasized most frequently. They are lying, stealing, murder, immorality and various forms of malicious behavior. To justify our particular list we might even turn to the listing of the works of the flesh in Galatians 5:19-21.

All of the previously mentioned actions need to be recognized for what they are—sin. Yet, at the same time we must not overlook other sinful actions and attitudes which are equally condemned by God. They not only separate a person from God but also provoke His anger and judgment. This can be readily seen when reviewing the judgment God sent on Israel (2 Kings 17) and Judah (2 Kings 25). Usually we discuss how their idolatry and hypocritical worship spurred God

to such destruction of His own people. Often overlooked are the rebukes for their social injustice against the poor, the widowed and the orphaned.

Listen to the words of Amos as he thunders against Israel: "Hear this word, you cows of Bashan on Mount Samaria, you women who oppress the poor and crush the needy. . . . Hear this, you who trample the needy and do away with the poor of the land" (4:1; 8:4, *NIV*).

As the Book of Isaiah opens, we read of the right way to live: "Learn to do well; seek judgment, relieve the oppressed, judge the fatherless, plead for the widow" (1:17). However, several verses later we read of what was actually taking place: "Thy princes are rebellious, and companions of thieves: every one loveth gifts, and followeth after rewards: they judge not the fatherless, neither doth the cause of the widow come unto them" (v. 23).

One last quote from the prophets: "If ye oppress not the stranger, the fatherless, and the widow, and shed not innocent blood in this place, neither walk after other gods to your hurt: then will I cause you to dwell in this place, in the land that I gave to your fathers, for ever and ever" (Jeremiah 7:6, 7).

In the New Testament the need for social justice appears as well. Hear Jesus' denunciation of the religious leaders: "Woe unto you, scribes and Pharisees, hypocrites! for ye devour widows' houses, and for a pretence make long prayer: therefore ye shall receive the greater damnation" (Matthew 23:14).

The previous verses are just selected examples of what the Word of God speaks concerning the believer's obligation to seek for social justice. When the Bible mentions people specifically for their disregard of social justice, they are people of power—power which came to them by either their political/religious position or wealth. That doesn't mean people of other classes and positions are exempt from the problem. It simply indicates those who are more prone to disregard social justice as they advance their own agendas. We see this very plainly in today's lesson as Ahab, the king, takes advantage of Naboth, a common landowner.

So that none of us thinks we are unaffected by the problems of social injustice due to our not having position or wealth, the words of James need our consideration: "Pure religion and undefiled before God and the Father is this, To visit the fatherless and widows in their affliction, and to keep himself unspotted from the world" (James 1:27).

Not only does today's lesson emphasize the need for social justice, but it further reveals the character of King Ahab and his queen, Jezebel. Wickedness never hides itself in only one area of an individual's life. It creeps into all areas of life.

I. COVETOUS DESIRE
(1 Kings 21:1-6)

A. The Request (vv. 1, 2)

(1 Kings 21:1 is not included in the printed text.)

2. And Ahab spake unto Naboth, saying, Give me thy vineyard, that I may have it for a garden of herbs, because it is near unto my house: and I will give thee for it a better vineyard than it; or, if it seem good to thee, I will give thee the worth of it in money.

The story begins with the initial dialogue between Naboth and King Ahab. Naboth's importance stems from his ownership of a piece of land in Jezreel. Located at the base of

Mount Gilboa, this property apparently was located very close to Ahab's summer palace. Like many other kings, he apparently had several palaces and the prestige that went with them, thus enabling him to have not only a change in venue but in weather.

Ahab chose to personally speak to Naboth rather than send a representative of the court. No specific reason for his direct contact is given in Scripture. Maybe Ahab thought that a personal visit would be very impressive and thus guarantee the deal being consummated. Or, the proximity of the property may have allowed for a spontaneous meeting.

Ahab got to the point immediately. He wanted Naboth's vineyard so he could use it for a vegetable garden, emphasizing its nearness to his home. Ahab offered Naboth a choice of payment. He could choose between receiving a vineyard of greater value or the cash price. It was completely up to Naboth.

This request was simple and aboveboard. The covetous nature of it could not be seen initially.

Ahab's request reminds us of Samuel's prediction prior to Israel's receiving a king. He warned that the king would want their vineyards (see 1 Samuel 8:14).

B. The Response (vv. 3-6)

(1 Kings 21:5, 6 is not included in the printed text.)

3. And Naboth said to Ahab, The Lord forbid it me, that I should give the inheritance of my fathers unto thee.

4. And Ahab came into his house heavy and displeased because of the word which Naboth the Jezreelite had spoken to him: for he had said, I will not give thee the inheritance of my fathers. And he laid him down upon his bed, and turned away his face, and would eat no bread.

no negotiation

Without hesitation Naboth offered his response. He was not impressed by the king's personal request. He did not want a better vineyard or even the cash value. A much higher principle guided him. And for that reason he refused. But instead of saying a simple "no" or "thanks but no thanks," this God-fearing man invoked the name of the Lord as he refused. His personal wishes or wants were out of the picture. What mattered was God's requirements. Naboth pointed out that he could not allow the title of this land to exchange hands.

There are several Old Testament passages which provide the basis for the refusal. Leviticus 25:23-28 paints a broad picture, but the beginning line of verse 23 lays the foundation: "The land shall not be sold for ever." Not to be overlooked is Numbers 36:7: "For every one of the children of Israel shall keep himself to the inheritance of the tribe of his fathers."

Ahab's response to Naboth's refusal indicates the covetous nature of the request and his inherent evil heart. Apparently he understood the reason Naboth said no, but Ahab's handling of it was so immature. There were no loud exclamations or uttered threats. Ahab simply returned to his house in a sullen, angry state. But it did not end there. He went to bed, turned his face to the wall, and refused to eat. He portrayed the depressed or sorrowful person who shrinks away from responsibility and wants no communication with anyone. We might rationalize this type of pouting from a little child, but not from a grown adult who was reigning as the king over 10 tribes of Israel!

Jezebel entered the picture and asked the normal questions of a concerned wife. First, she inquired as to the reason for his sullenness. Then, she wanted to know why he was fasting. We could guess that Jezebel assumed that some major reversal or kingdom crisis was at hand for her husband to react in such a manner.

Or maybe she had seen him pout over trivia before.

Ahab told his wife the basic details of his encounter with Naboth. It almost reminds us of a little boy sharing with his mother how he has been mistreated. Summarized, the account was simply this: "I asked. I even gave him choices. He said no!"

How different this situation is from the time when King Hezekiah turned to the wall. This came after the prophet's message that the king's illness was terminal and he should set his affairs in order (Isaiah 38:1, 2). Hezekiah in righteousness separated himself for the purpose of intercessory prayer. But instead of getting alone to pray, King Ahab was merely pouting.

II. ABUSE OF POWER
(1 Kings 21:7-16)

A. The Plan (vv. 7-10)

(1 Kings 21:8-10 is not included in the printed text.)

7. And Jezebel his wife said unto him, Dost thou now govern the kingdom of Israel? arise, and eat bread, and let thine heart be merry: I will give thee the vineyard of Naboth the Jezreelite.

Jezebel's response to her husband begins with an interesting question. The *New International Version* renders it, "Is this how you act as king over Israel?" (v. 7). There was a definite undertone of rebuke in her response. Eastern monarchs as wicked as Ahab would let nothing stand between them and their wishes. Very likely Jezebel could not understand his sullen attitude. The king should be taking the steps necessary to secure the desired vineyard regardless of Naboth's refusal.

Rather than waiting for Ahab to gather himself and take action, Jezebel assumed control of the situation. Her actions may have been partly motivated by affection for her husband. However, we must not overlook the aggressiveness of this wicked woman and her

Jezebel - controlling

desire to dominate. Notice her directives to Ahab. She wanted him to get up, eat and cheer up. The situation would change shortly. The vineyard would be his.

Beginning with verse 8, we see a carefully crafted plan. There does not appear to be any major time lapse between the cheering of her husband and the beginning of her sinful scheme. All of her planning would have been useless except for the willingness of others to be instruments of sin and death along with Jezebel. She may have paid them, or they may have been in her debt for a previous favor. Whatever the motive, they complied.

controlling

Using the official seal of the king, Jezebel sent official letters to the leading men of Jezreel. The directions were explicit. The leaders were to proclaim a special day of fasting. Then on that day during a special gathering, Naboth was to be given a prominent place among the people. However, at some point two scoundrels were to suddenly charge him with blasphemy. They would charge that he had cursed both God and the king. Then, in accordance with the law of Moses, Naboth would be taken out of the city and stoned.

Consider six aspects of the queen's plot. First, she incorporated people who would have had an opportunity to see Naboth's lifestyle and thus appear to be credible witnesses by virtue of their proximity. Second, the ordering of a fast for the entire city would make it appear as though a heavy load of guilt was hovering over them. Third, the securing of two witnesses would preserve the appearance of justice as required by the Law (Deuteronomy 19:15; Numbers 35:30). Fourth, the charge of blasphemy against God would secure Naboth's death (Leviticus 24:16; Deuteronomy 17:2-7). Fifth, charging Naboth with blasphemy against the king and God were not separate crimes. Since the king was God's representative on earth, to curse him was equivalent to cursing God. Sixth, Naboth appeared to be a godly man concerned about the Law, but he was surrounded by individuals of sinful attitudes and actions.

B. The Production (vv. 11-14)

(1 Kings 21:11-13 is not included in the printed text.)

14. Then they sent to Jezebel, saying, Naboth is stoned, and is dead.

Verses 11-13 describe a staged production. Jezebel wrote the script, then the nobles and elders followed through as actors. They accomplished everything exactly as the queen designed it. Evil triumphed and a good man perished.

The message sent to Jezebel was simple and matter-of-fact: "Naboth is stoned, and is dead." It is reminiscent of the message Joab sent to David after staging Uriah's death. He told of archers shooting from the walls and killing some of David's soldiers. Then he added, "And thy servant Uriah the Hittite is dead also" (2 Samuel 11:24).

In the case of Naboth's death, as with that of Uriah, the motivation behind the death was hidden. Life would go on as usual. But that's the deception of sin. It blinds individuals to the truth of God's knowing and seeing everything.

C. The Possession (vv. 15, 16)

15. And it came to pass, when Jezebel heard that Naboth was stoned, and was dead, that Jezebel said to Ahab, Arise, take possession of the vineyard of Naboth the Jezreelite, which he refused to give thee for money: for Naboth is not alive, but dead.

16. And it came to pass, when Ahab heard that Naboth was dead, that Ahab rose up to go down to the vineyard of Naboth the Jezreelite, to take possession of it.

With the dastardly deed accomplished, all that was left to be done was Ahab's taking possession of the desired property. Since it was Jezebel who promised him the property and arranged Naboth's execution, she was the one to notify her husband of its availability. Her words were simple: "Get up and take possession of Naboth's vineyard, which he refused to sell to you." Not only did Ahab now have the property, but he didn't have to pay any money for it. But later he would pay for it in a far greater manner.

Jezebel included one other fact. She pointed out that Naboth was no longer alive. On the one hand it simplified the situation. This man would not be around to protest the acquisition or continue to be a thorn in the flesh. Left unspoken was the manner of his death. Could it be that Ahab was so sheltered and naive not to know there had been underhanded dealing? Could he possibly believe that his wife, Jezebel, had nothing to do with Naboth's timely death and property availability? It's very doubtful that Ahab could stand innocent. Besides, hadn't her previous words to him indicated she would get the vineyard for him? AHAB did not care

The charge of blasphemy made Naboth's property available to Ahab from another perspective as well. Since blasphemy was seen as an act of high treason, the guilty party's property could be confiscated. Though no Mosaic law or principle stated this, there is a principle which was adapted. According to Deuteronomy 13:16, the property of those guilty of blasphemy forfeited their property to the Lord. This led to the king's confiscating the property of those found guilty of being a traitor in the kingdom.

Ahab followed Jezebel's advice and took possession of the vineyard. One can only speculate on his emotional state. Could he possibly have the same joy in possession now if he would have either paid for it or traded for it? However, since the Bible describes Ahab as the worst king of Israel to this point, what would the life of Naboth be to such person so steeped in sin and idol worship?

III. CONDEMNATION AND COMPASSION (1 Kings 21:17-29)

A. The Confrontation (vv. 17-19)

17. And the word of the Lord came to Elijah the Tishbite, saying,
18. Arise, go down to meet Ahab king of Israel, which is in Samaria: behold, he is in the vineyard of Naboth, whither he is gone down to possess it.
19. And thou shalt speak unto him, saying, Thus saith the Lord, Hast thou killed, and also taken possession? And thou shalt speak unto him, saying, Thus saith the Lord, In the place where dogs licked the blood of Naboth shall dogs lick thy blood, even thine.

Elijah's task as God's prophet to a wicked monarchy in Israel sometimes placed him in a perilous situation. Once again, in a crisis of evil, God called him into action with a definite message for King Ahab. He directed the prophet to meet Ahab in the vineyard of the deceased Naboth. The phrase "which is in Samaria" is better translated as "who rules in Samaria." Ahab, the king who ruled from his throne in Samaria, was still at the summer palace in Jezreel.

Is there a particular pattern God follows in confronting sinners with their sin? In the case of Ahab and Jezebel, God sent Elijah within what appears to be only days after Naboth's execution. God confronted Adam and Eve within the day of their disobedience. But in the case of David's adultery with Bathsheba and murder of

I didn't ask

her husband, God allowed months to pass. David took Bathsheba as his wife after she completed her time of mourning. And it was not until after their child was born that God sent Nathan to confront and expose David's sin. The principle which stands forth is that God rebukes the sinner, but He chooses the timetable according to His sovereign will.

God's message for Ahab cut immediately to the problem. Elijah was to identify the king as a murderer and property seizer. This emphasized the king's responsibility. He could have stopped Jezebel. He could have declared that Naboth and his vineyard were to be left alone. However, he did not. Now he stood directly responsible for murder as a result of his allowing it to take place.

The despicable nature of events demanded retribution of like nature. Elijah was to declare that in the very place where the dogs licked Naboth's blood, they would also lick Ahab's blood. This brief statement speaks volumes. First, it indicates Ahab would not die a natural death from old age while residing in the palace. Instead, there would be some form of violence causing his blood to be poured out. Second, the picture of dogs licking his blood meant they would have access to his body. Remember, dogs in this era were considered the equivalent of wild, vicious animals. All in all, Ahab did not have a promising future.

B. The Condemnation (vv. 20-24)

(1 Kings 21:20-24 is not included in the printed text.)

When Elijah approached Ahab in the vineyard, the battle lines were quickly drawn. The king greeted the prophet as "mine enemy." (This is a much stronger exchange than at an earlier time, when Ahab described Elijah as being the "troubler of Israel"

[1 Kings 18:17, NIV]. Equal to the task and intent on his mission, Elijah immediately changed the focus. He pointed out that the reason for this meeting was Ahab's selling himself to do evil (21:20).

Ahab and Jezebel's actions would now result in God's punishment of them and their family. Every male in Ahab's household would die, including freemen and bondmen. His dynasty would be exterminated just like those of two previous kings in Israel. Jeroboam, the son of Nebat, was the first king of the northern 10 tribes when came the division into northern and southern kingdoms. He perverted Israel's worship in an attempt to keep his citizens from feeling the need to go to Jerusalem. As a result, through the prophet Ahijah, God foretold of a day when dogs and birds would feed on his descendants (14:10, 11).

Baasha became the instrument who destroyed Jeroboam's dynasty. In turn, his sinfulness provoked God's anger. His descendants would suffer the same fate of being consumed by the dogs and birds (16:4). This points to the consistency of God's judgment on the leaders of His people when they neglected righteousness and chose evil. It should not have come as a surprise to Ahab when he heard of God's intended future for his household.

Ahab's descendants were going to experience the same judgment as those of the past. Those killed in the city would become food for the dogs, while those dying in the fields would be consumed by the birds (21:24).

Verse 23 promised a specific judgment for Jezebel. Since she spearheaded the plot against Naboth, God took special note of her punishment. Like the males in the dynasty, she too would be consumed by the dogs. But notice the location. It would happen outside the wall of Jezreel.

Naboth would have been stoned outside the city. Apparently she would die and be consumed in a like location, if not in the same spot. We know from 2 Kings 9:30-37 that this prophesy was fulfilled. There is a real sense of justice here. God's harshest judgment comes against those who knowingly pervert His law and harm the innocent. That's social justice.

C. The Conciliation (vv. 25-29)

(1 Kings 21:25, 26 is not included in the printed text.)

27. And it came to pass, when Ahab heard those words, that he rent his clothes, and put sackcloth upon his flesh, and fasted, and lay in sackcloth, and went softly.

28. And the word of the Lord came to Elijah the Tishbite, saying,

29. Seest thou how Ahab humbleth himself before me? because he humbleth himself before me, I will not bring the evil in his days: but in his son's days will I bring the evil upon his house.

Verse 25 begins with a statement placing Ahab on the top of the pyramid of evil. It is in accord with the description of him in 16:33, "Ahab did more to provoke the Lord God of Israel to anger than all the kings of Israel that were before him."

The distinctiveness of Ahab's wickedness can be seen by the statement of "which did sell himself to work wickedness in the sight of the Lord" (21:25). No wonder social justice was not seen in his actions. No wonder idolatry flooded his nation. He literally sold himself to unrighteousness for its very temporary reward.

Though the specific details of the marital relationship between Ahab and Jezebel are not revealed in Scripture, there are sufficient hints to see her as the catalyst in his life. The last phrase of verse 25, "whom Jezebel his wife stirred up," is also translated as "urged on by Jezebel his wife" (NIV). Surely Ahab's marriage and following his wife's desires were part of the sellout. Maybe there are similarities here with the influence Delilah had over Samson.

Verse 26 emphasizes the distinct abomination of Ahab's actions. In complete disregard and disobedience to the first two commandments, he allowed idolatry to permeate God's people. Encouraging the establishment of foreign gods placed Israel in the same category as the nations which God had decreed for destruction. Remember Deuteronomy 20:17, 18: "But thou shalt utterly destroy them; namely, the Hittites, and the Amorites. . . . That they teach you not to do after all their abominations, which they have done unto their gods; so should ye sin against the Lord your God."

With this picture of Ahab's despicable condition in mind, it is amazing to see his actions beginning in verse 27. Hearing of God's judgment to be poured out against himself, his wife and his family, the wicked king responded with fear and conviction! Immediately he exhibited the signs of sorrow and repentance. He tore his clothing and exchanged the finery of the robes of royalty for the harsh texture of sackcloth. He also began to fast. However, this time his fasting was not done in sullenness for not having his way. Even when he went to bed, he continued to wear the garments of repentance. Also, his daily demeanor lost all swagger and personal pride. Instead, he now exhibited a demeanor of submissive meekness and humility. What a change!

The Scriptures do not indicate how much time went by until the word of the Lord came again to Elijah. The message from God did not take away the announced judgment, but did delay it. God honored the humble, repentant spirit of Ahab and decreed the judgment for sin would take place after the king's death. This did not mean the dogs wouldn't lick his blood. However, it did indicate that the destruction of Ahab's dynasty would take place with the next generation.

This part of the account of Ahab's life reminds us that even the worst sinner is eligible for God's forgiveness if he or she will come in repentance. How can we forget that the entire city of Nineveh followed their king in sorrowful repentance after hearing Jonah's message of doom? No one is too evil for the cleansing power of God. Thus, it becomes our duty to continue praying for the salvation of even the most despicable of sinners.

Ahab's story also teaches that forgiveness of one's sins does not mean that the impact of previous actions will just be wiped away. Naboth was dead, as were his sons (see 2 Kings 9:26). This could not just be brushed away as though it never happened. The God who responds to repentance also administers justice.

This lesson ends with a path of conciliation. Ahab chose to recognize God's sovereignty and to admit his own sinfulness. As a result of his repentance, God honored him to the point where justice was also fulfilled.

GOLDEN TEXT HOMILY

"INASMUCH AS YE HAVE DONE IT UNTO ONE OF THE LEAST OF THESE MY BRETHREN, YE HAVE DONE IT UNTO ME" (Matthew 25:40).

When Jesus made this profound statement, He identified who "the least of these" were. He named the hungry, the thirsty, strangers, people needing clothing, the sick, and those in prison. Then He put Himself in the category of "the least" by saying however we treat them is how we are treating Him.

Jesus knew what it was to be hungry and thirsty, for He fasted 40 days in the wilderness.

Jesus knew what it was to be a stranger, for He invaded this world to save us, yet "his own received him not" (John 1:11).

Jesus knew what it was to need clothing, for His clothes were stolen from Him as He was taken away to be crucified.

Jesus knew what it was to suffer physically; He received the lash of the whip across His back, the sting of the thorns in His head, and the agony of the nails in His hands and feet.

Jesus knew what it was to be imprisoned, for His body was sealed inside in a cave tomb as He awaited His resurrection.

No wonder Jesus can identify with those He calls the least, and no wonder He calls us to reach out to them. The message is plain and practical: Jesus wants us to minister to the needs of people as if we were directly serving Jesus himself.

Who are the hungry and thirsty we can serve?

Who are the strangers in our community whom we can befriend?

How can we serve the sick among us?

How can we reach out to those in prison?

Jesus is calling; we must respond.—**Lance Colkmire**

SENTENCE SERMONS

SOCIAL JUSTICE is commanded by God.

—Selected

THE CHRISTIAN'S GOAL is not power but justice.

—Charles Colson

OF ALL FORCES, violence is the weakest.

—Gobineau

EVANGELISM APPLICATION

EFFECTIVE EVANGELISM MUST BE ACCOMPANIED BY SOCIAL JUSTICE.

Jesus did not come as a crusader against every social injustice evident in Palestine during His lifetime. He could not. That would have kept Him from accomplishing the primary purpose for coming in human flesh. It may have even brought attention from the Roman officials.

But at the same time Jesus demonstrated concern for those who were victims of social injustice. Of special note was the attention He directed toward the impoverished.

A true concern for people will never allow us to simply evangelize their souls while disregarding their physical plight. How can we speak of God's love and care without also being His hand of provision? How can we intercede for God to help the needy and not give of our own supplies?

Surely we can't. The love of God and truth of the gospel shines more effectively when heard *and* seen.

ILLUMINATING THE LESSON

In 1984, Ron Sider's book *Rich Christians in an Age of Hunger* was released. Chapter 1 includes a historical example of social injustice on a global scale.

"When oil prices tripled in 1973, farmers in the developing world could not afford the oil needed to run irrigation pumps for the new strains of grain [developed in the '60s]. Nor could they afford the necessary fertilizer which had increased in price by 150 percent between 1972 and 1974.

"Tragically, poor harvests in North America, Europe, the U.S.S.R. and Japan combined with unexpectedly large U.S. sales of grain to the U.S.S.R. to almost triple the cost of grain for export in the same short period. When poor nations searched desperately for grain to feed their hungry masses in 1974, they had to pay two and a half times as much as two years earlier. . . . For some of the millions of people who were already spending 80 percent of their budget on food, there was only one possible outcome—starvation."

DAILY BIBLE READINGS

M. Help the Less Fortunate.
Deuteronomy 15:7-11

T. God Loves Righteousness.
Psalm 11:1-7

W. Do Justice.
Micah 6:6-8

T. Works of Mercy Rewarded.
Matthew 25:34-40

F. Share With Those in Need.
Acts 11:27-30

S. Impartiality Commanded.
James 2:1-9

TRUTH SEARCH:
Creatively Teaching the Word

Aim: Students will pray for those in various realms of leadership.

Items needed: Marker board, marker, paper, pencils

FOCUS

Write these words on the board: *nuclear power, fire, wind, water, guns.* Ask students to describe harmful ways each of the items can be used. Next, discuss how each one may be used for good.

Not unlike fire, wind, or nuclear power, a leader's power can be used to do harm as well as good. Today we are going to discuss how leaders sometimes abuse the power they have been given. We will also discuss a Christian's responsibility to leaders.

EXPLORE

Read 1 Kings 21:1-29 aloud. Then divide the class into two groups. Assign one half of the class verses 1-16. Assign the other half verses 17-29. The answers to the discussion questions should be read aloud to the entire class and further discussion encouraged.

1 Kings 21:1-16

1. Why did Ahab want Naboth's vineyard?

2. Why did Naboth refuse his offer?

3. How did Ahab respond to this refusal?

4. Explain Jezebel's plan to get Naboth's vineyard.

5. What was the false charge brought against Naboth?

6. Does Scripture indicate that Ahab knew the details of Jezebel's plan? Do you think he did? Why or why not?

7. Was her plan successful?

1 Kings 21:17-29

1. How did Elijah learn of the situation regarding Naboth's vineyard?

2. How did God plan to punish Ahab for his actions (v. 19)?

3. How did Ahab greet Elijah? Why do you think he greeted him this way (v. 20)?

4. What did Elijah proclaim as Ahab and Jezebel's punishments (vv. 20-24)?

5. What does the history lesson in verse 25 tell us about Ahab?

6. What does Elijah's response to God's impending judgment teach us about how leaders should respond when "caught in the act" (v. 27)?

7. How did God respond to Ahab's humility? Why?

RESPOND

Ask the students to give additional Biblical and historical examples, as well as examples of current events, of leaders who abused their power. For example:

Biblical: King David and Bathsheba; Haman's plot to kill the Jews.

Historical: Hitler's plan to extinguish the Jews; Stalin's attempt to suppress Christianity in Russia; Yugoslavia's attempt at ethnic cleansing during its civil war.

We all probably know someone in the church, at our jobs, or in the world of politics who has abused their position of authority. Our job as Christians is to pray for our leaders to use their authority wisely and with humility.

Select three individuals to take turns leading in prayer for people in the following groups: church leaders, community business leaders, and political leaders.

Pursuing God's Best

Study Text: 2 Kings 2:1-22
Objective: To appreciate the wisdom of pursuing spiritual excellence and follow Christ.
Time: Around 854 B.C.
Place: Primarily the Jordan River
Golden Text: "I press toward the mark for the prize of the high calling of God in Christ Jesus" (Philippians 3:14).
Central Truth: God's best for us is to follow Christ faithfully.
Evangelism Emphasis: Seeking God's best for our lives will enhance our witness of Christ.

PRINTED TEXT

2 Kings 2:2. And Elijah said unto Elisha, Tarry here, I pray thee; for the Lord hath sent me to Bethel. And Elisha said unto him, As the Lord liveth, and as thy soul liveth, I will not leave thee. So they went down to Bethel.

6. And Elijah said unto him, Tarry, I pray thee, here; for the Lord hath sent me to Jordan. And he said, As the Lord liveth, and as thy soul liveth, I will not leave thee. And they two went on.

8. And Elijah took his mantle, and wrapped it together, and smote the waters, and they were divided hither and thither, so that they two went over on dry ground.

9. And it came to pass, when they were gone over, that Elijah said unto Elisha, Ask what I shall do for thee, before I be taken away from thee. And Elisha said, I pray thee, let a double portion of thy spirit be upon me.

10. And he said, Thou hast asked a hard thing: nevertheless, if thou see me when I am taken from thee, it shall be so unto thee; but if not, it shall not be so.

11. And it came to pass, as they still went on, and talked, that, behold, there appeared a chariot of fire, and horses of fire, **and parted them both asunder; and Elijah went up by a whirlwind into heaven.**

14. And he took the mantle of Elijah that fell from him, and smote the waters, and said, Where is the Lord God of Elijah? and when he also had smitten the waters, they parted hither and thither: and Elisha went over.

15. And when the sons of the prophets which were to view at Jericho saw him, they said, The spirit of Elijah doth rest on Elisha. And they came to meet him, and bowed themselves to the ground before him.

19. And the men of the city said unto Elisha, Behold, I pray thee, the situation of this city is pleasant, as my lord seeth: but the water is naught, and the ground barren.

20. And he said, Bring me a new cruse, and put salt therein. And they brought it to him.

21. And he went forth unto the spring of the waters, and cast the salt in there, and said, Thus saith the Lord, I have healed these waters; there shall not be from thence any more death or barren land.

22. So the waters were healed unto this day, according to the saying of Elisha which he spake.

DICTIONARY

mantle (MAN-t'l)—2 Kings 2:8—Besides the tunic which was worn on the body, the Israelites wore an outer garment—the mantle—which was loosely wrapped over the tunic. Prophets apparently wore a mantle that would immediately identify their office.

LESSON OUTLINE

I. FOLLOWING FAITHFULLY

  A. The Test

  B. The Crossing

II. SEEKING SPIRITUAL EMPOWERMENT

  A. The Request

  B. The Response

  C. The Ascension

III. MINISTERING IN THE SPIRIT

  A. The Mantle

  B. The Ministering

LESSON EXPOSITION

INTRODUCTION

This lesson records the transition of the prophetic leadership from Elijah to Elisha. Unlike other individuals whose ministry ended due to death or advancing age, Elijah's ministry saw a dramatic conclusion. In His sovereignty, God plucked him directly from earth to be with Himself. In place of a death process, there were horses of fire and a chariot of fire to carry Elijah to his eternal destination. He became one of only two individuals in Scripture not to see physical death.

The miraculous aspects of this event can cause us to miss the special characteristics and actions of the second man, Elisha. This special man of God did not just pop on the scene without any introduction or preparation. At the time of this transition in ministry, he was serving as Elijah's assistant.

Elisha's service to Elijah came as a result of a divine call. While Elijah hid in Horeb after fleeing the wrath of Jezebel, God gave three directions. He was to anoint three men to specific positions. The first two would become kings over separate areas. Then there was Elisha, who was to be anointed as Elijah's successor (1 Kings 19:15, 16).

The Scriptures include a brief description of that calling. In just a few moments Elisha changed from a farmer capable of plowing with oxen and overseeing other workers in the field to being the attendant to God's most powerful prophet (1 Kings 19:19-21). At that point Elisha probably did not know what God intended for him.

It is good that God usually informs us of most of His will on a need-to-know basis. Premature revelation of many details would hinder His purpose. Otherwise we would be overwhelmed by His intentions. Why? Sometimes our faith isn't at the point where we can believe God could do such great things through and for us. Other times may find us in a point of questioning and rebellion. We might think, *Lord, You want me to do what and where?* But when He leads us step-by-step and gradually unfolds His will, we can walk with obedience and confidence!

I. FOLLOWING FAITHFULLY
  (2 Kings 2:1-8)

A. The Test (vv. 1-6)

(2 Kings 2:1, 3-5 is not included in the printed text.)

2. And Elijah said unto Elisha, Tarry here, I pray thee; for the Lord hath sent me to Bethel. And

Elisha said unto him, As the Lord liveth, and as thy soul liveth, I will not leave thee. So they went down to Bethel.
6. And Elijah said unto him, Tarry, I pray thee, here; for the Lord hath sent me to Jordan. And he said, As the Lord liveth, and as thy soul liveth, I will not leave thee. And they two went on.

Verse 1 pinpoints Elijah and Elisha's location as they began their last journey together. Gilgal, located southwest of Shiloh and on the road to Jericho, provided a remarkable geographic picture. *Ellicott's Bible Commentary* describes it as follows: "From this spot the mountain land of Gilead, the Great Sea, and the snowy heights of Hermon were all visible, so that the prophet could take from there a last look at the whole country which had been the scene of his earthly activity."

God revealed His intent for that day to a variety of people. Both Elijah and Elisha knew of it, but initially neither spoke directly of it to the other. The prophet began the day by informing his assistant of his need to go to Bethel. He specifically asked Elisha to remain at Gilgal. However, Elisha would allow nothing to separate them.

Why did Elijah ask his assistant to stay in Gilgal? One suggestion is that this was the first step in a three-part test of Elisha.

Elijah and Elisha made the short trip to Bethel, where the sons of the prophets came out to meet them. These individuals were probably being trained for the possibility of being used in the prophetic ministry. Since the prophetic office was not hereditary, we know these individuals did not necessarily come from a family where the father was a prophet. When they were in Elisha's company alone, they presented their question.

Was he aware that today God would take his master away? Not only did he answer in the affirmative, but he asked them not to speak of it.

Notice the patience in Elisha's approach. He willingly restrained himself until his master spoke of the event.

At Bethel, Elijah made the second request of the day for Elisha to stay while he traveled on. This time he asked Elisha to stay at Bethel while he went down to Jericho. Once again, Elisha said that as long as God lives and Elijah lives, he would not allow a separation.

From Bethel, Elijah and Elisha walked to Jericho. Once again the resident company of prophets spoke to Elisha concerning God's taking his master that very day. Again Elisha said that he knew. And he did not want them to speak of it.

As the time to leave arrived, Elijah made the third request for Elisha to remain. Again, Elisha refused to leave Elijah.

This first phase of the whole story emphasizes that being a faithful follower does not exempt us from God's testing. God's testing of Abraham by asking him to sacrifice Isaac is a classic case (Genesis 22). Our years of faithfulness simply provide more opportunities for us to demonstrate our love and commitment to God. Psalm 66:10 further states the reality of testing: "For thou, O God, hast proved [tested] us: thou hast tried us, as silver is tried."

B. The Crossing (vv. 7, 8)

(2 Kings 2:7 is not included in the printed text.)

8. And Elijah took his mantle, and wrapped it together, and smote the waters, and they were divided hither and thither, so that they two went over on dry ground.

Though Elijah and Elisha walked together as they left Jericho, they were followed at a distance. Fifty of the prophets from the Jericho company stationed themselves at a location to see how the crossing of the Jordan would be accomplished (v. 7). There was no fording place there, so how would they get across? We can only speculate of the thoughts that may have been crossing their minds. Maybe this would be the place where God would take the esteemed prophet of Israel. However, instead they witnessed a present miracle which mirrored one of the past—the opening of the Jordan River.

Taking his outer mantle or cloak, which was symbolic of his prophetic position, Elijah rolled it up and then hit the waters of the Jordan with it. When the Red Sea was opened through the ministry of Moses, it occurred with the stretching out of his rod (Exodus 14:16, 21). The rod stood as one of the shepherd's tools or weapons. In the case of Elijah, the mantle spoke of his role. This reminds us of the value of symbolism. It helps us keep a clear perspective of both the person and the event.

Notice the description of what took place. The water divided to both the left and the right. A wall of water formed on both sides. Only a divine miracle could produce such a positioning of the water.

When God accomplishes a miracle, it includes the details. There would be no wading through a muddy river bottom. Instantaneously, a dry path formed between the walls of water. Not only did this duplicate the Red Sea crossing but also the miracle of the Israelites crossing the Jordan River as they entered the Promised Land (Joshua 3:17).

Can you imagine being one of the 50 prophets standing there and seeing this miracle unfold? Even more so, what would it have been like to be an Elisha walking through the Jordan on dry ground?

II. SEEKING SPIRITUAL EMPOWERMENT (2 Kings 2:9-12)

A. The Request (v. 9)

9. And it came to pass, when they were gone over, that Elijah said unto Elisha, Ask what I shall do for thee, before I be taken away from thee. And Elisha said, I pray thee, let a double portion of thy spirit be upon me.

After crossing the Jordan River, the conversation between Elijah and Elisha took a new turn. Instead of testing his assistant again, Elijah asked a major question. What did Elisha want Elijah to do for him prior to being taken by God? It is quite similar to the occasion when God asked Solomon, "Ask what I shall give thee" (1 Kings 3:5).

Elisha's answer had to be immediate. Elisha's inherent quality of character and spiritual maturity assured a response which would be of assistance to others instead of simply grasping for personal benefit.

Elisha's request to receive a double portion was not a greedy grasping for power or position. He was not asking to be twice as powerful as Elijah or to perform twice as many miracles. This request needs to be understood in terms of the inheritance system. Unlike other cultural systems where the eldest son took all or the estate was equally divided between the sons, in the Oriental system the eldest son received a double portion. For example, if there were six sons, the estate would be divided into seven shares, with the oldest son getting two shares.

In this response Elisha was asking to be considered as the eldest son of the prophet and thus receive a double portion of Elijah's spirit. This can be interpreted as a desire to be Elijah's spiritual heir. Elisha's desire spoke volumes concerning the life and ministry of Elijah. Elijah had what Elisha wanted.

B. The Response (v. 10)

10. And he said, Thou hast asked a hard thing: nevertheless, if thou see me when I am taken from thee, it shall be so unto thee; but if not, it shall not be so.

Elijah's response gives no hint as to his opinion concerning the nature of the request. Whether or not he found pleasure in Elisha's desire did not enter into the equation. The issue at hand dealt with the one who would make it come to pass. Granting this petition was not in Elijah's hands. He knew of God's directing him to anoint Elisha, but a double portion went far beyond that. No wonder he stated this was a difficult thing.

Though Elijah did not seem to know the mind of God on this matter, he did know the particular setting when it would be known. The prophet indicated if Elisha saw his being taken, then the desire would come to pass.

One caution came with the promising words. Failure to be with Elijah at the moment of his departure would negate this request. In view of how closely Elisha had followed Elijah throughout the day and from place to place, we might wonder why the caution. First, it is always appropriate to remind even the most dedicated believer of the consequences of failure. Every believer needs to concentrate on the task at hand and not become complacent in doing good. Second is the Biblical pattern for showing the full picture. It's like the Deuteronomic principle. Obedience brings blessings, but disobedience brings cursings and judgment.

Did Elisha understand who would be the true giver of his request? He must have. Surely after working with Elijah he knew that the prophet's greatness did not reside in himself but in God.

C. The Ascension (vv. 11, 12)

(2 Kings 2:12 is not included in the printed text.)

11. And it came to pass, as they still went on, and talked, that, behold, there appeared a chariot of fire, and horses of fire, and parted them both asunder; and Elijah went up by a whirlwind into heaven.

God's evidencing Himself through the use of natural phenomena can be seen repeatedly in Scripture. When He was about to give the Commandments to Israel at Mount Sinai, there was a marvelous demonstration of phenomena. First came thunder and lightning with a thick cloud over the mountain. Then there was an earthquake. When God descended on the mountain, smoke ascended as though there were volcanic activity (Exodus 19:16-19).

Later, when God appeared to Elijah at Horeb in "a still small voice," He first sent a strong wind that shattered the rocks. Then an earthquake followed. Lastly, fire appeared from nowhere (1 Kings 19:11, 12).

In our present text, as Elijah and Elisha were walking and talking, God dramatically appeared using the forces of nature and a display associated with the special revelation of God. Exactly what this whirlwind looked like in terms of its breadth and velocity isn't known. Perhaps it was like a cyclone or a small tornado. However, the distinctive difference was one of picking up Elijah without bringing any harm or injury to Elisha.

In this whirlwind appeared a chariot of fire and horses of fire. They literally drove between the two men, separating them. Elijah ascended into heaven through the whirlwind while Elisha remained. What an experience! Elisha saw his prophetic mentor being taken into the presence of God—not by death but by divine transportation.

Elijah responded by crying out, "My father, my father" (v. 12). This expresses how Elisha viewed Elijah as his spiritual father. This further defined his earlier request of receiving a double portion of Elijah's spirit. It stood forth not only as a request but what might be expected of a son to desire.

Elisha's tearing of his garments expressed his extreme sorrow. Yes, the dramatic revelation of God's taking Elijah would have spiritual impact. For the moment, however, Elisha dwelt on his personal loss. His spiritual father was gone from this life. Notice how carefully the scripture indicates the finality of the parting. They would not see each other again in this life.

III. MINISTERING IN THE SPIRIT
(2 Kings 2:13-15, 19-22)

A. The Mantle (vv. 13-15)

(2 Kings 2:13 is not included in the printed text.)

14. And he took the mantle of Elijah that fell from him, and smote the waters, and said, Where is the Lord God of Elijah? and when he also had smitten the waters, they parted hither and thither: and Elisha went over.

15. And when the sons of the prophets which were to view at Jericho saw him, they said, The spirit of Elijah doth rest on Elisha. And they came to meet him, and bowed themselves to the ground before him.

God took Elijah to Himself, but the prophet's mantle remained behind on the ground. Try to imagine what it must have been like. One moment Elisha was experiencing the phenomena of a divine event with all its visible evidences. And then, it was all over. Gone were the horses of fire, the chariot of fire and Elijah. All that was left behind was a personal covering.

Notice Elisha's reaction to the situation. He did not remain there mourning the separation from Elijah or the brevity of this divine encounter, because He understood what the presence of the mantle implied. Picking it up, he walked back to the Jordan River and stood on its bank. Then, in the same manner as Elijah, he smote the water with the mantle. Here was a man of action who apparently believed his request had been answered even though there had been no verbal confirmation.

Elisha accompanied his action with a special question: "Where is the Lord God of Elijah?" As the successor of Elijah, it would be appropriate for him to be able to recross the Jordan in the same manner as the initial crossing. And he did. The waters opened and divided on each side, enabling him to walk over on dry ground. Not only did this confirm God's intention for Elisha, but it became a statement to the 50 prophets from Jericho who had been watching.

Immediately upon coming into the presence of the watching prophets, Elisha received their homage. They bowed to him in recognition of his being their spiritual leader and father. What a change! In the morning he worked as Elijah's assistant. In the evening, as the day ended, he stood as the leader of the prophets. This transition was not just a matter of chance. It represented divine appointment on God's part with human preparation and steadfastness on Elisha's part. We can apply that same principle to individuals today. God wills distinct activities and positions for His children. But they will not be accomplished without the individuals making the necessary commitment.

God's confirming Elisha's position of leadership by a miracle was not unprecedented. When Joshua took over the leadership of Israel, he also followed in the shadow of a great man. He too was an assistant who received the top job. God enabled Joshua to receive the nation's respect through a leadership event similar to Moses' early days. "The Lord said unto Joshua, This day will I begin to magnify thee in the sight of all Israel, that they may know that, as I was with Moses, so I will be with thee" (Joshua 3:7). Moses had led Israel through the Red Sea, and now Joshua would lead them through the Jordan River at flood stage.

B. The Ministering (vv. 19-22)

19. And the men of the city said unto Elisha, Behold, I pray thee, the situation of this city is pleasant, as my lord seeth: but the water is naught, and the ground barren.

20. And he said, Bring me a new cruse, and put salt therein. And they brought it to him.

21. And he went forth unto the spring of the waters, and cast the salt in there, and said, Thus saith the Lord, I have healed these waters; there shall not be from thence any more death or barren land.

22. So the waters were healed unto this day, according to the saying of Elisha which he spake.

Even though the men of Jericho accepted Elisha as the new spiritual leader and believed Elijah had been taken by God, they apparently did not grasp the totality of what took place. Verses 16 and 17 indicate their pressing Elisha to allow them to send out a search party. Perhaps they were concerned that Elijah's body was lying somewhere after God had taken his spirit. Elisha initially refused their request. Finally, their persistence persuaded him to agree to allow them to look. For three days the 50 men looked unsuccessfully. Upon their return, Elisha reminded them that he

had told them not to go on this hopeless expedition.

After this event, Elisha apparently remained at Jericho for a period of time during which the people complained about the bad water. Its poor quality created a problem and made it unfit for producing vegetation. This situation provided another opportunity for the prophet to be accredited in the eyes of the people as Elijah's successor.

Beginning with verse 20, we see how Elisha ministered to their need. The method reminds us that God, through His servants, may use a variety of means to accomplish the desired result. Elisha asked for a dish of salt, which he then poured in the water supply. The salt in itself would not be sufficient to purify the water. Instead it symbolically represented God's healing the water supply of its putrid composition. The salt spoke of the power of God to renew and to bring life to that which previously was both harmful and unproductive.

Notice the word of the Lord which Elisha spoke in verse 21. The changing of the water's condition was not temporary. Rather, this water supply had been healed and would continue to produce good, sweet water like that of other wells in the area. What a ministry to the people of Jericho!

GOLDEN TEXT HOMILY

"I PRESS TOWARD THE MARK FOR THE PRIZE OF THE HIGH CALLING OF GOD IN CHRIST JESUS" (Philippians 3:14).

In the ancient games of Greece, with which the Philppians would have been very familiar, the race was a common sport and the winner's prize was a laurel wreath. The runners strained every muscle and earnestly pressed forward that they might win the prize, which was usually presented by some dignitary or noble person.

In the Christian life, Paul was pressing with a deeper intensity so he might win the prize that comes from the hand of Jesus Christ. The Christian race is called "the high calling," which suggests the exalted life of devotion and service to which we are called. The word *press* indicates that it will not be an easy way but that we must exert diligent effort to attain our goal.

In 1 Corinthians 9:24-27, Paul again compares the Christian life with a race, emphasizing that all who run the race can obtain the prize—"a crown that will last forever" (v. 25, *NIV*).—**Charles W. Conn**

SENTENCE SERMONS

GOD'S BEST for us is to follow Christ faithfully.

—**Selected**

A SAINT is not a man without faults, but a man who has given himself without reserve to God.

—**Brooke Westcott**

INTEGRITY has no need of rules.

—**Selected**

EVANGELISM APPLICATION

SEEKING GOD'S BEST FOR OUR LIVES WILL ENHANCE OUR WITNESS OF CHRIST.

Any activity that furthers our spirituality and demonstrates God's lordship in our lives positively impacts the quality of our witness. There's no way possible for us to be actively seeking God's best without its impacting both our inner person and the message of Christ which radiates to others.

If we want to improve our witness for Christ, we must actively seek to fulfill His will in our life to the fullest degree possible.

ILLUMINATING THE LESSON

Immediately upon his conversion, Attorney Charles Finney became willing to preach the gospel. The very next morning he refused to handle a case for which he had been retained. His explanation was, "I have a retainer from the Lord Jesus Christ to plead His cause, and I cannot plead yours."

This demonstrates a pattern for ministry which Finney followed for the rest of his life. Instead of settling for the goods of this world, he would strive for God's best.

DAILY BIBLE READINGS

M. Choosing Moral Excellence.
   Genesis 39:1-10
T. Asking for Understanding.
   1 Kings 3:5-12
W. Desiring God's Presence.
   Psalm 63:1-11
T. Seek God's Kingdom.
   Luke 12:22-32
F. Seek to Edify.
   1 Corinthians 14:6-12
S. Seek Eternal Things.
   Colossians 3:1-10

TRUTH SEARCH:
Creatively Teaching the Word

Aim: Students will pray for God to use them to continue the work of their spiritual forefathers.

Items needed: Marker board and markers

FOCUS

Ask the students to name 10 individuals of previous centuries that made great achievements in government, science, education, music or the arts. Write these names on the marker board. Beside each name write something that person achieved. Next, ask the class to describe how advancements have been made on those achievements. Also ask the class how it would have affected future societies if no future advancements were made on those achievements.

Today we are going to discuss continuing the work that our forefathers in the church started.

EXPLORE

Have a student read 2 Kings 2:1-10. Discuss these questions:
• *Three times Elijah told Elisha to stay behind. Each time Elisha refused. A popular interpretation says Elijah was merely testing Elisha's loyalty. Another interpretation says Elijah was humbled by the fact he was going to be taken by God and did not want witnesses. Which of these do you think is most likely? Why? Is there a third possibility?*
• *How do you think Elijah, Elisha, and the company of the prophets knew of Elijah's impending rapture?*
• *What did Elisha ask of Elijah? What do you think "a double portion of thy spirit" implies (v. 9)?*

Have a student read verses 11-22, then discuss these questions:
• *How was Elijah taken?*

• *What was the first miracle Elisha performed after Elijah's rapture (v. 14)?*
• *Compare that with the miracle performed by Elijah in verse 8.*
• *In what ways were these two miracles symbolic?*
• *How did the company of the prophets from Jericho respond to Elisha's miracle (v. 15)?*
• *What was Elisha's second miracle?*
• *Was Elisha immediately carrying on the work of Elijah?*

RESPOND

Erase the names off the marker board. Write the following list of great church leaders on the board and their accomplishments:
• **Stephen:** Stood firm in the face of persecution
• **Martin Luther:** Broke ties with the Roman Catholic Church and reaffirmed that salvation is by grace through faith alone
• **John Wesley:** Promoted the doctrine of sanctification and founded the Methodist movement
• **David Livingstone:** Pioneer missionary to Africa
• **Shearer Schoolhouse and Azusa Street revival participants:** Founders of the Pentecostal Movement in modern society

Ask the class how the church today would be different if these leaders had not been used by God.
• *How will our children's lives be affected if we allow the work of our spiritual forefathers to go unfinished?*

Lead the class in the following prayer: "Father, thank You for those men and women who made it possible for us to believe as we do. Move upon us by Your Holy Spirit to continue the work of the church. Make us shining examples for future generations. Amen."

Choose a Life of Integrity

Study Text: 2 Kings 5:1-27
Objective: To acknowledge that ministry to others must not be abused and maintain integrity.
Time: Around 852 B.C.
Place: Samaria and the Jordan River
Golden Text: "The integrity of the upright shall guide them: but the perverseness of the transgressors shall destroy them" (Proverbs 11:3).
Central Truth: Integrity is essential in Christian service.
Evangelism Emphasis: Integrity in relationships with the unsaved will help point them to Christ.

PRINTED TEXT

2 Kings 5:1. Now Naaman, captain of the host of the king of Syria, was a great man with his master, and honourable, because by him the Lord had given deliverance unto Syria: he was also a mighty man in valour, but he was a leper.

9. So Naaman came with his horses and with his chariot, and stood at the door of the house of Elisha.

10. And Elisha sent a messenger unto him, saying, Go and wash in Jordan seven times, and thy flesh shall come again to thee, and thou shalt be clean.

11. But Naaman was wroth, and went away, and said, Behold, I thought, He will surely come out to me, and stand, and call on the name of the Lord his God, and strike his hand over the place, and recover the leper.

12. Are not Abana and Pharpar, rivers of Damascus, better than all the waters of Israel? may I not wash in them, and be clean? So he turned and went away in a rage.

14. Then went he down, and dipped himself seven times in Jordan, according to the saying of the man of God: and his flesh came again like unto the flesh of a little child, and he was clean.

15. And he returned to the man of God, he and all his company, and came, and stood before him: and he said, Behold, now I know that there is no God in all the earth, but in Israel: now therefore, I pray thee, take a blessing of thy servant.

16. But he said, As the Lord liveth, before whom I stand, I will receive none. And he urged him to take it; but he refused.

20. But Gehazi, the servant of Elisha the man of God, said, Behold, my master hath spared Naaman this Syrian, in not receiving at his hands that which he brought: but, as the Lord liveth, I will run after him, and take somewhat of him.

25. But he went in, and stood before his master. And Elisha said unto him, Whence comest thou, Gehazi? And he said, Thy servant went no whither.

26. And he said unto him, Went not mine heart with thee, when the man turned again from his chariot to meet thee? Is it a time to receive money, and to receive garments, and oliveyards, and vineyards, and sheep, and oxen, and menservants, and maidservants?

27. The leprosy therefore of Naaman shall cleave unto thee, and unto thy seed for ever. And he went out from his presence a leper as white as snow.

DICTIONARY

Naaman (NAY-uh-mun)—2 Kings 5:1—Commander of the army of the king of Aram (Damascus).

Abana (ah-BAN-ah)—2 Kings 5:12—This river came from the northwest and flowed through Damascus.

Pharpar (FAR-par)—2 Kings 5:12—A river flowing into Damascus from the south.

Gehazi (geh-HAY-zye)—2 Kings 5:20—Servant of Naaman.

LESSON OUTLINE

I. A SEEKER FOR HELP

   A. The Need for a Cure

   B. The Need for the Right Person

II. MINISTRY NOT FOR SALE

   A. The Frustration of Humility

   B. The Desire to Compensate

III. MAINTAIN INTEGRITY

   A. The Temptation of Materialism

   B. The Judgment for Deceit

LESSON EXPOSITION

INTRODUCTION

This lesson ends the eight-lesson segment on learning from incidents in the lives of Samuel, Elijah and Elisha. This selection from the ministry of Elisha provides a thought-provoking story with an amazing variety of characters. In Syria (Aram) an unnamed slave girl gave witness of a cure for her master, Naaman, who was commander of the Syrian army.

Then, moving to Israel, we find three very different characters. Initially, we see the king of Israel, whose greatest fear was that the king of Syria was attempting to pick a quarrel. In contrast, Elisha stood as the messenger of God and offered healing, with the only condition being obedience. Then there is Gehazi, Elisha's servant. He demonstrated the struggle for integrity which the temptation of money can stimulate.

No other event in Elisha's ministry includes such a variety of topics for consideration while emphasizing the marvelous miracle of healing from leprosy. To begin with, there is the reality of disease. It affects individuals without regard for their status in life. Then we see the impact of one person's witness of hope. Next comes the difficulty an individual may encounter when desiring God's deliverance but questioning the means of attaining it. Finally there is the emphasis on integrity.

As a result of the diverse characters and topics included, this lesson brings a real challenge to both the teacher and students. It will be so easy to sidetrack on a variety of interesting subjects. Try to keep focused on the main topic of integrity.

What is integrity? One way to offer a definition is to compare *reputation* and *integrity*. *Reputation* is what or who people think you are, while *integrity* is what or who you really are. But also consider this three-step definition: (1) integrity is playing by the rules (there's more); (2) integrity is playing by the rules when no one else does (there's one more step); (3) integrity is playing by the rules when you're playing alone.

Dr. Vijai Sharma, a Tennessee psychiatrist, wrote: "All human beings care very much about integrity. In what way? They want everybody else to have it. Integrity is what we look for most in the other person. Even a criminal preparing to commit a crime wants integrity in his or her accomplice."

He continued by saying that we want our leaders and partners to "have absolute integrity so we can trust them. But, how many of us earnestly work on becoming a person of absolute integrity ourselves?"

As we work through today's lesson, one principle needs to stand in the forefront: Integrity doesn't just happen in our lives. But rather, it is a matter of choice and personal effort. Any time we neglect its development or continual maintenance, we can assume it will decline and eventually be lost.

I. A SEEKER FOR HELP
    (2 Kings 5:1-9)

A. The Need for a Cure (vv. 1-6)

(2 Kings 5:2-6 is not included in the printed text.)

1. Now Naaman, captain of the host of the king of Syria, was a great man with his master, and honourable, because by him the Lord had given deliverance unto Syria: he was also a mighty man in valour, but he was a leper.

The passage begins with an introduction of Naaman. On one hand, Naaman's life appeared to be the epitome of success. On the other hand, he suffered from a devastating disease. Even while standing forth as the defender of his country, he personally needed help.

Naaman held the prestigious position of commander in chief of the Syrian forces. He served his country with distinction by having led his forces in victory against surrounding nations. And he personally stood out as a brave warrior. He knew how to plan military strategy but also knew what it meant to be in battle as a soldier.

The contrast comes at the end of verse 1. Naaman suffered from leprosy. The exact nature of his leprosy cannot be stated since the term represents a wide variety of skin diseases. Regardless of its severity, this disease provided a dilemma in his life. In Syria lepers were not separated from the general population as was the rule in Israel. This enabled Naaman to occupy such a politically powerful position and be in close association with the king. But daily he had to deal with the personal problems associated with leprosy.

The potential for relief came from an unlikely source. In one of his raids into Israel, Naaman's soldiers brought home a captive Israelite girl. She became the personal servant to Naaman's wife. Though her name is not given, her character stands out. In view of the circumstances, no one could really blame her if she had no compassion for Naaman, master of the household. He was the one responsible for her being captured from Israel and placed in service in a foreign country. Instead she displayed a heart of concern by expressing her desire for Naaman's healing.

This young servant told Naaman's wife, "If only my master would see the prophet who is in Samaria! He would cure him of his leprosy" (v. 3, *NIV*). She did not merely suggest the possibility of recovery, but assumed it would be the automatic result of Naaman's visiting Elisha. What was the basis for her strong faith? Had she previously experienced the ministry of Elisha? On those questions we can only speculate.

Can you imagine what it was like for Naaman's wife to hear there was hope for a cure? Surely she delivered the message of hope immediately. In turn, Naaman took the news to his lord, the king. Verse 5 indicates the close relationship between the king and his commander in chief. The king urged him to go. All was to be gained and nothing lost by such a venture. The king said he would send a letter to the king of Israel (King Joram). This would most likely be a letter of introduction as well as a directive to be of whatever assistance Naaman would need in his quest for health.

Not knowing what to expect or the price to be paid, Naaman went well prepared. He carried an exceptionally large sum of money in the form of silver and gold. The silver was worth about $20,000 and the gold $60,000. Naaman also brought 10 sets of clothing. More than likely, the initial plan was to present this as a gift to the king of Israel in turn for his bringing health to Syria's chief military leader.

Verse 6 indicates that both the Syrian king and Naaman assumed the king of Israel would be the chief player in the healing. Not only did Naaman go to the royal residence, but the letter said to the king, "I am sending my servant Naaman to you so that you may cure him of his leprosy" (v. 6, NIV).

B. The Need for the Right Person
   (vv. 7-9)

(2 Kings 5:7, 8 is not included in the printed text.)

9. So Naaman came with his horses and with his chariot, and stood at the door of the house of Elisha.

Naaman's arrival with his letter of introduction caused King Joram some very tense moments. Upon reading the letter he immediately tore his clothing. This demonstrated the tremendous alarm which he sensed. He knew he lacked the power to cleanse this leper. Apparently he did not even think about who could be of assistance. His focus was on what might be unfolding here from a military standpoint. This visit from Naaman might be the point from which hostilities between Syria and Israel would heighten. The logical end would be armed conflict, and Israel would lose. No wonder the king responded in this manner. He foresaw the grief which was to come.

In the time of the king's despair, Elisha stepped into the picture. Having heard of the king's actions of despair, he sent word to the king. The means by which the prophet heard is not given. However, word of this dilemma surely had spread, and Elisha was a leading citizen of the kingdom. Besides, the Lord could have told him just as easily.

Notice the content of Elisha's message. The question "Why have you torn your robes?" (v. 8, NIV) was in reality a reproof or rebuke of the king. How could he so easily have forgotten or overlooked the ministry of the prophets in the land? The question was followed with the directive to send Naaman to him. But it did not end there. He emphatically stated the final result—this Syrian commander would know there was a prophet in Israel. Interpreted, it meant Naaman would encounter the power of God working through His minister, the prophet Elisha.

Verse 9 sets the stage for what followed. Naaman left the residence of Joram and presented himself at the home of Elisha. This verse indicates Naaman's willingness to go and to do what was necessary up to this point. He now stood at the door in expectation.

II. MINISTRY NOT FOR SALE
    (2 Kings 5:10-16)

A. The Frustration of Humility
   (vv. 10-13)

(2 Kings 5:13 is not included in the printed text.)

10. And Elisha sent a messenger unto him, saying, Go and wash in Jordan seven times, and thy flesh shall come again to thee, and thou shalt be clean.

11. But Naaman was wroth, and went away, and said, Behold, I thought, He will surely come

out to me, and stand, and call on the name of the Lord his God, and strike his hand over the place, and recover the leper.

12. Are not Abana and Pharpar, rivers of Damascus, better than all the waters of Israel? may I not wash in them, and be clean? So he turned and went away in a rage.

Naaman had no background in how God works, but as an important member of the Syrian court he understood protocol. It would be normal for him to expect a certain level of respect to be given to a man of his importance and position. Because of this, he came close to missing out on the blessing of God's healing.

This part of the story demonstrates the frustration we incur when presupposing how God should intervene in our behalf. Like Naaman, we might follow the protocol of the world and expect God to do the same. Or there can be the tendency to put God in the box of previous occasions. Since He worked one way in the past, we expect His future working to be exactly the same.

In verse 10 we see how Elisha's ministry did not become bogged down in the mire of status and position. As Naaman stood outside the door, the prophet viewed him as a leper needing healing. Naaman's rank never entered the setting. That is one reason Elisha did not bother with personally receiving Naaman. He was not concerned about making an acquaintance and exchanging small talk. His ministry was to exalt God whom he served. With that in mind, he did nothing more than send out his servant with a message.

The unusual message was for Naaman to go to the Jordan River and dip in it seven times. If he followed these guidelines, his flesh would be free from leprosy. The requirement was not difficult or time-consuming. All it involved was obedience and humility. However, for Naaman those were two major obstacles.

Immediately Naaman left in a rage. His anger burned both from the treatment and the message. Verse 11 states what Naaman expected in contrast to what took place. First, his expectation of the prophet appearing personally did not materialize. He knew Elisha's failure to come to the door was not because of Naaman's leprosy. Instead, it was his choice of operation. Second, Naaman's expectation of the prophet verbally calling on God in the presence of him and his entourage did not occur. In fact, there was no prayer, no special sacrifice, and no ceremony. Third, his expectation of the prophet's waving his hand over the leprosy and its instantly disappearing did not happen. How disappointing!

Naaman demonstrated the difficulty we may find ourselves in when we predetermine how a certain spiritual event should take place. Frequently we want the demonstrative when God chooses a quieter means. Or, we may want the result of God's intervention without having the necessary inner attitude which should accompany it. Sometimes we might want to choose a different location.

Location was part of Naaman's protest. Why should he dip (wash) in the muddy Jordan River? There was no history of its having a medicinal value. He compared the Jordan with rivers back home. Of the two named, the Abana, known now as the Barada, is easily identified. The Pharpar could be referring to a river some 10 miles southwest of Damascus. The waters of the Abana were clear, and some attributed medicinal qualities to it. More than likely the waters of the Pharpar were similar due to Naaman's lumping them together.

The commander's logic contained a major flaw. If these rivers were so powerful, why had he not already utilized them for healing his leprosy? This emphasizes his problem with submission and humility.

Fortunately for Naaman, his servants were wise and looking after his best interests. Notice their approach. Addressing him as "my father" (v. 13) reveals the nature of their relationship with him. Instead of making a statement of disbelief or disapproval, they asked a thought-provoking question: "If the prophet had told you to do some great thing, would you not have done it? How much more, then, when he tells you, 'Wash and be cleansed'!" (v. 13, *NIV*). The success of this approach is seen in the next verse.

B. The Desire to Compensate
   (vv. 14-16)

14. Then went he down, and dipped himself seven times in Jordan, according to the saying of the man of God: and his flesh came again like unto the flesh of a little child, and he was clean.

15. And he returned to the man of God, he and all his company, and came, and stood before him: and he said, Behold, now I know that there is no God in all the earth, but in Israel: now therefore, I pray thee, take a blessing of thy servant.

16. But he said, As the Lord liveth, before whom I stand, I will receive none. And he urged him to take it; but he refused.

Naaman recognized he had everything to gain and nothing to lose by doing what the prophet said. So he swallowed his pride, calmed his outrage, and proceeded to the Jordan. Verse 14 records Naaman's following the directions as given. After the seventh dip he received complete healing. The extent of this healing can be seen in the description. His skin now looked as healthy and pure as a young boy's. In other words, he had not looked like that since his youth.

Immediately Naaman and all his attendants returned to Elisha's home. When Elisha came out to meet Naaman, the conversation did not emphasize the physical miracle. Instead, it zeroed in on the spiritual event, which is of greater importance. Naaman expressed his recognition that the God of Israel was the only God in all the earth.

The thought of a god being associated to a particular place may be the reason behind Naaman's request for as much soil from Israel as two mules could carry (see v. 17). We can only speculate, but it would seem that he intended to worship God while standing or kneeling on this ground. Notice his commitment to personally worship only the Lord God while rejecting all other gods. However, he did ask for one exception to be considered (v. 18). Apparently his position required that at times he be present or assist the king of Syria at some of the official occasions of worship at the temple of Rimmon. Rimmon was the sun god, supreme deity of the Syrians. At this point Naaman was not ready to proclaim his sole commitment to the Lord God of Israel.

The second action of Naaman was the expression of his desire to present a gift to Elisha in recognition or compensation for his services. In the natural world this seems the normal as well as expected thing to do. The leprous man now stood wholly healthy. And as a man of means and position, some expression of thanks would surely be appropriate. But Elisha refused. Even though Naaman urged the acceptance, the prophet remained resolute. Why?

No specific reasons for Elisha's refusal are given; however several would seem logical. First, he was not going to allow any misconceptions to arise as to how this miracle transpired. God, not Elisha, was the miracle worker. Second, Elisha's ministry of miracles was not for sale. Third, the accumulation of a quick "bankroll" never should be a goal or result of ministry.

III. MAINTAIN INTEGRITY
(2 Kings 5:20-27)

A. The Temptation of Materialism (vv. 20-24)

(2 Kings 5:21-24 is not included in the printed text.)

20. But Gehazi, the servant of Elisha the man of God, said, Behold, my master hath spared Naaman this Syrian, in not receiving at his hands that which he brought: but, as the Lord liveth, I will run after him, and take somewhat of him.

The Biblical account tells little about Gehazi. We do know he was a servant to the prophet Elisha. His inclusion in the account of the Shunammite woman (2 Kings 4) indicates a long-time relationship as an assistant to Elisha. He was with Elisha before the woman's conception of a son, and he went out to meet her a number of years later as she came to the prophet after the boy's death. Gehazi was not a novice to the principles of ministry. Yet, that never makes anyone immune from temptation.

Shortly after Naaman and his company left, there arose within Gehazi a desire for the gifts which Elisha refused. Why should they be taken back to Syria after having been brought as presents for the healing of the commander? Gehazi decided to get some of the goods for himself. Immediately he ran and overtook Naaman. As soon as Gehazi was recognized, Naaman stopped the group and came down from his chariot. His leaving the chariot showed respect to the person whom Gehazi represented. Normally a man of Naaman's position would remain seated while the servant delivered his message.

Naaman asked, "Is all well?" (v. 21). Gehazi responded in the affirmative, then stated the reason for his being there. He presented a very convincing lie. Supposedly two young prophets, possibly pupils of Elisha, had just arrived and were in need. So the request was for two suits of clothing and 75 pounds (one talent) of silver.

The craftiness of Gehazi's request made it so logical. Elisha wouldn't receive anything for himself, but to help the neediness of others was a different matter. No wonder Naaman accepted the request without question. Besides, he probably saw this as a means of indirectly compensating the prophet. There was no reason to expect deception from Gehazi since he was the prophet's servant.

Naaman not only gave the two sets of clothing and one talent of silver, but insisted on sending a second talent as well. Then he had two of his personal servants go with Gehazi to carry them. Gehazi accepted this help. But when they came to "the tower" (5:24)—a well-known hill—before coming into the city, Gehazi personally took the gifts, sent the men back to Naaman, and then stored his ill-gotten gain in his house.

Supposedly no one knew how Gehazi had traded his integrity for clothing and money. But what Gehazi did not know was the final cost of the trade.

B. The Judgment for Deceit (vv. 25-27)

25. But he went in, and stood before his master. And Elisha said unto him, Whence comest thou, Gehazi? And he said, Thy servant went no whither.

26. And he said unto him, Went not mine heart with thee, when the man turned again from his chariot to meet thee? Is it a time to receive money, and to receive garments, and oliveyards, and vineyards, and sheep, and oxen, and menservants, and maidservants?

27. The leprosy therefore of Naaman shall cleave unto thee, and unto thy seed for ever. And he went out from his presence a leper as white as snow.

The next time Gehazi presented himself for service to Elisha, the prophet questioned him. This probably happened on the same day. "Where have you been?" is not asked a day or two later. This question arises when one is absent from his assigned duties or normal location. Without hesitation Gehazi responded that he had not been anywhere.

In verse 26 Elisha revealed his knowledge of the truth concerning Gehazi's activities. Elisha had experienced everything that transpired between Naaman and Gehazi at the very time it occurred. Elisha did not have just a revelation of knowledge. Instead, in spirit he had traveled the path with his greedy servant. The *New International Version* translates part of Elisha's response like this: "Was not my spirit with you when the man got down from his chariot to meet you?"

Elisha's next question was a statement about ministry. There never should be any time when selfishness and greed invade the prophetic office. This will result in disregard and contempt for spiritual ministry. Scandal occurs when a man or woman in ministry sacrifices integrity for personal gain.

This temptation is not confined to ministers who are experiencing difficult financial situations. It may come just as readily to those who are prospering. The temptation becomes one of wanting more and becoming like others who have an abundance of earthly possessions. Notice the listing in verse 26 of all the items which were possessions of the wealthy. Did Gehazi hope to add some of those items to his personal ownership?

Without allowing a time for explanation or repentance, Elisha passed God's sentence on Gehazi. Naaman's leprosy became his immediate plague. Was this too harsh? Maybe, if it were only because of greed. But his sin included the misuse or abuse of the prophet's name. This type of misrepresentation to Naaman, who had just found faith in the God of Israel, justified the curse of leprosy on Gehazi and his descendants.

GOLDEN TEXT HOMILY

"THE INTEGRITY OF THE UPRIGHT SHALL GUIDE THEM: BUT THE PERVERSENESS OF THE TRANSGRESSORS SHALL DESTROY THEM" (Proverbs 11:3).

There are two key words in this verse: *integrity* and *perverseness*. Let's look at the definitions and the potentials of each one.

Integrity is defined by Webster as "the quality or state of being complete or undivided," while *perverseness* is translated as "duplicity" by the *New International Version*. In other words, the person of integrity lives a transparent life that is devoted to a set of unchanging standards. Meanwhile, the perverse person lives a wishy-washy, go-with-the-flow, inconsistent life.

By those definitions, it is obvious that we live in a perverse world where only the few lead lives of integrity.

Where are these two lifestyles headed? The person of integrity is actually guided by his integrity. He has predetermined his course of action—to live an undivided, purpose-driven life—and nothing will sway him.

However, the perverse are called "transgressors" because they have no standards to live by. In the end, their duplicity shall destroy them.—**Lance Colkmire**

SENTENCE SERMONS

INTEGRITY is essential in Christian service.

—**Selected**

WHY IS IT that men know what is good but do what is bad?

—**Socrates**

THERE IS NO SUBSTITUTE for character. You can buy brains, but you cannot buy character.

—**Robert A. Cook**

EVANGELISM APPLICATION

INTEGRITY IN RELATIONSHIPS WITH THE UNSAVED WILL HELP POINT THEM TO CHRIST.

Why should anyone believe the truth of the gospel if Christians fail to be individuals of integrity? Personally, I can't think of a single reason. Can you?

Being eventually becomes more important than *speaking*. That's because who we are will impact what we do. Our deeds then either support our words or they undermine what we have been saying.

When we are honest in our business dealings and fulfill our promises, we earn speaking rights. On the opposite side, nothing hinders the gospel more than our attempts to witness when we are lacking in our own integrity.

Our challenge is to strive to be individuals of integrity so we can be Christlike in our witness.

ILLUMINATING THE LESSON

In ancient China, the people desired security from the barbaric hordes to the north. So they built the Great Wall of China. It was too high to climb over, too thick to break down, and too long to go around. Security achieved.

The only problem was that during the first 100 years of the wall's existence, China was invaded three times. Was the wall a failure? Not really—for not once did the barbaric hordes climb over the wall, break it down, or go around it.

How did they get into China? The answer lies in human nature. They simply bribed a gatekeeper and then marched right in through a gate. The fatal flaw in the Chinese defense was placing too much reliance on a wall and not putting enough effort into building character into the gatekeeper (Michael P. Green, *Illustrations for Biblical Preaching*).

DAILY BIBLE READINGS

M. Man of Integrity Chosen.
     Numbers 27:15-23
T. Integrity in Action.
     Job 29:7-17
W. Example of Integrity.
     Jeremiah 35:5-14
T. Lack of Integrity Condemned.
     Matthew 23:13-15, 23-26
F. Leaders With Integrity Chosen.
     Acts 6:1-7
S. Integrity in Ministry.
     2 Corinthians 4:1-5

TRUTH SEARCH:
Creatively Teaching the Word

Aim: Students will examine their lives for traces of pride and then ask God for deliverance and forgiveness.

Items needed: Marker board, markers, index cards and pencils

FOCUS

Write the following five statements on the board:

A. I find that I am right more often than wrong.

B. I generally do, or want to do, tasks by myself because I feel I am the only one that can do them correctly.

C. I am secretly bothered when others receive more attention/ praise/ recognition than me.

D. When I am wrong I have a difficult time admitting it.

E. I normally do not receive instruction well, particularly when it comes from someone I view as inferior (in position to me).

Give an index card to each student, and ask them to write the letters A-E to represent the five statements. Then they are to write a number from 1-10 next to each letter. A "1" will indicate that they strongly disagree with the statement. A "10" will indicate that they strongly agree with the statement. All answers are confidential.

EXPLORE

Ask the students to put the index cards away. Have a volunteer read 2 Kings 5:1-16. Then lead the entire class in a discussion based on the following questions:

• *How was Naaman viewed by those who either knew him personally or knew of him?*

• *Why was Naaman well known?*

• What was *Naaman's problem?*

• *How did Naaman learn about a possible solution?*

• *Based on the king of Israel's response in verse 7, how did he interpret the king of Aram's letter?*

• *At first, how did Naaman respond to Elisha's instructions? Why?*

• *What had Naaman expected?*

• *What argument changed his mind?*

• *How did Naaman respond to the healing?*

One of Naaman's problems was pride. His accomplishments had caused his countrymen to hold him in high esteem. This elevated stature seems to have caused him to be too proud to follow a Hebrew prophet's simple instructions.

We, not unlike Naaman, may also develop an unhealthy sense of pride based on our accomplishments and the attention we may receive from them.

RESPOND

Have the students refer back to the statements listed on the marker board and their index cards. Allow them to review the questions and their ratings. **If, after examining your ratings of these statements, you have discovered that you may have a problem with pride, pray silently with me. Let us ask God to deliver us from pride and forgive us of our sins.**

"Father, please deliver us from the pride of sin. We recognize that You resist pride and welcome humility. Please forgive us for allowing pride to grip us and drive us farther from You. Thank You for Your cleansing power. Amen."